The Letters to Timothy and Titus

THE PILLAR NEW TESTAMENT COMMENTARY

General Editor

D. A. CARSON

The Letters to TIMOTHY *and* TITUS

Robert W. Yarbrough

William B. Eerdmans Publishing Company
Grand Rapids, Michigan

APOLLOS
London, England

Published 2018 in the United States of America by
Wm. B. Eerdmans Publishing Co.
4035 Park East Court SE, Grand Rapids, Michigan 49546
www.eerdmans.com
and in the United Kingdom by
APOLLOS (an imprint of Inter-Varsity Press)
36 Causton St, Westminster, London SW1P 4ST, England
www.ivpbooks.com

Printed in the United States of America

27 26 25 7 8 9 10

ISBN 978-0-8028-3733-2

Library of Congress Cataloging-in-Publication Data
Names: Yarbrough, Robert W., author.
Title: The letters to Timothy and Titus / Robert W. Yarbrough.
Description: Grand Rapids : Eerdmans Publishing Co., 2018. |
Series: The Pillar New Testament commentary | Includes bibliographical references and index.
Identifiers: LCCN 2018007807 | ISBN 9780802837332 (hardcover : alk. paper)
Subjects: LCSH: Bible. Pastoral epistles—Commentaries.
Classification: LCC BS2735.53 .Y37 2018 | DDC 227/.8307—dc23
LC record available at https://lccn.loc.gov/2018007807

British Library Cataloguing in Publication Data
A catalogue record for this book is available from the British Library.
ISBN 978-1-78359-733-8

For Bernie

γυνὴ πιστὴ καὶ συνεργὸς ἐν τῷ εὐαγγελίῳ

Contents

THE LETTER OF 2 TIMOTHY

THE LETTER OF TITUS

INDEXES

List of Tables

Editor's Preface

Commentaries have specific aims, and this series is no exception. Designed for serious pastors and teachers of the Bible, the Pillar commentaries seek above all to make clear the text of Scripture as we have it. The scholars writing these volumes interact with the most important informed contemporary debate but avoid getting mired in undue technical detail. Their ideal is a blend of rigorous exegesis and exposition, with an eye alert both to biblical theology and to the contemporary relevance of the Bible, without confusing the commentary and the sermon. The rationale for this approach is that the vision of "objective scholarship" (a vain chimera) may actually be profane. God stands over against us; we do not stand in judgment of him. When God speaks to us through his word, those who profess to know him must respond in an appropriate way, which is certainly different from a stance in which the scholar projects an image of autonomous distance. Yet, this is no surreptitious appeal for uncontrolled subjectivity. The writers of this series aim for an even-handed openness to the text that is the best kind of "objectivity" of all. If the text is God's word, it is appropriate that we respond with reverence, a certain fear, a holy joy, a questing obedience. These values should be reflected in the way Christians write. With these values in place, the Pillar commentaries will be warmly welcomed not only by pastors, teachers, and students, but by general readers as well.

* * *

When Bob Yarbrough and I served on the same faculty, he was a cherished friend not only for his dry sense of humor and his skill with a chain saw, but for his habit of thinking about everything—everything!—in theological terms. That same personality (minus the skill with the chain saw) repeatedly surfaces in this commentary. Commentaries focus on different things, of course. This one devotes a great deal of thought and care to the meaning of words; in that sense, it is a rather old-fashioned commentary (and none the worse for that).

Equally, however, it penetratingly traces the line of thought in passage after passage and thus proves wonderfully fresh and sometimes innovative. This theologically and ethically rich commentary will prove to be a choice companion for years to come for pastors and scholars working their way through the Pastoral Epistles.

D. A. Carson

Author's Preface

I wish to express my gratitude for Professor Don Carson's invitation to write on Paul's so-called Pastoral Epistles (hereafter PE) for the esteemed Pillar New Testament Commentary Series. Thanks are also due to the William B. Eerdmans Publishing Company and its editors over several years, including Milton Essenburg, James Ernest, Trevor Thompson, and Craig Noll for their encouragement and patience in awaiting my completion of this project. For both Don's and Trevor's hands-on editorial pointers and suggestions, I am deeply in debt; my thanks for the miscues from which you spared me. The same goes doubly for Craig's painstaking scrutiny, improvements, and sometimes uncanny discovery of miscues. Remaining errors and inadequacies are my sole responsibility.

While this is a commentary based on the Greek text, its English exposition is based on the New International Version (2011), in part because of its continuing widespread use both in the US and abroad, in part because of its learned and creative attempts to arrive at fresh and linguistically justified renderings. Even when I opt for a different translation or shade of meaning, I find the NIV is a consistently fruitful discussion partner in the never-ending task of doing justice to the ancient Greek original in today's varied (and always changing) linguistic, social, political, and ideological settings.

As this commentary took shape, I realized I was gravitating toward focus on word meanings—not on etymologies of words or on "concepts" behind words (both criticized generations ago by James Barr),[1] but on words used in the PE with parallels (or lack of such) in contemporary documents.

1. James Barr, *The Semantics of Biblical Language* (London: Oxford University Press, 1961). Barr rightly stressed that "the real bearer of the theological statement is the large complex like the sentence, in which are used words having a certain semantic function" (265). For Barr's ongoing importance, see, for example, Douglas J. Moo, *We Still Don't Get It: Evangelicals and Bible Translation Fifty Years after James Barr* (Louisville: Evangelical Theological Society, 2014); Stanley E. Porter, *Linguistic Analysis of the Greek New Testament* (Grand Rapids: Baker Academic, 2015), 66, 87, 119.

It is now easy to go beyond reference to BDAG and quickly (with software) to ransack not only all NT and LXX documents but also Philo, Josephus, the Apostolic Fathers (AF), the Apologists, and Epictetus (for starters) to see how a word was used in the rough time frame of the composition of the PE. The results of these searches inform the exposition below; data are often amassed in footnotes to allow readers access for their own weighing of the evidence. Often it will be seen that PE usage of words is remarkably resonant with usage in Paul's ten other canonical epistles. Sometimes it is the anomalous nature of the word choice of the PE, in the context of the larger Pauline corpus, that stands out.

Sometimes the results of special attention to synchronic word usage was simply verification of BDAG. Sometimes it was a different connotation or translation than BDAG (or the NIV or other translations) proposes. Nearly always there was gain in what might be called semantic depth, for a word's function in other literary contexts (or absence from them) often sheds significant light on its function in a PE passage. Context, not word meaning in isolation, remains king for exegetical understanding and translation. But the validity of construing the larger literary unit (the sentence) cannot transcend defensible apprehension of the sentence's constituent parts (each word).

From personal experience in the West and observation of serious Bible readers and church leaders on other continents (esp. eastern Europe, Africa, and Asia), I am aware that readers of the PE often ponder the individual words (with respect to, e.g., qualifications for church leaders; see 1 Tim 3; Titus 1). Few things are more frustrating in a commentary than to be looking for help with details and to find instead breezy generalizations about some overarching message (or today, "story") taking no discernible account of at least the most distinctive individual words. While I am deeply interested in overarching meanings (or a narrative line) and have sought always to detect and highlight them, I have also tried to interpret "from below" via lexicographical focus based on observation of actual concurrent usage, along with constant consideration "from above" of the larger discourse patterns and flow.

In that commentary writers (unless they are hermits, and sometimes even then) write as members of communities, their finished work testifies to the support of various groups. I am conscious of the aid and often prayerful solicitude of fellow faculty at Trinity Evangelical Divinity School and now Covenant Theological Seminary over the years this commentary took shape. The administration of both institutions provided sabbatical leave, for which I am grateful. They also provided teaching assistants; among these, Craig (now Dr.) Long stands out in compiling extensive bibliography for my research. Previously, Melissa Ross and Ling Luo amassed and updated information from *New Testament Abstracts* and other sources that was equally invaluable. L. Timothy (now Dr.) Swinson put his shoulder to the wheel by devoting his

Trinity PhD dissertation to a PE topic; I am grateful for the stimulation of his investigations and delighted in the publication that resulted.[2] My current teaching assistant Brandon Flynn deserves recognition for compiling the biblical and extrabiblical indexes.

Over the past decade four churches have assisted my growth in the grasp of pastoral ministry: Khartoum Evangelical Church, Sudan; St. Mark Lutheran Church, Lindenhurst, IL; St. Paul's Evangelical Free Church, St. Louis, MO; and Central Presbyterian Church, also in St. Louis. Pastors who have taken interest in my work, given input to my thinking, and exemplify ideals upheld in the PE include Terry Breum, Bill Shields, Mark Friz, and lifelong friend Glen Land. I would be remiss not to mention also the respective secrets (humanly speaking) of their success and friends to me in their own right: Janet (an ordained pastor herself), Lisa, Gayle, and Joyce. For married ministers, not just success but merely survival (neither to be taken for granted in the pastorate) is profoundly a partnership.

In that vein, I dedicate this commentary to my wife, Bernie, particularly in view of her modeling of so much of what the PE call for, from care of widows (1 Tim 5:3) to self-sacrifice for other relatives (5:8), to distinguished marital commitment (Titus 2:3–5), not seldom in the shadow of adversity. Further effort to detail grounds for gratitude could not fail to be pitiful understatement.

2. L. Timothy Swinson, *What Is Scripture? Paul's Use of Graphe in the Letters to Timothy* (Eugene, OR: Wipf & Stock, 2014).

Abbreviations

AB	Anchor Bible
ABD	*Anchor Bible Dictionary.* Edited by David Noel Freedman. 6 vols. New York: Doubleday, 1992
adj.	adjective
AF	Apostolic Fathers
AfBCS	Africa Bible Commentary Series
AMP	Ampified Bible
ANF	*Ante-Nicene Fathers*
ANTC	Abingdon New Testament Commentaries
AsBCS	Asia Bible Commentary Series
ASV	American Standard Version
AV	Authorized Version
BAR	*Biblical Archaeology Review*
BDAG	Danker, Frederick W., Walter Bauer, William F. Arndt, and F. Wilbur Gingrich, *A Greek-English Lexicon of the New Testament and Other Early Christian Literature.* 3d ed. Chicago: University of Chicago Press, 2000
BDF	Blass, Friedrich, Albert Debrunner, and Robert W. Funk. *A Greek Grammar of the New Testament and Other Early Christian Literature.* Chicago: University of Chicago Press, 1961
BFCT	Beiträge zur Förderung christlicher Theologie
BNTC	Black's New Testament Commentaries
BRG	Blue, Red, and Gold Letter Edition
BTB	*Biblical Theology Bulletin*
BZNW	Beihefte zur Zeitschrift für die neutestamentliche Wissenschaft
CEB	Common English Bible
CEV	Contemporary English Version
ChrCent	*Christian Century*
CJB	Complete Jewish Bible
CNTUOT	*Commentary on the New Testament Use of the Old Testaament.* Edited by G. K. Beale and D. A. Carson. Grand Rapids: Baker Academic, 2007

CSB	Christian Standard Bible
CurTM	*Currents in Theology and Mission*
DLNT	Disciples' Literal New Testament
DPL	*Dictionary of Paul and His Letters*. Edited by Gerald F. Hawthorne, Ralph P. Martin, and Daniel G. Reid. Downers Grove, IL: InterVarsity Press, 1993
DRA	Douay-Rheims 1899 American Edition
DSS	Dead Sea Scrolls
EBR	*Encyclopedia of the Bible and Its Reception*. Edited by Hans-Josef Klauck et al. Berlin: de Gruyter, 2009–
EDB	*Eerdmans Dictionary of the Bible*. Editor-in-Chief David Noel Freedman. Grand Rapids: Eerdmans, 2000. Electronic text hypertexted and prepared by OakTree Software, Inc. Version 3.6.
EGGNT	Exegetical Guide to the Greek New Testament
EJT	*European Journal of Theology*
EKKNT	Evangelisch-katholischer Kommentar zum Neuen Testament
ERV	Easy-to-Read Version
ESV	English Standard Version
EvQ	*Evangelical Quarterly*
EXB	The Expanded Bible
FS	Festschrift
GELS	Muraoka, Takamitsu. *A Greek-English Lexicon of the Septuagint*. Leuven: Peeters, 2009
Gk.	Greek
GNC	Heinrich Walter Cassirer. *God's New Covenant: A New Testament Translation*. Grand Rapids: Eerdmans, 1989
GNT	Greek New Testament
GNV	Geneva Bible
GW	God's Word (Modern English Bible version)
HCNT	*Hellenistic Commentary to the New Testament*. Edited by M. Eugene Boring, Klaus Berger, and Carsten Colpe. Nashville: Abingdon, 1995
HCSB	Holman Christian Standard Bible
HTA	Historisch-theologische Auslegung
IBC	Interpretation: A Bible Commentary for Teaching and Preaching
IBMR	*International Bulletin of Mission(ary) Research*
ICB	International Children's Bible
ICC	International Critical Commentary
ISV	International Standard Version
JB	Jerusalem Bible
JBL	*Journal of Biblical Literature*
JETS	*Journal of the Evangelical Theological Society*
JSNT	*Journal for the Study of the New Testament*
JSNTSup	Journal for the Study of the New Testament Supplement Series
JTS	*Journal of Theological Studies*

JUB	Jubilee Bible 2000
KJ21	Twenty-First-Century King James Version
KJV	King James Bible
L&N	Louw, Johannes P., and Eugene A. Nida, eds. *Greek-English Lexicon of the New Testament: Based on Semantic Domains.* 2nd ed. New York: United Bible Societies, 1989
LEB	Lexham English Bible
LEH	Lust, Johan, Erik Eynikel, and Katrin Hausbie, eds. *Greek-English Lexicon of the Septuagint.* Rev. ed. Stuttgart: Deutsche Bibelgesellschaft, 2003
LNTS	Library of New Testament Studies
LSJ	Liddell, Henry George, Robert Scott, and Henry Stuart Jones. *A Greek-English Lexicon.* 9th ed., with revised supplement. Oxford: Clarendon, 1996
LXX	Septuagint
MEV	Modern English Version
MM	Moulton, James H., and George Milligan. *The Vocabulary of the Greek New Testament: Illustrated from the Papyri and Other Nonliterary Sources.* 1930. Repr., Peabody, MA: Hendrickson, 1997
MS(S)	manuscript(s)
MT	Masoretic text
NA^{27}/NA^{28}	Nestle-Aland *Novum Testamentum Graece.* 27th/28th ed.
NABRE	New American Bible Revised Edition
NASB	New American Standard Bible
NCBC	New Century Bible Commentary
NCV	New Century Version
NEB	New English Bible
NET	New English Translation
NETS	A New English Translation of the Septuagint
NICNT	New International Commentary on the New Testament
NIDB	*New Interpreter's Dictionary of the Bible.* Edited by Katharine Doob
NIDNTT	*New International Dictionary of New Testament Theology.* Edited by Colin Brown. 4 vols. Grand Rapids: Zondervan, 1975–78
NIDNTTE	*New International Dictionary of New Testament Theology and Exegesis.* Edited by Moisés Silva. 5 vols. Grand Rapids: Zondervan, 2014
NIGTC	New International Greek Testament Commentary
NIRV	New International Reader's Version
NIV	New International Version (2011 edition)
NIV84	New International Version (1984 edition)
NLT	New Living Translation
NLV	New Life Version
NPNF^{1}	*Nicene and Post-Nicene Fathers*, Series 1
NSBT	New Studies in Biblical Theology
NTD	Das Neue Testament Deutsch

NTE	New Testament for Everyone
NTG	New Testament Guides
NTOA/SUNT	Novum Testamentum et Orbis Antiquus/Studien zur Umwelt des Neuen Testaments
NTS	*New Testament Studies*
NTT	New Testament Theology
NW	*Neuer Wettstein: Texte zum Neuen Testament aus Griechentum und Hellenismus.* Edited by Georg Strecker and Udo Schnelle. Vol. 2/2: *Texte zur Briefliteratur und zur Johannesapokalypse.* Berlin: de Gruyter, 1996
OSHT	Oxford Studies in Historical Theology
PE	Pastoral Epistle(s)
pl.	plural
Presb	*Presbyterion*
PSB	*Princeton Seminary Bulletin*
RBL	*Review of Biblical Literature*
RGRW	Religions in the Graeco-Roman World
RNT	Regensburger Neues Testament
RSV	Revised Standard Version
SBL	Society of Biblical Literature
SD	Studies and Documents
SHBC	Smyth & Helwys Bible Commentary
sing.	singular
SJT	*Scottish Journal of Theology*
THNTC	Two Horizons New Testament Commentary
TJ	*Trinity Journal*
TLB	Tree of Life Bible
TLV	Tree of Life Version
TLZ	*Theologische Literaturzeitung*
TNTC	Tyndale New Testament Commentaries
TRu	*Theologische Rundschau*
TynBul	*Tyndale Bulletin*
VOICE	The Voice Bible
WBC	Word Biblical Commentary
WE	Worldwide English (New Testament)
WEB	World English Bible
WUNT	Wissenschaftliche Untersuchungen zum Neuen Testament
ZECNT	Zondervan Exegetical Commentary on the New Testament
ZIBBC	Zondervan Illustrated Bible Backgrounds Commentary

Bibliography

COMMENTARIES

The commentaries listed here are cited in the footnotes by author and page number only.

Aquinas, T. *Commentaries on St. Paul's Epistles to Timothy, Titus, and Philemon*. Translated and edited by C. Baer. South Bend, IN: St. Augustine's Press, 2007.

Barrett, C. K. *The Pastoral Epistles in the New English Bible*. Oxford: Clarendon, 1963.

Bassler, J. *1 Timothy, 2 Timothy, Titus*. ANTC. Nashville: Abingdon, 1996.

Baugh, S. M. "1 & 2 Timothy, Titus." Pages 42–109 in *1 & 2 Thessalonians, 1 & 2 Timothy, Titus*. By J. A. D. Weima and S. M. Baugh. ZIBBC. Grand Rapids: Zondervan, 2002.

Belleville, L. "1 Timothy." Pages 25–123 in *1 Timothy; 2 Timothy, Titus; Hebrews*. By L. Belleville, J. C. Laansma, and J. R. Michaels. Cornerstone Biblical Commentary 17. Carol Stream, IL: Tyndale House, 2009.

Berger, K. *Kommentar zum Neuen Testament*. 2nd ed. Gütersloh: Gütersloher Verlagshaus, 2012.

Bernard, J. H. *The Pastoral Epistles*. 1899. Repr., Grand Rapids: Eerdmans, 1980.

Brox, N. *Die Pastoralbriefe*. 4th ed. RNT 7/2. Regensburg: Pustet, 1969.

Calvin, J. *The Second Epistle of Paul the Apostle to the Corinthians and the Epistles to Timothy, Titus and Philemon*. Translated by T. A. Smail. Edited by D. W. Torrance and T. F. Torrance. Grand Rapids: Eerdmans, 1964.

Collins, R. F. *1 & 2 Timothy and Titus*. New Testament Library. Louisville: Westminster John Knox, 2002.

Davies, M. *The Pastoral Epistles*. NTG. Sheffield: Sheffield Academic Press, 1996.

Dibelius, M., and H. Conzelmann. *The Pastoral Epistles*. Translated by P. Buttolph and A. Yarbro. Hermenenia. Philadelphia: Fortress, 1972.

Gloer, W. *1 & 2 Timothy–Titus*. SHBC. Macon, GA: Smyth & Helwys, 2010.

Guthrie, D. *The Pastoral Epistles*. Rev. ed. TNTC. Leicester: Inter-Varsity, 1990.

Hanson, A. T. *The Pastoral Epistles*. NCBC. Grand Rapids: Eerdmans, 1982.

Hofmann, J. C. K. von. *Die Briefe Pauli an Titus und Timotheus*. Vol. 6 of *Die heilige Schrift neuen Testaments zusammenhängend untersucht*. Nördlingen: C. H. Beck'schen Buchhandlung, 1874.

Jeremias, J. *Die Briefe an Timotheus und Titus*. NTD 9. Göttingen: Vandenhoeck & Ruprecht, 1934.

Johnson, L. T. *The First and Second Letters to Timothy*. AB 35A. New York: Doubleday, 2001.

———. *Letters to Paul's Delegates: 1 Timothy, 2 Timothy, Titus*. The New Testament in Context. Harrisburg, PA: Trinity Press International, 1996.

Kelly, J. N. D. *The Pastoral Epistles*. BNTC. 1963. Repr., Peabody, MA: Hendrickson, 1998.

Knight, G. W., III. *The Pastoral Epistles*. NIGTC. Grand Rapids: Eerdmans, 1992.

Köstenberger, A. *Commentary on 1–2 Timothy and Titus*. Biblical Theology for Proclamation Series. Nashville: Holman Reference, 2017.

Krause, D. *1 Timothy*. London: T&T Clark, 2004.

Laansma, J. "2 Timothy, Titus." Pages 125–302 in *1 Timothy; 2 Timothy, Titus; Hebrews*. By L. Belleville, J. C. Laansma, and J. R. Michaels. Cornerstone Biblical Commentary 17. Carol Stream, IL: Tyndale House, 2009.

Long, T. G. *1 & 2 Timothy and Titus*. Belief: A Theological Commentary on the Bible. Louisville: Westminster John Knox, 2016.

Marshall, I. H., with P. H. Towner. *The Pastoral Epistles*. ICC. Edinburgh: T&T Clark, 2004.

Montague, G. T. *First and Second Timothy, Titus*. Catholic Commentary on Sacred Scripture. Grand Rapids: Baker Academic, 2008.

Mounce, W. D. *Pastoral Epistles*. WBC 46. Nashville: Nelson, 2000.

Neudorfer, H.-W. *Der Brief des Paulus an Titus*. HTA. Witten: Brockhaus, 2012.

———. *Der erste Brief des Paulus an Timotheus*. 2d ed. HTA. Witten: Brockhaus, 2012.

———. *Der zweite Brief des Paulus an Timotheus*. 2d ed. HTA. Witten: Brockhaus, 2017.

Ngewa, S. *1 & 2 Timothy and Titus*. AfBCS. Grand Rapids: Zondervan, 2009.

Oden, T. C. *First and Second Timothy and Titus*. IBC. Louisville: Westminster John Knox, 1989.

Quinn, J. D. *The Letter to Titus*. AB 35. New York: Doubleday, 1990.

Quinn, J. D., and W. C. Wacker. *The First and Second Letters to Timothy*. Grand Rapids: Eerdmans, 1999.

Ramsay, W. R. *Historical Commentary on the Pastoral Epistles*. 1909–11. Repr., Grand Rapids: Kregel, 1996.

Ryken, P. *1 Timothy*. Reformed Expository Commentary. Phillipsburg, NJ: P&R, 2007.

Saarinen, R. *The Pastoral Epistles, with Philemon and Jude*. Brazos Theological Commentary on the Bible. Grand Rapids: Brazos, 2008.

Schlatter, A. *Die Briefe an die Thessalonischer, Philipper, Timotheus und Titus*. Erläuterungen zum Neuen Testament 8. Stuttgart: Calwer, 1964.

———. *Die Kirche der Griechen im Urteil des Paulus: Eine Auslegung seiner Briefe an Timotheus und Titus*. 2nd ed. Stuttgart: Calwer, 1958. 1st ed., 1936.

Spencer, A. B. *2 Timothy and Titus*. New Covenant Commentary Series. Eugene, OR: Cascade, 2014.

Towner, P. H. "1–2 Timothy and Titus." Pages 891–918 in *Commentary on the New Testament Use of the Old Testaament*. Edited by G. K. Beale and D. A. Carson. Grand Rapids: Baker Academic, 2007.

———. *The Letters to Timothy and Titus*. NICNT. Grand Rapids: Eerdmans, 2006.

Trebilco, P., C. Caradus, and S. Rae. *2 Timothy and Titus*. AsBCS. Singapore: Asia Theological Association, 2009.

Trebilco, P., and S. Rae. *1 Timothy*. AsBCS. Singapore: Asia Theological Association, 2006.

Twomey, J. *The Pastoral Epistles through the Centuries*. Blackwell Bible Commentaries. Chichester: Wiley-Blackwell, 2009.

Wall, R. W., with R. B. Steele. *1 & 2 Timothy and Titus*. THNTC. Grand Rapids: Eerdmans, 2012.

Witherington, B., III. *A Socio-Rhetorical Commentary on Titus, 1–2 Timothy, and 1–3 John*. Vol. 1 of *Letters and Homilies for Hellenized Christians*. Downers Grove, IL: IVP Academic, 2006.

Wright, N. T. *Paul for Everyone: The Pastoral Letters; 1 and 2 Timothy and Titus*. 2nd ed. London: SPCK, 2004.

Zehr, P. M. *1 & 2 Timothy, Titus*. Believers Church Bible Commentary. Scottdale, PA: Herald Press, 2010.

ANCIENT SOURCES

Epictetus. GREEK: based on Epictetus, *Enchiridion*; *Dissertationes*. Edited by Henricus Shenkl, 1916 ed. *Discourses* raw text from BIKITHEKE, el.wikisource.org. Includes *Enchiridion* and *Discourses* 1–4. Morphologically tagged by Rex A. Koivisto. © 2016 OakTree Software, Inc. Version 4.0. ENGLISH: *All the Works of Epictetus*. Including *Enchiridion*, *Arrian*, and *Discourses* 1–4. Translated by Elizabeth Carter, 1758. Edited by Rex A. Koivisto. © 2016 OakTree Software, Inc. Version 4.0.

Josephus. GREEK: 1890 Niese edition. ENGLISH: *The Works of Flavius Josephus, Complete and Unabridged*. © 1987 by Hendrickson Publishers, Inc., Peabody, MA. Electronic text hypertexted and prepared by OakTree Software, Inc. Version 1.8.

Philo. GREEK: The Norwegian Philo Concordance Project. © 2005 Peder Borgen, Kåre Fuglseth, Roald Skarsten. Morphological tagging extensively revised and updated by Rex A. Koivisto; further revised with the help of Marco V. Fabbri. Updated portions © 2009 OakTree Software, Inc. Version 3.6. ENGLISH: *The Works of Philo, Completed and Unabridged*. Trans. C. D. Yonge. Copyright © 1993 by Hendrickson Publishers, Inc. Electronic text prepared by Oaktree Software, Inc. Version 1.2.

SECONDARY SOURCES

Aageson, J. W. *Paul, the Pastoral Epistles, and the Early Church*. Peabody, MA: Hendrickson, 2008.

Achtemeier, P., J. Green, and M. Thompson. *Introducing the New Testament: Its Literature and Theology*. Grand Rapids: Eerdmans, 2001.

Akin, D. L. "The Mystery of Godliness Is Great: Christology in the Pastoral Epistles." Pages 137–52 in *Entrusted with the Gospel*. Edited by A. J. Köstenberger and T. L. Wilder. Nashville: B&H Academic, 2010.

Arnold, C. *Ephesians*. ZECNT. Grand Rapids: Zondervan, 2010.

———. *Ephesians: Power and Magic*. Grand Rapids: Baker Books, 1992.

Asamoah-Gyadu, J. K. Review of *New Centers of Global Evangelicalism in Latin America and Africa*, by S. Offutt. *IBMR* 40.2 (2016): 192–93.

Balla, P. *The Child-Parent Relationship in the New Testament and Its Environment*. WUNT 155. Tübingen: Mohr Siebeck, 2003.

Ballor, J. "The Biblical View of Work." *The City*, Spring 2014, 25–38.

Barclay, J. *Paul and the Gift*. Grand Rapids: Eerdmans, 2015.

———. Review of *Paul and the Faithfulness of God*, by N. T. Wright. *SJT* 68.2 (2015): 235–43.

Barnett, P. W. *Jesus and the Logic of History*. NSBT 3. Downers Grove, IL: IVP Academic, 2001.

———. *Paul: Missionary of Jesus*. After Jesus 2. Grand Rapids: Eerdmans, 2008.

Barrett, M. *God's Word Alone: The Authority of Scripture; What the Reformers Taught . . . and Why It Still Matters*. The 5 Solas Series. Wheaton, IL: Crossway, 2016.

Barrs, J. *Delighting in the Law of the Lord: God's Alternative to Legalism and Moralism*. Wheaton, IL: Crossway, 2013.

Bassler, J. "A Plethora of Epiphanies: Christology in the Pastoral Letters." *PSB* 17 (1996): 310–25.

Bates, M. W. *Birth of the Trinity: Jesus, God, and Spirit in New Testament and Early Christian Interpretations of the Old Testament*. Oxford: Oxford University Press, 2015.

Batten, A. J. "Neither Gold nor Braided Hair (1 Timothy 2:9; 1 Peter 3:3): Adornment, Honour, and Gender in Antiquity," *NTS* 55.4 (2009): 484–501.

Baugh, S. M. "A Foreign World: Ephesus in the First Century." Pages 25–64 in Köstenberger and Schreiner, *Women in the Church*, 3rd ed.

Baur, F. C. *Paul, the Apostle of Jesus Christ: His Life and Works, His Epistles and Teachings*. 2 vols. Peabody, MA: Hendrickson, 2003.

Bauspiess, M., C. Landmesser, and D. Lincicum, eds. *Ferdinand Christian Baur und die Geschichte des frühen Christentums*. WUNT 333. Tübingen: Mohr Siebeck, 2014.

Bellah, R. N., et al. *Habits of the Heart: Individualism and Commitment in American Life*. 3rd ed.; Oakland: University of California Press, 2007.

Belleville, L. "Christology, the Pastoral Epistles, and Commentaries." Pages 317–36 in *On the Writing of New Testament Commentaries: FS Grant Osborne*. Edited by S. E. Porter and E. J. Schnabel. Leiden: Brill, 2013.

Belluck, P. and J. Cochrane, "Unicef Report Finds Female Genital Cutting to Be Common in Indonesia." *New York Times*, February 4, 2016, www.nytimes.com/2016/02/05/health/indonesia-female-genital-cutting-circumcision-unicef.html?_r=0.

Belz, M. "Numbers Matter." *World Magazine*, February 18, 2017, 32.

Berry, D. L. *Glory in Romans and the Unified Purpose of God in Redemptive History*. Eugene, OR: Pickwick, 2016.

Blankenhorn, D., D. Browning, and M. S. Van Leeuwen, eds. *Does Christianity Teach Male Headship? The Equal-Regard Marriage and Its Critics*. Grand Rapids: Eerdmans, 2004.

Blomberg, C. *The Historical Reliability of the New Testament*. Nashville: B&H Academic, 2016.

Bolt, P., and M. Thompson, eds. *The Gospel to the Nations: Perspectives on Paul's Mission: FS Peter O'Brien*. Leicester: Apollos, 2000.

Bonhoeffer, D. *Life Together: A Discussion of Christian Fellowship*. New York: Harper & Row, 1954.

Bonk, J. "Ecclesiastical Cartography and the Invisible Continent." *IBMR* 28.4 (2004): 153–58.

Boring, M. E., K. Berger, and C. Colpe, eds. *Hellenistic Commentary to the New Testament.* Nashville: Abingdon, 1995.

Brinkmann, B. Review of *Die Kirche der Griechen im Urteil des Paulus*, by A. von Schlatter. *Scholastik* 12 (1937): 291.

Bruce, F. F. *A Mind for What Matters.* Grand Rapids: Eerdmans, 1990.

———. *Paul: Apostle of the Heart Set Free.* Grand Rapids: Eerdmans, 1977.

Burk, D. "New and Old Departures in the Translation of Αὐθεντεῖν in 1 Timothy 2:12." Pages 279–96 in Köstenberger and Schreiner, *Women in the Church*, 3rd ed.

Byrd, A. *No Little Women: Equipping All Women in the Household of God.* Phillipsburg, NJ: P&R, 2016.

Calvin, J. *Institutes of the Christian Religion.* Translated by F. L. Battles. 2 vols. Philadelphia: Westminster, 1960.

Campbell, C. *Advances in the Study of New Testament Greek: New Insights for the Reading of the Greek New Testament.* Grand Rapids: Zondervan, 2015.

———. *Basics of Verbal Aspect in Biblical Greek.* Grand Rapids: Zondervan, 2008.

———. *Paul and Union with Christ: An Exegetical and Theological Study.* Grand Rapids: Zondervan, 2012.

Carson, D. A., ed. *The Enduring Authority of the Christian Scriptures.* Grand Rapids: Eerdmans, 2016.

———. *The Intolerance of Tolerance.* Grand Rapids: Eerdmans, 2013.

———. *Jesus the Son of God: A Christological Title Often Overlooked, Sometimes Misunderstood, and Currently Disputed.* Wheaton, IL: Crossway, 2012.

Carson, D. A., and D. Moo. *An Introduction to the New Testament.* 2nd ed. Grand Rapids: Zondervan, 2005.

Carson, D. A., P. T. O'Brien, and M. A. Seifrid, eds. *The Complexities of Second Temple Judaism.* Vol. 1 of *Justification and Variegated Nomism.* WUNT 2.140. Grand Rapids: Baker Academic, 2001.

Cochran, P. D. H. *Evangelical Feminism: A History.* New York: New York University Press, 2005.

Cole, G. *The God Who Became Human: A Biblical Theology of Incarnation.* NSBT. Downers Grove, IL: IVP Academic, 2013.

Cook, M. *Forbidding Wrong in Islam.* Cambridge: Cambridge University Press, 2003.

Cooper, J. W. *Panentheism—the Other God of the Philosophers: From Plato to the Present.* Grand Rapids: Baker Academic, 2006.

Cooper, M., and J. Cabellero. "Reasoning through the Creation Order as a Basis for the Prohibition in 1 Timothy 2:12." *Presb* 43.1 (2017): 30–38.

Couser, G. A. "'Prayer' and the Public Square: 1 Timothy 2:1–7 and Christian Political Engagement." Pages 277–94 in *New Testament Theology in Light of the Church's Mission: Essays in Honor of I. Howard Marshall.* Edited by J. Laansma, G. Osborne, and R. Van Neste. Eugene, OR: Wipf & Stock, 2011.

———. "'The Testimony about the Lord,' 'Borne by the Lord,' or Both? An Insight into Paul and Jesus in the Pastoral Epistles (2 Tim 1:8)," *TynBul* 52 (2004): 295–316.

Cowan, S., and T. Wilder, eds. *In Defense of the Bible: A Comprehensive Apologetic for the Authority of Scripture.* Nashville: B&H, 2015.

Croy, N. C. Review of *The Myth of Persecution: How Early Christians Invented a*

Story of Martyrdom, by Candida Moss. *RBL* 10 (2013), www.bookreviews.org/pdf/9158_10095.pdf.

Danker, F. W. *The Concise Greek-English Lexicon of the New Testament*. Chicago: University of Chicago Press, 2009.

Dau, I. M. *Suffering and God: A Theological Reflection on the War in Sudan*. Nairobi, Kenya: Paulines Publications Africa, 2002.

Davidson, B. W. "Narcission: The Root of All Hypocrisy in the Theological Psychology of Jonathan Edwards," *JETS* 57.1 (2014): 135–45.

Deines, R. *Acts of God in History: Studies towards Recovering a Theological Historiography*. Edited by Christoph Ochs and Peter Watts. WUNT 317. Tübingen: Mohr Siebeck, 2013.

———. "Did Matthew Know He Was Writing Scripture?" 2 pts. *EJT* 22.2 (2013): 101–9 and 23.1 (2014): 3–12.

Doering, L. *Ancient Jewish Letters and the Beginnings of Christian Epistolography*. WUNT 298. Tübingen: Mohr Siebeck, 2012.

Doriani, D. *Women and Ministry: What the Bible Teaches*. Wheaton, IL: Crossway, 2003.

Dorrien, G. *Kantian Reason and Hegelian Spirit: The Idealistic Logic of Modern Theology*. Chichester: Wiley-Blackwell, 2012.

Edwards, J. "Archaeology Gives New Reality to Paul's Ephesus Riot." *BAR* 42.4 (2016): 24–32, 62.

Elliott, J. H. "Jesus Was Not an Egalitarian: A Critique of an Anachronistic and Idealist Theory." *BTB* 32.2 (2002): 75–91.

Elliott, J. K. *The Greek Text of the Epistles to Timothy and Titus*. Studies and Documents 36. Salt Lake City: University of Utah Press, 1968.

Elliott, M. *Faithful Feelings: Emotion in the New Testament*. Leicester: InterVarsity, 2005.

Elwell, W., and R. Yarbrough. *Encountering the New Testament*. 3rd ed. Grand Rapids: Baker Academic, 2013.

Evans, C. A. *Ancient Texts for New Testament Studies*. Peabody, MA: Hendrickson, 2005.

Fee, G. *Pauline Christology: An Exegetical-Theological Study*. Peabody, MA: Hendrickson, 2007.

Fellows, R. "Name Giving by Paul and the Destination of Acts." *TynBul* 67.2 (2016): 247–68.

Fiorenza, E. S., ed. *Feminist Biblical Studies in the Twentieth Century*. Atlanta: SBL, 2014.

Folmar, K. *The Good Portion: The Doctrine of Scripture for Every Woman*. Fearn, Ross-shire, Scotland: Christian Focus, 2017.

Frey, J. *Von Jesus zur neutestamentlichen Theologie: Kleine Schriften II*. Edited by Benjamin Schliesser. WUNT 2.368. Tübingen: Mohr Siebeck, 2016.

Fung, R. Y. K. "Charismatic versus Organized Ministry? An Examination of an Alleged Antithesis." *EvQ* 52 (1980): 195–214.

Gire, K. *Shaped by the Cross: Meditations on the Sufferings of Jesus*. Downers Grove, IL: IVP Books, 2011.

The Greek-English New Testament. 28th ed. Wheaton, IL: Crossway, 2012.

Greene-McCreight, K. *Feminist Reconstructions of Christian Doctrine*. New York: Oxford University Press, 2000.

———. "United in Suffering: Martyrdom as Christian Vocation." *ChrCent*, September 30, 2015, 30–34.

Grim, B. J., and R. Finke. *The Price of Freedom Denied: Religious Persecution and Conflict in the Twenty-First Century*. Cambridge: Cambridge University Press, 2011.

Grudem, W. *Evangelical Feminism: A New Path to Liberalism?* Wheaton, IL: Crossway, 2006.

Haanen, J. "How We Lost the Craftsmen." *The City*, Spring 2014, 39–45.

Hagner, D. *The New Testament: A Historical and Theological Introduction*. Grand Rapids: Baker Academic, 2012.

Hamilton, J. "Does the Bible Condone Slavery and Sexism?" Pages 335–48 in *In Defense of the Bible*. Edited by S. Cowan and T. Wilder. Nashville: B&H, 2013.

Harris, M. J. *Jesus as God: The New Testament Use of Theos in Reference to Jesus*. Grand Rapids: Baker Books, 1992.

———. *Prepositions and Theology in the Greek New Testament*. Grand Rapids: Zondervan, 2012.

———. *Slave of Christ*. Nottingham, UK: Apollos, 1999.

Harrison, P. N. *The Problem of the Pastoral Epistles*. London: Oxford University Press, 1921.

Harvey, A. E. *Is Scripture Still Holy? Coming of Age with the New Testament*. Grand Rapids: Eerdmans, 2012.

Haykin, M. Review of *The Myth of Persecution: How Early Christians Invented a Story of Martyrdom*, by Candida Moss. *The Gospel Coalition*, August 25, 2014, www.thegospelcoalition.org/article/the-myth-of-persecution.

Hays, C., and C. Ansberry. *Evangelical Faith and the Challenge of Historical Criticism*. London: SPCK, 2013.

Hellerman, J. H. *Philippians*. EGGNT. Nashville: B&H, 2015.

Hellholm, D., T. Vegge, Ø. Norderval, and C. Hellholm, eds. *Ablution, Initiation, and Baptism: Late Antiquity, Early Judaism, and Early Christianity*. 3 vols. BZNW 176. Berlin: de Gruyter, 2011.

Herzer, J. "Abschied vom Konsens? Die Pseudepigraphie der Pastoralbriefe als Herausforderung an die neutestamentliche Wissenschaft." *TLZ* 129.12 (2004): 1268–81.

Hill, C. "'The Truth above All Demonstration': Scripture in the Patristic Period to Augustine." Pages 43–88 in *The Enduring Authority of the Christian Scriptures*. Edited by D. A. Carson. Grand Rapids: Eerdmans, 2016.

———. *Who Chose the Gospels?* Oxford: Oxford University Press, 2010.

Hock, R. "Paul's Tentmaking and the Problem of His Social Class." *JBL* 97.4 (1978): 555–64.

Hübner, J. "Revisiting the Clarity of Scripture in 1 Timothy 2:12." *JETS* 59.1 (2016): 99–117.

Issler, K. "Exploring the Pervasive References to Work in Jesus' Parables." *JETS* 57.2 (2014): 323–39.

Jacobsen, D. *Global Christianity: An Introduction to Christianity on Five Continents*. Grand Rapids: Baker Academic, 2015.

Jenkins, P. *The Next Christendom: The Coming of Global Christianity*. 3rd ed. Oxford: Oxford University Press, 2011.

———. "When Does Faith Become Fraudulent?" *ChrCent*, August 3, 2016, 45.

Jennings, J. N. "Hostility against Mission." *IBMR* 39.2 (April 2015): 57–58.

Jeon, P. *To Exhort and Reprove: Audience Response to the Chiastic Structures of Paul's Letter to Titus*. Eugene, OR: Pickwick, 2012.

Jeremias, J. Review of *Die Kirche der Griechen im Urteil des Paulus*, by A. von Schlatter. *TLZ* 62 (1937): 415–17.

Jipp, Joshua. *Saved by Faith and Hospitality*. Grand Rapids: Eerdmans, 2017.

Johnson, A. F., ed. *How I Changed My Mind about Women in Leadership: Compelling Stories from Prominent Evangelicals*. Grand Rapids: Zondervan, 2010.

Johnson, Ian. *The Souls of China: The Return of Religion after Mao*. New York: Pantheon, 2017.

Johnson, T., G. Zurlo, A. Hickman, and P. Crossing. "Christianity 2017: Five Hundred Years of Protestant Christianity." *IBMR* 41.1 (2017): 41–52.

Keener, C. *The IVP Bible Background Commentary*. 2nd ed. Downers Grove, IL: IVP Academic, 2014.

———. *Miracles: The Credibility of the New Testament Accounts*. 2 vols. Grand Rapids: Baker Academic, 2011.

Kiesling, E. C. "On War without the Fog." *Military Review* 81.5 (2001): 85–87.

Kim, S. *Paul and the New Perspective: Second Thoughts on the Origin of Paul's Gospel*. Grand Rapids: Eerdmans, 2002.

Klinker–De Klerck, M. "Dissertation and Monograph Summary." *Journal for the Study of Paul and His Letters* 3.2 (2013): 263–67.

———. "The Pastoral Epistles: Authentic Pauline Writings." *EJT* 17.2 (2008): 101–8.

Knight, G. W., III. *The Faithful Sayings in the Pastoral Letters*. Grand Rapids: Baker Books, 1979.

Knopf, R. Review of *Die Briefe an die Thessalonicher, Philipper, Timotheus und Titus*, by A. Schlatter. Theologische Rundschau 9 (1906): 62.

Köstenberger, A. "Theodor Zahn, Adolf Harnack, and Adolf Schlatter." Pages 163–210 in *Prevailing Methods before 1980*, vol. 1 of *Pillars in the History of Biblical Interpretation*. Edited by S. Porter and S. Adams. Eugene, OR: Pickwick, 2016.

Köstenberger, A., and Raymond Bouchoc. *The Book Study Concordance of the Greek New Testament*. Nashville: B&H, 2003.

Köstenberger, A., L. Kellum, and C. Quarles. *The Cradle, the Cross, and the Crown: An Introduction to the New Testament*. 2nd ed. Nashville: B&H Academic, 2017.

Köstenberger, A., and M. Kruger. *The Heresy of Orthodoxy: How Contemporary Culture's Fascination with Diversity Has Reshaped Our Understanding*. Wheaton, IL: Crossway, 2010.

Köstenberger, A., and T. R. Schreiner, eds. *Women in the Church: A Fresh Analysis of 1 Timothy 2:9–15*. 2nd. ed. (Grand Rapids: Baker Books, 2005); 3rd ed. (Wheaton, IL: Crossway, 2016).

Köstenberger, A., T. R. Schreiner, and H. S. Baldwin, eds. *Women in the Church: A Fresh Analysis of 1 Timothy 2:9–15*. Grand Rapids: Baker Books, 1995.

Köstenberger, A., and T. Wilder, eds. *Entrusted with the Gospel: Paul's Theology in the Pastoral Epistles*. Nashville: B&H, 2010.

Köstenberger, M. E. *Jesus and the Feminists: Who Do They Say That He Is?* Wheaton, IL: Crossway, 2008.

Kruger, M. "First Timothy 5:18 and Early Canon Consciousness: Reconsidering a Problematic Text." Pages 680–700 in *The Language and Literature of the New Testament: Essays in Honour of Stanley E. Porter's Sixtieth Birthday*. Edited by L. Dow, C. Evans, and A. Pitts. Leiden: Brill, 2017.

———. *The Question of Canon: Challenging the Status Quo in the New Testament Debate*. Downers Grove, IL: IVP Academic, 2013.

Kuligin, V. *Snubbing God: The High Cost of Rejecting God's Created Order*. Wooster, OH: Weaver Book Company, 2017.

Legaspi, M. *The Death of Scripture and the Rise of Biblical Studies*. OSHT. Oxford: Oxford University Press, 2010.

Levine, Amy-Jill, ed., with M. Blickenstaff. *A Feminist Companion to the Deutero-Pauline Epistles*. Cleveland: Pilgrim Press, 2003.

Levine, L. I. *The Ancient Synagogue: The First Thousand Years*. New Haven: Yale University Press, 2005.

Licona, M. *The Resurrection of Jesus: A New Historiographical Approach*. Downers Grove, IL: IVP Academic, 2010.

Linnemann, E. *Biblical Criticism on Trial: How Scientific Is "Scientific Theology"?* Translated by R. Yarbrough. Grand Rapids: Kregel, 2001.

Lohr, J. "He Identified with the Lowly and Became a Slave to All: Paul's Tentmaking as a Strategy for Mission." *CurTM* 34.3 (2007): 179–87.

Lucas, S. *For a Continuing Church: The Roots of the Presbyterian Church in America*. Phillipsburg, NJ: P&R, 2015.

Lütgert, W. *Die Irrlehrer der Pastoralbriefe*. BFCT 13.3. Gütersloh: Bertelsmann, 1909.

Luther, Martin. *Luther's Works*. Vol. 28: *Commentaries on 1 Corinthians 7, 1 Corinthians 15, Lectures on 1 Timothy*. Edited by H. C. Oswald. St. Louis: Concordia, 1973.

Mangold, W. *Die Irrlehrer der Pastoralbriefe*. Marburg: Elwert'sche Universitäts-Buchhandlung, 1856.

Mare, H. "The Pauline Work Ethic." Pages 357–69 in *New Dimensions in New Testament Study*. Edited by R. N. Longenecker and M. C. Tenney. Grand Rapids: Zondervan, 1974.

Markschies, C. *Hellenisierung des Christentums: Sinn und Unsinn einer historischen Deutungskategorie*. Forum Theologische Literaturzeitung 25. Leipzig: Evangelische Verlagsanstalt, 2012.

Marshall, I. H. "The Pastoral Epistles in Recent Study." Pages 268–312 in *Entrusted with the Gospel*. Edited by A. J. Köstenberger and T. L. Wilder. Nashville: B&H Academic, 2010.

Martin, D. *Biblical Truths*. New Haven: Yale University Press, 2017.

Mathews, A. P. *Preaching That Speaks to Women*. Grand Rapids: Baker Academic, 2003.

McClymond, Michael J. *The Devil's Redemption: A New History and Interpretation of Christian Universalism*, 2 vols. Grand Rapids: Baker Academic, 2018.

McRay, J. *Archaeology and the New Testament*. Grand Rapids: Baker Books, 1991.

Metzger, B. M. *A Textual Commentary on the Greek New Testament*. London: United Bible Societies, 1975.

———, ed. *A Textual Commentary on the Greek New Testament*. 2nd ed. Stuttgart: Deutsche Bibelgesellschaft, 1994.

Mitchell, M. "John Chrysostom," Pages 571–77 in *Dictionary of Major Bible Interpreters*. Edited by D. McKim. Downers Grove, IL: IVP Academic, 2007.

Moo, D. J. *We Still Don't Get It: Evangelicals and Biblical Translation Fifty Years after James Barr*. Louisville: Evangelical Theological Society, 2014.

Morgan, C., and R. Peterson, eds. *Fallen: A Theology of Sin*. Wheaton, IL: Crossway, 2013.

Morgan, J. "Global Trends and the North American Church in Mission: Discovering the Church's Role in the Twenty-First Century." *International Bulletin of Mission Research* 40.4 (2016): 325–38.

Morris, L. *The Apostolic Preaching of the Cross.* 3d ed. Grand Rapids: Eerdmans, 1965.

Moss, C. *The Myth of Persecution: How Early Christians Invented a Story of Martyrdom.* San Francisco: HarperOne, 2013.

Moule, C. F. D. *An Idiom Book of New Testament Greek.* 2nd ed. Cambridge: Cambridge University Press, 1994.

Murray, I. H. *Jonathan Edwards: A New Biography.* Edinburgh: Banner of Truth Trust, 1987.

Mutschler, B. *Glaube in den Pastoralbriefen: Pistis als Mitte christlicher Existenz.* WUNT 256. Tübingen: Mohr Siebeck, 2010.

Naselli, A. *From Typology to Doxology: Paul's Use of Isaiah and Job in Romans 11:34–35.* Eugene, OR: Pickwick, 2012.

Naselli, A., and J. Crowley. *Conscience: What It Is, How to Train It, and Loving Those Who Differ.* Wheaton, IL: Crossway, 2016.

Neuer, W. *Adolf Schlatter: A Biography of Germany's Premier Biblical Theologian.* Translated by R. Yarbrough. Grand Rapids: Baker Books, 1995.

———. *Adolf Schlatter: Ein Leben für Theologie und Kirche.* Stuttgart: Calwer, 1996.

Noll, M. *From Every Tribe and Nation: A Historian's Discovery of the Global Christian Story.* Grand Rapids: Baker Academic, 2014.

———. *The New Shape of World Christianity.* Downers Grove, IL: InterVarsity Press, 2009.

Noll, M., and C. Nystrom. *Clouds of Witnesses: Christian Voices from Africa and Asia.* Downers Grove, IL: IVP Books, 2011.

Oden, T. C. *A Change of Heart: A Personal and Theological Memoir.* Downers Grove, IL: IVP Academic, 2014.

———. *Ministry through Word and Sacrament.* New York: Crossroad, 1989.

Offutt, S. *New Centers of Global Evangelicalism in Latin America and Africa.* Cambridge: Cambridge University Press, 2015.

Ortlund, D. *Zeal without Knowledge: The Concept of Zeal in Romans 10, Galatians 1, and Philippians 3.* LNTS 472. London: Bloomsbury, 2012.

Osten-Sacken, T. von der, and T. Uwer. "Is Female Genital Mutilation an Islamic Problem?" *Middle East Quarterly* 14.1 (2007): 29–36.

Pao, D. "Let No One Despise Your Youth: Church and the World in the Pastoral Epistles." *JETS* 57.4 (2014): 743–55.

———. *Thanksgiving: An Investigation of a Pauline Theme.* NSBT 13. Leicester: Apollos, 2002.

Park, M. Sydney. *Submission within the Godhead and the Church in the Epistle to the Philippians.* LNTS 361. London: T&T Clark, 2007.

Payne, P. B. *Man and Woman, One in Christ.* Grand Rapids: Zondervan, 2009.

Peacore, L. D. *The Role of Women's Experience in Feminist Theologies of Atonement.* Eugene, OR: Pickwick, 2010.

Pennington, J. *The Sermon on the Mount and Human Flourishing: A Theological Commentary.* Grand Rapids: Baker Academic, 2017.

Perry, G. R. "Phoebe of Cenchreae and 'Women' of Ephesus: 'Deacons' in the Earliest Churches." *Presb* 36.1 (2010): 9–36.

Pietersma, A. *The Apocryphon of Jannes and Jambres the Magicians.* RGRW. Leiden: Brill, 1994.

Pitts, A., and J. Tyra, "Exploring Linguistic Variation in an Ancient Greek Single-Source

Corpus: A Register Design Analysis of Josephus and Pauline Pseudonymity." Pages 257–83 in *The Language and Literature of the New Testament: Essays in Honour of Stanley E. Porter's Sixtieth Birthday.* Edited by L. Dow, C. Evans, and A. Pitts. Leiden: Brill, 2017.

Porter, S. E. *The Apostle Paul: His Life, Thought, and Ideas.* Grand Rapids: Eerdmans, 2016.

———. "Family in the Epistles." Pages 148–66 in *Family in the Bible: Exploring Customs, Culture, and Context.* Edited by R. S. Hess and M. D. Carroll R. Grand Rapids: Baker Academic, 2003.

———. *Linguistic Analysis of the Greek New Testament.* Grand Rapids: Baker Academic, 2015.

———. *Verbal Aspect in the Greek of the New Testament, with Reference to Tense and Mood.* New York: Peter Lang, 1989, 1993.

———. "What Does It Mean to Be 'Saved by Childbirth' (1 Timothy 2.15)?" *JSNT* 49 (1993): 87–102.

———. *When Paul Met Jesus: How an Idea Got Lost in History.* Cambridge: Cambridge University Press, 2016.

Poythress, V. S. "The Meaning of μάλιστα in 2 Timothy 4:13 and Related Verses," *JTS* 53 (2002): 523–32.

Pryse, A. *Hidden Truth.* Morrisville, NC: Lulu Publishing Services, 2016.

Qureshi, N. *No God but One: Allah or Jesus?* Grand Rapids: Zondervan, 2016.

Raichur, A. *Biblical Attitudes toward Work.* Rev. ed. Karnataka, India: All Peoples Church & World Outreach, 2007.

Rainey, A. F., and R. S. Notley. *Carta's New Century Handbook and Atlas of the Bible.* Jerusalem: Carta, 2007.

Reiser, M. "Erziehung durch Gnade: Eine Betrachtung zu Titus 2,11–14." *Erbe und Auftrag* 69 (1993): 443–49.

Rengstorf, K. Review of *Die Kirche der Griechen im Urteil des Paulus*, by A. Schlatter. *Pastoralblätter für Predigt, Seelsorge und kirchliche Unterweisung* 79 (1936/37): 636–37.

Riesner, R. *Paul's Early Period: Chronology, Mission Strategy, Theology.* Translated by D. Stott. Grand Rapids: Eerdmans, 1998.

Ripkin, N., with G. Lewis. *The Insanity of God.* Nashville: B&H, 2013.

Robinson, J. *Redating the New Testament.* Philadelphia: Westminster, 1976.

Salas, R. C. "A Christian Feminist Hermeneutics of the Bible." Pages 161–78 in *Feminist Biblical Studies in the Twentieth Century.* Edited by E. S. Fiorenza. Atlanta: SBL, 2014.

Sanders, E. P. *Paul.* Minneapolis: Fortress, 2015.

Sandom, C. *Different by Design: God's Blueprint for Men and Women.* Fearn, Ross-shire, Scotland: Christian Focus, 2012.

Sanneh, L. "Global Christianity and the Re-education of the West." *ChrCent,* July 19–26, 1995, 715–18.

———. *Summoned from the Margin: Homecoming of an African.* Grand Rapids: Eerdmans, 2012.

Scharf, G. *Let the Earth Hear His Voice: Strategies for Overcoming Bottlenecks in Preaching God's Word.* Philipsburg, NJ: P&R, 2015.

Schlatter, A. *Einführung in die Theologie.* Edited by Werner Neuer. Stuttgart: Calwer, 2013.

———. *Einleitung in die Bibel.* 4th ed. Stuttgart: Calwer, 1923.

Schmeller, T. *Der zweite Brief an die Korinther: 2 Kor 7,5–13,13).* EKKNT 8/2. Neukirchen-Vluyn: Neukirchener Theologie, 2015.

Schnabel, E. J. "The Muratorian Fragment: The State of Research." *JETS* 57.2 (2014): 231–64.

———. *Paul and the Early Church.* Vol. 2 of *Early Christian Mission.* Downers Grove, IL: InterVarsity Press, 2004.

———. *Paul the Missionary: Realities, Strategies, and Methods.* Downers Grove, IL: IVP Academic, 2008.

———. "Paul, Timothy, and Titus: The Assumption of a Pseudonymous Author and of Pseudonymous Recipients in the Light of Literary, Theological, and Historical Evidence." Pages 383–403 in *Do Historical Matters Matter to Faith?* Edited by J. Hoffmeier and D. Magary. Wheaton, IL: Crossway, 2012.

Schnelle, U. *Apostle Paul: His Life and Theology.* Translated by M. Eugene Boring. Grand Rapids: Baker Academic, 2005.

———. *The History and Theology of the New Testament Writings.* Translated by M. Boring. Minneapolis: Fortress, 1998.

Schottroff, L., and M. Wacker, eds. *Feminist Biblical Interpretation: A Compendium of Critical Commentary on the Books of the Bible and Related Literature.* Grand Rapids: Eerdmans, 2012.

Schreiner, T. R. "An Interpretation of 1 Timothy 2:9–15: A Dialogue with Scholarship." Pages 164–225 in Köstenberger and Schreiner, *Women in the Church,* 3rd ed.

———. *Interpreting the Pauline Epistles.* 2nd ed. Grand Rapids: Baker Academic, 2011.

———. *New Testament Theology.* Grand Rapids: Baker Academic, 2008.

Schreiner, T. R., and A. B. Caneday. *The Race Set before Us: A Biblical Theology of Perseverance and Assurance.* Downers Grove, IL: InterVarsity Press, 2001.

Seccombe, D. *The King of God's Kingdom.* Milton Keynes: Paternoster, 2002.

Severance, D. L. *Feminine Threads: Women in the Tapestry of Christian History.* Fearn, Ross-shire, Scotland: Christian Focus, 2011.

———. *Her-Story: 366 Devotions from Twenty-One Centuries of the Christian Church.* Fearn, Ross-shire, Scotland: Christian Focus, 2016.

Shortt, R. *Christianophobia: A Faith under Attack.* Grand Rapids: Eerdmans, 2012.

Siebenthal, H. V. *Griechische Grammatik zum Neuen Testament.* Gießen: Brunnen, 2011.

Simut, C. *F. C. Baur's Synthesis of Böhme and Hegel: Redefining Christian Theology as a Gnostic Philosophy of Religion.* Leiden: Brill, 2015.

Smith, C. S. *God's Good Design: What the Bible Really Says about Men and Women.* Kingsford, NSW, Australia: Matthias Media, 2012.

———. *Pauline Communities as "Scholastic Communities": A Study of the Vocabulary of "Teaching" in 1 Corinthians, 1 and 2 Timothy, and Titus.* WUNT 2.335. Tübingen: Mohr Siebeck, 2012.

Sowell, T. "The Real History of Slavery." Pages 111–69 in *Black Rednecks and White Liberals.* San Francisco: Encounter Books, 2005.

Still, T. "Did Paul Loathe Manual Labor? Revisiting the Work of Ronald F. Hock on the Apostle's Tentmaking and Social Class." *JBL* 125.4 (2006): 781–95.

Stott, J. R. W. *The Message of 1 Timothy and Titus: Guard the Truth.* The Bible Speaks Today. Downers Grove, IL: InterVarsity Press, 1996.

Stout, S. *Preach the Word: A Pauline Theology of Preaching Based on 2 Timothy 4:1–5.* Eugene, OR: Pickwick, 2014.

Strachan, O., and K. Idleman. *Risky Gospel: Abandon Fear and Build Something Awesome.* Nashville: Nelson, 2013.

Strachan, O., and D. A. Sweeney. *Jonathan Edwards: Lover of God.* Chicago: Moody, 2010.

Sunquist, S. *The Unexpected Christian Century: The Reversal and Transformation of Global Christianity, 1900–2000.* Grand Rapids: Baker Academic, 2015.

Sweeney, D. A. *Jonathan Edwards and the Ministry of the Word.* Downers Grove, IL: IVP Academic, 2009.

Swinson, L. T. *What Is Scripture? Paul's Use of Graphe in the Letters to Timothy.* Eugene, OR: Wipf & Stock, 2014.

Thompson, J. *Pastoral Ministry according to Paul: A Biblical Vision.* Grand Rapids: Baker Academic, 2006.

Towner, P. H. *The Goal of Our Instruction.* JSNTSup 34. Sheffield: Sheffield Academic, 1989.

Tracy, S. "What Does 'Submit in Everything' Really Mean? The Nature and Scope of Marital Submission." *TJ* 29.2 (2008): 285–312.

Treggiari, S. "Marriage and Family in Roman Society." Pages 132–82 in *Marriage and Family in the Biblical World.* Edited by K. Campbell. Downers Grove, IL: InterVarsity Press, 2003.

Turcan, R. *The Cults of the Roman Empire.* Translated by A. Nevill. Oxford: Blackwell, 1996.

Turner, N. *Syntax.* Vol. 3 of *A Grammar of New Testament Greek.* Edinburgh: T&T Clark, 1963.

Verbrugge, V., and K. Krell. *Paul and Money: A Biblical and Theological Analysis of the Apostle's Teachings and Practices.* Grand Rapids: Zondervan, 2015.

Via, D. O., and R. A. J. Gagnon. *Homosexuality and the Bible: Two Views.* Minneapolis: Fortress, 2003.

Wallace, D. B. *Granville Sharp's Canon and Its Kin.* New York: Peter Lang, 2009.

———. *Greek Grammar beyond the Basics.* Grand Rapids: Zondervan 1996.

———, ed. *Revisiting the Corruption of the New Testament.* Grand Rapids: Kregel, 2011.

Walls, A., and C. Ross, eds. *Mission in the Twenty-First Century: Exploring the Five Marks of Global Mission.* Maryknoll, NY: Orbis Books, 2008.

Walton, S. Review of *Pauline Communities as "Scholastic Communities": A Study of the Vocabulary of "Teaching" in 1 Corinthians, 1 and 2 Timothy, and Titus,* by C. S. Smith. RBL 10 (2014).

Ware, T. *The Orthodox Church.* London: Penguin Books, 1997.

Wells, S. "The Banality of Pastoral Failure." *ChrCent,* June 25, 2014, 35.

Wenham, D. *Paul: Follower of Jesus or Founder of Christianity?* Grand Rapids: Eerdmans, 1995.

Weymouth, R. "The Christ-Story of Philippians 2:6–11." PhD diss., University of Otago, Dunedin, New Zealand, 2015.

Wilckens, U. *Kritik der Bibelkritik.* Neukirchen-Vluyn: Neukirchener Theologie, 2012.

Williams, R. H. *Stewards, Prophets, Keepers of the Word: Leadership in the Early Church.* Peabody, MA: Hendrickson, 2006.

Wilson, M. *Biblical Turkey: A Guide to the Jewish and Christian Sites of Asia Minor.* Istanbul: Ege, 2010.

Winter, B. *After Paul Left Corinth: The Influence of Secular Ethics and Social Change.* Grand Rapids: Eerdmans 2001.

———. "The 'New' Roman Wife and 1 Timothy 2:9–15: The Search for a *Sitz im Leben.*" *TynBul* 51.2 (2000): 285–94.

———. *Roman Wives, Roman Widows: The Appearance of New Women and the Pauline Communities.* Grand Rapids: Eerdmans, 2003.

Witherington, B., III. *The Paul Quest: The Renewed Search for the Jew of Tarsus.* Downers Grove, IL: InterVarsity Press, 1998.

Wolters, A. "ΑΥΘΕΝΤΗΣ and Its Cognates in Biblical Greek." *JETS* 52.4 (2009): 719–29.

———. "An Early Parallel of Αὐθεντεῖν." *JETS* 54.4 (2011): 673–84.

Wright, G. E. *The God Who Acts: Biblical Theology as Recital.* London: SCM, 1952.

Wright, N. T. *The Day the Revolution Began: Reconsidering the Meaning of Jesus' Resurrection.* New York: HarperOne, 2016.

———. *Paul and His Recent Interpreters.* Minneapolis: Fortress, 2015.

———. *Paul and the Faithfulness of God.* 2 vols. London: SPCK, 2013.

———. *The Resurrection of the Son of God.* Minneapolis: Fortress, 2003.

Yarbrough, R. "Adam in the New Testament." Pages 33–52 in *Adam, the Fall, and Original Sin.* Edited by H. Madueme and M. Reeves. Grand Rapids: Baker Academic, 2014.

———. "Familiar Paths and a Fresh Matrix." Pages 227–77 in Köstenberger and Schreiner, *Women in the Church*, 3rd ed.

———. "The Kingdom of God in the New Testament: Mark through the Epistles." Pages 125–51 in *The Kingdom of God.* Edited by C. Morgan and R. Peterson. Wheaton, IL: Crossway, 2012.

———. "Paul and Salvation History." Pages 297–342 in *The Paradoxes of Paul.* Edited by D. A. Carson, P. T. O'Brien, and M. A. Seifrid. Vol. 2 of *Justification and Variegated Nomism.* Tübingen: Mohr Siebeck, 2004), 297–342.

———. Review of *Miracles: The Credibility of the New Testament Accounts*, by C. Keener. JETS 55.4 (2012): 878–82.

———. *The Salvation Historical Fallacy? Reassessing the History of New Testament Theology.* History of Interpretation 2. Leiden: Deo, 2004.

———. "Schlatter on the Pastorals: Mission in the Academy." Pages 295–316 in *New Testament Theology in Light of the Church's Mission: Essays in Honor of I. Howard Marshall.* Edited by J. Laansma, G. Osborne, and R. Van Neste. Eugene, OR: Wipf & Stock, 2011.

Yiwu, L. *God Is Red: The Secret Story of How Christianity Survived and Flourished in Communist China.* Translated by Wenguang Huang. New York: HarperOne, 2011.

Young, F. *The Theology of the Pastoral Epistles.* NTT. Cambridge: Cambridge University Press, 1994.

Zamfir, K. *Men and Women in the Household of God: A Contextual Approach to Roles and Ministries in the Pastoral Epistles.* NTOA/SUNT 103.Göttingen: Vandenhoeck & Ruprecht, 2013.

Introduction

I. THE PASTORAL HERITAGE AND THE PASTORAL EPISTLES: EIGHT THESES

Serious readers of the Pastoral Epistles (hereafter PE) often study them for insight into the pastoral task. Each of the three PE presents itself as counsel to church leaders serving in a pastoral or pastoral oversight capacity. In each, "a 'shepherd' writes to 'shepherds' and addresses them squarely in their ecclesial shepherd capacity."[1] But what is a pastor? What exactly does Paul (authorship and other questions of introduction will be discussed below) hope to encourage in his original readers? One commentator notes, "The Pastorals contain valuable counsel not found elsewhere in the New Testament on how to administer and teach in the church."[2]

While the pastoral task varies with times, locations, confessions, persons, and other variables, that same commentator, Thomas Oden (1931–2016), has helpfully distilled eight conclusions on the care of souls in what he calls "the classical pastoral literature."[3] His observations are all the more trenchant in light of his personal story,[4] which in this respect mirrors that of the apostle Paul. Oden's academic convictions and religious views were at odds with Scripture and historic Christian teaching until well into his teaching career. But then he had a drastic change of heart. Like Paul, he realized he was resisting and in fact opposing the truth as revealed by the very God he claimed to serve. He began to rethink and restudy the primary sources of Christian testimony

1. Brox, 9. Translations of German works in this commentary are mine unless otherwise noted.

2. Oden, 16.

3. Thomas Oden, *Ministry through Word and Sacrament* (New York: Crossroad, 1989). Oden focuses on patristic, medieval, and Reformation sources, noting that in more recent times many of the classical texts on pastoral care "have fallen into disuse" (1).

4. See Thomas Oden, *A Change of Heart: A Personal and Theological Memoir* (Downers Grove, IL: IVP Academic, 2014).

through the centuries, beginning with Scripture and extending into the church fathers and beyond. With the aid of this altered vision, Oden surveyed church history to rethink the rudiments of pastoral care.

The eight rubrics at which Oden arrived[5] are brought into dialogue below with the PE as a means of giving contour to what this commentary finds in the PE and what the PE, for their part, have contributed over the centuries (and still offer today) in terms of the instruction and exhortation of pastoral leaders and workers.[6] Of course pastors in classical pastoral ministry have drawn from the whole of the Bible, not just or even primarily the PE. And the PE do not address all eight of Oden's conclusions with equal thoroughness. Moreover, as will be argued below, the PE are less about ministry than they are about God himself and Christ, who made and makes him known. There are points of difference and tensions between Paul's own original convictions and testimony in the PE, the initial receptions of the PE by Timothy at Ephesus and Titus on Crete, and the appropriation of those writings in subsequent eras and locales of ecclesial history. Still, Oden's conclusions furnish a structure for thinking of the pastoral heritage in a variegated yet unified manner and for identifying ways the PE interface with it, whether by way of confirmation or by way of contrast. Oden's rubrics also serve to remind of the breadth of the duties entrusted to pastors and pastoral workers. These responsibilities involve far more than the most obvious and visible action of presiding over a weekly public meeting and preaching.

1. "Pastors owe a duty not only to care for the flock, but to care for themselves . . . in the sense of feeding and nurturing one's own soul." Paul's letters to Timothy are explicit that Timothy must give attention to his own beliefs and behaviors. "Watch your life and doctrine closely," Paul writes. "Persevere in them, because if you do, you will save both yourself and your hearers" (1 Tim 4:16).[7] Desultory or occasional close attention is insufficient: "Be diligent in these matters; give yourself wholly to them, so that everyone may see your progress" (1 Tim 4:15). Stagnation or a poor example is to be avoided. Other examples of Paul's concern that Timothy not be oblivious to his own needs and duties are abundant:

> Train yourself to be godly. (1 Tim 4:7)
>
> Devote yourself to the public reading of Scripture, to preaching and to teaching. (1 Tim 4:13)

5. Conveniently summarized in Oden's *Ministry through Word and Sacrament*, 226–27.

6. In the past, some (e.g., Ernst Käsemann) have viewed early church organization as spontaneous and charismatic, not organized and to an extent hierarchical, as implied in the PE. For a strong rebuttal of this view, see R. Y. K. Fung, "Charismatic versus Organized Ministry? An Examination of an Alleged Antithesis," *EvQ* 52 (1980): 195–214, esp. 206–10 ("The Ministry in the Pastorals").

7. Unless otherwise noted, all biblical quotations in this commentary are from NIV (2011).

Keep yourself pure. (1 Tim 5:22)

Present yourself to God as one approved. (2 Tim 2:15)

Paul's relationship with Titus as reflected in the epistle to him is not as transparently personal as his tie with Timothy. There could be many reasons for this difference, from Paul's mood when he wrote, to the chemistry between Paul and Timothy that may not have been present vis-à-vis Titus at the times of composition of the respective letters, to Paul's ties with Lois and Eunice (2 Tim 1:5), which may have created a soft spot in his heart for their grandson and son Timothy, to the brevity (for whatever reason) of Paul's letter to Titus compared with the pair of canonical letters to Timothy, to Titus's strength of character—perhaps he was a more seasoned and stable Pauline coworker and did not attract or need the seemingly more personally targeted counsel that 1–2 Timothy contain.

Still, at the center of Titus is Paul's directive, "In everything set [the young men] an example by doing what is good. In your teaching show integrity, seriousness and soundness of speech that cannot be condemned" (2:7–8). Titus is Paul's "true son" (1:4), in whom Paul placed great confidence to identify leaders and defend the faith in a challenging environment (ch. 1), to admonish the faithful in view of Christ's appearing (ch. 2), and to stress high and holy truths "so that those who have trusted in God may be careful to devote themselves to doing what is good" (3:8). Paul assumed that Titus fully shared and deeply understood the heart and soul of Paul's gospel conviction and missiological passion. If he expends fewer words urging care for himself than he wrote to Timothy, it is probably not because he felt this was unimportant for Titus but because he did not see in Titus the same vacillation and angst-unto-tears (see 2 Tim 1:4) that he observed in Timothy. Or perhaps conditions on Crete were not tempting Titus to cut and run like Timothy may have felt pressured to do at Ephesus (1 Tim 1:3). Paul's letter itself is a means for Titus to care for himself in the sense of feeding and nurturing his own soul. It was no doubt avidly pored over by Titus to extract from it all he could for that purpose—and perhaps commended, directly or indirectly, to congregations he oversaw as well.

Support glimpsed in the PE for Oden's call for pastoral self-care, however, should not overshadow a countervailing truth: Paul did not practice or envision a pastoral self-understanding that may be common in a Western setting saturated in what has been called expressive individualism.[8] Yes, Titus and Timothy should be self-aware before God, exercising vocational, spir-

8. See R. N. Bellah et al., *Habits of the Heart: Individualism and Commitment in American Life*, 3rd ed. (Oakland: University of California Press, 2007).

itual, and moral responsibility. But this self-awareness does not mean self-indulgence, much less self-centeredness, both acute temptations in a sensual and narcissistic age. The pastoral role as Paul describes it is not a safe space for therapeutic self-actualization but a demanding and sometimes bruising vocation. Oden's "feeding and nurturing one's own soul" should be seen in the light of Paul's example of often forgoing his own rights, becoming a servant of all, exercising studied self-control, and subjugating his own body lest selfish interests cancel the integrity of his own preaching (1 Cor 9:15, 19, 25–27; see his appeal to Timothy in 2 Tim 2:3: "Share [with Paul] in suffering as a good soldier of Christ Jesus").

2. "Pastoral care occurs not only in individuated conversation but also through preaching, a public task intrinsic to the care of souls." The PE may be thought of as a form of "individuated conversation" from Paul to a pair of coworkers. They may be appreciated as such. But they reflect the existence and aim at the refinement of a community brought into being and sustained by kerygmatic[9] and didactic[10] proclamation.

The elaborate opening verses of Titus state programmatically that God's eternal redemptive promises were announced through Paul's preaching; they were "at his appointed season . . . brought to light through the preaching entrusted to me by the command of God our Savior" (1:3). The ecclesial activity Titus oversees will in part be a continuation of that kerygmatic ministry. This focus on preaching is confirmed by how the précis of Titus's duties to members of the church (ch. 2) is bookended by what he is to speak (see 2:1, 15; NIV "teach," Gk. *lalei*, "say, speak"). This speaking was not limited to a formal activity called preaching, but preaching was surely a primary means of Titus achieving the goals Paul sets for him.

Paul summarizes his aims for Timothy with the command that he "preach the word; be ready in season and out of season; reprove, rebuke, and exhort, with complete patience and teaching" (2 Tim 4:2). These commands and counsel not only prescribe preaching but describe its optimal frequency (continuous), key intents (reproof, rebuke, and exhortation), and delivery requirements (through patience and instruction). Timothy had grown up hearing preaching in the synagogue. He had observed Paul and others preaching and had engaged in preaching for years. Neither epistle to Timo-

9. That is, the good news of Jesus Christ was heralded (Gk. *kērygma*, what is preached, heralded).

10. That is, early Christianity was not merely a spiritual (charismatic) religious or social movement but an enterprise centered on teaching and learning. See Claire S. Smith, *Pauline Communities as "Scholastic Communities": A Study of the Vocabulary of "Teaching" in 1 Corinthians, 1 and 2 Timothy, and Titus*, WUNT 2.335 (Tübingen: Mohr Siebeck, 2012). A didactic (related to Gk. *didaskō*, "I teach") stress is consistent with the gospel picture of Jesus, who first formed a community of "disciples" (learners) nurtured by his teaching (*didachē*).

thy is or should be expected to constitute a homiletics guide. But Christian assemblies were led by those "whose work is preaching and teaching" (1 Tim 5:17). Like the Shema, which calls God's people to "hear" (Deut 6:4), Paul affirms that saving faith arises from listening to a word proclaimed (Rom 10:17; Gal 3:2, 5). Accordingly, Paul writes, "Until I come, devote yourself to the public reading of Scripture, to preaching and to teaching" (1 Tim 4:13). Even if the PE are not a homiletics guide, they are certainly a motivational refresher in the imperative and substance of sound and sustainable pastoral proclamation.

3. "Soul care occurs within a community whose primary corporate act is the praise of God's care." This worshiping body provides the necessary matrix for individuals to receive the Christian nurture, encouragement, and instruction they require. Since the PE are not a book of church order, they do not prescribe formal corporate activities (which surely became a fixture in the Pauline churches) as does, for example, the Didache, with its instructions on baptism (ch. 7), fasting (ch. 8), the Eucharist (ch. 9), formal prayers of thanksgiving (ch. 10), and assembly for worship (ch. 14). Still, the PE are suffused with a spirit of praise, its close cousin gratitude, also with pastoral care and worship, all with a view toward building up Christ's body.

The second person plural (not sing.) closing of all three PE is a reminder that, even in writing to individuals, Paul has the whole church in mind (1 Tim 6:21; 2 Tim 4:22; Titus 3:15). Paul's overt doxologies (1 Tim 1:17; 6:16; 2 Tim 4:18) give formal expression to the reverent corporate regard for God intrinsic to the early church's roots in the synagogue (where praise in the form of the Psalms was sung) and in the Scriptures, hallowed among Jesus and his followers. That the worshiping community, the church, is at the core of Paul's PE counsel is clear from references to *ekklēsia* (congregation, fellowship, church) in 1 Timothy (see 3:5, 15; 5:16).[11] When Paul writes Titus to "appoint elders in every town" (1:5), this action is for leadership in Christian assemblies.

In short, the gospel mandate embraced by Paul with missionary zeal[12] translated into an ecclesial commission for those building on the foundation Paul established (see 1 Cor 3:10). The PE, while written to individuals, are written for the flourishing of churches. Believers who benefit most from the PE are those who accept and develop their identity not only as individual elements (such as sodium, a highly reactive metal, or chlorine, a toxic gas in high concentrations) but as a united compound (such as sodium chloride, or common table salt).

11. NIV contains "church" also in 1 Tim 5:17, but there it is inferred from the context.

12. See Eckhard Schnabel, *Paul the Missionary: Realities, Strategies, and Methods* (Downers Grove, IL: IVP Academic, 2008); Peter Bolt and Mark Thompson, eds., *The Gospel to the Nations: Perspectives on Paul's Mission: FS Peter O'Brien* (Leicester: Apollos, 2000).

4. "Soul care is mediated powerfully through sacramental actions, the first of which is the ministry of beginnings—baptism." Of Oden's eight conclusions pertaining to classical pastoral literature and care, this is one of two with marginal explicit grounding in the PE. Adolf Schlatter wrote that one of the most important themes of church-historical study is "the difference between biblical and ecclesial Christianity."[13] It is possible that sacramental convictions that develop in church history do not always find secure grounding in early church doctrine and practice.

Yet, in broad terms the PE document a community unquestionably defined in part by acts such as baptism, which was in any case prescribed by Jesus (Matt 28:19–20) and practiced in the early church (mentioned over two dozen times in Acts). Paul was baptized (Acts 9:18). Timothy as a "disciple" (Acts 16:1) can be assumed to have been baptized, along with others who had become "disciples" in Lystra (Acts 14:30; Paul may refer to the beginnings of Timothy's faith in 1 Tim 1:18; 2 Tim 1:6). There would not have been clusters of Christians in Ephesus (Timothy's domain) or Crete (Titus's field of labor) had people not believed the gospel and been baptized.[14] Whether this act was "sacramental" depends on definitions and need not be debated here. What can be affirmed is that the kinds of understandings and practices addressed in the Didache (see Oden's thesis 3 above), which included baptism and other ritual acts, can be attested in New Testament documents as a whole and were surely factors, in some form or other, in the Ephesian and Cretan churches. Pastors reading the PE today will often find at least indirect insight into their ecclesial practices such as baptism, the theology that undergirds it, and the spirituality and ethical responses that characterize the baptized life. Scholarly scrutiny of baptism in the early Christian era references the PE at over thirty places.[15]

The PE also offer salutary correction to later church custom. For example, when the church becomes so preoccupied with itself that it loses Pauline theocentricity (see sec. II. below), or when its own concerns and autonomy supplant the authority of Christ in Scripture, whom the church purports to confess,[16]

13. Adolf Schlatter, *Einführung in die Theologie*, ed. Werner Neuer (Stuttgart: Calwer, 2013), 137.

14. For baptism at the founding of the church in Ephesus, see Acts 19:5.

15. See index (vol. 3) of D. Hellholm, T. Vegge, Ø. Norderval, and C. Hellholm, eds., *Ablution, Initiation, and Baptism: Late Antiquity, Early Judaism, and Early Christianity*, 3 vols. (Berlin: de Gruyter, 2011).

16. Oden (16) addresses this corrective function when commenting on the importance of Scripture for theological reflection and church practice today: "It may trouble some to take this [i.e., "how the Spirit is addressing us through the Scripture"] as a strict procedural premise, but even those whom it troubles cannot deny that this is a premise that has prevailed in consensual historic Christianity."

the PE serve to call the church back to its roots, possibly via repentance and behavioral or doctrinal change.

5. "The quintessential Christian pastoral act is one of feeding: eating and drinking, receiving spiritual nourishment for our souls." Oden continues: "No pastoral act is more central to the care of souls than the Supper where the resurrected Christ is present at table with the community. Confession is intrinsically connected with holy communion."[17]

Like baptism (see rubric 4), the formal administration of bread and cup associated with 1 Cor 11:17–34 and Gospel parallels is not attested in the PE. Just as other Pauline writings except for 1 Corinthians are virtually silent on the practice, so the PE do not address it. But also as in the case of baptism, it can be assumed that believers celebrated "the Lord's death until he comes" (1 Cor 11:26) through a regular observance that came to be termed an ordinance or sacrament. By way of analogy, it may be assumed that prayer was a regular activity under Timothy's and Titus's leadership, though it is barely mentioned in the PE (see 1 Tim 2:1–2, 8; 4:5; 5:5). Singing and praise, surely fixtures in congregational meetings, are likewise not mentioned. The PE take up salient points of concern and conflict; there is no need to rehearse settled custom.

While it would be fruitless to try to wring evidence of explicit baptismal or communion practice out of the PE, it is reasonable to observe that the PE do contribute to a Christocentric orientation (see sec. IV below) that gives impetus to the varying communion practices found in later churches. Ancient churches gathered in Christ's name, reaffirmed his lordship under prophetic or pastoral proclamation including exposition of the Scriptures, and sealed reception of the preached word by ingesting the communion elements (likely bread and drink from a common meal at first, with an eventual shift to a format less susceptible to abuse, possibly in light of apostolic warning; see 1 Cor 11:20–22, 33–34; cf. Jude 12) that called Christ to mind and in some understandings mediated his grace. The PE capture the dynamics of first-generation believers founding communities in which baptismal and communion practices began to establish themselves and take on definition (variously parsed subsequently).

Oden's mention of "penitential confession" is also not foreign to the PE, as Paul's frequent reference to aberrant beliefs and actions are implicit calls for acknowledgment of wrongdoing and invitations for reform. Paul frankly acknowledged his own grave transgression (1 Tim 1:12–16; cf. Titus 3:3). Pastors must have assumed some role in overseeing the progress of their members in such matters of nurture and even discipline (a ubiquitous concern in the PE) requiring the acknowledgment of and turning (repentance) from sin.

17. Oden, *Ministry through Word and Sacrament*, 154.

6. "The pastor is a teacher of the soul, educating the soul toward behavioral excellence. . . . If the care of souls is the pedagogy of the inner life, then the pastor must develop the art of teaching." Two concerns are foremost in this statement: behavior and teaching. As for behavior, Titus contains multiple exhortations for believers to perform good works (e.g., 2:7, 14; 3:14). The letters to Timothy are studded with imperatives (over ninety total) that call for action, either by Timothy or his hearers or both. Pastors longing for behavioral change in their own lives and among their parishioners will find the PE to be richly suggestive for both motives and outcomes.

As for the pastoral task of explaining and instilling the doctrines of the Christian faith, the importance of this concern is indicated by nearly three dozen occurrences of words such as "teach," "teacher," or "teaching" in the PE. In the early church overall, pastors were "shepherds of God's flock" (1 Pet 5:2; cf. Acts 20:28) under the Chief Shepherd (1 Pet 5:4; cf. Heb 13:20; 1 Pet 2:25; Rev 7:17), who distinguished himself in his earthly course not least by teaching. He founded a community of disciples, which means pupils, learners. Such emphasis on instruction does not make the church an academy, but it does make serious followers of Christ fervent hearers and ready thinkers, grateful for pastoral leaders who can expand their horizons in understanding the Scriptures and all they convey about God, the world, and the Christian mandate. Pastors also help provide structures in which God's people can live out what they come to understand, often gaining wisdom from pastoral example.

In the PE, the concern for pedagogy that instructs the mind and thereby nourishes the soul is epitomized by some nine references to "sound" or "healthy" teaching, doctrine, or faith (1 Tim 1:10; 6:3; 2 Tim 1:13; 4:3; Titus 1:9, 13; 2:1, 2, 8; see more on "sound doctrine" in sec. IX.D below). Perhaps no other Pauline letters furnish more direct and succinct instruction for why and what pastors must teach if they wish to remain faithful to the New Testament's dominical (i.e., having to do with Jesus the *dominus* / *kyrios* / Lord) and apostolic charge to them.

7. "The care of souls occurs not only individualistically, but extends to institutional nurture and accountability, and beyond the parameters of the congregation to the nurture of community in the parish, the civil sphere, the *polis*, and ultimately to the world." This conclusion, like the previous one, is also twofold: pertaining to the nurture and accountability of the church, and then pertaining to the interface between church and its social nexus, both local and extended.

Regarding the nurture and accountability of the church beyond the level of individuals, the PE deal with these issues whenever they promote love, *agapē*. This Greek word occurs ten times in the PE, testifying to an attribute of God that, when he bestows it on humans through faith in Christ, becomes a powerful glue for mutual compassion, social adhesion, self-sacrifice for the sake of others, and missional outreach. In 1 Timothy this divinely given love was "poured out" on Paul at his conversion (1:14). It is a means of grace for women (2:15). It is an imperative for Timothy (4:12; 6:11). A pastor who embraces and catalyzes such love in a congregation will go far toward extending the nurture and accountability it creates. This result will come about, in part, through the repudiation of the love of money among leaders (3:3) and congregants (6:10) alike, along with other idolatries.

In 2 Timothy, love is a gift of the Spirit, along with power and self-discipline, that makes boldness in ministry possible (1:7). Along with faith, it enables appropriation of apostolic teaching (1:13). Through pursuing it, "the evil desires of youth" can be circumvented (2:22). Without divine love, people will be "lovers of themselves" and "lovers of money," a recipe for community dysfunction (3:2). The absence or distortion of love (3:3) is of a piece with persons becoming "lovers of pleasure rather than lovers of God" (3:4), a fatal passion if such a mentality engulfs a congregation, with Demas serving as a possible example: his love became set on "this world" (4:10). Paul's model over decades previous was quite different and love-affirming (3:10).

Love is a factor in Titus, too. It appeared in Christ's coming (3:4) and is therefore available through faith to elders (1:8) and those under their care (2:2, 4).

Across the PE, the nurture and accountability that are intended to flourish in the Ephesian and Cretan congregations are promoted by the pastoral administration of God's gift of love, along with rejection and correction of its subversion by unholy blandishments.

Regarding the nurture of community beyond the parameters of the congregation, the PE, by shaping community-minded enclaves at the microcosmic level, condition persons to display social openness and interactive potential beyond the confines of church geography and relationships. To be closed to the wider world by a sense of indifference, hostility, or superiority is proscribed; there should be cooperation with "rulers and authorities" and graciousness toward all (Titus 3:1–2). Prayer in the church should be offered "for all people," including possibly hostile government authorities (1 Tim 2:1–2), for the God of the church "wants all people to be saved and to come to a knowledge of the truth" (1 Tim 2:4). God is not just savior in the church; he "is the Savior of all people" (4:10), who need to be called to faith by those who already possess it. Such observations serve as de facto prods to missionary outreach.

The horizons of compassion in the churches implied in the PE render them not faith ghettoes but staging points for lives of integrity that will be a positive social force to uplift family, local community, and sociopolitical networks beyond. Yet, they will not merely aid and abet conditions outside the church but often will challenge them, as when slaves are exhorted to behavior that will "make the teaching about God our Savior attractive" (Titus 2:10; cf.

1 Tim 6:1–2). Locales populated with believers from all walks of life, if they are possessed of the marks of grace limned in the PE, will tend to make social spheres at all levels more reflective of God's "kindness and love" (Titus 3:4). This positive projection does not preclude the likelihood that, because of social resistance, leaders and laity alike will suffer in the process (2 Tim 3:12). What God approves and promotes in the church, and sanctions as a centrifugal activity (such as mission, attempts at social reform, and even simple benevolences such as food distribution and medical care), may well be condemned, opposed, and even criminalized by those hostile to Christian expression, as can be observed around the world currently.[18]

8. "Soul care requires the support of the laity through voluntary gifts grounded in biblical imperatives, rather than on a fee-for-service basis. . . . When pastoral abuses occur, they require rigorous inquiry which presumes innocence and seeks procedures for fair hearing and due process." This conclusion addresses, first, the issue of mercenary motivation. The PE present a pastoral model of freedom from the love of money (1 Tim 3:3), which in turn produces people encouraged to practice generosity (1 Tim 6:17–19) and selfless care for those in real need among them such as widows (1 Tim 5). Pastors and people alike are content with what God has granted them (1 Tim 6:6–8), a lesson learned earlier by Paul himself (Phil 4:11–12) and dramatized by his self-support and refusal to receive funds from most churches in most settings (see Acts 20:33–35; 1 Cor 9:12; 2 Cor 2:17; 7:2; 11:9; 12:14–17; 1 Thess 2:5).

Then there is the issue of church discipline, particularly of its leaders. The PE recognize how often those in the church go astray, including those in oversight roles. Hymenaeus and Alexander could be examples (1 Tim 1:20; cf. 2 Tim 2:16–18). Paul's appeals to Timothy to stay on the straight and narrow may be expressions of apprehension that his loyalty to the faith could be compromised amid the pressures he faced. Paul gives graphic directions for the reward but also reproof of church elders (1 Tim 5:17–25). Even if Titus's ministry is scoffed at (Titus 2:15), he is to discern and, after due admonition, excommunicate a person making trouble in the church (3:10–11).

More could be said about the interface of the PE with Oden's conclusions regarding the care of souls in the classical pastoral literature. The above should suffice to remind of numerous ties, along with some dislocations, between the PE of the earliest Christian generations and the pastoral mandate in subsequent eras, as it has been variously understood and practiced. Whatever its envisioned form, that mandate is the motivation that drives many to the PE to

18. J. N. Jennings, "Hostility against Mission," *IBMR* 39.1 (2015): 57–58. The whole issue of this journal "focuses on Christian communities and God's people of mission who suffer hostile attack by those who consciously and explicitly oppose Jesus Christ and Christian mission" (58).

find resources for pastoral labor in its myriad manifestations in the twenty-first century. This is a time seeing the effects and feeling the demands of unprecedented numerical growth in the church worldwide.[19] The need for wise and godly pastors has not decreased since Paul's time—quite the contrary. The counsel of the PE along the lines sketched above (and others too) is needed, then, like never before.

II. HISTORY, EXEGESIS, AND THEOLOGY: THE PRIMACY OF GOD IN THE PE

The PE urge pastoral leaders named Timothy in the city of Ephesus and Titus on the island of Crete to commend and defend the Christian faith in congregations over which they have oversight. While each of the three letters reflects a historical setting, that setting is widely disputed. And since over the last few generations (with roots going back to ca. 1800) a majority of scholarly interpreters reject Paul's authorship of the PE, any proposed "historical" setting is necessarily speculative. For if we know few details of the scenario proposed in patristic sources,[20] in which Paul is released from his first Roman imprisonment and pens the PE before (or during: 2 Tim) a second and final imprisonment prior to his martyrdom, we have no concrete knowledge at all of pseudo-Pauline persons or locations making up Pauline "schools" to which many seek to attribute the PE, under the assumption that Paul did not write them. Nor, in this scenario, is it clear just who may have been addressed. Both author and audience are, according to the consensus, fictive.[21] Jens Herzer has pointed out the quandary this poses:[22] many scholars are agreed that the PE (1) are rightly viewed as a homogeneous trio of documents[23] that (2) were

19. For survey, see Douglas Jacobsen, *Global Christianity: An Introduction to Christianity on Five Continents* (Grand Rapids: Baker Academic, 2015); Scott Sunquist, *The Unexpected Christian Century: The Reversal and Transformation of Global Christianity, 1900–2000* (Grand Rapids: Baker Academic, 2015); S. Offutt, *New Centers of Global Evangelicalism in Latin America and Africa* (Cambridge: Cambridge University Press, 2015). See also T. Johnson, G. Zurlo, A. Hickman, and P. Crossing, "Christianity 2017: Five Hundred Years of Protestant Christianity," *IBMR* 41.1 (2017): 41–52. Growth has also been meteoric in the Roman Catholic communion.

20. See, for example, Eusebius, *Ecclesiastical History* 2.22.1–2.

21. For a brief summation of features of the consensus, see Christopher Hays and Christopher Ansberry, *Evangelical Faith and the Challenge of Historical Criticism* (London: SPCK, 2013), 154–56.

22. Jens Herzer, "Abschied vom Konsens? Die Pseudepigraphie der Pastoralbriefe als Herausforderung an die neutestamentliche Wissenschaft," *TLZ* 129.12 (2004): 1268–81.

23. Note, for example, how they are lumped together, at least for discussion purposes,

not written by the apostle Paul. But there is no consensus among major scholarly commentaries (particularly in German) regarding a positive historical or geographic location for either the composition of the PE or their reception.[24]

This commentary will take Paul to have been the author of the PE (see sec. X.B below). Throughout, I seek to avoid the situation described by Linda Belleville in which "theological analysis of the Pastoral Epistles . . . has suffered from a one-sided emphasis on the question of authenticity."[25] She notes that some major recent commentaries—she mentions those by Mounce, Knight, Witherington, and Marshall with Towner—devote inordinate attention to the authorship question. Others (rejecting Paul's authorship) place the PE a generation or more after Paul's death and focus on the ecclesial or social setting of the PE. In such presentations, statements about Christ are just traditional formulations, and the PE as a whole are about social organization. They describe the times of the AF, not the early church. She mentions commentaries in English by Dibelius and Conzelmann, Easton, Hanson, Oden, and Scott, and a number of others in German by Brox, Hasler, Merkel, Oberlinner, and Roloff that follow these trends. Belleville concludes, "While most commentaries note that Christology in some form is central to the Pastorals, there is little detailed attention given to it" (though she gives some credit to commentaries by Marshall and Towner on this score).[26]

Belleville, however, could have extended her worthwhile point. The main concern of the PE, if what the author mentions most frequently and foundationally is any indication, is not simply Christ (though he is undoubtedly central) but more broadly God. This is not to dispute the obvious fact that throughout church history, going back at least to the Muratorian Fragment (latter half of second century), the PE were seen as germane to church organization and practice: "[Paul also wrote] out of affection and love one [letter] to Philemon, one to Titus, and two to Timothy; and these are held sacred in the esteem of the Church catholic for the regulation of ecclesiastical discipline."[27]

---

in C. Blomberg, *The Historical Reliability of the New Testament* (Nashville: B&H Academic, 2016), 394–407. See also similar treatment in the section entitled "The Structured Transmission of Leadership Services and Apostolic Tradition: The Model of the Pastoral Letters," in J. Frey, *Von Jesus zur neutestamentlichen Theologie: Kleine Schriften II*, ed. B. Schliesser, WUNT 2.368 (Tübingen: Mohr Siebeck, 2016), 759–63. As will be seen below, however, a minority of commentators are presently calling for due regard of each PE separately.

24. Herzer, "Abschied vom Konsens?," 1280.

25. Linda Belleville, "Christology, the Pastoral Epistles, and Commentaries," in *On the Writing of New Testament Commentaries: FS Grant Osborne*, ed. S. E. Porter and E. J. Schnabel (Leiden: Brill, 2013), 317. See also James W. Aageson, *Paul, the Pastoral Epistles, and the Early Church* (Peabody, MA: Hendrickson, 2008), 11n32.

26. Belleville, "Christology," 318–19.

27. Eckhard Schnabel, "The Muratorian Fragment: The State of Research," *JETS* 57

This perception of the PE is evident in other patristic-era sources, including Ambrosiaster, Cassiodorus, Chrysostom, Didymus, John of Damascus, Pelagius, and Theodoret.[28] But another function was intertwined with it: the refutation of aberrant teaching and practice by the presentation of what is true and good. That is, we must give attention to what the PE say about divine truth—starting with God himself—as revealed in Scripture. Such truth is the focus of the PE themselves, as the accompanying table illustrates. It will be seen that God (or the Son of God) is far and away the major point of focus and assertion in the PE. And many sentences talk about God (or Christ) without using a name for him: instead there is (in English translation) a pronoun.

Table 1. Significant Greek words in the PE[29]

1 Timothy (1,591 words total)	2 Timothy (1,238 words total)	Titus (659 words total)
1. *theos* (God) 22	*kyrios* (Lord) 16	*theos* (God) 13
2. *pistis* (faith) 19	*theos* (God) 13	*ergon* (work) 8
3. *kalos* (good) 16	*Iēsous* (Jesus) 13	*pistis* (faith) 6
4. *Christos* (Christ) 15	*Christos* (Christ) 13	*sōtēr* (Savior) 6
5. *Iēsous* (Jesus) 14	*pistis* (faith) 8	*anthrōpos* (person, man) 5
6. *pistos* (faithful) 11	*logos* (word) 7	*kalos* (good) 5
7. *anthrōpos* (person, man) 10	*alētheia* (truth) 6	*logos* (word) 5
8. *gynē* (woman, wife) 9	*didōmi* (I give) 6	*agathos* (good) 4
9. *didaskalia* (teaching) 8	*ergon* (work) 6	*didaskalia* (teaching) 4
10. *eusebeia* (godliness) 8	*anthrōpos* (person, man) 5	*Iēsous* (Jesus) 4

(2014): 238. Schnabel argues convincingly for the second-century date, which has been disputed since the middle of last century.

28. Lloyd Pietersen, "Epistles, Pastoral," *EBR* 7:1095.

29. Word counts are from Andreas Köstenberger and Raymond Bouchoc, *The Book Study Concordance of the Greek New Testament* (Nashville: B&H, 2003). Some figures (such as the number of words in each PE) are from searches using Accordance 11 and the word-count function in Microsoft Word for Mac 2011, 14.6.6.

1 TIMOTHY (1,591 WORDS TOTAL)	2 TIMOTHY (1,238 WORDS TOTAL)	TITUS (659 WORDS TOTAL)
11. *logos* (word) 8	*hēmera* (day) 5	*hygiainō* (I am healthy) 4
12. *chēra* (widow) 8	*oida* (I know) 5	*charis* (grace) 4
13. *alētheia* (truth) 6	*charis* (grace) 4	*Christos* (Christ) 4
14. *ergon* (work) 6	*agapē* (love) 4	
15. *kyrios* (Lord) 6		
16. *agapē* (love) 5		
17. *anēr* (man, husband) 5		
Names/words for divinity: 57 of 1,591 total (3.58%)	Names/words for divinity: 55 of 1,238 total (4.44%)	Names/words for divinity: 27 of 659 total (4.10%)

Preponderance of God-language does not mean that other concerns are not also important. Bernhard Mutschler, for example, has thoroughly investigated "faith" and "believing" in the PE.[30] A collection of essays on Paul's theology in relation to the PE treats topics such as ecclesiology, ethics, mission, salvation, and stewardship in the PE.[31] Still, a *theo*logical approach to the PE corpus, with *theos* (God) at the center, is justified, since, unlike many modern theologians who do not think in terms of a God outside of the created universe who materially affects matters within it, including history,[32] Paul did believe in such a God. It is fair to say that the language in his epistles depicts him as enthralled with this Being to whom, he argued, he personally owed infinitely much (see, e.g., 1 Tim 1:12–17), and who in his view holds the world's only ultimate hope in his hands.

It is accordingly reasonable to regard theology, the substance of Christian faith and its proper exercise, as at least as justifiable a dominant focus in

30. Bernhard Mutschler, *Glaube in den Pastoralbriefen: Pistis als Mitte christlicher Existenz*, WUNT 256 (Tübingen: Mohr Siebeck, 2010).

31. Andreas Köstenberger and Terry Wilder, eds., *Entrusted with the Gospel: Paul's Theology in the Pastoral Epistles* (Nashville: B&H, 2010).

32. See John Cooper, *Panentheism—the Other God of the Philosophers: From Plato to the Present* (Grand Rapids: Baker Academic, 2006). See also Gary Dorrien, *Kantian Reason and Hegelian Spirit: The Idealistic Logic of Modern Theology* (Chichester: Wiley-Blackwell, 2012), for exposition of how (German) philosophical constructs supplanted God in theological discussion. Key names in Dorrien's treatment are Kant, Hegel, Schelling, and Schleiermacher.

studying the PE as the rarified social or speculative "historical" reconstructions that are common. "The theology of the New Testament," including the convictions articulated in the PE, is "no mere epiphenomenon superimposed upon history (as *Geschichte*), but is part of the chain of cause and effect which prompted all the characters in the story, Jesus too."[33] PE theology and first-century history intertwine, despite the strong (and largely dominant) trend in Western historiography in recent centuries to divorce the two.[34] An introduction to detailed commentary on these epistles does well to characterize and reflect on their theological representations, since this is a primary concern of the documents themselves (see table 1 above).

But what is Christian faith? As a clear and widespread articulation of core Christian belief across cultures and communions through the centuries, it is hard to improve on the so-called Apostles' Creed. An analysis of the PE using this historic confession of faith as a heuristic aid will afford a useful summary of the overarching content of the PE in anticipation of additional introductory discussion and verse-by-verse commentary later on.

33. See Robert C. Doyle's refutation of NT scholar Morna Hooker's (and theologian Maurice Wiles's) view that there is no connection between "history" and "biblical teaching on creation and fall," or between history and "the incarnation and 'Godness' of Jesus" ("The Uniqueness of Christ, 'Chalcedon,' and Mission," in Bolt and Thompson, *The Gospel to the Nations*, 352). In fact, in Hooker's outlook (352), "the Bible's teaching on redemption in general" has no historical backing in the proper sense. Accordingly, a historical reconstruction of the times and teachings associated with the PE would be one in which a transcendent God and an incarnate Jesus would play no material role. Doyle convincingly disputes some bases of this outlook, which runs quite counter to Paul's and that of other biblical writers (353).

34. A process ably summarized by Michael Murrmann-Kahl, "Historiography V.B: Modern Europe," *EBR* 11:1147–53. In connection with Leonhard Goppelt he mentions an "older interpretive strategy of salvation history (as with Johann Christian Konrad von Hofmann, Theodor Zahn, Johann Tobias Beck, Adolf Schlatter, and Oscar Cullmann)" that attempts "to reconstruct NT theology as a sequence of divine saving works throughout history" (1151). This matrix of understanding the relation between history and theology informs this commentary, though included in those "divine saving works" is the production of Scripture, which interprets the meaning of those works and enables conveyance of that meaning across cultures, language barriers (through translation), and generations. For this heritage in NT (and OT) scholarship, see Robert Yarbrough, *The Salvation Historical Fallacy? Reassessing the History of New Testament Theology* (Leiden: Deo, 2004). For a recent attempt to formulate a historiography that does justice to the complexity of the issues, see Roland Deines, *Acts of God in History: Studies towards Recovering a Theological Historiography*, ed. Christoph Ochs and Peter Watts, WUNT 317 (Tübingen: Mohr Siebeck, 2013), especially ch. 1: "God's Role in History as a Methodological Problem for Exegesis" (1–26).

III. GOD THE FATHER IN THE PE

Affirming Trinitarian understanding of God (not absent from earlier Pauline letters: see 2 Cor 13:13),[35] the Apostles' Creed epitomizes biblical teaching in three statements. The first: *I believe in God the Father Almighty, Maker of heaven and earth.*[36]

Every chapter of the PE contains explicit reference to God (*theos*). In fact, *theos* appears more frequently than any other noun in the PE: twenty-two times in 1 Timothy and thirteen times each in 2 Timothy and Titus. This God is called "Father" (*patēr*) in the opening of all three epistles (1 Tim 1:2; 2 Tim 1:2; Titus 1:4). He is "Almighty" (sovereign, ruler over all) in that he is the eschatological "righteous Judge" (2 Tim 4:8) and the "eternal King" (1 Tim 1:17; 6:15) over a kingdom (2 Tim 4:1, 18)[37] that encompasses heaven and earth and extends, where humans are concerned, even to conferral of eternal life (Titus 1:2; 3:7). His identity as Creator, implicit in any reference to God by a writer such as Paul, who so ubiquitously affirms the God revealed in the Old Testament, is highlighted particularly in 1 Timothy.

A. God the Father in 1 Timothy

In 1 Timothy it is God whose command made Paul "an apostle of Christ Jesus" (1:1). This same God is "our Savior" (1:1; also 2:3; 4:10). Along with "Christ Jesus our Lord," he is the source of the "grace, mercy and peace" (1:2) Paul wishes for Timothy. God exercises management (see 1:4: *oikonomia*) over a household

35. On this passage and "the divine Triad" in Paul generally, see Gordon Fee, *Pauline Christology: An Exegetical-Theological Study* (Peabody, MA: Hendrickson, 2007), 591–93. Thomas Schmeller, *Der zweite Brief an die Korinther: 2 Kor 7,5–13,13*, EKKNT 8/2 (Neukirchen-Vluyn: Neukirchener Theologie, 2015), 405, states that "one cannot really call this 'Trinitarian,' because in that case one would expect a different order [God the Father first, Schmeller thinks] and a determination of the relation between the three members." But this statement is imposing on Paul what Schmeller supposes Paul should have said. The history of interpretation is justified to see in this regard what Schmeller admits it has found there: "the starting point of Trinitarian thought" (406). If Jesus spoke as John's gospel records or as Matt 28:19–20 claims, then there is Trinitarian rootage in Jesus's self-consciousness as well. See Matthew W. Bates, *Birth of the Trinity: Jesus, God, and Spirit in New Testament and Early Christian Interpretations of the Old Testament* (Oxford: Oxford University Press, 2015).

36. Forms of the Apostles' Creed proliferate in printed and online sources; these forms vary little whether in their Roman Catholic or their various Protestant renderings. I cite here the form found in *Trinity Hymnal* (Atlanta: Great Commission Publications, 1990), 845.

37. For comments on the kingdom of God in Paul, including the PE, see R. Yarbrough, "The Kingdom of God in the New Testament: Mark through the Epistles," in *The Kingdom of God*, ed. C. Morgan and R. Peterson (Wheaton, IL: Crossway, 2012), 143–49.

(*oikos*), which is the church (3:15; cf. 3:5). Paul blesses this God because of the "glorious gospel" he entrusted to Paul (1:11). Paul accords God "honor and glory for ever and ever" because he is "the King eternal, immortal, invisible, the only God" (1:17). In the polytheistic world of the Pauline Gentile churches, the God of whom Paul speaks is the starkly singular God well known from Old Testament narrative (e.g., Gen 1) and commandment (e.g., Exod 20:3: "You shall have no other gods before me"). In Paul's own words, "There is one God" (1 Tim 2:5).

This God is the creator who made all things, among them marriage and food, "which God created to be received with thanksgiving by those who believe and who know the truth" (4:3). God gives life to all things that have it (6:13). Admittedly Paul views lives filled with "the word of God and prayer" (4:5) as integral to God-honoring enjoyment of creation's bounty.

God is not a philosophical postulate or category of human consciousness or self-projection but "the living God," upon whom believers rightly set their hope (4:10; 5:5). The rich in particular are urged to vest all hope in God and not their earthly wealth (6:17). God takes pleasure and personal interest in each individual of his household, the rich and the poor, as the example of families who care for their widows shows (5:4). He is the stern transcendent witness over Paul's admonitions to Timothy as Paul addresses his young charge "in the sight of God" (5:21; also 6:13). He has a reputation ("name"), a magnificent and incomparable identity, that is to be reverenced (6:1), especially by a pastoral leader such as Timothy, whom Paul terms "a man of God" (6:11: *anthrōpos theou*; see also 2 Tim 3:17), a designation reserved in the Old Testament for figures such as Moses (Deut 33:1), Samuel (1 Sam 9:7, 14), David (Neh 12:24), and other seers and prophets. This phrase is never used elsewhere in the New Testament, throwing into sharp relief the theocentric existence Paul writes to confirm and promote in Timothy.

God is central in 1 Timothy and other PE in passages that do not actually use the word "God." For example, the theological climax of 1 Timothy is Paul's concluding doxological statement preceded by mention of Christ's return (6:14), which "God will bring about in his own time—God, the blessed and only Ruler, the King of kings and Lord of lords, who alone is immortal and who lives in unapproachable light, whom no one has seen or can see. To him be honor and might forever. Amen" (6:15–16). The word "God" does not appear here in the Greek text but is rightly and necessarily present in English translation, since "God" is implied as the subject of the Greek verbs.

B. God the Father in 2 Timothy

God is no less prominent in 2 Timothy. Explicit references to God in this letter are concentrated in the opening verses. Paul is an apostle "by the will of God"

(1:1), who is the source of the "grace, mercy and peace" that Paul affirms for Timothy (1:2). Paul thanks God (1:3) for Timothy and affirms the gift Timothy received from God (1:6). God gifts all believers with "a spirit of power, of love and of self-discipline" (1:7) and can enable Timothy to join with Paul "in suffering, by the power of God" (1:8).

God has sent forth a saving word that "is not chained" (2:9) and that sets the agenda and furnishes the resources for Paul's perseverance as he serves "even to the point of being chained like a criminal" (2:8). God is to be at the center of Timothy's ministry, as he is to warn quarreling parishioners "before God" of the error of their ways (2:14) and thereby to present himself "to God" unashamed and competent in his handling of God's true word (2:15). In the face of false teaching about central matters such as the resurrection (2:18), "God's solid foundation stands firm" (2:19). Attesting to this fact are two uses of the word "Lord" (*kyrios*) to refer to God (2:19), unusual in the PE, where "Lord" generally refers to Christ (see below).

Timothy's confidence in ministry has its basis largely in the fact that God can "grant repentance" to those in error, "leading them to a knowledge of the truth" (2:25) and enabling them to "escape from the trap of the devil, who has taken them captive to do his will" (2:26). Satan and evil can ensnare and destroy people, but God is sovereign over the evil one's designs, even in an age where people are pleasure-lovers (*philēdonoi*) rather than "God-lovers" (*philotheoi*; 3:4).

In the end, Paul makes the core of his appeal in 2 Timothy "in the presence of God" (4:1) along with "Christ Jesus." It will be seen below that what is predicated of one in the PE is also very largely shared by the other.

C. God the Father in Titus

Of the thirteen occurrences of "God" in Titus, six come in the first seven verses. Does the abject godlessness that Paul attributes to the Cretans in general (1:12–13, 16) prod him to call Titus's attention all the more to the one true God's relevance and centrality?

Paul opens his epistle with the reminder that he is "a servant of God" (*doulos theou*; 1:1), entrusted with a message "by the command of God our Savior" (1:4). But this ministry is not merely interaction between Paul and God. It rather relates closely to "the faith of God's elect" (1:1), based on promises from "God, who does not lie" (1:2). From this same God Paul wishes Titus "grace and peace" (1:4). At the center of Paul's counsel to Titus will be directions for appointing pastoral overseers who can serve effectively directing "God's work" (1:7)[38] in the Cretan congrega-

38. But *theou oikonomon* in this verse may refer to Titus as "God's worker" or steward; see commentary below.

tions. This work will be arduous, because in the churches are many who "claim to know God, but by their actions . . . deny him" (1:16). Not all confession of God is authentic, accounting for much of Paul's instruction both to Titus and to Timothy.

In the Cretan congregations, a key need is for young women to conduct themselves is such a way that "no one will malign the word of God" (2:5). Older women's mentorship is likewise vital, as is Titus's service to the older women, who (like the older men) require equipping so they can pass gospel lore and graces along to peers and to the next generation. Slaves too have a role to play in making "the teaching about God our Savior attractive" (2:10). God's salvation-bearing grace has appeared to all persons (2:10) and encourages believers to live in expectation of the appearing "of our great God and Savior, Jesus Christ" (2:13), Paul here blurring the line between Father and Son by using a customary title for the former to refer to the latter. A few verses later Paul reverts to speaking of God alone as Savior (3:4). The final reference to God the Father in Titus comes as Paul characterizes Christian believers as "those who have trusted in God" (3:8).

IV. GOD THE SON IN THE PE

The second major division of the Apostles' Creed is *I believe in Jesus Christ, his only Son, our Lord, who was conceived by the Holy Spirit, and born of the virgin Mary. He suffered under Pontius Pilate, was crucified, died, and was buried; he descended into hell. The third day he rose again from the dead. He ascended into heaven and is seated at the right hand of God the Father Almighty. From there he will come to judge the living and the dead.* The PE are replete with references to Jesus: there is no chapter in the PE that lacks explicit mention of him.

A. Jesus in 1 Timothy

In 1 Timothy the phrase "Christ Jesus" occurs twelve times, and "Jesus Christ" twice (6:3, 14). "Christ" occurs alone, without an accompanying "Jesus," in 5:11. Four times "Lord" (*kyrios*) is added to "Christ Jesus," heightening his already exalted status (1:2, 12; 6:3, 14). Once "Lord" is used of the Son with no further designation: "The grace of our Lord was poured out on me abundantly" (1:14).

If Paul is the author of the PE, such terms and titles signified a human (eerily transformed)[39] with whom he had had personal interchange. At

39. That is, he had been publicly executed, but then he reappeared alive and in bodily form.

the very least, Paul encountered Jesus in risen form on the Damascus Road (Acts 9:5), shortly after which Acts depicts Paul as preaching in Damascus synagogues that "Jesus is the Son of God" (9:20) and "proving that Jesus is the Christ" (9:22). Barnabas confirms, in Luke's account, that Saul "preached fearlessly in the name of Jesus" directly after his Damascus Road encounter (9:27). Paul's focus was not a concept or even distant divine being but a person defined and known by an earthly and historical existence and career.

Paul's personal knowledge of Jesus can probably be traced back earlier than the Damascus encounter. It is hard to imagine that Saul of Tarsus had no knowledge of Jesus of Nazareth during the latter's earthly ministry, if Gospel accounts of the stir Jesus caused are even remotely accurate. To draw only from Matthew's account: people went out to hear Jesus's forerunner, John, "from Jerusalem and all Judea and the whole region of the Jordan" (3:5). Once Jesus began preaching, "news about him spread all over Syria. . . . Large crowds from Galilee, the Decapolis, Jerusalem, Judea and the region across the Jordan followed him" (4:24–25). After the Sermon on the Mount, "large crowds followed him" (8:1). As Jesus preached and healed, "news of this spread throughout" the various regions (9:26). On one occasion, "such large crowds gathered around him that he got into a boat and sat in it, while all the people stood on the shore" (13:2).

It is unnecessary to belabor the point. If Saul/Paul was resident anywhere from Tarsus to Judea (and perhaps even beyond) during Jesus's lifetime and was a mainstream rabbinic student and teacher (which there is no reason to deny), it is hard to imagine that he never had at least enough knowledge of Jesus to be impressed that this controversial but in the end to Paul laudable figure had laid down his life to save even hardened, hateful opponents like Saul (see 1 Tim 1:12–16). Firsthand knowledge of the man and the movement he sparked conditioned Paul's sense of connection with him following his death and resurrection.[40] This personal history should not be forgotten while analyzing words referring to Jesus in the PE. Particularly if Paul wrote them, they are not just words.

Paul is an apostle of "Christ Jesus," who is also "the hope" of Paul and Timothy and all who have trusted him (1 Tim 1:1). Along with God the Father, Christ Jesus is the source of "grace, mercy and peace" (1:2). He empowers Paul for ministry (1:12). In him are "faith and love" (1:14). He came into the world to save the very worst of transgressors, most notably Paul (1:15), for whose sake Jesus displayed "his unlimited patience as an example for those who would believe on him and receive eternal life" (1:16). He is the "one mediator between God and men, . . . who gave himself as a ransom for all men" (2:5–6).

40. See Stanley Porter, *When Paul Met Jesus: How an Idea Got Lost in History* (Cambridge: Cambridge University Press, 2016).

He is relevant not just to apostles who encountered him; deacons, too, "who have served well gain an excellent standing and great assurance in their faith in Christ Jesus" (3:13). Analogous bright prospects lie before Timothy, whom Paul reminds: "If you point these things out to the brothers, you will be a good minister of Christ Jesus, brought up in the truths of the faith and of the good teaching that you have followed" (4:6). In contrast to this positive response to Christ, younger widows who are put on the list for church support run the risk of letting their "sensual desires overcome their dedication to Christ" (5:11), a contingency Paul gives instructions to circumvent.

As seen above, Paul's charge to Timothy is extended "in the sight of God and Christ Jesus" (5:21), as the young leader opposes and seeks to correct those who do "not agree to the sound instruction of our Lord Jesus Christ" (6:3). Jesus's example of unwavering confession "before Pontius Pilate" (6:13) should put backbone in Timothy "to keep this command without spot or blame until the appearing of our Lord Jesus Christ" (6:14). He is a figure of the past, the present, and the future all at once.

His present and future stature, as risen Lord and returning Judge, are at center stage in 1 Timothy and in fact all the PE. But his earthly identity and accomplishment are far from minimized. For one thing, every one of the fourteen occurrences of "Jesus" is a reminder of the man from Nazareth, so named because of an angelic appearance to his ostensible father Joseph (Matt 1:20–21). This Jesus "came into the world" (1 Tim 1:15) and showed "unlimited patience" (1:16). He "gave himself a ransom" (2:6), an obvious reference to the cross. His work on earth comprises a great "mystery of godliness" (3:16): "He appeared in a body, was vindicated by the Spirit, was seen by angels, was preached among the nations, was believed on in the world, was taken up in glory." Here Paul covers the whole of Jesus's earthly accomplishment in one sweeping flourish culminating in his ascension.

Certain teachings or actions of Jesus are likewise evoked if not explicitly referenced in 1 Timothy. Paul's concern about proper regard for the law of Moses (e.g., 1:7–11) is foreshadowed by Jesus's constant sparring with various priestly and rabbinic leaders (e.g. Mark 11:27) and their associates (e.g., Mark 12:13, 28) over this same topic. Paul's sense of women's strength as learners (1 Tim 2:11–12) and ministers particularly to other women in the church (see Titus 2:3–5) is anticipated by Jesus's instruction and deployment of his female followers, who served alongside though not over their fellow male disciples. Paul's assessment of all foods as clean (1 Tim 4:4) was a doctrine whose foundation was laid by Jesus (e.g., Mark 7:18–19). The same could be said of Paul's defense of marriage in the same passage, as Jesus too hallowed this institution as God-given (e.g., Matt 19:4–6). Paul's instruction on care for widows (1 Tim 5) was foreshadowed by Jesus's outreach to disenfranchised women, including those who had lost their husbands, among whom was possibly his own mother.

Paul likely cites words of Jesus alongside Old Testament Scripture (5:18) and reflects Jesus's teaching in counseling Timothy how to handle accusations of transgression within a congregation (5:19–20). Paul's instruction on use of wealth (6:6–10, 17–19) parallels Jesus's frequent teachings on the subject, which are perhaps best summed up in his command to "store up for yourselves treasures in heaven, where moth and rust do not destroy, and where thieves do not break in and steal. For where your treasure is, there your heart will be also" (Matt 6:20–21). Paul echoes this instruction in telling Timothy to teach the rich to "lay up treasures for themselves as a firm foundation for the coming age" (1 Tim 6:19). We have already mentioned Paul's reference to Jesus's confession before Pontius Pilate as relevant for Timothy's own confessional readiness.

In the end, of all that the Apostles' Creed affirms regarding "Jesus Christ, his only Son, our Lord," the only details lacking explicit mention in 1 Timothy are "conceived by the Holy Spirit, and born of the virgin Mary," along with "he descended into hell" (which many think is not affirmed in Scripture anywhere). Major features of the whole sweep of Jesus's coming, earthly life, death, resurrection, ascension, and return are present in this PE alone. So are particular aspects of Jesus's teaching.

B. Jesus in 2 Timothy

Every time Paul mentions "Jesus" in 2 Timothy, it is in conjunction with the word "Christ." Twelve times Paul writes "Christ Jesus." In 2:8 he writes "Jesus Christ." But neither word occurs without the other in their total of thirteen occurrences.

Second Timothy gets off to a strongly Christocentric start. Paul is "an apostle of Christ Jesus . . . according to the promise of life that is in Christ Jesus" (1:1), from whom Paul can also bid Timothy "grace, mercy and peace" (1:2). Grace is not just a greeting but a gift, "given us in Christ Jesus before the beginning of time" (1:9). Moreover, this grace "has now been revealed through the appearing of our Savior, Christ Jesus" (1:10). Timothy is to uphold Paul's teaching "with faith and love in Christ Jesus" (2:1). Paul calls him to emulate Paul in enduring hardship "like a good soldier of Christ Jesus" (2:3). This is not some ideal Hellenistic savior-figure but the historical person of Jewish ancestry who was "raised from the dead, descended from David" (2:8). Through him, the elect "obtain the salvation that is in Christ Jesus, with eternal glory" (2:10).

Yet, this salvation will not come without cost. "Everyone who wants to live a godly life in Christ Jesus will be persecuted" (3:12). But Timothy has the means to stand firm and prosper because from infancy he has "known the holy Scriptures," which impart wisdom "for salvation through faith in Christ Jesus" (3:15). There is every incentive for Timothy to persevere because Paul admonishes him "in the presence of God and of Christ Jesus, who will judge the living and the dead" (4:1)—and Paul has already reminded Timothy that "if we disown him, he will also disown us" (2:12).

A substantial set of verses in 2 Timothy refers to Jesus as "Lord" (*kyrios*). The word does not occur in Titus, and usually when it appears in 1 Timothy, it is in conjunction with the additional words "Christ Jesus" (four times; see discussion above). But in 2 Timothy "Christ Jesus our Lord" appears just once. Yet, fifteen other times Paul speaks of "the Lord."

It will be reserved to the commentary below to determine, if possible, precisely which of these "Lord" references is to the Father, which to the Son, and which to God generically. In 2 Timothy it seems likely that "Christ Jesus" is near to hand for Paul at least when he speaks of "Lord" in 1:8, 16, 18a; 2:7, 24. In other "Lord" passages Paul may have God in all his fullness in mind, without in any way diminishing the particular functions and ministries of God as either Father, Son, or Spirit: 1:18b; 2:19, 22; 3:11; 4:8, 14, 17, 18, 22. Yet, explicit reference to Jesus even in some if not most of these verses can perhaps not be ruled out. The words of the Apostles' Creed *Jesus Christ, his only Son, our Lord* find strong resonance in 2 Timothy.

No proper title for Jesus appears at all in 2 Tim 1:12: "I know whom I have believed, and am convinced that he is able to guard what I have entrusted to him for that day." But this verse likely refers to him.

References to Jesus's life and teaching (a few already touched on above) are less frequent in 2 Timothy than in 1 Timothy (in part because the former is considerably shorter). But they are nonetheless present. Paul mentions the incarnation and the fact that Jesus "destroyed death and has brought life and immortality to light through the gospel" (1:10). Destroying death may draw on accounts of Jesus's numerous resuscitation miracles, his defeat of the devil, his own resurrection from the dead, or some combination of these. Bringing "life and immortality to light through the gospel" could refer to the salutary effects of Jesus's own preaching of the good news, to the enlivening and enlightening work of the gospel preached by Jesus's followers like Paul, or to both. In any case, Paul reminds Timothy of the life Jesus lived on this earth.

Jesus's life and ministry are at the forefront of one of Paul's key hortatory remarks (2:11–13): "If we died with him, we will also live with him; if we endure, we will also reign with him. If we disown him, he will also disown us; if we are faithless, he will remain faithful, for he cannot disown himself." There are at least hints here of Jesus's death, resurrection, and ascension and heavenly reign. When it comes to disowning Jesus and being disowned by him, possibly Paul draws on knowledge of Judas's duplicity and Jesus's handing him over to his own self-destructive wiles. With "if we are faithless, he will remain faithful" Paul could easily be referring to the night Christ was betrayed, when all the disciples fled, a night of which Paul was certainly aware (1 Cor 11:23).

It is also easy to imagine Jesus's influence in Paul's counsel (2 Tim 2:2) to make disciples who will in turn make disciples of others (cf. Matt 28:19–20).

The writer of 2 Timothy no less than the writer of 1 Timothy proceeds from an insider's knowledge of and loyalty to a "Jesus Christ" resembling "God's only Son, our Lord" as extolled in the Apostles' Creed.

C. Jesus in Titus

Titus, the shortest of the PE,[41] has correspondingly the fewest references to Jesus. There are four references to "Jesus Christ" (1:1; 2:13; 3:6) or "Christ Jesus" (1:4). These passages refer to Paul's apostleship at Jesus's command, the "grace and peace" that he grants, and his role as Savior. Jesus is implicated in the preaching that God entrusted to Paul (1:3) and that Paul passes along to others (1:9). Paul's concern for erroneous Jewish teachings (1:10, 14) have their correlate in Jesus's disputations with his countrymen over their law and traditions. People who claim to know God but by their deeds deny him (1:16) were warned against already in Jesus's sermons (Matt 7:21). The prominence of the act, ministry, and substance of teaching in Titus (e.g., Titus 1:9, 11; 2:1, 3, 4, 7, 9, 10, 12, 15) is reminiscent of Jesus's example of calling and making disciples. The notion of readiness for the return of Christ (2:13; 3:7) is found by many in Jesus's teachings about the coming of the Son of Man (e.g., Matt 24–25). Paul's directions for dealing with divisive members of a congregation (3:10) echo counsel set forth much earlier by Jesus (Matt 18:15–17).

While references to Jesus are not numerous or extensive in Titus, those that are present do not differ materially from what is found in 1–2 Timothy. The PE taken together testify solidly to a Jesus preached by Paul and taught about by Timothy and Titus in their churches, who is very much like the figure confessed in the Apostles' Creed.

V. GOD THE SPIRIT AND HIS FRUIT IN THE PE

The third major division of the Apostles' Creed is *I believe in the Holy Spirit, the holy catholic church, the communion of saints, the forgiveness of sins, the resurrection of the body, and the life everlasting. Amen.* Mention of the Spirit in the PE is far more sparing than mention of the Father and the Son, but by no means lacking. And the other five items of this segment of the Apostles'

41. The word counts in Greek for the three books: 1 Timothy, 1,591; 2 Timothy, 1,238; Titus, 659.

Creed—church, communion, forgiveness, resurrection, eternal life—are not only common but prominent in the PE. For example, without a Spirit-induced "church" there is no need for a pastor, and these are the "Pastoral" Epistles. So the PE themselves as a whole are eloquent witness to the "Lord" whose Spirit constitutes the church and who for Paul is one with the Father and the Son. Since in Pauline theology it is in part the Spirit's work to bring about things like the one universal church, fellowship, forgiveness of sins, resurrection, and eternal life, we refer to "the Spirit and his fruit" (see Gal 5:22) in this section to summarize the items mentioned in the third portion of the Apostles' Creed.

A. The Spirit in the PE

In 1 Timothy, Christ "was vindicated by the Spirit" (3:16), and Paul asserts that "the Spirit clearly says that in later times some will abandon the faith and follow deceiving spirits and things taught by demons" (4:1). In 2 Timothy the "spirit of power, of love and of self-discipline" (1:7) is likely to involve the divine Spirit, since the charismatic gift he imparts is mentioned in the preceding verse. This is confirmed by explicit reference a few verses later: "Guard the good deposit that was entrusted to you—guard it with the help of the Holy Spirit who lives in us" (1:14). However *theopneustos* be defined in 3:16 ("All Scripture is *God-breathed*"), the Spirit's influence is part of the mix in inscripturation of God's word, the *pneu-* in *theopneustos* coming from the *pneuma* (Spirit) of the Lord, who for Paul *is* the Lord (2 Cor 3:17). In Titus, Paul writes that God "saved us through the washing of rebirth and renewal by the Holy Spirit, whom he poured out on us generously through Jesus Christ our Savior" (3:5–6). It is unnecessary, and would have been pedantic, for Paul to lecture his seasoned coworkers on pneumatology; these stray and random allusions confirm that the author of the PE sees the Holy Spirit at work in a pervasive way in the world, in the church, and in personal Christian experience in a manner very much like one encounters in other Pauline letters.

B. The Spirit's Work in the PE

The work of the Spirit as articulated in the Apostles' Creed is a prominent feature of the PE. The table below matches the Spirit's work on the left with the content and various verses in the PE on the right.

Table 2. The work of the Holy Spirit in the PE

Work of the Spirit	Passages in the PE
holy catholic church	Throughout, since *all* the verses of the PE are directed to the leaders of *churches* that make up the one body of Christ in Pauline understanding (Rom 12:5; 1 Cor 12:13; Eph 4:4). See also 1 Tim 2, regulating *church* worship; 1 Tim 3 and Titus 1, setting forth standards for *church* leaders; 1 Tim 4, with instructions for conduct by *church* members; 1 Tim 5, giving counsel for ministry to various groups in the *church*; 1 Tim 6, summing up how Timothy must "guard what has been entrusted to [his] care" (v. 20), which is the *church* and its leadership. "The holy catholic church" is ubiquitous in the PE as a chief object of Paul's concern. See also occurrences of "church" in the NIV (1 Tim 3:5, 15; 5:16, 17).
communion of saints	Again, throughout. The *communion* with God and other believers enabled by sound teaching and godly behavior enjoined on Timothy and Titus, and to be passed along to parishioners, is a pervasive focus of the PE. One tribute to this dynamic is the "communion of saints" displayed throughout the PE between Paul and his two addressees, who share the *koinōnia* (communion, fellowship) of Christian experience and ministry with Paul.
forgiveness of sins	Implied, e.g., by references to *sōzō* (to save: 1 Tim 1:15; 2:4, 15; 4:16; 2 Tim 1:9; 4:18; Titus 3:5), *sōtēr* (savior: 1 Tim 1:1; 2:3; 4:10; 2 Tim 1:10; Titus 1:3, 4; 2:10, 13; 3:4, 6); *sōtēria* (salvation: 2 Tim 2:10; 3:15); *sōtērios* (saving: Titus 2:11).
resurrection of the body	Mentioned in 2 Tim 2:18. Implied for the elect (2 Tim 2:10; Titus 1:1) in "life everlasting" below; also in references to judgment, leading to everlasting life before or away from God (1 Tim 5:24; 2 Tim 1:12, 18; 2:12; 4:1, 8, 18) at a time ushered in by the appearing of Christ (1 Tim 6:14–15; 2 Tim 1:10; 4:1, 8; Titus 2:13). Every mention of Christ "raised from the dead" (2 Tim 2:8) is also a reminder to believers of their resurrected life with him, presently and in the age to come (2 Tim 2:11).
life everlasting	1 Tim 1:16; 4:8; 6:12, 19; 2 Tim 1:1, 10; 4:8, 18; Titus 1:2; 3:7.

Another way to depict the work or fruit of the Spirit in the PE is to look for elements of the Spirit's work as Paul depicts it in Gal 5:22. Again, a table can portray this usage graphically more easily than discourse alone.

Table 3. The fruit of the Holy Spirit in the PE

Fruit (work) of the Spirit	Passages in the PE (NIV)
love	1 Tim 1:5, 14; 2:15; 4:12; 6:10, 11; 2 Tim 1:7, 13; 2:22; 3:3, 10; Titus 2:2, 4; 3:4, 15
joy	2 Tim 1:4
peace	1 Tim 1:2; 2 Tim 1:2; 2:22; Titus 1:4
patience	1 Tim 1:16; 2 Tim 3:10; 4:2
kindness	Titus 3:4
goodness	No explicit references (but see Titus 3:4 ESV), though the quality denoted by the word is far from absent.
faith, faithfulness	1 Tim 1:2, 4, 5, 12, 14, 19; 2:7, 15; 3:13; 4:1, 6, 12; 5:8, 9; 6:10, 11, 12, 21; 2 Tim 1:5, 13; 2:13, 18, 22; 3:8, 10, 15; 4:7; Titus 1:1, 2, 4, 13; 2:2; 3:15
gentleness	1 Tim 3:3; 6:11 (also 2 Tim 2:25 ESV)
self-control	No explicit references in NIV, but see (under "self-control") 1 Tim 2:9, 15; 2 Tim 1:7; 3:3 ESV; under "self-controlled" 1 Tim 3:2; Titus 1:8; 2:2, 5, 6, 12 ESV). In either NIV or ESV, this is clearly a desideratum for Timothy and Titus, as well as for their parishioners in the face of pressures to abandon the respective duties God has placed on them.

It is obvious that the PE do not contain some choreographed reproduction of Pauline "fruit of the Spirit." Two of the fruits do not even appear explicitly in the PE. "Kindness" appears just once and refers to God's disposition in the incarnation; "joy" is what Paul will feel if and when Timothy reaches him in prison. Three times "peace" occurs in Paul's trademark epistolary greeting.

But there are numerous passages in which the Spirit's work, which for Paul is manifested as believers purpose to "live by the Spirit" (Gal 5:16) and "keep in step with the Spirit" (Gal 5:25), is evident in the PE, thereby serving as a calling card of the Spirit's presence. An example is 2 Tim 2:22, where Timothy is told to "pursue righteousness, faith, love, and peace," three of which are "fruit of the Spirit" in the table above. Some considerable portion of the "love, which comes from a pure heart and a good conscience and a sincere faith," mentioned in 1 Tim 1:5 is attributable primarily to the Spirit in Pauline understanding.

It is unthinkable that Paul would separate the Spirit from "the grace of our Lord" that "was poured out on me abundantly, along with the faith and love that are in Christ Jesus" (1:14). Perhaps the majority of the references in table 3 refer to communicable attributes of God that, in Pauline understanding, are accessible to believers through faith in Christ and the work of the Spirit. That is, we could say that there are a couple of dozen passages in the PE where the Spirit may be said to be assumed or even shown at work.

VI. PAUL AS *WORKING* PASTOR: EXPOSING AN OPEN ETHICAL SECRET

A. Introduction

The previous sections have argued for the centrality of the triune God for Paul's thought and life, as well as for reading the PE with optimal comprehension.[42] But there is another side to the Paul who vested so much in God (and vice versa; see 1 Tim 1:11; Titus 1:3). There is also the Paul whose grasp of God moved him to the herculean labors out of which arose the churches he (with others) founded and the epistles he composed. God's mighty work in Christ resulted in Paul working mightily. Below we explore this dimension of Paul's achievement and its reflection in the language of the PE.

Udo Schnelle has written that Paul "belongs to the small group of human beings of the last two thousand years whose life and thought have made lasting changes in the world."[43] There is an important but underreported key for understanding how Paul achieved this distinction. Ben Witherington III exemplifies the neglect of this key.[44] He helpfully and insightfully examines Paul as a writer and rhetor, a prophet and apostle, a realist and radical, an anthropologist and advocate, a storyteller and exegete, and finally an ethicist and theologian—a dozen roles in all. But none of them is "pastor."

As a founder of and leader in many church settings, and as a mentor to a generation of church leaders in the era of Timothy and Titus, Paul should be given credit for this aspect of his calling, activity, and achievement. It is no small part of what gives him credibility as he writes the pastoral letters

42. This section is adapted from ch. 11 of Brian S. Rosner, Andrew S. Malone, and Trevor J. Burke, eds., *Paul as Pastor* (London: Bloomsbury, 2018), 143–58; used by permission.

43. Udo Schnelle, *Apostle Paul: His Life and Theology*, trans. M. Eugene Boring (Grand Rapids: Baker Academic, 2005), 598.

44. Ben Witherington III, *The Paul Quest: The Renewed Search for the Jew of Tarsus* (Downers Grove, IL: InterVarsity, 1998).

under investigation in this commentary. It also helps explain why through the centuries both leaders in churches and those of the rank and file have prized these writings. They model and minister what Oden (sec. I above) has termed classical pastoral care. Paul's footprint in Scripture and history is wider ranging and more variegated than merely pastoral. But a sizable component of the persona revealed in writings of his era, including his own writings, discloses a pastoral thinker and practitioner.

To highlight Paul's pastoral side is in no way to call in question the perhaps equally significant sense in which Paul's identity is more fully captured by our term "missionary," as stressed, for example, in Eckhard Schnabel's *Paul the Missionary: Realities, Strategies, and Methods*, or in Paul Barnett's *Paul: Missionary of Jesus*.[45] Yet, the title "missionary" in our day may be as different from what Paul was and did, precisely, as the term "pastor" in today's widely varying settings is from Paul in his various gambits and duties. Possibly no single title or role in itself can capture or exhaust Paul in his complexity, versatility, and sometimes obscurity regarded from two millennia hence. The term he most favored for himself seems to have been *apostolos* (apostle). But there was a pastoral edge to the work of that office as it unfolded in the early decades of church formation.[46] Given Paul's extensive teaching and preaching as *apostolos*, and his care of souls in *ekklēsiai* (churches), and the evangelism he performed everywhere he went that grew out of or resulted in the planting of *ekklēsiai*, we are surely justified in looking to the *Pastoral* Epistles for clues regarding his *pastoral* outlook.

The italics in this section's title point to a dimension of the Pauline pastoral style and praxis that is easily overlooked in reading Paul. Paul's "open ethical secret" (this section's subtitle) is that he had a ferocious work ethic. In important respects it distances him from those who might seek to understand him and the PE today. Let us consider here the examples of academicians, ministers, and students.

Academicians may tend to view Paul primarily in terms of ideas or rational concepts (in important respects this approach goes back to F. C. Baur, on whom more below). Moreover, even if they note Paul's alleged trade, many professors have little experience of manual labor in their upbringing or background. Paul as a manual laborer, or artisan if one prefers, may seem an irrelevance. Most books on Paul say little to nothing about how demanding physical work may have conditioned his writings.

Second, Christian ministers contain in their ranks some of the hardest-working persons on earth, but some have a reputation, at least in the United

45. Schnabel, *Paul the Missionary*; P. W. Barnett, *Paul: Missionary of Jesus*, After Jesus 2 (Grand Rapids: Eerdmans, 2008).

46. Apostolic figures like James, Cephas, and John (Gal 2:9; cf. 1:19) seem also to have served as pastors in the Jerusalem church.

States, for laziness, inordinate love of eating, and other unseemly sensual excesses associated with idleness in the sense of too much time on their hands. This impression is not always unfounded stereotyping.

Finally, students who study Paul in the West hail from cultures that increasingly disdain manual labor and prize good times, winning the lottery, leisure, and living for the weekend, church attendance not envisioned.[47] Few professors in Bible schools or seminaries have not despaired over students who have more time for social media and online games, which are viewed not as luxury but necessity, than for their studies, which are viewed not as a once-in-a-lifetime opportunity but a formality to be endured, with as little intellectual expenditure as possible. Those who teach not only in the West but in developing nations marvel at the contrast: Western students with unlimited access to learning opportunities, bored and distracted with it all; Christian women and men in impoverished and sometimes persecution-plagued regions, zealous to learn and willing to make any sacrifice to travel where learning is available.

It will be argued below that what Paul modeled and counseled in his letters to Timothy and Titus reflects an embrace of arduous labor at many levels and in many ways. The PE are a fertile resource for restoring in the academic mind, for pastoral practice, and to student expectation a healthy regard for regular and rigorous work as an effect of the grace that the Pauline gospel announced. His grand and deep theological vantage point (see sections II–V above) did not originate from, or result in, thinking and living abstracted from the workaday world but one fully enmeshed in one of its most essential enterprises for human flourishing: arduous labor. His life and teaching reflect the conviction of the proverb: "All hard work brings a profit, but mere talk leads only to poverty" (Prov 14:23).

We will look first at work and Paul's work ethic in each of the three PE. We will then assess a recent exchange on this topic before offering final observations.

B. The Prominence of Work in the PE

Paul Barnett has rightly noted, referring to Paul's tentmaking: "It is clear that Paul's work was physical and arduous. Paul writes of 'labor and toil . . . we worked night and day' (1 Thess 2:9; also 2 Thess 3:8; Acts 20:35) and of 'working with our own hands' (1 Cor 4:12; also Acts 20:34). We gain an impression of one

47. See, for example, Jordan Ballor, "The Biblical View of Work," and Jeff Haanen, "How We Lost the Craftsmen," *The City*, Spring 2014, 25–38 and 39–45. For a pastoral statement on work from the perspective of a developing nation, see Ashish Raichur, *Biblical Attitudes toward Work*, rev. ed. (Karnataka, India: All Peoples Church & World Outreach, 2007).

whose daily life was characterized by hard physical labor, which began before sunrise."[48] Yet, Paul worked not only at tentmaking to sustain himself but at ministry to glorify God. Long ago F. C. Baur observed that Paul displayed "a spirit involved in a great struggle, in the throes of a travail which cannot be accomplished save with labour and conflict and high spiritual energy."[49] At every turn in the PE, we observe this combination of hard physical labor for subsistence, generated by a restless spirit that could not be content with half-measures or casual effort. In a perusal of the PE I noted the fingerprints of Paul's work ethic at twenty-nine places in 1 Timothy, twenty-four in 2 Timothy, and fifteen in Titus, for a total of sixty-eight references. All of these passages cannot be explicated here but we can touch on many of them in at least general terms.

1. Pointers toward a Work Ethic in 1 Timothy

Work is a primary orienting expectation for ministry in 1 Timothy. A career pilot for a major airline once wrote, "The cost of learning to fly professionally has always been the same: it takes everything you've got."[50] A conscientious pilot guiding an aircraft with hundreds of lives depending on his or her competence and concentration is not unlike the apostle Paul leading the early church in its formative decades. In 1 Tim 4:7b–10 we glimpse the epicenter of Paul's conception of pastoral leadership as he urged it on Timothy. It involves great effort, "everything you've got" in the pilot's words:

> Train [*Gymnaze*] yourself to be godly [*pros eusebeian*]. For physical training is of some value, but godliness has value for all things, holding promise for both the present life and the life to come. This is a trustworthy saying that deserves full acceptance. That is why we labor and strive, because we have put our hope in the living God, who is the Savior of all people, and especially of those who believe.

"Train yourself" calls on Timothy to exercise diligence. A form of the same word (from *gymnazō*)[51] appears in Heb 5:14 to describe those "who by constant use have *trained* themselves to distinguish good from evil." Hebrews 12:11 speaks of "a harvest of righteousness and peace for those who have been *trained*"—we might translate "whipped into shape"—by divine *paideia* (discipline).

48. Paul Barnett, "Tentmaking," *DPL* 926.

49. F. C. Baur, *Paul, the Apostle of Jesus Christ: His Life and Works, His Epistles and Teachings*, 2 vols. (Peabody, MA: Hendrickson, 2003), 2:269.

50. Paul Andrews, letter to the editor, *Flying* 141.7 (2014): 10.

51. For this word's athletic associations, see *NIDNTTE* 1:610.

As for being "godly" (see 1 Tim 4:7 cited above), godliness (*eusebeia*) is prominent in the PE, with ten of its fifteen NT occurrences found there, and eight of those in 1 Timothy (see sec. IX.B below). This godliness is not an automatic pastoral attribute, even for a Timothy with divine gifting through the laying on of apostolic hands (2 Tim 1:6). The grace he has received in the gospel impels him to athletic-like effort (note *gymnazō*) toward appropriation of a quality—hard-won godliness—that will serve him in good stead not only now but in the eschaton.

Therefore Paul writes, generously including Timothy, "We labor and strive" as the result of hope set on the living God. Toil is required to reach the goal of godliness. Hope in God results not in escapism or passivity awaiting the future but in a proactive posture toward grasping godliness in ministry. This resolve applies to Paul's ministry as he addresses Timothy and to Timothy's as he fights to "stay there in Ephesus" (1 Tim 1:3). As anyone with pastoral experience can attest, to "stay there" in a ministry where circumstances have become adverse is even more work than the pastoral task is already. Paul did not give up on Corinth but diligently strove (by his epistles and repeated presence there) to salvage their gospel commitment. He exhibited the same tenacity—for the sake of "effective work"—in Ephesus: "But I will stay on at Ephesus until Pentecost, because a great door for *effective work* has opened to me, and there are many who oppose me" (1 Cor 16:8–9). He calls for the same labor-intensive steadfastness from Timothy.

Paul's favored self-designation *apostolos* (1:2) implies subjugation to another—a grace that children of Adam and Eve find difficult if not odious. One used to hear routinely in North American preaching, "The hardest instrument in the orchestra is *second* violin," the idea being that support roles lack glamor and therefore interested applicants.

In this age of self-prioritization one hears it markedly less. *Apostolos* was not a term of glory and prestige in Paul's usage, like one might think of "bishop" or "cardinal" or "megachurch pastor" today, but one whose variegated connotations would include the idea of being a workhorse tasked with the unpleasant (see 1 Cor 4:9–13; 2 Cor 4:7–11). In fact, Paul summarizes the apostolic burden using the participle *synergountes*—apostles are "God's *coworkers*" (2 Cor 6:1). When Paul speaks of "God's work" (ESV "the stewardship from God") in 1 Tim 1:4, he casts Timothy as a worker in God's household (cf. 3:15).

Regarding 1 Tim 1:5, the competence to exercise love in the Christian mode with pure heart and good conscience and unaffected faith requires a long apprenticeship and an occupational commitment to self-abnegation. The same is true for "holding on to faith and a good conscience" in 1:19. The acquisition of these qualities for deployment in pastoral relationships is arduous and elusive. Pastors find themselves challenged constantly to love as they know they are called to, to live so as to keep their conscience relatively clean, and to embrace the historic faith with humility yet a fervor that commends it to those who look to the pastor for stability. The pastor who does not wince inwardly at the reminder of the deeply demanding and often bruising growth process in these directions has not progressed very far in them.[52]

When Paul speaks about "the law" in 1:8, he surely has in mind the Torah. Paul had spent a good bit of his life under Gamaliel learning that law (Acts 22:3) and its corollaries, as Timothy in a less formal and intense way had been instructed by his mother and grandmother (2 Tim 1:5; 3:14–15). There can be no proper regard for God's law in the gospel ministry of the pastorate without the labor required to understand it and the discipline acquired by striving to appropriate its lessons. A bonus here is that, as one works to learn Torah, Torah teaches work as a noble human endeavor: "Six days you shall labor and do all your work" (Exod 20:9). This is not punishment, for "the LORD God took the man and put him in the Garden of Eden to work it and take care of it" (Gen 2:15). Even after the fall, humans glorify God with their lives primarily through their everyday work. Gamaliel III (early third century) commended "study of the Torah combined with some secular occupation, for the labor of them both puts sin out of one's mind. All study of the Torah which is not combined with work will ultimately be futile and lead to sin" (Pirqe ʾAbot 2:2).[53] The law, Paul tells Timothy, is among other things a measurement tool for recognizing things "contrary to the sound doctrine" (1 Tim 1:10), an invaluable skill and ongoing project in pastoral labor.

Paul's work ethic did not come from nowhere. He came to God's *diakonia* (service, 1:12), a transparent term of employment in the sense of servitude, from his zealotry as "a blasphemer and a persecutor and a violent man" (1:13). But he received mercy (1:16), which set in motion a transformation that would shift not the zeal of Paul's labor but its direction. He would now apply might and main for Christ's renown rather than for the honor of his former religion and his vain boasting in it.

The glorious doxology of 1:17, which was instrumental in Jonathan Edwards's conversion and industrious commitment to God, segues into a metaphor designed to rally Timothy to readiness to receive Paul's apostolic charge to him: "fight the battle well" (1:18). To read Julius Caesar's *Gallic Wars* is to be reminded of the physical demand of plying Roman-era weapons and the exhausting regimen of carrying baggage and digging breastworks for encampments. Soldiering was the hardest of labor. This military metaphor, then, is not a call for violence but for things like intensity in action, endurance of adversity, bravery in the face of intimidation, and all-out effort to surmount obstacles.

52. Note, for example, the insightful remarks in Samuel Wells, "The Banality of Pastoral Failure," *ChrCent*, June 25, 2014, 35.

53. Barnett, "Tentmaking," *DPL* 925.

Chapter 2 of 1 Timothy calls twice for prayer, the most sublime of Christian activities but also one of the most demanding, mentally and physically. The dozing disciples with Jesus in Gethsemane illustrate the weakness of the flesh against the high demands of praying, here in 1 Timothy for all people, including those in high positions (2:1–2). Paul instructs Timothy to engage men in prayer rather than allowing them to languish in rancor and bickering (2:8). It is natural for men to harbor bitterness and join factions; it is hard work to find the spiritual space to replace skirmishing with supplication and other prayer forms (2:1). Around the world I have found it rare to encounter men in church who abound in prayer, and I struggle with it myself. Not only must Timothy pray in exemplary fashion, his pastoral calling is to lead others toward this challenging and elusive discipline. Here as throughout the PE, an overlooked aspect of the hard work of pastoral labor is setting high goals. Paul is not going to countenance prayerless assemblies, to avoid which requires pastoral intentionality, action, and bucking the default trend of the male demographic, which does not include proactive prayerfulness.

To "live peaceful and quiet lives" in 2:2 may not sound like work, but "lives" translates *bios*, a word for livelihood or everyday existence. For all but the highest classes in the Roman world, this *bios* meant work. Jesus's parable in Luke 17:7–10 would have resonated with many, as a servant or shepherd slaves all day, gets his master's meal first at the end of it, and doesn't even get a thank you. Not just the ethos of ministry and godliness called for work in Paul's outlook; the adversities of daily living in the Roman world, dramatized by what we would consider brutally brief life spans, called forth from those in Christ a demeanor and practices that mortified the flesh and honored God. Taken seriously, this expectation is a mandate for toil—sanctified and potentially joyful to be sure, but toil nonetheless.

Embedded in chapter 2 is Paul's insistent reference to his appointment as preacher, apostle, and teacher of Gentiles (v. 7). To sustain these roles over some three decades against the opposition Paul faced was a herculean task. But Paul had the moral authority to stand behind his claim that he was not lying because of his faithful labor. The preaching Paul did was often under tumultuous circumstances. As an apostle, he traveled by land some 8,700 miles and almost that many by sea.[54] That's over 500 miles a year for over thirty years. Teaching would often have been difficult and perhaps even distasteful in some ways for a man steeped in Jewish scruples reaching out to subgroups who may have demonized Jews like Paul. There was innate hostility to overcome on both sides. Paul persevered, furnishing Timothy a template for facing his own rigors at Ephesus, a place where Paul had once engaged in the enigmatic

54. Eckhard Schnabel, *Paul and the Early Church*, vol. 2 of *Early Christian Mission* (Downers Grove, IL: InterVarsity Press, 2004), 1288.

task of wrestling wild beasts (1 Cor 15:32). Wrestling may be entertaining to watch, but Paul was not describing a leisure activity or even a spectator sport.

The restraint, summons to be learners, and eschatological hope called for from women in 2:9–15 are work (see commentary below for explication). Qualifications for church officers (3:1–13) assume people of ambition, diligence, and productivity measured by high standards; the slothful need not apply. The word translated "aspires" in 3:1 bespeaks drive and striving, not tentative willingness. In 4:1–5 the work of affirming godly marriage and licit use of God's gifts would be a constant challenge in a cultural setting of self-indulgence and anti-Christian religious myth-making (see 4:7a). Timothy's only hope for pastoral effectiveness will lie in his identity as "a good minister [*diakonos*] of Christ Jesus, nourished on the truths of the faith and of the good teaching that [he has] followed" (4:6). Paul describes here the outcome of years of Timothy's learning and practice of the hard work of ministry under the tutelage of Paul.

First Timothy 4:11–16 contains a collage of effort-images that underscores the arduousness of what Paul places before Timothy: command, teach, let no one despise, set an example, devote yourself, do not neglect your gift, practice these things, immerse yourself in them, keep a close watch on yourself, persist. The outcome is glorious: by doing so "you will save both yourself and your hearers" (4:16). But just contemplating Paul's slate of duties for Timothy leaves one weary. Nothing short of divine enabling[55] would suffice for Timothy to implement this agenda with the verve Paul demanded and had modeled for him.

Thus far I have touched on just fifteen of the twenty-nine places in 1 Timothy where I believe one can speak of Paul's work ethic, whether in his own self-understanding as a servant of Christ, in his expectation for Timothy and other church workers, or both. We can survey the remaining data in rapid succession. In chapter 5 Paul again commends the hard work of self-restraint, this time in Timothy's dealings with older men, older women, and younger women. In 1 Tim 5:3–8 Paul calls on the church to "give proper recognition to" certain widows, which is not just symbolic respect but also material provision. This commitment will require congregational work to supply. Widows' children and grandchildren are expected to shoulder this load themselves. Self-indulgence on the part of widows is condemned, while the labor of night-and-day prayer by widows is commended. Verses 9–16 continue with more commendation of working widows and condemnation of idlers. Those who can, should support widows in their own families themselves, leaving the church free to care for those who are truly needy.

First Timothy 5:17–21 touches on the work of congregational direction, the labor of preaching and teaching, and the prickly necessity of ecclesial dis-

55. Such enabling points back to the theocentric foundation discussed in sections II–VI above.

cipline, a work widely abandoned in churches in our times because it does require such foresight and effort. In 5:22–25 we note the work of discernment, moral restraint, and spiritual integrity in the form of Timothy's personal purity, dietary discipline (extending to proper use of wine), and practical application of eschatological hope.

Finally, chapter 6 points to Paul's work ethic and affirmation of this ethic in others as he calls on slaves to render model service to their masters and vice versa (vv. 1–2), exhorts Timothy again to the work of teaching and exhorting (v. 2b), commends contentment with basic "food and clothing" (v. 8), and warns of the pitfall of the pursuit of plenty (vv. 9–10) rather than working for treasure that endures, like Jesus called for (Matt 6:19–20). In 6:11–12 Timothy is summoned with one of the rare omega-vocatives ("O man of God" ESV) in the Pauline corpus[56] to the labor of fleeing material fixation and pursuing the fruit of gospel grace and the Spirit's fruit. Timothy should fight, take hold, keep (6:12–14), words commending diligence and effort. People of means in Timothy's congregation should "do good," "be rich in good deeds," "be generous and ready to share," not in a mechanical way as buying divine favor but in view of the age to come, taking "hold of the life that is truly life" in the here and now (6:18–19). This commitment involves the work of future hope but also delayed gratification, a vanishing discipline in consumerist and digital wallet societies.

The dramatic conclusion of the epistle is a second omega-vocative, calling Timothy this time to the work of guarding the deposit and holding the line of resistance against a *gnōsis* that has subverted the faith of some (6:20). Perhaps they failed to work hard at the Christian faith and so were never really confirmed in it.

2. *Pointers toward a Work Ethic in 2 Timothy*

In 2 Tim 1:3 Paul speaks of serving God and praying night and day. I have known many pastors over the years who did not give the impression that they labored intensely in prayer, and only a few of whom I am sure they did. Willingness to work by itself will not guarantee quality prayer, but absence of that willingness will ensure either superficial prayer or the hypocrisy of affecting intense prayer communion but not actually engaging in it. In 1:7 God is said to confer a spirit of self-expenditure, revealing itself in power, love, and self-control. This is not a power that exploits others but one that elevates them, often at the pastoral caregiver's expense. That same dynamic is present in love and self-control. These are qualities that in Christ promote others, not

56. See also Rom 2:1, 3; 9:20; 11:33; Gal 3:1; 1 Tim 6:20.

self. Self-control, mentioned frequently in the PE,[57] should be highlighted as a difficult task, one that requires work to exercise. The reason so many people lack it is their failure to apply themselves to the rigors of exercising it, or perhaps even their unwillingness to seek from God the resources that would make possible the necessary change of will.

In 1:8 Paul writes of power from God that makes possible cosuffering for the gospel, Timothy joining with Paul in the thankless labor of undergoing harassment or the threat of same for the gospel's sake. We should not underestimate the steely discipline, which I suspect can arise only from a life of proactive appropriation of grace leading to habitual bodily faithfulness, which is needed to serve the gospel to the point of suffering in the Pauline sense. Mariam Ibrahim in Khartoum, Sudan, might qualify as a contemporary example.[58] From her first arraignment she was adamant in her Christian confession, nor did she seem to waver under the threat of lashings and execution. Such determination and steadfastness do not arise in Christian lives of lazy compliance with some easy religious scruples. Followers of Jesus whose lives mark them out for persecution and who persevere in it are modeling a focus and pattern of God-oriented selfless actions that typify the work ethic that reverberates everywhere in the PE.

Paul and Timothy have been saved and called, 1:9–12 states, not because of works but for work—that is, the work of preacher-apostle-teacher. For Timothy to "keep the pattern of sound teaching" he observed and receives from Paul is work, as is guarding the deposit (1:13–14). In 1:16–18 Paul commends Onesiphorus because of his work on Paul's behalf.

There are few verses in chapter 2 that do *not* remind of Paul's work ethic. In 2:1–2 Timothy's reception of "the grace that is in Christ Jesus" will result in teaching others so compellingly that the taught will do likewise. Chapter 2:3–7 amounts to another locus classicus for this topic, as the call is to suffer (a work in reward for previous work already treated above), which is illustrated by soldier and athlete and farmer. Timothy will fall short of his charge of discipling and serving to the point of suffering absent the whole-self devotion in the laborious fashion implied by this collage. Even Paul's final flourish in v. 7 to give thought points to the labor of reflection and abiding in a posture where "the Lord" is able to "give . . . insight" because Timothy is willing to be drawn further into his intense, self-mortifying role.

57. See also 1 Tim 2:9, 15; 3:1; 2 Tim 1:7; 3:3; Titus 1:8; 2:2, 5, 6, 12.

58. In 2014 this Sudanese Christian physician was arrested and charged with adultery for her marriage to a Christian man. Though her (Muslim) father had deserted the family when she was a girl and she was reared as a Christian by her mother, Islamic courts determined that, by their law, she should receive two hundred lashes and then suffer death by hanging unless she returned to her father's religion. She refused. Eventually she was allowed to leave Sudan and be united with her husband in the United States.

Remembering Jesus Christ (2:9), who worked himself into the grave but was rescued from it, will help Timothy here. So may Paul's example of enduring everything for the eventual redemption of the elect (2:10). As Timothy labors in reminding and charging the Ephesian believers, his goal is no less than to present himself to God as approved, "a worker who does not need to be ashamed" (2:14–15). Such a worker will find the restraint to recuse himself from "godless chatter" (2:16; cf. 2:23). He will experience ongoing cleansing, set apart, ready for every good work (2:20–21). He will be inclined to flee youthful *epithymiai* (desires) and to pursue faith, love, and peace along with others of pure heart (2:22). The chapter closes with a portrait of the daily pastoral labor of "the Lord's servant [*doulos*]," a fourfold mandate of kindness to everyone, teaching, enduring evil, and correcting opponents not harshly or triumphalistically but humbly (2:24–26). Here the hardest work for Timothy might have lain in overcoming the temptation just to quit putting up with the bother and to return some of that evil with justly deserved retaliatory ministry. How many ministers preach sermons that are engineered to "give it to" certain people in the congregation?

In chapter 3, vv. 1–9 depict a Zeitgeist of indulgent self-seeking rather than laboring for God's kingdom. Verses 10–11 praise Timothy's diligence thus far in endorsement by emulation of Paul's life of aggressive engagement of gospel entailments, going all the way back to the first missionary journey. These travels witnessed a legacy of labor, but also of the Lord's deliverance. Bearing Paul's precedent in mind, Timothy can "continue" (*menō*) in his doctrinal and scriptural understanding (3:14–16). This endurance will lead to the "good work" (3:17) on which the PE, like Christ in the Gospels, place such a high premium.

In chapter 4 we find a charge with the ultimate incentive to get and stay busy—the presence of God and his Son (4:1). Specific foci of pastoral labor are cited: preach, be ready, reprove, exhort, exercise patience, instruct (4:2). Verse 5 summarizes action items, including "the work of an evangelist"; vv. 6–8 point to Paul's ongoing work of carrying on, clinging to the favorable outcome that awaits. Verse 17 underscores the Lord's work in supporting Paul that he might complete his work. In v. 21 Timothy is entrusted with assignments—work. But there is hope (v. 18) in that "the Lord will rescue . . . from every evil work [*ergon*]" (my translation). One reason Paul insists on a life that is work-rich is that Christians are called to return evil with good (Rom 12:17; 1 Thess 5:15), and it seems the devil and his bunch never slumber. Against the demonic onslaught of evil deeds abounding in this fallen world, God juxtaposes the plethora of good works of the saints. No saint abounds in good works without a work ethic that generates selfless labor.

3. Pointers toward a Work Ethic in Titus

Paul's epistle to Titus shows that Paul's stress on theologically grounded pastoral labor, intensive and extensive, in 1–2 Timothy is not an aberration. This emphasis continues in Titus. In the first chapter Paul greets Titus not only as an *apostolos* (apostle) but first of all as a *doulos* (slave), underscoring service for the sake of others at the behest of Another. If Paul calls Titus to selfless labor for Christ's sake, it will be only what Paul practices himself. Verse 3 speaks of Paul's preaching, a body of work of which we have only sketches in Acts. Even that much is enough to be reminded how arduously Paul labored to further the message entrusted to him. Analogous to Paul's mandate, Titus receives one now himself (v. 5): set things in order and appoint elders—not any old way, but as Paul has directed. The qualifications for these elders represent a character sketch of an engaged, self-sacrificial congregational servant leader (vv. 6–9). The picture is also of a person willing to go to great lengths in the study of Christian doctrine so that he may teach it. He will also toil toward the costly appropriation of gospel graces rendering him "not overbearing, not quick-tempered, not given to drunkenness, not violent, not pursuing dishonest gain. Rather, he must be hospitable, one who loves what is good, who is self-controlled, upright, holy and disciplined" (vv. 7–8). In contrast, vv. 10–14 give a portrait of lack of restraint, laziness, and opportunism, markers of either no work ethic or a diabolical one. Verses 15 and 16 detail the unsavory character of figures who are significantly "unfit for doing anything good."

For his part, Titus in 2:1 and 15 is told to be on continual watch for opportunities to turn people in right directions by his habits of discourse. Translations say "teach," but the verb is the imperative of *laleō*, better understood as Titus's speech in all his pastoral and other interpersonal dealings. In 2:2–10 Paul affirms that all demographics in the church, including Titus himself, should model godly discipline and zeal for what is right. This behavior will enable them to "make the teaching about God our Savior attractive" (v. 10), living lives that, by their comprehensive attention to honoring God and suppressing the godless impulses of Cretan normalcy, make a statement by the discipline and effort of good works. Next, 2:11–14 underscores that God's grace "teaches" or "trains" (ESV) recipients to transformational, God-directed effort, with the end-game again good works. Verse 15 is a précis of the pastoral labor agenda: exhort, rebuke, stand tall in the industrious pastoral role.

Titus 3:1–3 details more pastoral labor, with a view to good work in light of an indolent and errant past of which all are guilty. Remarkable is the attitude change implied in v. 3, which calls for frank admission that, however despicable people around them may be, Christians at some point were no better. This comment opens the way for vv. 4–8 with their commendation of divine grace and direction for Titus to press these matters so that believers "may be careful to devote themselves to doing what is good" (v. 8). Verses 9–10 touch on the work of church discipline. Finally, in 3:12–14 Titus is called to various duties, as are the Cretan believers, who need to "devote themselves to doing what is good, in order to provide for urgent needs and not live unproductive lives" (v. 14).

C. Paul as Worker: Contemporary Discussion

In the last couple of generations important discussion of Paul's manual labor goes back to various publications by Ronald Hock. An example is his 1978 *JBL* article "Paul's Tentmaking and the Problem of His Social Class." Hock argued that Adolf Deissmann was right to surmise that Paul's tentmaking was significant in determining his social class. But whereas Deissmann viewed Paul as a laborer who embraced his trade, Hock follows William Ramsay in suggesting that Paul was aristocratic in outlook.[59] He carried out his manual labor, we might say, holding his nose. "Paul's choice of language to refer to his work reflects not the attitude of the typical artisan, as Deissmann would have us believe, or of the working rabbi who was taught to 'love labor,'[60] as many scholars would lead us to expect, but rather the snobbish and scornful attitude so typical of upper class Greeks and Romans."[61]

In 2007 Joel Lohr published an article in *Currents in Theology and Mission* entitled "He Identified with the Lowly and Became a Slave of All: Paul's Tentmaking as a Strategy for Mission." Lohr largely accepts Hock's portrait of Paul's low view of work but argues that Paul did it for strategic reasons. First, by tentmaking he could "identify with the lowly and . . . exhort the socially elite to do the same." Second, Paul viewed this as a form of imitating Christ. Finally, "Paul's refusal of financial support proves to be his solution to possible obligatory relationships in Corinth and aids his overall objective, to remove divisions and unify the body there."[62]

Hock's view was called in question, however, in a 2006 *JBL* article by Todd Still entitled "Did Paul Loathe Manual Labor? Revisiting the Work of Ronald F. Hock on the Apostle's Tentmaking and Social Class." Still notes that Hock immerses Paul too exclusively in a Hellenistic setting. When Jewish

59. R. Hock, "Paul's Tentmaking and the Problem of His Social Class," *JBL* 97.4 (1978): 564.

60. Hock's reference here is to Pirqe 'Abot 1:10.

61. Hock, "Paul's Tentmaking," 562.

62. Quotes in this and preceding sentences from J. Lohr, "He Identified with the Lowly and Became a Slave to All: Paul's Tentmaking as a Strategy for Mission," *CurTM* 34.3 (2007): 179.

sources and a wider range of New Testament texts are considered, a different picture emerges. Still thus objects to Hock's portrait, presents a Paul less negative toward manual labor and laborers, and concludes:

> A final, if unintentional, implication of Hock's ascribing to Paul a snobbish attitude toward his trade is that it portrays the apostle as a deeply conflicted and decidedly hypocritical individual. On Hock's reading, even as Paul enjoined his converts to lead a life of humility as graphically exhibited by Christ and himself (see esp. 2 Cor 11:7; Phil 2:3,8), he harbored an aristocratic hubris against manual labor and, by extension, manual laborers. As it happens, the Paul that Hock gives us is not so much a servant at work as a snob toward work; he is not so much an apostle who condescends as a condescending apostle.[63]

In my view, overall Still gets the better of this interchange. We should not romanticize the hard and dirty work that Paul's tentmaking or leatherworking or both involved. But neither should we ascribe to Paul a calculating cynicism or deep hidden resentment toward such labor. The Paul who speaks so much of labor in serving Christ in the PE comports well with a Paul who applied to ministry the same hard-nosed work ethic that would have been necessary to survive as an artisan in that social setting. The Christlike selflessness and utter lack of mercenary or entitlement thinking involved in working hard to pay one's own way so that one may work hard to serve others in the gospel are features of Paul's everyday practice not to be overlooked.

D. Concluding Observations

In a critical climate where the PE are largely isolated from the historical Paul, any work ethic teased out of the rhetoric of the PE is just as fictive as the rest of the PE. In many circles today, however, warrant for viewing the PE as pseudonymous or allonymous is felt to be unconvincing (see sec. X.B below). Late in Paul's life, if that be the right setting for the PE, the Paul of the gospel of grace is adamant regarding the necessity of arduous human labor for the body of Christ to realize its potential, especially insofar as its leaders are concerned.[64] Three observations may be offered in conclusion. I will apply them respectively to the hypothetical academician, pastor, and student mentioned in the introduction of this section.

63. T. Still, "Did Paul Loathe Manual Labor? Revisiting the Work of Ronald F. Hock on the Apostle's Tentmaking and Social Class," *JBL* 125.4 (2006): 793.

64. Köstenberger (507–8) recognizes this dimension of the PE.

The academician. Paul's work ethic in the PE calls for methodological repentance. Since at least F. C. Baur, Paul has been read as an idealist philosopher. "The great distinguishing characteristic which appears everywhere in the apostle's writings is the innate impulse, springing from the very roots of his nature, towards rational speculative contemplation."[65] Accordingly, the essence of his message is not Christ's person and work but speculative ideas. The question in the wide realms of scholarship that have followed in this academic tradition has only been, Which ideas? Baur thought Kantian and Hegelian ones, ideas forming themselves inexorably in Paul's psyche and manifesting themselves in his epistles, just like Hegel's god called *Geist* manifests itself in historical phenomena.[66] Paul's theology is all about human consciousness, not God and Christ and revealed Scripture and truth and commandments in any cognitively knowable ways. Baur wrote of "faith, love, and hope as the three *momenta* of Christian consciousness."[67] For Baur these virtues are all abstractions.[68]

A couple of generations later, Rudolf Bultmann (1884–1976, widely regarded as the most influential NT scholar of the twentieth century) followed suit, changing the substance of that consciousness from Baur's idealism to one in step with language popularized by the philosopher Martin Heidegger. A generation after Bultmann, Udo Schnelle in more recent times analyzes Paul not for the putative substance of Christian belief (*fides quae*) and its historical basis, even in his accepted letters, and the empirical grounds for this faith[69] but for "the Pauline dynamic of meaning formation."[70] To Schnelle's credit, he recognizes that Paul writes of God, not human consciousness. But this divinity is a "symbolic world" God. Human consciousness gets smuggled back in, as freedom becomes the holy grail of the human quest.[71] For Paul, was it not the glory of God, or perhaps union with Christ? In Schnelle, love becomes "the ground of all being." For Paul, if we speak in such terms, that ground would be the God who created all things, not some feeling or affection associated with

65. Baur, *Paul, the Apostle of Jesus Christ*, 2:275–76.

66. See Yarbrough, *Salvation Historical Fallacy?*, 11–13, for Baur's explanation of how ideas in a dialectical process of self-generation created the impression of Jesus's resurrection for Paul. He was not announcing the reality of a witnessed, historical event but telling a tall tale as a means of expressing a rational conviction of which he had become convinced.

67. Baur, *Paul, the Apostle of Jesus Christ*, 2:228.

68. For a reasonable and telling hypothesis regarding Baur's outlook, see Corneliu Simut, *F. C. Baur's Synthesis of Böhme and Hegel: Redefining Christian Theology as a Gnostic Philosophy of Religion* (Leiden: Brill, 2015). Simut's thesis helps explain why Baur moves so effortlessly from statements of biblical writers based (they argue) on observed events, remembered speech, and enscripturated truths to timeless ideas and states of consciousness.

69. This approach comes across as disdain for "myths" in the PE; see 1 Tim 1:4; 4:7; 2 Tim 4:4; Titus 1:14.

70. Schnelle, *Apostle Paul*, 598.

71. See Baur, *Paul, the Apostle of Jesus Christ*, 2:272.

God. For Schnelle, Paul, not Christ, "was and is the standard-bearer of this conception" of the love at being's ground.[72] But Paul proclaimed a gospel that was not a conception, and he was an apostle, not a saving-conception conceiver. He preached not himself or his ideas but Christ crucified (1 Cor 1:23).

As Gary Dorrien has shown,[73] mainstream Protestant thought since the Enlightenment and still today takes its bearings far more from Kant, Schelling, Hegel, and Schleiermacher than from biblical writers, even when purportedly explaining what the biblical writers say. This practice has had pervasive effect in biblical studies and vests far more confidence in idealist hermeneutics than is warranted. Many assume idealist outlooks without naming the philosophers who have bequeathed them to post-Christian academic thought.[74]

The distance between the *working* apostle-pastor of the PE and Baur's "apostle" who "recognized no other principle as having authority for him but his own immediate self-consciousness"[75] is too vast to try to bridge here. It may be a project worth pursuing for restoring a Paul in biblical studies whose Christ is larger and more tangibly demanding than much "critical" thought grants.

The pastor. Paul's work ethic in the PE may solve for the pastor what we might term the Schnabel Enigma. In his book *Paul the Missionary*, Eckhard Schnabel notes that twelve reasons have been advanced for the success of the early church's missionary outreach—success in the sense that the church arose and survived and still exists.[76] The enigma is that none of these twelve "historical" explanations, or any combination of them, suffices to explain the persistence of the Christian faith and believing communities.[77] Schnabel

72. Schnelle, *Apostle Paul*, 603.

73. Dorrien, *Kantian Reason and Hegelian Spirit.*

74. See, for example, Ulrich Wilckens, *Kritik der Bibelkritik* (Neukirchen-Vluyn: Neukirchener Theologie, 2012), 27–60, for a summary of how philosophical considerations, not historical or empirical ones, have exerted undue influence in German biblical studies, with results persisting to the present and producing international effects. Interpreters and philosophers he cites most prominently include Schleiermacher, D. F. Strauss, F. C. Baur, Kant, Hegel, Nietzsche, and Troeltsch.

75. Baur, *Paul, the Apostle of Jesus Christ*, 2:272.

76. Schnabel, *Paul the Missionary,* see esp. 360–73.

77. These twelve factors are (1) "the generally favorable conditions of the Pax Romana"; (2) "the rational critique of polytheism by Platonist and Stoic philosophers"; (3) "the disintegration of the Greek city-state"; (4) "the Hellenistic ruler cult," which "introduced the concept of a god-man"; (5) "the decline of pagan religiosity, especially in the third century A.D."; (6) the effectiveness of the church in addressing "status inconsistency"; (7) "the feelings of anxiety, insecurity, and helplessness" that the Christian message alleviated; (8) "the Christian view of life after death"; (9) "miracles and exorcisms"; (10) "the courage of the Christian martyrs"; (11) "the ideal of brotherly love and the praxis of Christian charity"; and (12) "the historical foundation of the Christian faith." Schnabel points out the inadequacy of any (or any combi-

rightly points to Paul's belief in the power of God for gospel advancement,[78] not immanent material or ideological factors or forces. Paul's prayer was key in actualizing this power. But what pastor doesn't believe in God's power and answered prayer? Yet, most still wish in their churches more of Paul's missionary effectiveness.

The elephant in the room here is what the power of God looks like when it gets hold of his people. Yes, in response they pray. But from the PE, we could argue that God's power and people's prayer are presuppositions for Timothy and Titus in their leadership roles. Given these factors, now they and their congregations find grace in the gospel to execute. They act, work, preach, teach, evangelize, mediate, challenge, rebuke, discern, guard, exercise restraint, suffer, and embrace myriad other tasks and dispositions that the gospel calling effects in them. And their active zeal can and by God's grace will mobilize others to similarly activated lives.

In a word, Paul as pastor in the PE reinforces in pastors, not the sufficiency of human effort for gospel flourishing, but the necessity of that effort. Is it possible that Protestant disdain for the high view of works in Catholic and liberal churches tempts evangelical leaders to underestimate the power of God and prayer to incite God's people not only to deep piety but also to hard labor in expression of that piety? Does well-meaning emphasis on *sola gratia* fail to convey the cost of discipleship in Western social settings that prize leisure and disdain hard work, hardship, and the self-abnegation Jesus called for and Paul echoed (see, e.g., 2 Tim 2:3)? Or in the event Bible believers do work hard, are they out of touch with Paul's rootedness in the living God (see secs. II–VI above)?[79] Many such questions could be posed.

The student. Many theological students work hard and effectively. Others work hard and ineffectively. Some fail to work. Many struggle with the relationship between grace and works and the place of work in their communion with God and in their present vocation as students. Nothing said in this section should be construed as advocating a thoughtless activism, workaholism, or other forms of barren busyness.

It is possible, however, that a culture of self-indulging idolatries, along with other factors like increasingly compromised Western educational sys-

---

nation) of these factors in providing an adequate explanation for the success of the missionary movement set in motion by Paul.

78. Schnabel, *Paul the Missionary,* 371–73.

79. Pastor Colin Smith laments "a diminished version of Christianity that is often found among people" diligent in Christian practices but who have yet to comprehend or experience "the great truth of union with Christ." Such a version of Christianity "majors on disciplines, and tends to produce a wooden, joyless attempt at discipleship that often lacks any real intimacy with God." See "Q and A with Rev. Colin Smith," *Christian Union: The Magazine* 15.3 (Summer 2016): 13.

tems, blind many students to the work ethic assumed by apostolic writers, and for that matter modeled in Jesus's teaching and life, as Klaus Issler has pointed out.[80] It would be another study to reflect on the forms this problem takes and how to address it. But many of those who preach and teach and publish probably need to.

This section closes with two inspirational images that commend the depth of commitment to work glimpsed in the PE. Both images are from sport, somewhat of an irony, since sport can be one of those idolatries that detracts from productive human labor. Pursued aright, however, it may constitute redemptive labor, as play and competition are surely gifts latent in a "very good" creation (Gen 1:31). And sport may offer useful lessons. Moreover, in its place it can surely be (like many other recreational pursuits; e.g., mountain-climbing) a laudable modeling of a work ethic in its own right. Many who have been or are athletes (some of whom go on to become ministers and scholars) can testify that the enterprise of athletic training and competition has been a means of common grace that taught them a work ethic that might never have surfaced in them under the tutelage of church or academy alone.

One image is in a Gatorade advert.[81] Dwayne Wade, a US National Basketball League superstar, is pictured in workout garb swigging a liter of orange elixir. Black perspiration stains the back of his gray sleeveless jersey. On second look, one realizes the sweat stains form an outline of the NBA championship trophy.[82] The caption: "Sweat says it all." While this is not quite the core message of the PE, it is a valid application of that message as seen in Paul's life and teaching in the PE, to which too many who read Paul may be foreign.

Another image, this one a word picture. In June 2014 a great African American baseball player died, Tony Gwynn. He was only fifty-four. Oral cancer, probably from chewing tobacco, felled him. *New York Times* reporter Tyler Kepner wrote a tribute entitled "In a .338 Lifetime Average, Every Day Counted." And then this subtitle: "Tony Gwynn's 2 Hitting Secrets: Work and More Work."

Kepner notes that many scoffed at Gwynn's intensity and rah-rah approach as melodrama and overkill.

> In 1994, while on his way to the fifth of his eight National League batting crowns, [Gwynn] spoke passionately about the attitude of the modern player.

80. See Klaus Issler, "Exploring the Pervasive References to Work in Jesus' Parables," *JETS* 57.2 (2014): 323–39.

81. See inside back cover of *Sports Illustrated*, June 30, 2014.

82. Other versions of the same ad feature tennis great Serena Williams. Her sweat-stained shirt reveals a silhouette of the Wimbledon trophy.

> "They just feel like stuff is supposed to happen to them," he said. "They're not going to have to work for it. And that bugs me because I know how hard I had to work to get where I got. Sometimes they sit there in amazement at why I come out here every day [to practice]. But I cannot let their way of thinking into my head."

The reporter concludes, "For Gwynn, the thrill was in the pursuit of perfection in a job built around failure." The greatest ever Major League baseball hitters, it should be noted, fail two-thirds of the time. Gwynn stands among the all-time greats in that sport with a batting average of just .338.

A central proponent of what Leon Morris called "the apostolic preaching of the cross"[83] was going to encounter a lot of failure. Paul did. Yet, he seems largely to have fulfilled God's will for him by grace. But it was also by the pursuit of Christ's perfection with a habit, an ethic, of major-league-level work. Readers of the PE may reasonably regard this effort (along with its deeply theological grounding) as one of the most profound and enduring legacies of these relatively brief letters.

VII. PLACES AND THEIR CONNECTION WITH THE PE

Less significant than theology or human labor in response, but still relevant to understanding the PE, is geography. Ephesus is a prominent part of the landscape in what Paul writes to Timothy, who allegedly serves there (1 Tim 1:3; 2 Tim 1:18; 4:12). Titus carries out his duties on the island of Crete. A brief characterization of each location is in order, along with comments on possible ties between place and the PE.

A. Ephesus

Details of a two- or three-year ministry by Paul at Ephesus are found in Acts 19, which recounts how the church there first came into being. Apollos had been active in Ephesus prior to Paul's arrival (Acts 18:24). Acts depicts a later memorable address there as Paul's so-called third missionary journey drew to a close (Acts 20:16–38). A port city at the mouth of the Cayster River on the Aegean Sea, Ephesus was the capital of the Roman province of Asia in what is now extreme western Turkey. Its population in the first century may have been near 250,000.[84]

83. Note Morris's book by that name (3rd ed.; Grand Rapids: Eerdmans, 1965).
84. Mark Wilson, *Biblical Turkey* (Istanbul: Ege, 2010), 200.

It included wealthy civic leaders of both sexes, called Asiarchs, some of whom Paul counted as friends (Acts 19:31). The fame of Ephesus was not only political and commercial: it was the center for worship of the pagan goddess Artemis (Diana). It was also known as a center of occult (magic) practices. An important study has correlated the pagan spiritual atmosphere with Paul's christological language in Ephesians.[85] The temple dedicated to Artemis was considered one of the seven wonders of the ancient world. Like smaller sister cities Pergamum and Smyrna, Ephesus was home to a temple for worship of the Roman emperor and his family.

If religious life was dominated by emperor worship, idolatry, and the black arts of occultism and spiritism, moral life was typical of a Greco-Roman city: a large brothel stood at one of the major intersections.[86] Excavations have uncovered an impressive amphitheater seating 24,000 people (see Acts 19:29). Irenaeus, a second-century church leader, reports that the apostle John resided and ministered there late in the first century.

One scholarly consensus has it that the historical value of Acts with regard to Ephesus is minimal. "Acts 19 is not a rich source for its narrated time, the mid-first century CE." Paul's letters to Timothy are equally dubious, since "Ephesus" is "part of the literary fiction" that many scholars regard the PE to be.[87]

Others defend the general and often detailed veracity of Acts.[88] Eckhard Schnabel's study deserves special mention in this regard.[89] He shows the plausibility of a broad seven-point outline within which to envision the history of the church at Ephesus (which, he notes, still needs to be written in detail):[90]

1. Paul's farewell speech before the elders of the Ephesian church at Miletus (Acts 20:17–36).
2. Paul's letter to the Ephesians (or simply the Ephesian letter, if, as many hold, it was circular).

85. Clinton Arnold, *Ephesians: Power and Magic* (Grand Rapids: Baker Books, 1992); see also his *Ephesians*, ZECNT (Grand Rapids: Zondervan, 2010), 30–41.

86. See map in John McRay, *Archaeology and the New Testament* (Grand Rapids: Baker Books, 1991), 251. For more detailed archaeological discussion, see Renate Pillinger, "Ephesus I: Archaeology," *EBR* 7:1008–15. In the central section of the same volume, note also plate 14, a second- or third-century fresco from Ephesus depicting Paul and Thekla.

87. Both quotes from Stephan Witetschek, "Ephesus II: Early Christian Sources," *EBR* 7:1016.

88. Note Rainer Riesner's response to Gerd Lüdemann in Riesner, *Paul's Early Period: Chronology, Mission Strategy, Theology*, trans. D. Stott (Grand Rapids: Eerdmans, 1998), 327–33. See also the summary offered by historian Paul Barnett, *Paul: Missionary of Jesus*, 208–10.

89. See Schnabel, "Missionary Work in the Province of Asia," in Schnabel, *Paul and the Early Church*, 1197–1231.

90. Schnabel, "Missionary Work in the Province of Asia," 1230.

3. 1 Timothy, in which Timothy is presumed to be in Ephesus.
4. 2 Timothy, which refers to Onesiphorus as Paul's coworker in Ephesus (2 Tim 1:18).
5. The letter to the Ephesian church in Rev 2:1–7.
6. The NT's Johannine corpus (Gospel and Letters of John; Revelation), perhaps written by John at Ephesus.
7. Ignatius of Antioch's letter to the Ephesian church (ca. AD 113).

While little of this information correlates directly and significantly with details of the language of 1–2 Timothy, the point is that it is both profitable and plausible to regard the real (not a fictive) city of Ephesus as recounted in the authentically historical account of Luke in Acts[91] to be the primary geographic background for understanding the first two of the PE as written to Timothy at Ephesus by Paul. Under this assumption, and drawing on numerous literary, epigraphic, and other resources, S. M. Baugh has given an able practical account of Ephesus and dynamics at work there at the time Timothy received his first letter from Paul.[92] He describes the historical setting (27–32), civic institutions (32–34), religious institutions (34–41), women in antiquity (41–44), and women at Ephesus (44–60), going on to highlight aspects of life relevant especially to women in that city at that time (priestesses of Artemis, childbirth, adornment, women and education).

Baugh concludes that, in most ways, Ephesus in Paul and Timothy's day was "a typical Hellenic society" (60). There is nothing in the sources (or in the NT) to suggest that Paul thought he was addressing an extraordinary location or situation, or that women addressed in 1 Tim 2 would have seen "Paul's exhortation to modesty and humility as unusual or necessarily unpalatable, even if they had earlier served as priestesses in pagan cults" (62). Ideals like modesty and devotion to husbands were not unique to Paul (though his christological basis is distinct to his Christian, as opposed to Jewish or Hellenistic, outlook), and Paul can be seen, actually, as more liberal in his regard for women than, for example, Plutarch, who writes on women and marriage around the same time. Baugh's summary of Paul's counsel to women is as follows:

> After reminding the wealthy women of Ephesus in particular about true piety in contrast to outward show, Paul anticipates that such women might

91. See, at the popular but scholarly informed level, James R. Edwards, "Archaeology Gives New Reality to Paul's Ephesus Riot," *BAR* 42.4 (2016): 24–32, 62.

92. S. M. Baugh, "A Foreign World: Ephesus in the First Century," in *Women in the Church: An Interpretation and Application of 1 Timothy 2:9–15*, ed. Andreas Köstenberger and Thomas Schreiner, 3rd ed. (Wheaton, IL: Crossway, 2016), 25–64. Page numbers in the text are to this article.

> misunderstand their inherited, worldly privileges to imply that they could step outside their divinely ordered role in the new covenant community. He points them instead to their distinct, profound, and significant roles in the church as those who hold the high calling of the general office in Christ's body and calls them, like all believers, to adorn this vocation with lives of grateful service. (64)

"Like all believers" in the citation above is key. They are who Timothy serves as a church leader, and it is for their pastoral care and direction that Paul writes two letters to Timothy at Ephesus. He singles out women only briefly; most of what he says in the letters pertains (as seen above) to God and the relevance of his work in Christ for the lives of all his followers in the church and thereby for all the world.

In the commentary below, reference is made as frequently as possible to contemporary literary, historical, or cultural sources or factors that shed light on the text. Like all the cities in which the NT speaks of Pauline churches, Ephesus posed challenges for proactive and mission-minded Christian expression. Yet, 1–2 Timothy should not be dissolved into their social setting, about which considerable is known in general but little can be reconstructed in particular. That limitation throws the reader of these epistles back onto the primary matters on which Paul speaks, and to which readers today still have access: the knowledge of God in Christ in social settings, then and still today, beset by sin, unbelief, and opposition to Christ's reign, both inside and outside the church. Paul's claim and experience is that the gospel he commends to Timothy succeeds in rolling back darkness with its light, as both epistles testify was underway at Ephesus, with analogies around the world at present.

B. Crete

Crete is a large island (over 3,000 square miles) lying south of Greece and southwest of modern-day Turkey. Presently its population is over 600,000. On three sides the Mediterranean Sea laps its shores. To its north lies the Aegean Sea, for which Crete serves as a southern boundary. It was home to the ancient Minoan civilization. Greek mythology associated Crete with King Minos, the Labyrinth constructed by Daedalus, the fearsome Minotaur who inhabited the Labyrinth, and Theseus who slew it. Crete is associated with Caphtor in the OT (Deut 2:23; Jer 47:4). Amos 9:7 calls it the land of origin of the Philistines. The island was therefore rich in cultural associations and identity.[93] It

93. Note references in A. F. Rainey and R. S. Notley, *Carta's New Century Handbook and Atlas of the Bible* (Jerusalem: Carta, 2007), 13, 27, 66, 174, 177, 194, 240, 244, 246, 249.

was conquered by Rome in the first century BC and was part of the Roman administrative district (province) of Cyrene on the North African mainland.

How did Christian congregations arise there? "There were large Jewish communities on Crete." Pilgrims from Crete were in Jerusalem on the Day of Pentecost and heard the gospel message in their own language (Acts 2:11). These individuals could have been Jews, converts to Judaism, or a mixture. They could have taken the Christian message back to Crete with them, in which case churches might have begun by the early AD 30s. Alternately, "a mission to Crete would have been a logical project for the early Jewish Christian missionaries" associated with the spread of the church in the first half of Acts.[94] In that case, the church would date to the later 30s or 40s.

Or perhaps in the late 50s "Paul's witness in Crete while on his way to Rome the first time (Acts 27) had formed an embryonic church, which he would naturally have wished to firmly establish upon his release" from Roman imprisonment.[95] Paul was freed by AD 63 or so, visited the island and took stock of its needs, and left Titus there to extend the work (Titus 1:5) while Paul journeyed on to Nicopolis in western Greece (3:13).

The fact is that we lack secure knowledge of the founding of churches on Crete. If Paul is writing to Titus in the 60s for the purpose of establishing pastors, it may seem unlikely that the church would have already been in existence for a decade or more; training and appointing elders is a first order of business when churches are planted (see Acts 14:23). So a founding by unknown means within not many years of Paul's writing is plausible.

An alternative is that the church was in reality much older, but that it had stagnated at some point after its implantation. In this scenario, it had a respectable beginning but then degenerated so seriously that Paul found it necessary to enlist Titus in attempting to stir up a fresh start or at least renewal of zeal for the fundamentals. Perhaps the church was already in its second generation by the 60s, and dead nominalism with its telltale ethical symptoms had become a problem. This scenario would account for the ground-level activity of training pastors urged by Paul in Titus, but at the same time the presence of rebellion and deception in the church understood as having a fairly lengthy history.

We do not know enough about Crete or its inhabitants to say much more about them or their cultural setting than what can be inferred from Paul's letter. We only know that classical references and ruins still testify today to numerous vibrant towns and cities there in Paul's time: their modern names on maps are Khania, Epano Palaiokastro, Rethymnon, Makryteikhos, Limin Khersonisos, Xidas, Elounta, Ierapetra, Gortyna.[96]

94. Both quotations in this paragraph are from Schnabel, *Paul and the Early Church*, 1284.

95. Baugh, 97. It was about 800 miles from Rome to Crete.

96. Schnabel, *Paul and the Early Church*, 1284–86.

They would all have been fields white unto harvest to the missionary vision of Paul (cf. John 4:35).

The last-named city, Gortyna, is mentioned in 1 Macc 15:23 as a city with a Jewish quarter. An ancient inscription attests to a woman named Sophia who held the post of "elder and ruler of the synagogue."[97] Local tradition makes Titus the first bishop of Gortyna,[98] and there is verifiable record of a bishop in the second century named Philippos. Nearly a dozen Christians from the city were martyred under Decius's persecution circa 250.

There is much we do not know about Crete in the 60s when Paul wrote. Nothing that is known about the geography or history of the period, or that is present in Paul's letter to Titus, rules out the plausibility of Paul writing an epistle of this character to a pastoral coworker named Titus at this time and place in the history of the early church.

VIII. PEOPLE IN THE PE

In addition to God (secs. II–V above), the labor of ministry (sec. VI), and key locations (sec. VII), the three main players in the PE merit attention. Less is known about them than we wish. But this gap simply means that we should be all the more careful in laying out the historical data that we do have. Then we can begin study of the PE with as grounded and clear a concept as possible regarding who we are dealing with in the broader scope of early church beginnings, including especially Paul's labor of spreading the good news of God's work in Christ, which was key to the eventual success of these beginnings.

A. Titus

"Titus" appears fourteen times in the NT. Only two of these references occur in the PE: the greeting in Paul's Epistle to Titus (1:4), and the information that "Crescens has gone to Galatia, and Titus to Dalmatia" (2 Tim 4:10). These references can be taken to indicate that Titus was an active Pauline coworker near the end of Paul's life.

But Titus's involvement with Paul goes back prior to Paul's composition of Galatians (ca. AD 48). For there Paul writes, "Then after fourteen years, I

97. All information and citations in this paragraph are from Schnabel, *Paul and the Early Church*, 1286.

98. For a photo of ruins of a church in Gortyna built in the sixth century, see *NIDB* 1:789.

went up again to Jerusalem, this time with Barnabas. I took Titus along also" (Gal 2:1). This comment indicates that, around AD 47,[99] when Paul (at that time still Saul) and Barnabas met with "those esteemed as pillars" in Jerusalem (Gal 2:9), Titus was present. Not only was he present, but he was close enough to the innermost Pauline circle that his lack of circumcision became an issue: "Yet not even Titus, who was with me, was compelled to be circumcised, even though he was a Greek" (Gal 2:3). Unlike Timothy, who was regarded as Jewish, Titus was not. And from this early period of his involvement with Paul, Titus had to contend with Jewish "false believers" who understandably sought to force their hallowed rituals on non-Jews like himself (Gal 2:4). Paul and Titus stood up to their faulty theological understanding and practical demands so that doctrinal fidelity might be upheld for the sake of the church: "We did not give in to them for a moment, so that the truth of the gospel might be preserved for you" (Gal 2:5). Some of these same dynamics, like false believers and Jewish-based challenge to Pauline teaching, will be seen in Paul's epistle to Titus. They are anticipated by nearly two decades in the events Paul describes in Galatians.

Other NT references to Titus cluster in 2 Corinthians, dating some ten years after Galatians. He is deeply involved in negotiations between Paul and the Corinthian congregation regarding their rocky relationship with Paul, along with their contribution for the believers in Judea (the Jerusalem collection). Titus comforts Paul (2 Cor 7:6), is refreshed by the Corinthians' responsiveness (7:13), and helps urge the Corinthians to full participation in the collection (8:6). In all this, and to commend Titus, Paul calls him "my partner and coworker" (8:23). He points out to the Corinthians that Titus did not exploit them but rather walked "in the same footsteps by the same Spirit" as Paul. This is not quite as high as the praise he gives to Timothy in another setting (Phil 2:19–22), but it comes close.

Who was Titus? If Paul's Epistle to Titus is written late in Paul's life (mid-60s), he was a Pauline coworker with nearly two decades of ministry experience in various settings. He is not a novice but someone who, Paul thought, could readily put into practice and expand on the sketchy remarks that make up the short epistle that goes by his name. Paul and Titus's long association and their shared background as native Hellenistic Greek speakers could help account for the workmanlike brevity of the Epistle to Titus, as well as the sometimes challenging vocabulary and unexplained allusions. They had been facing these things, sometimes together and sometimes at a distance, for many years. Paul could write idiomatically as one deeply committed and informed Jesus-follower to another because that is what both were and had been for a sizable share of their adult lives.

99. So, for example, Barnett, *Paul: Missionary of Jesus*, 137, 136.

B. Timothy

Timothy's name is stated four times in the PE (see commentary).[100] In Acts he is introduced as a "disciple" in Lystra "whose mother was Jewish and a believer but whose father was a Greek" (16:1). Evidently he was among those affected by the promulgation of the gospel message through Paul and Barnabas during the so-called first missionary journey (Acts 13–14).

Paul requested Timothy's involvement along with Silas in his ministry team as the second missionary journey began. For this role his circumcision was required, in Paul's judgment, in order not to offend Jews Paul wanted to reach with the gospel (16:3). Following this procedure and the time required for recovery, Timothy took part in the work of delivering the results of the Jerusalem Council (Acts 15): "As they traveled from town to town, they delivered the decisions reached by the apostles and elders in Jerusalem for the people to obey" (16:4). Timothy's earliest assignment with Paul involved mediation of apostolic teachings among Gentile churches, something still at the core of his mandate when he receives 1 and 2 Timothy. His dual citizenship, so to speak, in the Hellenistic world on the one hand as a native of Lystra and, on the other among the Jewish people in the Diaspora, suited him ideally for this assignment. He would have an insider's feel for the Abrahamic heritage fulfilled in Jesus, according to the gospel affirmed in Acts 15, yet strong points of contact with the Greek world of his own father and the region of his upbringing.

As the Acts account of the spread of the gospel unfolds, "Paul and his companions" (Acts 16:6) included Timothy, who evidently took part in founding the church begun in connection with witness to Lydia and other women at Philippi. He must have languished in the background (perhaps huddling terrified) when Paul and Silas were seized, flogged, and jailed overnight (Acts 16:24–34). Luke uses the same phrase "Paul and his companions"[101] to describe Paul, Silas, Timothy, and others making their way to Thessalonica (Acts 17:1) following the Philippians adventure. They were driven from Thessalonica to Berea, where trouble arose just as it had in Thessalonica. Paul had to be sent away to Athens for his own safety. Luke records that the Berean "believers immediately sent Paul to the coast, but Silas and Timothy stayed at Berea. Those who escorted Paul brought him to Athens and then left with instructions for Silas and Timothy to join him as soon as possible" (Acts 17:14–15). Clearly, Timothy was a right-hand man to Paul in times of tense gospel outreach and even possible physical harm. References to his possible fearfulness in the PE need to factor in the earlier valor implied in various Acts accounts.

100. 1 Tim 1:2, 18; 6:20; 2 Tim 1:2.

101. In both Acts 16:6 and 17:1, "Paul and his companions" are inferred as the subjects of plural verbs (*diēlthon* in 16:6, *ēlthon* in 17:1), with no stated subjects in Greek.

From Athens Paul traveled to Corinth (Acts 18:1) and met up with Aquila and Priscilla (v. 2). In Paul's early days here, tentmaking and reasoning in the synagogue (vv. 3–4), Silas and Timothy "came from Macedonia" (v. 5) and caught up with Paul. "Paul stayed in Corinth for a year and a half, teaching them the word of God" (v. 11). Presumably Timothy was present and witness to much or all that took place during that stretch of time. Timothy is not mentioned as Paul returned to the church at Antioch, marking the end of the so-called second missionary journey (v. 22). Yet, he may well have been with Paul all along, since once the third missionary journey gets underway (v. 23) and Paul spends over two years at Ephesus (19:10), he dispatches "two of his helpers, Timothy and Erastus, to Macedonia, while he stayed in the province of Asia a little longer" (19:22).

Timothy's central role in assisting Paul has by this time lasted the better part of a decade. As the third missionary journey draws to a close and Paul sweeps through Macedonia prior to his final return to Jerusalem, Timothy finds himself in distinguished company: Paul "was accompanied by Sopater son of Pyrrhus from Berea, Aristarchus and Secundus from Thessalonica, Gaius from Derbe, Timothy also, and Tychicus and Trophimus from the province of Asia" (Acts 20:4). He was part of a perhaps burly entourage of men entrusted to help Paul deliver the cash offering to the Judean churches that Paul and the Gentile churches had been collecting for years (the celebrated Jerusalem collection; see 1 Cor 16:1–3; 2 Cor 8–9). This is the last mention of Timothy in Acts, though he may well have been present for the events described at Miletus and then Jerusalem leading up to the time of Paul's arrest (Acts 21:27–36).

Another glimpse of Timothy is afforded in Paul's letters. In chronological order of these letters' appearance,[102] Timothy's name is found as follows:

Table 4. References to Timothy in Paul's epistles, chronologically arranged

Passage	Mention of Timothy
1 Thess 1:1 (ca. AD 50–51)	Paul, Silas and *Timothy*, To the church of the Thessalonians in God the Father and the Lord Jesus Christ: Grace and peace to you.
1 Thess 3:2	We sent *Timothy*, who is our brother and coworker in God's service in spreading the gospel of Christ, to strengthen and encourage you in your faith.

102. Dates are adapted from Stanley E. Porter, *The Apostle Paul: His Life, Thought, and Ideas* (Grand Rapids: Eerdmans, 2016), 53–60.

Passage	Mention of Timothy
1 Thess 3:6	But *Timothy* has just now come to us from you and has brought good news about your faith and love. He has told us that you always have pleasant memories of us and that you long to see us, just as we also long to see you.
2 Thess 2:1 (ca. 51–52)	Paul, Silas and *Timothy*, To the church of the Thessalonians in God our Father and the Lord Jesus Christ.
1 Cor 4:17 (ca. 55)	For this reason I have sent to you *Timothy*, my son whom I love, who is faithful in the Lord. He will remind you of my way of life in Christ Jesus, which agrees with what I teach everywhere in every church.
1 Cor 16:10	When *Timothy* comes, see to it that he has nothing to fear while he is with you, for he is carrying on the work of the Lord, just as I am.
2 Cor 1:1 (ca. 56)	Paul, an apostle of Christ Jesus by the will of God, and *Timothy* our brother, To the church of God in Corinth, together with all his holy people throughout Achaia.
2 Cor 1:19	For the Son of God, Jesus Christ, who was preached among you by us—by me and Silas and *Timothy*—was not "Yes" and "No," but in him it has always been "Yes."
Rom 16:21 (ca. 56–57)	*Timothy*, my coworker, sends his greetings to you, as do Lucius, Jason and Sosipater, my fellow Jews.
Phil 1:1 (ca. 61–62)	Paul and *Timothy*, servants of Christ Jesus, To all God's holy people in Christ Jesus at Philippi, together with the overseers and deacons.
Phil 2:19	I hope in the Lord Jesus to send *Timothy* to you soon, that I also may be cheered when I receive news about you.
Phil 2:22	But you know that *Timothy* has proved himself, because as a son with his father he has served with me in the work of the gospel.
Col 1:1 (ca. 61–62)	Paul, an apostle of Christ Jesus by the will of God, and *Timothy* our brother.
Phlm 1 (ca. 61–62)	Paul, a prisoner of Christ Jesus, and *Timothy* our brother, To Philemon our dear friend and fellow worker.

In table 4 above, Timothy's name appears in eight of Paul's letters. He is of course addressed in two of the PE. That leaves only three Pauline letters in which Timothy is not named: Galatians, Ephesians, and Titus. Few early church figures were as privy to Paul's movements and teachings over the years. The lone rival in this respect may have been Luke. Perhaps no other person, including Luke, had been so closely complicit in Paul's evangelization and church maturation labors. (Luke seems to have been a ministry observer, analyst, chronicler, and [as a physician] personal assistant; Timothy actually shared Paul's call to gospel service and rendered sometimes risky service in the trenches.) Paul's two letters to Timothy are a matchless testimony to Paul's convictions regarding the relevance of God and the gospel to his younger charge in trying circumstances—as Paul's own circumstances tended to be (see 2 Cor 11:23–12:9; 2 Tim 1:8, 12), and as ministry situations in all places and times may turn out to be (2 Tim 3:12).

C. Paul

For purposes of this commentary, the main points of importance of Paul will emerge from exegesis of the PE. It is neither possible nor necessary to attempt an overview of his life and teachings here.[103] But a few observations are in order by way of anticipation and explanation of how Paul will be approached below.

In terms of identity and role, Paul can be understood as a theologian (but see below), a missionary (or gospel herald: see 1 Tim 2:7; 2 Tim 1:11),[104] a discipler or teacher,[105] a mentor in the sense of a father figure,[106] a church planter, a pastor or pastoral overseer, an exegete,[107] and ultimately a martyr.

103. For a rudimentary presentation of my reading of Paul, see W. Elwell and R. Yarbrough, *Encountering the New Testament*, 3rd ed. (Grand Rapids: Baker Academic, 2013), 235–53. More recently, and among a vast literature, significant works include Porter, *The Apostle Paul*; E. P. Sanders, *Paul* (Minneapolis: Fortress, 2015); N. T. Wright, *Paul and His Recent Interpreters* (Minneapolis: Fortress, 2015); J. Barclay, *Paul and the Gift* (Grand Rapids: Eerdmans, 2015). Regarding the magnum opus by N.T. Wright, *Paul and the Faithfulness of God*, 2 vols. (London: SPCK, 2013), see the review by J. Barclay in *SJT* 68.2 (2015): 235–43, which highlights fault lines between major players on the English-language scene. For an older but perennially valuable study for Bible-teaching pastors, see F. F. Bruce, *Paul: Apostle of the Heart Set Free* (Grand Rapids: Eerdmans, 1977). See also Schnabel, *Paul the Missionary*. Both Bruce and Schnabel take Paul's claim to be an apostle with due seriousness.

104. See Köstenberger, 363–85, esp. 385: "The theology of the [PE] is firmly embedded in the Pauline mission."

105. 1 Tim 2:7; 2 Tim 1:11; 2:2; 3:10.

106. 1 Cor 4:15; Phil 2:22; 1 Thess 2:11.

107. Highlighted by D. Martin, *Biblical Truths* (New Haven: Yale University Press, 2017), 1–2, though he mistakenly reduces what Paul draws on to "text," while in reality Paul viewed it as more than that: Scripture is not "simply its own voice" (1) but a message and words given by a personal, living, and beneficient God revealed in his Son.

Paul calls himself a slave (*doulos*), but only three times explicitly.[108] More commonly his servile self-label is servant (*diakonos*).[109] Yet, most frequently of all, over two dozen times, the term he favors to characterize himself is apostle (*apostolos*).

For Paul, this is not a term of exaltation. He makes it clear that the apostolic calling and task was nothing to be sought, since, in his words:

> God has put us apostles on display at the end of the procession, like those condemned to die in the arena. We have been made a spectacle to the whole universe, to angels as well as to human beings. We are fools for Christ. . . . We are weak. . . , we are dishonored! To this very hour we go hungry and thirsty, we are in rags, we are brutally treated, we are homeless. We work hard with our own hands. When we are cursed, we bless; when we are persecuted, we endure it; when we are slandered, we answer kindly. We have become the scum of the earth, the garbage of the world—right up to this moment. (1 Cor 4:19–13)

Paul offers a briefer but analogous profile elsewhere (2 Cor 4:7–12). His sufferings (see esp. 2 Cor 11:23–33) are hard to overestimate as indicators of the nature and veracity of his message: "From now on, let no one cause me trouble, for I bear on my body the marks of Jesus" (Gal 6:17). Or as he wrote to Timothy, "You, however, know all about my . . . persecutions, sufferings—what kinds of things happened to me in Antioch, Iconium and Lystra, the persecutions I endured" (2 Tim 3:10–11). To be an apostle was to be humiliated and often harmed above the norm in the era of the rise of the early church. It was also, in nearly all cases, an eventual death sentence.

Yet, for this very reason, "apostle" is an indispensable rubric under which to understand Paul. First, it conveys his sense of call by and subordination to Jesus, who appeared to him and converted him to his cause.[110] An apostle was bound to represent not himself but the one who sent him. Second, it expresses the status Paul (or in actuality his writings) enjoyed over the centuries in Christian interpretation, until historical criticism arose and denied him

108. Rom 1:1; Phil 1:1 (with Timothy); Titus 1:1.

109. Self-references to Paul as *diakonos* with thing or person served (if stated): 1 Cor 3:5; 2 Cor 3:6 (of a new covenant); 6:4 (of God); 11:23 (of Christ). In Eph 3:7; Col 1:23, 25 Paul is *diakonos* of the gospel.

110. On Paul's conversion, see S. Kim, *Paul and the New Perspective: Second Thoughts on the Origin of Paul's Gospel* (Grand Rapids: Eerdmans, 2002), which draws on Kim's earlier work highlighting Paul's conversion; P. O'Brien, "Was Paul Converted?," in *The Paradoxes of Paul*, vol. 2 of *Justification and Variegated Nomism*, ed. D. A. Carson, P. T. O'Brien, and M. A. Seifrid (Grand Rapids: Baker, 2004), 361–91.

(and the rest of Scripture) divine origin and authority.[111] Third, it reminds us of Paul's privileged status as one who saw and conversed with the risen Jesus (1 Cor 9:1), received a unique commission (Acts 9:1–20), worked miracles (Acts 14:3, 9–10),[112] and was even transported into heaven—as he put it, "in the body or out of the body I do not know—God knows" (2 Cor 12:2). More particularly, he "was caught up to paradise and heard inexpressible things, things that no one is permitted to tell" (2 Cor 12:4). It was after this incident that he most likely wrote to Timothy and Titus. While the PE do not appear to violate the divine gag order placed on Paul, many who pore over the PE feel they draw on a depth of pastoral wisdom and theological understanding consistent with someone rooted in nothing short of a heavenly vision (see, e.g., 1 Tim 3:16). All of these experiences feed into who Paul was and what he wrote as an apostle. M. Kruger has helpfully summarized what this meant in the early church and can reasonably be affirmed by Christ-followers today: "Early Christians held the belief that the apostles were Christ's authorized agents to deliver and transmit the new message of redemption. Although the apostles did this orally, they also began to write their message down (2 Thess 2:15). Thus, documents that were regarded as containing apostolic teaching would have been viewed as authoritative right from the beginning and would not have needed to wait for later ecclesiastical developments [for their de facto recognition as sacred Scripture]."[113]

The miracles associated with Paul's ministry and contributing to its recognition (see, e.g., Gal 3:5) deserve special mention for those interested in Paul's writings for preaching and other aspects of gospel ministry. In an age when many academic and professional interpreters deny Paul's authorship of the PE, reject the possibility of sacred Scripture (which Paul very much affirmed: see, e.g., Rom 3:2),[114] affirm an apophatic theology because of rejection of Scripture as revelation and defend from Scripture what Scripture calls immoral,[115] and not surprisingly reject the miracles reported in Scripture, doubt can arise that teaching what the PE teach is much use—scholarly interpreters discount it all (starting with the first word of each the three PE: "Paul"). If the documents are uniformly wrong about their earthly author, what is the likelihood they have anything sure to say about the invisible transcendent God (1 Tim 1:17), a cosmic moral order, and eternal salvation that people could trust?

111. See, for example, M. Legaspi, *The Death of Scripture and the Rise of Biblical Studies* (Oxford: Oxford University Press, 2010).

112. See also Acts 15:12; 20:9–12; 28:8; Rom 15:19; 2 Cor 12:12.

113. M. Kruger, *The Question of Canon* (Downers Grove, IL: IVP Academic, 2013), 77; for broader discussion, see 67–76.

114. For example, A. E. Harvey, *Is Scripture Still Holy?* (Grand Rapids: Eerdmans, 2012). Harvey's answer is negative.

115. So, for example, Martin, *Biblical Truths*.

A helpful resource for some troubled by contemporary skepticism might be Craig Keener's magisterial two volumes on the subject.[116] Biblical miracles and documented correlates today should not be set aside as irrelevant to Scripture interpretation, or as evidence that biblical writers were superstitious dreamers who told whoppers as history. For Keener, miracles (ancient and modern) also do not justify replacing the message of the cross and the resurrection with triumphalist appeal to signs and wonders. What they do justify is calling attention to the God who (if biblical miracles are real) works miracles, and to his saving *logos* that Scripture constitutes and conveys. As Wilckens points out, "Denial of miracles by 'historical criticism' in accordance with 'reason' is at its core a *denial of the reality of the biblical God* himself."[117] Affirmation of apostolic heralds like Paul with the miracles they worked is a salutary step toward affirmation of the God who across the sweep of Scripture makes himself known and in fact actually saves[118] in conjunction with unusual mighty acts.

Since this God sent Christ and since Christ called apostles like Paul, Paul gains credibility as a trustworthy and authoritative source when viewed alongside other New Testament figures empowered by Jesus to perform the unusual (i.e., miracles) in the course of proclaiming gospel redemption. The PE are not so much church order manuals as interpersonal testimony and counsel to coworkers from a man elevated by God and ordained to be heeded, if it is God and Christ whom PE readers seek. While any number of themes and issues are pertinent to a full understanding and presentation of Paul and his thought,[119] the notions that God called him through the risen Jesus Christ, commissioned him to take the gospel to the majority non-Jewish ethnicities of the Roman Empire, and inspired writings from his hand are significantly undergirded by the miracles with which historical sources associate him, miracles that Keener has shown should not be facilely dismissed by appeal to Hume, ancient worldviews, or modern science.

Paul would be the first to underscore that he preached Christ, crucified and risen, not miracles in the abstract. But he is just as adamant that, without

116. Craig Keener, *Miracles: The Credibility of the New Testament Accounts*, 2 vols. (Grand Rapids: Baker Academic, 2011). For a review, see R. Yarbrough, *JETS* 55.4 (2012): 878–82.

117. Wilckens, *Kritik der Bibelkritik*, 19 (italics in original).

118. Christ's incarnation, sinless life, atonement, resurrection, and ascension, each attested in and central to Paul's writings and teachings, are all miraculous.

119. Major themes in Elwell and Yarbrough, *Encountering the New Testament*, 235–53: God, evil, the law, Abraham and his heritage, revelation and Scripture, Messiah, redemption, the cross, resurrection, the church, ethics, last things. In Porter, *The Apostle Paul*, "major themes" are divided into "fundamental beliefs" (96–107: God, Jesus Christ, Holy Spirit, grace, faith) and "developed beliefs" (107–33: justification, the law in relation to Christ's work, reconciliation, sanctification, salvation, God's triumph, gospel, church, Jesus's death and resurrection). Books on Paul multiply these categories.

miracles like the resurrection, the gospel message is false and in vain (see 1 Cor 15:12–19). As fundamental a Christian exercise as prayer assumes divine action, past and ongoing, of a miraculous nature (Rom 8:26–27).[120]

The Paul of the PE deserves the careful attention that commentary writing and reading imply, because offsetting his self-understanding as worst of sinners (1 Tim 1:15) is his status alongside other Christ-sanctioned spokespersons with a message essential for personal and world redemption. Paul's PE contribute substantially to understanding and administration of that message. He is not a theologian by normal definition, for he is not, sheerly by his own best lights, constructing a derivative body of belief; rather, he is being used by God to provide primary sources rooted in special divine self-disclosure for subsequent theologians, including pastoral practitioners. In its own way, such revelatory insight (or "truth," if one prefers) is miraculous (2 Tim 3:16; 2 Pet 1:20–21). And if it is true, it justifies readers in looking to the PE, not just as sources for reconstructing the thinking of an antiquated and often (by current standards) mistaken Paul, but with the hope and anticipation that, through those sources, they will encounter God in Christ as Paul did.

IX. KEY TERMS AND PHRASES IN THE PE

As already noted, the PE are dominated by references to God and Christ, with Spirit mentioned less often but assumed. Four additional words or word groups also bear mention. They characterize the PE in more explicit fashion than they do some other Pauline writings. To avoid repetition in the commentary, these expressions are given summary treatment here. They are discussed in their respective contexts in the verse-by-verse portion of the commentary.

A. Savior, Salvation

Four words in the *sōtēr-* word group are found in the PE: *sōtēr* (savior), *sōtēria* and *sōtērion*[121] (salvation), and *sōtērios* (saving, salvific).[122] They are also found in most other Pauline writings with the exceptions of 1 Corinthians, Galatians, Colossians, and Philemon, as the following table indicates:

120. In the PE, see 1 Tim 2:1, 8; 4:5; 5:5; 2 Tim 1:3.

121. This neuter form is listed as a substantive with *sōtērios* in BDAG 986. It occurs only in Eph 6:17: "the helmet of salvation."

122. For the verb *sōzō* (I save; twenty-nine times in Paul, seven times in the PE), see discussion in the commentary at 1 Tim 1:15; 2:4, 15; 4:16; 2 Tim 1:9; 4:18; Titus 3:5.

Table 5. Occurrence of *sōtēr-* words in the PE

Letter	Total hits[123]	Hits per 1,000 words
Romans	5	0.70
2 Corinthians	4	0.89
Ephesians	3	1.24
Philippians	4	2.45
1 Thessalonians	2	1.35
2 Thessalonians	1	1.22
1 Timothy	3	1.89
2 Timothy	3	2.42
Titus	7	10.62

In 1 Timothy God is called "Savior" three times (1:1; 2:3; 4:10). In 2 Tim "Savior" occurs once (2 Tim 1:10). Twice Paul writes of "the salvation that is in Christ Jesus" (2 Tim 2:10) or "through faith in Christ Jesus" (2 Tim 3:15). In Titus, "Savior" predominates, referring to God (1:3; 2:10; 3:4), to Christ (1:4; 3:6), and once to both, equating them: "our great God and Savior, Jesus Christ" (2:13). The sole remaining *sōtēr-* word group usage is in 2:11: "For the grace of God has appeared that offers salvation [*sōtērios*] to all people." This is more correctly translated, "For the saving grace of God has appeared to/for all people," because (1) Paul does not use the common noun for salvation (*sōtēria*) found eighteen times in his writings and (2) *sōtērios* in 2:11 is a feminine adjective, modifying grace, and is not neuter, as in Eph 6:17, where it serves as a noun.

G. Wieland canvasses numerous commentaries that find in this usage indicators of non- or pseudo-Pauline authors at work.[124] He more plausibly shows that the outlook connoted by these words in the PE meshes well with Paul's usage elsewhere.[125] This outlook points to "a salvation-historical framework" through which God's saving benefits in Christ are "universally

123. The search was conducted for all four words.

124. G. Wieland, "The Function of Salvation in the Letters to Timothy and Titus," in Köstenberger and Wilder, *Entrusted with the Gospel*, 153–55.

125. So also, for example, Witherington, 103–5, who argues for Luke's involvement in the composition of the PE.

available" but only "received by those who believe the gospel and orient their lives to its eschatological promise and present ethical demands." This same general outlook appears in distinctive form appropriate to the varying setting of each PE. God's (or Christ's) salvation urges readers in 1 Timothy "to resist inward-looking, restrictive tendencies within the church and hold to a gospel universal in scope," in 2 Timothy "to continue faithful ministry of the gospel despite opposition and apparent setbacks," and in Titus to "nurture missionary communities whose lifestyle would serve as a demonstration of the saving efficacy of the message of God's grace."[126]

In sum, "salvation" is as fundamental to the PE as it is to Romans: "For I am not ashamed of the gospel, because it is the power of God that brings salvation" (Rom 1:16). What is heightened in the PE is reference to the noun *sōtēr* (savior),[127] found in Paul outside the PE only in Eph 5:23 and Phil 3:20. Yet, God is personal *sōtēr* ("my savior") at least ten times in the LXX[128] and "Savior" in the broader sense dozens more times. Paul's usage in the PE is consistent with the OT view of God as one who cares and rescues all who long for his deliverance and call on his name. What stands out is the close and comprehensive extension of this word from referring to God to referring also to Jesus Christ.[129]

B. Godliness

A noun translated "godliness" (*eusebeia*) is found ten times in the PE and only five times elsewhere in the NT.[130] A cognate verb[131] and adverb[132] also appear, for a total of thirteen occurrences of *euseb-* stem words in the PE. Since words from this group are found only nine times elsewhere in the New Testament,[133] many seek an explanation for their concentration in the PE. Marshall with Towner chronicles a long history in German exegesis of trying to link the use

126. Wieland, "The Function of Salvation in the Letters to Timothy and Titus," 171, 172.

127. As noted by I. H. Marshall, "The Pastoral Epistles in Recent Study," in Köstenberger and Wilder, *Entrusted with the Gospel*, 309. For additional discussion, see Collins, 308–18.

128. See NETS at Pss 24:5; 26:1, 9; 61:3, 7; Sir 51:1; Pss Sol 16:4; Mic 7:7; Hab 3:18; Isa 12:2.

129. For more extended treatment of the salvation motif in the PE, see Köstenberger, 431–36.

130. PE: 1 Tim 2:2; 3:16; 4:7, 8; 6:3, 5, 6, 11; 2 Tim 3:5; Titus 1:1; elsewhere: Acts 3:12; 2 Pet 1:3, 6, 7; 3:11.

131. *Eusebeō* (to live in a godly way): "But if a widow has children or grandchildren, these should learn first of all *to put their religion into practice*" (1 Tim 5:4).

132. *Eusebōs*: "In fact, everyone who wants to live *in a godly manner* in Christ Jesus will be persecuted" (2 Tim 3:12); "[God's grace] teaches us in order that . . . we might live soberly, righteously, and *in a godly manner* in the present age" (Titus 2:12 NIV slightly adapted in both cases).

133. Acts 3:12; 10:2, 7; 17:23; 2 Pet 1:3, 6, 7; 2:9, 3:11.

of *eusebeia* in the PE with "pagan ethical thought" suggestive of "a compromise with the world" by adoption of a "bourgeois" ethic.[134]

Uses of *euseb-* words in the New Testament outside the PE show that notions associated with these words were not foreign to early Christian discourse from early on. Other words and notions admittedly take precedence, notably names for God and Christ and then the words "grace" and "faith." Viewing the *euseb-* words, and especially "godliness" (*eusebeia*) in the PE in the overall context of the New Testament corpus, Marshall with Towner concludes that "*eusebeia* expresses a strongly Christian concept of the new existence in Christ that combines belief in God and a consequent manner of life."[135] It is not known for sure why the PE use the term with relative frequency. Did earlier New Testament writers tend to avoid the term because of its association with pagan ethics? Did the rare use of *eusebeia* in the canonical Old Testament condition the early Christian community to favor other expressions?[136] Did Paul in the PE, writing to close associates, feel free to use the term without fear that Timothy or Titus would interpret it outside the robustly theological and christological nexus from which all of Paul's language drew its meaning? Was something analogous at work in Petrine usage?[137]

What can be said is that, like fine wine and cheese, *eusebeia* pairs well with the emphasis in the PE on God and Christ as "savior." From the divine side comes powerful and personal deliverance, "the mystery from which true godliness [*eusebeia*] springs" (1 Tim 3:16). This grace enables and calls for full-scale and heartfelt response on the human side: "Train yourself to be godly [*pros eusebeian*]" (1 Tim 4:7). "But you, man of God, flee from all this, and pursue righteousness, godliness [*eusebeia*], faith, love, endurance and gentleness" (1 Tim 6:11). It also contributes to an essential pastoral critical faculty: "having a form of godliness [*eusebeia*] but denying its power. Have nothing to do with such people" (2 Tim 3:5). It is important to avoid bogus godliness, a truth that is as basic to Christian practice and confession as the nearly two dozen references to hypocrisy and hypocrites in the Gospels, to say nothing of ubiquitous references to misguided religiosity in the Old Testament.

PE usage of "godliness" is distinct but well within the semantic range of other, overlapping New Testament expressions describing the practical Christian life in communion with God through faith in Christ.[138] Collins understates in noting that PE usage "deviates somewhat from that of other Hellenistic

134. Marshall, with Towner, 136.

135. Marshall, with Towner, 144.

136. Among canonical Old Testament books, *eusebeia* is found in only Prov 1:7; 13:11; Isa 11:2; 33:6. It occurs in fifty-four other LXX passages, with all but one of these in the Maccabean corpus, mostly 4 Maccabees.

137. 2 Pet 1:3, 6, 7; 2:9, 3:11.

138. For additional discussion, see, for example, Witherington, 99–102.

moralists."[139] Compared with Hellenistic moralism's assumptions, the use of *euseb-* words in the PE belongs in a distinct, substantially more promising class.

C. Trustworthy Sayings

A unique feature of the PE is five passages containing the words *pistos ho logos* ("the word is faithful"), translated in each case by NIV as "Here is a trustworthy saying" (1 Tim 1:15; 3:1; 2 Tim 2:11) or "This is a trustworthy saying" (1 Tim 4:9; Titus 3:8).[140] Twice elsewhere Paul uses a similar construction: *pistos ho theos* ("God is trustworthy"; 1 Cor 1:9); *pistos ho kalōn hymas* ("The one who calls you is trustworthy"; 1 Thess 5:24). But the precise and repeated phrase found in the PE stands out.

Commentators concur that this rhetorical flourish functions like "amen" did in Jesus's Gospel sayings (e.g., Matt 5:18: "Truly I tell you . . .").[141] Paul uses the words to preface something that Timothy or Titus can and should take with utmost seriousness, to the point of appropriating personally and completely.[142]

Perhaps the fullest characterization of the phrase's significance is provided by P. Towner. He argues that, against the backdrop of false teaching that is calling his message and authority in question, Paul uses "trustworthy saying" as a "technique" that, "in one motion, rearticulates his gospel (and corresponding aspects of teaching), asserts its authenticity and apostolic authority, and alienates the opposing teaching." Towner discerns a polemical tone in the expression, since the views of those whom Timothy and Titus need to challenge are not "trustworthy."[143]

While there are a few parallel expressions in literature outside the New Testament, the PE contain the first use of these words in the history of Hellenistic Greek that could be called formulaic. Rhetorically, it is clear that Paul uses the words for emphasis, like idiomatic English expressions that arise, are heard for a while, and then die off, to be replaced by new ones: "You can take this to the bank"; "This much is clear. . . ."; "I'll tell you one thing for sure. . . ." It is not as if other things Paul writes in the PE are untrue or untrustworthy, but at certain points Paul wants veracity underscored. T. Swinson's finding in a thorough study deserves mention: the expression (in 1 Tim 1:15) "serves as an affirmation of the worth and merits of the gospel message and teaching

139. Collins, 126 (fuller discussion in 122–26). Collins writes "other" because he calls the PE author "the Pastor," does not view him as Paul, and accordingly places the writer on exactly the same plane as other moralizers of the era.

140. For in-depth treatment, see G. W. Knight III, *The Faithful Sayings in the Pastoral Letters* (Grand Rapids: Baker Books, 1979).

141. Johnson, *First and Second Letters to Timothy*, 180; Collins, 43.

142. See Knight, 100.

143. Towner, *Letters*, 143–45.

mentioned previously, meaning that this message also stands as *God's* faithful word." Or with reference to 1 Tim 3:1, "the 'sound teaching,' the gospel word, is 'faithful,' and [Timothy and the church at Ephesus] may rely on it."[144] Truth matters, and what Paul writes as an apostle contains and conveys it for certain.

D. Sound Doctrine

A final distinctive PE usage to be considered here involves forms of two words (*hygiainō*, "to be healthy"; *hygiēs*, "healthy") associated with physical well-being in other New Testament contexts.[145] In the PE they refer to the soundness of Christian teaching.

Table 6. The soundness of teaching in the PE

Passage	Reference to "healthy" (sound, true, correct) teaching (or faith or speech)
1 Tim 1:10	. . . or the sexually immoral, for those practicing homosexuality, for slave traders and liars and perjurers—and for whatever else is contrary to the sound doctrine [*tē hygiainousē didaskalia*].
1 Tim 6:3	If anyone teaches otherwise and does not agree to the sound instruction [*hygiainousin logois*] of our Lord Jesus Christ and to godly teaching.
2 Tim 1:13	What you heard from me, keep as the pattern of sound teaching [*hygiainontōn logōn*], with faith and love in Christ Jesus.
2 Tim 4:3	For the time will come when people will not put up with sound doctrine [*tēs hygiainousēs didaskalias*]. Instead, to suit their own desires, they will gather around them a great number of teachers to say what their itching ears want to hear.
Titus 1:9	He must hold firmly to the trustworthy message as it has been taught, so that he can encourage others by sound doctrine [*tē didaskalia tē hygiainousē*] and refute those who oppose it.
Titus 1:13	This saying is true. Therefore rebuke them sharply, so that they will be sound in the faith [*hina hygiainōsin en tē pistei*].
Titus 2:1	You, however, must teach what is appropriate to sound doctrine [*tē hygiainousē didaskalia*].

144. Swinson, *What Is Scripture?*, 53, 58.

145. Matt 12:13; 15:31; Mark 5:34; Luke 5;31; 7:10; 15:27; John 5:6, 9, 11, 14, 15; 7:23; Acts 4:10; 3 John 2.

Passage	Reference to "healthy" (sound, true, correct) teaching (or faith or speech)
Titus 2:2	Teach the older men to be temperate, worthy of respect, self-controlled, and sound in faith [*hygiainontas tē pistei*], in love and in endurance.
Titus 2:8	. . . and soundness of speech [*logon hygiē*] that cannot be condemned, so that those who oppose you may be ashamed because they have nothing bad to say about us.

Dibelius and Conzelmann detect here a "singular use of these words" that constitutes a "problem." They find it "highly unlikely that in his old age Paul would have designated his gospel with other formulas."[146] This forms part of the argument that Paul did not write the PE.

From a philological viewpoint, however, the use of "healthy" as a metaphor for true, correct, or sound ideas is common in the era. In the history of ancient Greek language, "by the time of Paul," this world group "was used widely both for conditions of virtue and for the teaching that cultivated such conditions, among both Greco-Roman moral teachers" like Plutarch and Epictetus "and Hellenistic Jewish moralists" like Philo and Josephus.[147]

Epictetus serves as a good example. In his *Discourses* he uses *hygia*-stem words both in bodily health contexts (3.13.21; 3.20.4; 3.23.30) and in religious and moral settings:

> If what the philosophers say is true [*hygies*] . . . we must not look for it anywhere without. (1.11.28)

> And if [the gods] exist, but take no care of anything, in this case also how will it be right [*hygies*] to follow them? (1.12.5)

> But in the first place that which has been determined ought to be sound [*hygies*]. (2.15.2)

> The propositions which are true [*hygiesi*] and evident are of necessity used even by those who contradict them. (2.20.1)

> Have we then all sound [*hygiē*] opinions, both you and your adversary? (3.9.5)

146. Dibelius and Conzelmann, 24.

147. Johnson, *First and Second Letters to Timothy*, 172.

Over a dozen other passages could be cited just in this author. Dibelius and Conzelmann argue that Paul would have been violating some kind of protocol by using "these common expressions designating rational speech and opinions with reference to his gospel," finding it "very improbable, since nothing of the sort appears in the genuine epistles."[148] However, since "sound, true, correct" is a common meaning of the word at the time, if Paul wanted to describe apostolic teaching or doctrine, or faith rooted in that doctrine, using *hygia*-stem words, there is no compelling reason to deny that he could have done so. Every Pauline writing contains words and usages not present in his other writings. As Berger points out,[149] if contrasting use of words rules out common authorship, then there can be *no* genuine Pauline writings, for even undoubted "Pauline" writings diverge substantially from each other in word choice, imagery, themes, and other particulars.

Paul's characterization of teaching and faith using *hygia*-stem words simply "integrates it into the more comprehensive picture of mental and intellectual health" and "a behavioral or action-oriented interpretation of doctrine."[150] It responds to what Paul sees as the disasters resulting from unhealthy (or unsound) teachings (and related practices) in the air in Ephesus and Crete. It prioritizes antidotes that will tend toward more wholesome outcomes and serve as barriers against what weakens, sickens, and may even destroy. The importance of sound doctrine in Paul's pastoral pedagogy, and in the ministries of Timothy and Titus that Paul writes to promote, receives more explanation in the exposition below of passages containing *hygia*-stem words.

X. QUESTIONS OF INTRODUCTION

A. The Orientation of This Commentary

PE commentaries with lengthy discussions of formal "introductory" matters are common. Such discussions may occupy a fifth or more of a commentary.[151] Witherington's introduction is 22 percent of the whole, Hanson's 26 percent, Johnson's 29 percent, and Bernard's 43 percent.

The introduction to this present commentary devotes somewhat fewer pages to matters deemed preliminary, summary, or otherwise usefully pre-

148. Dibelius and Conzelmann, 25.

149. Berger, 792.

150. Saarinen, 40.

151. That is, issues commonly dealt with in New Testament introductions such as authorship, date, provenance, historical situation, recipients of the document, and related matters.

explanatory of the verses that make up each of the PE. This is in line with commentaries like those by Knight (11 percent), Towner (11 percent), Marshall with Towner (13 percent), and Kelly (14 percent).

This commentary has prescinded, then, from lengthy direct discussion of formal introductory matters. To repeat information willy-nilly would be to reproduce what is already available in abundance in other commentaries and New Testament introductions. In the sections above, rather, I have emphasized the contribution of the PE to the historic pastoral task, the theological substance of the PE in Trinitarian perspective, Paul's exemplary and herculean effort sustained over the better part of four decades to live out his gospel convictions, key places and persons dominant in the PE as they stand written, and selected key terms.

In the preceding discussion, however, this commentary's working position on the main introductory matters has emerged. The apostle Paul is taken to have been the author. The recipients are the Timothy and Titus mentioned elsewhere in the New Testament. We leave open the extent to which the letters were composed (1) personally, solely, and directly to them but then survived because of their relevance to wider ecclesial audiences right down to today; or (2) ostensibly to Timothy and Titus but in actuality to the communities they served—coming from Paul, the letters would lend authority to his associates as they sought to implement the counsel of the letters in sometimes resistant settings. As long as they are seen in apostolic in origin (as described in sec. VIII.C above), either understanding can be adopted productively. Or the two can be combined.[152]

We also leave open the question of exactly when the PE were written. It seems most likely, and is assumed for discussion's sake, that all three were written following Paul's release from a second imprisonment following the time described at the end of Acts 28. But scholars have made cases for 1 Timothy and Titus to have been written at some point during previous travels by Paul. Since we do not attempt to define the historical setting of the PE too precisely, or describe the opponents and false teaching implied in the PE in great detail,[153] it does not seem necessary to mount a strong defense of a par-

152. As in Johnson, *First and Second Letters to Timothy*, 41, with n. 86, who notes this was also the approach of J. D. Michaelis in the early nineteenth century.

153. The attempt has a long history; see, for example, W. Mangold, *Die Irrlehrer der Pastoralbriefe* (Marburg: Elwert'sche Universitäts-Buchhandlung, 1856), who even at that time says that the identity of the false teachers and teaching addressed in the PE "has already been decided by most, and by the most important, authorities" (v). See also W. Lütgert, *Die Irrlehrer der Pastoralbriefe* (Gütersloh: C. Bertelsmann, 1909); Brox, *Die Pastoralbriefe*, 31–42. Towner, *Letters*, 41–50, gives the matter thorough airing and arrives at the loose conclusion that parallels to the PE opponents are best sought "in the Pauline mission history," that is, in Paul's other letters, as well as in Acts, "not in later Gnostic movements." Also, the problems take different forms in Ephesus than in Crete.

ticular era or year when they were written. If Paul wrote 2 Timothy, then it is evident that he finished it shortly before his expected death, perhaps during a second Roman imprisonment as tradition holds. But the settings of 1 Timothy and Titus relative to Paul's life and travels are more difficult to establish. Other commentaries and New Testament introductions make valiant but as yet inconclusive attempts.

This commentary is sympathetic to Towner's remark that the "Pastoral Epistles" label has become so fraught with baggage that the label is better avoided. In the commentary below, we follow Towner in seeking to do justice to "both the individuality of the letters and their cluster relationship." Yet, for the sake of ease of reference, especially in dialogue with established scholarship, we use "PE" with much more frequency than Towner. We trust that the exposition allows each letter to "retain its status [and 'stature'] as an independent literary unity."[154] When we speak of them in combination or in the aggregate, we seek to enhance what they assert, individually and as a distinct component of the whole Pauline corpus, rather than write them off as a sub-Pauline corpus originating in a setting or circle that did not really grasp the historical Paul's genius or message. We hope this avoids, for example, the unhappy result seen in a book on Paul's view of pastoral ministry, in which not even one verse from any of the PE is cited.[155] The same absence of the PE is evident in N. T. Wright's study of the atonement, which, despite hundreds of references to Pauline writings, appears to lack reference to a single verse from the PE.[156]

B. The Authorship Question

We noted above (citing Belleville; see p. 12) the undesirability of allowing the authorship question to overshadow the weightier matters constituting the substance and message of the PE. Yet, precisely because a certain vein of scholarship has long pushed this issue to the forefront,[157] a more than passing accounting of it is required here. Below we sketch the current consensus, a historic affirmation of Pauline authorship from the twentieth century that still speaks to the twenty-first, and an emerging rival hegemony.

154. Towner, *Letters*, 88–89.

155. According to the Scripture index in J. Thompson, *Pastoral Ministry according to Paul: A Biblical Vision* (Grand Rapids: Baker Academic, 2006), 167–74. Three sentences appear to summarize the contribution of the PE to the book's theme (28).

156. N. T. Wright, *The Day the Revolution Began: Reconsidering the Meaning of Jesus' Resurrection* (New York: HarperOne, 2016).

157. For eighteen centuries, Pauline authorship was never doubted by the churches' intellectual leaders; even in the last two centuries, many have doubted the doubters.

1. The Status Quo

For a wide-ranging assessment of recent PE commentaries and numerous other PE studies and issues, see H. Marshall's panoramic survey.[158] Johnson has produced a valuable history of interpretation of 1–2 Timothy (within which the reception history of Titus may also be placed).[159] He shows the extent to which the non-Pauline authorship of the PE is a hypothesis, not a proven or (he thinks) provable fact. Yet, in scholarship stretching back to ca. 1800 in Germany, that hypothesis came to assume the status of unquestionable truth: "The inauthenticity of the Pastorals increasingly becomes a matter of dogma."[160] By the end of the twentieth century, for mainstream Western scholarship the PE had effectively "been removed not only from the Pauline corpus, but from anything more than purely formal canonicity."[161]

In recent times, even a relatively conservative New Testament scholar such as D. Hagner sides with "the arguments against Pauline authorship."[162] He draws this conclusion based on considerations of language and style, the apparent church organization reflected in the PE, their theology and ethics, and the portrait of Paul they present. There is another more covert factor at work: on the one hand, Hagner asserts that the theology of the PE "manifestly" does not contradict Paul's theology. On the other, he finds it "ludicrous that while women in the modern world can be prime ministers, presidents, governors, legislators, mayors, military officers, and CEOs, they are denied positions of leadership, to which they believe they are called by God, only in the church," in part based on teachings in the PE.[163] At least portions of the PE must be rejected as from Paul to satisfy Hagner's stringent dual demand.

U. Schnelle offers a largely overlapping set of considerations that for him eliminate the possibility that Paul wrote the PE: the historical situation of the PE (it cannot be squared with either Acts or Paul's letters); the PE "reflect the problems of the third Christian generation"; "exceptional linguistic features"; and differences in theology from the known Pauline letters. Schnelle concludes that "the overwhelming majority of exegetes regard the Pastorals as pseudepigraphical writings."[164] He concedes that there are dissenters, naming T. Zahn,

158. Marshall, "The Pastoral Epistles in Recent Study," 268–312.

159. Johnson, *First and Second Letters to Timothy*, 20–54.

160. Johnson, *First and Second Letters to Timothy*, 52, citing over a dozen works as examples.

161. Johnson, *First and Second Letters to Timothy*, 54.

162. D. Hagner, *The New Testament: A Historical and Theological Introduction* (Grand Rapids: Baker Academic, 2012), 614. Similarly, P. Achtemeier, J. Green, and M. Thompson, *Introducing the New Testament: Its Literature and Theology* (Grand Rapids: Eerdmans, 2001), 464.

163. Hagner, *The New Testament*, 615–22, 622n21, 636n59.

164. U. Schnelle, *The History and Theology of the New Testament Writings*, trans. M. Boring (Minneapolis: Fortress, 1998), 328–32, 331.

A. Schlatter, W. Michaelis, B. Reicke, and J. van Bruggen. But he fails to interact with their arguments. An unmentioned dissenter, E. Linnemann, has subjected each of Schnelle's objections to scrutiny. In sometimes brusque and crochety language she succeeds at showing there is generally less to Schnelle's claims than meets the eye.[165]

To return to Hagner, this scholar concludes, "Most important, the Pastorals breathe a different atmosphere." Here Hagner endorses the Dibelius thesis that the PE "reflect a conventional, 'bourgeois' Christianity—self-conscious, domesticated, institutionalized, finding its place in the world."[166] Hagner does not interact with work by Johnson and Towner[167] that prompts Pietersen to suggest that "the scholarly consensus post-Dibelius may need to be reexamined."[168] A subsequent study by M. Klinker–De Klerck has confirmed that claims of the PE reflecting a "bourgeois Christianity" (*christliche Bürgerlichkeit*) lack support in the ethical instruction of 1 Timothy and Titus.[169] Various writers in another volume show that Dibelius's outlook is not present in the PE as far as their soteriology, ethics, and missions outlook, either.[170]

Pietersen's summation of where things stands currently is apt: "The scholarly consensus has been to treat these letters as corpus written by a pseudonymous author (with a minority advocating the authenticity of 2 Timothy)." Yet, he also notes that some (he mentions Johnson and Towner) "have insisted that each letter should be treated separately and have argued for authenticity of Pauline authorship."[171]

165. E. Linnemann, *Biblical Criticism on Trial*, trans. R. Yarbrough (Grand Rapids: Kregel, 2001). On the alleged high number of hapax legomena in the PE, see 104; 1 and 2 Corinthians have a higher percentage than Titus, and Romans (12.38%) has a percentage comparable to 1 and 2 Timothy (13.94% and 13.57%, respectively). On the historical setting of the PE and church organization, see 128–32. On the allegedly non-Pauline theology of the PE, see 150–51. On the "churchy" (*kirchlich*) nature of Timothy's faith, see 153–54. For a rebuttal of both Schnelle and arguments advanced by P. N. Harrison (*The Problem of the Pastoral Epistles* [London: Oxford University Press, 1921], 31–32, 36–37), see 74–91. For more elegantly stated and sweeping responses to the majority position, see Johnson, *First and Second Letters to Timothy*, 81–90.

166. Hagner, *The New Testament*, 622.

167. Their PE commentaries constitute running refutation of the Dibelius thesis. See also Towner, *The Goal of Our Instruction*, JSNTSup 34 (Sheffield: Sheffield Academic, 1989).

168. Pietersen, "Epistles, Pastoral," *EBR* 7:1098.

169. See M. Klinker–De Klerck, *Herderlijke regel of inburgeringscursus? Een bijdrage aan het onderzoek naar de ethische richtlijnen in 1 Timoteüs en Titus* [Pastoral rule or lesson on assimilation? A contribution to the research on the ethical instructions in 1 Timothy and Titus] (Zoetermeer: Boekencentrum Academic, 2013; Ph.D. dissertation from University of the Reformed Churches in Kampen, the Netherlands), summarized in M. Klinker–De Klerck, "Dissertation and Monograph Summary," *Journal for the Study of Paul and His Letters* 3.2 (2013): 263–67.

170. Köstenberger and Wilder, *Entrusted with the Gospel*, 168, 238–39, 251, 267.

171. Pietersen, "Epistles, Pastoral," *EBR* 7:1093–94.

2. A New Look on Paul's Authorship of the PE?

After L. T. Johnson made his shift from affirming PE pseudonymity to arguing for Pauline authorship,[172] he observed in 2001 that E. Ellis's "mild optimism" in a 1961 publication regarding a possible "turn of scholarly opinion in favor of authenticity has not been vindicated."[173]

But Johnson's is not quite the voice in the wilderness now that it was then. Already in 2008 Klinker–De Klerck was chronicling a shift in the wind.[174] Although the inauthenticity hypothesis still holds sway, she finds numerous commentaries[175] and other studies have emerged to challenge the hegemony. Parallel to Klinker–De Klerck, Carson and Moo canvassed and assessed a great deal of scholarship surrounding pseudonymity and New Testament documents including the PE. They underscore the difficulty of the issues involved: "The entire complex apparatus of technical scholarship and historical criticism, not to say theology and worldview, impinge on an interlocking web of judgments that bear on the question of whether or not there are pseudepigrapha among the New Testament documents." Yet, they show that "the search for parallels to justify the view that the intended readers of some New Testament documents would have understood them to be pseudonymous, so that no deception took place [by their acceptance as genuine], has proved a failure."[176] They go on to assess thoroughly what they view as the main issues regarding PE authorship—vocabulary and wording (including P. N. Harrison's contentions), rhetorical style, historical problems, false teachers, church organization, and theology. In a reserved but searching manner they affirm Pauline authorship.

A. Köstenberger's chapter on the PE in *The Cradle, the Cross, and the Crown: An Introduction to the New Testament* comes to the same conclusion as do Carson and Moo on the authorship and pseudonymity questions.[177] Twelve

172. See Johnson, *Letters to Paul's Delegates*, 2–3. Johnson writes that, while he formerly shared the majority position, "when I tried to communicate to students the logic underlying" that view, "I could not make it convincing." Hence, he adopted "the traditional position as the more elegant and reasonable hypothesis." Still, he concedes "the impossibility of demonstrating the authenticity of" the PE (*First and Second Letters to Timothy*, 91).

173. Johnson, *First and Second Letters to Timothy*, 54.

174. M. Klinker–De Klerck, "The Pastoral Epistles: Authentic Pauline Writings," *EJT* 17.2 (2008) 101–8.

175. For Klinker–De Klerck's summary of the inauthenticity arguments, see her "Pastoral Epistles," 102–3. In 106n2 she mentions commentaries by Fee (1988), Knight (1992), Mounce (2000), Johnson (2001), Towner (2006), and Witherington (2006).

176. D. A. Carson and D. Moo, *An Introduction to the New Testament*, 2nd ed. (Grand Rapids: Zondervan, 2005), 337–53, 345, 350.

177. A. Köstenberger, L. Kellum, and C. Quarles, *The Cradle, the Cross, and the Crown: An Introduction to the New Testament*, 2nd ed. (Nashville: B&H Academic, 2017), 715–58.

years after Carson and Moo, Köstenberger's remarks and arguments,[178] significant in themselves, point to other fresh studies that directly or indirectly confirm the plausibility of Pauline authorship. One is an essay by E. Schnabel that opens, "Despite the pressure of majority opinion, the assumption of the pseudonymity of the letters to Timothy and Titus (called Pastoral Epistles) has weaker support than the assumption of authenticity." He continues: "Literary, theological, and historical evidence supports Pauline authorship, particularly when the three letters are evaluated separately rather than as a corpus." Following lengthy examination of these three points of debate, Schnabel concludes that the stakes are high, not insignificant as some suggest. He concludes, "As the evidence that has been surveyed demonstrates, there are good reasons to accept the Pauline authorship of these three letters."[179]

As an example of Schnabel's argumentation, regarding literary arguments he notes three objections to Paul's authorship of the PE based on language and style: (1) the PE diverge from the vocabulary of Paul's other letters, (2) the PE diverge from the style (length of sentences, syntax) of Paul's other letters, and (3) the PE diverge from the manner of argumentation found in Paul's other letters.[180]

In response, Schnabel sketches nine countervailing observations, grounded by discussion and often by significant supporting works and discussion in footnotes.[181]

1. The PE "are too small for (stylo)statistical analysis" because of insufficient number of words, both in the PE and in Paul's corpus generally. The limited database does not permit valid quantitative findings.
2. The majority opinion's reliance on vocabulary comparison is distorted by unjustified comparison of the PE as a group with the other Pauline epistles as a group.
3. All Pauline letters, not just the PE, contain clusters of words not found in some or any other Pauline letters.
4. The assumption that an author has a single unvarying style holding steady over decades and despite occasion, recipient, or subject matter is demonstrably false.[182]

178. They are augmented considerably in Köstenberger, 14–24.

179. E. Schnabel, "Paul, Timothy, and Titus: The Assumption of a Pseudonymous Author and of Pseudonymous Recipients in the Light of Literary, Theological, and Historical Evidence," in *Do Historical Matters Matter to Faith?*, ed. J. Hoffmeier and D. Magary (Wheaton, IL: Crossway, 2012), 403.

180. Schnabel, "Paul, Timothy, and Titus," 386–87.

181. See Schnabel, "Paul, Timothy, and Titus," 387–91.

182. A point verified by ongoing investigation; see A. Pitts and J. Tyra, "Exploring Linguistic Variation in an Ancient Greek Single-Source Corpus: A Register Design Analysis of

5. The dialogical mode selected by Paul in his *Hauptbriefe* (undoubted epistles), such as Romans, 1 and 2 Corinthians, and Galatians, sets them apart, not just from the PE, but from other equally accepted Pauline letters like Philippians and 1 Thessalonians; PE divergence from the *Hauptbriefe* does not necessarily mean they are non-Pauline.
6. The stylistic profile of Paul's language varies in part because of influence from Old Testament, confessional, and liturgical sources, or his decision in some letters to forgo reference to such sources.
7. Binary conception of authorship (i.e., either "Paul" or "not Paul") ignores the variables introduced by dictation, amanuenses, and possible influence by named coworkers (with effects on wording?) such as Sosthenes, Timothy, and Silas. (Only the PE, along with Romans and Ephesians, name Paul alone as their author.)
8. "The difference between (conceptual) orality and (conceptual) writing" plays an unvalued role in differences between the PE and other Pauline letters.
9. "The earliest church fathers . . . never doubted" Paul's authorship of the PE and were native Greek speakers much closer to Paul in the history of the Greek language than were German scholars beginning ca. 1800. These fathers' "sense of 'style' was surely on a par with that of modern scholars, who learn Greek in artificial classroom settings as teenagers or later in life and who never attain the fluency of a native speaker."

Schnabel's conclusion based on the above is that stylistic differences between the PE and other Pauline letters are "a matter of judgment," not a priori proof that the first word of each of the PE ("Paul") is a manifest misnomer disproven by literary observation. "The language of the Pastoral Epistles, despite some distinctive characteristics, renders Pauline authorship neither impossible nor implausible."[183]

Another source pointing to the increasing tenability of pushback against the majority view of the non-Pauline origin of the PE is the relevant chapter in Porter's introduction to Paul.[184] He mentions the standard sticking points raised by those who reject Paul's authorship:

1. the epistolary form (the PE are viewed as community letters, that is, letters to churches, and not real letters to individuals)
2. the literary style

Josephus and Pauline Pseudonymity," in *The Language and Literature of the New Testament*, ed. L. Dow, C. Evans, and A. Pitts (Leiden: Brill, 2017), 257–83.

183. Pitts and Tyra, "Exploring Linguistic Variation," 391.

184. Porter, *The Apostle Paul*, 409–42.

3. the substance or content of the letters
4. the challenge of fitting the PE into a Pauline chronology
5. the alleged absence of the PE from writings of the apostolic and sub-apostolic fathers.

With respect to (1), Porter calls in question the Dibelius-Conzelmann claim that 1 Timothy is less personal than 2 Timothy. He shows that the formal literary criteria indicate otherwise. Regarding 2–4, Porter shows that none of these objections suffices to demonstrate the "firm or indisputable basis" for rejecting Pauline authorship.[185] In the course of the discussion Porter points out that evidence is insufficient to prove precisely when Paul might have written the PE. But neither the period described in Acts nor the time afterward can be ruled out. Hence, "nothing in the chronological issues themselves" renders Paul's authorship implausible,[186] however much we might desire more varied and secure empirical corroboration. In fact, J. Robinson claims that "the very difficulty of squaring" the PE "with any itinerary deducible from Acts or the other Pauline epistles is a strong argument for their authenticity." A pseudonymous writer clever enough to produce the PE would surely have connected them more overtly with chronological or geographic details in Acts, in the other Paulines, or both. He proposes a chronology in which the PE were written in the 50s.[187]

Regarding (5) above, Porter notes that since B. Weiss (1887), who showed the likelihood of the use of the PE by those fathers, "important evidence [has been] slighted." Ignatius and Polycarp both cite the PE. Neither Marcion's rejection of the PE nor their absence from P[46] proves that they were not known and circulating well before the middle of the second century. Porter concludes: "The supposed weak attestation of the Pastoral Epistles is far from conclusive; in fact, there is evidence of their existence." After showing the weakness of standard arguments against Paul's authorship, Porter mounts a concluding positive case in light of chronology and internal evidence.[188]

In summary, this section has shown increased and continuing advocacy for Pauline authorship of the PE. Other studies could be mentioned. S. Walton observes that, in C. S. Smith's important monograph on the theme of Christian teaching and learning, "there is very great commonality between 1 Corinthians and the Pastorals, a point that might give pause to some arguments for the

185. Porter, *The Apostle Paul*, 412, 413–17.

186. Porter, *The Apostle Paul*, 417, with reference to evidence cited in Weiss's *A Manual of Introduction to the New Testament*.

187. J. Robinson, *Redating the New Testament* (Philadelphia: Westminster, 1976), 72, 84, 352.

188. Porter, *The Apostle Paul*, 418, 419, 423–31.

Pastorals being deutero-Pauline."[189] Blomberg has mounted a spirited defense of Pauline authorship in connection with broader questions of the New Testament's veracity.[190] While much current literature may give the impression that the non-Pauline option is beyond dispute, Johnson mentions six commentaries in the late nineteenth century that defended Paul's authorship, by Fairburn (1874), Beck (1879), Ellicott (1883), Plummer (1888), Bernard (1899), and Stellhorn (1899). He mentions twenty-seven more authors advancing the same position in the twentieth century: Weiss (1902), Belser (1907), Ramsay (1909–11), White (1910), Knabenbauer (1913), Brown (1917), Hilliard (1919), Parry (1920), Meinertz (1923), Wohlenberg (1923), Lock (1924), Loewe (1929), Gardner (1936), Molitor (1937), Boudou (1950), Ambroggi ([1953]), Guthrie (1957), Schlatter (1958), Knappe (1959), Kelly (1963), Spicq (1969), Ward (1974), Jeremias (1981), Oden (1989), Holtz (1992), Ramos (1992), Towner (1994), plus one by coauthors Lea and Griffin (1992).[191]

It is therefore significant that T. Long (who rejects Pauline authorship) writes: "The question of who wrote the Pastoral Epistles, once fairly settled, has opened up again in New Testament scholarship."[192] Given the resilience of the Pauline option as demonstrated in the nearly three dozen commentaries over recent generations, and intensification of pro-Pauline arguments since the turn of this century, it seems unwarranted to insist that rejection of Pauline authorship should be viewed as the only intellectually responsible position. Johnson has described the process by which doubting Paul's authorship became a dogmatic position.[193] Robinson explains the phenomenon in a related domain, the dating of New Testament documents. Describing the field of New Testament studies broadly over many generations, he asserts: "Each new student enters a field already marked out for him by datelines which modesty as well as sloth prompts him to accept, and having accepted to preserve. The mere fact that 'New Testament introduction' tends to occupy his earliest and most inexperienced years has a formative effect, for good or for ill, on all his subsequent work."[194] Johnson's observation bears contemplating: "An observer is tempted to suggest that the expulsion of the Pastorals was the sacrifice required by intellectual self-respect if scholars were to claim critical integrity and still keep the Paul they most wanted—and needed."[195]

189. S. Walton, review of *Pauline Communities as "Scholastic Communities": A Study of the Vocabulary of "Teaching" in 1 Corinthians, 1 and 2 Timothy, and Titus*, by C. S. Smith, *RBL* 10 (2014).

190. Blomberg, *Historical Reliability of the New Testament*, 394–407.

191. Johnson, *First and Second Letters to Timothy*, 49, 49–50.

192. Long, 11.

193. Johnson, *First and Second Letters to Timothy*, 42–54.

194. Robinson, *Redating the New Testament*, 350.

195. Johnson, *First and Second Letters to Timothy*, 48.

This section has raised the question whether "a new look on Paul's authorship of the PE" has arisen. In some ways, it surely has. Yet, the majority view in which non-Pauline authorship is simply assumed is still in vogue. Long gives exactly two sentences in his commentary to the Pauline possibility.[196] J. Twomey states, "The Pastoral Epistles are . . . in the view of a scholarly consensus which this commentary accepts, pseudepigraphical."[197] The reading he offers is not what the book's title might be taken to suggest—a history including description of how all Christian interpreters read the PE until the German Enlightenment—but a judgment on the history of interpretation in favor of decided bias against claims favoring Paul's authorship.

R. Saarinen's commentary is in much the same vein. In the course of dispensing with the authorship issue on one page, he mentions Mounce and Johnson, who defend Paul's authorship, but only to commend Mounce's bibliography and Johnson's history of interpretation. Towner's extensive work on the PE over the last three decades is nowhere cited in the book. Saarinen defends his decision to reject Paul's authorship with the sentence, "As the leading Lutheran (Roloff), Catholic (Oberlinner, Weiser, Collins) and evangelical (Marshall) commentators can all combine pseudonymity with their own high appreciation of this Pauline legacy, I can side with them on this issue." He does offer the following to readers committed to Pauline authorship: "Given the concentration on theological exposition" in his commentary, his presentation "would not be dramatically changed even if I would affirm Paul's authorship."[198] This stance ignores the ethical issue (which presumably affects the credibility of the putative theology of the PE) raised by documents strongly claiming to be from Paul and insisting "I am telling the truth, I am not lying" (1 Tim 2:7)—but which actually do deceive the reader at the most personal and direct level of misrepresenting the writer's true identity.[199] A writer melodramatically depicting his imminent execution and invoking God's presence in doxology (2 Tim 4:17–18) is, if he is making it all up, not only deceiving but on the verge of blasphemy.

By way of identifying the better option for purposes of this commentary—Pauline authorship of the PE or the view still preponderant in much

196. Long, 11.

197. Twomey, 2.

198. Saarinen, 22, 23.

199. Wall, with Steele, 6, scoffs at this reasoning, which he dismisses as "often heard among conservatives"; he rejects with scare quotes such "deception" arguments, although he does mention as the best defense the book by T. L. Wilder, *Pseudonymity, the New Testament, and Deception* (Lanham, MD: University Press of America, 2004; new ed. forthcoming). I find Wilder's study more convincing than Wall's dismissal. To Wall's credit, he does state (5) that he is unconvinced by the majority position that rejects Paul's authorship. He accepts apostolic (and even Pauline?) authorship, but on canonical and not historical grounds (7).

scholarship—two more considerations will be offered. First, in the next section, a fresh exposition of arguments for Paul's authorship will be presented. It is fresh in the sense that it comes from almost wholly untranslated sources, and from a scholar (Adolf Schlatter, 1852–1938) widely regarded as significant but overlooked in the history of New Testament studies.[200] It will give a flavor, limited in scope but illustrative in coverage, for a classic affirmation of Paul's authorship in a scholarly setting where this position had already been widely abandoned and marginalized. It may give fresh impetus for new appreciation of analogous views today. Second, in the closing section, we will cite developments in global Christianity and their possible relevance to this discussion.

C. A Pre-New Look Vantage Point

1. *Origin and Nature of the PE*

The introduction to Schlatter's more scholarly PE commentary lists over five dozen linguistic parallels between the PE and the other Pauline letters.[201] Such evidence does not of course prove Pauline authorship,[202] as impressive lists of non-Pauline usage in the PE can easily be generated and are standard fare in commentaries.[203]

Schlatter, however, counters that lists of non-Pauline words are also not the last word in disproving Pauline origin. Rather, "the decisive weight falls on the exposition; if separation of the letters from Paul makes them into a riddle for which there is no explanation, the linguistic distinctiveness of the PE cannot separate them from Paul."[204] Schlatter wishes to show

200. For a useful summary of Schlatter in his historical context, see A. Köstenberger, "Theodor Zahn, Adolf Harnack, and Adolf Schlatter," *in Prevailing Methods before 1980*, vol. 1 of *Pillars in the History of Biblical Interpretation*, ed. S. Porter and S. Adams (Eugene, OR: Pickwick, 2016), 163–210. For biographical information, see W. Neuer, *Adolf Schlatter: A Biography of Germany's Premier Biblical Theologian*, trans. R. Yarbrough (Grand Rapids: Baker Books, 1995); more extensively, W. Neuer, *Adolf Schlatter: Ein Leben für Theologie und Kirche* (Stuttgart: Calwer, 1996).

201. Schlatter, *Die Kirche der Griechen*. His more popular exposition was *Die Briefe*.

202. As a reviewer of even Schlatter's popular-level PE commentary observes, Schlatter "indicates that doubts about Pauline authorship are not foreign to him" (R. Knopf, review of *Die Briefe an die Thessalonicher, Philipper, Timotheus und Titus*, by A. Schlatter, *TRu* 9 [1906]: 62).

203. Much of this section is adapted from R. Yarbrough, "Schlatter on the Pastorals: Mission in the Academy," in *New Testament Theology in Light of the Church's Mission*, ed. J. Laansma, G. Osborne, and R. Van Neste (Eugene, OR: Wipf & Stock, 2011), 295–316; used by permission.

204. Schlatter, *Die Kirche der Griechen*, 17.

merely that the case for Pauline authorship is not utterly groundless even from a linguistic viewpoint. There are numerous instances of Pauline turns of phrase and diction, "over 70 literal points of contact with other Pauline letters in fact (most of all Romans and 1–2 Corinthians)."[205] These are not of the contrived and stilted sort one finds in, say, the apocryphal Epistle to the Laodiceans, much of which was manifestly cribbed from the canonical Philippians. They are often divergent enough not to qualify as slavish imitation of Paul, yet similar enough to raise the seeming likelihood of a common mind and hand.

This line of thought suggests to Schlatter the need to take a careful look at the historical setting, since vocabulary alone hardly settles the matter. Like most commentators, Schlatter concedes that the PE do not fit in the life and movements of Paul as described in Acts. And yet, "regarded in themselves, their references fit together seamlessly."[206] The details of the PE are consistent with a time after Paul's release from his first imprisonment,[207] a release that he stated he expected (Phil 1:25). And the conditions Paul describes in the PE, along with the language he uses,[208] are different from those reflected in his earlier epistles, which comports with a later time of composition.[209] Schlatter notes that the only direct contradiction between the PE and the other ten Pauline letters is at 1 Tim 2:5, where Jesus is the mediator, whereas in Gal 3:19, 20 it is Moses. Yet, he dryly observes, "The points of contact are so numerous that those who reject Pauline authorship must ascribe to their author not only familiarity with Paul's typical ecclesial language but also an intimate knowledge of the Pauline epistolary corpus."[210] Historically speaking, it is more likely that Paul is the author of all of this material than that he was not, which would mean that unknown writers skillfully and comprehensively mastered and mimicked his voice in often precise detail at an early juncture, without leaving any evidence of their existence, much less identity in the annals of early church history and literature.

The issue of different language is significant enough for us to show one of the ways Schlatter viewed things; his words will be quoted at length. How does he explain the shift in vocabulary from Paul's earlier letters to the PE? The following is not all of Schlatter's explanation, but it gives the flavor of his shrewd approach to the problem (recall that he wrote during the era of Hitler's consolidation of power):

205. As Neuer observes (*Adolf Schlatter: Ein Leben*, 796).

206. Schlatter, *Einleitung in die Bibel*, 420.

207. See Schlatter, *Die Kirche der Griechen*, 21.

208. Schlatter, *Einleitung in die Bibel*, 420.

209. Few suggest that the PE precede the undoubted Pauline letters.

210. Schlatter, *Die Kirche der Griechen*, 16, a point noted also by B. Brinkmann, review of *Die Kirche der Griechen im Urteil des Paulus*, by A. von Schlatter, *Scholastik* 12 (1937): 291.

> How a shift in verbal usage arises we are experiencing vividly through the changes that our language has recently undergone. Today a number of words have become somewhat common which earlier we used rarely, or only with other connotations: *Führer, Führung, Boden, Blut, Rasse, Rassenseele, Erbgang, Brauchtum.*[211] But also key terms in church language have received new application: "faith" in relation to government authority, "fellowship" in relation to the German people, "confession" as a problem in "fellowship" with the German people. In addition there is the virtual elimination of Latin-based words. This shift in language arises not because we have changed but because those to whom we speak have changed. . . . The question posed by the new words of the PE is: do they point to new situations and aspirations of the church? Much had taken place during the more than five years of Paul's imprisonment and separation from the churches; this may be glimpsed from his writings to the Corinthians and the Romans, as well as from the Prison Epistles. It is true that the Prison Epistles are not vastly separate from the PE temporally; but Paul's situation had substantially altered: now he is in touch with the churches not only through friends and messengers but by his physical presence. He himself interacts with those who contradict him. Of the words in the PE that point to controversy—ζήτησις, ἐκζήτησις, μῦθος, γενεαλογίαι, ψευδώνυμος γνῶσις, κενοφωνία, λογομαχία, ἀντιθέσεις, αἱρετικός, τετύφωται, ἐξέστραπται, πίστεως ἀστοχῆσαι, περὶ τὴν πίστιν [ἐ]ναυάγῆσαι, αὐτοκατάκριτος—it is certain that they are not new words coined by the writer but rather terms brought into play by those he must engage. Likewise, the new words making up the list of qualifications for overseers and policies for widows conform to the conditions that are now current in the congregations.[212]

It is not possible or necessary to document all of Schlatter's arguments for the linguistic plausibility of Paul's authorship of the PE. Just the brief excerpts above bear out Neuer's statement that Schlatter's case for Paul's authorship is not just "repetition and preference for arguments traditionally brought forth for 'genuineness'"; rather, it consists of "a plenitude of independent observations on the language and content of the letters."[213] It should also be noted that Schlatter's late-life affirmation of Pauline authorship of the PE represents a shift

211. Readers may recognize these words as connected to Nazi ideology. *Führer* as a title for Hitler should be obvious; the other words mean "leadership, soil, blood, race, soul of the [Aryan] race, inheritance, usage." On *Rassenseele* and *Brauchtum,* see Cornelia Schmitz-Berning, *Vokabular des Nationalsozialismus* (Berlin: de Gruyter, 1998), 524 and 616.

212. Schlatter, *Die Kirche der Griechen,* 16–17.

213. Neuer, *Adolf Schlatter: Ein Leben,* 796.

of conviction (like L. T. Johnson's mentioned above) from the earliest viewpoint of his career.[214] Evidently, his studies over the decades convinced him of this position, versus his simply continuing to hold a traditionally grounded conviction about non-Pauline authorship.

The bulk of Schlatter's exposition in his NT introduction relates the themes of the PE to a plausible Pauline ministry following his first imprisonment, a ministry with many points of contact to Jesus and to Paul's earlier letters, yet also with many disconnects, appropriate to the new and altered states of affairs he has encountered in Ephesus and evidently hears about in Crete as he writes to Titus. Schlatter's comments on 1 Tim 1 give a flavor of his understanding of the historical rootedness of the PE overall. These letters are both personally and ecclesially directed:

> The first epistle to Timothy states that Timothy has been left behind in Ephesus, where his main concern must be repudiation of false doctrines (ch. 1). The damaging nature of the doctrines moving through the local congregations is shown by how they are degenerating into vacuous chatter. As a result, the purpose of the divine law is being overlooked and twisted. On both points Timothy is reminded, concisely and graphically, of the leading truths that govern every word that is spoken in the worship gatherings of the congregation. All Christian admonition has love as its goal, love rooted in a pure heart, a good conscience, and unfeigned faith. Whatever does not serve this goal is chatter, even if it promotes itself with lofty claims of spirituality relating to God and his mysteries. The purpose of the law is to deal with evildoers and to judge their wicked works; it is not to be used to hinder the righteous and restrict the gospel. With its administration of the law and the fight against evil, the church, through what has happened to Paul, receives forever the rule because of which it remembers his apostolic calling, through which in a distinctive manner the grace of Jesus was manifest. In service to this grace Timothy is to conduct himself as a good soldier, unlike a few of Paul's earlier coworkers who suffered shipwreck in their faith.[215]

In sum, whereas for the majority non-Pauline conception of the PEs the "historical" setting of the PE is a speculative, undetermined place and time (probably around the onset of the second century) related to no concrete congregations, location, or known author, Schlatter reads the PE as an artifact of Paul's final years of apostolic ministry based on linguistic, literary, and concrete historical considerations.

214. Note sources cited in Yarbrough, "Schlatter on the Pastorals," 296–97.

215. Schlatter, *Einleitung in die Bibel*, 414–15.

2. *Theology of the PE*

For Schlatter, the PE are dominated by direct connecting lines not only to Paul but to Jesus: "The admonition of the PE is not separate from the person and work of Jesus."[216] And: "The church is a unity and encompasses all believers in Jesus."[217] While many explain the PE from a hypothetical scenario decades after Paul's death, Schlatter's reconstruction grows out of the life of Paul and Paul's convictions about Christ, the God who sent him, and the gospel message that by the Spirit makes him known savingly to sinners, foremost Paul himself (see 1 Tim 1:15). Or to put it another way, while the historical Paul is a shadowy background figure for majority exposition, which typically devotes much space to showing disconnects between Paul and the PE, for Schlatter not only Paul but even Jesus plays a significant role, perhaps not surprising, since the PE are replete with references to Jesus—no chapter in the PE lacks explicit mention of him. Even Schlatter's popular-level exposition of Titus (which contains only four explicit references to "Jesus Christ" [1:1; 2:13; 3:6] or "Christ Jesus" [1:4]) mentions Jesus frequently.[218] Schlatter's scholarly PE commentary overall mentions Jesus with respect to at least these topics: his resurrection, his message, his messianic office, his patience, his history, his grace, his coming, his mediatorial role, his sending, and his death. Schlatter also notes ties between Jesus and the Spirit, the law, the church, and his word.[219]

This brief summary of Schlatter's work may help explain reviewer recognition that Schlatter's PE exposition is user-friendly from a pastoral-preaching perspective and that it is theologically oriented. Neuer notes that the significance of Schlatter's major PE commentary lies in its "mature *theological* interpretation: Erlangen NT scholar Jürgen Roloff pointed out decades later" that in this work "there are valuable formulations of polished theological wisdom on almost every page."[220] We note just four passages in Schlatter's exposition of Titus where such wisdom is glimpsed.

In Titus (as in 1 Timothy), according to Schlatter, "faith arises from full apprehension of the truth" (244).[221] Schlatter here has in mind Paul's opening remark that parallels "the faith of God's elect" with "their knowledge of the truth" (Titus 1:1).[222] In Titus 1:2, as Paul speaks of "the hope of eternal life,"

216. Schlatter, *Einleitung in die Bibel*, 424.

217. Schlatter, *Die Kirche der Griechen*, 14.

218. See Schlatter, *Die Briefe*, 245, 252, 257, 259, 260, 261, 264, 265, 267, 268, 270.

219. See references collected in Schlatter, *Die Kirche der Griechen*, 274.

220. Neuer, *Adolf Schlatter: Ein Leben*, 798.

221. In this section, parenthetical page numbers refer to Schlatter's *Die Kirche der Griechen*. For more on this "full apprehension of the truth," see 175–76.

222. In this section, citations from Titus are from the ESV.

Schlatter observes that "man cannot conjure up this hope with his own ideas or moods, for it requires secure basis in God's action. It can only arise from the facts [*Tatsachen*] associated with God's sovereign reign" (245). The pastoral wisdom on display here is that Christian faith requires basis in fact. This view has been widely denied in Teutonic (and derivative) scholarship since Kant, for which facts and Christian faith are typically adjudged to be at least in tension and probably in antithesis. For Schlatter, however, the truth of the gospel message advanced in the PE is of a piece with the historical verities surrounding its earliest proclamation. This commonsense pastoral insight is of course quintessentially Pauline (see, e.g., 1 Cor 15:14), as is Paul's position advanced in Titus that believers "are not chosen because they believe but believe because they are chosen, which is the same view voiced in Romans" (176) in Schlatter's estimation.

When Paul speaks of those who "must be silenced since they are upsetting whole families by teaching for shameful gain what they ought not to teach" (Titus 1:11), Schlatter cautions that "the overseer is not to silence these people through dictatorial means." He should rather appeal to believers' conscience with "the word that calls to repentance with the suasive force of truth" (250). This directive is supported by Titus 1:9, 14. The theological wisdom here involves understanding of the importance of the inner life and how that life can be disturbed by "empty words divorced from the gospel" if these words gain subversive force in Christian households and relationships. The antidote is not sterile and formal opposition but pastoral correction that enables true apostolic faith to make whole those in families whose initially sound gospel convictions have been maliciously upset (186).

Different locales pose varying threats to faithful gospel appropriation (251). Strategies to offset these threats and to offer ongoing faithful representation of apostolic truth must therefore be sensitive to local conditions. The situation on the island of Crete (Titus 1:12–16) indicated how challenging Titus's work there would be (251). Paul did not offer Titus facile formulas for quick success. "Irresolute handling" of harmful Cretan distinctives "would only exacerbate those evils" (251).[223] A patient, firm, and positive pastoral administration of true Christian teaching would be necessary, one that mediated "redemption from evil" and thereby the experience of "how Christ is given to bring about righteousness and sanctification" (252). "Whether the congregations there would come to affirm teaching that was healthy or sick would depend on how thorough and earnest their repentance turned out to be" (252; see Titus 1:15–16). The pastoral wisdom here is wide-ranging but involves understanding of contextualization and the nuances of real-world ministry of the Christian message in complex, often hostile social settings.

223. Schlatter notes (186n2) the parallel with "reprove them severely" in 2 Cor 13:10.

Schlatter's grasp and explanation of the religious psychology at work in Titus 1:15 ("To the pure, all things are pure, but to the defiled and unbelieving, nothing is pure; but both their minds and their consciences are defiled") are clear and distinct. On the one hand, the way to purity is found when a person "is cleansed in his inner living core [*Lebensgestalt*], a cleansing attained by the one who has been made whole through his faith" (252). On the other, Schlatter unpacks carefully why those who reject the full cleansing of the gospel message necessarily defile all they regard: "Impurity is inherent in them, specifically in the two inner functions that dominate the human condition [*Lebensstand*], thinking and making judgments. These functions are defiled, as people deploy them in connection with other people and life generally; they are directed downward into darkness. Likewise people's conscience is robbed of peace and condemns them. . . . The inner condemnation that ensues prevents peace with God and blocks faith that is certain of his grace" (253). Here is a principled and sensitive dissection of the human condition, both as to its healthy existence through faith in Christ and as to its pathological status when Christ's restorative work through reception of the apostolic message has been hampered.

Elsewhere Schlatter plausibly relates healthy inner spiritual life to the teaching of Jesus, "who said that the contrast between clean and unclean was not through external things but in the heart of man through the desires that arise in him" (187). Aspects of Titus 1:15–16 are also shown to relate directly to Pauline convictions in known Pauline writings (187–89). The following is but a portion of how Schlatter unpacks the inner working of the soul among the "defiled and unbelieving" described in Titus 1:15–16:

> Every religious undertaking presupposes a knowledge of God. Those whose methods of salvation stand in opposition to the message of Jesus object that they know God.[224] But their confession of God occurs only through words, while their actions are not formed by their knowledge of God; their actions do not arise either out of the fear of God or out of that faith that submits to him. They thereby deny God. They cannot behave any differently, for what they are internally is despicable [*abscheulich*].[225] They do not obey the instruction offered to them, and when something good needs to be done, they are completely useless.[226] Through these [negative] results the new methods of salvation [advanced by the Cretan teachers] prove the exclusive saving force of the Christ and the saving power of his word. It is evident that only he is able to lead us out of the denial of

224. Schlatter here references (188n1) parallel Greek phrases in Gal 4:8; 1 Thess 4:5; Rom 1:21.

225. Schlatter relates (188n2) the Greek word *bdelyktoi* to its cognate in Rom 2:22.

226. Schlatter relates (189n3) the Greek word *adokimoi* to parallels in 1 Cor 9:27; 13:5–7.

> God to establish us in faith in God. Separated from him, yes, there can be a knowledge of God. However, it is nullified by sinful desire, and the distinguishing mark of guilt attaches to its striving against God. (188–89)

Passages like the four singled out above, in which both exegetical-historical acumen and theological-pastoral awareness are intertwined, are easily multiplied in Schlatter's exposition of Titus. Here are a few examples briefly summarized: first, in Paul's age-specific counsel in Titus 2, Schlatter highlights what holy living looks like and calls for, namely, showing that believers live constantly in the conviction that "they stand continually in the presence of God" (254).[227] Second, with respect to the high and holy calling of the older women (Titus 2:3–5), Schlatter comments on the necessity of Titus and other pastoral leaders not working extensively with women in their personal family affairs; that is something women attend to most effectively among themselves (255). Third, the reception of the gospel is dramatically influenced, for good or ill, by its effects on women in congregations. "The pagan populace had low regard for the daily tasks of women and observed closely how believing Christian women conducted themselves" (256). For that reason, "the comportment of the women will determine the impression about the divine Word that is formed in the city" (255). Fourth, frequently repeated in all of Schlatter's PE exposition is the conviction that the task of being a Christian is not about some special knowledge or the effecting of peculiar experiences of divine grace; it lies rather in the daily actions and relationships that fill everyday life—a direct point of contact between Paul and Jesus (257).

A fifth and final example is perhaps most illustrative of Schlatter's theologically rich and pastorally suggestive PE exposition. With respect to how "the grace of God . . . [trains] us to renounce ungodliness and worldly passions, and to live self-controlled, upright, and godly lives in the present age" (Titus 2:11–12), Schlatter calls attention to how grace mediates divine defeat of such passions and replacement with God and desire for him:

> Grace frees us from these desires, and although the whole world furtively embraces them and is driven by them, we acquire through grace the power to condemn these desires and close ourselves off against them. Because God pulls us away from our godlessness and does not hand us over helplessly to our appetites, but gives us mastery over them, he acts upon us as the Grace-Bestowing One [*der Gnädige*]. This brings about a way of life, free from deluded passion and grounded in sensibleness and sobriety, that grants people what we owe them and God his honor. And all this is

227. In each of these examples, more thorough explication appears in *Die Kirche der Griechen*, at the respective verses.

> precisely God's benevolent, fatherly intention for us. Yes, the present world order is not the abiding one; it stands in profound opposition to the divine will. Nevertheless, through the illumination, stimulation, and training of God's grace, we are set free from this form of the world and given a desire that far transcends this world. (258–59)

3. Significance of the PE in Church-Historical Perspective

In much current interpretation, the church today rightly grasps the PE only to the extent that it separates them from Paul's authentic writings and distances itself from much core PE counsel. For Schlatter the opposite is the case. Since he does not view the authentic writings and views of the historical Paul as in tension with and often antithetical to the PE, Schlatter's exegesis encourages a maximalist appropriation of the theology and ethics propounded in the PE for the present time.

Of course "present time" and its attendant circumstances vary for each generation of readers and their local settings. But one of Schlatter's most avid students and distinguished intellectual descendants, K. H. Rengstorf (1903–92), aptly characterized the significance of Schlatter's view of the PE in the volatile, Nazi-dominated atmosphere in which his scholarly PE commentary was first published. In Schlatter's reading, "the [Pastoral] Epistles discuss matters that are highly pertinent precisely for our generation." Among currently pressing issues that Rengstorf finds addressed in Schlatter's treatment are the questions of (1) "how the congregation of Jesus should conduct its own internal affairs," (2) "what legitimate church discipline looks like," and (3) "what constitutes an informed and responsible relation between the church and the state." The point at which Rengstorf notes the relevance of Schlatter's exposition most fully "at precisely this time of painful disruption within the German Protestant church and its theology" lies in Schlatter's "indefatigable summons to the sources of Christian knowledge and Christian life."[228] Rengstorf elaborates:

> Regarding the PE and their contemporary significance, we refer simply to this: the PE battle against the burgeoning intellectualization of the Christian proclamation which was becoming visible in the Hellenistic congregations. Closer investigation, meanwhile, indicates that the author of PE did not share our sense of the meaning of the term "doctrine." Wherever *didaskalia* ["teaching"] and related terms are used (cf. 1 Tim 1:3 and elsewhere), abstract dogma is not in view but rather instruction for

228. Rengstorf, review of *Die Kirche der Griechen im Urteil des Paulus*, by A. Schlatter, *Pastoralblätter für Predigt, Seelsorge und kirchliche Unterweisung* 79 (1936/37): 636–37.

> the ordering of everyday life (ethics). This [ethics] too is an extension of Jesus's teaching (1 Tim 6:3), so includes within itself "gospel" (in contrast to "myth") and "doctrine" (in contrast to heterodoxy). The goal of the PE, accordingly—and this is in keeping with saving work of God (1 Tim 1:1, 15)—is not merely a religious community having "a doctrine" in common but a compliant religious community that is willing and ready to perform good works.[229]

In addition, Rengstorf points out that Schlatter, in full awareness of the critical questions,[230] succeeds in situating the PE within the internal and external history of the growing early church and not only within the life of Paul.[231] The commentary accounts for both the history and the theology of the PE in their original setting in a way that makes their message pertinent for the present day. In the same vein J. Jeremias noted the contemporary aptness of the commentaries Schlatter published in his closing years, including this PE commentary; they all hold "significance for New Testament scholarship as well as for the preaching of the church."[232]

D. Pauline Authorship of the PE in Global Christian Perspective

The preceding discussion has established the vexed nature of the authorship question. Disagreement can be found on virtually every assertion made on opposing sides. One might despair of arriving at a clear personal decision one way or the other.

Perhaps help lies in looking outside the fusty confines of the in-house debate among PE exegetes with the help of interdisciplinary insight and less cultural myopia. For a generation, missiologists such as Andrew Walls, in concert with formidable historical studies by the likes of Philip Jenkins and Lamin Sanneh, have been confirming the contention voiced by J. Morgan: "A global shift of Christianity has been largely ignored by the North American media and academia, yet it may have been the most significant religious event of the twentieth century."[233] Or as J. Bonk put it more than a decade earlier:

229. Rengstorf, review of *Die Kirche der Griechen*, 637.

230. See also B. Brinkmann, review of *Die Kirche der Griechen im Urteil des Paulus*, by A. Schlatter, *Scholastik* 12 (1937): 291: the commentary is "in general objective, though lacking proper scholarly apparatus. Yet, the exhaustive knowledge of the author [i.e., Schlatter] is evident everywhere."

231. Rengstorf, review of *Die Kirche der Griechen*, 637.

232. J. Jeremias, review of *Die Kirche der Griechen im Urteil des Paulus*, by A. Schlatter, *TLZ* 62 (1937): 415. See Jeremias, 3–4, for his defense of Pauline authorship of the PE.

233. See, for example, A. Walls and C. Ross, eds., *Mission in the Twenty-First Century*

"The greatest surge in the history of Christianity occurred in Africa over the past one hundred years, and indeed continues its breathtaking trajectory into the twenty-first century."[234] The effect of this shift has made little discernible impact in the methods and conclusions of mainstream New Testament scholarship in general, much less on the PE in particular. Sanneh stated already in 1995 that theological education goes on today in the West "largely uninterested in Christianity's unprecedented expansion around the world." He added, "Standard theological sources and methods have failed to show any awareness of the Copernican shift that has taken place in the religious map of the world."[235]

Perhaps that shift calls for hermeneutical adjustment. As I was reminded in an email from an Egyptian national on Palm Sunday 2017 in the final days of writing this commentary:

> The Christians of Egypt are being slaughtered inside their churches again. An explosion occurred this morning inside a Coptic Orthodox church in the northern city of Tanta during Palm Sunday services. Our hearts are broken. As of this moment we are told that 27 died and many more injured. Then just minutes ago an explosion occurred outside the main Orthodox church in our city of Alexandria apparently as people were leaving the mass. The Pope himself was inside and we are told he is ok. At least 8 people have died, including three security officers, but it is early to assess the full situation. Reports of ambulances rushing to scene.

Estimates of Christians dying (mainly at the hands of religionists holding what the PE would call false doctrine and especially deficient Christology) range from just over three persons per day to something over two hundred.[236]

(Maryknoll, NY: Orbis Books, 2008), especially Walls's concluding essay, "Afterword: Christian Mission in a Five-Hundred-Year Context" (193–204). See P. Jenkins, *The Next Christendom: The Coming of Global Christianity*, 3rd ed. (Oxford: Oxford University Press, 2011). Orientation into the life and writings of L. Sanneh is found in his autobiography: *Summoned from the Margin: Homecoming of an African* (Grand Rapids: Eerdmans, 2012). See J. Morgan, "Global Trends and the North American Church in Mission: Discovering the Church's Role in the Twenty-First Century," *IBMR* 40.4 (2016): 330; see also M. Noll, *From Every Tribe and Nation: A Historian's Discovery of the Global Christian Story* (Grand Rapids: Baker Academic, 2014).

234. J. Bonk, "Ecclesiastical Cartography and the Invisible Continent," *IBMR* 28.4 (2004): 154.

235. L. Sanneh, "Global Christianity and the Re-education of the West," *ChrCent*, July 19–26, 1995, 715, 716.

236. The organization Open Doors recently tallied 1,207 Christians martyred per year, or about 3.3 per day. They limit their count to eyewitness accounts. The Center for the Study of Global Christianity at Gordon-Conwell Theological Seminary estimates 90,000 per year, or 247 per day. They include all who die as the result of being Christians, including those killed in war (e.g., in northern Nigeria at the hands of Boko Haram). For details, see See M. Belz,

It is evident that the world has changed since the days of F. D. E. Schleiermacher (1768–1834), who is often credited with beginning the tradition of denying Paul's authorship of the PE.[237] He joined many others in what came to be the liberal project of abandoning historic Christian convictions (often by redefinition of terms like revelation, inspiration, miracle, prophecy, the operation of grace, and ultimately even God) to make them more acceptable to the faith's "cultured despisers" in his native Germany and gradually far beyond. People disturbed by murdered Christians and understanding their lives to be linked with theirs are justified in having different priorities from Schleiermacher's.

An important hermeneutical question is how much our methods and interpretation should be tailored so as not to offend skeptics who accept few to none of the Christian's Bible-revealed truths to begin with. If it is primarily the agnostic guild that guides,[238] a fictional PE author and creative conception of the contents of the PE may prove compelling. Schleiermacher's concern and confidence are understandable in the age of Enlightenment Christendom having Europe as its substantial international center. In 1800, fully 85 percent of the world's Protestants were in Europe, and 12 percent in North America. The figure for Africa was 0.1 percent. Christianity then was truly and profoundly Western.

Things look different in 2017, when only 11 percent of the world's Protestants are in North America, 16 percent in Europe, 18 percent in Asia, and 42 percent in Africa. By 2050 (when Christian martyrs are projected to swell from today's 90,000 to 100,000 annually), North America is projected to have 8 percent of the world's Protestants, Europe 10 percent, Asia 17 percent, and Africa 53 percent.[239]

Readers of the PE thinking in global terms may, like Oden cited at the beginning of this introduction or Schlatter as described in the previous section, find it attractive to read the PE as they represent themselves, as the canon

---

"Numbers Matter," *World Magazine*, February 18, 2017, 32; Johnson, Zurlo, Hickman, and Crossing, "Christianity 2017," 50.

237. Schleiermacher wrote: "It is not the person who believes in a holy writing who has religion, but only the one who needs none and probably could make one for himself" ("On the Essence of Religion," 1799, quoted in Legaspi, *The Death of Scripture and the Rise of Biblical Studies*, v). No wonder Schleiermacher could dispense with Paul's authorship of the PE.

238. For the rise and character of much of the guild, see Legaspi, *The Death of Scripture and the Rise of Biblical Studies*. For its ground rules (such as denial of miracles, esp. including Jesus's resurrection, rejection of his death understood as an atonement for human sin, understanding of Jesus as no more than a moral teacher, rejection of "church" as a necessary factor in the thought and life of enlightened Christians), see Wilckens, *Kritik der Bibelkritik*, 18–24.

239. All figures in this and the preceding paragraph appear in Johnson, Zurlo, Hickman, and Crossing, "Christianity 2017," 41–52.

presents them, as they have been read by most believers through the centuries, and as the global church that believes the Bible, and is often dying because of it, still reads them. Going back to the 1970s, *The New Oxford Annotated Bible with the Apocrypha* discouraged readers from thinking of Paul as the PE author.[240] But as Jenkins observes, "The dominant current in emerging world Christianity is traditionalist, orthodox, and supernatural."[241] Andrew Walls adds, "Lands that were once at [the church's] heart are now on the margins, others that were on the margins are now at its heart."[242] Even a stalwart opponent of Pauline authorship of the PE, Jörg Frey, concedes that the classic Western "historical-critical" paradigm does not bear the same binding hermeneutical authority "in other cultural contexts," so that in those contexts "other approaches can in increasing measure be regarded as more or less legitimate."[243] The global church has been deeply impacted by Western critical voices; perhaps it is time for interpreters even in the West to grant fresh respect for "other cultural contexts," whether those around the world today or those of the nineteen centuries during which the PE were read as Pauline. It is probably neither ignorance nor obscurantism that explains why the *Africa Study Bible*,[244] with some 350 contributors (many with academic PhDs) from fifty countries, presents the PE as written by Paul.

Globally, many would affirm Mark Noll's missiological observation that "Scripture comes alive with new force when it is read as the book of God for all believers everywhere, as well as the book of God that speaks most directly to me in my particular time and place."[245] It is no great stretch to interpret the PE affirming Paul as their author when one's field of vision broadens to include, not only the evidence and construals presented by current specialists, but also the witness of world and historic Christianity.

240. *The New Oxford Annotated Bible with the Apocrypha* (New York: Oxford University Press, 1973), 1440. Admittedly it conjectures that the PE were a product of "a loyal disciple of Paul." But how loyal could that have been, when Paul had warned against pseudepigraphic letters in his name (2 Thess 2:2) and often added greetings in his own hand (1 Cor 16:21; Gal 6:11; Col 4:18; 2 Thess 3:17) to underscore the authenticity of his letters?

241. Jenkins, *The Next Christendom*, 8; see also 217–20.

242. Walls, "Afterword," 202.

243. Frey, *Von Jesus zur neutestamentlichen Theologie*, 52n108.

244. Printed in India and published in 2017 by Oasis International Limited and Tyndale House Publishers, Carol Stream, IL, USA. See *Africa Study Bible*, 1778, 1792, 1803.

245. Mark Noll, *The New Shape of World Christianity* (Downers Grove, IL: InterVarsity Press, 2009), 198.

The Letter of
1 TIMOTHY

The Text and Title of 1 Timothy

The Greek text that forms the basis for most modern-language translations of 1 Timothy is that of Nestle-Aland, now in its twenty-eighth edition.[1] This is a stable and reliable text, for 1 Timothy is attested most prominently by sixteen uncials (ℵ A C D F G H I K L P Ψ 048 0241 0262 0285) and by the same eleven minuscules (33 81 104 365 630 1175 1241 1505 1506 1739 1881) and two lectionaries (*l* 249 *l* 846) that likewise contain 2 Timothy and Titus. These twenty-nine texts are "consistently and frequently cited" in the Nestle-Aland apparatus.[2] Numerous additional Greek (and Latin) witnesses could be listed, but they would add nothing significant to this sizable collection of ancient documents deemed foundational by specialists in the field for determining with relative certainty what the original author of 1 Timothy composed.[3]

In the NIV 2011 translation, there are no footnotes pertaining to the Greek text of 1 Timothy. That is, there is no significant dispute about the wording of the original manuscript of this epistle for basic translation purposes. Textual critics still debate the precise original wording of the Greek text of 1 Timothy in some nineteen places.[4] In fifteen of these, the United Bible Societies assigns an A rating in their four-letter system of A (virtually certain) to D (evidence is divided). At these fifteen junctures,[5] though there is textual vari-

1. *The Greek-English New Testament*, 28th ed. (Wheaton, IL: Crossway, 2012). The virtually identical text appears in *The Greek New Testament*, 5th rev. ed. (Stuttgart: Deutsche Bibelgesellschaft, 2014).

2. *The Greek-English New Testament*, xxvii. For the listing of witnesses in 1 Timothy, see xxix.

3. In recent years a few scholars have stressed the uncertainty of our knowledge of the original texts of the New Testament writings. For a sample response to this minority but significant voice, see, for example, Daniel B. Wallace, ed., *Revisiting the Corruption of the New Testament* (Grand Rapids: Kregel, 2011).

4. See Barbara Aland et al., eds., *The Greek New Testament*, 4th rev. ed. (Stuttgart: Deutsche Bibelgesellschaft, 2001), 713–24.

5. 1 Tim 1:1, 4, 15, 17; 2:1, 7; 3:1; 4:16; 5:18; 6:5, 7, 9, 17, 19, 21.

ation, there is unanimity regarding the original wording. In two cases (1 Tim 1:4; 5:16) the committee assigns a B rating, and in two other cases (5:10; 6:13) a C rating. Commentary below will discuss variants when these are significant for the interpretation of the passages in which they occur.

Neither the Nestle-Aland nor the UBS text cites evidence for the original title of 1 Timothy. This information is available, however, in *A Textual Commentary on the Greek New Testament*.[6] There are nine different titles. "Timothy" appears as the recipient in them all. The main variation is due to scribal speculation on where Paul was when he wrote the epistle. Scribal notations suggest Laodicea, Nicopolis, and even (in some Bohairic Coptic manuscripts) Athens. Whatever these titles say, the first two verses of the epistle set forth the author and the recipient. Paul's precise location when writing (or dictating) the epistle is hardly decisive for its interpretation and in any case cannot be determined based on ancient manuscript information.

Overall, text-critical data are consistent with a view that 1 Timothy could have been composed by Paul to Timothy within the general time frame of Paul's known life span.

Outline of 1 Timothy

- I. Greeting (1:1–2)
- II. Rallying Timothy's Resolve (1:3–20)
  - A. Timothy Charged to Oppose False Teachers (1:3–11)
  - B. The Lord's Grace to Paul (1:12–17)
  - C. The Charge to Timothy Renewed (1:18–20)
- III. Order in Church and Life (2:1–6:2a)
  - A. Instructions on Worship (2:1–15)
  - B. Qualifications for Overseers and Deacons (3:1–13)
  - C. Reasons for Paul's Instructions (3:14–4:16)
    - 1. Conduct in God's Household and Its Basis in Christ (3:14–16)
    - 2. Pro-creation Ethics for the Last Days (4:1–5)
    - 3. True Godliness in Pastoral Ministry (4:6–10)
    - 4. Standing Orders for Timothy (4:11–16)
  - D. Subgroup Care: Widows, Elders, Slaves (5:1–6:2a)
    - 1. Overarching Principle (5:1–2)
    - 2. Widows: General Policies (5:3–8)
    - 3. Widows: Enlistment Rules (5:9–10)
    - 4. Younger Widows (5:11–15)
    - 5. Personal Caregivers of Widows (5:16)

6. B. M. Metzger, ed., *A Textual Commentary on the Greek New Testament*, 2nd ed. (Stuttgart: Deutsche Bibelgesellschaft, 1994), 577–78.

            6. Elders (5:17–20)
            7. For Timothy: An Aside (5:21–25)
            8. Slaves (6:1–2a)

IV. Final Clarification and Exhortation (6:2b–21)
    A. False Teachers and the Love of Money (6:2b–10)
    B. Final Charge to Timothy (6:11–21)

Commentary on 1 Timothy

I. GREETING (1:1–2)

Paul's greeting in 1 Timothy may come across as laconic and even formulaic.[1] Whereas the greeting to Titus is lengthy and theologically rich and the greeting in 2 Timothy includes a flourish regarding "the promise of life that is in Christ Jesus," 1 Timothy's opening words may seem flat and prosaic.

Yet, the 1 Timothy opening is longer than eight other Pauline prescripts[2] and the same length as Paul's opening words to the Colossians. In the extant Pauline corpus, openings in which Paul writes at some length or in detail are limited to his greetings in just three epistles: Galatians, Titus, and (longest of all) Romans (see table 24 "Pauline Prescripts" below). There is in fact a wealth of fact and lore contained in 1 Tim 1:1–2.[3]

1. Dibelius and Conzelmann state, "The duty of the exegete, once he has declared a work 'inauthentic,' is to set out to answer the question why these 'epistles' were written, and why they were written in their present form" (154). Since they view the PE as non-Pauline, their commentary (like many others) labors to explain them as non-Pauline creations, and indeed as mock epistles (hence "epistles" in scare quotes in the sentence quoted here). The present commentary views the PE as Pauline and will seek to explain them as actual letters to men in real ministry positions. Also, emphasis will be placed more on *what* they say (which the text conveys) than on *why* it was said (which is, after all, paratextual—it must be sought alongside or behind the text and is more easily missed, misunderstood, or manufactured by the interpreter).

2. That is, the prescripts of 1–2 Corinthians, Ephesians, Philippians, 1–2 Thessalonians, 2 Timothy, and Philemon.

3. Krause, 29, sees the proper names here as part of "the ruse of the intimate communication between Paul and Timothy." Like Dibelius and Conzelmann, she views both "Paul" and "Timothy" as fictitious constructs of an unknown author or authorial community.

[1] *Paul, an apostle of Christ Jesus by the command of God our Savior and of Christ Jesus our hope,* [2] *To Timothy my true son in the faith: Grace, mercy and peace from God the Father and Christ Jesus our Lord.*

1 Paul follows the letter-writing style of his historical and social location in beginning this epistle: he states his name. (On Paul, see Introduction, VIII.C.) Other elements of a typical prescript were the addressee's name (in this case, Timothy), a greeting, a blessing, and a prayer.[4] In this epistle (as in Titus, but not in 2 Timothy), Paul dispenses with the prayer, proceeding immediately to the counsel of v. 3. Observations of similarities between Paul's and other letters should not obscure the extent to which his letters are "remarkable" in that he "Christianizes the secular Hellenistic letter form," not missing "an opportunity to enrich his readers with spiritual knowledge and a sense of worship."[5] He also draws on Jewish convention, with novel results.[6]

Despite the evident close personal ties between Paul and Timothy that this letter immediately reveals (note "my true son," v. 2), it opens on an official-sounding note: the writer is "an apostle." While this term should not be saddled with a uniform and highly technical meaning every time Paul uses it, it is fair to observe that, with it, Paul here places himself among a select few in Christianity's founding era who possessed "specific leadership credentials and tasks."[7] Paul's apostolic qualifications include seeing the resurrected Jesus (1 Cor 9:1; note Acts 1:22), being chosen and sent by God and Christ to play a unique role in the gospel's spread (Gal 1:1, 15), and performing "the marks of a true apostle, including signs, wonders and miracles" (2 Cor 12:12).

"By the command" stresses that Paul was not self-selected but was called.[8] It may also hint at a sense that he had no choice in God's grand scheme of things.[9] The Greek stresses God's initiative and authority in the command more than NIV indicates. "By" translates *kata*, which is rightly understood as introducing "the norm which governs" something.[10] N. T. Wright and some

4. On Paul and his letters more broadly, see "Letters in the Hellenistic World," in Hagner, *The New Testament*, 410–18; L. Doering, *Ancient Jewish Letters and the Beginnings of Christian Epistolography*, WUNT 298 (Tübingen: Mohr Siebeck, 2012).

5. Hagner, *The New Testament*, 412.

6. Doering, *Ancient Jewish Letters*, 428.

7. Jeannine Brown, "Apostle I: New Testament," *EBR* 2:472.

8. For rich reflections on God's call, see Luther, 217–18.

9. Aquinas, 6, makes the application here that "prelates are held by the necessity of precept to those things which are of their office."

10. BDAG 512. See §B5aδ, where 1 Tim 1:1 is listed alongside other verses (Rom 8:28; 16:26; Titus 1:3) in which *kata* occurs where "the norm is at the same time the reason, so that *in accordance with* and *because of* are merged" (italics in original). But to construe either sense as instrumental "by" (the sense suggested by NIV) goes against the semantics of *kata* with the accusative. The

translations render "according to the command."[11] That something was a divine command[12] that Paul associates with both God and Christ. The former he calls Savior (on "Savior," see Introduction, IX.A), as he also does in other PE passages.[13] In the PE Paul also calls Christ the Savior.[14] This free alternation reveals Paul's conviction that Jesus as the Christ shared fully in the Father's divinity.[15] In antiquity "many gods were described as 'saviors.'"[16] Paul and Timothy, however, stand in a heritage in which there is but one such God, the God of Abraham, who has revealed himself in Christ.

With his opening words Paul communicates to Timothy that they serve a cause far greater than themselves: indeed, they serve the mysterious manifold personage who is "savior" in a world rife with gospel opposition. He is also "our hope,"[17] where such opposition may have tempted Timothy to fall into hopelessness. Paul speaks of "hope" to Titus as well (Titus 1:2; 2:13; 3:7). Timothy's challenging assignment at Ephesus (see 1:3) will benefit from the conviction that the apostolic gospel he ministers goes forth under the auspices of God who rescues and Christ who confers a sense of confidence in the future that is so strong that it transforms the present. "For the Christian, history is neither static nor cyclical but dynamic, the theater of God's creative and redemptive work ever moving toward the fulfillment of God's purposes."[18] Such a perspective grounds hope.

---

conflicting suggestion (BDAG 383) that "κατ᾽ ἐπιταγήν *in accordance w. the command*" may be rendered with an instrumental "*by command*" assigns a meaning to *kata* that belongs to other prepositions (like *dia*). It may in some sense be true that Paul's apostleship was *by* (or *by means of*) God's command, but this is not quite the point that "according to God's command" seeks to make. See also *kata* in 1:11, which NIV translates as "that confirms to." A norm is in view, not the means.

11. Wright, 3; ASV, LEB, NASB, WEB.

12. The same word for a command is used a total of seven times by Paul: see also Rom 16:26; 1 Cor 7:6, 25; 2 Cor 8:8; Titus 1:3; 2:15. Barrett (*Pastoral Epistles*, 38) comments that "the word is used of divine oracles." Krause, 32, observes that "the term announces that" what this epistle contains flows "directly from one who has been commanded by God."

13. 1 Tim 2:3; 4:10; Titus 1:3; 2:10; 3:4.

14. Christ is "savior" in Eph 5:23; Phil 3:20; 2 Tim 2:10; Titus 1:4; 3:6. Jesus Christ is called "God and Savior" in Titus 2:13.

15. Noted also in Ryken: "A command from the Father is also said to be a command from the Son, and vice versa. Therefore, the Son must be equal in power and authority to the Father. Jesus is God" (4). But not God the Father; for the importance of the distinction, see, for example, N. Qureshi, *No God but One: Allah or Jesus?* (Grand Rapids: Zondervan, 2016), 14.

16. C. Keener, *The IVP Bible Background Commentary*, 2nd ed. (Downers Grove, IL: IVP Academic, 2014), 603.

17. See Col 1:27, where Christ is the glorious "hope" in or among the Colossians. Dibelius and Conzelmann (13, with n. 2) point to six passages in the AF where Christ is called "our hope." But in only one of these is Christ called "hope" in conjunction with God the Father: "Farewell in God the Father and in Jesus Christ, our shared hope" (Ign. *Eph.* 21:2).

18. Gloer, 104.

Witherington suggests that v. 1 "helps to establish Paul's ethos so that the arguments carry weight in part because of whom they come from."[19] But there is nothing here about Paul's ethos, just an assertion of God's edict. That the edict led to an ethos is certain. What Paul seeks to impress on Timothy from the outset is not, however, about Paul, his style, his policies, or his custom. It is rather about God and even more prominently "Christ Jesus" (words repeated twice)—of the fifteen words in the Greek of v. 1, six of them are names or titles for the being Paul identifies as God. This usage establishes a strong theocentric platform from the outset for the letter's observations, commiserations, and directives.

2 Timothy is Paul's "true son." By rendering *teknon* as "son" rather than "child,"[20] NIV takes a liberty that makes Paul sound more sexist to some contemporary readers than his usage here justifies. The sense of "true" is genuine, legitimate. Paul applies the same adjective to an unknown "true companion" (Phil 4:3)[21] and to Titus (Titus 1:4). Paul was instrumental in Timothy's evangelization in his home town of Lystra (Acts 14:6; 21; 16:1–2) and enlistment in the gospel cause (Acts 16:3–4). In that sense Paul is a father figure for Timothy. Elsewhere he calls Timothy "our brother and coworker in God's service in spreading the gospel of Christ" (1 Thess 3:2; see also Phlm 1). The relationship was not only paternal: it was also fraternal.

Timothy is Paul's true child "in the faith," which parallels his statement that Titus was his true child "according to a common faith" (Titus 1:4 WEB). Paul acknowledges a body of belief that constitutes the core of Christian faith (see the apostolic "pattern of teaching" [Rom 6:17]). This core includes "shared commitment to the same Lord, Jesus"[22] but goes further to include the wide range of theological, soteriological, ecclesial, and other convictions to which the PE attest. He and Timothy are like father and son in their shared affirmation of God, the saving truths revealed in Scripture (see 2 Tim 3:15), the good news of Christ and his redemptive work, and numerous ethical entailments. This faith is not merely mental conviction, for as Schlatter notes, "The 'believing' through which one became a child of Paul gave form to the entire volitional faculty of the one believing."[23] The will and therefore behavior were transformed; it was more than just intellectual conviction. Paul served Jesus, who posed the discomfiting question, "Why do you call me, 'Lord, Lord,' and do not do what I say?" (see Luke 6:46). On this basis, Paul will have much to

19. Witherington, 187.

20. BDAG 994–95, does not offer "son" as a gloss for *teknon*. Rightly, Wright, 3: "my true child in the faith."

21. For discussion, see J. H. Hellerman, *Philippians*, EGGNT (Nashville: B&H, 2015), 231–32.

22. Johnson, *The First and Second Letters to Timothy*, 159.

23. Schlatter, *Die Kirche der Griechen*, 26.

say about what Timothy and his parishioners should do, not simply what they should think, believe, or confess.

Paul invokes God's blessing of "grace, mercy, and peace" on Timothy. Knight helpfully summarizes this distinctive though not unique (see 2 Tim 1:2) greeting. Grace expresses "God's ongoing forgiveness and enabling"; mercy, his "sympathy and concern"; and peace, "his tranquility and stability within and among" Timothy and fellow church members.[24] This is not, however, simply Paul's human good wishes. He pronounces this threefold blessing as an apostle authorized to articulate the divine will and good news (see 1 Thess 2:13). So special gravity attaches to the words "from God the Father and Christ Jesus our Lord," for Paul has been in the heavenly presence of which he speaks (2 Cor 12:1–7) and from which God's benefits flow.

Taken together, vv. 1–2 attest powerfully to Paul's theocentric and christocentric vision. While it is natural and fruitful to focus on Paul, Timothy, their biographies, their social setting, their or the gospel's opponents, and any number of other temporal and background factors, Paul's rhetoric makes merest mention of writer and recipient, majoring rather on the deity. He is named first as "Christ Jesus," which words also complete v. 2, except that "our Lord" is added, clinching his co-ownership of "the name that is above every name" (Phil 2:9). A major key to unlocking Paul's mentality as he writes (or dictates) is his overwhelming and distinct sense of God (dominant in vv. 1–2) and how Paul and Timothy stand united in their mission on his behalf in Christ's name.

II. RALLYING TIMOTHY'S RESOLVE (1:3–20)

"The first chapter of 1 Timothy is also a complete literary unity."[25] Paul turns immediately to his apparent primary concern: Timothy should not veer from or waver in his present duties in Ephesus (v. 3). This stabilizing exhortation is needed because of "certain people" purveying "false doctrines," a recurring theme in the letter.[26] Paul points to the baleful outcome of deviant "speculations" (v. 4) and affirms what is central to the Christian message and pastoral mission with which Timothy is entrusted (v. 5).

The rest of the section is devoted to review of what aberrant teachers are advancing (v. 6), apparently in the proximity of the church or churches

24. Knight, 67.

25. Saarinen, 31.

26. Bassler (38) notes similarity to the abrupt opening of Galatians, an epistle that likewise addresses the problem of figures Paul viewed as jeopardizing the integrity of the gospel message.

over which Timothy has oversight. It is true that "there is no indication that those who were spreading false doctrine were outsiders,"[27] but neither is there indication that they were accepted congregational leaders. They may have been quite on the fringe but with influence over some in the congregation through personal relationships or other means, of which commentators at this remove have no knowledge. Much controversy surrounds "the law" (see vv. 7–10),[28] which confirms that part of the problem surrounds misunderstanding, distortion, and misappropriation of Old Testament teaching and lore thrown in (note the genealogies in v. 4), apparently with an admixture of Greco-Roman views (note "myths," v. 4).[29] Such an amalgam would not be surprising at a cultural crossroads like Ephesus. Timothy's work, like Paul's, is based on "sound doctrine" that "conforms to the gospel" (vv. 10–11). This section serves, on that basis, to debunk teaching that is unsound so that the true proclamation and instruction can flourish in Timothy's personal life (like it does in Paul's), as well as among those to whom he administers pastoral care.

A. Timothy Charged to Oppose False Teachers (1:3–11)

> [3] *As I urged you when I went into Macedonia, stay there in Ephesus so that you may command certain people not to teach false doctrines any longer* [4] *or to devote themselves to myths and endless genealogies. Such things promote controversial speculations rather than advancing God's work—which is by faith.* [5] *The goal of this command is love, which comes from a pure heart and a good conscience and a sincere faith.* [6] *Some have departed from these and have turned to meaningless talk.* [7] *They want to be teachers of the law, but they do not know what they are talking about or what they so confidently affirm.* [8] *We know that the law is good if one uses it properly.* [9] *We also know that the law is made not for the righteous but for lawbreakers and rebels, the ungodly and sinful, the unholy and irreligious, for those who kill their fathers or mothers, for murderers,* [10] *for the sexually immoral, for those practicing homosexuality, for slave traders and liars and perjurers—and for whatever else is contrary to the sound doctrine* [11] *that conforms to the gospel concerning the glory of the blessed God, which he entrusted to me.*

27. Trebilco and Rae, 9.

28. "We see then that there is a very significant crisis in the church at Ephesus" (Trebilco and Rae, 9).

29. For the range of possibilities regarding "myths and . . . genealogies" (v. 4), see the excursus in Dibelius and Conzelmann, 16–17.

3 "As I urged you" implies that Paul has previously broached this topic with Timothy. Paul recalls a scenario in which he and Timothy were together at Ephesus, after which Paul departed for Macedonia, traveling to the north and west. Now Timothy is on his own, or at least without Paul's direct assistance. The word translated "urged" (from *parakaleō*) has a range of meanings from cheerful encouragement (e.g., 1 Thess 3:2) to stern admonition (e.g., Phil 4:2). It occurs in every Pauline letter except Galatians and is used by Paul a total of fifty-four times, eight times in the PE.[30]

"Stay there" is a command in English; the Greek is a little more oblique. It could be translated, "Like I urged you to stay on at Ephesus when I went to Macedonia, [so I urge you again now], in order to command certain people." In technical terms, instead of an imperative Paul uses an infinitive ("to stay on"), and Timothy can infer that Paul is, in effect, refreshing his standing orders.[31] This wording fits the frequent Pauline pattern of tactful suasion (on display, e.g., in Philemon and perhaps Rom 14) rather than heavy-handed direct decrees, which in turn points to Paul's conviction that Christ and his Spirit unite believers and guide them, so leaders (like Paul) should create space to impress and direct rather than rely on domineering tactics, even by an apostle. From the outset this approach gives 1 Timothy the feel of one side of the discussion between two parties about a situation and how it should be handled rather than a superior talking down to an underling and prescribing his next moves.

Timothy's continued tenure at Ephesus has a distinct purpose: "to put a stop to heretical teaching at Ephesus."[32] Three expressions stand out: Timothy's commission to "command," "certain people," and "false doctrines."

The word translated "command" is used twelve times by Paul, five of these uses in 1 Timothy.[33] Jesus used the same word when he sent out the Twelve (Matt 10:5), when he commanded a crowd to be seated (Matt 15:35; cf. Mark 8:6), and when commanding an unclean spirit to depart (Luke 8:29).[34] The other two congregations who received letters in which Paul spoke of "commands" with this word are Corinth and Thessalonica.[35] The former setting boasted wayward members, and the latter, new converts; both may have been factors at Ephesus, requiring Timothy to be proactive and directive in his pastoral labor, not merely encouraging and didactic.

"Certain people" corresponds to the "some" in v. 6 and perhaps also the "some" of v. 19, Hymenaeus and Alexander among their number (v. 20). They are

30. See also 1 Tim 2:1; 5:1; 6:2; 2 Tim 4:2; Titus 1:9; 2:6, 15.

31. That is, the sentence exhibits anacoluthon; see H. V. Siebenthal, *Griechische Grammatik zum Neuen Testament* (Gießen: Brunnen, 2011), §292e.

32. Barrett, *Pastoral Epistles*, 39.

33. See also 1 Tim 4:11; 5:7; 6:13, 17.

34. For use of the word in other sources (LXX, Philo, AF), see Quinn and Wacker, 61.

35. See 1 Cor 7:10; 11:17 and 1 Thess 4:11; 2 Thess 3:4, 6, 10, 12.

known less by name or biographical details in 1 Timothy than by their misrepresentations of the gospel, which Paul repeatedly leans on Timothy to address. In coming verses it is evident that part of their misunderstanding (or willful distortion) surrounds the Old Testament and its moral teaching (see esp. vv. 7–9). What is frustrating to commentators, though it perhaps speaks well of Paul's respect for others and restraint,[36] is that he says so little about them, citing them with the vague indefinite pronoun (see also 4:1; 5:15, 24; 6:10, 21; see table and discussion of *tines* ["some"] at 5:15). Paul used the same convention in his other writings.[37]

"Teach false doctrines" (see also 6:3) corresponds to one Greek word: *heterodidaskalein*. Evidently a word Paul coined (see BDAG 399),[38] it means teaching that deviates from a standard. For Paul to write this word implies that there were doctrinal norms in place already in the mid-first century; they did not first develop over the course of generations and reflect mainly a Hellenistic degeneration or powerful Roman hegemony as Adolf von Harnack, Walter Bauer, and others have argued.[39]

Here Paul's quarrel seems to be the substance of what is taught rather than the activity—it was not that "some" were teaching but that what they were teaching was aberrant. Marshall notes that it may seem "surprising that the first and principal task of Timothy is to deal with false teaching," but that is what the situation called for. As Marshall points out, it is "analogous to what happens in Galatians."[40] This corrective and any necessary polemical function may be latent in Jesus's commission to make disciples by teaching them to keep (not merely learn or nod agreement with) "all things whatsoever [*panta hosa*]" he commanded (Matt 28:20 KJV). No setting inhabited by humans is going to be readily amenable to, let alone compliant with, the full range of Jesus's challenging and comprehensive expectations. Ephesus as Paul and Timothy knew it certainly was not.

4 Paul continues his programmatic summary of why it is important that Timothy remain at Ephesus. Verse 3 spoke of false teaching; v. 4 gives examples of aspects of that teaching.

There is the danger that either the false teachers, their followers, or both will promote interest in "myths."[41] This word appears five times in the NT, four

36. Note the command in Titus 3:2. Cf. Eph 5:3; some things (including, presumably, people) "must not even be named among you, as is proper among saints."

37. Rom 3:3, 8; 1 Cor 4:18; Gal 1:7; 2:12.

38. See also Quinn and Wacker, 62.

39. See A. Köstenberger and M. Kruger, *The Heresy of Orthodoxy* (Wheaton, IL: Crossway, 2010). For background, see, for example, Christoph Markschies, *Hellenisierung des Christentums: Sinn und Unsinn einer historischen Deutungskategorie*, Forum Theologische Literaturzeitung 25 (Leipzig: Evangelische Verlagsanstalt, 2012).

40. Marshall, with Towner, 365.

41. For background and history of the word's usage, see *NIDNTTE* 3:343–47.

of them in the PE (see also 1 Tim 4:7 ["godless myths"]; 2 Tim 4:4; Titus 1:14 ["Jewish myths"]). Peter contrasts the narrative of Jesus's life, including such astonishing events as the transfiguration, with "cleverly devised myths" (2 Pet 1:16 ESV) that might either discredit or displace the saving truth of Christ's coming and accomplishment. All cultures have underlying or overarching narratives by which they interpret their existence. When this sense is valid, we might call it history. The more it is a purely imaginative construal, the more we may think of it as a story, with more or less verisimilitude. In the Hellenistic world of Paul's time, so-called myths were understood as fables or far-fetched tales, often involving the gods.[42] The NT uses of the word (all in the pl.) cast them as falsehoods, not only because they are untrue (in contrast to biblical narrative as NT writers understood it) but because of their pernicious effects, promoting immoral behavior in some cases and extreme asceticism in others. Focus on such myths would hardly have promoted respect for biblical claims regarding God and the redemptive good news surrounding Christ. It is understandable that Paul would advise Timothy to make sure that the oil of such exotic tales was not being mixed with the water of historically grounded gospel teaching and practice in the church.

Alongside the distraction of myths were "endless genealogies." (See discussion at Titus 3:9 of this commentary.) Keener thinks that reference might be to "expansions of biblical genealogies, as in some Jewish works from this period, or perhaps false postbiblical attributions of ancestry."[43] Berger speaks of the convictions of Pharisaic and early rabbinic opponents.[44] Paul's frequent mention of the law in coming verses may reflect the false teachers' preoccupation with the books of Moses,[45] but by "law" Paul could have been speaking about the OT corpus in general. What is clear is that Paul, like Jesus, rooted the good news of redemption in a creation-fall-redemption narrative that resulted in all followers of Jesus, Jew and Gentile, becoming children of Abraham.[46] It would be necessary for the rival construals of religious truth that Timothy faced at Ephesus to assert alternate salvation histories. This aim is likely what Paul refers to, with "endless" signaling either the voluminousness of their speculation, the futility of their efforts, the worthlessness of their conclusions compared to the eyewitness reportage undergirding gospel claims, or some combination of all three. Marshall is helpful in showing the dubiousness of scholars' continuing fascination with Gnosticism as an explanatory factor lying behind Paul's reference,[47] unless

42. See Towner, *Letters*, 109–10.

43. Keener, *Biblical Background Commentary*, 603.

44. Berger, 795.

45. So Marshall, with Towner, 366.

46. Acts 13:26; Rom 9:8; Gal 3:7.

47. Marshall, with Towner, 366. See, for example, Hanson, 57. Opposing the Gnostic connection from the side of German scholarship is Neudorfer, *Erster Brief an Timotheus*, 59. He

one locates the date of 1 Timothy well into the second century. Nor is Paul likely to have in mind Marcionites or Proto-Montanists.[48]

Paul wants Timothy to discourage attention to myths and genealogies because they "promote controversial speculations." "Speculations" is a rare word appearing nowhere else in the NT. BDAG (303) affirms it is found only in Christian writings of the era; it is absent, for example, from Philo, Josephus, and the AF. But Paul's meaning is clear, as he uses it to describe what "myths and endless genealogies" encourage and lead to: baseless inferences and convictions. In modern-day terms, it would be like imagining what aliens from other galaxies or zombies might mean for everyday life and redemption. The concern of the gospel and its servants like Paul and Timothy is not fantasy but rather "God's work" (*oikonomia*). This term probably refers to God's work of redemption in the world, particularly in the church itself (called God's *oikos* [household] in 1 Tim 3:15).[49] God has given ample knowledge of this redemption in Scripture and in history; it does not require intuitive divination or mystical imagination to discern.

Moreover, this "work" is said to be "of faith." This expression is probably shorthand for how integral "faith" is to reception of and participation in the divine "work." The gospel reveals a "righteousness of God" (the centerpiece of God's saving work, as Paul explains it) "that is by faith from first to last" (Rom 1:17). This phrase refers to personal trust in what God has made known, not construction by human speculation or proposals of what might conceivably be true. The down-to-earth focus of the religion the gospel promotes, as opposed to the fantasies Paul's seeks to discourage, becomes apparent in the next verse.

5 "The goal of this command" may seem to come out of the blue. What command? And who is talking about a goal? These questions are answered by a glance back at v. 3, where Timothy is urged to "*command* certain people not to teach false doctrines any longer." Verse 4 expands on variations of the false doctrine and their effect, and v. 5 turns to the desired effect ("the goal") of the true doctrine Paul *commands* Timothy to uphold. In a sense this is also the goal, or one could also say purpose, of this entire epistle.

In other words, Timothy is being tasked not just with opposing error but with creating space for the flourishing of "love" (*agapē*).[50] Here is a major

---

points to recent German scholarship trending away from the Gnostic hypothesis in connection with the Ephesian letter. See also Köstenberger, 58n12.

48. See Lloyd Pieterson, "Epistles, Pastoral," *EBR* 7:1095.

49. BDAG 697 suggests the meaning "program of instruction, *training* (in the way of salvation)." But the first attestation of this meaning among Christian writers is Clement of Alexandria. More likely is the sense of the divine design or plan, or administration of that plan, found in other passages where Paul uses this word (1 Cor 9:17; Eph 1:10; 3:2, 9; Col 1:25).

50. For the role this verse and teaching played for important commentators like Augustine, Aquinas, Calvin, and Kierkegaard, see Twomey, 22–23. Neudorfer, *Erster Brief an*

point of contact between Paul and Jesus, as Jesus said of the commands to love God and neighbor, "All the Law and the Prophets hang on these two commandments" (Matt 22:40). Paul ("apostle of Christ Jesus," v. 1) wrote similarly, "Love is the fulfillment of the law" (Rom 13:10). A difference between Paul and Jesus at this point is that the four Gospels represent Jesus speaking of "love" (*agapē*) primarily as a verb (sixty-three occurrences); the noun *agapē* appears in the Gospels only eight times. With Paul the stress is reversed: his thirteen canonical writings all contain the noun *agapē*, which he uses seventy-one times. He uses the verb (*agapaō*) only thirty-four times (and it is absent from Philippians, 1 Timothy, Titus, and Philemon). What Jesus speaks of primarily as an activity (drawing especially on the verbal formulations in Deut 6:5 and Lev 19:18?), Paul echoes (when he uses the verb) but also (with the noun) reifies—it is a reality rooted in God and Christ that transforms believers' lives when they receive the gospel, and that progressively marks their lives as they live that gospel out.

For Paul this is love distinguished by a threefold origin. First, it is "from a pure [*katharos*][51] heart." Paul affirms that Christ died "to redeem us from all wickedness and to purify [*katharizō*] for himself a people" (Titus 2:14; see also Eph 5:26). Believers are accordingly called to "purify [themselves] from everything that contaminates body and spirit, perfecting holiness out of reverence for God" (2 Cor 7:1). Because of the inner change that Christ effects, Paul knows that believers have an inner sanctum into and through which the divine presence exudes the central divine characteristic of love (see Rom 5:5; 1 Cor 13) through believers' dispositions and resulting actions.

Second, it is from "a good conscience."[52] Luther calls this "a beautiful text. 'The aim' is not to increase questions and to leave consciences unsure

---

Timotheus, 61, notes that mention of love, in conjunction with mention of "hope" and "faith" in previous verses, completes the triad of 1 Cor 13:13. For human flourishing as central to Jesus's mission and teaching, see J. Pennington, *The Sermon on the Mount and Human Flourishing* (Grand Rapids: Baker Academic, 2017).

51. On *katharos* (pure), see commentary on Titus 1:15.

52. On "conscience" (*syneidēsis*), see commentary on 2 Tim 1:3; Titus 1:15. The contention of Dibelius and Conzelmann (18–20) that a pseudo-Pauline reference here to conscience reveals a degradation from an "eschatological understanding of the world into a view that . . . the world is going to remain as it is" (20) has two problems: (1) it erects a false dichotomy, and (2) it requires a de-eschatologizing of all that Paul writes elsewhere in this epistle, whose Christology and soteriology both presuppose the eschatology-enriched outlook that is found in Paul's other letters as well. To "believe in [Christ Jesus] and receive eternal life" (1:16) and to understand the present as "later times" (4:1) are but two examples of the keen eschatological consciousness informing Paul's discourse. Or consider 5:21: "I charge you, in the sight of God and Christ Jesus and the elect angels. . . ." The world is not going to continue "as it is" but faces certain final judgment. On the "eschatological aspect" in the PE, see also Quinn and Wacker, 13; Köstenberger, 512–27.

after all their difficulties but to bring consciences to the point that they know this for sure."[53]

As Paul writes elsewhere, the love believers express should be "sincere" (Rom 12:9) and not feigned or phony. But such love requires a sense of forgiveness of one's own sins (and hence liberation from a bad conscience, a sense of condemnation: see Rom 8:1) and the resources of divine grace to enable the exercise of a love of divine origins (see, e.g., 2 Cor 5:14). Integral to believers' expression of love, then, is the "good conscience" that faith in Christ's finished work establishes and promotes. Attention to myths and genealogies, in contrast, is not apt to minister redemptively to the conscience, however much mastery of esoteric knowledge may satisfy the intellect or fortify one's sense of religious readiness. Optimal exercise of love would therefore be hampered.

Third, it is from "a sincere[54] faith." This is already the third time "faith" (*pistis*) has appeared in 1 Timothy, where it is found a total of 19 times (33 times in the PE total; 142 times in all Paul's writings). Here Paul uses "faith" to denote the believer's personal trust in Christ through the gospel message. The goal of the Pauline and apostolic instruction is not merely "love," however understood, but specifically the love engendered by personal trust in the God who came so that believers might receive and express his love. Such trust is what Paul means by "a sincere faith." It is rooted in gospel truth and so is not a self-deluding sham or arbitrary, perhaps benighted religious commitment. It connects the believer with God and so is not contrived but sincere, authentic by virtue of the reality of the God in whom faith is placed.

6 While v. 5 lays down the positive plank on which Paul will build throughout the letter, v. 6 joins vv. 3–4 and v. 7 in detailing the wrongheadedness of people whose presence at Ephesus constitutes a challenge to the ministry Timothy is charged to uphold and extend. Their error is twofold.

First, "some have departed from these." This "some" (*tines*, certain people) corresponds to the same term in v. 3 (see table and discussion at 5:15). "From these" means from the pure heart, good conscience, and sincere faith mentioned in the previous verse. "Departed" translates a form of *astocheō*, a word that occurs elsewhere in the NT only at 1 Tim 6:21 and 2 Tim 2:18 (see discussion of this word there). In the LXX it is used twice to mean "miss out" on something.[55] In the AF there is talk of "those who have gone astray [*tous astochēsantas*] and denied Jesus by their words or by their actions" (2 Clem. 17:7). The Didache (15:3) admonishes, "If anyone wrongs [*astochounti*] his or her neighbor, let no one speak to that person, nor let that one hear a word from you, until he or she repents." The concept and the word itself are not

53. Luther, 224. With "the aim," Luther refers to "the goal" mentioned in 1 Tim 1:5.

54. On "sincere" (from *anhypokritos*), see commentary on 2 Tim 1:5.

55. Sir 7:19 (a good wife); 8:9 (the wise things that the aged say).

uncommon in moral and religious discourse of the period.[56] As every pastor knows, people's religious paths can meander. Paul calls attention to instances of this problem at Ephesus.

At issue is not only what people "have departed from" but what their new preoccupation is: they "have turned to meaningless talk." "Turned to" translates a form of a word found in four other NT passages.[57] "Meaningless talk" (*mataiologia*) is a NT hapax, though the noun form (*mataiologos*) occurs in Titus 1:10. The family of words in the NT containing the *matai-* prefix (denoting something futile or vain; BDAG lists eight such words) is found frequently in the LXX and elsewhere in the NT and "is used mostly to condemn what is opposed to God and his commandments."[58] The gospel offers a transformed heart and life (v. 5), but the "some" of v. 6 find more appeal in vacuous alternatives. Keener comments that Judaism of that era and "most philosophers condemned empty, worthless talk, including arguments about words and the verbal skills of wordy rhetoricians unconcerned with truth."[59] Paul follows suit, with the important difference that he points instead not to his own religion or rhetoric but to Christ.

7 Later in the epistle Paul will commend those who aspire to be congregational leaders (3:1). Here, however, he is not thrilled about the "some" (v. 6) who now "want to be teachers of the law." It is unfortunate to speak here of "castigating opponents" with "stock forms of slander," a charge that implies that the modern commentator knows Paul's charges are false, overwrought, or both.[60] The only other two NT uses of this word (*nomodidaskalos*, teachers of the law) refer to (1) men who taught the Mosaic law in Jesus's setting alongside the Pharisees (Luke 5:17) and (2) Gamaliel, who instructed Saul prior to his conversion (Acts 5:34; 22:3). Such teachers were men of great learning who were held in high esteem by their communities, and with good reason: they were reigning experts in God's written self-revelation, which Paul extolled as

56. It is absent from Philo but occurs three times in Josephus (*Jewish War* 2.159; 4.116; 5.61).

57. That is, *ektrepō*, used to describe turning to follow after Satan (1 Tim 5:15), turning away from "godless chatter" (6:20), and turning "aside to myths" (2 Tim 4:4). The use of this word in Heb 12:13 is more anatomical or medical in nature.

58. *NIDNTTE* 3:247.

59. Keener, *Bible Background Commentary*, 603. For Cicero's critical comments on philosophers' verbal wheel-spinning with respect to the gods, see *Nature of the Gods*, 1.1–5.

60. Twomey, 23. In fact, Paul's charges are both vague and understated. He does not revel in detail or vent spleen in ways that would qualify as either castigation or slander (unless one has very thin skin). In Twomey's defense, he doesn't think Paul wrote the PE and that the discourse is, accordingly, fictitious. But that makes the charge of slander even more dubious: why charge a fictional writer with slandering others who are presumably also fictional constructs? Cf. 29, where Twomey speaks of those who "slander" the "imagined characters" of Alexander and Hymenaeus (1 Tim 1:20).

the Jews' greatest gift: "the very words of God" (see Rom 3:1–2). Paul, like Jesus, was in his way a "teacher of the law" by virtue of how often he referenced it (see, e.g., *DPL* 630–42). Paul's warning here to Timothy is not an expression of alarm that some would value and spread the truth of Moses's or other OT writings, for he upheld those writings himself, seen in the light of Christ.

Paul's apprehension is that these law-teacher wannabes are deficient in understanding ("they do not know [*noeō*]").[61] Their ignorance regarding revelatory matters is twofold, as denoted by a neither-nor construction (*mēte . . . mēte*) in which "a preceding negatived item [i.e., not knowing the law] is divided into its components" (BDAG 649). First, "They do not know what they are talking about." The image is almost amusing: here are people presenting themselves as learned expositors of holy writ who, however, are actually clueless. "They do not know" the law but apparently do not know that they do not know. Second, neither do they understand the inferences they draw from the law—"what they so confidently affirm." This charge is understandable and in fact inevitable, given that their grasp of the law itself is faulty. It is hard not to be reminded here of the contrasting representations of Torah reflected in the standoff between Jesus and purported Moses-experts in John 5:39–47.

8 Paul hastens to clarify that the abuse or twisting of the law mentioned in v. 7 is not the fault of the law. The explanatory function of v. 8 is seen in two ways. First, the second word of v. 8 (*de*), although not translated in NIV, is a conjunction[62] or a particle[63] (depending on the grammarian), which indicates that v. 8 will shed light on v. 7. Second, Paul's opening "we know" (*oidamen*) appears frequently in Paul's writings to introduce an assertion of agreed-on theological truth.[64] If Paul's language in v. 8 reflects usage like that in table 7, below, he is not presenting new information to Timothy but drawing on the same kind of assumed or established understanding of which he reminded his Roman and Corinthian readers in other epistles. Timothy does not require fresh education but merely review. One reason Paul could write "we know" to Timothy is because he was in Paul's proximity when he used this idiom in the Roman and Corinthian settings.[65]

61. Paul uses *noeō* (I grasp, perceive, understand) five times in all (see also Rom 1:20; Eph 3:4, 20; 2 Tim 2:7), always referring to insight into divine matters. Dibelius and Conzelmann, 21, detect here "the typical interweaving of speculation and ascetic observance which is related to an appeal to the OT."

62. See D. Wallace, *Greek Grammar beyond the Basics* (Grand Rapids: Zondervan 1996), 669.

63. BDAG 213.

64. Not included in table 7 are Paul's two other uses of *oidamen* (Rom 8:26; 2 Cor 5:16), which have a different rhetorical force.

65. Timothy and Romans: Rom 16:21; Timothy and the Corinthians: 1 Cor 4:17; 16:10; 2 Cor 1:1, 19.

Table 7. Paul's assertions and agreed-on theological truths

Paul's assertion	Agreed-on truth
Rom 2:2 Now we know that	God's judgment against those who do such things is based on truth.
Rom 3:19 Now we know that	whatever the law says, it says to those who are under the law.
Rom 7:14 We know that	the law is spiritual; but I am unspiritual, sold as a slave to sin.
Rom 8:22 We know that	the whole creation has been groaning as in the pains of childbirth right up to the present time.
Rom 8:28 And we know that	in all things God works for the good of those who love him.
1 Cor 8:1 We know that	"We all possess knowledge."
1 Cor 8:4 We know that	"An idol is nothing at all in the world" and that "There is no God but one."
2 Cor 5:1 For we know that	if the earthly tent we live in is destroyed, we have a building from God.

"The law is good [*kalos*]" in v. 8 echoes Paul's statement in Rom 7:16. He is probably speaking of the OT in its entirety and not simply Torah or the legal portions within it. Paul's view of the OT has been intensely discussed and disputed over the past century.[66] Even if he is speaking of the Torah in particular, "at no point does Paul deny, even by insinuation, the divine origin of the Torah or its authority when properly understood."[67] Paul confirms to Timothy the same high view of the old covenant literary corpus that Jesus modeled in his wide-ranging and reverent dependence on "Moses and all the Prophets" (Luke 24:27), restated a few verses later as "the Law of Moses, the Prophets and the Psalms" (Luke 24:45)—in other words, the whole OT. This sweeping view of the revered truth and status of the entire OT would have been instilled in Paul and Timothy alike by their synagogue upbringing.

The problem with the "some" of vv. 6–7 who "have departed" from valid gospel understanding (note again "certain people" teaching "false doctrines" in v. 3) is not their appeal to the OT. It is rather how they are interpreting and

66. For bibliography, see *NIDNTTE* 3:419–20.
67. *NIDNTTE* 3:412.

applying it. "What is at issue . . . is not the intrinsic value of the law itself but its results in the lives of those to whom it is addressed (or not addressed)."[68] For as v. 8 asserts, "the law is good if one uses it [*autō*, dative] properly."[69] "Properly" (*nomimōs*) is wordplay involving "law" (*nomos*). Many English translations reflect this etymology by translating "law" and "lawfully."[70] Epictetus illustrates the use of "properly" with his statement, "God says to you, 'Give me a proof that you have exercised according to the rules [*nomimōs*].'"[71] Paul's concern is that the OT "be used in ways that conform to its nature and purpose. It is not the basis for speculation (1:4) or for salvation (Rom 3:20)."[72] "The Law is abused when I assign to the Law more than it can accomplish. Good works are necessary and the Law must be kept, but the Law does not justify."[73]

Paul clearly rules out what the false teachers Timothy is facing are claiming. But what is "lawful" use of God's law? Paul explores this question in the next three verses.

9 Paul asserts two things: (1) there is a class of individuals, "the righteous," to whom the law does not apply, or does not apply in the same way it applies to others; and (2) the law does apply in a direct and authoritative way to others. Both of these claims call for analysis.

"We also know" (v. 9) continues in the vein of the "we know" of v. 8.[74] Paul is not revealing new information to Timothy but bringing knowledge they both share to bear on the situation at hand. With "the law is not made," Paul uses a verb (*keimai*) found four times elsewhere in his writings. The word does not mean "made" in the sense of created or produced but rather in the sense of being placed, designated, established, or even destined, as other examples show. Paul's other uses of *keimai*:

> For no one can lay any foundation other than the one already *laid*, which is Jesus Christ. (1 Cor 3:11)
> Even to this day when Moses is read, a veil *covers* their hearts. (2 Cor 3:15)
> The latter do so out of love, knowing that I am *put here* for the defense of the gospel. (Phil 1:16)
> . . . so that no one would be unsettled by these trials. For you know quite well that we *are destined* for them. (1 Thess 3:3)

68. Köstenberger, 74.

69. The verb translated "uses" (from *chraomai*) takes its object in the dative. *Chraomai* is used eleven times in the NT, nine of those in Paul; see also 1 Cor 7:21, 31; 9:12, 15; 2 Cor 1:7; 3:12; 13:10; 1 Tim 5:23.

70. For example, KJV, ESV, GNV, WEB.

71. Epictetus, *Discourses* 3.10.8 (my translation). See also MM 429.

72. Ngewa, 20.

73. Luther, 232.

74. *Oida* is the lexical form for both expressions.

In every case, an outworking of divine purpose is implied, not independent of human agency but sovereign within and over that agency. It is accordingly reasonable to surmise that in 1 Tim 1:9 Paul refers to the deployment or effect of the law (or OT) in the light of God's purpose for that body of writings.

"For the righteous" is in emphatic position. In Pauline terms, a "righteous" (*dikaios*) person is one who has been declared righteous through faith in Jesus Christ (Rom 3:24, 26). Even more explicitly, "No one will be declared righteous in God's sight by the works of the law; rather, through the law we become conscious of our sin" (Rom 3:20). The law evokes awareness of guilt, but human adherence to it cannot produce the righteousness that God demands. This understanding contrasts, for example, with Paul's near contemporary Philo, who wrote, "The law has been delivered [*keitai*] to us 'to pursue righteously what is righteous,' that we may attain . . . righteousness."[75] Paul's writings reveal contrasting convictions. Wright's translation "people who are in the right" is Philonic rather than Pauline.[76]

Paul is therefore reminding Timothy that God did not give the law as the means for guilty people to establish their righteousness by obeying God's commands.[77] Rather, the OT in its richness and fullness relates the history of creation, fall, and redemption in a way that centers on God and his saving promises, culminating in Christ's coming, person, and work. In this account humans are transgressors in need of divinely bestowed forgiveness and new life through trust in their Redeemer, not moral agents with the potential to redeem themselves by their dogged faithfulness to what God requires of them in his law.

Paul's frequent appeal to the OT in his writings demonstrates their continuing importance for the believer. At the same time, statements like "a person is justified [i.e., declared righteous] by faith apart from the works of the law" (Rom 3:28) confirm what 1 Tim 1:9 asserts: the law was not given, and does not exist today, "for the righteous," that is, in order for people to attain or even maintain a righteous standing solely by means of living up to God's written commands. Torah rightly received has always administered God's promise and through it his grace.[78]

75. Philo, *The Worse Attacks the Better,* 18 (my translation).

76. Wright, 7.

77. Cf. Luther, 234–35: "It is the good use of the Law to restrain and reveal sin; but it is misuse thereof to say that it takes away sin. . . . It is Christ who removes sin and justifies."

78. Of course Paul's understanding had formerly been that of his Jewish contemporaries and their understanding of Torah, of whom Paul writes: "The people of Israel, who pursued the law as the way of righteousness, have not attained their goal. Why not? Because they pursued it not by faith but as if it were by works" (Rom 9:31–32). In other words, Paul argues, they thought obedience to Torah would earn the blessing promised by God's covenant rather than the covenant promise, received by faith, giving rise to obedience in the hearer.

Such a misunderstanding or misuse of the law may well lie behind Paul's terse "we also know that the law is made not for the righteous." He and Timothy agree on a fundamental point at which the false teachers (vv. 3, 6) are going astray. What, then, is the law's purpose? We should not expect here, and do not find, a comprehensive account of all the implications of the OT or the Torah for those under its verdict (i.e., the whole world; see Rom 3:19). Rather, Paul gives a composite sketch of lawbreakers who need the good news that transcends what the law requires (full compliance with God's commands) but cannot by itself establish (because of human nature and behavior in the wake of the fall).

Paul starts with four pairs of transgressors to whom the law *does* apply,[79] in contrast, quite possibly, to the ideas the false teachers are circulating. Perhaps they were not calling out such transgressors as they should have been. In Hellenistic thought there was the view that "the one who does no wrong is in no need of law."[80] More broadly, Philo wrote, "There is no need of addressing either command, or prohibition, or recommendation to the man who is perfect, and made according to the image of God; for the perfect man requires none of these things; but there is a necessity of addressing both command and prohibition to the wicked man."[81] Scripture however sees all humans as subject to the law's standards and (because of sin) condemnation. Whatever the particular views of the false teachers, they err if they downplay what Paul is about to highlight.

There is probably not a lot to be gained in lingering long over possible fine shades of meaning in the descriptors found in 1 Tim 1:9–10. Yet, each deserves more than a mere passing glance. "Lawbreakers" (from *anomos*) appears in Paul elsewhere (1 Cor 9:21; 2 Thess 2:8) to describe people bereft of God's revealed written guidance or in willful rebellion against it. The same word is used in Isaiah's prophecy that the Suffering Servant would be numbered "with the transgressors [*meta anomōn*])" (Isa 53:12, quoted in Luke 22:37). "Rebels" is found also in Titus 1:6 ("disobedient") and 1:10 ("rebellious people"). Its only other NT occurrence is Heb 2:8 (referring to things "not subject to" God's creation order). Paul's point is that the law has something vital to say to those who break it and flaunt its strictures with impunity.

In Pauline parlance elsewhere, the "ungodly" are those whom God justifies (Rom 4:5) and for whom Christ died (Rom 5:6), assuming they will receive

79. Rhetorical boost is achieved with the first five words in the list beginning with the Greek letter alpha.

80. Sentence of Antiphanes (408/405–334/331 BC); see M. Eugene Boring, Klaus Berger, and Carsten Colpe, eds., *Hellenistic Commentary to the New Testament* (Nashville: Abingdon, 1995), 499.

81. Philo, *Allegorical Interpretation* 1.94.

the gospel message. Of course they will not if false teaching hides from such persons their benighted state, Christ's solution to their plight, or both. The "ungodly" are paired with the "sinful" (from *hamartōlos*), a word frequent (forty-five times) in the NT overall but found sparingly (eight times) in Paul.[82] A few verses later Paul will underscore that it is those who are "sinners" whom Christ came to save (1 Tim 1:15)—making it all the more important that the law's identification of such persons be presented and understood. Those not brought face to face with their sinful state are unlikely to seek, much less find, the only remedy for it.

A third pair of typical evildoers identified by the law is "the unholy and irreligious." The former (from *anosios*) is found elsewhere in the NT only in 2 Tim 3:2. In the LXX, the positive form *hosioi* ("holy ones") appears frequently to denote those who are upright before God; its Hebrew equivalent is *ḥăsîdîm.*[83] Paul uses a word that describes persons bereft of this status or drive. He correlates these "unholy" persons with others he terms "irreligious." The latter term (from *bebēlos*)[84] describes Esau (see Heb 12:16) in his dedication to this-worldly matters and disregard for matters pertaining to God and his promises.[85]

Paul's description of a final pair of transgressors moves from the awful to the heinous: "those who kill their fathers or mothers," whom Paul additionally terms "murderers." At this point one observes that Paul's list begins to track with the order of the Ten Commandments.

The Decalogue calls for:	Paul says the law condemns:
Fifth commandment: honor parents	those who kill their fathers or mothers
Sixth commandment: do not murder	murderers
Seventh commandment: do not commit adultery	the sexually immoral, those practicing homosexuality
Eighth commandment: do not steal	slave traders
Ninth commandment: do not bear false witness	liars and perjurers

82. Rom 3:7; 5:8, 19; 7:13; Gal 2:15, 17; 1 Tim 1:15. In Rom 7:13 it does not denote a sinner but is used as an adjective to refer to sin.

83. See *NIDNTTE* 3:557–58.

84. Used elsewhere in the NT only in the PE (1 Tim 4:7; 6:20; 2 Tim 2:16) and in Heb 12:16.

85. For the same word and theme in Philo with regard to Esau, see *NIDNTTE* 1:502–3.

"A high estimation of motherhood and parenthood can be traced everywhere in antiquity,"[86] so murder of either parent is a crime of unspeakable evil. The law commands honor of parents (Exod 20:12; Deut 5:16), moral teaching seconded by Jesus (Matt 15:4; 19:19; also Eph 6:2), which obviously forbids their killing. "Murderers" is a NT hapax and refers to manslayers of any kind, including but not limited to those who take a parent's life. Scripture condemns murder in the Decalogue (Exod 20:13; Deut 5:17) and elsewhere in the OT (e.g., Ps 10:8; Prov 28:17; Jer 7:9; Hos 4:2), as does the NT (e.g., Matt 15:19; 19:18; Rom 13:9; Jas 2:11; 1 John 3:12).

10 Paul continues the litany with five more unsavory descriptors. It should be underscored that this is not Paul lashing out at behavior or individuals who do not meet his personal approval. It is not what certain Western discussions have tagged as hate speech. Paul believes that all (including himself, "the worst of sinners" [1 Tim 1:16]) have violated God's law and stand in danger of his judgment. But the same law that condemns can also lead to something immeasurably better: forgiveness and new life in Christ. "So the law was our guardian until Christ came that we might be justified by faith" (Gal 3:24). In "God's household" the church, in which Timothy ministers (1 Tim 3:15), the stress needs to be on Christ and proper use of the law (1:8), not the twisted understanding that the false teachers are evidently pressing (1:7).

To underscore the difference between law in its primarily negative application and the gospel-centered reference to it that one observes in Paul's writings, he continues to list groups whom the law (without reference to Christ) condemns. First in v. 10 are "the sexually immoral" (from *pornos*). The word is used mainly by Paul among NT writers, though not only by him.[87] It refers to anyone who engages in sex acts prohibited by Scripture. Obvious examples would be sex for hire (prostitution); sex outside of marriage (fornication), whether casual ("hook-up") or habitual (noncommittal cohabitation); sex by married persons with someone not their spouse (adultery); as well as same-sex relations, incest, and bestiality.

God's law calls persons created in his image to the highest good of lifelong fidelity to an opposite-sex companion. It prohibits what is unholy in God's sight and ultimately degrading of the body and destructive of society. This prohibition is for the sake of hallowing the opposite-sex covenantal union established before sin entered the world (Gen 1–2). Hebrews 13:4 captures God's revealed intent and warning: "Marriage should be honored by all, and the marriage bed kept pure, for God will judge the adulterer and all the sex-

86. *NIDNTTE* 3:297.

87. *Pornos* in Paul: 1 Cor 5:9, 10, 11; 6:9; Eph 5:5. Elsewhere in the NT: Heb 12:16; 13:4; Rev 21:8; 22:15. It occurs only once in the LXX (Sir 23:17) and the AF (Polycarp, *Phil.* 5:3), not at all in Josephus, and only once in Philo (*Allegorical Interpretation* 3.8).

ually immoral." Paul writes elsewhere regarding all (including believers) who engage in illicit sexual relations: "The Lord will punish all those who commit such sins, as we told you and warned you before. For God did not call us to be impure, but to live a holy life" (1 Thess 4:6–7). This outlook is reflected in Jesus's inclusion of sexual immorality alongside other grave sins: "For out of the heart come evil thoughts—murder, adultery, sexual immorality, theft, false testimony, slander" (Matt 15:19). The entire Bible presents a united front on the issue of sexual immorality.

A subgroup of the "sexually immoral" to which Paul has just referred is "those practicing homosexuality" (from *arsenokoitēs*, a male who has sex with another male).[88] The other NT use of the word *arsenokoitēs* is in 1 Cor 6:9. This is one behavior among many that marks those who are strangers to God's transforming grace: "Do not be deceived: Neither the sexually immoral nor idolaters nor adulterers nor men who have sex with men nor thieves nor the greedy nor drunkards nor slanderers nor swindlers will inherit the kingdom of God" (1 Cor 6:9–10). Paul describes this behavior among both women and men in Rom 1:24–27. "Jesus's and Paul's views on love and grace reinforce, rather than reject, the need for strong commandments against sexual immorality, including same-sex intercourse."[89] There can be forgiveness for homosexual actions, but this assumes that someone is "washed . . . sanctified . . . justified in the name of the Lord Jesus Christ and by the Spirit of our God" (1 Cor 6:11), with corresponding transformed desire and changed behavior. Paul's instruction regarding both same-sex and opposite-sex transgression, given "by the authority of the Lord Jesus," is worth recalling: "It is God's will that you should be sanctified: that you should avoid sexual immorality," adding a few verses later, "Anyone who rejects this instruction does not reject a human being [i.e., Paul] but God, the very God who gives you his Holy Spirit" (1 Thess 4:2–3, 8). As difficult as sensual restraint and redirection of desire (toward God rather than self-indulgence) may be, "God did not call" believers "to be impure, but to live a holy life" (1 Thess 4:7).

Paul next lists "slave traders." Another translation could be "kidnapper" (BDAG 76). As the table above indicates, this crime would violate the commandment not to steal. The tie between stealing and kidnapping was acknowledged in rabbinic teaching.[90] It was a capital offense in the Torah (Exod 21:16; Deut 24:7). It exists today in seamy trafficking of the young for sexual

88. For an extended explication of the homosexuality issue in biblical and Pauline perspective, see Neudorfer, *Erster Brief an Timotheus*, 74–80. For the English-language debates and major contributions, see Köstenberger, 76–78.

89. Robert Gagnon in D. O. Via and R. Gagnon, *Homosexuality and the Bible: Two Views* (Minneapolis: Fortress, 2003), 88.

90. Gloer, 117, referring to Mekilta of Rabbi Ishmael (*Ba-Hodesh* 8:5).

purposes.[91] The next words "liars and perjurers" are violations of the ninth commandment, which bars bearing false witness.

Paul could no doubt have continued at length by naming transgressions Timothy might encounter at Ephesus, and regarding which the false teachers would be spreading misunderstanding. But he has waxed specific enough to make his point. These behaviors, and "whatever else is contrary to[92] the sound doctrine,"[93] are beneath the intent and transformational capacity of the gospel message he and Timothy have been spreading together for over a decade (see next verse).

11 This verse gives added definition to "sound doctrine" in v. 10. NIV places no comma at the end of v. 10, which encourages a reading that restricts Paul's reference to doctrine "that conforms to the gospel." Most translations place a comma, semicolon, or period at the end of v. 10, which has the effect of making v. 11 applicable to all that Paul has just said: the law is good if used as God intends (v. 8), but its role for those declared righteous through faith is quite different than for those whom it is primarily designed to address and confront (vv. 9–10), all "according to" or "in line with the gospel" (*kata to euangelion*, v. 11).

Verse 11 can, then, be understood as summing up the basis for all that Paul has said in vv. 8–10. He has reasoned based on what "conforms to the gospel concerning the glory of the blessed God." There is a parallel here with 1 Cor 15:1, where Paul sums up all he has been saying to the Corinthians by referring back to the gospel he first preached to them. This good news relates to Christ's death in fulfillment of the Scriptures and his bodily resurrection to lordship at the Father's right hand. Whatever issues arise in the household of faith, there are resources for addressing them in the gospel good tidings and its inexhaustible applications.

Few words are more central to Paul's writing than "gospel" (*euangelion*).[94] The word occurs in Paul some sixty times and in every Pauline writing except Titus. It appears on Paul's lips in Acts 20:24 as a summary of his life's very purpose: "However, I consider my life worth nothing to me; my only aim is to

91. For a moving depiction, see Allyn D. Pryse, *Hidden Truth* (Morrisville, NC: Lulu Publishing Services, 2016).

92. "Contrary to" translates *antikeimai* (to oppose), a word found elsewhere in the NT only in Luke (13:17; 21:15) and Paul (1 Cor 16:9; Gal 5:17; Phil 1:28; 2 Thess 2:4; 1 Tim 5:14).

93. On "sound doctrine," see commentary Introduction, IX.D. Contrary to Dibelius and Conzelmann, 25, this emphasis should not be pitted against the "pneumatic" thinking that they think marks "the true Paul." This is not a "shift toward rationalism" betraying a non-Pauline mind but a characterization of apostolic teaching quite in line with the *didaskalia* (teaching) explicitly mentioned in other Pauline passages (Rom 12:7; 15:4; Eph 4:14; Col 2:22) and set forth tacitly across the whole span of his epistles.

94. For details, see, for example, *NIDNTTE* 2:309–10.

finish the race and complete the task the Lord Jesus has given me—the task of testifying to the good news [*euangelion*] of God's grace." It is therefore entirely consistent that he would appeal to it here.

This is a gospel "concerning the glory of the blessed God." God's glorious good news is not exhausted in the law's prohibitions of unholy behaviors. It points rather to God in his ineffable splendor, which Paul will praise in doxological form shortly (v. 17). Like "gospel," "glory" (*doxa*) is a signature Pauline expression, occurring in every Pauline writing except for Philemon.[95]

His heavenly grandeur is incomparable; "blessed God" surely relates to his unique and "privileged" status (BDAG 610). "Blessed" (*makarios*) occurs nearly seventy times in the LXX but nearly always with reference to people, who are blessed if they know God's salvation (Deut 33:29), trust in God (Ps 84:12), walk in his light (Ps 89:15), or otherwise benefit from personal relationship with him. "Blessed" likewise always refers to people in the AF (forty-three occurrences). Paul's description of God as "blessed" has more ties with Hellenistic sources such as Philo than with the Greek OT.[96] In contrast, given the wide-ranging and profound ways that those who know the OT God are *makarios*, it is no great stretch to praise as "blessed" the source of all such benefit.

Calling God "blessed" is plausible especially in light of Paul's personal tie with this God, who "entrusted" the gospel and its ministry to Paul.[97] The "which"[98] in NIV's "which he entrusted to me" refers back to the gospel, not to "God" or "glory." The use of the verb for "believe" (*pisteuō*) in the passive voice is limited to Paul in the NT, as table 8 indicates:

Table 8. Passive voice occurrences of *pisteuō* (be believed, entrusted)

Passage	*Pisteuō* (be believed, entrusted)
Rom 3:2	The Jews *have been entrusted* with the very words of God.
Rom 10:10	For it is with your heart that you believe. (lit. For with the heart [the gospel message] *is believed.*)

95. Elsewhere in the PE: 1 Tim 1:17; 3:16; 2 Tim 2:10; 4:18; Titus 2:13. More broadly, see Donald L. Berry, *God's Glory in Romans and the Unified Purpose of God in Redemptive History* (Eugene, OR: Pickwick, 2016).

96. Noted in *NIDNTTE* 3:206–7.

97. Krause, 38, polemicizes against the text here, which she views as a fictional creation, and charges, "Remarkably Paul has been transformed in this construction from one who proclaims the gospel (as he states throughout his letters), to one who guards it." But "entrusted" is consistent with one who "guards," and as table 8 shows, there is nothing non-Pauline about God entrusting the gospel message to Paul.

98. On the construction, see M. Harris, *Prepositions and Theology in the Greek New Testament* (Grand Rapids: Zondervan, 2012), 233.

Passage	*Pisteuō* (be believed, entrusted)
1 Cor 9:17	If I preach . . . I am simply discharging the trust *committed* to me.
Gal 2:7	They recognized that I *had been entrusted* with the task of preaching the gospel.
1 Thess 2:4	We speak as those approved by God *to be entrusted* with the gospel.
2 Thess 1:10	Our testimony to you *was believed.* (ESV)
1 Tim 1:11	the gospel . . . with which I *have been entrusted* (ESV)
1 Tim 3:16	The mystery . . . *was believed on* in the world.
Titus 1:3	the preaching *entrusted* to me by the command of God our Savior

For Paul, God entrusts his people with his saving word (see Rom 3:2 in table 8; see also Rom 9:4–5). As a Hebrew himself (2 Cor 11:22; Phil 3:5), Paul continues in this line, but with the important qualification that, unlike many Jews of his generation (and since), he sees "the light of the knowledge of God's glory displayed in the face of Christ" (2 Cor 4:6). Christ has fulfilled the law and is the law's terminus (Rom 10:4). As Timothy wrestles with pseudoexperts in God's law at Ephesus, the gospel message entrusted to Paul and Timothy remains their plumb line, their lifeline in their respective personal relationships with God, their mutual commitment and central focus in life, and their confirmation that in the apparent church tensions and conflicts at Ephesus involving among other things the law, they (rather than the false teachers) are honoring Christ as Lord. "It's a great thing to know that one has the very sure and infallible Word of God" in the gospel.[99]

B. The Lord's Grace to Paul (1:12–17)

The next six verses are framed by Paul's expression of gratitude to start (v. 12) and a concise but majestic doxology (v. 17) to conclude. In between, Paul discusses the wonder of the mercy he received in view of the opposition to God he formerly mounted. He sets forth the first of five "trustworthy sayings," emphatic statements of the gospel's goodness and force (v. 15; see also 3:1, 4:9; 2 Tim 2:11; Titus 3:8 see Introduction, IX.C). Paul advances one major reason

99. Luther, 239.

why it pleased God to show mercy to him, despite the dark segment of his life that had been devoted to thwarting the gospel's advance in any way possible.

> [12] *I thank Christ Jesus our Lord, who has given me strength, that he considered me trustworthy, appointing me to his service.* [13] *Even though I was once a blasphemer and a persecutor and a violent man, I was shown mercy because I acted in ignorance and unbelief.* [14] *The grace of our Lord was poured out on me abundantly, along with the faith and love that are in Christ Jesus.* [15] *Here is a trustworthy saying that deserves full acceptance: Christ Jesus came into the world to save sinners—of whom I am the worst.*
>
> [16] *But for that very reason I was shown mercy so that in me, the worst of sinners, Christ Jesus might display his immense patience as an example for those who would believe in him and receive eternal life.* [17] *Now to the King eternal, immortal, invisible, the only God, be honor and glory for ever and ever. Amen.*

12 In the previous verse Paul commended the gospel and the God who had entrusted him with it. Now he commends the person to whom Paul and Timothy have dedicated themselves, "Christ Jesus [their] Lord."

Paul expresses thanks with a distinctive expression (*charin echō*, I have gratitude) that appears only one other time in the NT (2 Tim 1:3). He gives thanks for the "strength" extended to him, using a verb cognate of the Greek word *dynamis* (power). "The Stoics equated God with a self-originating cosmic δύναμις that moves all things, and the gnostics hoped for redemption through their incorporation into the heavenly powers. People tried, above all through magic, to obtain a share in the powers of the supranatural world."[100] Paul, in contrast, found strength in Christ, crucified but risen. NT use of the verb for "strengthen" (*endynamoō*) found here is limited elsewhere to statements about (Acts 9:22) or by Paul (see also Rom 4:20 [referring to Abraham]; Eph 6:10; Phil 4:13;[101] 2 Tim 2:1; 4:17). Most frequently, as here, Christ is the active agent in Paul's fortification. The result is impressive, as Luther comments: "Anyone can let the spit fly in public and be considered a learned teacher. But to teach with this confidence is indeed a rarity."[102] Paul received a rare confidence owed to Christ and not clever manipulation of the law.

Why does Paul mention his strength and its source? Perhaps it is to remind Timothy of resources for his flourishing, too. Ministry is enervating,

100. *NIDNTTE* 1:776.

101. In Phil 4:13 Paul uses the present form of the participle (*endynamounti*). A few ancient MSS use this form in 1 Tim 1:12. But the aorist form *endynamōsanti* has better external support and fits the context better.

102. Luther, 240.

particularly when opposition arises. There is temptation to fall back on natural means and draw on native capacities. Paul knows that there is no future in such a response; the self without divine enabling is no match for problems like false teachers, their often seductive doctrines, and the confusion they create in lives, households, and eventually congregations. There is hope only in the one who can transform and uphold the self, flawed as it is because of its rootage in error and unbelief, and transform congregations or at least critical minorities within them. Paul is a prime example of such transformation. What God did for Paul, he can certainly do for Timothy.

What God did was to regard Paul as "trustworthy" (*pistos*), an assertion with a direct parallel in 1 Cor 7:25:[103] Paul is "one who by the Lord's mercy is trustworthy [*pistos*]." God knew his intentions for Paul from his mother's womb (Gal 1:15). He was eventually appointed[104] to God's service (*diakonia*) or ministry. God got him into his apostolic labor, just as God had worked in Timothy's life and brought him to the juncture at which he finds himself as he reads Paul's letter. As undeserving as Paul was (see next verse), God upheld him. Timothy should be no less confident of God's support.

13 Paul of all people should never have expected anything but a smackdown from God. Raised under rabbinic tutelage "according to the strict manner of the law of our fathers" (Acts 22:3) in Jerusalem, a place decried by Jesus as "the city that kills the prophets and stones those who are sent to it" (Matt 23:37) before he met his end there, Paul was a prime candidate for divine judgment on three counts (among others he could have mentioned). Dibelius and Conzelmann consider it "inconceivable that the terms 'blasphemer' and 'evil-doer' [NIV 'violent man'] could have been used by Paul in describing his past."[105] The explanation below seeks to show how plausible the characterization is.

He was, first, a "blasphemer." The word is used three times elsewhere in the NT, all in adjectival forms describing alleged blasphemous words by Stephen against Moses and God (Acts 6:11), abusive tendencies of godless people in the end times (2 Tim 3:2), and condemnatory declarations mouthed by false teachers but avoided by God's holy angels (2 Pet 2:11). Paul's self-designation is scathing. He well understands the mentality and misplaced zeal[106] that can fill those who think they are serving God by upholding Bible-based traditions with murderous passion (see John 16:2). "Paul came to see that he had, in fact, been wrong."[107]

103. So also Dibelius and Conzelmann, 26.

104. See parallel statements in 1 Tim 2:7; 2 Tim 1:11.

105. Dibelius and Conzelmann, 28.

106. Recall Paul's recollection in Gal 1:14: "I was advancing in Judaism beyond many of my own age among my people and was extremely zealous for the traditions of my fathers."

107. D. Ortlund, *Zeal without Knowledge* (London: Bloomsbury, 2012), 153; see also 170.

"Persecutor" translates *diōktēs*. The word appears in the NT only here. A cognate word used in the LXX (e.g., Exod 3:8) is found outside biblical writings describing a foreman at a quarry who is a virtual slave driver.[108] Paul's meaning could be he overloaded people with crushing religious duties he himself could not fulfill (see Matt 23:4). But he is likely speaking literally rather than figuratively. The resurrected Jesus accused Paul of persecuting him (Acts 9:5), and Paul recounts the stinging accusation and its basis repeatedly thereafter (Acts 22:4, 7–8; 26:11, 14–15; cf. 1 Cor 15:9; Gal 1:13, 23; Phil 3:6). His blasphemous character was matched by an activist commitment to bring physical force to bear against what he perceived as violation of God's commands and will.

"Violent man" translates *hybristēs*, a word cognate with our word "hubris." It occurs in the NT elsewhere only in Rom 1:30. Proud, arrogant people sometimes rise up in physical opposition against those they oppose.[109] God promised to send "violent men" (*hybristas*) to Babylon to avenge its violent treatment of Jerusalem (Jer 28:2 LXX). Middle East violence today (and indeed the world's violence everywhere) did not arise only in modern times but has an ancient heritage, which the NT recalls in its references to the protomurderer Cain (Heb 11:4; 1 John 3:12; Jude 11). A memorable portrait of Paul's former violent identity is afforded in Luke's account of Stephen's executioners entrusting their garments to Saul before hurling their stones (Acts 8:1).

Paul could have said more, but he has written enough to confirm how thoroughly unworthy he was of anything but the law's penalty, since he had broken it so flagrantly precisely in his religious zealotry. He exceeded the false teachers who were twisting the law at Ephesus in his violation of it. But something happened to him, which he now moves to underscore to Timothy. He is not a better man than the false teachers (nor is Timothy). But they have met the one who delivers from the potentially destructive effects of humans enforcing religious tradition and morality by their own best lights.

Verse 13 continues with a strong adversative (*alla*, but), turning the discourse firmly in the opposite direction. Paul had been a lawbreaker par excellence, *but* he "was shown mercy" (from *eleeō*). This verb appears some 132 times in the LXX, almost always describing God's sovereign benevolence, as in these words to Moses: "And he said, 'I will pass by before you in my glory, and I will call by my name 'Lord' before you. And I will have mercy on whomever I have mercy, and I will have compassion on whomever I have compassion'" (Exod 33:19 NETS). Paul was undeserving, but that is whom God delights to lift up when such people acknowledge their need to come to him: "Have

108. MM 166.

109. The cognate verb *hybrizō* denotes physical mistreatment in four of the five times it is used in the NT (Matt 22:6; Luke 18:32; Acts 14:5; 1 Thess 2:2). The other sense is "insult"; see Luke 11:45.

mercy on me, O Lord, because to you I will cry all day long" (Ps 85:3 NETS). Paul mentions God's merciful work in ten passages in his canonical writings.[110] God's merciful nature and deeds are axiomatic throughout the OT and Paul's letters. The same verb looms large in the Gospels, most often in the form of people crying to Jesus to "have mercy" on them.[111]

God extended mercy to Paul, appearing to him on the Damascus road when his life direction appeared to be steadfastly resistant. Paul states that this mercy was given "because I acted in ignorance and unbelief." This explanation could suggest the formula: to receive God's mercy, act in ignorance and unbelief. But Paul is probably not excusing himself,[112] nor is he propounding a distorted version of Luther's ironic counsel to Christians to "sin boldly." He is rather stating the truth he expresses elsewhere in different words: "Christ died for the ungodly" (Rom 5:6). As Jesus put it, "I have not come to call the righteous, but sinners" (Matt 9:13). This is not an invitation to sin, just an expression of the reality that all people are sinners (Rom 3:23) and that, "while we were still sinners, Christ died for us" (Rom 5:8). There could be hope for Paul, therefore, despite his "ignorance and unbelief."[113] This "unbelief" is another way of saying he "acted in ignorance," twisting things regarding which he should have known better—just like the false teachers.[114] Yet, through processes hidden to us in the economy of the NT text, three days after Jesus appeared to Paul (Acts 9:9, 17), a transformation began that is still underway as he pens or dictates these lines to Timothy. The following verse expands on what took place.

14 Paul connects his closing thought in v. 13 with the opening words of v. 14 with the conjunction *de* ("and" or "but," untranslated in NIV). He had acted faithlessly and indeed culpably (v. 13). But as the result of God's mercy, grace abounded.

While "mercy" and "grace" in some ways overlap, it is fair to view "mercy" more in terms of judgment waived and "grace" more in terms of positive blessing received. By metonymy, and reaching back into Homeric times, *charis* (grace) "is often used of the concrete favor or act of kindness bestowed on someone, thus approaching the sense 'gift.'"[115] In v. 14 Paul affirms

110. Rom 9:15 (twice), 18; 11:30, 31, 32; 1 Cor 7:25; 2 Cor 4:1; Phil 2:27; 1 Tim 1:16.

111. For example, Matt 9:27; 15:22; 17:15; 20:30–31.

112. As Hofmann (78) recognizes.

113. Paul is portrayed as using "ignorance" (*agnoeō*) twice in Acts (13:27; 17:23). He uses it sixteen times in his writings, often in the expression "Do you not know?" (= "Are you ignorant of the fact that . . . ?"; see Rom 1:13; 6:3; 7:1; 11:25; 1 Cor 10:1; 12:1; 2 Cor 1:8; 1 Thess 4:13). "Unbelief" occurs sparingly in the Gospels (Matt 13:58; Mark 6:6; 9:24; 16:14). In Paul it occurs outside of 1 Tim 1:13 only in Romans (3:3; 4:20; 11:20, 23).

114. Wright, 11, translates, "But I received mercy, because in my unbelief I didn't know what I was doing."

115. *NIDNTTE* 4:653.

this gift "of our Lord" (i.e., from Jesus Christ, or perhaps attained by him for sinners' sake) "was poured out . . . abundantly" on him.[116] Paul uses a word (*hyperpleonazō*) that describes a pouring out to overflowing.[117] Grace gushed across Paul's blasphemy and violence (v. 13) like water scouring offal from a polluted floor, cleansing him from those and all other transgressions.

It is a mark of gospel grace that it does not merely cleanse but confers a fullness that Paul sums up with "faith and love." "In Christ Jesus" likely points to "the role of Christ in mediating the work of God toward believers" and, more particularly, the state or condition under which believers receive this boon.[118] This faith and love are "conditioned by Christ in juxtaposition to false versions" of it, like those advanced in the rival construals of false teachers.[119]

15 The verse begins with something of a formula (see Introduction, IX.C) that occurs here and in four more PE passages (see also 3:1; 4:9; 2 Tim 2:11; Titus 3:8). With "Here is a trustworthy saying," at the very least Paul is telling Timothy: what I'm about to state is decisive, and you can bank on it.[120] Rhetorically, it functions somewhat like Jesus's "truly I say to you" in many Gospel passages.[121] Timothy ministers in a setting where unacceptable teachings are circulating. Paul's assertions, in contrast, deserve "full acceptance." "Acceptance" translates *apodochē*, which is found elsewhere in the NT only at 1 Tim 4:9, though it is not a rare word in the era.[122] It denotes reception of something. Paul is about to make a pronouncement that Timothy and those under his guidance should not discount or minimize under any circumstances but rather endorse and embrace. Neudorfer views this word as programmatically foreshadowing the missiological emphasis of the letter, which receives

116. For the motif of gift in Paul, see Barclay, *Paul and the Gift*. This massive and insightful study references the PE sparingly, however. Barclay does suggest that "grace" in 1:14 implies "clemency (on the sinful)"; cf. Rom 11:30–32.

117. This word appears only here in the NT. It appears once in the LXX (Pss Sol 5:16): "Happy [*makarios*, blessed] is the man whom God remembers in due proportion to sufficiency; if man has too much [*hyperpleonasē*], he sins" (NETS). The verb here means to receive more than is needed. It is absent from Philo and Josephus and occurs once in the AF (Herm. Mand. 5.2.5), where it describes an overflow of evil elements that displace the Holy Spirit in a person who gives way to an angry temper. Barclay, *Paul and the Gift*, lists "superfluity" as one of six "possible perfections of grace" found in Paul's use of the word (see, e.g., 70, 562). This connotation certainly is present here.

118. Constantine Campbell, *Paul and Union with Christ* (Grand Rapids: Zondervan, 2012), 94, calling attention to similar constructions in 2 Tim 1:1 and 2:10.

119. Campbell, *Paul and Union with Christ*, 92, with reference to Marshall, with Towner, 396.

120. Note Wright, 11: "Here is a word you can trust, which deserves total approval."

121. For example, Matt 5:18; 11:11; 16:28; in John's Gospel always doubled (e.g., John 1:51; 3:3; 5:24).

122. Over two dozen occurrences in Philo, about five in Josephus.

deeper explication in 2:4. Christ is the key to all and any human redemption, and he cannot be dissolved into some pluralistic "ecumenism of world religions," then or now.[123]

Paul's weighty declaration is that "Christ Jesus came into the world to save sinners." Why would he be stressing this point in this verse and in this entire section (vv. 12–17)? Perhaps the law-teachers (vv. 3, 6–7) were getting traction with impressive exposure and conviction of sin by their appeals to OT moral teaching and insistence on devotion to obedience under their supervision rather than Timothy's or Paul's with their Christ-faith-grace emphasis. Religious moralism has its appeal. Paul wants to shift the focus from what the law condemns to the sole savior of lawbreakers (everybody): Christ. What the law could never accomplish because of human weakness, God did. He condemned sin, not only by giving the law (though "the giving of the law" is one of God's great redemptive gifts),[124] but also by sending Jesus "in order that the righteous requirement of the law might be fully met in us" (Rom 8:4) through Jesus's self-sacrifice and sinners' reciprocal response.

Along with emphasis on Jesus's saving mission ("came into the world"), Paul stresses his effect: "to save." Paul uses this verb (*sōzō*) twenty-nine times, with seven of these occurrences in the PE.[125] While the word has broad connotations, an important aspect is rescue from divine wrath.[126] Lawbreakers who do not get turned around are on a collision course with God's judgment of their souls and misdeeds. But Jesus saves, however trite that can be made to sound or parodied it be by scoffers. It is neither trite nor ridiculous when God's universal condemnation of all persons through the law (Rom 3:19), to say nothing of their own consciences (Rom 2:14–16), is taken seriously, as Paul does. But the law's seriousness cannot be alleviated by fear of the law, submission to the law, or zealous promulgation of the law. Rather, its demands are met in Christ, according to Paul.

The law's undoubted glories (Rom 7:7, 12, 14, 22; 9:4; 2 Cor 3:7) are always bungled when humans try to base their hope on satisfying the law's demands—because they are "sinners." Paul uses the word sparingly,[127] but its meaning is clear: someone who fails to measure up to God's standards or demands, particularly as they were codified in Israel's Scriptures and their extension by Christ and his apostles. On the one hand, it seems self-denigrating to accept that label. On the other, it is precisely while and as people acknowledge they

123. Neudorfer, *Erster Brief an Timotheus*, 98.

124. See Rom 9:4.

125. See elsewhere in the PE at 1 Tim 2:4, 15; 4:16; 2 Tim 1:9; 4:18; Titus 3:5. Elsewhere, Paul uses the word in Romans, 1–2 Corinthians, Ephesians, and 1–2 Thessalonians.

126. See, for example, Rom 5:9: "Much more shall we be saved by him from the wrath of God."

127. Its other seven Pauline occurrences are Rom 3:7; 5:8, 19; 7:13; Gal 2:15, 17; 1 Tim 1:9.

are sinners that "Christ died for us" (Rom 5:8) sounds a note of hope. "Sinners" are condemned, but their status also qualifies them for membership among those whom Jesus transforms: "For just as through the disobedience of the one man the many were made sinners, so also through the obedience of the one man the many will be made righteous" (Rom 5:19). This action happens because Jesus "came to seek and to save the lost" (Luke 19:10)—that is, sinners; he did not come to exonerate or affirm those already righteous in their own estimation. As Jesus said elsewhere, "I have not come to call the righteous, but sinners to repentance" (Luke 5:32).

In his former days, "sinner" would have described Paul, who for that reason can list himself as "the worst" (*prōtos*, first). On a rogues' list, Paul was number one. He knows the damage that can be inflicted when law-convicted yet self-righteous persons take the reins of religious leadership, so that high morality or intense religiosity or both are looked to as salvific rather than the one whom the Father appointed to come "into the world to save sinners"—Christ Jesus. "Of whom I am the worst" is Paul signaling that, however well-versed in the law the false teachers at Ephesus might be, their expertise in the subject pales next to Paul's. And he knows, and wants Timothy to make no mistake, that the way they understand and represent the law is a dead end, because they fail to connect it to Jesus (see Rom 10:1–4).

16 In important ways this verse restates v. 13, in which Paul states, "[But][128] I was shown mercy." Verse 16 repeats, "But for that very reason I was shown mercy." Yet, the two verses differ significantly by virtue of what follows them. Verse 13 leads to a statement in v. 14 of *what* happened to Paul to change his life—grace, faith, and love were "poured out on" him. Verse 15 adds *who* was responsible for this—"Christ Jesus," who "came into the world to save sinners," Paul being among "the worst."

Verse 16 carries forward the idea of God's mercy coming to Paul. But it will go on to explain a significant reason for this action. God showed Paul mercy for the "very reason" that, precisely because he was "the worst of sinners," the "immense patience" shown him by Christ would serve as a powerful testimonial ever after. Just as Israel was shown favor not because of its numbers (Deut 7:7) or its righteousness (Deut 9:6) but was an example of God raising up something out of next to nothing (Deut 10:22; cf. Rom 4:17), God designed that Paul, the prototypical enemy of God, should serve "as an example for those who would believe in" Christ and thus "receive eternal life."

As in v. 13, "shown mercy" in v. 16 is a passive form of the verb meaning to have mercy on someone. It can be taken as a divine or theological passive, with God or Christ or both serving as the implied active agent of the favor that the grammatical subject ("I," i.e., Paul) receives.

128. NIV does not translate *alla* (but), which is present in the Greek text.

"Might display" in v. 16 translates a form of *endeiknymi* (show, demonstrate).[129] Paul uses the verb in eight other passages, five times to denote what people display or demonstrate (Rom 2:15; 2 Cor 8:24; 2 Tim 4:14; Titus 2:10; 3:2). But in three other passages forms of *endeiknymi* point to God's display of his aims or attributes. Romans 9:17 is a parallel to 1 Tim 1:16, as there God states to Pharaoh, "I raised you up for this very purpose, that I might display my power in you." Just as God had a purpose for Pharaoh, so he had one for Paul. Romans 9:22 depicts a theoretical show of God's wrath and power. Ephesians 2:7 explains why God raised Christ and seated believers with him in heavenly places: to "show the incomparable riches of his grace." God moving to make something known visibly or palpably is a familiar biblical and Pauline motif: he is "the God who acts."[130]

But in v. 16 it is not power, wrath, or riches of grace that "Christ Jesus" aims to show: it is "his immense[131] patience." "Patience" (*makrothymia*), like "display," is an expression found across other Pauline writings.[132] In a total of ten occurrences, thrice Paul speaks of divine patience, whether God's (Rom 2:4; 9:22)[133] or Christ's (1 Tim 1:16). Twice he speaks of human patience that draws directly from God (Gal 5:22; Col 1:11). The other five passages describe patience as a quality in the lives of those who trust in Christ (2 Cor 6:5; Eph 4:2; Col 3:12; 2 Tim 3:10; 4:2). The God who gave the law might easily be portrayed as bent on judgment. Paul is impressed by, and wants Timothy to note, God's signature attribute of patience, highlighted in the OT by the refrain that he is "slow to anger."[134]

Christ's display of "immense patience" in Paul's most undeserving case[135] serves as "an example[136] for those who would[137] believe in him and receive

129. Its middle voice form carries no special force; it was simply the form of the word used in the NT era (BDAG 331), even in semantic situations that called for the active voice.

130. See G. E. Wright, *The God Who Acts: Biblical Theology as Recital* (London: SCM, 1952), an important book from the era of the so-called biblical theology movement.

131. The Greek adjective (from *hapas*) is an intensive form of *pas* (all). It stresses the totality of something. NIV's "immense" rightly extends "all" to convey magnitude and scope. Other translations use different renderings to arrive at similar results: "endless" (CEB, CEV); "perfect" (ESV); "extraordinary" (HCSB); "utmost" (NET); "to the full" (*GNC*).

132. See also Rom 2:4; 9:22; 2 Cor 6:6.

133. Underscored by Neudorfer, *Erster Brief an Timotheus*, 89, who calls it a Pauline technical term for divine restraint in judgment.

134. Exod 34:6; Num 14:18, Neh 9:17; Pss 86:15; 103:8; 145:8; Joel 2:13; Jonah 4:2; Nah 1:3.

135. Highlighted by *en emoi* (in me), a dative of respect (cf. 1 Cor 4:6; 9:15; Harris, *Prepositions and Theology*, 121) intensified by *prōtō* (first, worst).

136. Greek *hypotypōsis* (pattern, prototype, standard). It appears in the NT elsewhere only in 2 Tim 1:13 (see discussion there).

137. A form of Greek *mellō*, a verb that depicts something that will happen in the near or distant future. Paul uses it fourteen times—ten times in reference to a future occurrence

eternal life." "Eternal life" is a pan-NT concern mentioned twenty-five times in the Gospels and nine times in Paul.[138] Paul knew law-keeping in itself would never attain this "gift of God in Christ Jesus our Lord" (Rom 3:23), which comes only to those who "believe in him."[139] Those who do venture such faith might with Paul discover the theological exhilaration expressed in the next verse.

17 Paul's recollection in previous verses of the mercy shown him culminates in a brief but potent doxology. "The terms of his praise size up the character of the God who has the capacity to make good on the stunning promise to save sinners for eternal life through Christ Jesus."[140]

Paul terms God "King"[141] and affirms his eternality. He "has no peer," for "He is the King of ages. With one wink of His eye He beholds the eyes and crowns of all kings in contempt. They are the kings of an hour."[142] Whereas creation and humankind within it are subject to temporality, God existed before all time and is not bound by it. This is, at least, the understanding of God that has been dominant over the centuries in classical Western theism. In this view God the Father "does not exist in time or as part of the cause-and-effect networks in terms of which creatures exist and relate within the world order. . . . God is eternal and immutable, even in relationship with his creation."[143] Modern theologians have largely abandoned this view, but biblical writers like Paul are best understood as affirming it. God towers over all time, times, and eternity itself as their sovereign.[144]

There was nothing unusual about a *basileus* (king) in Paul's day. The word occurs some 3,181 times in the LXX, 344 times in Philo, and 2,235 times in Josephus. Epictetus likens God to "a good king" (*Discourses* 1.6.40). But Paul speaks of the eternal King, distinguished from all rivals and facsimiles in three ways.

---

with eschatological associations (Rom 4:24; 5:14; 8:13, 18, 38; 1 Cor 3:22; Eph 1:21; 1 Tim 4:8; 6:19; 2 Tim 4:1), and three times referring to temporal events viewed in their imminent dimension (Gal 3:23; Col 2:17; 1 Thess 3:4). The usage here in 1 Tim 1:16 has both a this-worldly and an age-to-come tie.

138. Rom 2:7; 5:21; 6:22, 23; Gal 6:8; 1 Tim 1:16; 6:12; Titus 1:2; 3:7.

139. "Believe in him" is one of only four times in the NT where *pisteuō* (I believe) plus *epi* (upon) with a dative personal object appears (also Rom 9:33; 10:11; 1 Pet 2:6; all citations of Isa 28:16 LXX). The expression "denotes the placing of one's complete reliance and trust on a person (Christ) who affords a firm support or a solid foundation" (Harris, *Prepositions and Theology*, 235).

140. Wall, with Steele, 74.

141. A word (*basileus*) used elsewhere in Paul only in 2 Cor 11:32; 1 Tim 2:2; 6:15.

142. Luther, 249.

143. As Cooper argues in *Panentheism*, 15 and throughout.

144. Dramatized, for example, in Darius's decree that God is "the living God" who "endures forever," with no end to his kingdom and dominion (Dan 6:26), followed by the description of "the Ancient of Days," who to confers on "one like a son of man" everlasting "dominion and glory and a kingdom" (7:13–14).

First, God is "immortal" (*aphthartos*). "Glory and honor are not for the Roman emperor or the local politician, who has a limited period of rule, but for the King of all ages."[145] He is described with the same adjective in Rom 1:23. Paul uses the word to describe the Christian's everlasting heavenly reward (1 Cor 9:25: "a crown that will last forever") and the imperishable quality of the resurrected dead (1 Cor 15:52). By applying the word to God, Paul affirms his "imperviousness to corruption and death" (BDAG 156).

Second, God is "invisible" (*aoratos*). Paul notes the hiddenness of God (or aspects of his heavenly realms) elsewhere (Rom 1:20; Col 1:15, 16). As spirit and not a created being (John 4:24), God's invisibility is axiomatic to biblical writers; as he told Moses, "You cannot see my face, for no one may see me and live" (Exod 33:20). "No one has seen the Father except the one who is from God; only he has seen the Father" (John 6:46; cf. 14:9). Through faith in Christ, however, Paul has glimpsed this God and here extols his grandeur, for the gospel he and Timothy preach "displays the glory of Christ, who is the image of God" (2 Cor 4:4). This invisible God "made his light shine in our hearts to give us the light of the knowledge of God's glory displayed in the face of Christ" (2 Cor 4:6). Paul can revel in God's hiddenness, because Christ has brought to greater light what was formerly opaque by comparison.

Third, God is singular, "the only God [*monō theō*]." There is none like him, which is the basis for the first command of the Decalogue: "You shall have no other gods before me" (Exod 20:3). He and he alone is creator of the world and redeemer of his people. Hezekiah prayed, "You alone are God over all the kingdoms of the earth. You have made heaven and earth" (2 Kgs 19:15; cf. 19:19). He likewise implored God to "deliver us from [Sennacherib's] hand, so that all the kingdoms of the earth may know that you, LORD, are the only God" (Isa 37:20). L. Belleville rightly notes that Paul's God stands out "over against the polytheism of the non-Jewish world."[146]

In view of these and other properties of the regal God, "the blessed God" (1 Tim 1:11) whom Paul and Timothy serve (and whom the law-teachers at Ephesus seek to reduce to the proportions of their presentations), it is no wonder that Paul affirms his "honor and glory for ever and ever. Amen." R. F. Collins notes that "the language is performative. By pronouncing the doxology, the worshiper *gives* honor and glory to God."[147] Paul "amens" God's brilliance in two other places in the PE (6:16; 2 Tim 4:18 [see discussion there]) and repeatedly in Romans (1:25; 9:5; 11:36; 16:27). He ascribes glory to God with the same words that appear in 1 Tim 1:17 ("for ever and ever") in Gal 1:5 and Phil 4:20.

145. Zehr, 46.
146. Belleville, 39.
147. Collins, 46 (italics in original).

Verse 17 might be seen as little more than a pastiche from passages elsewhere that list divine qualities. In the flow of vv. 12–17, however, it makes sense to view them as a celebration of the divine largesse that had given Paul's life transcendent meaning for over thirty stressful years and that could also galvanize Timothy in his own daunting circumstances. Relatively recent church history demonstrates the potential of the vision Paul's confession permits. The memorable hymn by W. Chalmers Smith (1824–1908) draws on v. 17 with its opening words, "Immortal, invisible, God only wise."[148] Still earlier, in the spring of 1721 this verse worked powerfully in the life of Jonathan Edwards. As a seventeen-year-old he was pondering this very text. Later in life he recalled: "As I read the words [1 Tim 1:17], there came into my soul, and as it were diffused through it, a sense of the glory of the divine being; a new sense, quite different from anything I ever experienced before. Never any words of Scripture seemed to me as these words did. I thought with myself, how excellent a Being that was; and how happy I should be, if I might enjoy that God, and be wrapt up to God in heaven, and be as it were swallowed up in him."[149]

Schlatter notes that Paul's doxology is relevant to the apparent doctrinal disputes Timothy faces at Ephesus. "Only the proper stance to the law, only understanding of Jesus's message and certainty of his great grace, lead to such veneration of God."[150] Teachers who glory in the subtleties of their "speculations" (v. 4) and "meaningless talk" (v. 6) about the law would do well to weigh the brighter light of the mercy, grace, faith, and love "poured out . . . in Christ Jesus" (vv. 13–14). So would Timothy, who was charged with a higher message rooted in Paul's majestic vision.

C. The Charge to Timothy Renewed (1:18–20)

> [18] *Timothy, my son, I am giving you this command in keeping with the prophecies once made about you, so that by recalling them you may fight the battle well,* [19] *holding on to faith and a good conscience, which some have rejected and so have suffered shipwreck with regard to the faith.* [20] *Among them are Hymenaeus and Alexander, whom I have handed over to Satan to be taught not to blaspheme.*

148. See Wright, 14.

149. See Owen Strachan and Douglas Sweeney, *Jonathan Edwards: Lover of God* (Chicago: Moody, 2010), 32, citing *The Works of Jonathan Edwards*, vol. 16: *Letters and Personal Writings*, ed. G. Claghorn (New Haven: Yale Universit Press, 1998), 792–93. For a fuller report, see Iain H. Murray, *Jonathan Edwards: A New Biography* (Edinburgh: Banner of Truth Trust, 1987), 35–37.

150. Schlatter, *Die Briefe*, 130.

18 The Greek starts with conspicuous stress on "this command," which has the effect of harking back to v. 3 ("command certain people") and v. 5 ("the goal of this command"). Verses 6–17 have certainly not been just filler; Paul has affirmed problems Timothy faces (vv. 6–11) and resources for surmounting them found in God's mercy through grace that bestows faith and love (vv. 12–17). Timothy, like Paul, can look to and celebrate the ongoing glorious reign of "Christ Jesus" (vv. 12, 14, 15, 16) and "the King" he makes visible (v. 17).

Previous verses serve now to underscore a major intent for Paul's writing: to fortify Timothy as he executes a game plan that will require all the resources he can muster.

Two of these resources are visible in the remainder of v. 18. There is, first, Paul's personal support. Only here and in 6:20 does Paul address Timothy by name, using the vocative case (*Timothee*). This usage lends a poignant touch, enhanced by "my son" (Gk. *teknon*, child; see discussion at 1:2 above). They have been through a lot together, during which Paul has found Timothy to be remarkably pastoral, Christ-centered, dedicated, and in sync with Paul's gospel focus, as he reminds the Philippians (and again calls him "son"): "I have no one else like him, who will show genuine concern for your welfare. For everyone looks out for their own interests, not those of Jesus Christ. But you know that Timothy has proved himself, because as a son with his father he has served with me in the work of the gospel" (Phil 2:20–22).

Paul's support for Timothy, as well as the gravity of what he now calls on him to do, is confirmed also by the verb he uses (*paratithemai*, set before, entrust) when he writes "I *am giving* you this command." Other translations opt for a more distinct connotation ("am giving" is notably flat). Three examples: This charge I *entrust* to you (ESV); I am *setting before* you this instruction (LEB); I *put* this charge *before* you (NET). The LXX uses this word to describe how Moses conveyed God's words on Sinai to the people (Exod 19:7; 21:1; Deut 4:44) and how David entrusted his spirit to God (Ps 30:6 [5]). Paul's diction is little short of ceremonious when one combines his use of this word, his chosen word order, the vocative of direct address, and alliteration of the initial letter pi in the opening clause.[151] In some ways, in terms of what Paul wants to elicit from Timothy, the epistle begins here.

A second resource for Timothy's perseverance is "the prophecies once made [*proagousas*][152] about you." Little more is known about this event; later in the letter Paul will write, "Do not neglect your gift, which was given you through prophecy when the body of elders laid their hands on you" (4:14). Paul was evidently there on that occasion; later he will remind Timothy "to

151. *Parangelian* (command), *paratithemai* (giving), *proagousas* (once made), *prophēteias* (prophecies).

152. This participle is from *proagō*; see BDF §308.

fan into flame the gift of God, which is in you through the laying on of my hands" (2 Tim 1:6). Apparently, Timothy showed great promise, in terms of divine sanction and equipping, from early in his ministry and perhaps virtually from the outset. But calling and earlier convictions can be doubted (Matt 11:2; Col 4:17; 2 Tim 4:10; Heb 10:32; 2 Pet 1:9–10). Timothy needs to reaffirm God's steadfastness in the form of testimonies made by other believers—indeed, "the body of elders," on the occasion he was set apart for future service. That future, as Timothy reads Paul's letter, has arrived.

The fruitfulness of that future will depend to some degree on how Timothy appropriates the past: he is to "fight the battle well" in conjunction with "recalling" those prophecies made a decade or more ago. "Recalling" is an inference from the words *en autais*—"by them," that is, by the prophecies. The NIV rendering places emphasis on Timothy's powers of recollection, a tack taken by few other translators. Admittedly he must remember the occasion and its impact to draw benefit from it. But "by them" stresses the prophecies, not Timothy's memory. The prophecies represent God's promise and assurance, both greatly needed in the fog of ecclesial conflict.

For to "fight the battle well,"[153] a barely living metaphor for ministry under duress, will require the supernatural enablement and intervention that genuine "prophecies" would prepare one to expect. Paul relates ministry to soldiering, using the same verb (*strateuō*, to fight, serve as a soldier) elsewhere.[154] Later he will testify (using a different word but similar construction)[155] that he has "fought the good fight" (2 Tim 4:7). He is not asking of Timothy anything he has not weathered repeatedly himself. In one of Paul's earliest letters he spoke of congregations suffering oppression from both Gentile and Jewish quarters (1 Thess 2:14–16). Now at Ephesus Timothy must also reckon with internal dissent and challenge. Verse 19 details how Timothy may do so and why it is critical for him and for believers in general.

19 This verse continues the thought of v. 18. It begins by affirming a pair of strengths that will serve Timothy well. The first is "faith."[156] The second is "a good conscience."[157] NIV positions exercise of these qualities in unspecified parallel with "fight the battle well" in the previous verse. But the adverbial participle construction translated "holding on to" could imply more. Paul

153. For criticism of the NIV rendering, see Towner, *Letters*, 157n15. For both Qumran and Hellenistic background to the military imagery, see Dibelius and Conzelmann, 32–33.

154. 1 Cor 9:7; 2 Cor 10:3; 2 Tim 2:4.

155. That is, a cognate accusative. 1 Tim 1:18 could be translated, "that . . . you might fight the good fight." For the construction, see BDF §153; Wallace, *Greek Grammar*, 189–90.

156. For a similar construction, combining a form of *echō* (to have, hold) with "faith," see Matt 17:20; 21:21; Acts 14:9; Rom 14:22; 1 Cor 13:2; Jas 2:18.

157. For a similar construction, combining a form of *echō* with "conscience," see Acts 24:16; Heb 10:2; 13:18; 1 Pet 3:16.

might be specifying the means of fighting: "*by* holding on to faith and a good conscience." Or he could be pointing to the reason why such struggle holds promise: "*because* you hold on to faith and a good conscience."

Both qualities are highly prized in Paul generally and in the PE in particular. The noun "faith" (*pistis*) occurs 109 times in Paul apart from the PE and 33 times in the PE. Often it refers to *the* faith, the substance of what is confessed and believed (*fides quae creditur*).[158] Other times stress lies on the personal act of faith (*fides qua creditur*). The latter is likely Paul's emphasis here. Timothy's success in the strife, and Paul's optimism regarding his prospects, will be in part a function of his living trust in Christ.

Equally significant is "a good conscience." Both qualities are discussed above (see comments on 1:5), where Paul reminds Timothy that both are (along with love) the goal of "this command," which overshadows the whole of 1 Tim 1. Timothy will prevail in his mission at Ephesus as he permits the gospel message, as well as the living Christ it mediates, to effect in him the results he hopes to see produced in those he instructs and admonishes.

These qualities will also be critical in avoiding the ruin signaled by their lack. The "some" in v. 19[159] may well be connected with the false teachers and teaching against which Paul has already warned. There are individuals who "have rejected" the faith and good conscience that Paul commends.

"Rejected" translates a word (*apōtheō*) used six times in the NT, three of those in Acts, where it refers to a literal pushing aside of Moses (7:27) in a physical scuffle and then a rejection of his spiritual leadership by the wayward children of Israel in the exodus (7:39). Paul and Barnabas dramatically charge their synagogue audience with rejecting God's word (13:46), resulting in a historic shift in their mission so that they will henceforth target the Gentiles. Paul uses the same word twice in Rom 11, once in the rhetorical question "Did God reject his people?" (v. 1) and again with the insistence "God did not reject his people," adapting words from the LXX.[160] Usage in Josephus and Philo indicates the word often connotes a rash and violent dispersal of something or putting someone to flight. Paul may be understood as describing, not a less-than-perfect faith or a spiritual outlook not completely congruent with his own, but a determined or even vehement blockage. His implied critique in this verse is by no means petty.

158. For example, 1 Tim 3:9; 4:1, 6, 12; 5:8; 2 Tim 4:7; Titus 1:4, 13.

159. See table 21 and discussion of *tines* (some) at 5:15.

160. Either 1 Sam 12:22 or Ps 93:13 [MT 94:13]. In both passages, however, where the verb is future and the subject *kyrios* (Lord), Paul writes *theos* (God) and interprets the future retrospectively, as a prediction accomplished in Christ's finished work. For a comparable use of the word in Philo (who uses the word over two dozen times, though only once in a matter pertaining to faith or God), see *Virtues* 65: by "their laws and customs," the Jews "have rejected [*apōsamenois*] all errors about gods who have been created themselves [i.e., idols]."

Coupled with such rejection of faith and good conscience is "shipwreck with regard to the faith."[161] Here, because of the definite article "the" (*tēn*), Paul likely has in view not primarily the act or experience of personal faith but more the substance and content of true belief affirmed and confessed (*fides quae creditur*). When healthy personal faith and good conscience are shaky or even repelled, the consequences are calamitous—shipwreck.[162] "Suffered shipwreck" suggests personal loss, and such pitiable tragedy should not be minimized; shortly Paul will confirm that God "wants all people to be saved and to come to a knowledge of the truth" (2:4).

But with the *fides quae* in view, Paul may be alluding to the doctrinal destruction resulting from failure to arrive at true personal faith and good conscience (cf. Rom 9:31–32). He is not stressing victimhood but victimizing. These misunderstandings are in fact culpable and willful distortions that wreak havoc on what believers affirm and confess to their salvation—indicating that to follow their mistaken lead would be fatal betrayal of the means of grace embodied in the truth of the gospel (see Col 1:5). Paul refers to people like someone who receives the keys to an impressive new car and then promptly takes it out and wrecks it. The reckless driver may live to drive again, but the car is totaled. Timothy is up against persons at Ephesus whose religious bent—whose bogus belief and unredeemed conscience—would result in total wreckage of the apostolic conviction Paul and Timothy champion, were that possible.

Towner disputes that Paul might be asserting, in essence, that some are wrecking the faith.[163] Why does Paul not simply say they are destroying or denying the substance of Christian teaching? Perhaps it is because Paul views the assertions that together constitute true Christian faith (e.g., Christ's incarnation, divinity, and resurrection; see, e.g., 1 Tim 3:16) as indestructible. What those who reject faith and good conscience are attempting is unattainable. Their attempts could only backfire disastrously, and that is what has happened, in the end to their own detriment, though the intent was (and remains) to pose lethal challenge when it comes to the fundamental claims of true gospel belief (a legitimate way to view the connotation of *peri tēn pistin*).

161. For the construction *peri tēn pistin* (concerning the faith), see also 1 Tim 6:21; 2 Tim 3:8, the only other occurrences in the NT.

162. The only other NT use of the word is literal (2 Cor 11:25). Philo's five uses of the word include both the literal (*Change of Names* 215; *Dreams* 2.143; *Life of Joseph* 139) and the metaphorical (*Dreams* 2.147; *Embassy to Gaius* 371). It is not found in the LXX, Josephus, the AF, or the Apologists. Collins's statement (49) that "the verb is often used metaphorically in the Septuagint" needs correcting. He is likewise wrong in claiming it is found in Josephus, giving *Jewish Antiquities* 5.183, 12.355 as examples. Those passages rather use the word for "reject" (*apōtheō*), found earlier in the verse.

163. Towner, *Letters*, 159–60. So also, for example, Hofmann, 87.

20 Paul names names. Numbered among the shipwrecked, and perhaps shipwreckers, are "Hymenaeus and Alexander." Their identities are as enigmatic as the discipline to which Paul says he has subjected them.

Someone named Hymenaeus (the mythological Greek god of marriage) is also listed with a certain Philetus in 2 Tim 2:17–18. They are described as departing *peri tēn alētheian* ("from the truth") just as "some" in v. 19 shipwrecked *peri tēn pistin* ("with regard to the faith"). Here truth and faith may be regarded as near synonyms. Nothing more is known of Hymenaeus, and it is not clear that the one named in 1:20 is the same figure as the one in 2 Tim 2:17 (see comments there).[164] Yet, neither can their identification be ruled out.

"Alexander" is also mentioned. This is one of several by this name in the NT.[165] If he is different from the Alexander mentioned in 2 Tim 4:14, then what Paul says in v. 20 is all that is known. Like Hymenaeus, he has forsaken faith and a good conscience, with disastrous consequences viewed from the standpoint of the faith. See commentary below on 2 Tim 4:14–15, where the position is taken that both Hymenaeus and Alexander may be identified as the same ones about whom Paul warns Timothy here.

What is clear is that Paul has taken measures to place them in Satan's hands "to be taught not to blaspheme." The verb translated "be taught" (from *paideuō*) is used elsewhere by Paul to refer to restorative instruction rather than blind punishment or vengeance.[166] Paul's action is intended to bring or restore them to saving faith rather than allowing them to continue to misrepresent that faith, slander it, or otherwise speak evil of it, the sorts of meanings that attach to NT occurrences of "blaspheme."[167] As odious as their actions are, in a religion that teaches prayer and love for enemies (Matt 5:43), Paul is not resorting to a nuclear option or repaying evil with evil (Rom 12:17; 1 Pet 3:9). By such restraint, Paul will aid Timothy not only by checking these men's

164. Collins, 49, seems to assume they are not the same, possibly because he views both references as fictitious inventions of "The Pastor," whom he views as the (pseudonymous) author of the PE. Johnson, *First and Second Letters to Timothy*, 185, concludes that paucity of evidence makes determination either way impossible. Towner, *Letters*, 160, cautiously treats them as the same. Trevor Thompson ("Alexander 10: Coppersmith at Ephesus," *EBR* 1:738) regards arguments to equate the two as "not . . . wholly convincing" and "not persuasive."

165. See also Mark 15:21 (son of Simon of Cyrene and brother of Rufus); Acts 4:6 (a member of the high priest's family who helped question Peter and John); Acts 19:33–34 (an Ephesian Jew who became enmeshed in a riot caused by Paul's ministry there); 2 Tim 4:14–15 (a metalworker who opposed Paul).

166. See 1 Cor 11:32; 2 Tim 2:25; Titus 2:12. On the restorative process as administered in and by the church, see Wright, 16.

167. On Greek *blasphemeō*, see also 1 Tim 6:1; Titus 2:5; 3:2 (and comments in Titus commentary below). In Paul elsewhere: Rom 2:24; 3:8; 14:16; 1 Cor 10:30.

excesses but by giving Timothy an example of how to handle troublemakers in a constructive fashion.

The means Paul uses for the correction of Hymenaeus and Alexander is to hand them over to Satan (see under *paradidōmi*, hand over, in BDAG 762). Named thirty-six times in the NT (not counting references to "devil" or other monikers), this is one of only two references (the other is in 1 Tim 5:15) to *satanas* (also spelled *satan*; see BDAG 917) in the PE.[168] The obvious and sole close Pauline parallel involves a man in an incestuous relationship: "As one who is present with you in this way, I have already passed judgment in the name of our Lord Jesus on the one who has been doing this. So when you are assembled and I am with you in spirit, and the power of our Lord Jesus is present, hand this man over to Satan for the destruction of the flesh, so that his spirit may be saved on the day of the Lord" (1 Cor 5:3–5).

From these two passages it may be inferred that in grave cases of ethical or doctrinal lapse, and perhaps drawing on Job 2:6,[169] Satan was viewed as "God's agent in judicial administration."[170] Whereas congregations would normally have prayed for one another, there were evidently cases where petition would shift from divine protection to divine discipline (with Satan as God's agent). Sometimes harsh measures are required to wake people up (see 2 Thess 3:10–14). These men needed "to be taught not to blaspheme," a construction (divine passive) that "suggested to patristic interpreters that Paul meant God, not humans," would bring about the needed change.[171] If Hymenaeus and Alexander learn their lesson, there will be benefit to all concerned. That possibility, rather than some malicious or vengeful impulse, surely stands behind the strategy Paul has deemed expedient to employ here.[172]

168. For *diabolos*, see 1 Tim 3:6, 7; 2 Tim 2:26. The same word is used, but not of the devil per se, in 1 Tim 3:11; 2 Tim 3:3; Titus 2:3.

169. "The Lord said to Satan, 'Very well, then, he is in your hands; but you must spare his life.'" Cf. Twomey, 31: "Using Job's testing by Satan as a paradigmatic case, both Tertullian (*De fuga* 9.2, *ANF* 4:117) and Chrysostom (*Hom. 1 Tim.*, *NPNF*[1] 13:425) argue that the devil in fact does operate at the behest of God for the sake of the elect."

170. Collins, 50.

171. Johnson, *First and Second Letters to Timothy*, 186. In contrast, Krause, 45, views not God but "the letter writer" as "actively involved in who is saved and who is damned." This polemical treatment of the passage misses the restorative, not punitive, intent Paul expresses.

172. Note the pastorally rich and extended discussion in Ryken, 53–56.

III. ORDER IN CHURCH AND LIFE (2:1–6:2A)

1 Tim 1 is foundational in establishing Paul's counsel to Timothy (that he remain at Ephesus; 1:3), in confirming major impediments (misguided teachers and teaching; 1:4–11), and in recalling God's merciful intervention in the lives of misguided law-devotees (like Paul) in the past (1:12–17).

Assuming Timothy does remain and is not stampeded by the likes of Hymenaeus and Alexander (1:18–20), how should he go about his labors? What Christian graces should characterize people under his spiritual care? How should they behave, particularly in gathered worship? What sorts of leaders, pastoral and diaconal, are called for? What ought Timothy's personal priorities to be? What ministry challenges (e.g., involving widows, elders, slaves, and masters) require particular attention? Paul addresses these questions and others in this letter's bulk and core lying just ahead (2:1–6:2a).

A. Instructions on Worship (2:1–15)

A word is in order about the complexity of discussion of 1 Tim 2, particularly vv. 9–15. The literature on these verses is enormous.[173] A book in print since 1995, *Women in the Church*, is devoted entirely to just the passage 2:9–15. A second edition appeared with updates in 2005. A third edition, running to over 400 pages, appeared in 2016 with all chapters either new or completely revamped.[174] The chapter exegeting 2:9–15, by Thomas Schreiner, is sixty-two pages long. The bibliography compiled in this book fills some thirty pages. The treatment below cannot hope, and does not need, to cover the same ground with the same thoroughness.

This commentator's views of the all-important hermeneutical parameters that inform interpretation of the passage are found in successive editions of *Women in the Church*.[175] These chapters respond to a setting in which there are basically three approaches (with endless variations and permutations) to the passage. Daniel Doriani has provided a helpful and accurate table.[176]

173. See already in 1999 the list of studies in Marshall, with Towner, 436–37.

174. Andreas J. Köstenberger, Thomas R. Schreiner, and H. Scott Baldwin, eds., *Women in the Church: A Fresh Analysis of 1 Timothy 2:9–15* (Grand Rapids: Baker Books, 1995); Andreas J. Köstenberger and Thomas R. Schreiner, eds., *Women in the Church: An Analysis and Application of 1 Timothy 2:9–15*, 2nd ed. (Grand Rapids: Baker Books, 2005); 3rd ed. (Wheaton, IL: Crossway, 2016).

175. R. Yarbrough, "The Hermeneutics of 1 Timothy 2:9–15" (155–96 in the 1st ed.); "Progressive and Historic: The Hermeneutics of 1 Timothy 2:9–15" (121–48 in the 2nd ed.); "Familiar Paths and a Fresh Matrix: The Hermeneutics of 1 Timothy 2:9–15" (227–77 in the 3rd ed.).

176. See *Women and Ministry*, 3rd ed., 136.

Table 9. Three main positions toward Scripture and women

Critical feminist	The Bible is traditionalist. Its patriarchalism oppresses women; the Bible is wrong.
Evangelical feminist	The Bible is feminist. Its egalitarianism liberates women; the Bible is right.
Evangelical traditionalist	The Bible is traditionalist. Its advocacy of loving leadership lets women thrive; the Bible is right.

The first view above is informed by feminist hermeneutics.[177] It views a major aim of 1 Timothy, like the Bible and traditional Christianity itself, "to put women in their place by whatever means and to assert the superiority of men in a patriarchal system."[178] A typical outlook from this viewpoint would assert, "Rather than caring for individuals of the church," the author of 1 Timothy "is establishing the legitimacy of masculine authority in the church." The "interpretation of Genesis 2–3" found in 1 Tim 2:14–15 "is entirely driven by his need to establish his singular definition of authority within the church."[179]

In this view, 1 Tim 2:9–15 is "regarded as one of those parts of Scripture which are to be in effect rejected."[180] "One cannot avoid the conclusion that 1 Timothy is misogynic not only by modern standards, but also by the standards of many other New Testament writings."[181] This is a relatively new approach, whose history is unfolding.[182] Its dilemma is captured well in the following statement: "Feminist hermeneutics is profoundly paradoxical, since feminist interpreters must struggle against God as enemy with the help of God, and at the same time must reject the Bible as a kyriarchal authority while at the same time using the Bible as liberatory."[183]

177. For a sample critique of this spectrum of feminism's handling of a central doctrine, see Linda D. Peacore, *The Role of Women's Experience in Feminist Theologies of Atonement* (Eugene, OR: Pickwick, 2010).

178. Marshall, with Towner, 438. See also Towner, *Letters*, 199.

179. Krause, 66, 61–62.

180. Marshall, with Towner, 438.

181. Saarinen, 54.

182. From a sizable literature, for orientation, see Elisabeth Schüssler Fiorenza, ed., *Feminist Biblical Studies in the Twentieth Century* (Atlanta: Society of Biblical Literature, 2014); Luise Schottroff and Marie-Theres Wacker, eds., *Feminist Biblical Interpretation: A Compendium of Critical Commentary on the Books of the Bible and Related Literature* (Grand Rapids: Eerdmans, 2012). See also Amy-Jill Levine, ed., with M. Blickenstaff, *A Feminist Companion to the Deutero-Pauline Epistles* (Cleveland: Pilgrim Press, 2003).

183. Rosa Cursach Salas, "A Christian Feminist Hermeneutics of the Bible," in Schüssler Fiorenza, *Feminist Biblical Studies in the Twentieth* Century, 162.

Because this commentary (and the series in which it appears) attempts to provide a reading that comports with a historic Christian view of God and Scripture, it does not adopt this vantage point, which does not seem to do justice to the text on either historical or theological grounds. It also seems to ignore how many women, through the ages and around the world, have found the Bible and its message far more liberating than oppressing.[184] This largely Western, university-based hermeneutic seems out of touch with perhaps most women who are active in the church as Bible readers and believers worldwide. It also reduces much if not all of the PE to a target for polemical and adversarial reconstruction rather than a divine gift to the church for its benefit (see 2 Tim 3:16–17).

Rejection of this view is not necessarily a matter of "disregard for feminist biblical scholarship as it has emerged in academic discourse since the 1970s," a charge pinned by Suzanne Scholz on John Piper, Wayne Grudem, and others on "the complementarian Christian right." She levels similar objections against the late Catherine Clark Kroeger, Mary Evans, Lynn Cohick and others who publish with evangelically oriented companies like IVP and Baker, "within the boundaries of a sociotheologically conservative hermeneutics." True "feminist exegetes continue to combat . . . views on women, gender, and the Bible that they have been deconstructing for more than forty years."[185]

This commentary will not interact extensively with feminist exegesis in this vein, not to disregard it, but because like many others, this commentary author has not found feminist hermeneutics and the exegesis it tends to underwrite a fruitful avenue toward a historic Christian understanding of Scripture.[186] Readers can consult commentaries like those of Deborah Krause and Thomas Long for expositions that may try to salvage parts of the PE for use today but engage in frank critique of Scripture rather than deference to its affirmations at points where the PE and modern convictions are in conflict.[187]

184. In a popular devotional format, Diane Lynn Severance has collected 366 biographical vignettes that illustrate: *Her-Story: 366 Devotions from Twenty-One Centuries of the Christian Church* (Fearn, Ross-shire, Scotland: Christian Focus, 2016).

185. Scholz, "'Stirring Up Vital Energies': Feminist Biblical Studies in North America," in Schüssler Fiorenza, *Feminist Biblical Studies in the Twentieth Century*, 66.

186. For an informed, illuminating, and detailed interaction with feminist readings of 1 Tim 2:9–15, see Thomas Schreiner, "An Interpretation of 1 Timothy 2:9–15: A Dialogue with Scholarship," in Köstenberger and Schreiner, *Women in the Church*, 3rd ed., 164–225.

187. L. Portefaix, "'Good Citizenship' in the Household of God: Women's Position in the Pastorals Reconsidered in the Light of Roman Rule," in Levine, *Feminist Companion to the Deutero-Pauline Epistles*, 147–58, occupies a somewhat mediating position. She defends the author of 1 Tim 2 against the charge of misogyny. Instead, she argues that the author advocated a certain mien and behavior for women (and slaves) to avoid persecution during the reign of Trajan (AD 98–117), "aggravated by the activity of Gnosticizing heretical teachers" (157). Subsequently, admittedly, this passage has caused "oppression inside and outside the

The middle view in table 9 may be called evangelical feminist. Its hermeneutic is often termed egalitarian. It understands Jesus as supportive of its outlook,[188] though the viability of understanding Jesus as a protofeminist has been disputed.[189] In many ways it grew out of the first view (above) but attempts what it sees as a positive reading of a text like 1 Tim 2:9–15, mainly by viewing it as a response to conditions in Ephesus long ago,[190] so that the teaching it advances and practices it prescribes are no longer binding on the church today.

A history of the movement (which, like the first view above, is unfolding) observes a use of "the Bible to meet the perceived needs of the individual" and a "reliance on individual reason to judge the truth of scripture, without the assistance of an institutional and historical church."[191] The individually determined character of this approach is confirmed by an egalitarian apologetic for it: "The evangelical [feminist] position . . . understands that a fully authoritative Bible supports the freedom of women under Christ *without male supervision* to follow their God-given callings and special gifts of the Spirit, including full leadership ministries."[192] But it is doubtful that the *Pastoral* Epistles may be termed "fully authoritative" when readers are free to remove all church and (at least male) supervision from consideration at the same time as they profess to be "under Christ." *Pastors* (again, at least if they are male) are cut out of the picture by definition. But they and their exercise of leadership (not portrayed as brute authority, even in 1 Tim 2) are center stage in the PE.

The same historian observes an emphasis on "individual preference and rationality" in egalitarian circles, demonstrating that "even in evangelicalism" as typified by egalitarian readings, "authority has been minimized,"[193] at least authority as historically understood in the evangelical movement and indeed

---

church from late antiquity up to the present time" (158). But the original motivation was self-preservation, not misogyny.

188. See, for example, Philip B. Payne, *Man and Woman, One in Christ* (Grand Rapids: Zondervan, 2009), 57–59.

189. See John H. Elliott, "Jesus Was Not an Egalitarian: A Critique of an Anachronistic and Idealist Theory," *BTB* 32.2 (2002):75–91; Margaret Elizabeth Köstenberger, *Jesus and the Feminists: Who Do They Say That He Is?* (Wheaton, IL: Crossway, 2008).

190. For example, Gloer, 145: "If Paul's admonitions here are meant for such a situation, one could understand Paul's reticence to have [women] teach, but one must be careful not to apply them in churches where such problems do not exist." In other words, they are not valid in the modern West.

191. Pamela D. H. Cochran, *Evangelical Feminism: A History* (New York: New York University Press, 2005), 193.

192. Alan F. Johnson, ed., *How I Changed My Mind about Women in Leadership: Compelling Stories from Prominent Evangelicals* (Grand Rapids: Zondervan, 2010), 14 (italics in original).

193. Cochran, *Evangelical Feminism*, 193.

in the historic church until very recently in some quarters.[194] The PE are replete with appeal to authority as represented by God, Christ, the Spirit, and the Scriptures, and revealed to apostolic figures like Paul and those he taught, for the sake of "the church of the living God, the pillar and foundation of the truth" (1 Tim 3:15). The apparent anti-authoritarianism of the egalitarian hermeneutic[195] does not seem well-suited to give a sympathetic account of Paul's teaching of "the truth" as he presents it in 1 Tim 2.

Applied to 1 Tim 2:9–15, Marshall, a proponent of this view, argues: "Interpreters who are sympathetic to the ministry of women in teaching and church leadership today claim that the passage does not give a blanket condemnation of these activities, and argue that it is dealing with an unusual ecclesiastical situation that required unusual measures and/or that the teaching reflects a particular cultural situation and therefore should not be universalised."[196] While perhaps most would agree on the need for "the ministry of women in teaching and church leadership today" and also that the PE do not give "a blanket condemnation of these activities" by women, the culture-driven nature of this view is clear[197] (as is its caricature of the traditional view). It

194. This assessment is confirmed by M. E. Köstenberger, *Jesus and the Feminists*, 176: "Increasingly, evangelical feminists have been found to engage in a fundamental critique of the actual nature of authority and leadership in the church. . . . Their egalitarian outlook has resulted in the erosion of any meaningful notion of authority in the church, whether exercised by men or by women."

195. Observed, for example, in the essays of egalitarian contributors to David Blankenhorn, Dan Browning, and Mary Stewart Van Leeuwen, eds., *Does Christianity Teach Male Headship? The Equal-Regard Marriage and Its Critics* (Grand Rapids: Eerdmans, 2004). Their answer to the question posed in the book's title is no, though the answer given in Paul's writings is obviously yes.

196. Marshall, with Towner, 438–39.

197. David Scholer (in a reprint of a 1986 essay) attempts to deny the culture-driven nature of today's egalitarian (or evangelical feminist) readings; see "1 Timothy 2.9–15 and the Place of Women in the Church's Ministry," in Levine, *Feminist Companion to the Deutero-Pauline Epistles*, 98–121. He refers to Margaret Fell in 1666 and then to "36 defenses of women in ministry" from the nineteenth century who anticipated today's feminist exegesis (119). But where were such interpretations of 1 Tim 2 in the history of the church for the first millennium and a half of its existence, across the numerous locales and languages and cultures in which the church existed? It took culture shifts in the West, and apparently a social consciousness that favored primarily English speakers, for interpreters like Fell to propose interpretations previously unattested. Scholer's claim that "only the ill-informed could suggest that such exegesis depends on or even takes its initiative from secular feminism" (121) can be countered simply by the observation that there are precursors to the hermeneutical shifts formally labeled "feminist" by the 1960s and beyond, during which the secular impetus as defined at that time was often definitive. For "the three waves of feminism" (1830s, 1960s, 1990s), see M. E. Köstenberger, *Jesus and the Feminists*, 18–24 (with bibliography). It can be argued that secular impulses pervade all three waves to varying and at times unhelpful degrees.

breaks with (1) historic church practice (and biblical precedent)[198] at the point of pressing for ordination of women to the pastoral office, and (2) classic exegesis of the passage that understands it as binding on the church in the world at all times and places, and not simply reflective of cultural conditions that make the passage irrelevant for the church today. As R. T. France has stated, "It can hardly be denied that it was the changing nature and values of secular society which were the catalyst that led Christians to re-examine their understanding of the Bible on this issue."[199]

While evangelical feminists by definition are normally not part of mainline denominations, the pattern in these denominations of bracketing out (by declaring culturally outdated) larger and larger parts of the Bible's teaching on human sexuality is ominous for evangelicals who are following their lead on women's ordination. The pattern is ominous not only because the staggering loss of mainline membership has only accelerated in the decades since women's ordination has begun. Across the board in the mainline, affirmation of a hermeneutic friendly to LGBTQ conviction has tended to be the next move. Given the rapidity of change in societal views on marriage in the United States in recent years (where convictions on same-sex marriage, at least as enforced by US Supreme Court ruling, almost completely reversed in less than a generation), it would be naive to suppose that there might not be a similar sea change in churches where right now there is insistence that it could never happen.

Because egalitarian hermeneutics seems more indebted to the mood of the age in the West (and by its influence worldwide) than to the history, language, theology, and ecclesiology in the PE, this commentary will opt for a different interpretive approach.[200]

The third view in table 9 is often termed complementarian.[201] Towner appears to object to this wording, stating that "at the heart of this view (however such language hopes to soften the blow) is hierarchy." He therefore calls it "the traditional hierarchalist position."[202] It is doubtful, however, that any rational hermeneutical approach is altogether free of some prioritizing of values and affirmation of absolutes, even if they claim to be anti-absolute.

198. That is, there is no clear example of female pastors in the NT, despite Bassler's claim (72) that "in Paul's own churches . . . women played various leadership roles," citing however just Rom 16:1–2.

199. Cited in Johnson, ed., *How I Changed My Mind about Women in Leadership*, 15.

200. For extensive exegetical interaction with the egalitarian position as advanced by dozens of its proponents, see Schreiner, "An Interpretation of 1 Timothy 2:9–15," as well as the commentary below.

201. For works supporting this outlook, see Köstenberger and Schreiner, *Women in the Church*, 3rd ed., and esp. 164n3.

202. Towner, *Letters*, 199n17, 198.

Certainly there are powerful hierarchies at work in both critical feminist and evangelical feminist structures. The question is, Does an approach adopted let God as revealed in Scripture determine and permeate the hierarchy? Is an exegetical approach willing to allow the convictions that inform the hegemony it represents be relativized by the claims of the text it seeks to unpack? Oden raises a noteworthy point: "The actual subject of this paragraph [1 Tim 2:9–15] is extraordinarily deep-going theologically—not merely petty moralism or culture-bound moral advice. It ranges widely over subtle themes of the relation of outward and inward behavior; the nature of leadership and its relation to sexuality; and salvation history from the fall to redemption, from Eve to incarnation. Hence it is regrettable that some treat it only as a petty moral regulation so filled with sexual bias that it is disqualified from serious modern consideration."[203] Comments below will seek to avoid falling prey to peremptory dismissal of the passage.

In defense of a complementarian hermeneutic, it has not charged the Bible with wholesale error (unlike the first view above), and it can credibly claim to be in line with the church's own reading of 1 Tim 2 through the centuries (unlike the second view above, which underscores its rejection of this reading). A complementarian understanding, like its rivals, cannot answer every question addressed to it. It is also not monolithic, as there are many nuances and differences in the ways complementarian interpreters explain the passage, and even more variance in how they think the passage should be applied. Most important, most would agree that the church (composed as it is of sinners, men and women alike) has not always been either humane or biblical in its treatment of women. Refinements and at times repentance are an ongoing need in response to ongoing study and application of Scripture, which affirms maximal and not minimal initiation of and involvement in ministry by women.[204]

Yet, complementarian hermeneutics does not necessarily prevent the flourishing and ministry of women, as a nonfeminist reading of the history of the church shows,[205] and as women ably defending complementarian understanding of Scripture have argued.[206] As *Women in the Church* seeks to

203. Oden, 95–96.

204. This is a theme of Daniel Doriani, *Women and Ministry: What the Bible Teaches* (Wheaton, IL: Crossway, 2003).

205. See Diana Lynn Severance, *Feminine Threads: Women in the Tapestry of Christian History* (Fearn, Ross-shire, Scotland: Christian Focus, 2011).

206. See, for example, Carrie Sandom, *Different by Design: God's Blueprint for Men and Women* (Fearn, Ross-shire, Scotland: Christian Focus, 2012); Claire S. Smith, *God's Good Design: What the Bible Really Says about Men and Women* (Kingsford, NSW, Australia: Matthias Media, 2012); Aimee Byrd, *No Little Women: Equipping All Women in the Household of God* (Phillipsburg, NJ: P&R, 2016).

document, scholars with openness to complementarian-friendly conclusions have contributed substantially to scholarship in areas like lexicography[207] and the syntax of 1 Tim 2:12. This viewpoint will be reflected in the discussion below, though exegesis will not follow any rigid template, since there is not a single complementarian reading of 1 Tim 2 affirmed by all. Comments offered below are sure to stray at times from interpretations supported by other complementarian exegetes.

Paul begins the next major section (2:1–6:2a) with reminders of what should be priorities in worship. As Towner observes, starting with 2:1, Paul is "preoccupied with activities and behavior within the worship assembly."[208] It might seem at first that he is concerned simply with "instructions on prayer," which is how Johnson labels 2:1–7.[209] And if these verses appeared in isolation, such a reading would be reasonable. However, they segue into vv. 8–15, which make it clear that Paul's directions regarding prayer, while certainly relevant to everyday living, have particular application in a setting where men are in public prayer (v. 8; otherwise why would "anger and disputing" be mentioned?) and women are worshiping God (v. 8) and learning while pastoral care is being dispensed via instruction where both women and men are present (v. 12). Paul's remarks are best explained by the deduction, based on the statements found in this chapter overall, that he has in mind the ambience and practice of believers in their regular assemblies.[210]

This approach in no way rules out the application of insights found here to the lives of believers in the course of their everyday lives (so, e.g., to their prayer lives). "These are instructions of general validity offered directly to the worshiping community and its leaders."[211] There is always a mutually conditioning relationship between corporate behavior and its rationale for the body of Christ assembled, on the one hand, and on the other, for the inner lives and public practices of individual members of that body as they live as witnesses and servants of Christ in their respective settings. In 1 Tim 2, however, Paul's purview is more public worship attitude and practice than personal or individual behavior in the world at large.

207. Particularly with reference to the verb *authenteō* (exercise authority) in 2:12.

208. Towner, *Letters*, 190. So also Belleville, 43 ("The setting [of 1 Tim 2] is corporate worship") and most other commentators.

209. Johnson, *First and Second Letters to Timothy*, 188.

210. For an excellent analysis of the passage with a view to the meaning of the command to pray, see G. Couser, "'Prayer' and the Public Square: 1 Timothy 2:1–7 and Christian Political Engagement," in Laansma, Osborne, and Van Neste, *New Testament Theology in Light of the Church's Mission* 277–94. Couser concludes (293) that "this passage is Paul's call for the church to be the church."

211. Bassler, 49.

1 I urge, then, first of all, that petitions, prayers, intercession and thanksgiving be made for all people— 2 for kings and all those in authority, that we may live peaceful and quiet lives in all godliness and holiness. 3 This is good, and pleases God our Savior, 4 who wants all people to be saved and to come to a knowledge of the truth. 5 For there is one God and one mediator between God and mankind, the man Christ Jesus, 6 who gave himself as a ransom for all people. This has now been witnessed to at the proper time. 7 And for this purpose I was appointed a herald and an apostle—I am telling the truth, I am not lying—and a true and faithful teacher of the Gentiles. 8 Therefore I want the men everywhere to pray, lifting up holy hands without anger or disputing. 9 I also want the women to dress modestly, with decency and propriety, adorning themselves, not with elaborate hairstyles or gold or pearls or expensive clothes, 10 but with good deeds, appropriate for women who profess to worship God. 11 A woman should learn in quietness and full submission. 12 I do not permit a woman to teach or to assume authority over a man; she must be quiet. 13 For Adam was formed first, then Eve. 14 And Adam was not the one deceived; it was the woman who was deceived and became a sinner. 15 But women will be saved through childbearing—if they continue in faith, love and holiness with propriety.

1 Paul begins with a coordinating inferential conjunction (*oun*, NIV "then"),[212] confirming that what follows draws on what he has said in the previous chapter. The word translated "urge" has already occurred in 1:3 (see discussion there). It implies urgency but also encouragement. Paul is about to describe a positive priority. Its importance is underscored by "first of all."[213]

That priority is prayer.[214] As prayer is a prominent feature throughout the OT writings (climaxing, it could be argued, in the Psalter), it was also central in the synagogue, as Paul would have known from his Jewish religious heritage. In Lee I. Levine's magisterial *The Ancient Synagogue: The First Thousand Years*, prayer looms larger in discussion than any other single topic (even Torah, Sabbath, and Jerusalem) except for synagogue architecture (the

212. Paul uses the same word in the PE in 1 Tim 2:8; 3:2; 5:14; 2 Tim 1:8; 2:1, 21. It is absent from Titus. The same word appears with comparable frequency (about 2.5 times per 1,000 words) in all the other Pauline letters except for Romans, where it is more frequent (6.75), and 1–2 Thessalonians, where it is less common (1.35, 1.22).

213. The Greek phrase (*prōton pantōn*) is absent from the rest of the NT, the LXX, Josephus, and Philo. In the AF is found only in the Didache (5:1) and in Shepherd of Hermas (Vis. 5.5; Mand. 1.1; 6.2.4; 8.9; Sim. 5.3.6). It occurs once in the Apologists (Irenaeus, *Against Heresies* 4.20.2) and once in Epictetus (*Discourses* 2.13.6).

214. Luther (256) stresses respect for civil office and those who hold it. But Paul emphasizes prayer for all people, rulers included.

central focus of that book).[215] Gospel portrayals of Jews, John the Baptist (who taught his disciples to pray; Luke 11:1), and Jesus (particularly in Luke's Gospel) confirm the centrality of prayer in Jewish personal and public life. It is no less central in the NT and in the expression of relationship to God through faith in Christ that the gospel message mediates.

Paul stresses the need for all kinds of prayers for all kinds of people. As for prayers, he mentions "petitions, prayers, intercession and thanksgiving." These are overlapping terms (all pl. in Greek), not distinct and mutually exclusive modes of intersubjective dialogue with God. They describe what public prayers in the Ephesian congregations should consist of and contain.

Table 10. Words for prayer in 1 Tim 2:1

Number of times used in:	petitions (deēseis)	prayers (proseuchas)	intercession (enteuxeis)	thanksgiving (eucharistias)
NT	18	36	2	15
Paul (including PE)	12	14	2	12
PE only	3 (also 1 Tim 5:5; 2 Tim 1:3)	2 (also 1 Tim 5:5)	2 (also 1 Tim 4:5)	3 (also 1 Tim 4:3, 4)

It will be helpful to illustrate Paul's use of these words in other contexts. In table 11 below, three of the four words occur in one Pauline passage (Phil 4:6); in each verse, the appropriate word is in italics.

Table 11. Other occurrences of the words for prayer in 1 Tim 2:1

Prayer word	Passage
petitions *(deēseis)*	Do not be anxious about anything, but in every situation, by prayer and *petition*, with thanksgiving, present your requests to God. (Phil 4:6)
	Brothers and sisters, my heart's desire and *prayer* to God for the Israelites is that they may be saved. (Rom 10:1)
	And pray in the Spirit on all occasions with all kinds of prayers and *requests*. (Eph 6:18)

215. Levine, *The Ancient Synagogue* (New Haven: Yale University Press, 2005). In the index, see the references to prayer, the Amidah (the thrice-daily liturgical prayer), and the Shema.

Prayer word	Passage
prayers *(proseuchas)*	Do not be anxious about anything, but in every situation, by *prayer* and petition, with thanksgiving, present your requests to God. (Phil 4:6) And pray in the Spirit on all occasions with all kinds of *prayers* and requests. (Eph 6:18)
intercession *(enteuxeis)*	For everything God created is good, and nothing is to be rejected if it is received with thanksgiving because it is consecrated by the word of God and *prayer*. (1 Tim 4:4–5)
thanksgiving *(eucharistias)*	Do not be anxious about anything, but in every situation, by prayer and petition, with *thanksgiving*, present your requests to God. (Phil 4:6) For everything God created is good, and nothing is to be rejected if it is received with *thanksgiving*. (1 Tim 4:4)

The upshot of table 11 is that it would not be justified to draw distinctions in too fine a fashion between the words Paul uses in 1 Tim 2:1. The point is that there be an abundance of prayers appropriate to worship occasions and concerns, not a precise delineation of prayer types or techniques.

Not all the words, however, point to exactly the same thing. "Petitions" often are a request for God to grant something. "Prayers" is the most generic word Paul uses in this verse. "Intercession," while it can be a more general word for prayer, may denote prayer for another's sake when used (as here) with *eucharistia* (BDAG 339). "Thanksgiving" (pl. in Greek) describes expressions of gratitude and recognition of favors granted. Still, "the four words probably do not describe a liturgical menu, but merely categorize modes of prayer."[216]

Prayer is to be made "for all people." Paul will give prominent prayer targets in the next verse. Prayers should cast a wide net because of their far-reaching vital functions, among them:

1. to touch "*all* those in authority" and enable "*all* godliness and holiness" among believers (v. 2), and
2. to play a role in "*all* people" receiving salvation and knowledge (v. 3), because
3. Christ "gave himself a ransom for *all* people" (v. 6).

The vast dimensions (emphasized by italics) of God's ambitions for believers and their intercessory role in world redemption require that the church look to

216. Johnson, *First and Second Letters to Timothy*, 189.

him with large expectations and copious prayerful attentiveness. Many psalms and other OT prayers, Jesus's prayers, and prayers in Paul's letters offer a wide range of examples.

2 Just as Paul was gripped by the world-embracing scope of Christ's death, resurrection, reign, and return,[217] "Christians must see the embodiment of the gospel in our preaching and involvement in the world around us as a requirement of Christian existence."[218] God who reigns from on high can be expected to exercise his sovereignty over those at the top levels of earthly oversight, which includes "kings and all those in authority." Engagement with the world is implicit in making disciples of all nations (Matt 28:19), doing so under subjection "to the governing authorities" (Rom 13:1) when this is possible without disobeying God. Prayers for these individuals are an obvious need, particularly in an empire whose reign could be oppressive for marginal groups like the early Christians.

The word "king" could refer to the Roman emperor (John 19:15) or to relatively petty rulers at the local level (Acts 4:26; 25:13). God "the King of kings" rules over them all (1 Tim 6:15). Hence, prayer to God for them is appropriate, for "by [God] kings reign and rulers issue decrees that are just" (Prov 8:15). "In the Lord's hand the king's heart is a stream of water that he channels toward all who please him" (Prov 21:1). Such OT references apply first to Hebrew or Jewish conceptions of their own kings (as, e.g., King David or Solomon), but also to pagan rulers like Cyrus (Isa 45:1) and Nebuchadnezzar (Jer 43:10). In a similar vein, for Paul the God whom Christ mediates (1 Tim 2:5) holds no less sway over the full range of Roman overloads and their delegates. As Jesus said to the Roman governor Pilate, "You would have no power over me if it were not given to you from above" (John 19:11). This conception of God as Lord over all and able to influence all regimes, even if in given cases he should choose not to in ways his people ask, is perhaps closer to the surface of Paul's conviction than "an apologetic intent" informing the concern of the author of the PE that "the kinds of prayers . . . offered on behalf of authorities in the Hellenistic world were tainted by idolatry."[219] Prayers affirming a true understanding of God's law, Son, and mission dominate the discourse here rather than an intent to correct a pagan conception of prayer.

In its only other NT occurrence, Paul uses the word translated "authority" (from *hyperochē*) in a related sense of superior or lofty speech (1 Cor 2:1). But the same word for "persons of consequence" (MM 653) is widely attested in both Hellenistic and Jewish sources (BDAG 1034). A busy and influential

217. See 1 Tim 3:16 for allusions to most of these events; on Christ's future appearing (*epiphaneia*), see 1 Tim 6:14; 2 Tim 4:1, 8; Titus 2:13.

218. Towner, *Letters*, 190.

219. Collins, 51. More broadly, see Dibelius and Conzelmann, 36, who stress "the traditional character of the intercession for those in authority." Note also their excursus "Prayer for the Pagan Authority" (37–38).

city like Ephesus would be thick with them,[220] and in any case Paul and Timothy had encountered them in abundance over the years of their travels and ministry together. "All those in authority" underscores that prayers in this regard need to be thorough, not omitting any with relevance to individual and corporate Christian well-being and mission in the world.

Whereas false doctrines, myths, and "controversial speculations" had recently reared their ugly head at Ephesus (1:3–4), with disastrous consequences (1:18–20), Paul envisioned Timothy reaffirming a less tumultuous regimen for the flourishing of the Ephesian believers under his oversight. Turning aside from such extraneous confusion, Timothy and others could look to God in hopeful prayer for conditions propitious for the worship and mission to which they were called, which was not primarily wrangling with wrongheaded religionists. "That we may live peaceful and quiet lives in all godliness and holiness" (v. 2) gives the sense, although the Greek is singular ("a peaceful and quiet life"), which may include a corporate meaning favorable to Christian survival and missional presence in view, not the preoccupation of individuals with their own personal, God-sanctioned good fortunes. A similar phrase, "peaceful and calm life," is attested in a third-century source (MM 281). "Life" (or "lives" in NIV) is *bios*, daily living and the subsistence required for it. Paul likely wants prayers at Ephesus to aim for social, political, and economic stability conducive to everyone's well-being, that of Christians included. The international refugee situation that has persisted in the absence of such stability has been a tragic feature of the twenty-first-century world. The desirability of social order in any century, Paul's and Timothy's included, needs no belaboring at the present time, when chaos and genocide make headlines with staggering frequency. People regularly risk their very lives to flee conditions under which "peaceful and quiet life" has become impossible; the specter of death in a leaky refugee boat is less feared than the insanity of disorder, insecurity, deprivation, and sometimes lethal intimidation.

Paul envisions social order and stability not just for persons at large—this is not a letter to society but one to a pastoral overseer for the direction of churches—but also for Ephesian believers seeking to move forward with a gospel edge "in all godliness and holiness." On "godliness," see Introduction, IX.B; the word (*eusebeia*) recurs in the PE (see also 3:16; 4:7, 8; 6:3, 5, 6, 11; 2 Tim 3:5; Titus 1:1). Prayerful communion with the relational God Paul represents bespeaks a desire for participation in the graces he offers and a manifestation of them in daily life (a way to characterize *eusebeia*).

"Holiness" translates a word (*semnotēs*) rendered "respect" in 3:4 and "seriousness" in Titus 2:7 (see discussion there). As with "godliness," this quality should be seen in conjunction with an outworking of informed and dedicated prayer. Invoking God's presence and aid enhances the possibility of living "above what is

220. Recall the "Asiarchs," whom Paul befriended (with the aid of prayer?) in Acts 19:31.

ordinary and therefore [living in a manner] worthy of special respect" (BDAG 919 on *semnotēs*). But the "respect" Paul has in mind is not human accord but God's favorable regard. "This is good and pleases God," Paul will observe in the next verse.

3 By "this is good," Paul likely has in mind what he has been describing in vv. 1–2: a scenario in which assembled believers pray for all people and especially for those who oversee national and local affairs, then reap the benefit of social order conducive to the tasks God sets for his people. This is not the sole good noted by Paul; he uses *kalos* (good, beautiful, attractive) with a frequency in 1 Timothy that is approximated only in Titus.[221] The near-synonym *agathos* (good, right) is also noted below.

Table 12. The "good" (*kalos, agathos*) in 1 Timothy

Verse	Item or person termed *kalos*
1:8	the law (if used lawfully)
1:18	the battle Paul urges Timothy to fight (ESV "wage the good warfare")
2:3	prayer for those who rule and the social order conducive to productive godly lives that may result
3:1	serving as an overseer (pastor)
3:7	the necessary reputation (or testimony: *martyrian*) of a prospective overseer
3:13	the standing attained by those serving well as deacons
4:4	everything God created (regarded and used as he intends)
4:6	Timothy as a minister, if he is faithful in his duties
5:10	the deeds of the virtuous widow on the church's assistance roll
5:25	the deeds performed by church members
6:12	the battle Timothy is called on to wage ("Fight the good fight of the faith")
6:12	Timothy's "confession in the presence of many witnesses"
6:18	the works that Paul calls on rich people to perform in abundance

221. *Kalos* occurs 10.06 times per thousand words in 1 Timothy. Other rates of occurrence in the other seven of Paul's letters where *kalos* appears: Romans 0.7, 1 Corinthians 0.88, 2 Corinthians 0.45, Galatians 1.34, 1 Thessalonians 0.68, 2 Timothy 2.42, Titus 7.59. *Agathos* appears with greater frequency in Titus (6.07) than in any other Pauline letter.

Verse	Item or person termed *agathos*
1:5	conscience, a source of love
1:19	conscience, which some reject to their undoing
2:10	works performed by women who truly worship God
5:10	works performed by godly widows

Table 12 confirms that the God to whom believers at worship appeal in prayer is concerned with and promotes a lengthy list of beneficial outcomes. The life of faith to which the gospel calls does nor culminate in grim, dour duty (though it can feel like that at times); rather, it announces favorable prospects and forward movement. Prayer is not merely commanded but is a source of great good (*kalos, agathos*) across the whole spectrum of life in the church, and by God's working in response throughout the world.

Prayer and its outcomes are not merely "good" in the abstract: God smiles on prayer and those who offer it (v. 3: "This . . . pleases God our Savior").[222] Paul has already termed God "Savior" in 1:1 and will do so again in 4:10. He rarely uses the word outside of the PE (only Eph 5:23; Phil 3:20). When he does so in a setting like Ephesus, it may be to remind Timothy "what the title Messiah implied for the Jews and because it served to contrast the claims of the gospel with those of the imperial cult."[223] Modern readers who may be conditioned to think of the term "savior" in religious and even divine terms need to be reminded that it was also used extensively of human figures. "God our Savior," who is pleased by his people's prayers, is not a distant transcendent being whose pleasure is an appreciative but ultimately meaningless metaphor. Rather, "Savior" bespeaks personal agent, the living presence of someone[224]—frequently the only one who can make a difference in life's challenges and adversities. Paul has already expressed heartfelt indebtedness to him as the person who rescued, strengthens, and sustains him (1:12–17). The felt pleasure of *this* Savior, which prayer promotes, can furnish Timothy with motivation for its exercise as it surely did Paul.[225]

222. On Savior, see commentary Introduction, IX.A.

223. *NIDNTTE* 4:432.

224. Implied by *enōpion* ("in the presence of"); the Greek of v. 3 can be rendered "This . . . pleases/is acceptable in the presence of God our Savior." The word translated "pleases" (*apodekton*) occurs elsewhere in the NT only in 5:4; see commentary below.

225. See Towner, *Letters*, 176, for rich OT associations in Paul's language. Towner posits that Paul intends to convey that "prayer has replaced sacrifice for the messianic people of God, another subtle reminder to the Torah-based opponents who resist the shape of the New Age."

4 Paul's exhortation to prayer in worship continues to trend in a personal and interpersonal direction. Prayers of all appropriate varieties should be offered "for all people" (v. 1), for the higher-ups, whose decisions weigh heavily on prospects for everyone's orderly daily existence (v. 2), and for the assured approval and pleasure of "God our Savior" (v. 3). Verse 4 moves on seamlessly to the personal and beneficent intentions of this God in his capacity as Savior, meaning rescuer and deliverer. Prayer holds promise because of God's twofold will: (1) that all people be saved, and (2) that they arrive at knowledge of the truth.

With respect to "all people" (note repetition of the words in v. 1 and v. 6) being saved,[226] one likely stress, given the history of Paul's missionary efforts, is that God's saving promise fulfilled in Christ is not just for this or that people group but for all peoples, Jew and Gentile and any other people that could be named.[227] Close-knit groups can tend to become insular; it is a characteristic of Jesus's followers that they reach out to all because that is the scope of the soteriological interest of the God they serve. John Stott speaks of "the monopoly spirit of which we need to repent" and gives examples such as "racism, nationalism, tribalism, classism and parochialism, together with the pride and prejudice which are the cause of these narrow horizons."[228] Timothy must not let the scope of church prayer and evangelistic concern shrivel to a preferred people group.

Paul can hardly be taken to mean that all will, indeed, come to saving faith in Christ, or simply be forgiven in the end because God wills it. This interpretation would make his missionary intensity incomprehensible—why such effort if none can be lost?—and defy clear statements that God judges the ungodly who fail to seek forgiveness and new life in Christ.[229] With respect to Jews, for example, Paul writes that he labors "in the hope that I may somehow arouse my own people to envy and save some of them" (Rom 11:14). "Some of them" implies that not all will be saved. More broadly, Paul declared memorably, "To the weak I became weak, to win the weak. I have become all things to all people so that by all possible means I might save some" (1 Cor 9:22). Again he shows awareness that some, if not most, will resist the message he brings. God's saving intent was and continues to be realized in the wide-ranging offer of gospel grace in Christ to as many people and by as many means possible, not in the eventual redemption of every sinful soul on the planet.[230]

226. The infinitive (from *sōzō*) for "to be saved" is cognate with "Savior" (*sōtēr*) in the previous verse, producing the same rhetorical effect visible in English (Savior/saved), though easily overlooked in both languages. Cf. German *Retter* (Savior) and *retten* (to save).

227. See Marshall, with Towner, 426–27 for discussion of a range of other options.

228. John R. W. Stott, *The Message of 1 Timothy and Titus* (Downers Grove, IL: InterVarsity, 1996), 64.

229. For example, 2 Thess 1:8–10.

230. For a comprehensive investigation of the issue, see Michael J. McClymond, *The*

In close conjunction with the salvation God wills is "a knowledge of the truth."[231] The NIV selection of "a knowledge" reflects the lack of a definite article in Greek. Other translations render "the knowledge"[232] because this knowledge is made quite definite by virtue of a very particular God and the singular mediator who represents him (see next verse). Another way of expressing "knowledge of the truth" is "faith" understood as *fides quae creditur*, the body of truth that is believed (see discussion on 1:19 above).

In v. 4 overall Paul is describing God's zeal to see all people rescued from their plight of fallenness by means of understanding the gospel message (described in following verses). "To come to a knowledge of the truth" "is a technical phrase in the PE for coming to faith in Christ."[233] "Salvation has its cognitive side. . . . One hears and accepts the gospel message itself."[234] Classic narrative depictions of God's proactive saving that inform first-century Jewish thinkers like Paul and Timothy would be his search for Adam and Eve in Eden after the fall, his commission of Jonah to Nineveh, and the sending of his own Son. This "truth" is not a defensively held proprietary secret but a bulletin meant for promulgation for and to the "all people" who dot the landscape of this discourse.

How can Paul be so sure of this will? What is the source of his confidence and zeal? The next few verses help explain Paul's assurance.

5 This verse presents God in his sole and universal saving significance. For informed and effective prayer and worship, nothing is more needful than conviction of God and the means by which finite and sinful beings can enter his presence and make their requests "for all people" (v. 1), including the greatest (v. 2). In speaking of God and the mediator who makes him accessible, Paul provides grounds for this conviction.[235]

Regarding God, "there is one." Association with the seminal declaration of OT worship is likely: "Hear, O Israel: The LORD our God, the LORD is one" (Deut 6:4).[236] In a location like Ephesus, pagan temples abounded, and polytheism was the default popular belief. As Paul conceded to believers in a sister city, Corinth, "Indeed there are many 'gods' and many 'lords'" (1 Cor 8:5) as far as the Greco-Roman world was concerned. Paul emphasizes the

---

Devil's Redemption: A New History and Interpretation of Christian Universalism, 2 vols. (Grand Rapids: Baker Academic, 2018).

231. The "and" in v. 4 translates a *kai* that is explicative—"knowledge of the truth" explains how people come "to be saved." See Marshall, with Towner, 428n44.

232. So, for example, CEV, ESV, HCSB, KJV, TLV.

233. Marshall, with Towner, 428.

234. Zehr, 56.

235. "For" in v. 5 translates *gar*, which marks this sentence as giving a basis for what precedes.

236. Other explicit affirmations of "one God" include Mal 2:10, 15; Rom 3:30; Gal 3:20; Eph 4:6; Jas 2:19. On 1 Cor 8:6, see below. The concept is implicitly ubiquitous in both OT and NT.

contrarian truth that there is actually only one God. Monotheism is, for Paul, the foundation of world mission. That is what makes v. 4 a credible assertion: he is unique and sovereign above all others, so it makes sense to worship him and pray for "all people" and their entrance into saving truth, since that is his will. Paul writes to Timothy tersely, but years earlier he had explained more fully: "For us there is but one God, the Father, from whom all things came and for whom we live; and there is but one Lord, Jesus Christ, through whom all things came and through whom we live" (1 Cor 8:6). Master of all and mediator for all are inseparable, though distinguishable.

In tandem with the "one God" is the "one mediator between God and mankind." "Mankind" translates a form of *anthrōpos* (person, man, human), a word that is thematic in this section:

v. 1: prayers for "all *people*"
v. 4: "wants all *people* to be saved"
v. 5: "mediator between God and *mankind*"
v. 6: "ransom for all *people*"

No one is exempt; all humans on earth in all times and places exist by the creation and sustenance of the "one God." That is what makes "one mediator" so important. "One" signifies that he is as singular as the God he represents. "Mediator"[237] identifies him as a go-between. God is invisible and "lives in unapproachable light" (1 Tim 1:17; 6:16). How is communion in prayer with him and worship before him possible? The work of a mediator is necessary, "the man Christ Jesus."

While the word and concept "mediator" appear in OT and in secular Greek texts, NT teaching is distinct. "There is no true knowledge of God as Father apart from Christ's revelation."[238] Two passages make Jesus's mediating role explicit:

> Jesus said to him, "I am the way, and the truth, and the life. No one comes to the Father except through me. (John 14:6)

> All things have been handed over to me by my Father, and no one knows the Son except the Father, and no one knows the Father except the Son and anyone to whom the Son chooses to reveal him. (Matt 11:27)

Yet, "the apostolic writers do not at all view Jesus as a neutral third party seeking to negotiate an agreement," as is the case in the common use of the

237. Elsewhere in the NT the word appears in Gal 3:19–20; Heb 8:6; 9:15; 12:24.
238. *NIDNTTE* 3:287.

word. "Perhaps this factor explains why they rarely speak of him as a μεσίτης [mediator]. The mediatorship of Jesus Christ is *sui generis*."[239]

His uniqueness is underscored with "the man Christ Jesus." While Timothy's opponents might suppose that the law, or submission to it, could unite man and God, the whole tenor of the Gospels and the clear teaching of Paul himself were that the law could not bring humankind and God into a peaceable relation.[240] But why does Paul stress Jesus's humanity here instead of just giving his name or title?[241] One reason might be found in earlier Pauline teaching aired in Ephesus. It was precisely as a man, namely, a crucified one, that Christ made peace through the cross (Eph 2:13; cf. Col 1:20). This is the mediating act par excellence, authorizing access to God: "For through him we both have access to the Father by one Spirit" (Eph 2:18; cf. 1 Pet 3:18). "There is a strong link between the suffering and humanity of Christ in the early church."[242] These thoughts lead to a further consideration.

Another reason for Paul's stress on Jesus's humanity might be its doxological impetus when combined with the title "Christ Jesus." As man, he was humble, but by the titles conferred on him and won, he was exalted. In a discourse serving as a rallying call to worship in prayer, Paul's allusion to the mystery of Jesus's humiliation yet messianic exaltation contained in the words "Christ Jesus" is uncannily apt and could have evoked praise, gratitude, and awe in Timothy (and the Ephesian audience if these convictions were shared with them).

6 Corresponding to the strategic importance, uniqueness, and finally grandeur of Christ's person in v. 5 are the impact and timing of his central saving act.

"Ransom" (*antilytron*) appears only here in the NT, but it belongs to a cluster of some half-dozen words appearing there that convey the sense of redemption, deliverance, or release. A slightly different noun form appears in a central affirmation of the Gospels: "For even the Son of Man did not come to be served, but to serve, and to give his life as a ransom [*lytron*] for many" (Mark 10:45). Paul uses similar language in Titus 2:14: "who gave himself for us to redeem [from the verb *lytroō*] us" (see discussion there). Basically, Paul chooses here to view Jesus's saving act as an exchange. He gave one thing (him-

239. *NIDNTTE* 3:288.

240. For example, Rom 3:19–20.

241. Collins (61) holds that Christ's humanity "is a very important factor in the Pastor's [i.e., Paul's] theological scheme" for polemical reasons. He was protesting "the divinization of emperors" and expressing "his radically Jewish view of God—unique, dynamic, transcendent." But Paul puts emperors in their place by stressing God and his sole sovereignty, and the way he speaks of Jesus' humanity here does not separate him from but unites him with God, which is a radical departure from views of God held by most Jews in the first century.

242. Marshall, with Towner, 430.

self) in exchange for something else (a transformed situation "for all people"). His death was far more than a moral example;[243] it was a costly and complete self-sacrifice.

Perhaps the most striking element of the image is the flawless and exalted status of the one given, compared with the flawed recipients of the gift he offers. Scripture elsewhere marvels at such incompatability: "It was not with perishable things such as silver or gold that you were redeemed [from the verb *lytroō*] from the empty way of life handed down to you from your ancestors, but with the precious blood of Christ, a lamb without blemish or defect" (1 Pet 1:18–19). The wonder of this gift strikes another chord conducive to worship and prayer, a major theme of the discourse. Another note of wonder would be the asymmetry of the transaction, the saving act of a single individual sufficing to deal with the countless weight of transgressions committed by untold others (see Rom 5:12–20). The self-giving of the human yet exalted Son with its manifold doxological implications is a signature Pauline stress.[244]

In affirming Christ's self-sacrifice "for all people," Paul is not affirming universal salvation (see discussion of "who wants all people to be saved" in v. 4 above).[245] "All" can mean "every kind" or "all kinds" of something.[246] Paul may be stressing that Christ's ransom applies to whoever seeks it, Jew or Gentile. It has also been observed that "the Qumran background suggests that this term may refer to the elect eschatological community."[247] In that case, Paul (affirming a Christology lacking at Qumran) would be speaking of the full range of individuals included in "the elect,"[248] understood as those favored by God to respond to the saving message of Christ. This group would include "not only the Gentiles who have actually responded to the gospel but also pagan rulers who at the time might even be hostile" (see again v. 2).[249] Paul himself was an example of this future inclusion, as in v. 7 he will note that he did not seek or volunteer for his apostolic duties but "was appointed."

243. Note Luther's polemic: "Some people think that Christ's death has been set as an example, a type, an ideal of Christians. This is preaching scarcely half of Christ" (264).

244. See also Gal 1:4; 2:20; Eph 5:2, 25.

245. For concise but stinging critique of the idea of universal salvation as a defensible exegesis of Paul's "all people" references in this passage (so, e.g., Barrett, *Pastoral Epistles*, 51, with appeal to Barth), see Berger, 797, who observes, "Here also [as in v. 4], 'for all' amounts to an invitation for all who believe in him and are blessed by his substitutionary sacrifice." The act of belief is required to become a recipient of the blessing.

246. This use of "all" or "every" (*pas*) can be observed, for example, in Matt 23:27; Rom 1:29; 7:8; Eph 1:3.

247. *NIDNTTE* 3:184.

248. See 2 Tim 2:10; cf. Rom 11:7.

249. *NIDNTTE* 3:185. For logical ruminations on the divine will, see Aquinas, 25.

The rest of the verse comments on the attestation and timing of Jesus's ransoming act (i.e., the cross): "This has now been witnessed to at the proper time." Translators wrestle with the wording:

a testimony at the proper time (HCSB)

to be testified in due time (KJV)

revealing God's purpose at his appointed time (NET)

This is the message God gave to the world at just the right time. (NLT)

the testimony to which was borne at the proper time. (RSV)

The same words translated "at the proper time" in the NIV (*kairois idiois*) appear in 6:15 and in Titus 1:3. See table 25 and discussion of the Titus passage, where we conclude that this wording often connotes the aptness of the hour[250] rather than the chronological location of an event (see BDAG 497). Admittedly, since the ransom occurred in history, "at the proper time" is not a timeless declaration. But all five translations above concur, despite their different wording, that what Jesus did occurred at the juncture necessary. It was not a random event that caught the Father or the Son by surprise. Rather, it occurred at "a time uniquely fitted to the disclosure of history's meaning, a particular season in which the meaning of all other divine disclosures became essentially revealed."[251] "Proper time" refers to "the history of salvation" and is "a phrase which originally meant the time determined by God in the promises" made to his people.[252]

"Witnessed to" likely refers to the apostolic preaching of the gospel, the meaning that attaches elsewhere to the word Paul uses here (*martyrion*, witness, testimony; NIV renders the noun with a verbal expression). He speaks of "our testimony about Christ" (1 Cor 1:6) and "our testimony to you" (2 Thess 1:10), both times implying the gospel message of Christ crucified and risen. Paul also exhorts Timothy elsewhere: "So do not be ashamed of the testimony about our Lord or of me his prisoner" (2 Tim 1:8; see discussion there).

The connection between "witness" and the OT law should not be overlooked. Whereas at Ephesus the Torah was being misinterpreted, in the Torah facts were established by multiple (lit. "two or three") witnesses (Deut 17:6;

250. In Titus 1:3 and at Gal 6:9; 1 Tim 2:6; 6:15, Wallace, *Greek Grammar*, 157, suggests "something like 'at just the right moment.'"

251. Oden, 47.

252. Dibelius and Conzelmann, 43.

19:15). Jesus reaffirmed this principle (Matt 18:16, 20). Paul was among those who carried it forward into early church life (1 Cor 14:29; 2 Cor 13:1; 1 Tim 5:19; see also Heb 10:28). Whereas "witness" or "testimony" today can mean one's unique personal inner religious experience, its biblical usage points to shared, publicly observed phenomena, which is Paul's point in this verse. The false teachers can twist the law however they wish, but the plain, publicly attested truth is that Christ "gave himself as a ransom." There can be no gainsaying the fact, as Paul's insistences in the next verse underscore. This truth with its glorious implications "for all" contributes powerfully to the overarching mandate of this passage, namely, that Timothy and other believers be proactive in worship and especially wide-ranging prayer.

7 Paul affirms a major reason that he serves as a witness: he received a divine appointment. He also speaks of the capacities in which God has placed him to promulgate his testimony. If the relative truth of two positions is in the balance—the law-teachers troubling Timothy at Ephesus or the testimony of Paul, long shared by Timothy—there should be no question in Timothy's mind which direction to follow.

Paul was "appointed" (passive of *tithēmi*).[253] He uses similar language in 2 Tim 1:11 (see discussion there). He had a strong sense of God's hand on his life since conception (Gal 1:15). He was divinely called to his office (Rom 1:1; 1 Cor 1:1, 15:9); he did not seek it or volunteer for the assignment. The same lexical form underlies the statement that Paul and Barnabas were *appointed* as "a light for the Gentiles" (Acts 13:47, drawing on Isa 49:6, where the Servant of the Lord is appointed). Jesus "appointed" the Eleven (John 15:16). Paul describes God's action of designating gifted leaders and servants in the church using the same word (1 Cor 12:28; cf. 2 Cor 5:19). Paul has confidence in his message and his counsel to Timothy because of his deep conviction that what he stood for was God-ordained. Paul labored tirelessly, but behind that toil stood the choice and the grace of God (1 Cor 15:10). Paul was not an ideologue championing his own creative synthesis but a servant entrusted with a heavenly message.

The words "herald" and "apostle" confirm that Paul passes along what he has received (cf. 1 Cor 15:3), perhaps unlike the false teachers, who assert things they concoct (1 Tim 1:7). "Apostle" (used thirty-four times in Paul) stresses Paul's role as agent under the authority of another—in this case, Christ. "Herald" (*kēryx*) appears in the NT only once outside its two PE occurrences (see also 2 Tim 1:11; 2 Pet 2:5, referring to Noah as a "preacher" of righteousness). It is rare in the LXX.[254] It refers to someone making a public announcement, often at the behest of a sending official. Heralds were as much a part of life in

253. A "divine passive"—meaning God appointed him; so Collins, 62.

254. Gen 41:43; 4 Macc 6:4; Sir 20:15; Dan 3:4. It appears five times in Philo, eight in Josephus, four times in the AF, and twice in Epictetus.

the ancient world as a town crier in colonial America or a news outlet today. Combined with the claim of being "appointed," Paul, in using "herald," underscores that he is simply passing along a message entrusted to him by another, a fact touched on in other epistles that speak of the "revelation" given him (Gal 1:12; 2:2; Eph 3:3). What is distinct about Paul's herald role is its origin (God), substance (Christ crucified and risen), and unerring veracity (attested to by both human witnesses and God, who does not lie),[255] not that he is a man conveying a message.

Paul finds it necessary to insist he is telling the truth, a feature in other Pauline letters (Rom 9:1;[256] 2 Cor 11:31; Gal 1:20). Johnson suggests that Paul is countering the criticism of the law-teachers seeking to impose Torah on Ephesian Gentiles.[257] They seek to undercut Paul's advocacy of grace and faith in Christ as the proper response to the God who gave the law (see 1:12–17); Paul answers their tacit charge.

Another possibility is that he senses the pressure Timothy faces. The Roman world regarded polytheism as its religious foundation; Jews in some quarters favored the law with notable zeal (Rom 10:2).[258] In the heat of disputation and challenge, Timothy might feel pressure to fudge, to go along to get along. Or Paul might sense a susceptibility in Timothy—himself a born and now circumcised Jew (Acts 16:3) grounded deeply in the law (2 Tim 3:15)—to be swayed by Jewish arguments claiming to venerate what Timothy (following Paul)[259] would have agreed was God-given and holy writ. Perhaps Paul identified a psychological threat similar to the one encountered years earlier, not in Asia but in the neighboring Roman province of Galatia: "Those people [i.e., Paul's adversaries in the Galatian congregations] are zealous to win you over, but for no good. What they want is to alienate you from us, so that you may have zeal for them" (Gal 4:17). Paul's injection of a ludicrous hypothetical—that he is spouting lies and out of touch with what is true—would go against all that Timothy had observed and committed to in his years working with Paul. Even if things go downhill in the reception of Paul's message in Asian Ephesus—as

255. See Titus 1:2.

256. In Rom 9:1 Paul writes, "I speak the truth in Christ." The words "in Christ" made it into some ancient MSS in 1 Tim 2:7. But they are lacking in enough others that the shorter reading is apt to be original.

257. Johnson, *First and Second Letters to Timothy*, 197.

258. Recent scholarship emphasizes the variegated regard for the law in Judaism of the NT era. Monolithic representations of Jewish views of the law are to be avoided. Yet, a zealous regard for it by many Jews is undeniable. Among a vast literature, see D. A. Carson, Peter T. O'Brien, and Mark A. Seifrid, eds., *The Complexities of Second Temple Judaism*, vol. 1 of *Justification and Variegated Nomism*, WUNT 2.140 (Grand Rapids: Baker Academic, 2001). On nomistic enthusiasm, see Ortlund, *Zeal without Knowledge*.

259. So also Paul: Rom 7:7, 12, 14.

it seem they did (2 Tim 1:15)—Paul stands by his testimony. His outcry is a rhetorical jolt to brace Timothy in a setting where the message he lives and dies by might—in Paul's absence—seem at times counterintuitive in the extreme.

But in fact Paul is not only a recipient of a divinely given saving message, great though his gospel commission was, but "a true and faithful teacher of the Gentiles." Most translations construe the Greek more along the lines of "a teacher of the Gentiles in faith and truth" (HCSB) or (less frequently) "to teach the Gentiles this message about faith and truth" (NLT). Divergent translations aside, three points are indisputable.

First is *Paul's role as teacher.* As Claire S. Smith has shown, the early churches were "scholastic communities"; that is, teaching and learning were at the core of their group activity and identity.[260] This conclusion is entirely plausible, given Jesus's foundational role and identity as a shepherding figure (among other things, such as a prophet) who called disciples and sent them out to make disciples, with an effect that left a deep impression on Paul in his relation to Timothy: "And the things you have heard me say in the presence of many witnesses entrust to reliable people who will also be qualified to teach others" (2 Tim 2:2).

Second is *Paul's target: the Gentiles.* The word "Gentile" (*ethnos*) occurs fifty-six times in Paul and in all but four of his letters.[261] The shift in the spread of the gospel message from primarily Jewish hearers and regions to lands and peoples beyond the regions where Jesus walked is one of the most dramatic chapters in the rise of the church. It is highlighted, for example, in Peter's encounter with Cornelius (Acts 10–11), which paved the way (Acts 15:7) for Paul's eventual focus on non-Jewish peoples. Paul's mention of this expanded scope to Timothy balances Paul's roles (herald-apostle-teacher) with the more important fact of the vast population he was called to evangelize. Since Timothy is Paul's understudy, these words are effectively also a reminder to Timothy of his own mission.

Third is *Paul as "true and faithful."* That Paul was on target and dedicated in his instructional duties can hardly be doubted, which the NIV rendering underscores. Commentators point out, though, that, in view of the OT and Jewish background, Paul would have been thinking in terms of truth and faithfulness as qualities first of all of God, and then by extension of the message entrusted to his servants the prophets and apostles. Marshall concludes: "Thus faithfulness and truthfulness here are not human characteristics but rather the marks of the one whose ministry and authority originate in God."[262] Marshall's observation fits well with the direct rendering favored by most translations: "a

260. Smith, *Pauline Communities.*

261. It is lacking in Philippians, 2 Thessalonians, Titus, and Philemon.

262. Marshall, with Towner, 435.

teacher of the Gentiles in faith and truth [*en pistei kai alētheia*]."[263] Paul is not touting himself but subordinating his own importance to the true message of salvation through faith in Christ (see also the close association between truth, with faith in the gospel implied, and salvation in v. 4 discussed above).

8 Paul continues to remind Timothy of worship priorities. Verses 1–2 underscored prayer; vv. 3–7 centered on the work of God and Christ that makes prayer fruitful and worship possible. Verse 8 turns to key dispositions in worshipers. Just as v. 1 began with *oun* (therefore; translated "then" in NIV), v. 8 opens with the same conjunction. Paul is not, however, transitioning to a new subject (as in v. 1). He is rather refreshing the focus of his discourse, which is worship and prayer.[264] In vv. 3–7 he veered a little to the side; v. 8 and following pick up where v. 2 left off.

"Everywhere" conveys that this practice is prescribed for all congregations, or at least all those influenced by Paul.[265] This understanding is confirmed by the same expression used elsewhere by Paul.[266] It may be compared to his use of "all the churches" in other passages.[267] Paul directs this comment to "men," using a word that denotes adult males or husbands, depending on the context. This is a gender-specific directive. It does not mean women should not pray in worship; he knows they will, should, and do (see 1 Cor 11:5, 13). He rather identifies a point of weakness or need affecting men's prayers—anger. More will be said on this below.

"I want" translates a word (*boulomai*) used by Paul both in the PE[268] and elsewhere.[269] This is different from another word (*thelō*) that he uses much more frequently (sixty-one times) and that carries roughly the same lexical meaning. Paul tends to use *thelō* when speaking of a preference, desire, or intention.[270] *Boulomai* (as in v. 8) may be more appropriate to stating a settled

263. Harris, *Prepositions and Theology*, 121, sees the use of "in" (*en*) here as denoting respect: Paul's teaching was true with respect to faith and truth.

264. Marshall, with Towner, 443.

265. See Neudorfer, *Erster Brief an Timotheus*, 117.

266. *En panti topō*, "in every place," found elsewhere in the NT only at 1 Cor 1:2; 2 Cor 2:14; 1 Thess 1:8.

267. Rom 16:4, 16; 1 Cor 7:17; 2 Cor 8:18; 11:28. Collins, 65, is correct that "prayer was not to be restricted to a 'place of prayer.'" But Paul's point here is to underscore that this is a directive for churches everywhere. He is not making the obvious point that how men pray in congregational worship (without rancor; see below) is also true of how they should pray in other places.

268. He uses it a total of nine times. See also 1 Tim 5:14; 6:9; Titus 3:8.

269. 1 Cor 12:11; 2 Cor 1:15, 17; Phil 1:12; Phlm 13.

270. For example, 1 Thess 2:18: "For we *wanted* to come to you . . . but Satan blocked our way." Or 1 Tim 1:7: "They *want* to be teachers of the law." These expressions convey an intent that might or might not be successful. See 1 Tim 2:4: "who *wants* all people to be saved." This is God's general desire. It is not a settled determination of what will come to pass in every specific instance.

determination, as when the Holy Spirit distributes his gifts "just as he determines" (*bouletai*; 1 Cor 12:11). While the distinction should not be pressed, his usage here is consistent with the observation that Paul is not stating an idle wish but prescribing what Timothy needs to encourage as proper and necessary deportment by men in prayer. "To pray" in v. 8 is a verbal form of the noun translated "prayers" in v. 1.

Paul directs Timothy, then, to ensure that at Ephesus, as in churches everywhere, worshiping men (and by reasonable inference women, too) will pray. This might seem obvious, but if the modern world offers any analogies, observation teaches that it is quite possible for Christian worship to take place with very little in the way of prayer, or for prayers to be so perfunctory or formal as to be more expressive of distance from than of intimacy with God. Paul, like men of God before him, is conscious that integrity in prayer at worship, even assuming there is any, cannot be regarded as automatic. While prayer in Scripture is normally regarded positively, it is often seen to be corrupt. Paul's counsel here should not be regarded as stock blather; it rather connects with a long heritage of warnings regarding vain and wicked prayer.

Table 13, among other things, reminds us that Jesus's famed model prayer (the Lord's Prayer) emerged from a context warning against hypocritical and useless prayer (note references to Matt 6:5, 7; the Matthean Lord's Prayer is found in Matt 6:9–15). The lexical form of the noun or verb for prayer used in the LXX and NT is provided.

Table 13. Unholy prayer, futile prayer: An overview

Passage	Divine displeasure with unworthy prayers
Ps 80:4	How long, Lord God Almighty, will your anger smolder against the prayers [*proseuchē*] of your people?
Ps 109:7	When he is tried, let him be found guilty, and may his prayers [*proseuchē*] condemn him.
Prov 28:9	If anyone turns a deaf ear to my instruction, even their prayers [*proseuchē*] are detestable.
Isa 1:15	When you stretch out your hands to me [in prayer], I will turn away my eyes from you; even if you make many petitions [*deēsis*]. I will not listen to you, for your hands are full of blood. (NETS)
Isa 16:12	When Moab appears at her high place, she only wears herself out; when she goes to her shrine to pray [*proseuchomai*], it is to no avail.

Passage	Divine displeasure with unworthy prayers
Isa 44:17	From the rest he makes a god, his idol; he bows down to it and worships. He prays [*proseuchomai*] to it and says, "Save me! You are my god!"
Isa 45:20	Gather together and come; assemble, you fugitives from the nations. Ignorant are those who carry about idols of wood, who pray [*proseuchomai*] to gods that cannot save.
Lam 3:8	Even when I call out or cry for help, he shuts out my prayer [*proseuchē*].
Lam 3:44	You have covered yourself with a cloud so that no prayer [*proseuchē*] can get through.
Matt 6:5	And when you pray [*proseuchomai*], do not be like the hypocrites, for they love to pray standing in the synagogues and on the street corners to be seen by others.
Matt 6:7	And when you pray [*proseuchomai*], do not keep on babbling like pagans, for they think they will be heard because of their many words.
Matt 21:13	"It is written," he said to them, "'My house will be called a house of prayer' [*proseuchē*], but you are making it 'a den of robbers.'"
Mark 12:40	They devour widows' houses and for a show make lengthy prayers [*proseuchomai*]. These men will be punished most severely.
Luke 18:11–12, 14	The Pharisee stood by himself and prayed [*proseuchomai*]: "God, I thank you that I am not like other people—robbers, evildoers, adulterers—or even like this tax collector. I fast twice a week and give a tenth of all I get." . . . All those who exalt themselves will be humbled.

The passages in table 13 are a graphic reminder that prayer can be as much a sign of corruption and sickness of the soul as of godly appeal and peaceable communion with God and others. Paul knows that if men's attitudes are conducive to acceptable prayer, Timothy's pastoral leadership has hope of succeeding. But if prayer goes awry, approach to God in worship is imperiled.

"Lifting up holy hands" evokes a repeated OT image of godly men imploring God with outstretched arms:[271] Aaron (Lev 9:22), Ezra and the people

271. For extrabiblical parallels (in Josephus, AF, and Seneca), see Johnson, *First and Second Letters to Timothy*, 198.

(Neh 8:6), David (Pss 28:2; 63:4; 141:2). Of Jesus, Luke records, "When he had led them out to the vicinity of Bethany, he lifted up his hands and blessed them" (Luke 24:50). Uplifted hands signal appeal to God for his favor and readiness to regard others favorably. "Holy" implies the hearts of those lifting hands are right with God.

"Without anger [*orgē*] or [*kai*] disputing [*dialogismos*]"[272] acknowledges that rancor disrupts true worship. It signals unholy passion and division rather than the harmony with God and others that the gospel of reconciliation enables and calls for. Paul's concern is as basic to worship as what Jesus acknowledged in teaching on worship: "Therefore, if you are offering your gift at the altar and there remember that your brother or sister has something against you, leave your gift there in front of the altar. First go and be reconciled to them; then come and offer your gift" (Matt 5:23–24). Men ancient and modern often relish disagreement. They love to be right and will go to great lengths to vindicate themselves and disparage real or perceived foes. Road-rage incidents, almost always involving men, offer contemporary illustration. Self-righteousness easily forgets and may effectively contradict the assertion that "the anger of man does not produce the righteousness of God" (Jas 1:20 ESV).

Later in the passage (v. 12) it becomes clear that men are overseeing worship at Ephesus. It is critical that they not be permitted to set a tone of conflict and unholy one-upmanship inimical to the spirit of Christ by whom worship thrives. Since conflict was in the air because of the false teachers already warned about (1:6–7), Paul's directive is all the more timely. But given the missionary edge of gospel Christianity and the opposition to which it typically gave and gives rise,[273] there is probably no place or time where this directive does not bear repeating. Angry men passionate about being right are a primary threat to acceptable worship, as well as to the wider relational dynamics that should contribute to harmony in Christian homes and congregations.

9 While v. 8 singles out anger and disputing as unhealthy male tendencies, vv. 9–10 balance off this instruction with mention of a female tendency: unhealthy concern with bodily appearance. Just as in v. 8 Paul was not accusing all men of being hotheads, so here he is not accusing every woman of being vain. But as Paul wrote in another setting where dispute about the law was in the air because of troublemakers, "A little yeast works through the whole batch

272. The word *orgē* occurs nineteen times in Paul but only here in the PE. Many translations translate "and," the most common lexical meaning of *kai*. The Greek affirms that Paul may be warning against either or both expressions of aggression. *Dialogismos* is used elsewhere by Paul only at Rom 1:21; 14:1; 1 Cor 3:20; Phil 2:14. In other contexts the word is rendered positively as "reasoning," and in still others as "doubt" (BDAG 232–33).

273. In the contemporary setting, note Jennings, "Hostility against Mission," 57–58.

of dough" (Gal 5:9). It takes only a few strategically positioned angry men or glamour-obsessed women to set an unhealthy tone for a much larger group.

As noted above, Paul in v. 8 was not implying that it would be fine for women not to pray or to lift up unholy hands in prayer; he rather focused on a typical point of male downfall. With v. 9 he is not giving men permission to dress immodestly or ignoring the fact that men, too, may obsess about their appearance and worship their image in the mirror. He is rather singling out a way in which he is aware that women's priorities can be skewed, with godliness in a full and true sense (see v. 10) being crowded out by vanity (v. 9). Nor should it be supposed here that Paul is calling for ugliness and slovenliness as the necessary norms for feminine appearance in the church. He is not counseling that Christian women must "make sure they are always out of style."[274] He is simply affirming that women are as responsible for the integrity of God's people at worship as men are. If men may imperil that integrity by misplaced zeal, women may do so by undue attention to how they look.

Verse 9 begins with the word "likewise" (*hōsautōs*). Paul does not pedantically repeat the "Therefore I want" of v. 8; he rather uses "likewise" to represent the sentiment of that phrase. The clipped prose avoids the possible impression, created by more expansive English translations, that Paul is delivering a ponderous and sweeping command for women: "I want the women to. . . ." Rather, in as concise a fashion as possible, he affirms the truth—dignifying women rather than denigrating them—that they are as responsible for worship decorum as the men are. But Paul gauges they are less apt to be in the thralldom of anger and more likely to incline toward featuring their feminine charm via dress rather than their moral and spiritual seriousness via the appearance and behavior that true worship calls for (v. 10).

"Women" is sometimes translated "wives"; similarly, the word for men in v. 8 can also mean "husbands." In both verses Paul means people who are of age, that is, adults. In his setting that would mean from about early teens and up. Adult women should "dress modestly."

This is not a sudden interjection of prudery. Rather, the topic begun in 2:1 and refreshed in v. 8 (prayer in the context of group assembly for worship) continues. Men's unholy behavior and anger can sabotage it, and so can women's wardrobe excesses and the mentality that gives rise to them. "Modestly" renders a form of *kosmios*, a word appearing elsewhere in the NT only in 1 Tim 3:2: "Now the overseer is to be . . . respectable [*kosmios*]." This trait is equally important for men and women, but NIV is correct to translate it "modestly" for contextual reasons when it appears in conjunction with women and "cloth-

274. Ryken, 83. Luther waxes eloquent on contextual considerations in women's dress, and how often (without sin) elegance befits the occasion in varying customs and locales (273–75).

ing" (*katastolē*).[275] Paul accepts as a given that women at prayer and worship will devote attention to their appearance ("adorning themselves"). But their adornment should pass muster before a higher bar than contemporary fashion at Ephesus.[276] Presumably Paul had observed that misguided concern for appearance could be a snare for women who had come to faith. Possibly he was aware of conditions at Ephesus raising particular concern, but his stated scope of focus is "everywhere" (v. 8), not just in that city.

Women in prayer and worship should be attractive most of all in terms of "decency and propriety." The former word (*aidōs*) is a NT hapax. The latter (*sōphrosynē*) appears also in Acts 26:25 and 1 Tim 2:15. Taken together, the words do not conjure up the image of cloistered women in burkas but rather dress that is not ostentatious but appropriate to the worship of the God and Christ of whom Paul speaks so frequently in the PE. Hot-tempered men in worship is a contradiction in terms, and men everywhere have ways of projecting such aggression (v. 8), however religiously cloaked. Likewise, women in any locale have ways of assuring by their intentional appearance that they will contribute more to the sensual consciousness of people around them, or simply to awareness of their beauty real or imagined, than to a consciousness of holy God.

The "not with" clause uses four words to list three places where there may be temptation to go overboard:[277] coiffure (*plegma*, a NT hapax), jewelry, and luxurious dress. The list is not exhaustive but illustrative, just as "anger or disputing" is far from the only possible male violation in worship deportment.[278] The words translated "gold," "pearls," and clothes that are "expensive" appear only here in Paul's writings. Rather than suspicion that here a stealthy forger betrays his or her non-Pauline identity, Paul might receive credit for not being a petty moralist who characteristically thunders against women's fashion trends.

Towner, following Bruce Winter,[279] proposes such a setting for this verse. Paul (like 1 Pet 3:3–5) draws on a secular critique of a "new woman" issue that

275. NIV's "dress modestly" renders *en katastolē kosmiō* ("in/with modest clothing"). This translation follows from supplying a verb ("I also want the women . . .") where Greek lacks one ("Likewise [also] women . . .").

276. See Montague, 61 ("Women's Fashions in the Roman Empire").

277. Paul uses *mē* rather than the indicative *ou* (both meaning "not"), which could indicate the hypothetical rather than actual nature of the excess he describes. Or *mē* could presuppose an unstated imperative or infinitive ("not [to dress] with elaborate hairstyles . . ."), which would call for *mē*. Certainty here is not possible. But the ambiguity justifies caution against being too sure that Paul is inveighing against a known concrete abuse.

278. In some congregational settings, for example, deference to the rich man and contempt for the poor was a problem; see Jas 2:1–7 (where v. 2 speaks of a wealthy man [*anēr*] apparently being catered to by congregations and their leaders).

279. Bruce W. Winter, *After Paul Left Corinth: The Influence of Secular Ethics and Social Change* (Grand Rapids: Eerdmans 2001); idem, *Roman Wives, Roman Widows: The Appearance of the New Women and the Pauline Communities* (Grand Rapids: Eerdmans, 2003).

had emerged in the Roman world at this time.[280] This context cannot be ruled out.[281] Other commentators focus on Greco-Roman parallels to shed light on Paul's rhetoric (sparse though it be).[282] But we search Paul's writings in vain for anything but superficial quotations from this corpus.[283] Paul was a theologian of Christ and the OT Scriptures, where the tension between vain feminine charm and true godliness had a hoary pedigree by Paul's time in his own cultural history: "Charm is deceptive, and beauty is fleeting; but a woman who fears the LORD is to be praised" (Prov 31:30). Isaiah mocked "haughty" women of Zion "with ornaments jingling on their ankles" (Isa 3:16). His description of their finery makes Paul's references look dull and flat by comparison (3:18–23): "the bangles and headbands and crescent necklaces, the earrings and bracelets and veils, the headdresses and anklets and sashes, the perfume bottles and charms, the signet rings and nose rings, the fine robes and the capes and cloaks, the purses and mirrors, and the linen garments and tiaras and shawls." Like Paul, Isaiah's concern is not to demonize feminine fashion but to depict the hazard of ostensibly worshipful people stuck on cosmetic excess while oblivious to God. Hosea uses the trope of vain beauty to describe Israel in his day: "'I will punish her for the days she burned incense to the Baals; she decked herself with rings and jewelry, and went after her lovers, but me she forgot,' declares the LORD" (Hos 2:13). In Amos one finds the elegant but decadent "cows of Bashan on Mount Samaria" (Amos 4:1).

Paul may have drawn on both OT and (if Towner and Winter are correct)[284] contemporary secular resources in being sensitive to the possible correlation between women's undue concern for their appearance and the threat such an attitude might pose to worship integrity. He goes on to summarize a better approach and outcome.

10 Deeds trump decoration "for women who profess to worship God." Paul wants the women consumed with concern, not for fancy trappings, but for "good deeds." The basic thrust of the verse is clear. A closer look at subtle features of Paul's language is called for.

280. Towner, *Letters*, 205.

281. Yet, see the caution voiced by Alicia J. Batten, "Neither Gold nor Braided Hair (1 Timothy 2:9; 1 Peter 3:3): Adornment, Honour, and Gender in Antiquity," *NTS* 55.4 (2009): 497n73.

282. For example, Marshall, with Towner, 449–50; Johnson, *First and Second Letters to Timothy*, 201; Collins, 66–68.

283. See NA[28] 878; UBS[4] 901. Two of the possible places where Paul cites pagan writers are in speeches in Acts (17:28; 26:14), whose historicity many scholars dispute. One of the Pauline passages is Titus 1:12, which many scholars reject as Pauline. That leaves one definite reference (1 Cor 15:33) in the ten-letter Pauline corpus.

284. Cautioning against placing too much weight on either at this point is Schreiner, "An Interpretation of 1 Timothy 2:9–15," 172.

In Greek the word order runs (using the NIV's words) "but what is appropriate for women who profess to worship God, with good deeds." If the understood verb after "but" is "I want," so that it parallels v. 8 ("I want the men") and v. 9 ("I also want the women"), in v. 10 Paul wants something in contrast ("but"). In that case, Paul can be understood as saying, "But [I want] what is appropriate for women professing reference for God." Paul's concern, then, continues to be with worship, which could be imperiled by appearance preoccupations (v. 9). Worship, not self-display, is fitting for worshiping women.

"Appropriate" translates a form of *prepō*, a word used three other times in Paul:

> Is it *proper* for a woman to pray to God with her head uncovered? (1 Cor 11:13)
>
> But sexual immorality and all impurity or covetousness must not even be named among you, as is *proper* among saints. (Eph 5:3 ESV)
>
> You, however, must teach what is *appropriate* to sound doctrine. (Titus 2:1)[285]

Certain situations call for certain attitudes, responses, or behaviors. The worship setting that has been Paul's concern since 2:1 invites women to a higher plane than v. 9 warns about.

"Profess to worship God" might sound as if the women are not really worshiping but are just professing to do so. But this understanding would be mistaken. This elegant phrase translates an idiom in which "profess" (*epangellomai*) is defined as "to claim to be well-accomplished in someth., *profess, lay claim to, give oneself out as an expert in*."[286] These women are competent and well-versed in what constitutes Christian worship. What they are skilled in is *theosebeia*, a word found only here in the NT but seven times in the LXX,[287] with translations there in NETS like "piety," "godliness," and "the worship of God." Marshall points out that it "is equivalent to *eusebeia*, which defines genuine Christian existence as the combination of the knowledge of God and the behaviour which grows out of that knowledge."[288] It appears six times in the AF, once referring to godliness and the other times referring to the faith

285. See also discussion of *prepō* at this verse in the commentary.

286. BDAG 356 (italics in original).

287. Gen 20:11; 4 Macc 7:6, 22; 17:15; Job 28:28; Sir 1:25; Bar 5:4. It is found nine times in Philo (with similar meanings) but never in Josephus. Neudorfer, *Erster Brief an Timotheus*, 123, notes that Gen 20:11 LXX translates the Hebrew expression "fear of God." He explains the word as meaning "letting God be God and conducting oneself before him accordingly."

288. Marshall, with Towner, 451.

and practice of Christians, or their religion.[289] Pursuit of God in a way that befits his majesty is a prominent feature of OT and early Christian faith and life.[290] The women in 1 Tim 2:9–10 have set lofty goals and know the means of attaining them. It would be a pity if lower concerns frustrated their highest intentions.

What the NIV highlights with its word order ("but with good deeds") appears at the end of the verse, almost parenthetically, in NA[28], the text from which English translations are made: *di' ergōn agathōn*. Johnson comments that "the construction . . . is unexpected," adding, "The idea is that these are the practices that reveal the internal moral dispositions of the women."[291] It should be kept in mind that Paul's concern is with women's worship integrity before God and others, not moral behavior for its own sake.[292] "With good deeds" (which could be translated "by/through good deeds") in NIV runs the risk of reducing Paul's concern primarily to certain random and discrete acts of kindness, like Boy Scouts of former generations in the US helping an old lady across the street, remembering their official slogan, "Do a good deed[293] daily." But "good deeds" is a less than ideal rendering of what is often translated "good works," referring especially to fulfillment of divine commands.[294] Sinners are not saved by good works,[295] but the commandments that define them are good, holy, and—in numerous instances where Paul cites them—binding.[296]

It is better to see "with good deeds" not as how women should dress (NIV: "I also want the women to dress modestly, with decency . . . not with elaborate hairstyles . . . but with good deeds") but as a means through which they attain their potential for mature and practiced corporate worship of God, a plausible description of what Paul has in mind by "what is fitting for women truly acknowledging God" (my translation) in worship rather than abusing the worship occasion to make a fashion statement. Women's lives need to be centered on activities in accordance with Scripture and applications of it (i.e., good works) far more than on fine-tuning or showcasing their beauty. Just as men are urged to bring holy hands to worship, women are called to bring

289. Godliness: 2 Clem. 20:4. Religion: Diogn. 1:1; 3:3; 4:5, 6; 6:4.

290. Of course many more words and phrases express the reality to which *theosebeia* refers.

291. Johnson (*First and Second Letters to Timothy*, 200) translates "through good works."

292. Thus the contention in Dibelius and Conzelmann, 47, that this verse points to a post-Pauline "rational conception of Christianity" is misguided.

293. "Deed" was used decades ago; today the Scout website uses "turn," which sounds even more symbolic and ceremonial.

294. See discussion of good deeds/works at Titus 1:16.

295. Rom 4:2; 9:12, 32; 11:6; Eph 2:9.

296. Thus Paul venerates "the very words of God" given to Israel (the OT; see Rom 3:1) and "the receiving of the law" (Rom 9:4).

consecrated lives, two ways of saying the same thing. This is a deeper matter than "with good deeds" is apt to convey.

Admittedly, the line can be fine between overdressing or overspending on dress and looking nice. Also, dress and appearance standards vary widely with times, places, age, weather, social and economic levels, occupations of worshipers, denominations, role in worship activity, and other variables. This verse does not justify facile inferences about the definition and price range of "appropriate" (NIV) dress for worshipers. It does, however, remind readers that appearance and its motivations are not matters of indifference to God when his people assemble in Christ's name.

11 Verse 10 ended with Paul noting that truly godly women at worship should make good works, not overdone appearance, their priority. Paul now individualizes that general directive, moving from "women" to "a woman."[297] In worship, each individual woman is to "learn in quietness and full submission." This directive could be felt as a sexist put-down. Or it could be understood as affirming an important principle in congregational assembly: a major goal (alongside prayer; see previous verses) is didactic equipping and building up through the teaching and learning that takes place. Wright's heading over his translation of 1 Tim 2:8–15 is apt: "Women Must Be Allowed to Be Learners."[298] By comparison, there is no place for expending comparable energy impressing each other with clothes and accessories.

Paul takes seriously each woman's importance as a learner. "Scholars have often pointed out that this injunction represents an advance over some traditions in Judaism that forbade women from learning."[299] One is reminded of numerous incidents in the Gospels where Jesus took time for face-to-face instruction of women. Each one who came to Jesus and who became his disciple embarked on a pilgrimage of learning. Early church practice comported with this practice: "They devoted themselves to the apostles' teaching and to fellowship, to the breaking of bread and to prayer" (Acts 2:42). This verb describes not only men. Each woman was, and now also at Ephesus should be, taken seriously as a disciple, every bit as much as any man.

In v. 11 Paul can be viewed as putting his finger on three factors that may stand in the way of a woman growing in understanding so that, as she worships, she can progress toward her maximum potential in knowledge of God and facility in doing good works (v. 10). The first factor is learning. Paul

297. In principle, *gynē* (woman) could be translated "wife," but nothing in the context suggests Paul is limiting his remarks only to a married female.

298. Wright, 21.

299. Schreiner, "An Interpretation of 1 Timothy 2:9–15," 184. So also Trebilco and Rae, 56: "This represents a striking departure from the social attitudes of the day. Jewish women were generally not instructed in the Torah, and so were generally not able to teach each other."

wants no woman to neglect this core aspect of corporate worship. All four Gospels affirm that John the Baptist's movement attracted "disciples,"[300] and the Jesus movement followed suit (note Matt 28:18–20). To varying degrees, all of Paul's letters are didactic—they confirm or extend teachings (or doctrines) relevant to belief in and adherence to the gospel message. Teaching and learning are a steady emphasis in the PE (with Titus 2 emphasizing teaching by and of women). Second Timothy 2:2 epitomizes Paul's discipleship strategy: "And the things you have heard me say in the presence of many witnesses entrust to reliable people who will also be qualified to teach others." For a woman to worship aright, she must take her place in a community that enables and expects her to grow in faith by learning and eventually teaching what she learned to others as well. The gospel is not just something received once, like a tattoo, but a live communiqué that is learned and then transforms the learner (by the truth learned and the Spirit who applies it). Paul wrote to the Colossians that they "learned [*emathete*]" the gospel "from Ephaphras" (1:7); Paul wrote to the Ephesians about how they had "learned [*emathete*] Christ" (Eph 4:20).

In English "a woman should learn" (NIV) is an indicative declaration. In Greek it is a third person singular imperative: "Let a woman learn." The verb "learn" (*manthanō*) is cognate with the noun "disciple, learner" (*mathētēs*). Paul is not moralizing, propounding a general theory of what women should do. He rather continues to underscore for Timothy things that are essential for disciples of Jesus, men and women, in worship—the command is not first of all to women but to Timothy as the person responsible for oversight of Ephesian worship. The sense of Paul's command is "See to it, Timothy, that the woman who seeks to learn does so."

For the whole congregation, Paul is reminding Timothy that worship calls for prayerfulness (vv. 1–2) based on solid understanding of God and Christ's mission (vv. 3–7), in which the church participates, free from (for example) the bane of male combativeness and aggression (v. 8), as well as from the distraction of women's preoccupation with appearance (v. 9). Timothy is rather to ensure a worship setting in which a woman is encouraged to embrace her call as a disciple to learn.

After learning, the second factor important for promoting each woman's worship is an ambience that will enhance her learning: "in quietness." Contextually, at the very least this quality reaffirms the payoff of freedom from hot-headed male clamor (v. 8), as well as from the buzz of female appearance competition (v. 9), with women instead displaying spiritual and ethical seriousness (v. 10). But the words "in quietness" convey more than the sum benefit of previous verses.

300. Matt 11:2; Mark 2:18; 6:29; Luke 5:33; 7:18; 11:1; John 1:35; 3:25.

It is tempting, and in a Western setting perhaps unavoidable, that something like a repressive "Shut up!" will be read into Paul's words. But *hēsychia* (quietness, rest) rarely refers to a blanket prohibitive policy against spoken expression. Used only two other times in the NT, it refers once to the space afforded for Paul to be heard when he addressed a restless crowd (Acts 22:2).[301] BDAG (440) notes that "here such concepts as 'reverence,' 'devotion,' 'respect' may have some influence." This is attentive silence for the sake of giving someone a hearing.[302] In the case of v. 11, that someone would be the Ephesian church leader(s) instructing the congregation, and ultimately God or Christ, who are mediated through the gospel as it is taught. "The call then is not for total verbal silence from women, but for them to exhibit a peaceful and gentle attitude" in their task of learning.[303]

The other NT occurrence is 2 Thess 3:12. There, as in 1 Tim 2:11, there is a connection to working (cf. 1 Tim 2:10: "with good works"), as Paul writes, "Such people we command and urge in the Lord Jesus Christ to settle down [*meta hēsychia ergazomenoi*] and earn the food they eat." The Greek words convey not muteness (hence NIV does not translate "with silence") but orderly, industrious, and self-responsible labor in accordance with dominical and apostolic teaching. People freeloading off others will cause disturbance and unrest. Paul calls Thessalonian readers to pay attention to what will make for a stable and peaceful atmosphere in Christ's service rather than self-serving disruption.[304] In the same way, Paul calls on Timothy to see that each woman in the Ephesian setting is protected from distractions for the sake of the redemption afforded by teaching (and thus learning) able to save both Timothy and his hearers (see 1 Tim 4:16). An analogous situation might be Martha, "distracted by all the preparations that had to be made," in comparison with Mary, "who sat at the Lord's feet listening to what he said" (Luke 10:39–40). Here was *hēsychia*. Was it demeaning?

A third factor enhancing the learning mandate is denoted by "full submission." Again, in a Western setting, these are words that easily excite resent-

301. For a close parallel, see Josephus, *Jewish Antiquities* 5.235). He uses the word thirty-four times. Philo (who uses the word fifty-six times) notes the close association between learning and strategic silence: "Those who have learnt [*mathontes*] to speak have also learnt [*memathēkenai*] to be silent [*hēsychazein*], the same capacity teaching a man both lines of conduct. But those men who relate what they ought not, do not display the faculty of eloquence, but the weakness of their faculty of silence [*hēsychias*]" (*The Worse Attacks the Better* 102).

302. In Philo the word often connotes not verbal "silence" but social or situational "tranquility." See, for example, *Drunkenness* 97, 104; *Posterity of Cain* 108; *Agriculture* 132.

303. Trebilco and Rae, 56.

304. The LXX uses *hēsychia* (quiet) only twelve times but in three of those passages pairs it with *eirēnē* (peace): 1 Chr 4:40; 22:9; Ezek 38:11. *Hēsychia* is translated "peace" in 1 Macc 9:58 (NETS).

ment. The temptation is to read into them a patriarchal command for every woman to submit fully to any man. But to don those spectacles in reading this passage would be anachronistic. If the exegesis thus far is on the right track, then Paul has in mind a pastoral leader's (i.e., Timothy's) responsibility for each woman's worshipful learning, not her suppression, much less denigration.

"In full submission" translates *en pasē hypotagē*. One attempt to render this phrase is "They should listen to what men have to say" (NLV). Equally periphrastic is "being fully ready to obey" (ICB) and "being ready to cooperate in everything" (NCV). In an anti-authoritarian Western setting sensitive especially to perceived oppression of women, no option seems ideal.

TLV takes a more promising tack: "Let a woman receive training in a quiet demeanor *with complete respect for order.*" This wording conveys the dominical and apostolic order universal in the Pauline churches (see 1 Cor 14:40). It still requires explanation, but at least it avoids the impression that Paul is issuing men a carte blanche to demand women's wordless compliance at least in church matters and perhaps in all of life.

Explanations of the phrase should note that the word translated "submission" (used four times in the NT, and only by Paul) can have a positive connotation. Admittedly there is one use in a negative setting: in Gal 2:4–5 Paul assures his readers that he "did not yield in *submission* even for a moment" to "false brothers," in order that "the truth of the gospel might be preserved for" them (ESV). "Submission" to gospel subversion would be evil, as Paul recognizes, and is not an innate good. In contrast, in 2 Cor 9:13 Paul speaks of the Corinthians' "obedience" (*hypotagē*) shown in their "confession of the gospel of Christ" (NIV). This is not blind compliance but informed, purposeful, and personal response to God. In 1 Tim 3:4 Paul will mention the need for prospective overseers to have children who are *en . . . hypotagē*, meaning in subjection or obedience to parents (a reflection of the Decalogue). Subjection is not usually a bad word in biblical parlance;[305] it does not have to be in 1 Tim 2:11. *GNC* translates this phrase as follows: "In learning something a woman should do so in silence, showing herself submissive in every way."

There is also the question of to whom this "full submission" is rendered. Paul did not view his gospel as humanly given (Gal 1:11–12), and he was an apostle not by his own initiative but "by the command of God our Savior and of Christ Jesus our hope" (1 Tim 1:1). In the flow of 1 Tim 2, where the topic to

305. Note a primary finding of M. Sydney Park's important study *Submission within the Godhead and the Church in the Epistle to the Philippians* (London: T&T Clark, 2007), 185: "Submission, as portrayed in Philippians, is not the consequence of oppression or coercion. Rather, it is offered freely, and reflects the self-giving character of God in the salvation events (2.6–11). . . . Submission, on all three levels of relations, intradivine, God-believer and inter-believer, is intrinsic to the nature of soteriology, identity of the Godhead and consequently the identity of believers." This Pauline understanding suffuses 1 Tim 2 and lifts it above current gender debates.

this point has been worship, there is sparse contextual ground for reading Paul as calling on women to submit fully either to him or to Timothy.

Rather, "a woman" in worship is to be provided with a setting conducive to her discipleship calling to learn "in quietness," not disruption, and in "full submission" either to what she is being taught,[306] to God, who stands behind the Christian message and comes to his people by his Spirit through their hearing of it, or to both. The notion of women in general being in "full submission" to men in general is completely foreign to the discourse flow. Given the lengths Paul goes in his letters (including the PE) to inform, instruct, exhort, and elicit the fellowship of agreement with apostolic teaching (not demand mindless "full submission"), a reading imputing sexism to Paul either brings a tin ear to the passage or deploys an unhelpful hermeneutic of suspicion. Complementarian readings seeing a license for men to demand women's obeisance to them find just as little basis in the text contextually considered.

In sum, v. 11 is consistent with the discourse flow leading up to it. Paul counsels Timothy to make sure that in worship each woman finds space to attend to her mandate as a disciple to learn. This learning takes place as she turns away from the distractions sketched in v. 9 and takes seriously the implications of worshiping God through full attention to good works (v. 10). To know and do good works in worshipful relationship to God through Jesus, she is given, like every disciple, the means of grace of learning (v. 11). Timothy is to do all that is possible and necessary to provide a sphere of quiet for this learning to take place, along with encouragement of each woman to receive fully what she learns of God and from God, to whom in Christian worship each woman and man alike bends the knee through prayer. Paul, through the oversight Timothy and others will administer, appeals to her reverent mind for the sake of the good works to which women are called.

12 Paul continues his counsel to Timothy regarding women at worship, with the focus still on the representative individual learning woman of v. 11. In v. 12 Paul excuses her from direct responsibility for two signature activities of a congregational pastor: teaching and spiritual oversight. Both were modeled by Jesus, the epitome of pastoral leaders,[307] who above all called and taught disciples, and to that end led and watched over them. He taught them and served as their spiritual overseer, in the language of v. 12. This is a fair summary of the core of what a woman in community worship is indirectly charged[308] *not*

306. This submission would imply attention to and respect for pastoral teachers. See Schreiner, "An Interpretation of 1 Timothy 2:9–15," 187. Yet, ultimately pastoral teachers are ministers (servants) of God and his word, not the objects of women's terminal attention and worship. Church leaders who conflate submission to them with submission to God or Scripture tread hazardous ground.

307. See John 10:11, 14 ("the Good Shepherd"); 1 Pet 5:4 ("the Chief Shepherd").

308. Paul is addressing Timothy, not women or a woman.

to concern herself with when it comes to the congregation as whole, men and women. These duties, rather, are assigned to overseers (ch. 3).

"I do not permit [*ouk epitrepō*]"[309] is a tactful way of reminding Timothy of the division of labor that obtained in the congregational worship setting. The fact that *epitrepō* is present tense should not be pushed to signify that this is only Paul's current opinion or policy, which might well change: in plenty of other places he uses the present to convey standing, unaltering directives (e.g., Rom 12:1, 3; 15:30; 16:7; 1 Cor 4:14; 1 Tim 2:1).[310]

Paul wants each woman to be affirmed in her worshipful learning, free from unhealthy preoccupation with fashion (v. 9), intent on godliness as expressed in good works (v. 10). Verse 12 reveals that these works do not include the pursuit of church oversight as implied by the qualifications listed in the next chapter (and for Timothy this use confirms that Paul is not stating a new policy).[311] An expanded paraphrase of vv. 11–12 may be helpful as a guide to the explanation given below: "Let a woman at worship concentrate quietly on her calling as a disciple to learn—fully intent on what God has to teach her. That is to say, I do not want that woman to teach and exercise oversight over a man (that is your job as pastoral leader, Timothy, as well as men whom you and the church vet and appoint), but as I said, to have a quiet space for learning preserved for her when she is at worship."

It is widely agreed that this is the most controversial verse in 1 Timothy and perhaps in the PE overall. The main reason is likely its function, real or perceived, in limiting women's teaching and other church leadership involvement.[312] It is said to articulate a patriarchal understanding that is unacceptable among many who study and comment on the verse. Its face-value statement is simply unpalatable in modern Western society. Complementarians have been accused of vesting too much importance in this single, hard-to-interpret verse. Jamin Hübner makes this case. He examines "how the verse is handled in light of the traditional hermeneutical principle of interpreting obscure passages in light of the more clear" and concludes that complementarians are misguided in treating 1 Tim 2:12 "as a clear passage," suggesting they may do so "out of an effort to legitimize the ban on women pastors."[313]

309. Used also by Paul in 1 Cor 14:34; 16:7.

310. For extended discussion, see Schreiner, "An Interpretation of 1 Timothy 2:9–15," 188–90.

311. That is, male congregational leadership, like male headship in marriage, is ubiquitous in the early church, as attested by the NT. Definitive anticipations of it include the preponderance of male presence in the leadership of the OT faith community and Jesus's selection of a dozen men, not some proportion of both men and women.

312. The antipathy with which this verse is regarded by some is epitomized in Twomey, 45. This book prints a photo from a now defunct website (russelsteapot.com/know-your-bible) of a woman with black electrical tape in the shape of a cross on her forehead. The upright portion of the cross extends down her nose to her mouth, which is completely taped shut.

313. J. Hübner, "Revisiting the Clarity of Scripture in 1 Timothy 2:12," *JETS* 59.1 (2016): 99.

In this commentary I seek to show that the discourse flow, the unusual words Paul uses, and the argument he makes are tolerably coherent, given recent scholarship with which Hübner is unfamiliar,[314] within the framework of historic understanding of its teaching.

Regarding how hard the verse is to interpret, an anecdote and query may be permitted. Australian NT scholar Claire S. Smith tells of a new Christian, a university-aged woman in "an ethnic based church" who read 1 Tim 2 for the first time.[315] When asked whether she found it difficult, she replied, "No, it's easy. Paul is saying women shouldn't teach in church, because that's the way God wants it." It would be easy, Smith notes, to suppose that "her ethnic cultural background probably made it easier for her to do that." But Smith continues: "But can you see that the opposite might also be true—that *our* culture influences *our* reading of the text, and that many of the difficulties we find in it might exist because of *our* culture and *our* personalities and not because of the text itself?" Applying the doctrine of the clarity of Scripture to mean that egalitarian interpretation of 1 Tim 2:12 is mandatory may underestmate the effect of cultural background in egalitarian hermeneutics and exegesis.

Another reason for controversy is the presence of three major issues that play into exegesis, translation, and application of the verse: (1) the historical setting of Ephesus, (2) the meaning of *authenteō* ("assume authority over" in the NIV), and (3) the grammatical construction involving the expression "teach or . . . assume authority." Each of these matters has given rise to a sizable literature, too extensive to be canvassed and assessed here. Below we will characterize the issues and summarize the solutions at which the major study *Women in Church* has arrived.

The first issue is *the historical setting.*[316] Many commentators feel that Gal 3:28 is a normative declaration: "There is neither Jew nor Gentile, neither slave nor free, nor is there male and female, for you are all one in Christ Jesus." 1 Tim 2:12 seems to contradict this statement. The author (whether Paul or someone else) must be addressing, or pretending to address, a local setting unlike other locations, since Paul's genuine counsel is identifiable by its egalitarian orientation.[317] As Collins puts it, 1 Tim 2 ranks with other passages that "are ad hoc compositions whose essential import relates immediately and directly only to the

314. Included here would be the findings of authors in the third edition of Köstenberger and Schreiner, *Women in the Church*. Some of these findings are reviewed below.

315. Quotations in this paragraph are from Smith, *God's Good Design*, 24. Italics in quotations are Smith's. The paragraph largely follows Yarbrough, "Familiar Paths and a Fresh Matrix," 275.

316. See also Schreiner, "An Interpretation of 1 Timothy 2:9–15," 166–74. My comments above, however, are independent of Schreiner's remarks.

317. See, for example, F. F. Bruce, *A Mind for What Matters* (Grand Rapids: Eerdmans, 1990), 262–64 ("Women in the Church: A Biblical Survey").

situation that dictated their composition."[318] Marshall concludes that "there must, then, be special reasons for the prohibition [against women teaching] here."[319]

Doubtless there were special conditions at Ephesus; all historical settings have their distinctive features. But the question is whether the historical setting (real or fictive) at Ephesus was so different from other places and times that the counsel found in 1 Tim 2:12 has no relevance beyond its original location. Were there, for example, uneducated women at Ephesus or women teaching false doctrine or a gnostic heresy advocated by women at Ephesus that limited the applicability of what Paul writes to that particular setting?[320]

In response, it should be noted that, whether we view 2:1 or 2:8 as the head verse of this passage, both have a universal purview: "prayers . . . for all people" in v. 1, and "everywhere" (NIV) or "in every place" (ESV) in v. 8. The author gives no hint that his charge to Timothy (1:3, 5) is so specific to Ephesus that what he says about prayer and men and women in worship would not have applied in other settings. In fact, Johnson has shown how similar "the situation sketched by 1 Timothy" is to "that presented by 1 Corinthians."[321] Claire Smith's study makes the same point based on a different data set.[322] Paul is applying the policy and practice of apostolic churches everywhere to Ephesus, not formulating a specific set of guidelines for that setting alone. Collins observes, for example, that Paul's counsel in v. 12 "does not necessarily indicate that the Pastor's community was troubled by false teaching coming from a group of liberated and charismatic women," as some claim.[323]

Moreover, as S. M. Baugh has shown, "The search for a distinctive background" for 1 Timothy has "led to many fanciful reconstructions of Ephesus." In response, he shows that "Ephesus' society and religion—even the cult of Artemis Ephesia—shared typical features with many other contemporary Greco-Roman cities. Ephesus was thoroughly Greek in background and character and showed the beginnings of Roman influence. . . . Hence we have every reason to expect that when Paul restricted women from teaching and exercising rule through special office over a man, he applied it to 'every place' (v. 8)."[324]

There is, then, justification for viewing 1 Tim 2:12 as both distinctive (since Paul writes in and to a particular time and place to address distinct issues) and as universal in scope as any other NT epistle.[325] While there were

318. Collins, 75.

319. Marshall, with Towner, 455 (commenting on 1 Tim 2:12).

320. For documentation of and reasonable objection to these proposals, see Wayne Grudem, *Evangelical Feminism: A New Path to Liberalism?* (Wheaton, IL: Crossway, 2006), 171–91.

321. Johnson, *First and Second Letters to Timothy*, 144.

322. Smith, *Pauline Communities*.

323. Collins, 70.

324. Baugh, "A Foreign World," 60n100, 60–61.

325. So also, on canonical grounds, Wall, with Steele, 93.

undoubtedly issues facing Timothy relating to women at Ephesus that were unique as far as our precise knowledge base goes—especially as regards marriage (4:3) and widowhood (5:3–16)—Paul's counsel can be reasonably harmonized with his statements in other epistles, as well as with the narrative picture furnished in the NT and the Bible overall that describes and prescribes male responsibility for many of the leadership duties "in God's household" (3:15).

The second issue in understanding v. 12 is *the meaning of authenteō*.[326] In v. 12 teaching is paired with a word that has been assigned two basic meanings, one negative and one more neutral.

Table 14. The meaning of *authenteō*

Negative construals of *authenteō* (pejorative translations)	Neutral construals of *authenteō* (nonpejorative translations)
But I suffer not a woman to teach, nor to *usurp authority over* the man. (KJ21)	I do not permit a woman to teach or to *exercise authority over* a man. (ESV)[327]
I don't allow a wife to teach or to *control* her husband. (CEB)	I do not let women teach men or *have authority over* them. (NLT)[328]
Moreover, in the area of teaching, I am not allowing a woman to *instigate conflict toward* a man. (ISV)	
I do not permit a woman to teach or to *assume authority over* a man. (NIV)	
I never let women teach men or *lord it over* them. (TLB)	
But I do not allow a woman to train or *dictate to* a man. (TLV)[329]	
It's not my habit to allow women to teach in a way that *wrenches authority from* a man. (VOICE)	

326. For overview of discussion stretching back several decades, see Schreiner, "An Interpretation of 1 Timothy 2:9–15," 194–97.

327. "Exercise authority" is also found, for example, in AMP, LEB, NASB, NET, WEB.

328. "Have authority" is also found, for example, in ASV ("have dominion"), GNT, GW, HSCB, NKJV, RSV.

329. Cf. Wright, 22: "I'm not saying that women should teach men, or try to dictate to them."

The difference between the two translation emphases is clear. On the left, pejorative side, translators view *authenteō* negatively in the sense that power is wielded in an abusive way or initiated in an undesirable manner. Even more sensational translations have been proposed: "murder," "commit violence," "proclaim oneself author of a man."[330] None of these latter renderings has yet found its way into a major published translation. On the right side of the table, *authenteō* is viewed as denoting a neutral or positive pastoral activity.

In light of recent research by Al Wolters, the negative renderings should be rejected.[331] His very thorough canvassing of "cognates, immediate context, ancient versions, patristic commentary, and the broad use of the verb elsewhere" confirms that in this passage the word carries neither a negative nor an ingressive sense. Negative would imply an inappropriate or illicit exercise of power (as in TLB or TLV in table 14); ingressive would imply initiation of such exercise (as in ISV or NIV in table 14). He calls on BDAG and L&N to remove hints of these connotations, bringing them in line with the German lexicon on which BDAG is based but from which it has departed.[332]

Wolters's findings are extended by Denny Burk in an inquiry into the validity of the NIV's "assume authority" translation. He shows Linda Belleville's claim to be mistaken that the weight of translation history is solely on the side of a negative or pejorative translation of *authenteō*.[333] In careful interaction with the NIV Committee on Bible Translation, Burk argues that the change from the 1984 NIV's "have authority over a man" (i.e., noningressive and nonpejorative) to the present-day NIV's "assume authority over a man" (i.e., ingressive and apt to be understood pejoratively) is unfortunate. He concludes, in line with Wolters's philological findings, that in 1 Tim 2:12 *authenteō* "denotes the positive exercise of authority over men (not its abuse or wrongful assumption)."[334] It may seem "a reasonable conjecture . . . that the women at Ephesus . . . were trying to gain the advantage over the men

330. For references, see Grudem, *Evangelical Feminism*, 199–206.

331. See A. Wolters, "The Meaning of Αὐθεντέω," in Köstenberger and Schreiner, *Women in the Church*, 3rd ed., 65–115. Note also a pair of related, earlier studies by the same author: "ΑΥΘΕΝΤΗΣ and Its Cognates in Biblical Greek," *JETS* 52. (2009): 719–29; and "An Early Parallel of Αὐθεντεῖν," *JETS* 54.4 (2011): 673–84.

332. See Wolters, "The Meaning of Αὐθεντέω," 113, 114. "Ingressive" here is conveyed in the NIV rendering "assume authority."

333. D. Burk, "New and Old Departures in the Translation of Αὐθεντεῖν in 1 Timothy 2:12," in Köstenberger and Schreiner, *Women in the Church*, 3rd ed., 281–86.

334. Burk, "New and Old Departures in Translation," 296. Burk is not convinced by the NIV Committee's insistence that "assume authority" just means "to begin or take on authority" in a benign sense. This is a semantic possibility for "assume" in a nuanced English expression, but it is not compelling rendering for *authenteō* in 2:12, where contextually Paul appears to be ruling out a woman's filling that position, period.

by teaching in a dictatorial fashion,"[335] but the philology runs against the conjecture.

The third issue considered here is *the grammatical construction involving the expression "teach or . . . assume authority."* Andreas Köstenberger has shown that the Greek underlying NIV's translation "to teach or to assume authority over" follows a clear and consistent pattern.[336] There are two options, one positive and one negative. In the positive option, "two activities or concepts are viewed positively in and of themselves, but their exercise is prohibited . . . due to circumstances or conditions adduced in the context." In the negative option, "two activities or concepts are viewed negatively, and consequently their exercise is prohibited or . . . they are to be avoided."[337] Since "teaching" is a positive activity in the PE and in Paul's letters generally unless the context indicates otherwise, the exercise of authority Paul prohibits is not something sinister or excessive but positive, just like the teaching.

Furthermore, some translations and commentators try to combine the two actions in a sort of hendiadys—"teach in a way that wrenches authority from a man" (VOICE), or "teaching in a manner which is heavy-handed and abuses authority."[338] But such interpretations run against the pattern of the construction itself, in which the two activities overlap but remain distinct. Köstenberger concludes that, "in referring to two related activities in his prohibition, Paul is moving from a more specific activity (teaching) to a more general activity (exercising spiritual authority over men)."[339] Another way of understanding the two activities is as summarizing the pastoral task in a twofold manner: instruction and oversight. But the principle remains: these activities are discrete and do not merge into one. And in any case, "just as v. 11 was not a demand for all learning to be done in silence, as an unqualified absolute, but was concerned with women's learning in the midst of the assembled people of God, so also the teaching here has the same setting and perspective in view."[340] In other settings women's teaching is commended or mandated,[341] just as their vocal participation is assumed and affirmed (e.g., 1 Cor 11:5).

The last clause in v. 12, "she must be quiet," is translated brusquely in the NIV. Another understanding is possible. Just as Paul directed Timothy

335. Belleville, 61.

336. A. Köstenberger, "A Complex Sentence: The Syntax of 1 Timothy 2:12," in Köstenberger and Schreiner, *Women in the Church*, 3rd ed., 117–61. In the same volume, see also by Köstenberger, "Conclusion," 341–46, and "Appendix: LXX and First-Century Greco-Roman Syntactic Parallels to 1 Timothy 2:12," 347–61.

337. Köstenberger, "Conclusion," 342.

338. Witherington, 228, drawing on Marshall, with Towner.

339. Köstenberger, "Conclusion," 342–43.

340. Knight, 140.

341. See, for example, Titus 2:3–5; 2 Tim 1:5; 3:14, 15; Acts 18:25, 26.

to let each woman learn "in quietness" (*en hēsychia*) in v. 11, so at the end of v. 12 he repeats that women are be undisturbed (*en hēsychia*) in their learning rather than being tasked with the duties of pastoral instruction and oversight as exercised in corporate worship. "I do not permit" one set of duties, Paul writes, but he does mandate that each woman as an avid learner "be a quiet listener" (CEB), "remain at peace" (CJB), "listen quietly" (NLT), or "be in a quiet demeanor" (TLV). "She must be quiet" is wrongly understood as asserting that Paul's aim is reached when women are silenced, whether in worship or in some other setting where some male wishes. The passage teaches rather that Timothy is to see that, in the worship assembly, each woman's learning potential is encouraged and enhanced.[342] Wright helpfully summarizes (though his reference to Artemis is speculative): "Paul is saying, like Jesus in Luke 10, that women must have the space and leisure to study and learn in their own way, not in order that they may muscle in and take over the leadership as in the Artemis-cult, but so that men and women alike can develop whatever gifts of learning, teaching, and leadership God is giving them."[343]

13 "For" (*gar*) indicates that Paul is giving a reason for his counsel about women.[344] In mentioning Adam and Eve,[345] he seems to have Gen 2 in view, for his choice of "formed" (from *plassō*) reflects a distinct word found repeatedly there in reference to Adam's creation (Gen 2:7, 8, 15).[346] While Gen 1 stresses the unity of woman and man in creation with a broad, day-by-creation-day overview (vv. 26–28), Gen 2 reveals details of human origins. Adam was "formed first" (1 Tim 2:12; see Gen 2:7). Later, God purposed to furnish a "helper" (v. 18), taken not from the earth alone as was Adam (v. 7) but in some sense from Adam (v. 23: "she was taken out of man"). As Paul elaborates elsewhere, "Man did not come from woman, but woman from man; neither was man created for woman, but woman for man" (1 Cor 11:8–9). This is not necessarily Pauline patriarchy but a reasonable articulation of what the Genesis text describes.

Paul draws, then, on the protology, chronology, and teleology of Gen 1–2 to make application in his own time in Ephesus, reminiscent of Christ referring to the same chapters to make a point about the permanence of marriage

342. Cf. the intent behind Alice Mathews, *Preaching That Speaks to Women* (Grand Rapids: Baker Academic, 2003).

343. Wright, 25–26.

344. Arguments that Paul is not giving a reason for his teaching, just positing an example or illustration of what happens when women wrongly teach men, are unconvincing. See Schreiner, "An Interpretation of 1 Timothy 2:9–15," 200–201.

345. For broader reflections, see R. Yarbrough, "Adam in the New Testament," in *Adam, the Fall, and Original Sin*, ed. Hans Madueme and Michael Reeves (Grand Rapids: Baker Academic, 2014), 33–53 (on Adam in the PE, see 49–50).

346. So also Collins, 70–71.

in God's creation order (Matt 19:4–6). In an ecclesial and social setting where created gifts like food and marital sexuality were disparaged (1 Tim 4:1–3), "Adam was formed first, then Eve" is a declaration "that the creation order is still in effect."[347]

In that order, man and woman are equal in ontological standing before God, but not identical or interchangeable as to what God expects of them relative to their created sexual giftedness. Their simultaneous unity *and* diversity are stressed: "So God created mankind in his own image, in the image of God he created them [unity]; male and female he created them [diversity]" (Gen 1:27). The distinction between the two (evident, e.g., in the fact that in the biological family it is women who are mothers and men who are fathers) gives a basis for differing responsibilities in certain settings "in God's household, which is the church of the living God" (1 Tim 3:15). One of those settings is congregational worship. In this setting, tested men called overseers (see 1 Tim 3) are tasked with instruction and oversight as these responsibilities are administered in public assembly, just as in Gen 2 certain responsibilities were assigned to Adam, not Eve.[348] The godly woman who utilizes the worship setting to rest in God and learn is analogous to Eve before the calamity of Gen 3.[349] It is Timothy's task to preserve that space through those he advances to overseer rank and through his own diligence and example.

14 The connection between v. 13 and v. 14 is as tight as the connection between Gen 2 and Gen 3. Verse 13 argues from the prefall creation order (pronounced by God "very good," Gen 1:31) to justify a division of labor in the worship assembly that will permit the godly woman to focus on learning, leaving the pastoral teaching and oversight to the overseers. Verse 14 shows Paul's realism: Timothy and others at Ephesus inhabit a post-Edenic world order. Sin has entered, and with it came death (Rom 5:12), and thus the need for a second Adam to undo the effects of "the transgression of Adam, who was a type of the one who was to come" (Rom 5:14). Christ has come, and Paul and Timothy are ministers of the good news that God's people can live redeemed lives, despite Adam's original and their subsequent sin. First Timothy 2 outlines protocol for worship under the auspices of that sin-dispelling gospel.

347. Towner, "1–2 Timothy and Titus," 897.

348. Stressed and expounded by M. Cooper and J. Cabellero, "Reasoning through the Creation Order as a Basis for the Prohibition in 1 Timothy 2:12," *Presby* 43.1 (2017): 30–38.

349. For exposition and refutation of egalitarian claims that this text is unclear or not central to Paul's argument (M. Evans, G. Fee), that it nullifies logic and justice (S. Motyer), that redemptive history has moved on from Paul's circumstances (W. Webb), that Paul's argument is illogical (P. Hanson, P. Jewett), that Paul was speaking only of women who spread heresy or were uneducated (G. Bilezikian, B. Mickelsen, P. Payne, P. Zehr), that Paul is calling only for conformity to norms of his time (P. Towner), and many other objections, see Schreiner, "An Interpretation of 1 Timothy 2:9–15," 202–10.

The opening words of v. 14, however, seem at first nonsensical: "And Adam was not the one deceived." For Paul, Adam is the prototypical sinner. How can one sin without being deceived? Even if a man sins with his eyes wide open, so to speak, he is calculating that he can somehow get by with it, but Paul knows that "the wages of sin is death" (Rom 6:23). And actually, by adding the words "the one," the NIV slightly softens the Greek, which can be rendered, "And Adam was not deceived." This is a categorical declaration. Yet, elsewhere Paul writes that "by a man [i.e., Adam] came death," and "in Adam all die" (1 Cor 15:21, 22). Paul clearly viewed Adam as guilty of succumbing to the serpent's wiles along with Eve. Both were deceived. But in Eden, Eve took the lead.

This narratival observation suggests another translation. Paul's meaning is reasonably clear if vv. 13 and 14 are held in sufficiently close connection.[350] For then the word "first" (*prōtos*), which is in a prominent position in v. 13, applies likewise to v. 14. Adam *was* deceived, but he was not deceived *first*. A devil in the details of Gen 3 is that, whereas Adam was created first, had prior delegated jurisdiction over Eden, received Eve as his equal (but complementary, not identical) partner, and as the responsible primary caretaker should have resisted the serpent's advance for God's sake on behalf of both himself and Eve, the serpent found a way to subvert the one designed to be Adam's "helper" (Gen 2:18, 20). At a bad time and in an ill-advised fashion, Adam followed her lead (Gen 3:6). Yet, Adam is still held responsible for human sin: God approaches him first, not Eve, after they sin (Gen 3:9–12). In the NT overall, original sin is booked to Adam's account, not Eve's.[351]

Paul's observation in v. 14 is simply that the male leadership mandated in v. 12 is justified, not only in terms of a "very good" world (Gen 2; cf. 1 Tim 2:13), but also in a fallen world—in the wake of what Gen 3 describes about Eve running ahead of Adam, or Adam idly allowing (if he was present) the serpent to do his worst, or both. God will continue to redeem the world through men (like Adam) in the household of God leading in fulfilling his will, with women no less important ("in the Lord woman is not independent of man, nor is man independent of woman"; 1 Cor 11:11) but not identical in their public worship and pastoral duties. Timothy can be sure that worship will arrive at its God-intended effects with women learning rather than seeking to do what the overseers are charged with.

350. The *gar* ("For") at the beginning of v. 13 can be viewed as marking both v. 13 and 14 together (joined by the conjunctive *kai*) as an explanation for v. 12. Following Paul Barnett, Schreiner also accepts an implied "first" as part of the v. 14 discourse. See Schreiner, "An Interpretation of 1 Timothy 2:9–15," 214–15.

351. See Yarbrough, "Adam in the New Testament."

The language of v. 14 bears more scrutiny. Some hold that Paul's word choice implies a difference between Adam's being deceived (from *apataō*)[352] and Eve's (from *exapataō*)[353] being "*really* deceived."[354] It is more likely that the change is merely stylistic. In the LXX the woman uses *apataō* to describe what the serpent did to her (Gen 3:13). It is unlikely that Paul uses *exapataō* in 1 Tim 2:14 with a different meaning that would contradict the LXX. In 2 Cor 11:3 he uses *exapataō* to describe the serpent's deception of Eve, with no discernible special emphasis. The words are interchangeable.[355] As explained above, Paul's point is likely that Adam was not the first to fall to the deception that undid them both that day.

Eve "became a sinner" in the NIV rendering, which makes Paul sound more accusatory than is justified. Just as v. 14a says flatly "Adam was not [the first] deceived," v. 14b can be rendered "but the woman, being deceived, came/fell into transgression."[356] The noun "sinner" or "transgressor" is not used,[357] which comports with the explanation above: both were deceived, but Eve's misstep is pertinent to Paul's point in vv. 12–14, because he is describing the optimal focus (learning) of the godly woman in corporate worship, reminding Timothy (and through him the church) of the sad historical precedent of Eve evidently taking the lead in an unauthorized way. The result was unmitigated disaster. Paul wants Timothy to learn from that example and apply the lesson as he leads the women and men under his instruction and oversight.

352. Translated as "deceive" (NIV) in its other two NT occurrences (Eph 5:6; Jas 1:26). It is used thirty-eight times in the LXX (seventy-three times in Philo, thirty-six in Josephus, nine in the AF).

353. Translated as "deceive" (NIV) in its other five NT occurrences (Rom 7:11; 16:18; 1 Cor 3:18; 2 Cor 11:3; 2 Thess 2:3). It is used only once in the LXX (three times in Philo, twenty-one times in Josephus, twice in the AF). Clearly the compound form *exapataō* is the rarer form in these copora; Paul is the outlier in preferring the compound. But nowhere are marked differences in meaning observed. As Siebenthal observes (*Griechische Grammatik*, §185b), "Prepositional prefixes . . . often have no discernible effect on the meaning of the uncompounded form."

354. Collins, 71 (italics in original). Collins depends heavily on Jewish parallels (Philo, the rabbis) for his interpretation. Towner ("1–2 Timothy and Titus," 896) argues that Paul is *not* reflecting then-current "Jewish chauvinistic belief in the inherent gullibility of women." He concludes that Jewish chauvinism "is irrelevant to a discussion of the argument in 1 Tim 2."

355. Standard LXX lexica (LEH, *GELS*) define the words in similar terms. They offer more glosses for *apataō* because it is used far more widely and in varying contexts, requiring glosses like "divert," "cheat," "distract," and "seduce," in addition to "deceive" (LEH 61).

356. "Transgression" (*parabasis*) is found in Paul also at Rom 2:23; 4:15; 5:14; Gal 3:19. Its only other NT occurrences are Heb 2:2; 9:15.

357. This does not mean the NIV translation is wrong. It is only to question whether it is the best way to account for the features of the original language.

Discussions of v. 14 and verses preceding have become notoriously fractious since the rise of feminism.[358] Egalitarians who think Paul wrote the PE (many argue that he did not) seek ways to confine what Paul seems to be saying to another era by declaring it culturally outdated and no longer binding. Complementarians in recent years have sought to explain why Paul would write like as he did—he must have felt women were more easily deceived or men more capable of teaching. In the more distant past, commentators like Aquinas brought in notions from philosophers like Aristotle to furnish their theological anthropology, imputing ideas to Paul (often in the name of an alleged allegiance to "household codes") that are foreign to his teaching and practice.[359] Abuse of male power has too often been the result.

Yet, such interpretations do not rule out the validity of the qualified complementarian reading offered in this commentary. Paul's point as explained above is not to decertify women as teachers or leaders, nor is it to license men per se to instruct and rule. It is not to make assertions about human nature and the superiority or inferiority of one sex in relation to the other. It is rather to describe what Paul wants Timothy to promote as regular worship order. Overseers (see ch. 3) should do just that, and in the context of early church worship, it means that, while men and women alike offered prophecy and prayer (1 Cor 11:4–5), there came a time in the assembly when the pastoral leaders (men, according to the NT sources) instructed and no doubt exhorted, consistent with the mandate given to Titus: "These, then, are the things you should teach. Encourage and rebuke with all authority" (Titus 2:15). Or as he will tell Timothy: "Command and teach these things" (1 Tim 4:11). Those are real-time snapshots of "teaching and exercising authority" when it came to the corporate assembly. Women were to be attentive active learners in that setting. So were the men, laying anger aside (v. 8), counsel that applied to overseers, too, as they were required to be "not violent but gentle, not quarrelsome" (1 Tim 3:3). In fact, the whole congregation, leaders and followers, men and women, are "to be peaceable and considerate, and always to be gentle toward everyone" (Titus 3:2). Like other apostolic leaders, Paul grasped that "the anger of man does not produce the righteousness of God" (Jas 1:20 ESV).

What *will* produce that righteousness among those who seek it in the public assembly is learning what the gospel message teaches (see Rom 10:17). Verses 9–14 have described the scenario Timothy is to promote so that this

358. See detailed interaction with recent exegesis in Schreiner, "An Interpretation of 1 Timothy 2:9–15," 210–16. For background of the rise of the movement, see M. E. Köstenberger, *Jesus and the Feminists*; Cochran, *Evangelical Feminism*; Schüssler Fiorenza, ed., *Feminist Biblical Studies in the Twentieth Century*. Still valuable is also K. Greene-McCreight, *Feminist Reconstructions of Christian Doctrine* (New York: Oxford University Press, 2000).

359. On the dubious value of the "household codes" for PE interpretation, see Yarbrough, "Familiar Paths and a Fresh Matrix," 229–33.

learning may occur to the godly woman's advantage. Verse 15 completes Paul's counsel meant to ensure her highest attainment, both as an individual and as a collective of all the women in God's household: eschatological salvation.

15 Paul begins with "But she will be saved." The verb is singular (there is no stated noun; the subject is inferred from the verb form). NIV renders "But women will be saved," which may be because later in the verse, Paul shifts to the plural—"if they continue." NIV anticipates this shift by treating "she will be saved" as meaning "they will be saved," and then by replacing "they" with "women" for clarity. This is all defensible translation procedure. But the outcome obscures something important: the individuality of the woman envisioned in vv. 11–15a.

In v. 11, after mention of "good works" (v. 10, ESV), Paul shifted from talking about men and women as aggregates to picturing an individual woman. Perhaps he did so because "good works" are not abstractions but discrete, personally performed actions that require individual initiative, understanding, and follow-through. Every pastor knows the frustration of a group that supports a cause but from whose ranks no one will step forth and act. From a congregation whose women may be fiddling with their hair and clothes (vv. 9–10), Paul wants Timothy to zero in on individuals who are truly seeking God. One responsive, active learner will bring more honor and glory to God than any number of distracted, perfunctory churchgoers. Massaging the group-think is not enough; Timothy must aim at inspiring the engagement required for an individual woman to step into the opportunity to learn that can easily be squandered when Christians assemble.[360]

Another explanation for Paul's shift to the individual in v. 11 might be anticipation of his mention of Adam and Eve. For better or for worse, they set precedents that every believer either follows to their detriment or transcends. Paul wants Timothy to apply lessons from their personal experience (both prefall and postfall) in a way that will shape individual women.

In either case, as v. 15 opens, Paul's language indicates that he still has the individual woman in view, the godly woman intent on good deeds and truly worshiping God as shown in her readiness to learn. She "will be saved through childbearing."

"Will be saved" (note future tense) likely refers to eschatological salvation, which is how the word (*sōzō*) is used throughout the PE[361] and else-

360. This understanding, by the way, puts pressure on Timothy and those he appoints to make sure that the teaching offered be of substance. Too commonly, in the history of the church and today, a woman intent on learning in a worship service would encounter little of didactic substance because of the failure of pastors to present something more than standard sermonic rhetoric reflecting minimal study, rumination, ordered presentation, and Holy Spirit conviction.

361. See 1 Tim 1:15; 2:4; 4:16; 2 Tim 1:9; 4:18; Titus 3:5.

where in Paul.[362] After death, she will be in heaven. In a setting where life expectancy may have been thirty or under, and where death from childbirth was common, assurance of life after death would have been welcome news to any woman.[363]

The meaning of "childbearing" is clear: the act of having children. The noun occurs only here in the NT.[364] Paul uses the cognate verb in 1 Tim 5:14: "I counsel younger widows to marry, to have children, to manage their homes." But what does "saved through childbearing" mean?

Some have argued that Paul is referring to Christ's birth—he has in mind the *protevangelium* of Gen 3:15, which promises deliverance by the seed of woman. Others propose that Paul refers to bringing up children. Schreiner gives convincing rebuttals of both proposals.[365] Bruce Winter points to the wide range of words connected with bearing and rearing children and observes "there is no standard term." He follows W. M. Ramsay in proposing that the woman envisioned in v. 15 "would be saved through the raising of children rather than following her secular sisters who used contraception and/or abortions to avoid becoming a mother and to pursue instead adulterous dalliances—hence the reference to remaining in holiness."[366] While this explanation may be true, it is a lot to expect the reader to infer from three nondescript words translated "through childbirth." Also, Paul speaks of bearing children, not rearing them, for which other words were available, one of which Paul uses later in 1 Tim 5:10 (*teknotropheō*).

Stanley Porter is likely closer to the mark in observing what 1 Timothy overall implies about the Ephesian setting where Timothy finds himself. Myths and false doctrines are in the air (1:3), as are deceiving spirits and demons (4:1), resulting in prohibition by some of marriage and foods, which ought to be enjoyed (4:3–5). As a result, Paul confirms the legitimacy and importance of domestic matters like caring for widows (5:3–16). Porter concludes that ascetic excess in the Ephesian setting led Paul to stress that the very activities being minimized or maligned by false teachers (marriage and domestic life generally) are actually means of grace "for the woman who abides in faith, love and holiness," for "her salvation will come by the bearing

362. See Rom 5:9, 10; 9:27; 10:9, 13, 14, 26; 1 Cor 3:15; 7:16. The same word (*sōzō*) also refers to eschatological salvation in other passages not using the future tense.

363. For arguments that Paul was referring to some other kind of deliverance—safety in childbirth, freedom from the alleged limitations of vv. 11–12, spiritual preservation from Satan—see Schreiner, "An Interpretation of 1 Timothy 2:9–15," 217–18.

364. This word is absent from the LXX, Philo, Josephus, and the AF. These sources use other words to refer to childbearing.

365. Schreiner, "An Interpretation of 1 Timothy 2:9–15," 218–20.

366. Bruce Winter, "The 'New' Roman Wife and 1 Timothy 2:9–15: The Search for a *Sitz im Leben*," *TynBul* 51 (2000): 293.

of children."[367] This interpretation comports with Schreiner's conclusion that "the verse says what it appears to say on first glance."[368]

But more can be said. First, quite apart from the Ephesian setting, in any setting bearing children is a woman's distinct domain and privilege. Therefore Paul may use synecdoche here, citing a quintessential component of womanhood to represent the whole of a woman's identity and life. A woman will be saved by being a godly woman, not by denying her createdness in some ascetic fashion, or rejecting what the Scriptures relate about Adam, Eve, and their respective standings before God. It should also be recalled that "be fruitful and increase in number" is at the core of the creation mandate (Gen 1:22, 28). Whereas today pregnancy and childbirth may be dreaded, avoided (contraception), or rejected (abortion) for career or other reasons, in biblical perspective they are a blessing, as the whole heritage of Israel, and the phenomena of both literal and spiritual "children of Abraham," dramatize.

Second, in light of the proximity of mention of Eve in vv. 13 and 14, and with Gen 3 being the contextual background to Paul's reference to Genesis in v. 14, it is reasonable to suggest that in v. 15 Paul has in mind, not Gen 3:15 and the seed of woman, but Gen 3:16 and the curse of pain in childbearing, along with the woman's potential subjugation by the man. Few truths are more prominent in Paul's theology than that Christ redeems from the law's curse (Gal 3:13). Woman's salvation does not lie in seeking to deny the terms of the fall, to reinvent herself so those terms no longer apply (if that were possible), or to relate to her husband in a proactively combative fashion in self-defense. It lies rather in Christ, who can make the "curse" latent in womanhood and fertile marriage eternally fruitful precisely "through [*dia*] childbirth" and its agony, the bitter medicine pronounced in Gen 3:16.

But "saved through childbearing" receives additional definition in the last clause of the verse: "if they continue in faith, love and holiness with propriety." Paul shifts to the plural "they" because what he writes applies, after all, to all women who receive the gospel, not just the individual projected in vv. 11–15a. And the clause clarifies that salvation is not simply a matter of having a child. Nor is having a child necessary for a woman's salvation. Rather, Christ saves through faith as the gospel message is proclaimed and women hear, internalize, learn, and live it. Paul will now sketch with consummate brevity what that looks like.

"If they continue" underscores perseverance as a sign that women are on a trajectory terminating in eschatological salvation. "Faith"[369] is where the

367. S. Porter, "What Does It Mean to Be 'Saved by Childbirth' (1 Timothy 2.15)?," *JSNT* 49 (1993): 101, 102.

368. Schreiner, "An Interpretation of 1 Timothy 2:9–15," 221.

369. The word is used 19 times in 1 Timothy alone, 142 times in Paul's writing overall.

pilgrimage begins. It is the path women (like men) follow every day of their lives. It means personal and dynamic trust in God as he has revealed himself savingly in Christ. "Love" can be viewed as even greater than faith (1 Cor 13:13); certainly "faith" that does not result in love (and works that express love) falls short of the faith Paul has in mind, which is a faith that works (see v. 10; Gal 5:6;[370] Phil 2:12–13; 1 Thess 1:3).

"Holiness" is used eight times in Paul's writings but only here in the PE.[371] It is an attribute of God bespeaking his distinction from what he has made and his awful magnificence. The seraphim chanting "holy" around God on his throne give the sense (Isa 6:1–3). Isaiah's terrified response conveys the threat God's unmediated holiness poses for those guilty of sin against him (Isa 6:5)—which is every human.

But Paul wrote in 1 Tim 2:5 of a mediator. Through faith in him, Christ becomes "wisdom from God" for believers, which is to say, their "righteousness, holiness and redemption" (1 Cor 1:30). They become "slaves to righteousness leading to holiness" (Rom 6:19). They become "slaves of God," and what they "reap leads to holiness, and the result is eternal life" (Rom 6:22).

These references sketch the glory of what Paul tells Timothy the gospel brings to women who persevere in gospel graces like "faith, love, and holiness," to which he adds "with propriety." He used the word in v. 9 (see explanation above). Together with a half-dozen other related NT words, it refers to prudence and self-control. Sexual chastity is proposed as the connotation here,[372] but that is not evident from the discourse, though it is certainly an entailment of what Paul understands by "holiness" (see 1 Thess 4:3, 4, 7). What is evident is that the gospel message calls for and produces initiative, understanding (learning), commitment, and countercultural life choices for women who take that message seriously. Paul writes Timothy with detailed counsel for their sake, not because he fears or seeks to suppress them, or because unique conditions obtain at Ephesus, but because he takes them seriously as servants of, witnesses to, and coworkers for the same message that has worked eternal alteration in him.

B. Qualifications for Overseers and Deacons (3:1–13)

While ch. 2 focuses on worship "in God's household, which is the church" (3:15), ch. 3 moves to the character of those who qualify to be appointed to preside in that worship and oversee in that household. Neudorfer notes that

370. "Faith working through love" (ESV).

371. Rom 6:19, 22; 1 Cor 1:30; 1 Thess 4:3, 4, 7; 2 Thess 2:13.

372. *NIDNTTE* 4:445.

none of the qualifications or qualities about to be set forth are merely local or "just cultural" in nature,[373] raising the question of why many find it so easy to apply those labels to much of ch. 2.

Paul writes this letter to Timothy to dig in at Ephesus for the long haul (1:3), which calls for leadership development. Whatever Timothy must do, he needs coworkers to whom he can delegate key tasks, just as Paul over the years had delegated much to Timothy (and continues to do in this very epistle). Congregations in any time and setting undergo turnover, requiring leadership replacement. If there is growth, new leaders are needed. If there is conflict or moral failure and a leader must be dismissed, a successor must be sought. As the gospel message does its work among any sizable collection of individuals and families, people learn and grow and reach junctures where they are ready to move to new levels of responsibility in gospel promulgation (whether local or beyond) and pastoral care for others. Religious movements require leaders as catalysts and instructors and directors; Jesus as founder of the movement in which Paul finds himself spent much of his time and energy in leadership development, according to all four Gospels. Emphasis on leadership excellence and training is an underrated link between what Jesus set in motion and what Paul toiled to expand to new lands and levels.

It is a noble thing to aspire to congregational leadership (v. 1). Yet, aspiration alone is not a sufficient ground for appointment. Accordingly, in about a dozen verses Paul offers a composite sketch of traits and qualities that need to be evident in candidates. This should not be viewed as a comprehensive statement. It simply touches on high points. Timothy had been with Paul for a decade or more; he already knew a great deal about Paul's leadership expectations and had observed other coworkers of Paul in their strengths and weaknesses. What Paul writes in coming verses simply reminds Timothy of what he should definitely not overlook.

Not only overseers (vv. 2–7) but also deacons come into view (vv. 8–13). This is not because they hold the same position or perform identical functions (the overseer must teach, e.g., [v. 2], while nothing is said of this qualification regarding deacons or the women of v. 11). It is rather because both offices, overseer and deacon, are viewed as ministries (i.e., services) that require relatively advanced levels of doctrinal understanding, moral probity, personal discipline, marital integrity (if the person is married), parental skills (if blessed with children), respect in the broader community—and proven experience in all these matters.

Moreover, the overseer is responsible primarily for congregational teaching and oversight (epitomized in 2:12, implicit across the whole of all three of the PE). Yet, part of that oversight is the practical care with which deacons

373. Neudorfer, *Erster Brief an Timotheus*, 146.

have traditionally been associated. There may or may not be a direct line between the seven appointed to assist the Twelve in Acts 6, on the one hand, and the deacons working alongside the overseers in 1 Tim 3, on the other. In either case, however, most pastors find that "prayer and the ministry of the word" (Acts 6:4) inevitably occupy so much pastoral energy that they require skilled and spiritually gifted help to carry out the full range of ministries in the congregation(s) they oversee. This is not to mention the (typically far larger) ranks of lay congregational members whose wide-ranging witness and service constitute the bulk of what a church "does" in the course of a given week or season. It will be recalled that Paul had sought to establish at Ephesus a view of ministry in which pastor-teachers existed "to equip [Christ's] people for works of service [*diakonia*, related to the English word 'deacon']" (Eph 4:12).

In this scenario, trained diaconal assistance working in close conjunction with pastoral leadership becomes critical. The intertwined nature of what gospel ministry entails from both a pastoral and a diaconal vantage point probably explains why Paul includes both in his remarks in his direction and encouragement for Timothy's leadership training planning.

> [1]*Here is a trustworthy saying: Whoever aspires to be an overseer desires a noble task.* [2] *Now the overseer is to be above reproach, faithful to his wife, temperate, self-controlled, respectable, hospitable, able to teach,* [3]*not given to drunkenness, not violent but gentle, not quarrelsome, not a lover of money.* [4]*He must manage his own family well and see that his children obey him, and he must do so in a manner worthy of full respect.* [5]*(If anyone does not know how to manage his own family, how can he take care of God's church?)* [6]*He must not be a recent convert, or he may become conceited and fall under the same judgment as the devil.* [7]*He must also have a good reputation with outsiders, so that he will not fall into disgrace and into the devil's trap.* [8]*In the same way, deacons are to be worthy of respect, sincere, not indulging in much wine, and not pursuing dishonest gain.* [9]*They must keep hold of the deep truths of the faith with a clear conscience.* [10]*They must first be tested; and then if there is nothing against them, let them serve as deacons.* [11]*In the same way, the women are to be worthy of respect, not malicious talkers but temperate and trustworthy in everything.* [12]*A deacon must be faithful to his wife and must manage his children and his household well.* [13]*Those who have served well gain an excellent standing and great assurance in their faith in Christ Jesus.*

1 The verse begins with an expression that occurs here and in four other PE passages (see also 1:15; 4:9; 2 Tim 2:11; Titus 3:8; see also Introduction, IX.C). With three short words (*pistos ho logos*; "Here is a trustworthy saying") Paul breaks off the preceding discourse regarding worship deportment and moves to the related but different topic of congregational leadership. The expression has the effect of underscoring the truth and seriousness of what follows.

Most translations handle the next words (*ei tis*) as something like "if anyone"[374] or "if a/any man."[375] NIV avoids both "if" and "man" by opting for "whoever." In the seventeen other Pauline passages where "whoever" occurs in the NIV, there is only one passage with the identical wording *ei tis* (1 Cor 8:3). Most often "whoever" renders a definite article and a substantivial participle, as in 2 Cor 9:6; Gal 6:8 [twice] (*ho speirōn*, whoever sows) or Rom 13:2 (*ho antitassomenos*, whoever rebels). The NIV rendering pictures a wide-open appeal for applicants to the overseer position. Greek *ei tis* ("if a certain person") lends itself to a more restricted hypothetical understanding: not everyone would, could, or should entertain pursuit of this office. But "if someone does. . . ."

"Aspires" translates a form of *oregō* (I strive for, eagerly desire). Used only three times in the NT, its other positive use is in Heb 11:16: "Instead, they were longing [*oregontai*] for a better country—a heavenly one." It is suggested that "the writer is not speaking of inner emotional feeling divorced from reality. Rather, the will here is brought into line with a goal given by God."[376] This understanding would fit what Paul likely has in mind, which is not a dreamy-eyed advancement to a posh appointment but enlistment in a duty that is always exacting and often thankless. "I always see many of the sort who seize the office of teaching in contempt of all good works. They are looking for glory."[377]

Paul's understanding of "overseer" is glimpsed in Acts 20:28, where he addresses the "elders" (*presbyterous*) of the Ephesian church: "Keep watch over yourselves and all the flock of which the Holy Spirit has made you overseers [*episkopous*]. Be shepherds of the church of God, which he bought with his own blood." It is likely that "elders" and "overseers" are synonyms for the men who had been appointed (see Acts 14:23) to local congregational leadership, "shepherds of the church of God," as Acts 20:28 puts it. This leadership model "followed the synagogue model, which had elders."[378] It is worth noting that Christ is called "Shepherd and Overseer [*episkopon*] of your souls" (1 Pet 2:25). With Christ's precedent in mind, it can be said that "oversight means loving care and concern, a responsibility willingly shouldered; it must never be used for personal aggrandizement."[379] Paul's example, his counsel for Timothy and Titus, and the qualities called for in verses below confirm this observation.

374. For example, CEB, DLNT, ESV, GW, HCSB, ICB, LEB.
375. For example, KJ21, AV, BRG, GNT, KJV, MEV, NASB, NLV, TLB, TLV, WE, WEB.
376. *NIDNTTE* 3:538–39.
377. Luther, 282.
378. Zehr, 78.
379. *NIDNTTE* 2:251.

The pastoral office is "a noble task," *kalou ergou*,[380] which can be translated "a good work." See Titus 1:16 and table 26 for the seven references to good works in that epistle; see Introduction, VI.B, for "good works" in the PE. Paul mentioned good works in connection with the godly woman earlier (2:10). He commends them for others later in the letter (5:10 [twice], 25; 6:18). Obedience to what God commands is a priority for all who seek to follow Christ, because doing his will is their highest aim. A possible future elder should view his aspiration in that positive but somber light. It should not be viewed, for example, as just an intriguing career move, as a path to hoped-for self-fulfillment, or as a means of slaking thirst for influence over others.

2 This verse begins a riff that extends to the end of v. 6.[381] A comparable list is found in Titus 1:5–9. A word is in order about the literary, or rather nonliterary, style. In the NIV, vv. 2–6 are three sentences containing one hundred words. In Greek, there is one sentence with fifty-seven words. Why the striking difference? The answer lies in the fact that Paul does not write here in a flowing style, as he often does, but in rapid succession spits out a range of terse descriptions of what is and is not called for in prospective church leaders. He gives more of an inner-office memo than a polished employment ad or job description. This format reminds the reader that the traits called for are abbreviated and representative. Much more could be said. Modern readers should not let the smoothed-out and expanded English wording make them forget that Paul is only listing key reference points, not furnishing a full, balanced, and complete statement. The points are redolent of many other positive indicators, or red flags, that he will expect Timothy to recognize with any given candidate in view.

Paul begins with seven positive traits, all in v. 2. "Now" translates an inferential conjunction (*oun*): based on v. 1, and particularly because an overseer's (or a pastor's) duties constitute fulfillment of God's command ("a good work"; see previous verse), certain qualities are necessary (NIV: "the overseer is to be" certain things).

"Is to be" translates *dei* (it is necessary), a significant word in the PE. It conveys moral and often divinely demanded necessity, as table 15 indicates.

380. It is genitive because, like *oregō* ("aspires") earlier in the verse with the genitive *episkopēs* ("overseer") as its object, the verb *epithymeō* ("desires") takes its object in that case. Verbs of sensation and emotion or volition frequently takes genitive objects (Wallace, *Greek Grammar*, 132). See BDF §171.1.

381. English translations may break up Paul's intense sequencing for clarity.

Table 15. ***Dei*** **(it is necessary, must) in the PE**

Passage	Translation (NIV)	Comment
1 Tim 3:2	The overseer is to be [*dei*] above reproach	High standards are absolutely necessary.
1 Tim 3:7	He must [*dei*] also have a good reputation	The view from outside and not only from inside the church is important.
1 Tim 3:15	how people ought to [*dei*] conduct themselves	Practical outworking—conduct—is a chief aim of the gospel message.
1 Tim 5:13	saying things they ought not to [*ta mē deonta*]	Speech ethics are critical in the disciple's life.
2 Tim 2:6	The hardworking farmer should be [*dei*] the first to receive. . . .	Common sense, and possibly common grace, mandate the farmer's fair share from his labor.
2 Tim 2:24	And the Lord's servant [i.e., ministers like Timothy] must not be [*ou dei*] quarrelsome.	Timothy is forbidden to lapse into contentious behavior or an attitude resulting in it.
Titus 1:7	An overseer . . . must be [*dei*] blameless.	The same language as 1 Tim 3:2.
Titus 1:11	They must be [*dei*] silenced . . . teaching things they ought not [*ha mē dei*] to teach	Pastors must at times act decisively to counter untrue or destructive teachings affecting their flock.

While it would be trivializing to call Paul a stickler in some pedantic sense, table 15 reveals how, throughout the PE, he expresses a very definite sense of requisite order. This structured concept of leadership is consistent with his apostleship and ministry under Christ who is *Lord*, as "he must [*dei*] reign until he has put all his enemies under his feet" (1 Cor 15:28). That reign in earthly terms is particularly through his body the church. In about fifteen other passages outside the PE, Paul uses this same word, which often points to God's sovereignty behind the scenes and the blessed necessity this attribute places on those who fear and follow him.[382]

382. For example, "we must [*dei*] all appear before the judgment seat of Christ" (2 Cor 5:10).

In sum, "the overseer is to be" introduces more than a random wish list for the pastorally inclined do-gooder. It points to a quality and depth of godliness that are indispensable for the magnitude and gravity of pastoral labor that Paul models, expects of Timothy, and hopes to see replicated in generations to come at Ephesus and beyond.

Of the seven requirements in this verse, the first is "above reproach." The word (from *anepilēmptos*) is found elsewhere in the NT only in 5:7 and 6:14.[383] The idea is similar to "blameless" in Titus 1:6 (see commentary there). Paul did not affirm sinless perfection, and even Christ was reproached (Rom 15:3; Heb 13:13 ESV). Paul means the person should be of stellar character and free of obvious or provable black marks against his character.

Second, "faithful to his wife." See comments on the same expression in Titus 1:6. The Greek is explicit that the overseer is a male[384] who, if married, has a female wife to whom he is fully and exclusively dedicated.[385] It would be overreading to infer that Paul required overseers to be married. Jesus never married. Paul may have been married at some earlier point in life (rabbis were expected to be) but seems to regard marriage as a right he denied himself (1 Cor 9:5; cf. 7:7–8). The other apostles, including Peter, and "the Lord's brothers" (James and Jude) were married (1 Cor 9:5). Paul is envisioning the typical situation of a man who has come to the age or season of his life when he eligible to be, or seeks to become, an overseer. Paul is aware that following puberty and with the onset of adulthood there is a strong urge in both sexes for relational attachment. Paul also knows that God's provision from Eden onward for sanctification and direction of this noble drive is marriage (Matt 19:4–6). Most men of overseer age would have been married, or open to the possibility. If an overseer is not married, it does not mean he should not be an overseer: it means he should be celibate (1 Cor 7:7–8; cf. Matt 19:12).

Paul wants Timothy to affirm the overseer whose relationship with God is such that his commitment to his wife reflects the love and fidelity that the

383. It is absent from the LXX but found (with the spelling *anepilēptos*) twenty-nine times in Philo and once (with Philo's spelling) in the AF (Mart. Pol. 17:1), which speaks of "the greatness of Polycarp's martyrdom and the irreproachable character of his life from the beginning." It is absent (in either spelling) from Josephus.

384. *Andra*, man, male, husband. Wright's statement (29) that "Paul refers to the bishop throughout as a man" because "that's how Greek grammar normally refers to both genders together" is false.

385. An understanding as ancient as Theodore of Mopsuestia (ca. 350–428): "He who marries one wife, lives with her prudently, keeps to her, and directs to her the desire of nature" (cited in Dibelius and Conzelmann, 52). Less likely, Dibelius and Conzelmann argue, is the theory that Paul was speaking of either polygamy (see Wright, 27: "He must not have more than one wife") or a second marriage.

law requires[386] and that grace enables. Paul probably has in mind a candidate showing signs of loving his wife like Christ loved the church (Eph 5:25). Pastoral leadership "calls for integrity and fidelity to the marriage covenant."[387] The robust love for God and people that is the lifeblood of pastoral care should be fueled by the discipline and joy of married love in the pastor's personal life.

Third, "temperate." The same word is used in v. 11 and in Titus 2:2 (see discussion there). The word can refer to freedom from alcohol misuse, but Paul will mention that issue in v. 3. So here he likely has in mind a figurative meaning: the candidate should regard his calling and duties with sobriety rather than flippancy and should demonstrate self-control rather than impulsiveness, lack of concentration, or distracted behavior.

Fourth, "self-controlled." The same word appears also in Titus 1:8 (referring to aspiring overseers); 2:2 (referring to older men in the church); 2:5 (referring to what older women should teach the younger women to be); see discussion in these passages. There are no other NT references. Pastoral leaders should know their own minds and not be flighty or unstable. Ryken relates the term to decision-making ("Men who make vital decisions about the ministry of the church must be prudent") and to the control of appetites.[388]

Fifth, "respectable." The word occurs elsewhere in the NT only at 2:9, where in relation to women's dress it carried the sense of "modesty." With respect to an overseer, the sense is "having characteristics or qualities that evoke admiration or delight," so that a person is held in high regard (BDAG 561). While "respectable" may sound dull and prudish, Epictetus uses it to good effect to warn against the fallout of behaviors like adultery (*Discourses* 2.10.18) and failure to perform one's duty (2.7.36): one loses "respectable" standing. Such actions cause a person to be regarded as indecent and crass, which is not fitting for a pastoral leader. Paul wants overseers whose characteristic actions cause them to be held in high esteem.

Sixth, "hospitable." See discussion of this word (*philoxenon*) at Titus 1:8.[389] The only other NT occurrence is 1 Pet 4:9. The noun form (*philoxenia*) occurs only at Rom 12:13 (hospitality to other Christians) and Heb 13:2 (hospitality to strangers). To show hospitality to other believers is to show it to Jesus himself (John 13:20). Hospitable care for others, especially believers (see Gal 6:10), or lack thereof will be judged on the last day, according to Jesus (Matt 25:31–46). Church leaders need to set a tone of openness and receptivity toward all persons (see Titus 3:2).

386. See Exod 20:14, 17: "You shall not commit adultery. . . . You shall not covet your neighbor's wife."

387. Zehr, 79.

388. Ryken, 112.

389. See also David B. Howell, "Hospitality," *EDB*, 611–12.

Seventh, "able to teach." The only other NT use of the word (*didaktikos*) is at 2 Tim 2:24 (see discussion there). It is self-evident that a movement founded by a consummate teacher, whose followers were tasked with spreading his legacy by teaching others what he had taught them (Matt 28:18–20), would need skilled teachers at the helm. Paul had been teaching at least since Barnabas had discovered him and brought him to Antioch (Acts 11:25–26), if not indeed from the very time of his conversion (Acts 9:20). Timothy was expected to do likewise (2 Tim 2:2). Paul does not use the word *didaktikos* in Titus, but he calls for the same competence and explains how critical it is: the overseer "must hold firmly to the trustworthy message as it has been *taught*, so that he can encourage others by sound *doctrine* and refute those who oppose it" (Titus 1:9). As noted earlier in discussion of 2:11, teaching in tandem with the exercise of pastoral oversight are the two mainstays of shepherding the flock in Pauline and NT conception.

3 The previous verse spoke of seven desirable qualities Timothy should look for in an overseer. Now he lists four disqualifiers. First, "not given to drunkenness [*paroinon*]." The same prohibition is given in Titus 1:7 (see discussion there), the only other place the word occurs in the NT. But the perils of intoxication are graphically depicted elsewhere (Luke 12:45; 21:34; Rom 13:13; Gal 5:21; Eph 5:18; 1 Thess 5:7). They have no place in the life of an overseer, or any other serious disciple of Jesus for that matter.

Second, "not violent but gentle." As with the previous expression, "not violent" occurs in the New Testament elsewhere only in Titus 1:7 (see discussion there). Here, unlike in Titus 1:7, Paul offsets "not violent" with "but gentle" and then other positive traits. "Gentle" translates *epieikēs*, an adjective that occurs in four other NT passages (Phil 4:5; Titus 3:2; Jas 3:17; 1 Pet 2:18; in the last three passages NIV translates "considerate").

"Gentle" can conjure up the picture of a weak leader who blandly accepts whatever happens with a helpless smile. Neither Jesus nor Paul are depicted in this way in the NT writings. BDAG 371 offers insight here in explaining the noun form *epieikeia* as "the quality of making allowances despite facts that might suggest a reason for a different reaction." It then goes on to list glosses like "clemency, gentleness, graciousness, courtesy, indulgence, tolerance." MM 238 comments from numerous papyrological examples, "It will be seen that *epieikeia* is a very elusive term, and is by no means always . . . 'sweet reasonableness.'" Paul is calling for a magnanimity that rules out quick-tempered, mercurial reactions. But he by no means rules out the leadership steel and strategies that may be necessary to "fight the good fight of the faith" (6:12) and to "reprove, rebuke, and exhort" (2 Tim 4:2 ESV). "These, then, are the things you should teach. Encourage and rebuke with all authority" (Titus 2:15). "Evenhanded" and "measured" convey the sense.

Third, like "gentle," the word translated "not quarrelsome" (*amachos*) is listed as a positive trait in place of "not violent." Its only other NT occurrence is in Titus 3:2, where it is translated "peaceable" (see discussion there). In a world being shaken by the rise of militant Islam, the contrast is stark between the war-riven heritage of Muhammad, on the one hand, and on the other, of Jesus, who said, "My kingdom is not of this world. If it were, my servants would fight to prevent my arrest by the Jewish leaders. But now my kingdom is from another place" (John 18:36). Overseers in the church are not warlords, gang leaders, or cult figures whose repertoire includes physical intimidation and force. Their mission does not feature the sword (though there may be limited need for one: Luke 22:36, 38).

Nor are overseers quick to get bogged down in petty controversy, if a possible connotation of NIV's "not quarrelsome" be pressed: "But avoid foolish controversies and genealogies and arguments and quarrels about the law, because these are unprofitable and useless" (Titus 3:9). Paul would have been schooled in the wisdom of Proverbs: "It is to one's honor to avoid strife, but every fool is quick to quarrel" (Prov 20:3; cf. 15:18; 17:14, 19; 18:1; 26:17). Overseers are not polemical and pugnacious as a matter of course.

Fourth, like "gentle" and "not quarrelsome," the word translated "not a lover of money" (*aphilargyros*) is listed as a positive trait in place of "not violent." In the Titus 1:7 parallel, Paul forbids elders from "pursuing dishonest gain" (see discussion there). Hebrews 13:5 contains the only other NT use of the word: "Keep your lives free from the love of money and be content with what you have, because God has said. . . ." The love of money is dangerous and destructive of both self and community (see 1 Tim 6:10). "Like Adam and Eve's grasping after the forbidden fruit in the garden of Eden, a person's selfish amassing of material possessions suggests that life is no longer being accepted thankfully from the hand of God. Love of money erects a selfish dividing wall against God and our neighbors; it is the germ of total alienation from God."[390] Other NT passages depict lovers of money and their folly (Luke 16:14; 2 Tim 3:2; see discussion there). Greed is inconsistent with pure zeal for God, the saving gospel message, and the care of souls that should be the heartbeat of the overseer's inner life and therefore evident in his attitude toward income and spending.

4 This verse in conjunction with v. 5 makes explicit the close connection between family relations and rapport in the life of the overseer and his suitedness for congregational leadership (or not) on that account.

"His own family" (or household: *oikos*)[391] are the first words in Greek, setting up the logic of v. 5 in a lesser-to-greater sequence: if he fails here, what

390. *NIDNTTE* 4:608.

391. Here in the genitive, as *proistēmi* takes its object in that case, in line with the pattern for other verbs of ruling (Wallace, *Greek Grammar*, 134; BDF §177).

hope does he have for overseeing an entire congregation made up of many families plus others? Paul will give similar directives in v. 12 regarding deacons.

"Manage" translates *proistēmi*, which is used with this meaning in several other Pauline passages (Rom 12:8; 1 Thess 5:12 [ESV]; 1 Tim 3:12; 5:17). In other places Paul uses it to refer to giving assistance or being devoted to or intent on something (1 Thess 5:12 [NIV]; Titus 3:8, 14). Josephus and Philo use the word frequently with overtones of both supervision and protection.[392] Such an understanding fits well with v. 4, where the context points to measured oversight, not draconian rule or tyranny. "Well" (*kalōs*) underscores the quality and aptness of the management style and decisions of the household head. He is good at this; things are not in disarray because of neglect, incompetence, or harshness.

Regarding family health and the presence of Christian graces in home relationships, the overseer is to "see that his children obey him." The Greek is more oblique: "having children in subjection" (see BDAG 1042). This expectation is no more than an application of the Decalogue: "Honor your father and your mother, so that you may live long in the land the Lord your God is giving you" (Exod 20:12), which Paul had addressed earlier to the Ephesian church (Eph 6:2). On this basis came his admonition, "Children, obey your parents in the Lord, for this is right" (Eph 6:1; cf. Col 3:20). See discussion at Titus 1:6 on the closely related statement that an elder is to be "a man whose children believe and are not open to the charge of being wild and disobedient."

This is not a one-sided or top-down mandate, for earlier Paul wrote to Ephesus, "Fathers, do not exasperate your children; instead, bring them up in the training and instruction of the Lord" (Eph 6:4; cf. Col 3:21). Parental authority involves wise and nurturing guidance that will evoke devotion, affection, and loyalty in return. Paul assumed parental care and provision for children: "Children should not have to save up for their parents, but parents for their children" (2 Cor 12:14; cf. Prov 13:22). He gives a direct description of how "a father deals with his own children": "encouraging, comforting and urging you to live lives worthy of God, who calls you into his kingdom and glory" (1 Thess 2:11–12).[393] He expresses concern for the upbringing, welfare, and love of children (1 Tim 5:10; Titus 2:4). This disposition is the ethos of Israel: "As a father has compassion on his children, so the Lord has compassion on those who fear him" (Ps 103:13; cf. 127:3–4). The heavenly Father's love is the analogue and pattern for a godly earthly father.

The picture of an aspiring overseer Paul paints, then, is not of an exasperated, authoritarian husband roaring at his children, slapping them into

392. *NIDNTTE* 4:140.

393. Cf. Prov 23:24: "The father of a righteous child has great joy; a man who fathers a wise son rejoices in him."

subjection, or enforcing strict compliance when church people are present to keep up appearances. It is rather loving like a father "in a manner worthy of full respect." "Respect" (*semnotēs*) occurs only two other times in the NT; it is translated as "holiness" in 1 Tim 2:2 and as "seriousness" in Titus 2:7 (see discussion in commentary). NIV shapes the wording so that it is the father, or his leading, that attracts respect. But the Greek (*meta pasēs semnotētos*) could refer to the solemnity he exercises in exercising his parental prerogatives. He fathers "with full recognition of the holiness and seriousness of his trust." Many fathers (though doubtless too few) realize early on that good relations with children are as much a work of divine grace as is fruitful mutual marital love. Neither can be commanded—or rather, if they are only commanded and not drawn out by the father and husband's proactive care, affection, and self-sacrifice, things will be at best forced and strained.

This qualification, then, is not about a husband cracking the whip at home so he can bring the same people-taming talent to a congregation (a caricature to which translations may help give rise). It is rather about the love of the Father through the gospel for his people finding full and authentic expression in the real, daily, private life of a father and husband as requisite before he is considered for appointment to shepherding God's flock. Key congregational essentials are exercised first in the marriages and homes of church members, or it is sheer hypocrisy to pretend they exist on Sundays: forgiveness, care for others, prayer and regard for God's word, self-sacrifice, loving service, respect for others, listening to others, finding joy in what pleases others rather than oneself, making personal changes and forsaking sin for the sake of improved relations with other family members, in many cases seemingly endless delayed gratification, and much more. Paul writes to Timothy to cultivate congregations of real-life authenticity, not showcases for religious pretending. This task requires big men, not little autocrats.

5 This verse raises a parenthetical question whose answer is obvious: he can't.

On "manage his own family," see discussion on the previous verse. "God's church" (see more at 3:15) is a reminder that, while a congregation consists of people who in some ways administer their own affairs, in the end God is Lord over what they are and do, with Christ as head (1 Cor 11:3; Eph 4:15; 5:23; Col 2:10). In Paul's reckoning it requires a man of God—subservient to God, in touch with God, humble before God—to carry out God's pastoral bidding. It also requires an informed and competent man, someone who knows how to exercise his family oversight. To encourage disciples (learners) in the family, one must be a learner oneself.

"Take care of" sheds light on what Paul means by "manage," which it parallels. He does not mean self-directed, heavy-handed, or capricious management (a possible misunderstanding, e.g., of 2:12). "Take care of" translates a word (*epimeleomai*) that occurs elsewhere in the NT only at Luke 10:34–35.[394] The Good Samaritan "*took care of*" the hapless mugging victim (v. 34). He told the innkeeper, "*Look after* him . . . and when I return, I will reimburse you for any extra expense you may have" (v. 35). The background of this solicitude is found in v. 33: "When he saw him, he *had compassion* on him" (ESV). The words in italics can be brought to bear on what Paul has in mind in v. 5. The overseer manages out of compassion for the congregation's sake and its health and mission in God's service, not as his own fiefdom.

An aspiring overseer whose domestic life demonstrates his grasp of a selfless and compassionate dynamic has a basis for putting his nurturing executive abilities at the disposal of "God's church." If he does not—and it is Timothy's task to make this determination—he is not suited for the overseer position.

But there are other possible disqualifiers, and vv. 6–7 take them up.

6 "A recent convert" (*neophytos*; see English "neophyte") is a metaphor drawing on the image of something newly planted or sprouting (see LXX Pss 127:3; 143:12; Job 14:9; Isa 5:7). "No parallels can be found in Hellenistic ethics,"[395] possibly because conversion was not required to ply those ethics as it was for a pastoral leader to fulfill the requirements of his office. Paul knows that new believers are untested and unsuited for the responsibilities the overseer faces. Even persons who might otherwise seem qualified are not overseer material in the early stages of their assimilation into Christian confession and congregational living.

Paul reminds Timothy of a representative hazard faced by a new convert (no doubt he could have listed many). That person might "become conceited" (from *typhoō*). This word occurs elsewhere in the NT only at 1 Tim 3:6 and 6:4 (see discussion there). It was used widely outside the NT to describe people who were overly impressed with their own knowledge. For example, Philo (*Preliminary Studies* 127–28) describes a teacher who interprets a pupil's brilliance as the teacher's own achievement. That teacher "has puffed himself up [*tetyphōtai*] . . . and holds his head high, and draws his eyebrows and becomes full of pride. . . . [He is] full of pride, and to be puffed up with arrogance [*tetyphōsthai*] beyond all moderation." Josephus uses the word five times in much the same sense.[396] Arrogance and pride were as common in Paul's setting as today. They are obviously undesirable traits in a congregational leader.

Luther is frank about his own error here: "When I first became a monk, I was ready to take heaven by storm. . . . I had this fault when I first got into

394. The word appears thirty-nine times in Philo, frequently with the sense of "care for" or "cultivate" (e.g., *Cherubim* 118; *The Worse Attacks the Better* 33; *Husbandry* 153; *Planting* 97), including God "taking care of [*epimeloumenou*] his own flock" (*Change of Names* 115).

395. Saarinen, 64.

396. *Jewish War* 2.442; 7.80; *Life* 53; *Against Apion* 1.15; 2.255.

the Scriptures. Speculations seemed to me to be the very best ideas, and no one understood but me." He adds: "That's the way it is for those who are fresh newcomers in Scripture."[397] Paul might have added, "And in ministry." Either way, the zeal and confidence often present in inexperience can be outweighed by liabilities.

For example, as a result of pride, a neophyte could "fall under the same judgment as the devil." CEV puts this prospect more colorfully: "be doomed along with the devil." ERV suggests "condemned for his pride the same as the devil was." NASB renders "condemnation incurred by the devil." NET has "the punishment that the devil will exact." All these options (and others) are plausible attempts to do justice to a flat (and ambiguous)[398] expression combining "condemnation" (*krima*)[399] and a Greek genitive (*tou diabolou*, of the devil).

What they have in common is recognition that, quite apart from challenges like the vices named in v. 3, spiritual forces epitomized in Satan are arrayed against the church and its leaders. Paul warned the Ephesians earlier not to "give the devil a foothold" (Eph 4:27) and to arm themselves "against the devil's schemes" (Eph 6:11). Others in the congregation are likewise susceptible to his wiles (2 Tim 2:26; see discussion there).[400] Paul has already spoken of church (mis)leaders being "handed over to Satan" for disciplinary and restorative reasons (1:20). It would be a tragic waste of time for Timothy to appoint someone who would end up not only impeding ministry but become a disciplinary case in his own right by a calamitous fall.[401]

7 In Greek a new sentence begins here. Verses 1–6 give a view from within the faith community. As Paul prepares to shift from overseers to deacons (v. 8), he reminds Timothy of the importance of the view from outside the community. The new sentence underscores that he is no longer talking about the fresh convert but has rather shifted back to give a final specification for the overseer in general.

"He must also have a good reputation with outsiders." "Reputation" translates *martyria*,[402] which can here (with *kalēn*, good, admirable) be

397. Luther, 289–90.

398. Towner, *Letters*, 257.

399. Used twelve times in Paul: see also Rom 2:2, 3; 3:8; 5:16; 11:33; 13:2; 1 Cor 6:7; 11:29, 34; Gal 5:10; 1 Tim 5:12.

400. "The devil" (*diabolos*; all relevant Pauline references occur above) and Satan (*satanas*) are basically interchangeable names in Paul; he uses the latter slightly more often. For Paul's ten mentions of Satan by name, see Rom 16:20; 1 Cor 5:5; 7:5; 2 Cor 2:11; 11:14; 12:7; 1 Thess 2:18; 2 Thess 2:9; 1 Tim 1:20; 5:15.

401. Paul uses *empiptō* ("I fall into") elsewhere only in the next verse ("fall . . . into the devil's trap") and in 6:9 (of rich people who "fall into temptation").

402. *Martyria* (witness, testimony) occurs in Paul elsewhere only in Titus 1:13 (see statistics and commentary there).

thought of as "a good standing" (BDAG 619). Regarding "must" (*dei*), see discussion in v. 2 above. In principle, this requirement is not negotiable. "Outsiders" comes from *exōthen*, an adverb that can be used (as here) to refer to the location of a group (see also Epictetus, *Discourses* 3.22.28). It is used thirteen times in the NT but nowhere else of persons.[403] The more common term for outside persons is from *exō*, which Paul uses three times to stress the exclusive nature of congregational membership:

> What business is it of mine to judge those *outside* the church? Are you not to judge those inside? (1 Cor 5:12)
>
> Be wise in the way you act toward *outsiders*; make the most of every opportunity. (Col 4:5)
>
> . . . so that your daily life may win the respect of *outsiders* and so that you will not be dependent on anybody. (1 Thess 4:12)

Paul's usage is a reminder that the church has a public reputation to uphold, as well as its own in-house needs and standards. Sometimes people outside the church see matters more clearly than those inside (note Jesus's observation: "For the people of this world are more shrewd in dealing with their own kind than are the people of the light" [Luke 16:8]). Public perception may well furnish input that someone like Timothy at Ephesus needs to heed in leadership selection. Paul's counsel also assumes that there will be live connection between those inside and those outside the church. In settings where church communities or their members have grown isolated from "outsiders," this verse is a reminder that social separation (for which there is some justification in Paul's references to a "holy people") can be overdone and detrimental.[404]

Paul's concern is that the prospective overseer "not fall into disgrace and into the devil's trap." "Disgrace" (*oneidismos*) occurs in Paul elsewhere only in Rom 15:3 (a quotation of LXX Ps 69:9), where it is translated "insult." An overseer regarded as unsavory by reasonable "worldly" standards will bring reproach that reflects poorly on himself, on the congregation and its message, and even on God. Towner underscores that Paul's concern is most of all "the threat to the evangelistic mandate that would follow from the church falling into disgrace" by immoral or incompetent leaders.[405]

403. For persons the more common mention is *exō* (Mark 4:11; 1 Cor 15:12; Col 4:5; 1 Thess 4:12).

404. "Holy people" in Paul: Rom 1:7; 1 Cor 1:2; 2 Cor 1:1; Eph 1:1, 18; 3:18; 5:3; Phil 1:1; Col 1:2, 12; 2 Thess 1:10; Phlm 5.

405. Towner, *Letters*, 259.

The same word (*oneidismos*) refers to "insult" or "disgrace" in Hebrews (10:33, of noble persecuted believers; 11:26, of Moses, who "regarded disgrace for the sake of Christ as of greater value than the treasures of Egypt"; 13:13, of Christ, who suffered "outside the camp" so that believers might bear "the disgrace he bore"). Sometimes disgrace is the price of faithfulness to God and the gospel. Contemporary news events document the spectacle of ministers, however, whose disgrace is not from brave goodness but sin, even measured in non-Christian terms. Timothy should seek candidates who pass the test of valid secular assessment. And it is not enough merely that the candidate not be contemptible: "good reputation" implies affirmation, some form of community recognition of character and behavior.

NIV repeats "into" in v. 7, whereas the Greek does not. This nonrepetition could mean Paul views "disgrace" and "the devil's trap" as a single disaster viewed from two angles. Paul warns elsewhere about the traps of obsession with wealth (6:9) and of failing to repent and trust in Christ (2 Tim 2:26; see discussion there). These situations all amount to being overpowered and held in captivity like some animal snared by the devil. NIV's wording may support a two-stage or otherwise twofold understanding: "disgrace" and (possibly even more dire) "the devil's trap." Elsewhere (Rom 6:16–20) Paul writes of people being under one dominion (God's) or another (impurity, wickedness, sin). In addressing Timothy at Ephesus, Paul emphasizes that the "struggle is not against flesh and blood" alone but against spiritual forces (Eph 6:12), epitomized and personalized as "the devil." Perhaps this language "is a sign of the times."[406] But even if it is, judging from the magnitude and malice of diabolical wickedness in today's world, to say nothing of Scripture's testimony, it would be a mistake to minimize Paul's warning on the assumption that the church need no longer fear the devil or his effects.

8 "In the same way" signals that Paul is not leaving his topic totally behind but turning his attention to an analogous consideration.[407] He is moving from the overseer (spoken of in the sing. in both vv. 1–7, like the sing. "elder" in Titus 1:6–9) to "deacons" (pl.). The change in number might be arbitrary; more than one was needed for both positions. Or Paul might be viewing the overseer as a more demanding position with more stringent qualifications; deacons required high standards but not as high as overseers, and in the nature of the case they would be more numerous. A congregation needing only one or a handful of overseers (as the Jerusalem church appeared to have three: James, Cephas, and John [Gal 2:9]) might require many more deacons.

In the history of exegesis and church government, Acts 6 with the appointment of Stephen and six others has always seen as relevant to diaconal

406. Collins, 85.

407. See use of the same expression (*hōsautōs*, likewise) in Rom 8:26; 1 Cor 11:15; 1 Tim 2:9; 3:11; 5:25; Titus 2:3, 6. It also occurs nine times in the Synoptic Gospels.

definition and identity.[408] But they are not actually called deacons using the Greek word *diakonos*. That word refers to a "servant" in various senses and capacities in Paul's twenty-one uses of the word.

Table 16. *Diakonos* (servant, minister, deacon) in Paul

Passage	Translation of *diakonos*
Rom 13:4 (twice)	For the one in authority is God's *servant* for your good. But if you do wrong, be afraid, for rulers do not bear the sword for no reason. They are God's *servants*, agents of wrath to bring punishment on the wrongdoer.
Rom 15:8	For I tell you that Christ has become a *servant* of the Jews on behalf of God's truth.
Rom 16:1	I commend to you our sister Phoebe, a *deacon* of the church in Cenchreae.
1 Cor 3:5	What, after all, is Apollos? And what is Paul? Only *servants*, through whom you came to believe—as the Lord has assigned to each his task.
2 Cor 3:6	He has made us competent as *ministers* of a new covenant.
2 Cor 6:4	Rather, as *servants* of God we commend ourselves in every way.
2 Cor 11:15 (twice)	His [the devil's] *servants* also masquerade as *servants* of righteousness.
2 Cor 11:23	Are they [Paul's opponents] *servants* of Christ?
Gal 2:17	Is Christ then a *servant* of sin? (ESV)
Eph 3:7	Of this gospel I was made a *minister* according to the gift of God's grace.
Eph 6:21	Tychicus the beloved brother and faithful *minister* in the Lord.
Phil 1:1	Paul and Timothy, servants of Christ Jesus, to all the saints in Christ Jesus who are at Philippi, with the overseers and *deacons*.
Col 1:7	. . . Epaphras our beloved fellow servant [*syndoulou*]. He is a faithful *minister* of Christ on your behalf.

408. Kari Latvus, "Deacon, Deaconess," *EBR* 6:313: "The history of deacons is interwoven with the interpretation of Acts 6."

Passage	Translation of *diakonos*
Col 1:23	. . . the gospel . . . of which I, Paul, became a *minister*.
Col 1:25	. . . of which I became a *minister* according to the stewardship from God.
Col 4:7	Tychicus . . . is a beloved brother and faithful *minister* and fellow servant [*syndoulos*] in the Lord.
1 Tim 3:8	*Deacons* likewise must be. . . .
1 Tim 3:12	Let *deacons* each be the husband of one wife.
1 Tim 4:6	If you put these things before the brothers, you will be a good *servant* of Christ.

Diakonos, it can be seen in table 16, is a noun referring primarily to someone who performs a service or ministry. Most frequently, the reference is *not* to a church appointment or office per se. Examples (none translated above as "deacon") are a government official, Christ, Apollos and Paul, those who serve the devil (including Paul's opponents), Tychicus, Epaphras, and Timothy. These could be called nontechnical uses of the term.

Those termed "deacon" above are Phoebe, officials at Philippi, and deacons in 1 Tim 3:8, 12. These can be called "official" uses: they refer to a person occupying a recognized position in the church. Even if Acts 6 and the appointment of seven men to assist in serving widows is brought into the discussion, it may be surprising how little is known from the NT sources about specifics regarding the office of deacon. Much of what we think we know today likely stems from projecting back into early NT history the roles of deacons with which we are familiar from traditions that can be attested in full only much later. This does not mean contemporary discussion of deacons cannot make appeal to these (and other) Scriptures. It is simply to underscore that the explicit sources are quite limited. Applications made from them deserve to be careful and as modest as the amount of definite information available.[409]

Nevertheless, just as Paul appointed elders (or overseers) in churches founded ca. AD 50 (Acts 14:22), and just as there were both "overseers and deacons" in the church he planted at Philippi, it is reasonable that in 1 Tim 3 Paul has a similar bi-level church leadership structure in view. For deacons (v. 8), Paul first lists two desirable and then two undesirable qualities.

On the plus side is "worthy of respect" (from *semnos*). "Are to be" (an implied imperative) is imported (using "likewise") from the force of "must"

409. Johnson's comments on early church structure and order provide a helpful framework (*First and Second Letters to Timothy*, 217–25).

(*dei*) in v. 7. The same word *semnos* is translated "noble" in Phil 4:8. It is used of women or wives in 3:11 and Titus 2:2 (of older men; see discussion there). *NIDNTTE* combines the meaning of this word with *semnotēs* (in Paul elsewhere only at 2:2 and Titus 2:7) and concludes that in both cases reference "is always to honorable conduct."[410] Yet, the character producing the conduct can hardly be excluded. Other glosses offered by BDAG (919) for *semnos* are "dignified" and "serious." Ruled out would be behavior or attitudes that are frivolous and lack suitable focus in the service of God and the gospel. Deacons should be people with admirable traits and character.

A second positive desideratum for deacons is that they be "sincere." The Greek has more texture: *mē dilogous* (not double-talkers, i.e., saying one thing while meaning another; a hypocrite, dissembler). Polycarp (*Phil.* 5:2) uses the same word (probably paraphrasing this verse) in his description of deacons: "Similarly, deacons [*diakonoi*] must be blameless in the presence of his righteousness, as servants [*diakonoi*] of God and Christ and not of people. They must not be slanderers, not insincere [*mē dilogoi*], not lovers of money, but self-controlled in every respect, compassionate, diligent, acting in accordance with the truth of the Lord, who became a servant [*diakonos*] of all." Integrity before God in one's speech is emphasized in the Proverbs, in Jesus's teaching, in James's letter, and in Paul (e.g., Eph 4:15, 25, 29; 5:4). Harmful talk is a recurrent theme of the PE.[411] While "sincere" as a deacon qualification may refer to more than what someone says, "the mouth speaks what the heart is full of" (Matt 12:34; Luke 6:45). Deacons need to be characterized by probity of both heart and speech.

"Not indulging in much wine" is nearly identical to an admonition addressed to "the older women" in Titus 2:3 (see discussion there). All members of the church should lay hold of the grace of the gospel so as to rise above substance abuse; this behavior is all the more imperative for church-sanctioned figures like deacons. Even a secular writer like Epictetus recognized the necessity of abstemiousness in use of wine, though he also praised its legitimate enjoyment.[412]

"Not pursuing dishonest gain" is identical with a qualification for the elder in Titus 1:7 (see discussion there). Greed is condemned throughout the Scriptures, including Paul's writings.[413] Diaconal service calls for a generous spirit, not a grasping, selfish, and mercenary approach to life.

410. *NIDNTTE* 4:283.

411. 1 Tim 1:7; 3:11; 5:13; 6:4; Titus 1:10; 2:9.

412. Epictetus, *Enchiridion* 29.2; *Discourses* 3.15.3. "For the power of seeing and hearing, and indeed for life itself, and for the things which contribute to support it, for the fruits which are dry, and for wine and oil give thanks to God" (*Discourses* 2.23.5). This is the God of Stoicism, not the God of the OT and NT.

413. Rom 1:29; Eph 4:19; 5:3; Col 3:5; 1 Thess 2:5.

9 While it may be hard to establish formal ties between deacons in 1 Timothy and the seven chosen to serve in Acts 6, this verse is an excellent description of someone like Stephen, who, according to Luke's representation, spoke not only with the Spirit (Acts 6:3, 5, 10, 55) but also with "wisdom" (6:3, 10), deep faith (6:5), and "God's grace and power" (6:8; cf. 7:60). Surely these qualities would exemplify someone "keep[ing] hold of the deep truths of the faith with a clear conscience," as Stephen's conscience was so clear that he could call the Jerusalem leadership to account and maintain Jesuslike composure in a violent death. Saul of Tarsus, of course, witnessed this event (Acts 7:60–8:1). Historians can only speculate on how this incident might still inform Paul's thinking on the character of deacons decades later.

"Deep truths of the faith" translates words often rendered something like "the mystery of the faith" (*to mystērion tēs pisteōs*) in other English versions. NIV translates the same word *mysterion* as "mystery" in v. 16, its only other PE occurrence. Elsewhere Paul uses the word nineteen times, often to denote redemptive truths formerly concealed but now revealed in Christ's coming.[414] The concept bears comparison with the "common faith" spoken of in Titus 1:4 (see comments on the *fides quae creditur*, or core content of the Christian faith there). This is where Stephen's example is suggestive, as the sweep and sophistication of his christological biblical exposition and application (Acts 7:2–53) continue to occupy scholars' attention.[415] In any case, Paul's counsel to Timothy assumes that deacons are not just busy activists but also capable and informed in matters pertaining to Christian teaching, experience, and to some extent the Scriptures (OT and any then-recognized NT) themselves.

On "clear conscience," see comments on 1:3, 5, 19 above, as well as at 2 Tim 1:3 and Titus 1:15. The conscience might not be clear if a deacon is poorly grounded in Christian teaching, does not affirm it wholeheartedly, or is negligent in bringing his behavior into line with the implications of the gospel message and Christ's lordship. As the next verse makes clear, Paul has more in mind than passing a test on "the deep truths of the faith" with flying colors; he is concerned about the practical, demonstrated, public appropriation of those truths. Deacons "will often have to give advice and comfort, if they are not going to neglect their duties."[416] To function well requires good biblical and theological understanding, as well as ethical integrity.

414. See, for example, Rom 16:25–26; 1 Cor 2:7; Eph 3:3–9; Col 1:26. On "mystery" in the AF and LXX, see Quinn and Wacker, 273–74. For grounding of "mystery" in Jesus's teaching (and in the Old Testament, esp. Daniel), see D. Seccombe, *The King of God's Kingdom* (Milton Keynes: Paternoster, 2002), 324: "In speaking of the *mystery* of the kingdom of God, Jesus indicates that there are things about the kingdom which can only be known through revelation from God" (italics in original).

415. See, for example, *CNTUOT* 556–72.

416. Calvin, 229.

10 Verses 8–9 consist of five terms or phrases in Greek with no stated finite verb ("deacons are to be" [v. 8] and "They must hold" [v. 9] are inferred from the context). Verse 10, however, is a grammatically full sentence: "They must first be tested. . . ." Just as an overseer could not be a novice (v. 6),[417] so deacons must have a proven track record. Paul commends testing (*dokimazō*) of groups[418] and individuals;[419] the word occurs seventeen times in his writings, though only here in the PE. Timothy will need to observe and discern the mettle of diaconal candidates to establish their fitness, just as the church needs to "test" everything and "hold on to what is good" (1 Thess 5:21). To put it another way, it would be imprudent for untested persons to be inducted into the deacon position because of the damage they might cause to the church, to themselves, or to those they are called to serve.

"First" and "then" in v. 10 point to some season or process of assessment. "If there is nothing against them" renders a participial clause that could also be rendered "if they prove blameless" (HCSB), "if they are above reproach" (LEB), or "if they pass the test" (NLT). The key word here is *anenklētos*, discussed in full in connection with Titus 1:6 (see commentary), where it is a qualification for an elder. It means innocent of provable charges of sub-Christian belief or behavior, to put it negatively.[420] Positively, deacons should display lives that exhibit a full range and depth of Christian faith and practice. When and if Timothy establishes that they do, he can "let them serve as deacons." "Serve as deacons" translates a form of the word *diakoneō*; see discussion at v. 13 below.

11 The opening construction of this verse is identical to v. 8, except "the women" replaces "deacons." NIV (1984) translated "their wives," reflecting the facts that (1) the Greek can be translated either "women" or "wives" (there is no "the" or "their" in Gk.), and (2) many translators understand the discourse flow to imply reference to the wives of deacons (or of both deacons and elders).[421] Other translations find "women" here.[422] Jouette Bassler observes,

417. The opening words of the verse, *kai houtoi*, could be understood as "these [deacons] too," with "too" an oblique reference to the overseer whose testing and approval is presupposed throughout vv. 2–7. See NEB: "No less than bishops, they. . . ."

418. For example, 2 Cor 13:5: "Examine yourselves to see whether you are in the faith; test yourselves. Do you not realize that Christ Jesus is in you—unless, of course, you fail the test?"

419. For example, Gal 6:4: "Each one should test their own actions."

420. Aquinas (42) says this means not guilty of mortal sin but leaves room for venial sin based on 1 John 1:8. The Roman Catholic dogmatic categories are contestable, but the wisdom is sound that Paul does not have in mind sinless perfection.

421. "Wives" or "their wives" appears, for example, in KJ21, BRG, CJB, ESV, GNT, GNV, HCSB, ISV, LEB, NET, NLT, and others.

422. Among others: AMP, ASV, CEB, CEV, DRA, ERV, ICB, NABRE, NASB, NRSV, WEB.

"The women . . . may be women deacons, but the text is very cryptic and is open to other interpretations."[423]

What is clear is that Paul has moved from the overseer (vv. 1–7), to analogous requirements for deacons (vv. 8–10, 12–13), and now to "women" or "wives." In an era where church offices have increasingly opened to women, arguments for "women" being in view have proliferated, because it could imply that, even when speaking of "deacons," Paul already had female deacons in view, and possibly female overseers, too—and this verse would confirm their involvement in these offices from early in the history of the church. Hence Witherington quotes Thomas Oden favorably: "There can be no doubt . . . that these were women in ministry, requiring qualifications for service, whose qualifications were set rhetorically right beside those of male deacons."[424]

Johnson is just as certain, adding reference to Phoebe (Rom 16:1), whom Paul named "as a *diakonos* of the church at Cenchrae, so we know that he had no difficulty with women holding such a position."[425] This conclusion assumes, though, a technical meaning of the word (see table 16) that cannot be verified, though it also cannot be ruled out with evidence currently available. Gregory R. Perry[426] argues for a similar view in Calvin,[427] B. B. Warfield, Edmund Clowney, and others among theologically conservative Presbyterian groups. Belleville summarizes much current sentiment: whether the "women" of v. 11 are deacons or not, "Paul was singling out a group of women who served the church in a recognized leadership capacity."[428]

423. J. Bassler, "A Plethora of Epiphanies: Christology in the Pastoral Letters," *PSB* 17 (1996): 310–25 (here 325n1). Also stressing the passage's ambiguity is Dibelius and Conzelmann, 58: "The question whether the reference here is to deaconesses, or to the wives of deacons, can hardly be answered with certainty."

424. Witherington, 241, quoting Oden, 149. So also Neudorfer, *Erster Brief an Timotheus*, 150, who dismisses the alternative without comment or explanation.

425. Johnson, *First and Second Letters to Timothy*, 228–29. So also Towner, *Letters*, 266, with supporting arguments in 265–66n28. The dismissal there (with "predictably") of Mounce and Knight is unfortunate.

426. Gregory R. Perry, "Phoebe of Cenchreae and 'Women' of Ephesus: 'Deacons' in the Earliest Churches,'" *Presb* 36.1 (2010): 9–36.

427. This comment requires qualification: Calvin discerned two kinds of deacons (in Rom 12:8)—those who administered care of the poor, and those who actually performed the care. Men composed the former group, while women (for the sake of the care of widows and others with whom women can best connect) were part of the latter. See John Calvin, *Institutes of the Christian Religion*, trans. Ford Lewis Battles (Philadelphia: Westminster, 1960), 2:1061. Moreover, in commenting on 1 Tim 3:11, Calvin (229) is unequivocal: "He refers here to the wives of both bishops and deacons." Twomey, 59, also notes that Calvin did not view "the women" in 1 Tim 3:11 to be "officeholders in their own right."

428. Belleville, 75.

Others are sure of the opposite, as all the translations containing "wives" imply. Doriani gives a helpful summary of four major positions: (1) the women are "part of the general order of deacons," (2) "they are female deacons or deaconesses who correspond somehow to the male deacons," (3) they are "assistants to deacons" like the praiseworthy widows (1 Tim 5:9–10) and older women who train the younger (Titus 2:3–5), and (4) they are the deacons' wives. He observes that "all four views agree that women should be involved in diaconal work."[429] For that matter, Christian women *not* involved in formal diaconal work can profit from the counsel of v. 11, just like nonoverseer and nondeacon men can learn much from the qualifications for both of those offices (to which, after all, they might someday aspire).

In part because of the way v. 11 is sandwiched between vv. 8–10 and 12–13, where (male) deacons are clearly in view, it is defensible (though not necessary compelling) to understand v. 11 as the wives of deacons. There is here also a possible nod to wives of overseers, since "in the same way, deacons" (v. 8) affirms a close parallel between the two—and if deacons' wives are critical to the diaconal ministry, the same holds no less true for the wives of pastoral church leaders. If indeed Paul has deacons' (and overseers'?) wives in mind, this is another indication of his concern for the full engagement and benefit of women in the ministry of the church (see 2:11 on women learning).

"Worthy of respect" is the same word applied to deacons in v. 8. See comments there along with reference to discussion of related words and passages in the PE. What "worthy of respect" entails is enlarged on with three additional qualifications. First, "not malicious talkers [*diabolous*]." The same word is translated "slanderous" in 2 Tim 3:3 and (of the older women at Crete) "slanderers" in Titus 2:3 (see discussion in commentary).[430] Second, wives of deacons (and possibly of overseers) or women who are deacons should be "temperate." This word was applied to the overseer in v. 2 and to "the older men" in Titus 2:2, the only other Pauline uses of the word. See discussion of both passages in the commentary. Third, these women or wives should be "trustworthy [from *pistos*] in everything." "Everything" is a plural form in Greek and could be translated "all things." Faithfulness in everything requires faithfulness in particulars (cf. Luke 16:10–12). *Pistos* (faithful, trustworthy) is a significant adjective in the PE, occurring seventeen times. Five of those are the celebrated "trustworthy saying" passages.[431] Christ regarded Paul as "trustworthy" by his grace. In some PE passages the noun form of the word is rendered "believer" (e.g., 1 Tim 4:12; 5:16; 6:2).

429. Doriani, *Women and Ministry*, 180–83 ("Appendix II: Wives or Deaconesses in 1 Timothy 3:11").

430. See *NIDNTTE* 1:691–92 for additional concise discussion of the word.

431. 1 Tim 1:15; 3:1; 4:9; 2 Tim 2:11; Titus 3:8.

Paul gives, then, a concise characterization of traits necessary for women to take their place alongside their husbands (or other deacons) in the full scope of the ministry, for which 3:1–13 makes leadership provision (deacons being those who take the lead and bear the brunt in various service capacities). He could easily have omitted their mention. The fact that he did not reflects how instinctively he viewed them as integral to ministry infrastructure and execution. In my reading, they did not hold formal office, but it did not mean they did not constitute a major phalanx in the ministry initiatives of the Ephesian congregation(s). Doriani's reflections "An Alternate Vision of Leadership" and "Thriving in Our Places" summarize a much wider discussion that is suggestive for maximal engagement of women in diaconal (and) other church ministry today.[432]

It may bear underscoring that, just as men by their convictions and behavior can disqualify themselves for overseer or deacon appointment, in Paul's outlook, so can the women or wives of v. 11 do great harm to the church, their marriages, and themselves if they prove *not* to be "worthy of respect," *are* "malicious talkers," and are *not* "temperate and trustworthy in everything." Whatever their rights and responsibilities as Scripture sets forth, divine blessing on their endeavors depends on their success in finding the grace in the gospel to reflect such Christlikeness.

Under the assumption that the ungodly deportment of his wife would hinder a deacon's appointment, Aquinas inquires into the justice of this restriction. He observes that an ungodly wife would herself need care, rendering the husband less available for church duties. Also, men can be "corrupted by their wives." And finally, "many frequent the houses of the ministers of the Church," and Aquinas calls this "dangerous" if the wife is deficient in the ways Paul highlights.[433]

12 Paul returns to deacons. "Must be" is an impersonal rendering of an imperative addressed to Timothy:[434] "Let them [i.e., deacons] be faithful. . . ." In the same vein as he began in v. 8, Paul continues to sketch an optimal portrait of church officers who lead through the specialty of serving.

On "faithful to his wife," see discussion of parallel phrases in v. 2 and in Titus 1:6. This wording does not mean deacons had to be married: it is an assumption that adult men eligible to be considered as deacons will have pursued matrimony, as was customary in both Greco-Roman and Jewish cultures.

432. Doriani, *Women and Ministry*, 130–32. See also at the practical level Byrd, *No Little Women*; Smith, *God's Good Design*. For biblical veracity and authority from a woman's standpoint, see K. Folmar, *The Good Portion: The Doctrine of Scripture for Every Woman* (Fearn, Ross-shire, Scotland: Christian Focus, 2017).

433. Aquinas, 143.

434. Paul uses the word *estōsan*, the only present imperative third person plural form of *eimi* (to be) in the NT, apart from Luke 12:35.

Unmarried deacons would have been expected to be celibate and to exercise the same purity enjoined on Timothy (1 Tim 4:12; 5:2). Whatever one's marital status, serving as a deacon in a movement whose leader taught, "Anyone who looks at a woman lustfully has already committed adultery with her in his heart" (Matt 5:28) would call for a high level of maturity and integrity in both inner life and the outward expression of sensual and sexual drives.

On "manage his children and his household well," see comments on vv. 4–5 above, where similar language and concerns appear, though with the order switched: household (or "family") and then children in v. 4, children and then household in v. 12. It can hardly be stressed too often, in contemporary settings where "church" and home are separate places, that, in the NT setting, congregations met in homes. Double lives were not as easy to maintain as they are where people can live one way domestically, then be transformed to live out a church identity in another location, only to return to their domicile and lapse back into very different priorities and behavior. Paul calls for seamlessness and consistency as displayed in marital and parental performance. Unless the gospel message and instruction centering on love (cf. 1:5) does its work in the privacy of deacons' family relations, deacons' service to and on behalf of the congregation will be mechanical, forced, and possibly without the necessary support that God calls on all ministry in Christ's name to seek through prayer.[435]

It is too easy, however, to view v. 12 as a minefield with threats or as a stark punch list for ecclesial recognition. Viewed positively, as against false teaching apparently in the air at Ephesus, "God created" marriage, like good food, "to be received with thanksgiving by those who believe and who know the truth" (4:3). Marriage and children constitute blessings and sources of joy and strength. The tie between husband and wife is like that between Christ and the church (Eph 5:25–33). Paul wants deacons to serve with the affection and verve that grace enables, not out of a grimly conceived monogamy and exacting suppression of children's behavior. Managing one's "household well" draws from the deep springs of God's provision, wisdom, and commands that are evident throughout 1 Timothy. Love that abounds in a deacon's daily life is a primary practical source for the love his diaconal service will express for Christ's glory in the church.

13 In Greek the conjunction "for" (*gar*) joins this verse with the one preceding. Loving wife and children and negotiating home life well (v. 12) has its own rewards. It is requisite for diaconal service. But v. 13 puts icing on the cake: "For those 'deaconing' well will gain . . . ," it could be rendered. There is additional incentive, two aspects of which Paul mentions next. First, "those who have served well gain an excellent standing." "Well" is the same adverb

435. According to 1 Pet 3:7, men who mistreat their wives sabotage their own prayers. See more generally Ps 66:18.

(*kalōs*) that occurs eleven other times in Paul, four of them in 1 Timothy.[436] In the PE all uses pertain to the quality of service performed by church leaders. "Served" translates a form of *diakoneō*, a word used in the PE only here and in v. 10. These are the only places Paul uses it to connote diaconal service. His six other uses describe ministry more generally on the part of Paul (Rom 15:25; 2 Cor 3:3; 8:19, 20), Onesimus (2 Tim 1:18), or Philemon (Phlm 13). Such service in the deacon's role results in reward—the deacons will "gain."[437] In its other two NT uses this means gain with great effort (Luke 17:33) or at high cost (Acts 20:28). Here it denotes the result of faithful service in the deacon's position: "an excellent[438] standing."

"Standing" (*bathmos*) can carry the idea of rank or grade. Deacons' sacrifice to do the job right (vv. 8–19, 12) results in recognition. The Greek states explicitly "for themselves" (*heautois*). Deacons will increase in the "respect" that is needed for effective ministry (cf. mentions of "respect" in vv. 4, 8, 11). They will also be positioned to handle subsequent ministry opportunities with the support and trust of those who have observed this person's effective service in the past. There could also be a hint of a promise of eschatological reward here, a motivator in Paul's own faithful service (see 6:19; 2 Tim 4:8; Titus 3:7).

Second, faithful deacons also gain "great assurance in their faith in Christ Jesus." While pride and complacency are dangerous, justified (as opposed to delusional)[439] assurance is surely to be welcomed. Faithful diaconal service is a means to acquire it.

NIV's translation of "assurance" deserves comment. Paul uses the same word (*parrēsia*) seven other times, but in those cases NIV most frequently follows BDAG in conveying the notion of boldness (2 Cor 3:12; cf. Eph 6:19 "fearlessly"; Col 2:15 "public spectacle"; Phlm 8), frankness (2 Cor 7:4), or courage (Phil 1:20). BDAG does not list "assurance" as a gloss for *parrēsia*. It is possible that this is not exactly what Paul is promising. The offer may be of "abundant boldness," which might assume (or result in) some form of assurance but is not congruent or identical with it. Deacons should serve aggressively and sacrificially (i.e., "well"), not for the sake of assurance[440] (which, if they were successful, might tempt to them to take their foot off the gas, so to speak),

436. Rom 11:20; 1 Cor 7:37, 38; 14:17; 2 Cor 11:4; Gal 4:17; 5:7; Phil 4:14; 1 Tim 3:4, 12; 5:17.

437. From *peripoieō*, found thirty times in the LXX, sixty-one in Philo, thirteen in Josephus, thirteen in Epictetus, and nine in the AF. It is an example of a word common in other extant first-century writings but rare in the NT.

438. That is, "excellent" in the sense of *kalos* (good, attractive). The same word is translated "noble" in v. 1 and "good" in v. 7.

439. See, for example, Matt 7:21–23; 1 Tim 1:7; 4:2; Titus 1:16.

440. "Assurance" occurs only two other times in the NIV: in Heb 10:22 (translating *plērophoria*) and in Heb 11:1 (translating *elenchos*).

but to be equipped to continue to ramp up the level of their commitment and service. It is the difference between contentment with a plateau and fire in the belly to continue to be expended in Christ's service. Whatever the exact translation, Paul's word choice favors the latter notion.

"In their faith in Christ Jesus" similarly runs against many other translations that take the Greek to be speaking of "the faith" (*fides quae*) more than the deacons' faith (*fides qua*).[441] Most translations then define that faith by its object: "the faith that/which is in Christ Jesus."[442] NIV's "great assurance in their faith in Christ Jesus" risks conveying a self-referential emphasis that stands in tension with Paul's Christocentric theology and focus on what God does to save more than what man does to appropriate the benefit of God's saving act in Christ. See Paul's testimony (1:12–17) for Paul's customary theocentric emphasis.

In the end v. 13, however translated, gives Timothy grounds to commend diaconal service as bringing advantage to the one performing it, especially as regards (the or their) faith in Christ Jesus. This commendation is along with the obvious positive effects on those served, as well as witness to the care and provision of God, under whose direction such service is rendered.

C. Reasons for Paul's Instructions (3:14–4:16)

The next section constitutes the substance of the epistle in terms of specifics to Timothy personally. Chapter 1 stated and restated Paul's charge, touched on false teachers, and affirmed Paul's testimony in the light of God's mercy and majesty. Chapter 2 laid out worship priorities (like prayer), foundations (God and Christ), and protocol (attitudes and deportment). Chapter 3 dealt with leadership standards. None of these topics would be without immediate interest and appeal to Timothy, for they are all matters vital to ministry at Ephesus. But little has been aimed at Timothy directly except for 1:18–19.

Paul's angle of address is about to take a turn in Timothy's direction. In just 432 words (NIV; 277 in Gk.) Paul will confirm more fully (fleshing out the charges in 1:3, 18) why he is writing (3:14–15) and tarry in doxology (3:16) before warming to his topic in this section, which is primarily exhortation to Timothy. Paul underscores evil of eschatological proportions facing the church and how believers should respond (4:1–5). From there he embarks on a series of rich affirmations and admonitions aimed directly at Timothy (4:6–16).

441. See discussion of the distinction at Titus 1:4 in the commentary. Among other versions, seeing "their faith": CEV, ERV, EXB, GNT, GW, ICB, ISV, TLB.

442. For example, KJ21, AMP, ASV, BRG, CEB, DRA, ESV, GNV, HCSB, JUB, KJV, LEB, NASB, NET.

The final verse in the section is an apt summary: "Watch your life and doctrine closely. Persevere in them, because if you do, you will save both yourself and your hearers" (4:16). This is not hyperbolic. Congregations, especially in pioneer stages,[443] stand or fall by their leadership. It is easy for leaders to drift, err, or waver. Then the cause to which Paul and Timothy are committed is imperiled, for both Timothy and those he instructs will have run aground (see 1:19, where Paul likewise calls Timothy to persevere).

Such disaster can be avoided through the resources for godliness (including Timothy's) in Christ (3:16) and Timothy's diligence, devotion, and visible progress in response (4:15).

1. Conduct in God's Household and Its Basis in Christ (3:14–16)

> [14] *Although I hope to come to you soon, I am writing you these instructions so that,* [15] *if I am delayed, you will know how people ought to conduct themselves in God's household, which is the church of the living God, the pillar and foundation of the truth.* [16] *Beyond all question, the mystery from which true godliness springs is great:*
>
> *He appeared in the flesh,*
> *was vindicated by the Spirit,*
> *was seen by angels,*
> *was preached among the nations,*
> *was believed on in the world,*
> *was taken up in glory.*

14 Paul turns from overseers and deacons in the previous section to why he is writing.[444] The shift may be slightly more graceful in Greek, as Paul begins with *tauta soi graphō elpizōn elthein* ("these things[445] to you I am writing, although I am hoping to come . . ."). This wording signals directly that he is moving from his previous topic ("these things") to other matters. Such direct reference to his writing using precisely this form is not common in Paul, but it is not unprecedented.

Paul uses *graphō* (I write, am writing) five other times: 1 Cor 4:14; 14:37; 2 Cor 13:10; Gal 1:20; 2 Thess 3:17. In these passages one observes a raised level

443. Christianity at Ephesus was barely a decade old.

444. Twomey, 59, sees here "a play for epistolary verisimilitude." But if Paul is the author, he is simply stating a reasonable intention.

445. Mostly likely referring to the immediately prior discourse of 3:1–13, which verses, however, are also organically connected with what preceded them.

of intensity because of the setting or issues Paul addresses. For example, in Gal 1:20 he writes, "The things I am writing to you—I assure you before God I am not lying!" (my translation). Does *graphō* in 1 Tim 3:14 point to elevated emotion or concern? Perhaps Paul knows he is about to highlight present dire straits (4:1) and their implications. Elevated concern could have been what called forth the lofty vision and prose (3:16) that will precede Paul's warning. Witherington detects Paul writing "in haste" here "these telegraphic instructions."[446]

These are speculations. What is clear is that, wherever Paul is as he writes (or dictates), he has every intention of joining Timothy at Ephesus in the near future. Earlier believers at Ephesus had been shattered by the realization that "they would never see [Paul's] face again" (Acts 20:38; cf. v. 25); now Timothy can take heart that he might. Till then, there are critical matters Timothy needs to keep squarely before both him and those he instructs and oversees (see 4:6, 11).

15 Paul intends to be there soon (previous verse), but he might be "delayed." In that event, the matters already touched on in chs. 1–3, combined with the remainder of the epistle, will confirm Timothy in the guidance he needs to furnish.

That guidance starts with everyday living as disciples of Jesus, as Paul wants to remind Timothy "how people ought to conduct themselves in God's household," by which Paul means the voluntary association ("church")[447] that is devoted to "the living God," whose Son "came into the world to save sinners" (1:15). As the church at Ephesus receives teaching and oversight (2:11; cf. 4:11) from Timothy and other leaders, they need to make sure they "conduct themselves" in ways "the living God"[448] approves.

That is a plausible paraphrase of the thrust of v. 15. A closer look nuances the picture. Many translations prefer "how one ought to conduct oneself" or "how you ought to conduct yourself." In the Greek "people" does not appear. Paul writes "in order that you [sing.; i.e., Timothy] might know how it is necessary [*dei*] to conduct oneself [*anastrephesthai*]" (my translation). Both Greek words in brackets deserve close attention.

On *dei* (NIV "ought to"), see table 15 and comments on 1 Tim 3:2 above. Here in v. 15 it indicates that Paul is broaching a topic invested with high moral

446. Witherington, 245.

447. "Church" (*ekklēsia*) is mentioned in the PE only here and in 1 Tim 3:5; 5:16, 17. Paul assumes rather than argues for its composition and existence. His ecclesial teachings, to the extent we possess them, are aired in writings to recently founded congregations (see, e.g., 1 Cor 12; Eph 1–4), not in the PE, written to coworkers long involved in church planting and nurture. See the excursus on the church in the PE in Marshall, with Towner, 512–18.

448. The expression denotes "the God who is both alive and at work in the world and in the lives of people in both the Old and New Testaments" (Gloer, 161). See additional discussion at 4:10.

and perhaps even divine import. Paul was aware of divine sanction behind his counsel at times (e.g., 1 Cor 7:40; 2 Cor 2:17; Col 1:25 1 Thess 2:13), quite apart from the canonical consideration that his writings as Scripture are properly regarded as divine revelation in toto.[449]

Regarding *anastrephesthai* (NIV "to conduct themselves"), the word could as easily refer to how Timothy ought to conduct himself. That meaning would comport with "in order that you [sing., referring to Timothy] might know . . ." in conjunction with the rest of the chapter, which deals more with Timothy's conduct than that of people in the church in general.

What needs to be stressed is that a shallow moralistic understanding of "conduct themselves/yourself" should be resisted.[450] Johnson observes that *anastrephesthai* occurs in moral discourse to denote, not simply certain acts one performs, but, more important, one's "manner of life" as informed by "guiding principles."[451] This understanding is borne out by several of Epictetus's twenty-three uses of the verb[452] and cognate noun.[453] These words have their equivalents in OT, LXX, and Second Temple writings too; in NT occurrences, "the main point is to translate knowledge into practice," which is Paul's concern here. But as his testimony in 1:12–17 reminded, "turning to Christ . . . implies a simultaneous turning away from one's previous way of life, for which Christ frees and enables the believer."[454] Paul wants Timothy to minister a message that changes lives, not that confirms the complacent in a presumptuous status quo.

"God's household" (*oikos theou*) is also mentioned in Eph 2:19 and Titus 1:7 (see commentary), although with different Greek words. The idea is not that God is contained in a physical structure or that his presence is limited to just one certain place or people, for God is omnipresent. But from OT times God made his presence known to persons with such force that Jacob (after his dream at Bethel, which means "house of God") could say, "This is truly the house of God [*oikos theou*]!" (Gen 28:17 LXX, my translation). Rescued from "the land of Egypt, out of a house of slavery" (Exod 20:2 NETS), God's people are called to bring "the first products of your land . . . into the house of the Lord your God" (Exod 23:19 NETS; cf. Deut 23:18). "The house of God"

449. See, for example, Swinson, *What Is Scripture?* For broader framework, see D. A. Carson, ed., *The Enduring Authority of the Christian Scriptures* (Grand Rapids: Eerdmans, 2016); Matthew Barrett, *God's Word Alone: The Authority of Scripture* (Wheaton, IL: Crossway, 2016).

450. Many translations use the word "behave" or "behave yourselves," which in American English sounds inherently like a scolding parent.

451. *First and Second Letters to Timothy*, 231. Among extrabiblical writers he cites Polybius, Xenophon, Aristotle, and Josephus.

452. For example, *Enchiridion* 15.1; *Discourses* 1.7.3, 11; 1.29.44; 3.10.16.

453. *Discourses* 1.7.2; 9.11, 24; 22.13.

454. *NIDNTTE* 1:289–90.

is the place of worship in Jerusalem (2 Sam 12:20 LXX) and the tabernacle in the desert (1 Chr 6:48). It is the temple rededicated and rebuilt under Ezra and Nehemiah (Ezra 6:16–17; Neh 10:37–38). Isaiah spoke of "the last days" when "all the nations" will come to "the house of God" (Isa 2:2).

This millennia-long and often grandiose concept of God coming to and somehow dwelling among his people stands behind Paul's vision of the significance of Jews (like Timothy) and Gentiles together at Ephesus worshiping God through Christ (see next verse). The Ephesian congregation (or perhaps congregations) with Christ in its midst constitutes a divine dwelling place, an assembly ("church," *ekklēsia*) where "the living God" is known and worshiped. Quite in contrast are the Greco-Roman gods, who are figments of idolatry (1 Cor 8:5–6; Gal 4:8; cf. Acts 14:11; 19:26). They are effectively dead gods, despite their traditional affirmation in the Roman world. It is striking that Paul would view the (numerically) modest presence of at most surely just a few hundred believers at Ephesus as a locus of the presence of "the living God" in a Roman world dominated by such a contrasting religious consciousness. But both Paul and Timothy were part of an ancient Abrahamic heritage that was accustomed to being a minority presence in a world with contrasting loyalties.

Because of God's presence, his "household" and "church" under Timothy's leadership can also be called "the pillar and foundation of the truth." Paul uses the word "pillar" elsewhere only in Gal 2:9, to describe the Jerusalem pastoral stalwarts "James, Cephas, and John." The church as a "pillar" is a straightforward metaphor expressing its load-bearing role in upholding "the truth."[455] The church is likewise the "foundation." The word is used in the NT only here and may in fact have been invented by Paul.[456] In connection with "the truth," "pillar and foundation" likely points to the church's role (through their confession of Christ; see v. 16) in combatting soul-destroying error at Ephesus in the form of false teachers and their deleterious effects. Paul will shortly touch on this theme further (4:1–3). Perhaps in anticipation, he confirms for Timothy here that "truth" exists and that it matters, especially in issues relating to God, humans, sin, and salvation.[457] Luther offers this understanding: "As doctrine is, so also is life. If the doctrine is filled with lying, life is hypocritical. In the church doctrine is pure, and therefore life, too, so that the truth of both doctrine and life are preserved."[458]

455. Less relevant is God's presence in the "pillar" of Exod 13:21–22 and elsewhere; see Towner, *Letters*, 275.

456. *NIDNTTE* 2:88. The adjective form ("firm, steadfast") is found three times (1 Cor 7:37; 15:58; Col 1:23).

457. On "truth" (*alētheia*) in the PE, see discussion below at 2 Tim 2:25; 3:7–8. The word is used ten other times in the PE (see commentary at 1 Tim 2:4, 7 [twice]; 4:3; 6:5; 2 Tim 2:15, 18; 4:4; Titus 1:1, 14) for a total of fourteen references.

458. Luther, 303.

16 It is hard to avoid the impression that mention of "the truth" in v. 15, in conjunction with an upcoming allusion of demonic error (4:1–3) and the previous mention of false teaching (1:3, 7), helps account for mention of Christ in his fullness here. "The highest of the Christological moments in this letter is to be found in [this verse]."[459] In Christ's person and work lies the key to the strength and flourishing of the faith community Timothy oversees, along with its missiological edge.[460]

"Beyond all question" translates *homologoumenōs*, an adverb that for Paul could carry liturgical and confessional weight.[461] The idea is "in keeping with what we believe and confess about Jesus Christ," which is "truth," in contrast to all that may oppose him and those faithful to him. The adverb highlights the magnitude, excellence, and nonnegotiable veracity of the christological affirmations upcoming.

On "godliness," see commentary on Titus 1:1, as well as the Introduction, IX.B. On "mystery," see 1 Tim 3:5 and commentary above, the only other use of the word in the PE. It refers to redemptive truths formerly concealed but now revealed in Christ's coming. Whereas Ephesian residents had once sought to halt the gospel's spread with a riot rallying around the slogan "Great is Artemis of the Ephesians!" (Acts 19:34),[462] Paul seeks to exalt the greatness of another. There is a close connection between his coming and the presence of "true godliness"[463] on the part of his followers, which Paul wants Timothy to grow in and promote.

In six clauses Paul characterizes Christ's greatness. This mystery now made known in him may well be that "from which true godliness springs" (NIV), but the less defined "mystery of godliness" preferred by other translations[464] leaves room for the mystery to be all that Paul implies (and more) with the wide-ranging christological truths about to be affirmed.

459. Twomey, 61.

460. Stressed by Neudorfer, *Erster Brief an Timotheus*, 166.

461. So Towner, *Letters*, 276. In other contexts, related words appear in legal or academic/logical contexts.

462. See J. R. Edwards, "Archaeology Gives New Reality to Paul's Ephesus Riot," *BAR* 42/4 (July/August 2016) 24–32, 62.

463. "True" is absent from the Greek. It is virtually absent from the English-language translation tradition except in the 2011 NIV and associated renderings (NIRV, NIVUK). Godliness associated with the OT and NT God "who does not lie" would of necessity be "true" godliness (not false, or lying, or otherwise deceived or deceiving), so the adjective seems superfluous. Is the point perhaps to underscore the sincerity of this godliness, or perhaps its conformity to apostolic norms (cf. Rom 6:17)? In the other nine passages where "godliness" (*eusebeia*) occurs in the PE, NIV never adds "true."

464. For example, KJ21, ASV, AMP, BRG, CEB, DLNT, ESV, GNV, HCSB, JUB, NASB, RSV, TLV, WEB.

Many stress the hymnic,[465] traditional, or poetic origin or nature of the statement of the articles below,[466] but specifics of their origin (if Paul did not write them) are unknown. There is nothing in them that Paul could not have written,[467] or of which he shows no awareness in his other writings.[468] Appeal to "implicit teaching against Gnosticism found in the letter writer's quotation of the hymn"[469] is unnecessary to explain the passage.

1. "He[470] appeared in the flesh." On "appeared" (from *phaneroō*), see commentary on 2 Tim 1:10 and Titus 1:3, the only two other places the word is used in the PE. The word is "hardly attested at all prior to the NT."[471] Here it refers to Jesus's earthly appearing (see John 1:14), including the course of his entire life prior to his ascension. It includes his resurrection, which some think is at the core of the meaning of this clause.[472] Even if resurrection is the main point, the incarnation[473] is basic to it, and Paul's statement is reasonably viewed as broad enough to include either or both miraculous manifestations. Whereas the law-teachers (1:7) might point to the Torah as God's definitive self-disclosure, and ascetics (4:3) might demonize the bounty of God's created order, Paul's incarnational understanding of Jesus makes him, not the law, God's definitive self-disclosure. The incarnation likewise affirms rather than

465. Perhaps on the analogy of, and even with some indebtedness to, Phil 2:6–11; so Neudorfer, *Erster Brief an Timotheus*, 166. But the theory that the Philippians passage owes its origin to a pre-Pauline hymn can be questioned: see R. Weymouth, "The Christ-Story of Philippians 2:6–11" (Ph.D. dissertation, University of Otago, Dunedin, New Zealand, 2015), summarized in *Tyndale Bulletin* 67.2 (2016) 317–20. Caution is advised in assuming what cannot really be proven with respect to 1 Tim 3:16 as well.

466. For example, Krause, 79–81. Dibelius and Conzelmann, 61, note here the correspondence between "mystery" and "the rationalistic character of the teaching" found in the PE. But the opposite could be argued: these are all revealed, transcendent truths, not constructions of human rationality.

467. For Paul's robust awareness of Jesus' earthly life, see Paul Barnett, *Jesus and the Logic of History* (Grand Rapids: Eerdmans, 1997); Porter, *When Paul Met Jesus*. For the Jesus-Paul connection in their teaching, see D. Wenham, *Paul: Follower of Jesus or Founder of Christianity?* (Grand Rapids: Eerdmans, 1995).

468. On the verse, see esp. Daniel Akin, "The Mystery of Godliness Is Great: Christology in the Pastoral Epistles," in Köstenberger and Wilder, *Entrusted with the Gospel*, 137–52.

469. Krause, 82.

470. On the textual variant, see, for example, Quinn and Wacker, 295. The word translated "he" (the Gk. pronoun *hos*) was changed to "God" (*theos*) in some later NT MSS. Another scribal move was to read the neuter singular pronoun *ho*, which would refer back to "the mystery." *Hos* with Jesus understood as the antecedent is the most difficult reading and has the best MS support.

471. *NIDNTTE* 4:588.

472. See Collins, 108–9.

473. Presupposed in Paul in verses like 2 Cor 8:9; Gal 4:4; and other passages speaking of Christ coming or being sent from heaven.

minimizes creatureliness and activities integral to it like marriage and enjoyment of foods. There is rich theological truth here too: "The difference between God and man is very great, and yet in Christ we see God's infinite glory joined to our polluted flesh so that the two can become one."[474]

2. He "was vindicated by the Spirit." This phrase seems to echo Rom 1:4, where by the Spirit, Jesus was declared to be "the Son of God in power by his resurrection from the dead." BDAG 249 places the meaning of "vindicated" (from *dikaioō*) in a semantic field meaning "to demonstrate to be morally right, *prove to be right*." Although Christ came in the likeness of sinful humans (Rom 8:3), by the work of the Spirit he was delivered from the disgrace and shame of the sin he bore (2 Cor 5:21), remaining free from committing sin himself.[475] This is the only occurrence of "by the Spirit" (*en pneumati*) in the PE, but Paul uses the expression sixteen times elsewhere. (On the Spirit more broadly, see at 4:1 below.)

Table 17. "By the Spirit" (*en pneumati*) in Paul

Passage	The Spirit's function
Rom 2:29	Cleanses the heart: "circumcision is . . . of the heart, by the Spirit."
Rom 8:9; 14:17	Provides the sphere in which believers subsist: they "are not in the realm of the flesh but are in the realm of the Spirit, if indeed the Spirit of God lives in/among" them. . . . For believers, God's kingdom is not just "eating and drinking" but rather "righteousness, peace and joy in the Holy Spirit."
Rom 9:1	Testifies to truth-telling: Paul was telling the truth, which his conscience confirmed by the Holy Spirit.
Rom 15:16	Sanctifies the otherwise unworthy: the Gentiles became "an offering acceptable to God . . . by the Holy Spirit."
1 Cor 12:3[476]	Grants powers of discernment and expression to enable confession of "Jesus is Lord."
1 Cor 14:16	Enables praise of God.
2 Cor 6:3	Furnishes a means (or agent) for apostolic vindication.

474. Calvin, 233.

475. Cf. Aquinas, 47, who says as to his humanity Christ was "a justified [i.e., vindicated] spirit, because He was just, without any sin."

476. *En pneumati* occurs twice in this verse.

Passage	The Spirit's function
Gal 6:1	Furnishes means for the restoration of someone who errs, that is, "someone . . . caught in a sin."
Eph 2:22	Furnishes means for God to dwell among believers who are, as a result, "being built together."
Eph 3:5	Reveals the mystery of the gospel, which was made known "by the Spirit to God's holy apostles and prophets."
Eph 5:18	Fills and guides believers, helping them steer away from drunkenness and debauchery.
Eph 6:18	Furnishes means and a sphere in which believers pray ("Pray in the Spirit on all occasions").
Col 1:8	Furnishes a context and perhaps the means by which believers may love fervently.
1 Thess 1:5	Accompanies and drives home the gospel message: Paul's "gospel came to" the Thessalonians "not simply with words but also with power, with the Holy Spirit and deep conviction."

The occurrences above confirm that Paul views the Spirit as active on a broad front for the sake of the people of God. Such a perspective suggests a tie between "vindicated by the Spirit" and the incarnation, asserted in "appeared in the flesh": Christ not only fully manifested God as a human but was also upheld by God's Spirit, as table 17 shows is profoundly true for and among God's people. "Was vindicated by the Spirit" is as much a testimony to Jesus's real humanity as it is a snapshot of the intersection between Christology and pneumatology.[477]

3. He "was seen by angels." Since "angels" can also be translated "messengers," and since the risen Jesus appeared to followers whom he then sent out to spread gospel tidings (see, e.g., Matt 28:19–20; Luke 24:44–49; Acts 1:8), some propose that this clause refers to Jesus's postresurrection appearances to various witnesses (see also 1 Cor 15:5–8).

NIV "angels"[478] reflects the more widespread conviction that Paul does indeed have in mind heavenly beings (see 1 Tim 5:21, the only other occurrence of *angeloi*, angels, in the PE).[479] "When He was incarnate, many mysteries

477. For plausible additional connection between Jesus' vindication and Isa 53:11–12, see Collins, 109.

478. A lone English version translating "messengers" and not "angels" is DLNT.

479. For "angels" elsewhere in Paul, see Rom 8:38; 1 Cor 4:9; 6:3; 11:10; 13:1; 2 Cor 11:14; Gal 1:8; 3:19; 4:14; 2 Thess 1:7.

were made known to the angels which before they had not known."[480] Angels witnessed and announced Jesus's resurrection (Matt 28:2–7; Luke 24:4–9; John 20:11–13). They also surround the heavenly throne, where Jesus took his seat at God's right hand following his vindication from death (see Heb 1:3–4; 1 Pet 3:22; also Rev 5:8–14). Paul's point, then, is to invoke the angels' testimony to celebrate with Timothy "the mystery" that underlies the church under the aegis of its head, to whom all things, including angels, are subordinate.

4. He "was preached among the nations." On the word translated "preached" (from *kēryssō*), see 2 Tim 4:2, the only other PE occurrence of a word Paul uses over a dozen times outside the PE. With the cognate noun Paul terms himself a *kēryx* (preacher, herald; see 1 Tim 2:7; 2 Tim 1:11). The proclamation of Christ "among the nations" (from *ethnos*, a word connoting "Gentile[s]" to Pauline-era Jewish ears) evokes Jesus's frequent reference to this people group (the vast majority in the Roman world).[481] Most notably, Jesus's followers are to "make disciples of all nations" (see *ethnos*; Matt 28:19), and Paul is "apostle to the Gentiles" (Rom 11:13; Gal 2:8) and "a true and faithful teacher of the Gentiles" (1 Tim 2:7; see commentary above). Paul is basically citing the evangelization and church-planting developments at the center of which he and Timothy have labored. Christ as a light to the nations is a strong tie uniting OT prophets (see Isa 51:4; 60:3) and NT heralds like Paul. The proclamation of Jesus's person and work leading to human redemption (not just of God's chosen people the Jews but of humanity beyond) is the soteriological point of the previous three christological affirmations.

5. He "was believed on in the world." This statement complements the previous one. Proclamation that finds few takers is sometimes unavoidable (note the preaching of figures like Noah, Jeremiah, Jesus in many Gospel incidents and by some measures in his ministry as a whole, and Paul in places like Athens). But when the message is "believed on," redemption "in the world" proceeds as promised by God, who bids that people "hear" (Deut 6:4; Rom 10:17). Paul's use of a form of the verb *pisteuō*[482] (to have faith, believe) correlates with his stress elsewhere on believing and faith (*pistis*).[483] What has happened in the form of gospel reception across the Roman world in just a few decades since Jesus's appearing is glorious in itself[484]—but it also shows

480. Aquinas, 47. Calvin, 234, extends this: "Although they knew of the redemption of humanity, they did not know at first how it was to be accomplished, and it must have been concealed from them in order that the greatness of God's kindness might make them admire the more."

481. Forms of the word *ethnos* appear fifteen times in Matthew's Gospel, for example.

482. Occurring fifty-four times in Paul, six of these in the PE: 1 Tim 1:11, 16; 2 Tim 1:12; Titus 1:3; 3:8.

483. Occurring 142 times in Paul, 33 of these in the PE.

484. Aquinas, 47, comments from his vantage point in time and geography, "It is most amazing that through simple, poor and powerless men the whole world has been converted."

the bankruptcy of rival messengers and messages propounded by the false teachers at Ephesus. For it is not their message or theories that constitute "the mystery" underlying Christian congregations ("the church of the living God"; see v. 15). They are rather parasitic on and aberrations of what Paul here lauds.

6. He "was taken up in glory." Luke's Gospel refers to Jesus's ascension in advance (9:51) and as a completed event (24:51). Acts 1:9 describes the incident from another angle. "Glory" (*doxa*) "is an important christological term for Paul," but he also uses it widely in relation to believers.[485] Elsewhere Paul writes of Christ's presence in or among believers as their "hope of glory" (Col 1:27). While his reference here is undoubtedly christological in focus, it is not without ecclesial implications. It is fitting as a climactic descriptor of his work to establish the church. "Thus both in the world through the obedience of faith and in the Person of Christ a wonderful change was wrought, for He was exalted from the mean state of a servant to the Father's right hand that to Him every knee might bow"[486] in light of the mystery. "The thought of the victorious exaltation/ascension of Christ concludes the piece."[487]

2. *Pro-creation Ethics for the Last Days (4:1–5)*

> [1] *The Spirit clearly says that in later times some will abandon the faith and follow deceiving spirits and things taught by demons.* [2] *Such teachings come through hypocritical liars, whose consciences have been seared as with a hot iron.* [3] *They forbid people to marry and order them to abstain from certain foods, which God created to be received with thanksgiving by those who believe and who know the truth.* [4] *For everything God created is good, and nothing is to be rejected if it is received with thanksgiving,* [5] *because it is consecrated by the word of God and prayer.*

1 Paul continues to inform Timothy about the purpose of this epistle. Having reminded him of his ethical aim (3:14–15) and its christological basis (3:16), he now characterizes the times that define Timothy's ministry setting.

"The Spirit" is for Paul the Holy Spirit, mentioned five other times in the PE.[488] His activities vary, but among them is a revelatory function. His role within the Trinity is particularly prominent when it comes to the (for

485. Donald L. Berry, *Glory in Romans and the Unified Purpose of God in Redemptive History* (Eugene, OR: Pickwick, 2016), 3.

486. Calvin, 234.

487. Marshall, with Towner, 529.

488. 1 Tim 3:16; 2 Tim 1:7, 14; 4:22; Titus 3:5. Witherington comments (252n295) that "the range of function" of the Holy Spirit in the PE "in facts sounds very much like what we find in the earlier Paulines."

Paul) all-important resource of written Scripture (2 Tim 3:16). With the Spirit's aid, believers in general may speak (1 Cor 12:3) or praise God (1 Cor 14:16). It is the Spirit who enables believers' prayer (Rom 8:26). Paul's postconversion pilgrimage began, in Luke's telling, when Ananias confronted him with both a christological and a pneumatological summons: "Brother Saul, the Lord—Jesus, who appeared to you on the road as you were coming here—has sent me so that you may see again and be filled with the Holy Spirit" (Acts 9:17). Paul is aware that, as an apostle, he is capable of rendering judgments that are sanctioned by God's Spirit (see, e.g., 1 Cor 7:40). He discerns truths and trends that may elude the perception of others (see, e.g., Eph 3:2–6). This ability was presumably a factor in the course of action he took in dealing with Hymnaeus and Alexander (1 Tim 1:20).

By "the Spirit clearly says," Paul means he is stating what he is certain is true based on his communion with God by the Spirit and the wisdom that relationship imparts to him. He does not mean to be walling himself off from other sources of information like OT teaching and testimony, Jesus's end-time teaching perhaps known to Paul, input from other Spirit-gifted individuals including NT prophets,[489] and information gleaned from his own observation of the times, people, and movements. "Clearly" (*hrētōs*) is a NT hapax and is also absent from the LXX and the AF. But it is attested in the papyri (see MM), Philo (six times), Josephus (twice), and second-century writers like Irenaeus and Justin Martyr.[490] Paul feels that the guidance the Spirit gives, which he is about to convey, is compelling and undeniable.

"Later times" means right now (see discussion at 2 Tim 3:1), as Paul writes or dictates these lines.[491] These "times" arrived with Christ's coming (Heb 1:1–2), intensified with his resurrection and the Spirit's powerful manifestation (Acts 2:17, drawing on Joel 3:1), and continue until his return. Paul is about to describe, then, conditions as they will be but also already are. A book on contemporary preaching lists as a major hindrance to effective pulpit communication "Inadequate Contextualization to the Preaching Situation."[492] Paul wants to ensure that Timothy will not be ineffective because of a failure in discerning the times (cf. Matt 16:13). Eschatological awareness is key to pastoral readiness.

Timothy can expect rough sailing for two reasons. First, "some[493] will abandon the faith." They will depart from the core teachings of Jesus and the

489. See 1 Cor 12:28; 14:29, 32, 37; Eph 2:20; 3:5; 4:11; Acts 11:27; 13:1; 15:32; 21:10.

490. Cf. also Dibelius and Conzelmann, 64.

491. Guthrie, 103: "What is predicted of the future is conceived of as already operative in the present, so the words have specific contemporary significance."

492. Greg R. Scharf, *Let the Earth Hear His Voice: Strategies for Overcoming Bottlenecks in Preaching God's Word* (Philipsburg, NJ: P&R, 2015), ch. 7.

493. See table 21 and discussion of *tines* (some) at 5:15.

apostles, along with their OT foundations and necessary contemporary entailments. "When the faith is abandoned, the true image of Christ is suppressed or disfigured."[494] "The faith" corresponds to the "common faith" mentioned in Titus 1:4 (see discussion there of the *fides quae*) and "the faith" in 1 Tim 1:2.[495] Paul has already mentioned teachers who have gone astray in part because of misunderstanding the OT ("the law"; see 1 Tim 1:6–7). Others "have suffered shipwreck with regard to the faith" (1:19). The next verse will speak of "hypocritical liars," whose pernicious convictions must be identified and opposed (see also v. 6). By giving instructions for worship (ch. 2) and qualifications for church officers (ch. 3), Paul might give the impression that Timothy presides over a stable, business-as-usual setting. There are no such situations in pastoral work anywhere at any time, in light of the imminence of the end of the age (see Rom 13:11–12). Certainly at Ephesus Timothy must have no illusions regarding the difficulties that the progress of the gospel and the purity of the church will face. The pure milk of God's word and the gospel message are under constant threat of adulteration (see 1 Pet 2:1–3; Rom 16:17–18).

Second, the same people who "will abandon the faith" will also (and probably as both cause and consequence) "follow deceiving spirits and things taught by demons." Jesus warned against getting rid of "an impure spirit" but failing to fill the void with something spiritually pure and powerful (Matt 12:43). In that case, "the final condition of that person is worse than the first," to which Jesus added, "That is how it will be with this wicked generation" (v. 45).

Paul, also Timothy at Ephesus, inhabits that same "wicked generation," as does all the church prior to Christ's return. People may show a semblance of gospel reception, but convictions and practices inimical to "the faith" may easily come roaring back. "The demonic powers, though defeated on the cross, remain still at work amid the ruins of the history of sin."[496] "Follow" in v. 1 translates a form of *prosechō*. It occurs four other times in the PE, where NIV translates it "devote" (1 Tim 1:4; 4:13), "indulg[e] in" (3:8), and "pay attention to" (Titus 1:14). The faith that unites the church is easily decentered by closer attention to rival claims. It may well be that, by appealing to "deceiving spirits" and "demons," Paul is drawing on a "dualistic description of the final times . . . from postbiblical Judaism."[497] But Jesus taught this same view of things (e.g., in Mark 13; Matt 24); his input into Paul's thinking is no less possible. The end times, in one sense a prelude to glory, also feature a susceptibility to falling away, infatuation with non-Christian ideas and practices, and spiritual

494. Schlatter, *Die Kirche der Griechen*, 120.

495. So also Barrett, *Pastoral Epistles*, 67.

496. Oden, 58.

497. Collins, 113, referring to various passages in the DSS and OT pseudepigrapha.

deception. Paul will shortly give present examples relevant to Timothy. But first he will identify their human conduit.

2 V. 1 points to Paul's apocalyptic consciousness, epitomized in the statement that in the work of the gospel and the church, "our struggle is not against flesh and blood" but against spiritual powers of evil (Eph 6:12). But these powers exploit human means. Their claims and precepts are passed along "through hypocritical liars," which could also be translated "by the hypocrisy[498] of liars." The word translated "liars" (from *pseudologos*)[499] describes people who "like actors play parts so well that their words have the ring of truth" (BDAG 1096). Timothy's task is difficult because opposition to Jesus's lordship and the gospel's redemptive truth can be suave and sophisticated, demonic in conception, and polished in presentation.

In modern (and postmodern) times eminent biblical scholars (e.g., Rudolf Bultmann, Robert Funk and the Jesus Seminar, Bart Ehrman) have occupied places of cultural authority and taught against foundational factual claims found in the NT. Ulrich Wilckens has written of the profound bias against Christian truth claims that lies at the heart of the "historical-critical" reading of the NT that gained dominance in the West by the nineteenth century and continues unabated in many quarters still.[500] Many follow the lead of such movements because they make their case, it is felt, so persuasively. At the church level whole denominations have abandoned historic understanding of Scripture's theological representations and ethical demands, following instead the doctrines of secular philosophers, especially Kant, Hegel, and Schelling, with Schleiermacher also looming large.[501] A conservative North American church body has confessed its complicity in racism and social injustice at and since its founding in the 1970s; corrupt cultural values supported by misguided leaders hijacked biblical convictions and priorities.[502] Something akin to this process was already underway as Paul wrote to Timothy.

How does this departure from biblical teaching and its basis in historical fact happen? Historical events are never monocausal, but Paul singles out

498. The only other use of the word *hypocrisis* (hypocrisy) in Paul's writings is in Gal 2:13, describing the ill-advised behavior of Peter, Barnabas, and others.

499. The word is used only here in the NT.

500. *Kritik der Bibelkritik: Wie die Bibel wieder zur Heiligen Schrift werden kann* (Neukirchen-Vluyn: Neukirchener, 2012). On this subject more broadly, see D. A. Carson, "The Many Facets of the Current Discussion," in Carson, *The Enduring Authority of the Christian Scriptures* (Grand Rapids: Eerdmans, 2016), 3–40, esp. 4–14, who documents not only outright denials of Scripture's truth claims but "a rising number of students and scholars who seek to blur as many distinctions as possible" (14).

501. See, for example, Dorrien, *Kantian Reason and Hegelian Spirit.*

502. See Sean Lucas, *For a Continuing Church: The Roots of the Presbyterian Church in America* (Phillipsburg, NJ: P&R, 2015).

a significant contributing factor in the case or cases he has in mind: seared conscience.[503] On "conscience," see comments on 1:3, 5, 19 above, as well as at 2 Tim 1:3; Titus 1:15.[504] These individuals should be brought up short by their own inner sense of right and wrong. But it is possible to willfully disable that internal guidance device.[505] Alternately, if "have been seared" is understood as a divine passive, God has given these individuals over[506] to the rebellion against him they have pursued. The result is a burned-out, defunct moral compass (see Eph 4:19 for a possible hypothetical parallel). The image, however, may not refer so much to a disabled organ as to a conscience that is still very productive—but with perverse and destructive results. When the truth is abandoned (see v. 1), the results are never benign. The next verse cites representative examples.

3 A reasonable summary of the entire Bible's view of marriage is found in Heb 13:4: "Marriage should be honored by all." It is presented as God's means for human fulfillment of the creation mandate found in Gen 1:28: "God blessed them and said to them, 'Be fruitful and increase in number; fill the earth and subdue it.'" Christ endorsed marriage, not only indirectly at Cana (John 2) but by explicit teaching (Matt 19:4–8). While statements by Paul in 1 Cor 7 (like Jesus in Matt 22:30) confirm that marriage is a penultimate, not ultimate good (Timothy and Jesus did not marry, and Paul may not have married), trumped in some situations by higher kingdom concerns, overall Paul champions it,[507] in line with the general tenor of Scripture and the high view of life-long monogamous marriage associated with Christian tradition in its understanding of both Testaments.

Against this background, the scandal of forbidding marriage in v. 3 is understandable. Such a prohibition marks a break with a biblical mandate and heritage that is comparable to, say, Marcion's denigration of the OT and its God a few generations later (ca. AD 140). Pressed to the extreme, abstention from marriage would result in the extinction of any group practicing it consistently (unless children were intentionally produced out of wedlock, an arrangement that would mark a cult rather than a Christian enclave). It could easily encourage immorality because of people's inability to remain chaste in such an arrangement (see 1 Cor 7:5). Ryken points out that "self-denial is

503. NIV renders "as with a hot iron." This phrase helps dramatize the action of searing or cauterization implied in the perfect passive (or possibly middle) participle translated "have been seared" (*kekaustēriasmenōn*). But the very words are absent from the Greek text.

504. See also A. Naselli and J. Crowley, *Conscience: What It Is, How to Train It, and Loving Those Who Differ* (Wheaton, IL: Crossway, 2016).

505. This would imply a middle participle (see n. 503).

506. Cf. Rom 1:24, 26, 28. See also Isa 19:14: "For the Lord has prepared for them a spirit of error" (NETS).

507. See, for example, 1 Cor 7:10–11, 39; 9:5; 1 Thess 4:1–8; Eph 5:25–33.

often used as a way to become self-righteous."[508] It would be premature to blame the gnostics for the neglect of good creation, since "Christian striving for perfection can also lead to ascesis."[509] Wright suggests that some may have reverted to ascetic practices because of past pagan involvements in destructive behavior.[510] Verse 3 does not elaborate on the specific dangers Paul identifies. Perhaps it was a danger he and Timothy had encountered before, making further explanation unnecessary. To a fellow Jewish Christian like Timothy, it would be self-evident that these marriage-deniers have mounted an assault on a foundational good for human society both inside and outside the church. It also constitutes an attack on the freedom granted in the gospel from human prohibitions not sanctioned in the Scriptures themselves (see, e.g., Rom 14; Gal 5:13–15). Going beyond (and in this case against) "what is written" (1 Cor 4:6) into an ascetic approach to following Christ is fruitless on the face of it (see Col 2:20–22) and can lead only to negative outcomes.

Just as sinister is the order "to abstain from certain foods." Diet as regulated by OT food laws was already shown to have limited redemptive value by Jesus (Mark 7:14–19). Peter's vision of "unclean" foods, in conjunction with his revelation that the gospel transcends Jewish tradition that hallowed kosher eating, marks a major stage in the gospel's spread in Acts (see Acts 10:1–11:15; 15:7–11). Paul had tangled with misunderstandings of eating or not eating certain foods before (see, e.g., 1 Cor 8; 10:23–11:1). Romans 14 teaches a responsible approach to what is ingested, with room allowed for freedom of conscience, with due consideration for implications of one's actions for others (Rom 14:20). The overarching principle is that "the kingdom of God is not a matter of eating and drinking, but of righteousness, peace and joy in the Holy Spirit" (Rom 14:17). Parsing the matter from another angle, Paul writes that "food does not bring us near to God; we are no worse if we do not eat, and no better if we do" (1 Cor 8:8).

Towner points out how the words "abstain from certain foods [*brōma*], which God created to be received with thanksgiving," draw on Gen 9:3 LXX, in which after the flood God declares both animals and plants to be licit food (*brōsis*).[511] He also accounts for Paul's use of *ktizō* (to create) in place of forms of *poieō* in the Gen 1 LXX account. The former was the preferred term for denoting "create" in Paul's Hellenistic Jewish setting, as well as the NT itself.[512] The historical incident Paul draws on is still unmistakably the Genesis account.

508. Ryken, 163.
509. Saarinen, 76,
510. Wright, 43.
511. Towner, "1–2 Timothy and Titus," 898.
512. See Towner, "1–2 Timothy and Titus," with numerous references.

At the basis of Paul's consternation in v. 3 is the positive principle that marriage and foods are things that[513] "God created to be received with thanksgiving by those who believe and who know the truth." Of course all persons can enjoy them, but he is addressing a setting where professing believers are being misled, pressured into not partaking of what God has given to be enjoyed. In the next two verses Paul provides data that Timothy will need to combat this misinformation.

4 The initial word "for" (*hoti*) indicates that Paul is about to give the basis for his reasoning in the previous verse. "Everything God created is good [*kalos*]" "quite obviously"[514] draws on Gen 1:31: "God saw all the things that he had made, and see, they were exceedingly good [*kalos*]" (NETS). It is possible that Paul had word that false teachers were propounding a faulty reading of the early chapters of Genesis or were promoting behavior that assumed such a reading. This knowledge could have prompted Paul to reaffirm an interpretation more in line with the OT rightly understood, Jesus's teaching, and the nuanced combination of freedom and responsibility granted by the gospel message for those who receive it.

The principle Paul is expounding (latent already in v. 3) is that relationship *with* God sanctifies participation in the created order given *by* God. For Paul, of course, this relationship comes through faith in Christ (see 1:12–17). Paul uses marriage and foods as emblematic of the whole range of bounty God's created world furnishes. Relationship with God is underscored by the identical words "with thanksgiving"[515] found both here and in v. 3 (recall also Paul's proviso that the ones expressing gratitude are "those who believe and who know the truth" [v. 3]). Because Timothy and those he leads know fellowship with God as expressed in their gratitude for what he gives them (their "daily bread," to use the words of the Lord's Prayer), they do not need to be stampeded into desperate approaches to marriage and eating as a means of achieving religious sufficiency.

Related to this point of creation theology[516] is a christological and soteriological truth. Salvation is by Christ, not by abstention from foods or marriage. Paul polemicized in another context against "enemies of the cross of Christ," whose "god is their stomach, and their glory is in their shame" (Phil 3:18–19). "Stomach" here likely refers to food laws, and "shame" (a word that can connote "nakedness") likely refers to circumcision. Paul calls out

513. The underlying relative pronoun *ha* refers first of all to foods. But it is likely to include marriage as well; see Knight, 190; Johnson, *First and Second Letters to Timothy*, 240.

514. Towner's words in "1–2 Timothy and Titus," 898.

515. The same words (*meta eucharistias*) appear in Phil 4:6.

516. See Witherington, 254–55: "Paul offers a clear, positive creation theology that entails in this case the premises that both marriage and food are good gifts from God."

these "dogs" (false teachers) promoting "confidence in the flesh" rather than in Christ (Phil 3:2–3).

Verse 4 recalls Timothy to a high view of creation, not because foods and marriage (or sex) are salvific, but because human flourishing and redemption are granted by God's acceptance through Christ, not by human confidence in use (or rejection) of created things apart from faith in Christ. It is a reminder of the sufficiency of what Paul outlined in 1 Tim 3:16 (i.e., the sufficiency of Christ himself) to bring all God offers to those who seek him. It is also a bulwark against the false teachers alluded to in vv. 1–3.

"Nothing is to be rejected[517] if it is received with thanksgiving" assumes participation in marriage and foods in keeping with God's commands and human prudence. The statement does not sanction someone using illegal drugs (after they thank God) on the grounds that the Bible says "nothing is to be rejected." It does not legitimize extramarital sex[518] (or pornography) by someone who reasons that (1) they are married, and (2) they have thanked God. It does not give license for alcohol abuse or for eating to the point of obesity—"nothing is to be rejected" does not mean God will be unhappy if someone puts down the fork before maximum engorgement. Elsewhere Paul lists all kinds of "deeds of the flesh" that *are* to be rejected (see Gal 5:19–21). His positive counsel in v. 4 does not represent a change of heart regarding matters he clearly identifies as sin in other contexts.

5 In the concluding verse to this short subsection, Paul adds words that confirm and qualify two matters he has affirmed in the previous verse. First, there is a potential goodness in "everything God created." Elsewhere Paul affirms creation's flawed and groaning status (Rom 8:20–22). Creation after the fall is not without its limitations and perversities (like thorns and thistles: Gen 3:18). But there remains a thick vestige of original perfection as God-sanctioned provisions like marriage and foods are "consecrated" (from *hagiazō*). The same word is translated "made holy" in 2 Tim 2:21, the only other occurrence in the PE (see discussion there, including reference to Paul's seven other uses of the word). In the same way that God may save the very worst of persons (1 Tim 1:13–16), he can consecrate the seemingly mundane (marriage, eating). In Christ everyday activities can bring glory to God (1 Cor 10:31; cf. Col 3:17, 23) through his sanctifying or consecrating presence by faith (1 Tim 4:3).

Second, things are "consecrated" through the means of grace God provides. Why is Paul so adamant that marriage (which can be a source of woe) and food (which is not in itself salvific) not be disparaged? Paul is speaking in

517. On the use and meaning of this word (*apoblētos*; absent from LXX, NT, and AF), see Quinn and Wacker, 305, who render it "despicable."

518. Aquinas, 51, observes, "Indeed, he is stupid who gives thanks to God for fornication because God is not the agent of evil."

broad terms. He knows that a marriage can become problematic (1 Cor 7:15). He knows that in itself "food does not bring us near to God" (1 Cor 8:8). But Paul is reminding Timothy of two primary means of grace by which churches are founded and their members persevere: "the word of God and prayer." As he continues to issue instructions so that Timothy "will know how people ought to conduct themselves in God's household" (3:15), these two key aids stand out for commendation.

"The word of God" for Paul certainly extends to Scripture (Rom 3:4; 9:6). He also uses it to refer to the gospel message he proclaimed and its implications.[519] This combination—Scripture itself and the message it imparts—is part of what sets apart "everything God created" (v. 4) for rightful enjoyment by believers (v. 3) who receive God's good things "with thanksgiving" (vv. 3, 4).

In what ways do Scripture and its message sanctify things like marriage and foods? Paul does not stipulate here,[520] but several possibilities may be proposed, especially if references in other Pauline writings are considered.

1. They bring people into relationship with God (Rom 10:17).
2. They call people to gratitude for God and his gifts (1 Thess 5:18).
3. They teach proper regard for marriage (cf. 1 Cor 6:9–10) and for the blessing of other "everyday" things like foods (Rom 14:6), so that believers by neglect or abuse do not bring censure on themselves.
4. They uphold believers in a daily pursuit of God that keeps appreciation for his good gifts fresh (Eph 5:20) and that assures the enjoyment of these things will help fuel lives of worship, service, and mission, not a self-glorifying hedonism that might tempt believers to revel in the gift without corresponding delight in the Giver (see Rom 1:21).

A second gracious provision of God Paul mentions is prayer. The same word (*enteuxis*) is translated "intercession" in 2:1 (see discussion and table 10 there). In what ways does prayer (intercessory or otherwise) sanctify things like marriage and foods? First, prayer in the sense of crying out to God is or can be a component in all four points mentioned above. It works in tandem with seeking God in and by his word to live in a way that

519. See, for example, 1 Cor 14:36; 2 Cor 2:17; 4:2; Col 1:25; 1 Thess 2:13; 2 Tim 2:9. Johnson, *First and Second Letters to Timothy*, 242 adds that "the word of God" so understood "could include even the words of Jesus declaring the goodness of all food (Mark 7:1–23) and the sanctity of marriage in God's eyes (Mark 10:2–9)." Marshall, with Towner (*Pastoral Epistles*, 546), gives seven options for the meaning of "word of God" here and opts for "Gen 1:31 as the divine oracle by which God created the world and which once for all declares all food edible" and "a more general use of Scripture," including use of "scriptural language in grace before meals."

520. Cf. Barrett, *Pastoral Epistles*, 68: "The precise meaning of *it is hallowed by God's own word and by prayer* is not clear."

honors God in all aspects of life. Second, prayer is a (though not the only) means of determining God's will[521] in regards to matters like marriage and use of food. Both involve judgment calls along the way (e.g., whether to pursue or consent to a marriage; whether to eat in a given setting or to abstain for the sake of another's weakness) that call for prayer so that the best decisions are made. Third, prayer is a primary means of nurturing ongoing personal relationship with God (see, e.g., Eph 6:18–20); it has been shown above how integral this is (recall "with thanksgiving") to proper regard for God's good gifts. As Paul writes elsewhere, "Devote yourselves to prayer, being watchful and thankful" (Col 4:2). Fourth, prayer (as the Lord's Prayer reminds) pursued as Jesus instructed teaches petition for "daily bread," that is, nutritional necessities. Such prayer increases the likelihood that believers will receive food for what it truly is, an ongoing heavenly gift like the manna of old, rather than taking it for granted and growing cold toward God as a result of presumptuousness or resentment like that of Exodus-era Israel and, in their train, some in the Corinthian church (see 1 Cor 10:1–13).[522] Finally, prayer is a means of assuring an open door for the gospel message and its clear proclamation, key to God's purpose in calling followers into his kingdom and church where they enjoy things like marriage and food in order to live their lives individually and corporately on mission (Matt 28:19–20; Eph 4:12) for God's glory.

Knight sums up 4:1–5 well: "In short, the truth of the good creation of God, whose purpose is to provide for people's needs, coupled with an appropriate response and acceptance is the correct teaching and the antidote to the false teaching."[523]

3. *True Godliness in Pastoral Ministry (4:6–10)*

In a personal pastoral letter from an individual (in this case Paul) to an individual (in this case Timothy), it is reasonable to expect a healthy number of second person singular verbs. In 1 Timothy's 113 verses, there are forty-one such verbs.[524] This ratio suggests a communiqué that is neither heavy-handed (Paul is not inserting an explicit "you!" into every verse) nor distant (he is not composing an abstract treatise with no personal application to Timothy).

521. Modeled by Jesus in Gethsemane and by Paul, for example, in his exchange with God over his thorn in the flesh (2 Cor 12:8).

522. See Witherington, 255: "Eating while recognizing the source of our nourishment not only sanctifies . . . the act of eating, but also honors God the creator."

523. *Pastoral Epistles*, 193.

524. Based on an Accordance search of the Greek text. This does not count participles that are dependent on verbs and may be translated as verbs in English.

What is striking, however, about Paul's direct address to Timothy is its distribution. The number of second person singular verbs by chapter appears in table 18.

Table 18. Verses containing second person singular verbs[525] in 1 Timothy

Chapter	Occurrences
1	2 (vv. 3, 18)
2	0
3	1 (v. 15)
4	8 (vv. 6, 7, 11, 12, 13, 14, 15, 16)
5	10 (vv. 1, 3, 7, 11, 18, 19, 20, 21, 22, 23)
6	5 (vv. 2, 11, 12, 17, 20)

Table 18 indicates that, up to this point, Paul has addressed Timothy directly very sparingly, with only three second person verbs total prior to 4:6. From that point on to the end of the epistle, Paul will focus on application of what he has said earlier.

It will be observed that 4:6 marks a spike in Paul's direct appeal to Timothy. The significance of this distribution will emerge in the discussion below. It may be remarked in passing that the pattern implied in table 18 corresponds with a Pauline pattern observed in some of his letters to churches, in which (very generally speaking) he first lays a theological foundation and then proceeds to make practical application (see, e.g., Rom 1–11 and 12–16; Eph 1–3 and 4–6; Col 1–2 and 3–4).

> [6] *If you point these things out to the brothers and sisters, you will be a good minister of Christ Jesus, nourished on the truths of the faith and of the good teaching that you have followed.* [7] *Have nothing to do with godless myths and old wives' tales; rather, train yourself to be godly.* [8] *For physical training is of some value, but godliness has value for all things, holding promise for both the present life and the life to come.* [9] *This is a trustworthy saying that deserves full acceptance.* [10] *That is why we labor and strive, because we have put our hope in the living God, who is the Savior of all people, and especially of those who believe.*

525. Some verses contain more than one: there are a total of forty-one second-person singular verbs in the Greek text of 1 Timothy; they appear in just twenty-six verses.

6 By "these things" Paul has in mind the teaching of the immediately preceding verses: Christ's supremacy over all things (3:15), the distortions of religious thought and practice in the air (4:1–3a), and the goodness that inheres in God's creation and Christians' freedom to accept from God's hand the good gifts he offers (4:3b-5). If Timothy clarifies these matters, he will be serving "the brothers and sisters"[526] (i.e., the church) well. Luther calls this verse "a golden testimony eminently capable of comforting us. . . . It ties together everything that Paul teaches in this epistle."[527]

"If" is common in many translations and reflects a reasonable understanding of the adverbial participle *hypotithemenos* (here meaning "to point out").[528] But "if" can be interpreted as a sort of ultimatum or borderline warning of what Timothy had better do—or else.[529] Other translations are no less justified in understanding the participle to be implying means or attendant circumstance,[530] not condition: "In pointing out these things" (TLV, NASB); "By pointing out such things" (NET; cf. Mounce); "While pointing-out these *things*" (DLNT). If Paul is applying pressure, it is certainly cordial and diplomatic. He should probably be understood as reflecting collegial directness and zeal for Timothy's pastoral effectiveness rather than strong-arming Timothy or attempting to motivate by fear.

On "good" (*kalos*), see table 12 and discussion at 2:3 above. "Minister" is *diakonos* (see table 16 and discussion at 3:8 above). Pastoral leaders are servants, not commanding officers as in military understanding, nor even clerical functionaries as per later Christian history.[531] Yet, Timothy is a "minister of Christ Jesus." He is under Christ's authority, which gives him a certain derivative authority as he carries out the bidding of the Lord of the church. Paul thus spoke earlier of teaching and exercising oversight as fundamental to the pastoral office (2:12). Paul's use of the future tense here ("you will be") suggests optimism that Timothy will readily embody the counsel Paul gives and may imply he is already doing so.

526. NIV understands *adelphoi* ("brothers") as inclusive and expands to underscore. Other translations (like ESV, with "brothers and sisters" in an explanatory footnote) retain "brothers," or translate "brethren," or propose justifiable equivalents that avoid possible sexist connotations: "the believers" (GNT), "other followers" (CEV), "the Christians" (NLV).

527. Luther, 319.

528. The only other use of the underlying verb (*hypotithēmi*) in the NT is in Rom 16:14 (where it carries the meaning of "to risk"). In numerous uses in Philo (e.g., *Posterity of Cain* 12; *Preliminary Studies*, 85; *Life of Moses* 1:294), Josephus (e.g., *Jewish Antiquities* 1.50, 76), and Epictetus (e.g., *Discourses* 1.26.13; 2.2.21, 24), it carries the sense of "suggest" or "call attention to," not issue mandates.

529. Cf. Collins, 120: "proviso."

530. Cf. Johnson, *First and Second Letters to Timothy*, 242.

531. Towner, *Letters*, 303n5 comments, "I prefer to steer away from the 'ministerial' translation of the [NIV]."

Paul's optimism rests in part on what he knows fuels Timothy: he is "nourished"[532] on certain "truths" pertaining to "the faith" and "the good teaching that you have followed." "Followed"[533] could refer to the teaching or to both the faith and the teaching. The phrase "truths [*logois*, words] of the faith" begs to be connected with Paul's reference to "faithful words" or sayings elsewhere.[534] Timothy is informed in and loyal to the foundational tenets of Christian confession (some of which Paul touched on in 3:16). It is reasonable to surmise that he will encourage others in similar paths.

"The faith and . . . the good teaching" could be viewed as two ways of referring to the same body of beliefs. But repetition of the article *tēs* after "nourished on the truths" may suggest that Paul has in mind (1) theological and christological truths revealed by God, especially through Scripture, and (2) teaching based on those truths. It is more than just "intellectual grasp of the teaching,"[535] since in Paul's understanding it is a work of divine grace. Such teaching is "good" (*kalos*; see table 12 and discussion at 2:3 above) because it conforms to the Scriptures and to the standard of doctrine (see Rom 6:17) God has furnished for his people's understanding, faith, practice, and ultimately redemption. Viewing Paul's point as simply that Timothy is "loyal to Christ Jesus" and "loyal to Paul, his teacher" is not wrong,[536] but it fails to acknowledge how Christ and Paul most often validated *their* views: by the Scriptures (see 2 Tim 3:15). Paul is commending more than Timothy's personal loyalties.

7 In the same way that 4:1–3 implies that misguided creational (or anticreational) teaching is in the air, and that other passages in the letter have already referred to distortions of the law and myth (1:3–4, 6–7, 19), v. 7 implies the lamentable presence of "godless myths and old wives' tales" in Timothy and the Ephesian church's proximity. The Greek word order of v. 7[537] juxtaposes the myths and tales against the faith and good teaching of the previous verse.

532. The underlying verb *entrephō* is a NT hapax. It is not found in the LXX (though the related word *trephō* (to feed) occurs twenty-two times. Philo uses it nineteen times, frequently with the sense of the intellect or soul being "nourished" by resources coming from God, wisdom, or reason (*Allegorical Interpretation* 1.102; *Sacrifices of Cain and Abel* 33, 76). Johnson, *First and Second Letters to Timothy*, 243, points out that Philo speaks of "being trained by the holy writings" in two passages (*Embassy to Gaius* 195; *Special Laws*, 1.314). See also Dibelius and Conzelmann, 68.

533. The underlying word *parakoloutheō* (to follow) is found elsewhere in Paul only at 2 Tim 3:10 (see discussion there).

534. See commentary and discussion at 1:15; 3:1; 4:9; 2 Tim 2:11; Titus 3:8.

535. Dibelius and Conzelmann, 68.

536. Cf. Collins, 121.

537. In Greek v. 7 begins with the direct objects: "But godless myths and old wives' tales have nothing to do with."

The contrast is stark. "Have nothing to do with" (from *paraiteomai*) recurs in the PE (see 5:11; see also discussion at 2 Tim 2:23; Titus 3:10). Some ideas or proposals are so far beyond the pale of plausible that a pastor has no time or business giving them the dignity of extensive attention. This does not mean writing people off crudely (cf. Titus 3:2). But overall, Paul's view (and example)[538] is to focus on and promulgate the truths of Christ and the faith, not to be distracted with undue attention to aberrant beliefs. There are contemporary analogies, for example, in conspiracy theories, so-called urban legends, and endless issue-oriented (and often polemical) blogs and websites from which most pastors find it wise to recuse themselves.

Paul warns against "myths"[539] that are vile or profane (*bebēlous*;[540] NIV "godless") and foolish or silly[541] (*graōdeis*; NIV "old wives tales"). These accounts or tales are detestable and vacuous.[542] Irenaeus seems to be the earliest Christian writer besides Paul who uses *graōdeis*,[543] applying it to misguided religionists who "are really worthy of being mourned over" because of the false (gnostic) religion they seek to spread. They "perversely pull to pieces the greatness of the truly unspeakable power [i.e., Christian doctrine], and the dispensations of God in themselves so striking, by means of Alpha and Beta, and through the aid of numbers. But as many as separate from the Church, and give heed to such old wives' fables [*graōdesi mythois*] as these, are truly self-condemned; and these men Paul commands us, 'after a first and second admonition, to avoid' [Titus 3:10–11]."[544]

538. It is an ongoing source of scholarly frustration that Paul is not more specific about the names and views of his opponents. He tends to focus on what he holds to be true and redemptive rather than allow gospel detractors to set the agenda for his remarks or exhaust his energies in venting so as to profile them.

539. The Greek word *mythos* is found elsewhere in the NT in 1 Tim 1:4 (see commentary discussion there); 2 Tim 4:4; Titus 1:14; 2 Pet 1:16.

540. Found in four other passages of the NT (listed here with NIV translation): 1:9 "irreligious" people; 6:20 and 2 Tim 2:16 "godless chatter"; Heb 12:16 "godless" person (Esau).

541. So many translations: for example, AMP, ESV, HCSB, TLB, Mounce, RSV.

542. See Towner, *Letters*, 305: the heresy is "pagan in its thrust and insignificant in its contribution."

543. The root word *graōdēs* (an adj. that BDAG 207 defines as "characteristic of an elderly woman") does not occur in the LXX, elsewhere in the NT, Philo, Josephus, AF, or Epictetus. Quinn and Wacker, 374, call it "a term which conveys a sophisticated, literate contempt for that which cannot be taken seriously." The translation "old wives' tales" in today's climate injects for some a sexist aura into the discourse, whereas in antiquity (as in English today) it would be overinterpreting the expression to insist on attributing misogyny or ageism to this time-worn figure of speech and dead metaphor. It is unlikely that an ageist and misogynist Paul would have devoted so much energy to giving instructions on the care of widows, especially those over age 60 (1 Tim 5:2–16, especially v. 9).

544. Irenaeus, *Against Heresies* 1.16.3.

Timothy can and should transcend such speculations. "Rather, train yourself" is a forceful summons to an about-face. In fact, it is the first imperative in this epistle that is aimed at Timothy—earlier imperatives pertain to women (2:11) and to deacons (3:10, 12). There are some forty-three imperatives in the epistle;[545] since Paul has waited until this point to adopt this mode of address, it is clear that the verses and chapters ahead will be thick with strong admonition.

"Train yourself" (from *gymnazō*) combines a singular reflexive pronoun (*seauton*, yourself) with a metaphor drawing on athletic competition.[546] "Train" can connote rote conditioning (as in training a dog to fetch or a child to turn off the light when they leave a room). But as v. 8 will indicate with its reference to "physical training," Paul has in mind disciplines and pursuits that result in focus, stamina, and self-mastery in the face of competition (in this case, false doctrines and their proponents), fatigue (pastoral work wears one down), distractions (like all persons Timothy has to deal with evil in his own personal sphere), and other threats. The goal of Timothy's self-conditioning regimen is "to be godly" (*pros eusebeian*).[547] This could also be rendered "for godliness" (ESV) or (less likely) "in godliness" (HCSB). The means of attaining better pastoral conditioning will be the counsel Paul offers in the remainder of this letter, along with the godly practices already instilled in Timothy from his Jewish boyhood. "Godliness" (*eusebeia*) in biblical thinking is an inherent good, but Paul has specific reasons for the command to pursue it in a disciplined fashion like an athlete in training. They appear in the next verse.

8 Extending the exercise metaphor, Paul concedes the value of physical exercise. "Some" translates *pros oligon*, a prepositional phrase found elsewhere in the NT only in Jas 4:14: "You are a mist that appears for a little while [*pros oligon*][548] and then vanishes." The phrase means to a certain and limited extent, with the limitation perhaps viewed most of all as temporal: for a while. Paul is not disparaging physical exercise[549] or saying it is of negligible "value" (*ōphelismos*).[550] In an age of increasing obesity worldwide, from which clergy

545. Forty-one are present. The other two are aorist: 1 Tim 6:12 ("Take hold of the eternal life to which you were called"), 20 ("guard what has been entrusted to your care").

546. The other NT uses of the word: Heb 5:14; 12:11; 2 Pet 2:14.

547. On "godliness" (*eusebeia*), see commentary Introduction, IX.B.

548. In the LXX the expression is found in 4 Macc 15:27; Wis 16:6. In both cases it has temporal significance: for a short time. It also has temporal connotation in most of Philo's fifteen uses of the same prepositional phrase. The same is true in Josephus (twenty-three occurrences).

549. As does, for example, Aquinas (54), who relates it to fasting and other penal bodily deprivations and says "it is profitable for little namely, only for the illness of carnal sin." This seems out of touch with the flow of a discourse which has just cast aspersions on ascetic religion (vv. 3–4).

550. The word occurs elsewhere in the NT only at 2 Tim 3:16 (Scripture is "useful"); Titus 3:8 (the things Paul teaches are "profitable").

in many quarters have not escaped, Paul's words here should not be used to justify neglect of the body's need for regular vigorous activity. E. Schnabel reckons that Paul traveled at least 15,500 miles, of which some 8,700 was by land, much of that on foot.[551] Over a thirty-year period (early AD 30s-60s), Paul thus averaged close to 300 miles per year on foot and nearly the same distance on small boats, which were not luxury cruise ships—on rough seas they would have been more like riding a bucking bronco. He advises Timothy here from a framework of personal physical toughness,[552] with which Timothy as Paul's sometime travel companion would have been familiar.

Yet, there is something more valuable than physical conditioning and its beneficial outcomes: "godliness" (*eusebeia*; see Introduction, IX.B). Godliness is not just something for Timothy to affirm and commend: it has to suffuse his own being, which will not happen without rigorous self-discipline. There is literary symmetry between exercise being "of some value" (*pros oligon ōphelismos*) and godliness having "value for all things" (*pros panta ōphelismos*). The underlying logic, in lesser-to-greater fashion, is that, if arduous physical training is worth it, how much more is a life dignified and ennobled by the presence of divine attributes. Timothy should be willing to go to great lengths to attain this benefit.

For godliness holds "promise for both the present life" (just like exercise does), as well as for "the life to come." In the only other use of the word "promise" (*epangelia*) in the PE,[553] Paul speaks of "the promise of life that is in Christ Jesus" (2 Tim 1:1; see commentary). All of God's promises find their fulfillment in Christ (2 Cor 1:20). Paul writes to appeal to Timothy in his present circumstances at Ephesus. But he needs to see those circumstances in a christological, transtemporal light, too, that is, in view of "the life to come."

Elsewhere Paul voices the consolation of this promise for him and all others who live out their faith in Christ: "Now there is in store for me the crown of righteousness, which the Lord, the righteous Judge, will award to me on that day—and not only to me, but also to all who have longed for his appearing" (2 Tim 4:8). For the sake of Timothy's physical and spiritual self-discipline, then, and in support of his pastoral calling, Paul rallies him with the reminder of the eschatological implications of all that pastors do day after day. Timothy should expend effort worthy of an athlete in training to attain and maintain the godliness needed to excel in his pastoral duties. A portion

551. Schnabel, *Paul and the Early Church*, 1288.

552. Cf. 1 Cor 9:27 (Paul buffets his body and makes it his slave); 2 Cor 11:23–27 (Paul describes his deprivations over his years of missionary service, including the comment [v. 26] "I have been constantly on the move.").

553. It occurs in twenty-four other Pauline passages in four of his letters: Romans, 2 Corinthians, Galatians, and Ephesians.

of this effort will involve the iron determination needed to "have nothing to do with" the myths that are distracting some (v. 7). Schlatter well describes the form Timothy's focus needs to take: rejection of the myths "does not occur through giving laws to the church regarding what it needs to think, but rather by Timothy speaking to the church the message Jesus entrusted to it."[554]

9 For the third time in 1 Timothy,[555] Paul declares that the word (*logos*, NIV "saying") he writes is "trustworthy" (*pistos*). Does Paul refer to what he just wrote (most commentators),[556] or to what he is about to write (conceded by many as a possibility)?[557] The question may be posed too sharply. Paul may have in mind the intertwined central substance of vv. 6–10: the truth of the faith (v. 6); the inestimable value of God's promise and resulting possibility of relative human godliness with certainty of eternal life (v. 8); the living God (not some concocted chimera) in his saving regard for sinners "who believe" (v. 10), among whom are (most undeservedly) Paul and Timothy. These things, taken together, deserve Timothy's "full acceptance" as he ponders Paul's words and call to doctrinal integrity and renewed self-discipline in his personal life and pastoral duties.

"Deserves full acceptance"[558] repeats words found in 1:15. "Deserves" translates *axios* (worthy, deserving) and is found not only in the PE (see 5:18; 6:1) but also elsewhere in Paul,[559] for a total of eight Pauline occurrences. Marshall thinks the effect of Paul's saying is "to underline the importance of godliness for all believers."[560] Yet, in a section so centered on Timothy personally (see remarks under the heading "3. True Godliness in Pastoral Ministry [4:6–10]" above), one can wonder whether Timothy would have understood Paul's statement as applying primarily to others, not him. Also, with "Christ

554. *Kirche der Griechen*, 123.

555. See earlier 1:15; 3:1. On "trustworthy" sayings, see commentary Introduction, IX.C.

556. For example, Johnson, *First and Second Timothy*, 250, who nevertheless laments, "The preceding statement concerning a promise of life both now and in the future, therefore, seems to be the best possibility, even though it does not have any recognizable sapiential pedigree."

557. For example, Barrett, *Pastoral Epistles*, 70: "Neither alternative can be excluded as impossible." Cf. Luther, 324: "I feel that this passages refers to what goes before rather than to what follows. However, I do not fight over it."

558. "Acceptance" (*apodochē*) appears in the NT only here and in 1:15. It is absent from the LXX. For the combination of "worthy" (*axios*) and "acceptance" (*apodochē*), see Philo, *Flight and Finding* 129; *Rewards and Punishments* 13. It is also present in Justin Martyr (*Dialogue with Trypho* 3), as he writes: "Therefore it is necessary for every man to philosophize, and to esteem this the greatest and most honorable work; but other things only of second-rate or third-rate importance, though, indeed, if they be made to depend on philosophy, they are of moderate value, and worthy of acceptance."

559. Rom 1:32; 8:18; 1 Cor 16:4; 2 Thess 1:3.

560. *Pastoral Epistles*, 554.

Jesus" mentioned in v. 6, and "the living God" who is "Savior" dominating the final verse of the subsection (v. 10), it may be preferable to seek a theocentric theme to connect with Paul's "trustworthy saying" interjection. If so, it is God in Christ in his rock-solid relevance to the onerous pastoral task (requiring self-discipline) that Paul commends (of which "godliness" is an entailment), as the next verse confirms.

10 The exact logical connection with or progression from previous verses is difficult to nail down with certainty. It is possible that "that is why we labor and strive" harks back to and confirms Paul's imperative (v. 7) to "train yourself to be godly." That task requires maximum effort. Verse 8 gives the reason for that command, and v. 9 confirms the truths that justify Paul's imperative. Now in v. 10 Paul encourages Timothy by reminding him that it is not only he who must give himself rigorously to his calling; they each "labor and strive" side by side, though presently separated geographically. Whereas Paul used an athletic metaphor in v. 7, in v. 10 he shifts the image to generic arduous toil. Paul's expression highlights "the strenuous and fatiguing nature of missionary labors."[561] Like any effective leader, Paul is not calling on Timothy to make any sacrifice that Paul himself is not making. On "labor" (*kopioō*), see discussion at 2 Tim 2:6 (the "hard-working" farmer).[562] On "strive" (*agōnizomai*),[563] see discussion at 2 Tim 4:7; the word also appears in 1 Tim 6:12.

Such all-out effort is sustained by a firmly placed hope.[564] This hope is in "the living God" (see also 3:15). Paul, Timothy, and the church they serve are not sustained by legends or hoary Greek or Roman traditions (myths). Nor, despite their Jewish heritage, is their hope in God's law, despite their reverence for it seen in the light of its fulfillment in Christ. Their hope rests rather in the God who created the world and still currently sustains it, hence "living."[565] The expression "living God" occurs eleven other times in the NT.[566] For Paul (and

561. Belleville, 87.

562. The only other PE reference is 1 Tim 5:17 (elders who "work hard" in preaching and teaching).

563. Many ancient MSS contain *oneidizometha* ("we are being insulted") instead. The quality of the witnesses, the context, and Paul's usage (*oneidizō* is found in Paul elsewhere only at Rom 15:3) seem to favor *agōnizomai*.

564. Greek *ēlpikamen*, which can be understood as "we have hoped" or "we have set our hope." NIV "have put our hope" is notable for its restraint. Paul uses the verb elsewhere in the PE with God as the object in 1 Tim 5:5; 6:17. He uses the verb to denote hope in God (or Christ) in seven other passages: Rom 8:24, 25; 15:12; 1 Cor 13:7; 15:19; 2 Cor 1:10; Phil 2:19.

565. This wording could also reflect Paul's creation theology, on which he drew earlier (v. 4). The God who created all life is the living God.

566. The passages, with the speaker who calls God living (if not obvious): Matt 16:16 (Peter at Caesarea Philippi); 26:63 (the high priest adjuring Jesus); Acts 14:15 (Barnabas and Paul at Lystra); Rom 9:26 (Paul, quoting Hosea); 2 Cor 3:3; 6:16; Heb 3:12; 9:14; 10:31; 12:22; Rev 7:2.

other NT writers) God's dynamic personal presence is not only a theological conviction but a truth corroborated by their relationship to him by the Christ whom he sent and by the Spirit who constitutes God's living presence with his people as the Son makes intercession at the Father's right hand. No wonder Paul has such strong motivation, sustained now into the fourth decade of his post-Damascus walk with God through faith in Christ.[567] With the words "our hope" he includes Timothy in the circle of believers "who believe and know the truth" (v. 3) and are buoyed up by the consciousness of God and by their privilege of service in the will of God that results.

On God as "Savior," see commentary Introduction, IX.A. In the PE Christ is also called Savior (2 Tim 1:10; Titus 1:4; 2:13; 3:6); Father and Son share this glorious role. Calvin stresses the term's meaning here as "one who guards and preserves. [Paul's] argument is that God's kindness extends to all men."[568]

Regarding "of all people,"[569] see discussion of similar language in connection with Christ's role as "ransom" in 1 Tim 2:6. By adding "and especially[570] of those who believe," Paul confirms the position he establishes firmly elsewhere[571] that it is those who trust in Christ who are enabled to know him (and God) as their Savior in the deepest and ultimate sense. "Salvation for Paul is not a universalism in which everyone is saved. . . . Receiving salvation requires human response to Jesus Christ."[572] Yet, God and his reign are relevant to "all people" whom Timothy may encounter at Ephesus. Since the gospel targets not just the church for its encouragement (see, e.g., 1 Cor 15:1–11) but "all people" for their consideration and potentially their redemption,[573] God's status as Savior for and over "all people" is a basis for the deepest possible hope among those (like Paul and Timothy) charged to promulgate that gospel.

4. *Standing Orders for Timothy (4:11–16)*

In this last subsection of reasons for Paul's instructions" (3:14–4:16), the discourse is dominated by imperatives. Of the thirty second person singular

567. Paul writes 1 Timothy, presumably, in the AD 60s, after three previous decades of service beginning in the early AD 30s.

568. *Timothy, Titus and Philemon*, 245.

569. Aquinas (56) distinguishes between "bodily salvation" (i.e., physical provision and preservation) for all people, on the one hand, and "spiritual salvation" for those whom Aquinas calls "the good" or "the faithful" (corresponding to Paul's "those who believe"), on the other.

570. On Greek *malista* (especially), see commentary at Titus 1:10.

571. For example, with programmatic significance, in Rom 10:13 (drawing on Joel 2:32): "Everyone who calls on the name of the Lord will be saved."

572. Zehr, 100.

573. Stressed by Witherington, 257 (drawing on Bassler).

commands found in 1 Timothy, only two have appeared in the epistle so far (both in 4:7: "have nothing to do with" and "train yourself"). But in the next five verses, seven imperatives will occur. We have termed this section "standing orders" because the commands Paul issues, while related to Timothy's situation, are not overly situation-specific. They call for attitudes and actions that are in order for whatever tasks Timothy, or anyone in his pastoral position, faces, not just in the present moment but in the course of regular ministry over time.[574]

> [11] *Command and teach these things.* [12] *Don't let anyone look down on you because you are young, but set an example for the believers in speech, in conduct, in love* [575] *in faith and in purity.* [13] *Until I come, devote yourself to the public reading of Scripture, to preaching and to teaching.* [14] *Do not neglect your gift, which was given you through prophecy when the body of elders laid their hands on you.* [15] *Be diligent in these matters; give yourself wholly to them, so that everyone may see your progress.* [16] *Watch your life and doctrine closely. Persevere in them, because if you do, you will save both yourself and your hearers.*

11 "Command and teach"[576] echoes the twin basic duties that constitute the pastoral task as summarized in 2:12 (see also, with some expansion, Titus 2:15): teaching and spiritual oversight.[577] Here the order is reversed.

"Command" translates a form of *parangellō*. Its noun cognate *parangelia* (command, directive) is also present in 1 Timothy. In fact, the two words as Paul deploys them furnish the hortatory theme that unites the entire epistle, as table 19 indicates. The words denote things that must be done or take place; the tendency of some translations to render the noun as "instruction(s)" (e.g., 1 Thess 4:2; 1 Tim 5:7 NIV) is questionable. The sense is that of an order, not loose counsel, advice, or didactic instructions. "The solemn appeal to God and Christ" accompanying use of the word at times[578] "makes clear the nature of authority behind the apostolic

574. Zehr, 101, relates this to verbal aspect: "All these imperatives are present tense, implying that Timothy's response should be one of continuing action in the ongoing ministry."

575. Some ancient MSS insert *en pneumati* ("in the Spirit") after "in love." Scribes may have borrowed the extra words from Col 1:8. The shorter reading has better external support, but either reading is true to Paul's teaching.

576. Cf. 6:2 ("teach and insist on"); Titus 2:15 ("Declare these things; exhort and rebuke with all authority" [ESV]).

577. Collins comments (128), "Evangelization and teaching is [*sic*] [Timothy's] ministry." While that is true, "command" is not about evangelization but urging the truths and entailments of the faith on the faithful.

578. See, for example, 1 Thess 4:2 ("by the authority of the Lord Jesus"); 2 Thess 3:6 ("in the name of the Lord Jesus Christ"); 1 Tim 6:13 ("in the presence of God" [ESV]).

commands."[579] Or as Marshall states of the verb: "παραγγέλλω [*parangellō*] is used of authoritative instruction and commands by a church leader."[580]

Table 19. The verb and noun for "command" in 1 Timothy

Verse in 1 Timothy	Presence of "command"
1:3	Stay there in Ephesus so that you may *command* certain people not to teach false doctrines any longer.
1:5	The goal of this *command* is love.
1:18	Timothy, my son, I am giving you this *command* in keeping with the prophecies once made about you.
4:11	*Command* and teach these things.
5:7	*Command* these things as well. (ESV)
6:13	In the sight of God . . . I *charge* you.
6:17	*Command* those who are rich in this present world not to be arrogant.

Table 19 reveals that Paul's hortatory intent for the epistle is established in ch. 1. Timothy must "command certain people" to cease from their doctrinal misrepresentations (1:3). Positively, Paul's charge ("command"; 1:5) to Timothy is not polemical: at the core of the gospel imperative "is love [*agapē*], which comes from a pure heart and a good conscience and a sincere faith." In 1:18 Paul restates this instruction, relating it to weighty and memorable prophecies that evidently attended Timothy's launch into gospel service. Now in 4:11, after various instructions (regarding worship, ch. 2; overseers and deacons, ch. 3) and explanations, Paul again takes up this "command" theme. To a certain extent, the whole of 1 Timothy (in view of the three subsequent commands in chs. 5–6; see table 19) is Paul's command to Timothy regarding what he as pastor must stand for and instill in those he leads.[581]

Along with commanding, Timothy should "teach these things." "These things" is the direct object of both "command" and "teach." Paul likely refers

579. *NIDNTTE* 3:617.

580. *Pastoral Epistles*, 558–59.

581. The same verb and noun are found in Paul in eight other passages: 1 Cor 7:10; 11:17; 1 Thess 4:2, 11; 2 Thess 3:4, 6, 10, 12. The situations addressed in Corinth and Thessalonica bear similarities with Ephesus as implied in 1 Timothy.

primarily to what he just conveyed to Timothy (4:6–10), as supported by all he wrote in the letter up to that point. He wants Timothy to give instruction so that hearers can understand and implement what Paul testifies to and calls for. Timothy as a disciple of Jesus is called to train others to be disciplers (see 2 Tim 2:2). Even (especially) as a pastor, teaching is a primary activity; it is tragic that in many modern church settings "making disciples" has either been relegated to a parachurch specialty or ignored as a pastoral mandate.[582] See commentary Introduction, IX.D for more on "teaching" in the PE.

12 Two more imperatives confront Timothy in this verse. The first pertains to perception of his age, presumably by those he leads. Bassler find evidence here that the letter and its youthful recipient are a literary contrivance, out of sync with the "projected image" of Timothy found to this point in the letter of "a mature, responsible church leader."[583] But a historical explanation is also reasonable. If Timothy was just a teenager when Paul enlisted him in his mission in the early AD 50s (Acts 16:1–5), and if 1 Timothy was written in the mid-AD 60s, he is probably not yet thirty. In a very thorough study of this verse, David Pao concludes that Timothy's exact age is less important than the fact that he was not old (as was, e.g., Paul by comparison).[584] His age might tempt those dealing with him to fail to grant him the respect (Pao emphasizes "honor" in an "honor/shame" social outlook)[585] that his calling, office, and giftedness call for.[586]

In this setting, Timothy should not "let anyone look down on"[587] him because of his youthfulness. This reaction is hardly something Timothy could enforce or control by mere command; rather, his example will help people regard him as they ought (see second half of the verse). Paul's admonition is timely, because this epistle commissions Timothy to reaffirm his pastoral leadership on a number of fronts, some of them touchy (as in correcting false teaching). Paul knows that some will seize on his age as a pretext to resist his leadership. In addition, wariness of youthfulness is not necessarily groundless bias: the wizened frequently see matters more clearly than relative neophytes.

582. For a stirring call to pastors' teaching ministry and recognition of the resistance they face, see Wright, 48.

583. *1 Timothy, 2 Timothy, Titus*, 86. Cf. 92: "the fiction of Timothy's youth."

584. See David Pao, "Let No One Despise Your Youth: Church and the World in the Pastoral Epistles," *JETS* 57/4 (2014) 743–55 (here 749).

585. Pao, "Let No One Despise Your Youth," passim.

586. Neudorfer, *Erster Brief an Timotheus*, 180, quotes various scholars relying on ancient Jewish or Roman sources, which differ on the age range when a man is regarded as mature and no longer youthful (Jewish: 40–59; Roman: 30–45).

587. The root verb *kataphroneō* occurs in Paul three other times: Rom 2:4; 1 Cor 11:22; 1 Tim 6:2. In the NT, "the predominant use of this word group is in contexts dealing with lack of due respect for the words, works, ministers, and people of God" (*NIDNTTE* 2:645).

Yet, Paul is confident that Timothy is capable of a quality of work that will make his age irrelevant or at least minimize its deleterious potential. This command is, then, more a vote of confidence in Timothy to encourage him to be bold about his faithful pastoral labor than a prescription for dealing with detractors who are using Timothy's age as a pretext for downplaying his pastoral authority.

The preemptive antidote for unfounded contempt for youth is the "example" (*typos*) Paul commends. See discussion at Titus 2:7, where the same word is used, and where Titus (whose youth Paul does not mention as a problem) is told to set an example by good works and excellent teaching. The imperative translated "set" (from *ginomai*, be, become) is present tense in form.

While simplistic distinctions between present and other tense-forms are to be avoided, the aorist imperative of this verb is often used where an action is prescribed that will bring a situation to its conclusion.[588] If Paul had used an aorist here, by that measure he might be calling for a decisive, all-encompassing move or performance on Timothy's part that demonstrates a permanent alteration. But he uses the present, of which there are thirty-six examples (twenty-two of them in Paul) involving a form of *ginomai* in the NT. In this case the action commanded is most often ongoing in nature: "be [*ginesthe*] wise as serpents and innocent as doves" (Matt 10:16); "be [*ginesthe*] imitators of me" (1 Cor 4:16); "be [*ginesthe*] thankful" (Col 3:15). Only in Paul does this construction occur in the singular (as in 1 Tim 4:12), a form observed in four other passages. In each case the command (*ginesthō*) is clearly to bring about or perform something in an ongoing way: Rom 3:4 ("Let God be true"); 1 Cor 14:26 ("Let all things be done for building up" ESV); 1 Cor 14:40 ("But everything should be done in a fitting and orderly way"); 1 Cor 16:14 ("Do everything in love").

Applying this pattern to v. 12, Timothy would hear in Paul's command, not a directive to perform (or stage) a dramatic gesture that would make a compelling case for his maturity, but a call to comport himself among those he leads and serves ("for the believers") in a consistently exemplary way. Paul lists five domains to which Timothy may devote attention; the list is surely not meant to be exhaustive. At several points what Paul asks of Timothy is what he lists elsewhere as central in his own example.[589]

588. Of the nine aorist imperative uses of *ginomai* in the NT, all fit this description: Matt 6:10; 8:13; 9:29; 15:28; 26:42; Acts 1:20; Rom 11:9; 1 Cor 3:18; 1 Pet 1:15. Taking the Pauline example, when Paul prods the Corinthians with "If anyone among you thinks that he is wise in this age, let him become [*genesthō*] a fool that he may become wise," he is calling for a one-and-done adjustment, not an ongoing practice. A similar nuance is observed in the LXX's sixty-nine aorist imperatives of this verb. For example, all of God's "let there be" (*genēthētō* if sing., *genēthētōsan* if pl.) statements in Gen 1 are aorist. The action, once performed, is completed and not repeated.

589. See 2 Tim 3:10, which lists (among other things) Paul's teaching, way of life, faith, and love.

First, "in speech [*logos*]." For a pastor who preaches and teaches, the importance of verbal patterns and representations cannot be overestimated. For one thing, speech is a barometer of the heart: "For the mouth speaks what the heart is full of" (Matt 12:34).[590] Timothy needs to seek the proverbial purity of heart (Ps 51:10) that will permit his words to do justice to his subject matter (Scripture and the Christian message, among other things), holy calling, and prescribed duties (like preaching and teaching) that involve speaking.

Second, "in conduct [*anastrophē*]." The principle is as basic as Jesus's question "Why do you call me, 'Lord, Lord,' and do not do what I say?" (Luke 6:46). This is Paul's only use of this word in the PE,[591] but the importance of behavior that comports with confession is basic to Paul's teaching. Examples are numerous, for example, in ch. 3, where Paul cites numerous practical-life indicators of qualifications for overseers. Yes, they must be "able to teach" (3:2). But most of the other requirements involve conduct. Conduct is also implicit in the remaining verses of this subsection (4:13–15).

Third, "in love" [*agapē*]. "Love" is not one of the most frequently occurring significant words in the PE.[592] Yet, since it epitomizes the entirety of Paul's "command" to Timothy (1:5) and indeed the Christian message itself (1 Cor 13:13), it unsurprising that Paul lists it here. See commentary on 2 Tim 1:7 (where, as in 1 Timothy "love" is programmatic for the epistle).

Fourth, "in faith [*pistis*]." Elsewhere Paul makes clear the intertwined nature of love and faith (Gal 5:6): "The only thing that counts is faith expressing itself through love." Schlatter observes that situations constantly emerge in congregational life "in which questions arise regarding how to respond faithfully." In that case at Ephesus, assuming Timothy's positive example of love, believers "could see in Timothy how they ought to think and act in keeping with faith."[593]

Fifth, "in purity [*hagneia*]." See also 5:2, where Paul calls for "absolute purity," and 2 Tim 2:22 ("Flee the evil desires of youth"). Close interaction between members of the opposite sex takes place in congregational life and many ministry ventures. Such relationships must proceed without erotic drives finding improper expression. A pastor's example rooted in a chaste inner life is foundational. Timothy will need to draw on this purity in his service on behalf of widows struggling with "sensual desires" (5:11). Conversely, pastoral laxity or impurity can infect all that a congregation undertakes, to say nothing of

590. Recall also the attention devoted to speech in, for example, Proverbs and James.

591. It occurs elsewhere in Paul at Gal 1:13; Eph 4:22.

592. It appears in just nine other PE passages: 1 Tim 1:5, 14; 2:15; 6:11; 2 Tim 1:7, 13; 2:22; 3:10; Titus 2:2. The verb *agapaō* occurs just twice (2 Tim 4:8, 10) and carries little theological significance.

593. Schlatter, *Die Kirche der Griechen*, 129.

disastrous effects in the overseer's marriage and the church's public witness. Scripture, as well as the daily news, offers numerous cases of (supposed) secret sin by church leaders wreaking havoc in due course.

Through excelling in characteristics like the five above, Timothy can minimize gratuitous disregard because of his age. He can rather bring his youthful zeal and energy to bear on pastoral opportunities and challenges with the same "pure heart and . . . good conscience and . . . sincere faith" that Paul's "command" in this epistle calls for (see 1:5).

13 Paul writes, "Until I come." "The time is uncertain but not the fact" that he will presently arrive.[594] In the interim, Paul commends three emphases, to which Timothy should "devote" (from *prosechō*)[595] himself.

The first is "the public reading of Scripture." This practice in the church was carried over from the synagogue (and of course persists to the present).[596] A Scripture was read, and a speaker would expound it (see Luke 4:16–27; Acts 13:14–41). Scripture in its OT form was a constant basis for Jesus's teaching and preaching as recorded in the Gospels. Paul's letter to the Romans and passages in most of his other letters show how much his thought constituted exposition or application of Scripture. Both OT and some NT Scripture is expounded in the AF, showing how it was basic to the development of Christian thought and practice. Paul's letters would have quickly gained public recognition by being read before the congregation as per his own orders (Col 4:16).[597] Timothy should cultivate this practice, which naturally implies his own personal reading and reflection in preparation for public reading and exposition (see below). In a social setting where few could have afforded or owned copies of Scripture (which would have been scrolls at this point in history), public reading was a primary avenue of teaching what the Scriptures say. Because of its perceived heavenly origin (see 2 Tim 3:16) and edifying effect, it would also be a catalyst for worship.

The second emphasis enjoined on Timothy is "preaching" (*paraklēsis*). Based on Scripture reading, Timothy would encourage and exhort—*paraklēsis* occurs only here in the PE, but nineteen other uses in Paul give a good sense

594. Towner, *Letters*, 316.

595. Used five times in Paul, all in the PE: see 1:4; 3:8; 4:1 (discussion); Titus 1:14.

596. See Keener, *Bible Background Commentary*, 609, for numerous references to passages in Josephus and Philo that illustrate the role of Scripture in Jewish congregational life. Keener points out analogues in non-Jewish Hellenistic settings as well; on this point, see also Towner, *Letters*, 318n29.

597. Cf. Towner, *Letters*, 317: "The synagogue readings would have expanded naturally to include the stories in the Gospel tradition and the Pauline letters, as texts such as 2 Cor 7:8; Col 4:16; 1 Thess 5:27; and 2 Thess 3:14 suggest for the latter." Swinson (*What Is Scripture?*, esp. 101–11) has argued persuasively for the early (by ca. AD 60) regard for Luke's Gospel as Scripture in Christian circles.

of its meaning. Paul writes to the Romans that they can take heart "through the endurance taught in the Scriptures and the encouragement [*paraklēsis*] they provide" (Rom 15:4). While Timothy or those he oversaw likely engaged in one-on-one interaction with congregational members,[598] "preaching" addresses "the household of God, the church" (1 Tim 3:15) in its regular assembling. In terms of 1 Tim 2:12, the exercise of oversight takes place in significant measure through congregational leaders like Timothy administering the grace Scripture mediates through its exposition to the assembly.

A third emphasis is "teaching" (*didaskalia*; see commentary Introduction, IX.D) There is no "and" in Greek; the wording of the original can be understood as pointing not so much to a sequence or progression as to three intertwined and perhaps inseparable activities. Reading Scripture without further comment (preaching, teaching) would be incomplete and perhaps confusing. "Preaching" something other than the Scriptures, or preaching without instruction ("teaching") would be unfruitful. "Teaching" without the authoritative appeal implied in "preaching," and without dominical and apostolic understanding of the divinely given basis in Scripture, would resemble the misguided presentations Paul is writing to oppose and correct (see 1:3, 6–7; 4:1–2).

Verse 12, then, does not lay out new guidelines or propose innovative ministry strategies for Timothy at Ephesus as the church there faced confusing and contradictory doctrinal challenges and unacceptable practices (recall 4:3 on marriage and diet). He should rather be faithful to the long-established means of grace that over the centuries have earned Christians (also Jews) the appellation "people of the Book." Yet, this is not merely a bookish or academic exercise but one involving a called leader's dedication (see vv. 15–16 below) and Holy Spirit empowerment (see next verse).

14 This verse presupposes a historical scenario whose details are largely unattested elsewhere. Timothy's "gift" (*charisma*)[599] that he should not "neglect"[600] suggests a divine bestowal through the Holy Spirit of competencies essential to his ministry. "Was given" reflects a likely divine passive: the active agent was God.[601] "Through prophecy" may point to an event related to Timothy's reception of the gift, or perhaps to group recognition of that reception. In

598. Cf. "house to house" in Acts 5:42; 20:20; 1 Tim 5:13.

599. See *NIDNTTE* 4:660: the word (found seventeen times in the NT) is "found almost exclusively in the Pauline corpus" (but see 1 Pet 4:10) and is "his distinctive term for the manifold outworking of divine grace in individual Christians through the one Spirit."

600. "Neglect" translates a present imperative of *ameleō*, which occurs nowhere else in the NT. It is, however, attested four times in the LXX (2 Macc 4:14; Wis 3:10; Jer 4:17; 38:32) and is frequent in Philo (thirty-eight times) and Josephus (fifty times). It is used twice in the AF to refer to neglect of widows. See Ign. *Pol.* 4:1; Pol. *Phil.* 6:1. See also Diogn. 8:10.

601. So also Towner, *Letters*, 323.

connection with all this experience, "a group of elders laid hands on Timothy."[602] See 2 Tim 1:6 and commentary for more discussion; Paul urges Timothy in that passage "to fan into flame the gift of God, which is in you through the laying on of my hands."[603] Was Paul among that group of elders? Was his laying on of hands part of a different event or incident? Data for decisive solutions to such questions are sparse.

Reminding Timothy that a respected "body of elders" endorsed him might boost his confidence in the face of criticisms of his youth. Keener suggests the elders may have been the ones appointed by Paul at Lystra (Acts 14:21–23; 16:2–3). Keener also proposes that Timothy's gift was "probably teaching,"[604] which cannot be verified. Yet, given Timothy's teaching duties (4:13), his gifting must have served in support.

Marshall argues that the imposition of hands was "for the spiritual strengthening to carry out specific tasks and to develop a Christian character." He continues: "A general equipping of Timothy for ministry is meant. The Spirit who is already at work in him grants him further gifts for his ministry."[605] In other words, Paul does not have in mind Timothy's initial salvation experience. If a personal associate of an apostle must take care to recognize and utilize his gift, how much more followers in the same tradition centuries later?

As for Timothy's gift being given "through [*dia* with genitive sing. object] prophecy,"[606] Towner plausibly suggests "a reference to words of the Spirit spoken by a prophet(s) that confirm and identify Timothy's giftedness and thereby authorize his ministry in the community."[607] "Through" signals that the words were a means of recognition of Timothy's gift, not the cause of its bestowal.

What is clear is that, for all Paul's exhortation in this subsection for Timothy to apply himself, act, teach, and serve, at the same time he is interdependent with those represented by the elders who at some point authenticated his giftedness. He is not on his own but part of the church. He is, even more

602. Collins, 131. Collins proposes Acts 6:6 as a parallel, when the apostles "imposed hands on the seven disciples, who were then recognized as servants in the community." See also Acts 8:17; 9:17; 19:6.

603. For the apparent ceremony in the early church, see the excursus in Dibelius and Conzelmann, 70–71.

604. Keener, *Bible Background Commentary*, 610.

605. Marshall, with Towner, *Pastoral Epistles*, 565.

606. The object could also be accusative plural, in which case the meaning of *dia* would be "because of, on account of." Most commentators agree this interpretation would yield an obscure result. For more extensive discussion, including the synonymity of *dia* and *meta* in this verse, see Harris, *Prepositions and Theology*, 77. He understands *dia* as denoting "accompaniment as well as instrumentality."

607. Towner, *Letters*, 323.

importantly, dependent on God, who in Paul's reckoning is the sole recipient of any credit for gospel ministry creditably accomplished (see, e.g., 1 Cor 15:10; Eph 3:8). Since God is ever faithful,[608] Timothy can take heart.

15 Paul's exhortation continues and perhaps even ratchets up. Two imperatives take center stage, with an entailment associated with the second.

First, "be diligent[609] in these matters [*tauta*]" harks back to v. 11: "Command and teach these things [*tauta*]." The repeated *tauta* gives a bookend effect. Verses 11–14 list *what* Timothy needs to do; now v. 15 underscores the attitude and intensity *with which* Timothy needs to approach those things. Diligence is required for responsible ministry, quite apart from the unique challenges facing Timothy at this time. When it comes to the mandates Paul lays down in vv. 11–14, a lukewarm minister is a self-contradiction. Jesus's intensity regarding his duties and field of service comes to mind (John 2:17). Paul's testimony to his own intense focus (in an epistle that lists Timothy in the opening verse) gives Paul grounds for exhorting Timothy: "Besides everything else, I face daily the pressure of my concern for all the churches. Who is weak, and I do not feel weak? Who is led into sin, and I do not inwardly burn?" (2 Cor 11:28–29; cf. 1:1). In a sense Paul calls Timothy to no more than he expects of all believers: "Never be lacking in zeal, but keep your spiritual fervor, serving the Lord" (Rom 12:11). But ministers (like Timothy) are just believers, too. They require encouragement in the same paths as anyone else in the church.

Second, "give yourself wholly to them" essentially restates "be diligent in these matters." "Give yourself wholly" translates the present imperative of *eimi* (to be).[610] Paul wants Timothy to be "all in" in the sense of fully committed and engaged. While there is danger in taking oneself too seriously, there is also the opposite error of approaching a task too casually, lacking urgency and a due sense of that task's gravity. With his age and experience, Paul may have had a finer sense for the high stakes and pitched opposition Timothy was facing. Timothy may have been underestimating the concentration and effort that would be needed to overcome the odds stacked against him. Paul's repeated imperative (which he extends in the next verse) makes it seem he felt it necessary to shake Timothy awake almost as if from sleep. "Timothy is to . . . be immersed in what he has been taught and what gifts he has been given."[611] That he needed to be told may help explain the repetitiveness and overlap found in this subsection.

608. 1 Cor 1:9; 10:13; 2 Cor 1:18.

609. For the verb *meleta* (from *meletaō*) and its possible meanings, see Marshall, with Towner, *Letters*, 570n140.

610. BDAG 284 (3c).

611. Witherington, 260.

A reason for Timothy's diligence and devotion is "so that everyone may see [his] progress [*prokopē*]." There is a tension here with Jesus's warning: "Be careful not to practice your righteousness in front of others to be seen by them" (Matt 6:1). But the tension inheres in Jesus's own teaching: "Let your light shine before others, that they may see your good deeds and glorify your Father in heaven" (Matt 5:16). Paul uses the same word "progress" in Phil 1:12 (the "advance" of the gospel) and in Phil 1:25 (the Philippians' "progress and joy in the faith").[612] Growth and forward movement are signs of spiritual life and ministry effectiveness. Paul wants Timothy to exhibit both, movement and effectiveness.

Motive in this context is everything: Timothy would not be undertaking this ministry for the sake of personal gain, ego, or public acclaim. Rather, the motivation Paul has given still stands: to "set an example for the believers" (v. 12), as Timothy expends athlete-like effort in pursuit of godliness (v. 7) and as he labors and strives (v. 10). Verse 16 will give another reason—salvation of all involved. Timothy's credibility as a leader is another consideration: if a leader is not engaged in growing, how can he lead others in that direction? Still another consideration is simply the nature of healthy life in Christ, as Paul describes it in his own case: "Straining toward what is ahead, I press on toward the goal to win the prize for which God has called me heavenward in Christ Jesus" (Phil 3:13–14). Timothy's spiritual father, Paul (see 1:2), calls for Timothy to follow in the path he has established (cf. 1 Pet 2:2; 2 Pet 3:18; where the watchword is not progress but growth).

16 In a pattern similar to the previous verse, Paul exhorts Timothy with a pair of imperatives, the second essentially restating the first, followed by a statement of result.

The first command is for Timothy to "watch [his] life and doctrine closely." "Watch" translates a form of *epechō*, a word that can mean (1) hold on to something (as in Phil 2:16: "as you hold firmly to the word of life"), (2) be mindful of or attentive to, or (3) to stay somewhere for a time. Here the second of these meanings applies: Timothy should spare no effort in applying himself (*seautō*). "Watch your life" (NIV) is as defensible as other options: "Keep

612. There are no other NT occurrences. The noun is absent from the AF. But the verb (from *prokoptō*) is attested: "Let us . . . strive to advance [*peirōmetha prokoptein*] in the commandments of the Lord, in order that all of us, being of one mind, may be gathered together into life" (2 Clem. 17:3). The noun occupies a prominent place in various discussions on self-improvement and progress in Epictetus (nineteen occurrences; the verb occurs twenty times). For a synopsis of conceptions of "progress" in other philosophers of the day, see Collins, 131–32; Johnson, *First and Second Letters to Timothy*, 254. The verb *prokoptō* is found six times in the NT: Luke 2:52 (Jesus' growth in wisdom and stature); Rom 13:12; Gal 1:14 (Paul's advancement in Judaism); 2 Tim 2:16; 3:9, 13. The three uses in 2 Timothy refer to advancement of the ungodly in the wrong direction.

a close watch on yourself" (ESV); "Watch yourself" (GNT, Mounce); "Pay close attention to yourself" (NASB); "Be conscientious about how you live" (NET). Translations that are intentional in reflecting the reflexive pronoun ("yourself") may make Paul sound a little more foreboding (if he seeks to apply pressure) or apprehensive (if he fears for Timothy's steadfastness). Professors try to instill in students a sense of methodological self-consciousness; Paul wants Timothy to be ministerially self-aware. Schlatter observes that such awareness is crucial, "because Timothy draws that which he gives to others from that which he himself possesses."[613]

Guthrie thinks "watch your life" (NIV) "does not so well bring out the meaning," adding, "Moral and spiritual rectitude is an indispensable preliminary to doctrinal orthodoxy."[614] In this view, Paul is not so much saying Timothy should watch his life as that he should examine and guard his heart and soul, the inner person who must be right with God for one's observable life to be of use to God in pastoral labor. It is notoriously the case that the outward life of a minister (like the life of any professing Christian) can look one way and the inner reality be substantially different.[615] This possibility may be what Paul is trying to make sure Timothy comes to grips with.[616]

This watching or paying close attention applies not only to Timothy and his life (whether inner, outer, or both) but also to his "doctrine" (*didaskalia*, used nineteen times in Paul, with fifteen of these in the PE; see commentary Introduction, IX.D). It is not Timothy's doctrine in the sense that he owns it or devised it; it is not distinct to him but is shared with Paul and others in church leadership across the Roman world. Yet, it is his in the sense that he has a responsibility to be faithful to what he has received and how he builds on it (see 1 Cor 3:10). "Watch yourself how you act and what you teach" (NLV) captures well Paul's concern, which came into view as early as 1:3 when he pointed to false doctrine and ordered Timothy to stand firm on the teaching that is true.

In continuing parallel with v. 15, Paul moves from a first imperative ("watch") to a second: "persevere." "In them" is most naturally taken with "life and doctrine." Johnson translates "remain steady in both."[617] A quick checkup is not what Paul has in mind but consistent attention in the long run.

613. Schlatter, *Die Kirche der Griechen*, 131.

614. Guthrie, 111.

615. On some readings of Rom 7, this battle line exists in the life of every believer, as it did for Paul himself.

616. Cf. Jesus's warning to "teachers of the law" who fastidiously "clean the outside of the cup and dish, but inside . . . are full of greed and self-indulgence" (Matt 23:25), and who "look beautiful on the outside but on the inside are full of the bones of the dead and everything unclean" (Matt 23:27).

617. Johnson, *First and Second Letters to Timothy*, 254.

"Persevere" (from *epimenō*) translates a word found only here in the PE but eight other times in Paul, five of which are relevant here:[618]

> *Shall* we *continue* in sin, that grace may abound? (Rom 6:1 ASV)
>
> Consider therefore the kindness and sternness of God: sternness to those who fell, but kindness to you, provided that you *continue* in his kindness. . . . And if they *do* not *persist* in unbelief, they will be grafted in. (Rom 11:22–23)
>
> But it is more necessary for you that I *remain* in the body. (Phil 1:24)
>
> . . . if you *continue* in your faith, established and firm, and do not move from the hope held out in the gospel. (Col 1:23)

From the words above in italics, which translate forms of *epimenō*, a sense is gained for settings in which to remain or continue is clearly a good thing (and others where it is not). In v. 16 Paul expresses the same desire that he did earlier for believers at Rome and in Colossae. For churches to persevere, their pastors must do no less. As both the Romans and Colossians passages above in their if-clauses indicate, the full benefit of the redemption promised in the gospel depends on human perseverance.

Schlatter points here to the similarity with 1 Cor 9:22–27. Paul calls people to Christ "so that by all possible means I might save some" (v. 22). There is a practical sense in which the gospel herald is as salvific as the gospel message, for "how can they hear without someone preaching to them?" (Rom 10:14). As for himself, Paul writes, "I strike a blow to my body and make it my slave so that after I have preached to others, I myself will not be disqualified" (1 Cor 9:27). "There is no salvation for Paul without total devotion to his ministry." Yet, none of this is tantamount to synergism, "because the work can only be accomplished with that which has been bestowed as a gift of grace."[619]

When Paul writes, "I worked harder than all of them—yet not I, but the grace of God that was with me" (1 Cor 15:10), he expresses the same dialectic between human effort, on the one hand, and divine sufficiency and sovereignty, on the other (see also Phil 2:12–13). Theologically, sovereignty is supreme. God alone saves by his grace rooted in Christ's saving work. Phenomenologically, humans must act in response and persevere. It is the phenomenological truth that Paul stresses in v. 16.

618. In three cases the verb carries the sense of a person spending time somewhere: 1 Cor 16:7, 8; Gal 1:18.

619. Schlatter, *Die Kirche der Griechen*, 132.

Mention of Timothy's "hearers" is an indirect affirmation of the core of the pastoral task: the ministry of the word. As pastors (and believers they oversee) deploy that word, saving faith arises and is sustained in those who hear and receive it (see Rom 10:17). To encourage this process is why Paul has stressed teaching and preaching and doctrine in this subsection and elsewhere. On "save" (from *sōzō*; twenty-nine occurrences in Paul, seven of them in the PE), see commentary Introduction, IX.A. He has already used the word in 1:15; 2:4, 15 (see discussion above). These verses stress that Christ saves (1:15) and that God saves (2:4, 15 contain divine passives). Paul's monergistic understanding is highlighted in 2 Tim 1:9: "He has saved us and called us to a holy life—not because of anything we have done but because of his own purpose and grace. This grace was given us in Christ Jesus before the beginning of time."[620] Here Paul speaks from the theological perspective; salvation is solely God's doing. Yet, precisely because of God's foresight and faithful provision, in the direst of straits Paul can write, "The Lord will rescue me from every evil attack and *will bring me safely* [form of *sōzō*] to his heavenly kingdom" (2 Tim 4:18).

For this reason it makes eminent sense for Timothy to serve as if all depends on him. For precisely in doing so, he embraces the mandate of his mentor expressed in a letter in whose first verse the name of Timothy also appears:[621] "Work out *your own salvation* with fear and trembling, for it is God who works in you, both to will and to work for his good pleasure" (Phil 2:12–13 ESV).[622]

D. Subgroup Care: Widows, Elders, Slaves (5:1–6:2a)

In the United States there is a saying, "All politics is local." While national and international issues may be of utmost significance, there is a local dimension that flavors and ultimately defines (sometimes disastrously) any body politic in its essence and resulting actions.

This section of 1 Timothy could be taken to confirm that all pastoral ministry is personal. While lofty theological truths and doxological realities give impetus to pastoral labor, and while preaching itself can become impersonal speech-making, and while too often today pastoral positions bear crushing administrative responsibilities, the care of individual souls, and thereby the body of the church as a whole, is at the heart of serving as an undershepherd of the Great Shepherd Jesus Christ.

620. Much the same conviction is expressed in Titus 3:5.

621. See Phil 1:1: "Paul and Timothy, servants of Christ Jesus."

622. NIV omits the word "own," which seems required by *heautōn* in the text.

If Acts 20 is any indication, the pastoral heritage at Ephesus (where Paul called pastors "shepherds of the church of God"; Acts 20:28) that Paul began with his three-year stay there was founded through highly personal involvement and initiatives. He taught both "publicly and from house to house" (Acts 20:20). He did not spare himself, as he "served the Lord with great humility and with tears and in the midst of severe testing" (v. 19). By physical labor Paul's hands "supplied my own needs and the needs of my companions" so as not to burden the fledgling church. He could tell pastors at Miletus, "I am innocent of the blood of any of you" (v. 26), implying interpersonal dealings with each of them. This understanding of the scope of his ministry is confirmed as Paul reminds them, "For three years I never stopped warning each of you night and day with tears" (v. 31), reflecting a high level of personal commitment and emotional attachment. The scene of Paul's departure speaks eloquently to the personal rapport between Paul and those he had faithfully served: "When Paul had finished speaking, he knelt down with all of them and prayed. They all wept as they embraced him and kissed him. What grieved them most was his statement that they would never see his face again" (Acts 20:36–38).

In modern times, many pastors have experienced very different responses to their departure from a church—like glee and relief and even celebration (sometimes echoing the pastors' own sentiments). When there is wistful regret, as with Paul saying good-bye at Miletus, it is a tribute to pastoral care that has not only nobly held forth the word of truth but has also connected with persons in Christ one-on-one.

It is the one-on-one dimension of pastoral care that the section below highlights. Of course no pastoral care is hermetically sealed off from its other dimensions. Parts of what Paul will say in 1 Tim 5 will relate closely to other parts of 1 Timothy, the PE, the Pauline corpus, and the rest of Scripture. But in some ways 5:1–6:2a is strikingly distinct. No other portion of all the Bible has so much to say about the congregational care of widows. Other subgroups come into view as well. Paul's personal solicitude for Timothy also reemerges, as do theological pronouncements that transcend (though they are still relevant to) interpersonal pastoral care (e.g., 5:24–25). Timothy will be reminded that there is an irreducibly personal and interpersonal dimension to his calling. Without that application, the point of correcting false teaching (ch. 1), ensuring a blessed worship order (ch. 2), appointing qualified servant-leaders (ch. 3), and making sure his own commitment is as vigorous, measured, and wise as his best efforts by God's grace can make it (ch. 4) has been missed. As Neudorfer puts it, "Ethics is the testing ground of doctrine."[623]

623. Neudorfer, *Erster Brief an Timotheus*, 197.

1. Overarching Principle (5:1–2)

> [1]*Do not rebuke an older man harshly, but exhort him as if he were your father. Treat younger men as brothers,* [2]*older women as mothers, and younger women as sisters, with absolute purity.*

1 Paul segues easily from what Timothy should command and teach (4:6, 11) and the diligence with which he should perform his duties (4:15–16) to the people he is charged to instruct and oversee. He is not their overlord. Nor are they there for his misuse. All in the congregation, old and young, male and female, can expect their pastor's respect, empathy, and readiness to serve. Paul divides the people of God in a local church into four groups and cites the default approach for Timothy to adopt as he relates to them.

First are older men. Some understand Paul to speaking of a church "elder," that is, a pastoral leader or officer. Most translations accord with NIV's "older man"; the Greek word is the same for both. Given the way the same word comes up below (vv. 17–20), it is possible that in v. 1 Paul has in mind the mature (in contrast to the youthful) men under Timothy's leadership in general. Below (beginning in v. 17) Paul will single out a subset of this group.

Paul personalizes in v. 1 with "an older man" in the singular; the parallels with younger men and women in subsequent clauses confirm that this is a representative "older man." As a whole, Paul means men older than Timothy. But to do justice to the group, Timothy has to deal aright with each individual. By the same token, in coming clauses, where there are instructions for treatment of individuals, it will be understood that each is representative of their entire group.

It is easy for a younger church leader, whether from defensiveness or from an undue sense of self-importance, to deal impatiently with the elderly. (And to someone in their early twenties, people in their thirties can seem elderly, let alone the truly aged.) Also, the elderly are not above sin and may require confrontation.[624] But Paul warns against peremptory treatment. The word translated "rebuke" (from *epiplēssō*) is found only here in the NT, nor is it present in the LXX. But its meaning is clear from usage in other sources.[625] Rather than rebuke an older man under his spiritual care Timothy should "exhort" him like he would his father. (This command assumes a healthy relationship with one's father.)[626]

624. For Cicero's rebuke of the elderly (for luxury and vice), see Montague, 229.

625. That is, Philo (ten times), Josephus (fifteen times), Epictetus (four times), along with other Hellenistic sources (see BDAG; MM).

626. Cf. Epictetus, *Enchiridion* 31.4: "A father is reviled by a son, when he does not impart to him the things which he takes to be good." The same writer also voices what a good

"Exhort" (*parakalei*) can also mean encourage or comfort. The point is that, in contrast to harsh dismissal or correction, "the Lord's servant must not be quarrelsome but must be kind to everyone, able to teach, not resentful" (2 Tim 2:24; see commentary). This command could have been a real challenge when dealing with alpha males (or females), who may have tried to take advantage of Timothy if he showed them deference. Paul has already made it clear that Timothy must stand up to false teaching and teachers. But he speaks here not of those who are in error and trying to steamroll him but of those who seek (or are at least willing to accept) Timothy's encouragement.

Similarly, "younger men" deserve Timothy's gracious regard as if they were his brothers, which they are, inasmuch as God's household, the church, is a family (3:4–5, 15). "Younger" here means men younger than those regarded as older;[627] the dividing line would be fluid. Keener points out that, in light of Proverbs, "Judaism heavily emphasized concern for one's neighbor by offering and accepting correction." This concern would be all the more true of fellow family members. At the same time, Timothy's (and Paul's) Jewish roots "emphasized the necessity of private as opposed to public rebuke unless all attempts at private settlement failed."[628] Jesus reflects and extends this tradition (Matt 18:15): "If your brother or sister sins, go and point out their fault, just between the two of you. If they listen to you, you have won them over." Young men are notorious for swagger and arrogance, and doctrinal or moral conviction can bring out the worst in pride and self-importance. Timothy must take care not to repay evil with evil (Rom 12:17; see also 1 Pet 3:9) but overcome evil with good (Rom 12:21).

In all of these potentially prickly matters, Timothy's standing as overseer and teacher with responsibility before God for those under his care is not reduced. Paul's intention is simply to shape "how that authority will be expressed."[629]

2 There is no double standard here but perfect symmetry: older women and younger women deserve exactly the same respect as the corresponding male demographics.

As for older women, Paul's directive that they be regarded "as mothers" again draws on the notion that church members as members of God's household having one heavenly Father are like family members. A young man like

---

relationship assumes: "Is anyone a father? If so, it is implied that the children should take care of him, submit to him in everything, patiently listen to his reproaches, his correction" (30.1). Paul addresses Timothy not only in the light of the gospel but in recognizable continuity with conventions of their setting that the gospel does not contravene.

627. Towner, *Letters*, 331.

628. Keener, *Bible Background Commentary*, 610.

629. Towner, *Letters*, 331.

Timothy, accordingly, regards women who are older like he would (and evidently did) his own mother, Eunice (2 Tim 1:5; cf. Acts 16:1).

But there is an additional layer of tradition informing the discourse here. In Proverbs there is frequent emphasis on the respect to be accorded both father *and* mother. This balance stood in marked contrast to the paterfamilias concept of the Roman world, according to which fathers were uniquely privileged and empowered by comparison.[630] In Proverbs, while father and mother are sometimes distinguished, they are also frequently honored jointly. Often this equal regard is reflected in synonymous parallelism:

> Listen, my son, to your father's instruction and do not forsake your mother's teaching. (Prov 1:8)[631]

> For I too was a son to my father, still tender, and cherished by my mother. (Prov 4:3)

> The proverbs of Solomon: A wise son brings joy to his father, but a foolish son brings grief to his mother. (Prov 10:1)

> A wise son brings joy to his father, but a foolish man despises his mother. (Prov 15:20)

See also Prov 17:25; 19:26; 20:20; 23:22, 25; 28:24; 30:11, 17, where the same joint honoring is mirrored. Honoring older women as mothers, like honoring older men as fathers, might be difficult in a given situation. But it was an age-old precept in the Scriptures of the early church. A pastoral leader and equipper like Timothy must not forget this theological and social rule.

Younger women receive analogous regard. They are "sisters" in Christ. Paul adds a critical rider: "with absolute[632] purity [*hagneia*]." The same word occurs at 4:12 above (see discussion). The broader word group of which *hagneia* is part (see *hagnos*) was often used in the context of pagan religion to denote cultic purity. But in the early church, "the word group is used to express the moral purity demanded in the behavior of Christians." Since Christ is pure (*hagnos*), his followers may share that attribute via his righteousness (see 1 John 3:3). As they do, their "purity and integrity are . . . not merely human

630. See, for example, S. Porter, "Family in the Epistles," in *Family in the Bible: Exploring Customs, Culture, and Context*, ed. R. S. Hess and M. D. Carroll R. (Grand Rapids: Baker Academic, 2003), 154.

631. Nearly repeated in 6:20.

632. The Greek is a form of *pas* (all). "All purity" can be taken to mean as much as possible to the greatest extent Timothy can manage. (In this life, is any man totally free from the lure of lust?) "Absolute" is a good way to express this concept.

virtues: they indicate the relation of a person to God,"[633] because they come about through the work of Christ on their behalf appropriated by faith.

These considerations suggest that "with absolute purity" is not about moralism or some prudishness on Paul's part. Nor should it be regarded as sexist regard for woman as temptress (see Sir 9:2–9). Linda Belleville frames the issue wisely: "All the forms of propriety are to be observed when it comes to younger women. This is common sense. Even today it is a male pastor's or leader's relationship to the younger women of the church that is particularly prone to being misconstrued."[634] Furthermore, the problem may not be misconstrual but outright exploitation from either or both sides.

"With absolute purity" is rather an ethical entailment of a theological truth: the gospel brings cleansing from sin and union with God (or Christ),[635] who imparts his holiness to those who walk in relationship with him by faith. A pastor in particular should be advanced in the appropriation of a sensual discipline that makes possible chaste regard for those under his care because of the effect of a strong sense of the presence of God in his holiness.

This sensibility can be difficult to achieve and maintain in light of multiple factors. Today, pornography has had a major role in the erosion of moral and spiritual purity on the part of many. Promiscuous behavior in the past (at best) marks more and more of the lives of those entering ministry, to say nothing of those in churches, among whom are increasing numbers who are cohabiting, addicted to pornography themselves, or dabbling in other fashionable approaches to what Scripture calls immoral sexual expression. In some circles more and more "trans" ministers or ministerial candidates have declared themselves to be men or women when they were born the opposite.[636] Gender is declared to be nothing more than a social construct or individual preference rather than a gift of God conferred at conception (like it was at creation: Gen 1:27).

In such a climate, and with the rise of digital viewing and connecting possibilities, Paul's call for Timothy's God-sustained "purity" in his dealings with younger women is if anything more timely now than in any age of the church. Women ministers can take these things to heart in their dealings with men. With same-sex attraction becoming an increasing issue, there is challenge from yet another quarter. There are resources in the gospel for redemptive and upright pastoral regard for all others in all situations.

633. *NIDNTTE* 1:138.

634. Belleville, 96.

635. As representative of a large, relatively recent literature, see Campbell, *Paul and Union with Christ*.

636. On female-at-birth seminarians who have become men, see "People," *ChrCent*, July 20, 2016, 19. For one of their stories, see Brett Ray, *My Name Is Brett: Truths from a Trans Christian* (CreateSpace Independent Publishing Platform, 2015).

One way the moral steel called purity can be expressed is in the care of (both older and younger) widows, the subject of the next four subsections.

2. *Widows: General Policies (5:3–8)*

> 3 *Give proper recognition to those widows who are really in need.* 4 *But if*
> *a widow has children or grandchildren, these should learn first of all to put*
> *their religion into practice by caring for their own family and so repaying*
> *their parents and grandparents, for this is pleasing to God.* 5 *The widow*
> *who is really in need and left all alone puts her hope in God and continues*
> *night and day to pray and to ask God for help.* 6 *But the widow who lives*
> *for pleasure is dead even while she lives.* 7 *Give the people these instructions,*
> *so that no one may be open to blame.* 8 *Anyone who does not provide for*
> *their relatives, and especially for their own household, has denied the faith*
> *and is worse than an unbeliever.*

3 We have stressed above that this section of 1 Timothy illustrates the personal-care dimension of pastoral ministry. Not that only pastors should perform such care, but in a teach-and-exercise-oversight understanding of pastoral leadership (2:12; 4:6, 11), Timothy and those like him whom he appoints would be the point persons in facilitating it. It is important that it occupy a prominent place in their ministry outlook. Age-and-gender subgroups (see previous two verses) and now other significant categories of persons (i.e., widows) come in for Paul's particular attention.

Keener suggests that, in mentioning "widows," Paul "probably refers to an order of widows who served the church, as in second-century Christianity."[637] Johnson outlines feminist arguments for seeing what Paul says about widows as an example of patriarchal suppression.[638] Krause offers a sustained polemic against the passage, which in her reconstruction does not promote widows' welfare but relegates women without husbands "to a ghetto of widows."[639] While Johnson grants that "the evidence is sufficiently ambiguous and difficult to allow honest disagreement and to provide some support to the case made by such scholars," he finds their reconstruction (reflected in Keener's suggestion above) unconvincing.[640]

637. Keener, *Bible Background Commentary*, 610. He immediately adds parenthetically: "Commentators disagree on this point." For defense of an early order of widows, see B. Thurston, "1 Timothy 5:3–16 and the Leadership of Women in the Early Church," in Levine, *Feminist Companion to the Deutero-Pauline Epistles*, 159–74.

638. Johnson, *First and Second Letters to Timothy*, 270–72.

639. Krause, 108 (broader discussion in 96–109).

640. Johnson, *First and Second Letters to Timothy*, 271. Equally skeptical of the reconstruction is Bassler, 92.

Marshall likewise delves into the primary sources and arguments adduced by those who view this passage as another attempt of 1 Timothy "to reassert the domination of male leaders in the church" against a recognized order of female ministers who, the author felt, must be suppressed. After comparing this view to interpretations more shaped by first-century history and the text and less by feminist hermeneutics, Marshall summarizes the two options: one sees restriction of "the development of a female 'order' within the church." The other interprets Paul's directives regarding widows "in terms of concern to ensure that charitable care is properly directed." Marshall concludes that while in theory both concerns "could be present side by side," in actuality "there can be little doubt that the second interpretation is the correct one."[641] This is the interpretative framework that is adopted below.

A rough-and-ready translation of v. 3 is: "Honor the widows who really [*ontōs*][642] are widows." By "honor" (here a present imperative), Paul means "give what they are due."[643] The word could also be used of honor due the gods; see the next verse for the care of widows viewed as a religious or holy duty.[644] Across the Roman world, as in much of the world today, women whose husbands died could find themselves with no means of support, especially if children were not able or willing to lend a hand in their upkeep.[645] This was a social problem of the age that surfaced already in Acts 6:1–4. A congregation established for some time (as at Ephesus) should do no less for this needy subgroup than the prototype first church in Jerusalem. "Widows who are really in need" (NIV) would be those lacking resources or relatives with resources. Additional qualifications for recognition of widow status and church assistance are listed in following verses.

Why such sudden concern for just this subgroup? It may be assumed they were numerous in the church(es) under Timothy's jurisdiction. Otherwise it would be inexplicable that Paul spends so much time and space on the subject in this letter. In addition, three observations are worth noting.

First, other early pastoral leaders such as James made treatment of widows "in their distress" (along with orphans) as a barometer of church health

641. Marshall, with Towner, *Pastoral Epistles*, 574–81, here 576–77. So also Witherington, 266, esp. n. 364 (on the possibility of a formal order of ministering widows at this time in the early church).

642. The Greek word here is an adverb formed from the partciple *ōn* (to be). It conveys such adverbial meanings as "really, certainly, in truth" (BDAG 715).

643. See Eph 6:2 for a parallel: "Honor your father and mother." This is the only other place Paul uses the verb *timaō*. He uses the noun (*timē*, show of honor, respect) eighteen times, six of these in the PE. See 1 Tim 1:17; 5:17; 6:1, 16; 2 Tim 2:20, 21.

644. See BDAG 1004; Hofmann, 153.

645. It should be recalled that becoming a Christian often resulted in ostracism in both Jewish and pagan settings. Widows who confessed Christ as Lord might find no support from their born kinfolk, even if they had any.

and personal spiritual integrity. Their care (along with orphans) by the church, an intrinsic good (see below), was also necessary "to keep oneself from being polluted by the world" (Jas 1:27).

Second, Jesus cared for widows (e.g., Luke 7:11–17). He cited them in his parables (e.g., Mark 12:41–44; Luke 18:1–8). Given the dearth of references to Jesus's earthly father Joseph, it is possible that "widow" describe his own mother, whose care he arranged in the hour of his death (John 19:26). He criticized those in his own day who neglected the care of widows (Mark 12:40). Presumably some of the money over which Judas had jurisdiction went to widows among "the poor" (John 13:29).

Third, numerous OT passages underscore the ethical necessity for caring for widows.[646] Towner comments that Paul's teaching on widows in this section "taps into the rich tradition of God's special care for widows and orphans."[647] Evil people are characterized as those who "drive away the orphan's donkey and take the widow's ox in pledge" (Job 24:3; cf. 24:21; Ps 94:6; Isa 10:2; Jer 7:6; Ezek 22:25). Care for widows is an indicator of righteousness (Job 29:13; 31:16, 18). God himself is "a father to the fatherless, a defender of widows" (Ps 68:5; cf. 146:9; Prov 15:25). The prophets are vehement in their insistence on Israel's care for widows as an indicator of their fidelity to the God who brought them out of Egypt in their own helpless state (Isa 1:23; Jer 22:3; 49:11; Mal 3:5).

Given the OT theme of care for widows, and the way this concern echoed in Jesus's teaching and example and then subsequently in the early church, it is no great stretch to surmise that, if Paul and Timothy became aware of their presence in or near the Ephesian congregation(s), the gospel as proclaimed by Jesus from the outset[648] made it incumbent on the church to make their care a priority.

In contemporary discussion, if anything is remarkable about this verse and the passage following it, it is the lack of credit Paul receives for prioritizing the care of individual, elderly, godly widows (and the admonition of ungodly ones; v. 6), hardly a mark of institutionalizing the church or an expression of suppression of women.[649]

646. For example, Exod 22:22; Deut 10:18; 14:29; 16:14; 24:17; Zech 7:10.

647. Towner, "1–2 Timothy and Titus," 899.

648. See, for example, Luke 4:16–26, which suggests widows were a particular beneficiary of Jesus' message and presence, just as they were in Elijah's ministry.

649. See, for example, K. Nash in *EDB*, 1378. She sees in this passage evidence that "by the 2nd century . . . care of widows had become an institutionalized ministry. . . . Community leaders [like the author of 1 Timothy] thus assumed the responsibility of male relatives to regulate the sexuality of female family members and to determine the ministerial roles open to women." Nothing is said of meeting the possibly dire physical needs of true widows, let alone Paul's Christlike compassion for needy women.

4 This verse make clear part of what defines a widow "really in need" (v. 3). If a widow in the church (see v. 5) has "children or grandchildren," these individuals need to seize the learning-and-ministry opportunity that their needy elderly relative presents.

What is this opportunity? NIV's "put their religion into practice" translates a form of *eusebeō*, a word that "refers to a sense of awesome obligation arising within a system of reciprocity in which special respect is showed to those who have the greatest investment in one's well-being, such as deities and parental figures" (BDAG 413). In the only other NT use of the word, Paul speaks of the "UNKNOWN GOD" that the Athenians "worship" (Acts 17:23; emphasis in NIV). The Athenians sensed indebtedness to deities, even the unknown one. Their owed the god their highest devotion.

Paul uses the same word in v. 4 to direct children and grandchildren not to "worship" their household per se, but to recognize the holy duty[650] that relationship to Christ places upon family members. Godly widows are doubly family members: by blood and by faith. Relatives of widows should not expect the church to care for their widowed relative when they can do it by their own means. Paul rather commands Timothy:[651] "Let them learn first" (my translation) to honor their elderly female relative as she deserves, in God's household (cf. 3:15). Society may not value widows. Family members in the Christian community with a sense of linkage to the God of Scripture (see above) will be willing to "learn"[652] to do so as disciples of Jesus.

If "children or grandchildren" of a widow follow Paul's directive here, "by caring for their own family" (i.e., the widow), they are "repaying their parents" (if they are a child of the widow) "and grandparents" (if they are grandchildren). "Repaying" implies indebtedness. On the one hand, "children should not have to save up for their parents, but parents for their children" (2 Cor 12:14). But, on the other, when parents have done their work and reach their

650. See discussion of "honor" in the previous verse, a concept that could connote a theologically significant and not merely humanitarian gesture.

651. The Greek form is a third person imperative: Timothy receives a command that pertains to widows' children or grandchildren under his pastoral care. NIV "should learn" makes the imperative into an indicative. This wording could be taken as Paul's observation of what "should" take place, obscuring that he is issuing a command for Timothy to administer, not offering an advisory comment. Admittedly, renderings like "let them first learn" (ESV) can be read as if Paul wanted Timothy to grant permission, which is also wide of the semantics of the original. "Put their religion into practice" (NIV) may unwittingly promote religious moralism by undertranslating *eusebeō* (see previous paragraph). Paul commands follow-through of a learned and acknowledged holy duty (implicit in *eusebeō*), something likely sharper and better defined than "practice" of "religion."

652. From *manthanō*, the verb that is cognate with *mathētēs* ("disciple"). The word appeared earlier in 2:11 (see commentary there). Other PE uses: 1 Tim 5:13; 2 Tim 3:7, 14; Titus 3:14. Note also the pan-PE stress on the practice and content of teaching.

own time of need, the tables turn. Relatives of widows, if they are able, must seek means of sharing their God-granted provisions with the elderly relative who has given her whole lifetime for the sake of her descendants.

It is worth recalling that Paul's scruples here have rootage in a decadence Jesus decried among his contemporaries: "You say that if anyone declares that what might have been used to help their father or mother is Corban (that is, devoted to God)—then you no longer let them do anything for their father or mother" (Mark 7:11–12). Jesus named this practice for what is was: replacing Scripture (in this case the book of Isaiah and Moses's writings; see Mark 7:6, 10) with self-serving hermeneutics: "Thus you nullify the word of God by your tradition that you have handed down" (v. 13). Paul too will wax prophetic shortly (1 Tim 5:8) on the related topic of caring for widows. The concern articulated in this discourse, then, is at least as plausibly tied to Jesus (and OT teaching) as it is to some second-century ecclesial concern.

Paul adds a major motivation: "for this is pleasing to God." Nearly the same expression occurs in 2:3 (see commentary above). The ultimate warrant for Paul's word here is God himself, whether one thinks in ethical terms (see OT Scriptures on widows above) or in doxological terms of what will enable ongoing enjoyment of a sense of God's presence in the household of faith. God will not be honored and grace Christ's followers with his presence when those who profess faith stonewall a widowed relative if it in within their means to provide essential care.

5 Paul moves from the proper recognition of widows (v. 3) to the responsibility of family members to care for widows who are their relatives (v. 4). But he needs to clarify who qualifies to be regarded as a widow supported by the church ("really in need," v. 3). Verse 5 answers that question in two ways.

First, the true[653] widow, one who is "left all alone" (i.e., has no relatives as per v. 4), "puts her hope in God." The expression resembles the declaration in 4:10 that Paul and Timothy "have put [their] hope in the living God" (see also 6:17).[654] Towner notes the background for the expression in "the psalmists' dominant framing of Israel's faith and worship in terms of 'placing hope in YHWH.'"[655] She is truly a woman of faith. Celebrated biblical parallels like Ruth in the OT and Anna in the NT (Luke 2:36–38) come to mind as indefatigable devotees of God, despite the loss of their husbands. Of Anna it is said that "she never left the temple but worshiped night and day [*vukta kai hēmeron*],

653. Paul uses the same adverbial form of the present participle of *eimi* as in v. 3 (*ontōs*).

654. Outside the PE, see 1 Cor 15:19 (hope in Christ); 2 Cor 1:10 (hope in God). The use of the perfect tense form of *elpizō* in this theological sense is absent from the LXX, Philo, Josephus, and the AF. Justin Martyr uses it once (*Dialogue with Trypho* 11), but with the proposition *eis* rather than *epi* as in Paul. Hope in God using *elpizō* in other tenses and *epi* is frequent in the Psalms (LXX), as Towner points out (next note).

655. Towner, *Letters*, 341.

fasting and praying [*deēsesin*]" (Luke 2:37). This language echoes in the next clause of v. 5. Another NT example is the persistent importuning widow of Jesus's parable in Luke 18:1–8.

Second, the true widow, like Anna, "continues night and day [*vukta kai hēmeron*] to pray [or: "in prayers"; *tais deēsesin*] and to ask God for help." She is fully in sync with the congregational priority of prayerfulness (see 1 Tim 2:1–8) continually. "Night and day" describes Paul's own dogged consistency of admonishing (Acts 20:31), toiling (1 Thess 2:9; 2 Thess 3:8), and praying (1 Thess 3:10; 2 Tim 1:3). The true widow is apostle-like in her dedication to prayer.[656]

There is, then, a threefold qualification to this point for being regarded as a true widow: (1) bereft of family who could help, (2) exemplary in setting her hope on God, and (3) vigilant continual prayerfulness. Having lost one's husband is a necessary qualification, but not sufficient in itself to be able to look to the church for monetary (or equivalent) support.

6 If v. 5 is a definition and commendation of the true widow, v. 6 tersely[657] describes a widow who is godless by comparison. She "lives for pleasure." The verb (*spatalaō*)[658] occurs only twice in the LXX (Sir 21:15; Ezek 16:49) and not at all in Philo, Josephus, or Epictetus. It occurs three times in the AF, twice of sheep gamboling about (Herm. Sim. 6.1.6, 6.2.6) and once of people who, it is said, are like pigs (Barn. 10:3): "When [these people] are well off [*spatalōsin*], they forget the Lord, but when they are in need, they acknowledge the Lord, just as the pig ignores its owner when it is feeding, but when it is hungry it starts to squeal and falls silent only after being fed again." The widow of v. 5 thinks of little but the Lord; the godless widow of v. 6 seeks fulfillment in earthly plenty.

NIV's "lives for pleasure" may give the impression that the godless widow's error is sexual; the semantic range of uses noted above tends more in the direction of denoting material excess: she lives for the "pleasure" of luxurious living (see also Jas 5:5,[659] the only other NT occurrence). Yet, this might not rule out sexual insinuation too (a problem noted with respect to younger widows; v. 11), using charm as a means of attracting funding for expensive tastes. Paul has already touched on the problem of such tastes infecting some women at church gatherings (see 2:9).

656. Both of the words used for prayer in this verse also occur in 1 Tim 2:1, as well as in Phil 4:6 and Eph 6:18. NIV inserts "God" whereas the Greek wording runs "she remains in supplications and prayers." Presumably justification for inserting "ask God for help" is drawn from the connotation of the two words for prayer.

657. The verse contains five words in Greek; the NIV rendering runs to thirteen words.

658. The form actually used is a present participle. With the feminine singular definite article it can be translated "the widow who indulges in luxury," inferring "widow" from the context. NIV's rendering is equally reasonable.

659. "You have lived on earth in luxury and self-indulgence [*espatalēsate*]."

Verse 6 is possibly hyperbolic: Paul may envision a widow who is not truly in need or truly godly or even neither. Yet, she has wormed her way into the church's largesse for the sake of her own benefit (cf. 2 Thess 3:10–11). Her "pleasure" is not as heinous as can be imagined; it fact it might just be enough to get by on the church's nickel. But even this modest stipend is fraudulent, because it is undeserved, and because it soaks up resources that should benefit someone who truly qualifies. Hence the scathing language.

Whatever the exact nature of her transgression, this widow's show of living large is deceiving. "Even while she lives" translates a present participle of *zaō* (to live) as adverbial and concessive. She is not as alive as she looks. In fact, she "is dead."[660] Schlatter discerns here "Paul's well-known principle that a person dies when they give reign to their desire (Rom 7:9–10)."[661] This could continue a hyperbolic line of rhetoric (see previous paragraph). Or it could denote her spiritual condition: lacking real appetite for God like the godly widow (v. 5), she is in a moribund spiritual state. "Though physically living she is spiritually dead."[662] In either case, the result is grievous: "A life of self-indulgent luxury—particularly when others in the community are 'left all alone' without resources—is not mildly reprehensible, but a death to that life by which the community claims to live" in Christ.[663]

Twomey calls Chrysostom's message on this passage "particularly galling invective against women" because it sets before his listeners a binary choice: "obscene luxury or charity for the poor."[664] But perhaps Chrysostom knew some in his congregation needed this prod. Moreover, the entire Bible (which Chrysostom knew and preached well) calls for God's people to live for God, not pleasure, and to care for the poor. Chrysostom probably did a better job of modeling this in his own courageous ministry than most contemporary biblical commentators.[665] It is unwarranted to impugn Chrysostom's pastoral application of this verse by casting it as a misogynistic assault, especially after making no comment on Paul's commendation of the godly widow in v. 5.

660. The underlying verb *thnēskō* (die) is found only here in Paul. It is used eight other times in the Gospels and Acts.

661. Schlatter, *Die Kirche der Griechen*, 140.

662. Witherington, 268.

663. Johnson, *First and Second Letters to Timothy*, 262–3.

664. Twomey, 77.

665. Chrysostom compromised his health, for life, by living in a cave for two years while a young man, monastic style, and memorizing the New Testament. His sermons emphasize "especially almsgiving and great devotion to things spiritual, and away from aspects of their life and urban culture that he considers reprehensible, such as the theater and the racetrack" (M. Mitchell, "John Chrysostom," *Dictionary of Major Bible Interpreters*, ed. D. McKim [Downers Grove, IL: IVP Academic, 2007], 571–72). What Chrysostom said to women in his sermon on this passage was modeled in his life and preached to all alike.

7 As in v. 6, the language is compressed.[666] Regarding "Give the people these instructions" (NIV), see discussion of the verb and noun for "command" or "charge" at 4:11 above. The words *kai tauta parangelle* are better rendered something like "Command these things as well," as per table 19 at 4:11. This is "a strong and sharp apostolic command."[667] "These things" likely refers to the preceding instructions regarding widows.

This is the third of five commands to Timothy that dot and unite the epistle (see also 1:3; 4:11; 6:13, 17). Paul's words serve to underscore the importance of Timothy's management of the widow issue. He is an overseer, not a commandant, but with the expectation that Timothy will spare no effort to make sure that the church operates wisely, ethically, and proactively in this apparently critical area, Paul uses stiff language.

The reason he gives (second half of the verse) is "so that no one may be open to blame" (NIV). Another way of taking the Greek would be: "in order that they might be blameless [*anepilēmptoi*]." The word *anepilēmptos* (irreproachable) appears in the NT only here and at 1 Tim 3:2 (see discussion in commentary above) and 6:14. High ethical standards among Christians were critical to the spread of the gospel.[668] It is hard to rule out oblique reference to God's eschatological assessment as well.

Is Paul's "they" referring to the church (or the families in the church who care for widows)[669] in how they handle matters pertaining to the widows?[670] Or does "they" refer to the widows[671]—expressing Paul's concern for the reproach they may bring on themselves and, by extension, the church if they misuse the church's aid or possibly (as in v. 6) receive aid undeservingly? Either understanding is defensible. It is also possible that Paul intends Timothy to understand that both groups—the congregation caring for the widow and the widows being cared for—are called to maximum circumspectness. God's solicitude for widows (see commentary on v. 3 above) demands no less: in the household of God, God's house rules reign.

8 "Anyone" could be either masculine or feminine; it is impossible to determine whether Paul means "anyone in the congregation,"[672] "anyone in families with widows," or (least likely) "any widow."[673] What he says here may well be directed to all under Timothy's pastoral oversight. It is also a statement

666. This verse contains six words in Greek, fourteen in the NIV.

667. Marshall, with Towner, 589.

668. Keener, *Bible Background Commentary*, 611.

669. Marshall, with Towner, 589.

670. So Johnson, *First and Second Letters to Timothy*, 263.

671. So Collins, 140.

672. Collins, 139.

673. Marshall, with Towner, 589; Marshall thinks there is "an application to widows with families for whom they are responsible."

of general principle whose implications should not be restricted merely to this particular situation, since it draws on a truth (the sanctity of family relations, to the extent that family ties do not jeopardize an even higher call; see Jesus's sayings below) with points of contact throughout Scripture.

It is important that each person who ought to "provide for their relatives" do it. The "anyone" (sing.) conceives of this responsibility in terms of individual conscience. "Relatives" translates a form of *idios*, an adjective meaning "one's own" that here functions as a noun. It could refer to near or more distant relatives. "Their own household" is from a form of the adjective *oikeios* meaning "belonging to a household"; like *idios* it functions here as a noun.[674] It refers to relatives that are not distant but part of one's close family structure—the nuclear or extended family.

It seems that in v. 8 Paul looks back on vv. 3–7 and summarizes. Pinpoint definition of "anyone," "relatives," and "their own household" is difficult but also unnecessary. It's a little like the law-expert's question, "Who is my neighbor?" (Luke 10:29). Jesus's answer was: whoever sees another person in need. By extension, anyone who has relatives who are widows to some extent has responsibility to care for them.[675] This duty is all the more clear for close relatives (of one's "own household"), such as one's mother or mother-in-law or grandmother. Intertwined in the discourse of this verse is the further complication of dual family identity: there are family members by birth and marriage, and there is the (sometimes much closer) tie of family membership through rebirth by faith in Christ. Jesus made this point powerfully: family-of-faith ties are even more binding than sometimes misguided and splintered natural family demands. The recollections of Matthew and Luke are germane:

> While Jesus was still talking to the crowd, his mother and brothers stood outside, wanting to speak to him. Someone told him, "Your mother and brothers are standing outside, wanting to speak to you." He replied to him, "Who is my mother, and who are my brothers?" Pointing to his disciples, he said, "Here are my mother and my brothers. For whoever does the will of my Father in heaven is my brother and sister and mother." (Matt 12:46–50; Mark 3:31–35 is very similar)

674. See Gal 6:10 ("the family [*oikeious*] of believers"); Eph 2:19 ("members of the household [*oikeioi*] of God" ESV).

675. NIV "provide for" translates a form of *pronoeō*. It conveys the sense of giving thought beforehand and then following through with tangible care and provision. Paul uses the same word in Rom 12:17 and 2 Cor 8:21, the only other NT occurrences. For a LXX parallel, see Wis 6:7. Similar uses are frequent in Philo (twenty-four occurrences).

> Now Jesus' mother and brothers came to see him, but they were not able to get near him because of the crowd. Someone told him, "Your mother and brothers are standing outside, wanting to see you." He replied, "My mother and brothers are those who hear God's word and put it into practice." (Luke 8:19–21)

Paul's point in this entire subsection is that followers of Christ in God's household should not do less than conscientious pagans would on behalf of widows, a notoriously overlooked subgroup in whom God takes particular interest. If widows are in one's own family (whether natural or the family of faith Jesus speaks of above), family members should be all the more proactive in caring for them, so as not to burden the church (see also v. 16 below) whose purview must be widows "really in need" (vv. 3, 5).

Paul has harsh words for anyone who overlooks his or her responsibility in this matter: that person "has denied the faith and is worse than an unbeliever." Christian confession (summarized, e.g., in 3:16) that is genuine takes the form of lives that embody the concerns of the God in whom faith is purportedly placed. Widows (and orphans) are emblematic of the covenantal compassion of God (see commentary above on v. 3). To fail to step up to support them when ties of natural or spiritual family demand and when opportunity is present is to be doubly damned. For then one is proven to be a denier of the faith (by failing to validate faith in practice) and a hypocrite lacking the compulsion to care that even pagans often demonstrate. "Even unbelievers exercise filial piety. Christians should excel in the display of this civil virtue,"[676] which it could be argued Paul understands more as a spiritual grace.

3. *Widows: Enlistment Rules (5:9–10)*

> [9] *No widow may be put on the list of widows unless she is over sixty, has been faithful to her husband,* [10] *and is well known for her good deeds, such as bringing up children, showing hospitality, washing the feet of the Lord's people, helping those in trouble and devoting herself to all kinds of good deeds.*

Paul's articulation of personalized pastoral care continues. But just as family members (along with the larger family of family) are required to be conscientious in not neglecting widowed kin (vv. 3–8), Timothy needs to establish and administer a structure in which there is quality control, so to speak, over

676. Saarinen, 88.

which widows receive the church's no doubt limited aid. The next two verses give guidelines for that structure.

9 "No widow" sounds exclusionary and grudging. The Greek wording, however, is businesslike rather than grouchy: "Let a widow be enrolled [on the widows' aid list]. . . ." The command is to Timothy (or those to whom he delegates) for direction in policy-making and no doubt individual judgment calls. The third person singular (not pl.) command confirms that Paul envisions one-by-one assessments of individuals, reinforcing the motif of personal care that runs through this chapter. He is not talking about, because he does not conceive of, widows as a corporate abstraction when it comes to their presence in a local church.

The verb translated "put on the list" is a NT hapax but occurs frequently in other writings of the NT era. Here it means to be selected "for membership in a group" (BDAG 520). From the context we infer that the group consists of widows receiving church assistance.[677] Paul is not trying to keep widows off the list but to make sure that those who benefit from the gesture of God's care have some claim to care about God.

There is, first, an age restriction: sixty is the minimum. If they are younger than that, they likely have the vitality to fend for themselves. Or they can find a spouse and avoid becoming a ward of the church by that means (see v. 14). Second, there is a moral consideration. Just as a qualification for overseer (see 3:2; also 3:12 [deacons]; Titus 1:6) was to be "faithful to his wife" (or "a one-woman man" as an overliteral rendering might have it), a listed widow will have been "faithful to her husband" (or "a one-man woman"). She established a track record for love and faithfulness toward God by her life of love and faithfulness to her husband in the years they enjoyed together.[678] This covenantal stipulation will help church assistance be seen for what it is: not sterile humanitarian aid or the expression of some universal human right (as institutional care for the aged might be construed today), but the confirmation that the same God who gave the wife her husband and possibly children, and walked with her in the greener pastures of youth, is now there for her in the leaner years of old age. (It should be recalled that life expectancy in that setting was far below sixty.)

10 Verse 9 highlights external criteria. They are more or less matters of public record. Verse 10 shifts to the more subtle criteria of character and its outworking in demonstrations of love for others.

"Well known" translates a usage that occurs some dozen other times in the NT in which a form of *martyreō* (to testify, witness) denotes a strong

677. It is anachronistic to read into this some formal "order of widows" along lines visible in sources generations after Paul's death.

678. For Roman and Greek views of widows and remarriage, see Collins, 140.

endorsement of someone either by God or by God's people (note the preponderance of passive forms). Table 20 illustrates.

Table 20. Commendation (using a form of *martyreō*) of NT figures

Passage	Person(s) commended and commendation	Person(s) commending
Acts 6:3	. . . seven men from among you who *are known to be* [*martyroumenous*] full of the Spirit and wisdom.	the Jerusalem church
Acts 10:22	[Cornelius] is a righteous and God-fearing man, who *is respected* [*martyroumenos*] by all the Jewish people.	Jewish beneficiaries of Cornelius's support for their synagogue
Acts 16:2	The believers at Lystra and Iconium *spoke well* [*emartyreito*] of [Timothy].	believers who knew Timothy
Acts 22:12	[Ananias] was a devout observer of the law and *highly respected* [*martyroumenos*] by all the Jews living there.	Jews at Damascus who knew Ananias
Rom 3:21	But now apart from the law the righteousness of God has been made known, to which the Law and the Prophets *testify* [*martyroumenē*].	God via Scripture
1 Tim 5:10	. . . and *is well known* [*martyroumenē*] for her good deeds	acquaintances of the godly widow
Heb 7:8	The tenth is collected . . . by [Melchizedek] who *is declared to be* [*martyroumenos*] living.	God via Scripture
Heb 7:17	For it *is declared* [*martyreitai*]: "You [Melchizedek] are a priest forever. . . ."	God via Scripture
Heb 11:2	This [i.e., faith] is what the ancients *were commended* [*emartyrēthēsan*] for.	the people of God; God via Scripture

Passage	Person(s) commended and commendation	Person(s) commending
Heb 11:4	By faith [Abel] *was commended* [*emartyrēthē*] as righteous, when God *spoke well of* [*martyrountos*] his offerings.	God via Scripture
Heb 11:39	These [the OT saints in Heb 11] *were* all *commended* [*martyrēthentes*] for their faith.	God via Scripture
3 John 12	Demetrius *is well spoken of* [*memartyrētai*] by everyone—and even by the truth itself. We also *speak well of* [*martyroumen*] him, and you know that our *testimony* [*martyria*] is true.	believers who know Demetrius; God; the apostle John (and his circle?: "we")

Most of the examples in table 20 are not from Paul. But the table shows all of the examples from the NT that use a form of the verb *martyreō* (and in one case the noun: see 3 John 12 above) to point to someone "well known." More than mere public perception or word on the street is involved, unless 1 Tim 5:10 is an anomaly amid all other NT uses. The woman of v. 10 is among elite company indeed, as verified by her "good [from *kalos*] deeds" (see table 12 on *kalos* and *agathos*, both meaning "good," at 2:3 above).

"Deeds" at the beginning and end of v. 10 sounds staid and pedestrian; see discussion at 2:10 above on good works, as well as table 26 and discussion at Titus 1:16. The "deeds" by which a widow is assessed for possible inclusion on the list are, taken together, impressive and indicative of deep commitment to Christ and the body of Christ.

The sentence construction (on which more below) suggests that "is well known for her good deeds" is a general description, while the five clauses following the words "such as" mark specific examples. Each clause begins with the hypothetical marker *ei* ("if"; "such as" in NIV).

First, "bringing up children." This assumes she had children, just as ch. 3 assumes that prospective overseers and deacons will be adults with children, the dominant scenario for individuals past puberty in most cultures throughout history. In a setting where marriage itself is in dispute (4:3), this widow has shown a mother's selflessness over the long haul. According to Epictetus, the Greek philosopher Epicurus (died 270 BC) "ventures to say that we should not bring up children."[679] Doubtless in all places and times adults must wrestle

679. Epictetus, *Discourses* 1.23.7. In the same context (*Discourses* 1.23.3), Epicurus uses the word for "bring up children" (*teknotropheō*) that Paul uses in v. 10.

with whether to accord their children the attention they deserve and require, particularly if the goal (as it is in the church) is to "bring them up in the training and instruction of the Lord" (Eph 6:4). This widow has found grace in the gospel to honor God and her husband in her approach to her children.

Second, "showing hospitality." Openness to outsiders is a much-discussed issue in ancient cultures. See *NIDNTTE* 3:442–46 for discussion of "hospitality" among Greeks and Jews alike, as well as the many angles on it presented in the NT.[680] Paul commends the practice of hospitality to the church (Rom 12:13) and praises Gaius for demonstrating this grace (Rom 16:23). "Hospitable" should characterize the church's overseers (1 Tim 3:2; Titus 1:8). Over the years this widow has shown God's own care for the stranger.[681] Since Paul commended doing "good to everyone, and especially to those who are of the household of faith" (Gal 6:10 ESV), the widow's commendation may rest substantially on care for fellow believers as well, as the next clauses show.

Third, "washing the feet of the Lord's people." Washing feet was an ancient custom.[682] It was practiced in Jesus's time (Luke 7:44) and immortalized for Jesus's followers in the incident recorded in John 13, where Jesus washed his disciples' feet. Johnson suggests that Paul uses footwashing here to denote "the entire posture of service shown" to the church by the now-widowed woman.[683] "Lord's people" is *hagioi* (holy ones), a term used for believers as persons belonging and devoted to God. It appears in Paul's writings over a dozen times but only here in the PE.

Fourth, "helping those in trouble." "Those in trouble" may imply believers in dire straits because of their faith in Christ or service to Christ, since Paul often uses forms of this verb (*thlibō*) in this way.[684] "Helping" (from *eparkeō*) is a word used twice in v. 16 but nowhere else in the NT. But the wider word group with which it is associated found wide usage in OT and NT times.[685] The widow helped the destitute, of which there were many in a major Roman city like Ephesus, particularly among a marginalized group like the Christians, for whom Paul expected steady exposure to persecution (see 2 Tim 3:12).

680. See also and more strongly Joshua Jipp, *Saved by Faith and Hospitality* (Grand Rapids: Eerdmans, 2017).

681. Commended by Jesus, for example, in the account of the sheep and the goats (Matt 25:34–40). Care of strangers (a connotation of words in the "hospitality" group) was also an ancient Near East virtue (e.g., Lev 25:35; Job 29:16; 31:32).

682. See, for example, Gen 18:14; 19:2; 24:32; 43:24; Judg 19:21; 1 Sam 25:41; 2 Sam 11:8. For footwashing from antiquity through the Bible and into Christian history right up to today, see the contributions of various writers in "Footwashing," *EBR* 9:390–403.

683. Johnson, *First and Second Letters to Timothy*, 265.

684. See 2 Cor 1:6; 4:8; 7:5; 1 Thess 3:4; 2 Thess 1:6, 7. See also Heb 11:37 ("persecuted").

685. *NIDNTTE* 1:395–97.

Fifth, "devoting herself to all kinds of good deeds."[686] Whereas "good [*kalos*] deeds" at the beginning of v. 10 was plural, "all kinds of good [*agathos*] deeds" at the end of v. 10 is singular in Greek ("to every good deed/work").[687] Both in general and in specific cases and situations, this woman was proactive and took initiative in acts expressing faith in Christ and love for God as demonstrated in regard for other people. Literarily, this fifth clause in the series is parallel with the earlier four. But conceptually, it serves to summarize the first four and to place a bookend that corresponds to "good deeds" at the beginning of the verse. This is not a widow whose spirituality is merely contemplative or speculative; her life has been one of "devoting[688] herself" in concrete ways requiring arduous and selfless action.

Repetition of "good deeds" in v. 10 invites notice of the sentence construction. NIV's five gerunds (bringing up, showing, washing, helping, devoting) after "such as" might give a random feel—these are the kinds of things expected of the widow placed on the list. The gain here is real: it rightly implies that Paul is providing a representative composite sketch rather than a comprehensive list of particular actions. Yet, in Greek, the gerunds are indicative verbs following *ei* (if), which gives a feel of specificity, underscored by the fivefold repetition of *ei*, which expresses intensity and attention to detail on Paul's part. On the condition, not that she may have done things "such as" these, but that she definitely did perform them (and myriad others that Paul did not need to enumerate), a widow of this description is eminently deserving of the grace the church should extend to such individuals in the widow subgroup.

Paul's concise thoroughness would have placed Timothy on notice that this important largesse should not be squandered by falling prey to the squeaky-wheel syndrome (the persons who complain the loudest get attention), to the nepotism (regard for natural-family members when spiritual-family members may take precedence) that sometimes infects church practice, or to other malpractice rooted in a casual approach to a high and holy priority of a local congregation: doing what God enables to help those truly in need, in this case among the widowed.

686. On NIV's addition of "and" (not in Gk.) before "devoting," see discussion of v. 14 below.

687. See table 12 on *kalos* and *agathos*, words translated "good" in v. 10, at 2:3 above. On "deeds," see discussion at 2:10 above on good works; see also table 26 and discussion at Titus 1:16.

688. The verb *epakoloutheō* (follow, devote oneself to) occurs elsewhere only at 5:24 (with the meaning of "follow," NIV "trail behind") and 1 Pet 2:21 ("follow in his steps").

4. Younger Widows (5:11–15)

> [11]*As for younger widows, do not put them on such a list. For when their sensual desires overcome their dedication to Christ, they want to marry.* [12]*Thus they bring judgment on themselves, because they have broken their first pledge.* [13]*Besides, they get into the habit of being idle and going about from house to house. And not only do they become idlers, but also busybodies who talk nonsense, saying things they ought not to.* [14]*So I counsel younger widows to marry, to have children, to manage their homes and to give the enemy no opportunity for slander.* [15]*Some have in fact already turned away to follow Satan.*

11 Paul's concern for individuals continues, still on the topic of widows. "Some have in fact already turned away to follow Satan" (v. 15). This development gives urgency to the issue. In the previous subsection (v. 9) Paul gave a minimum age of sixty for enrollment on a list for receiving church relief where family means were inadequate or not forthcoming (see vv. 3–8). Now he sheds light on why that age consideration is necessary.

The first twelve words of v. 11 ("As for younger widows, do not put them on such a list") translate just four in Greek, which could be rendered, "Younger widows? Forget it!"[689] The subject on the table is which widows deserve church aid (v. 9). But Paul has evidently learned that this list and widows who are still of childbearing age (see v. 14) are incompatible. So he counsels Timothy to reserve the benefit afforded by being listed for older widows only.

The first reason for this policy involves younger widows' desire to marry. In itself this seems unobjectionable. But v. 12 will reveal that such a desire violates a pledge they have made, perhaps the pledge to remain wholly and solely dedicated to God as a condition of receiving church aid (v. 5). Paul has apparently observed a concession to wantonness in this. The verb *katastrēniaō* (give in to sensuous impulses) seems to be a word Paul coins by adding *kata-* (here likely an intensifying prefix)[690] to the less uncommon word *strēniaō* found in classical Greek sources, as well as in Rev 18:7, 9 (referring to Babylon's decadent sensuality).[691] "Their sensual desires overcome their dedication to Christ" is a fit description of the result. Marshall comments that the present tense "suggests that cases are already happening, as v. 15 confirms."[692]

689. The verb in v. 11a is *paraiteomai*, used only three other times in Paul (1 Tim 4:7; 2 Tim 2:23; Titus 3:10). In these three passages, NIV translates "having nothing to do with" or words very similar.

690. BDF §181 glosses "become wanton against."

691. Note also the cognate noun *strēnos* (sensuality, luxury) found in Rev 18:3: "the merchants of the earth grew rich from [Babylon's] excessive luxuries."

692. Marshall, with Towner, 599.

The young widows' desires are expressed in the wish to marry. Marriage would be honorable (v. 14), were it not for the pledge (v. 12). They should never have been pressured by constraints they could not bear by being placed on the list to begin with. Paul's counsel in v. 11 not to list them is, then, not some punitive move but a pastoral measure to support younger widows in a course of action best suited to their situation and human flourishing.

12 This verse confirms the trap into which some have apparently fallen. "They bring judgment on themselves"[693] is probably not eschatological rejection by God[694] but culpability because of sin. Their sin: "they have broken their first pledge." Paul uses the word translated "have broken" in similar ways elsewhere.[695] "Pledge" translates a form of *pistis*, which most often means "faith"[696] but can (as here) mean an oath or promise (see BDAG 818 [1b]). "First pledge" recalls the Ephesians' abandoned "first love" mentioned by John (Rev 2:4).[697] Jesus had warned, hyperbolically but still seriously, against ill-thought vows (Matt 5:34–36). Paul viewed vows as permissible, but they needed to be honored (Acts 18:18). God hears pledges and deals with people on the basis of what they promise him (Gen 31:13; Num 6:21; for exceptions see Num 30:5, 8). The principle is: "When a man makes a vow to the LORD or takes an oath to obligate himself by a pledge, he must not break his word but must do everything he said" (Num 30:2; see also Deut 23:21–23). It will be recalled that God honored Hannah's vow (1 Sam 1:11); it came at the high cost of dedicating her son to God's service. From OT wisdom comes the counsel: "It is a trap to dedicate something rashly and only later to consider one's vows" (Prov 20:25).

The exact nature of the younger widows' broken vows in v. 12 has not been preserved. But sensual desire (v. 11) has caused them to jettison a promise to which God is witness. This choice is not healthy for them or for the church. In itself this violation would be serious. But the next verse shows that the vow-

693. For parallel Pauline expressions, see, for example, Rom 13:2; 1 Cor 11:29, 34; Gal 5:10.

694. Interpreters who think "first pledge" refers to their faith in Christ will be more inclined to view Paul's reference as eschatological judgment. See, for example, Calvin, 258; Schlatter, *Die Kirche der Griechen*, 142–43.

695. See occurrences of *atheteō* (invalidate, reject) at Gal 2:21; 3:15; 1 Thess 4:8.

696. Towner favors taking it as "faith" here (*Letters*, 352). He thinks that Paul assumes marriage to unbelievers (disallowed by 1 Cor 7:39). When widows do this, their religion becomes that of their new (pagan or Jewish) husband. Then in v. 14 Paul assumes marriage to believers. This interpretation is all plausible. Yet, I find the "pledge" view of *pistis* slightly more preferable, in part because of the qualifier "first." If widows were simply leaving the faith, would "first" be necessary or likely? Would Paul imply their subsequent status is a second faith? But if they remarry, which involves a vow, that makes their earlier vow (to live as widows, and perhaps on the list) their "first." Also, if v. 12 refers to apostasy via remarriage, v. 13 seems too trivial by comparison to be relevant.

697. The reference is erroneously given as 2:3 in BDAG 818 (1.b).

breaking was part of a larger pattern of unfruitful and unbecoming behavior. None of this fits what belongs in "in God's household, which is the church of the living God, the pillar and foundation of the truth" (3:15).

13 Along with[698] vow-breaking, the younger widows also[699] *argai manthanousin* (learn to be idle/lazy/unproductive). NIV renders this clause as "they get into the habit of being idle." There is certainly grounding for that in the Greek. Yet, it obscures an association that is fruitful to observe: Paul's use of *manthanō* (learn) in the PE, bearing in mind the possible connection with the cognate noun translated "disciple," which means "learner." In 1 Tim 2:11 Paul wants women to *learn*; 1Tim 5:4 speaks of the priority of widows *learning*; 2 Tim 3:7 decries *learning* gone awry; 2 Tim 3:14 exhorts Timothy, "Continue in what you have *learned* and have become convinced of, because you know those from whom you *learned* it"; Titus 3:14 states programmatically, "Our people must *learn* to devote themselves to doing what is good." All this is quite apart from the even more pronounced stress in the PE on teaching, which only confirms the centrality of the discipleship motif.

This consistent underlying concern with learning justifies the conclusion that Paul is particularly unhappy (if not alarmed: see v. 15) because the discipleship/learning mandate incumbent on Jesus's followers including women (2:11) is being squandered. In fact, it is being subverted, for the problem is not that these widows are not learning; it is that their learning faculty is being deployed in vacuous directions. They are becoming students of indolence, not the good works that marks the godly widow (v. 10) and God's people in general. And whereas they ought to be going forth with the gospel, they are "going about from house to house" as purveyors of vapidity.[700] It is not clear whether these houses (or households) refer to the residences of their circle of friends and acquaintances or to various congregations meeting in homes. Either would be a loss for healthy Christian witness, to say nothing of being detrimental to these women and those pulled down by their garrulous traipsing about.

Paul's description moves from bad to worse. "And not only" translates *ou monon de*, a signature Pauline expression.[701] These peripatetic idlers become babblers (*phlyaroi*, perhaps implying "gossipy"; BDAG 1060) and snoopy

698. NIV "besides"; Greek *hama*. For other Pauline uses, see Col 4:3; 1 Thess 4:17; 5:10; Phlm 22.

699. Denoted by *kai*. There is also a *de* present; the rhetorical effect of *hama de kai* is something like "Moreover, at the same time they also. . . ." The wording implies careful engagement rather than casual or distant description.

700. Cf. 2 Thess 3:11.

701. Outside of Paul it occurs only once in the NT (Acts 19:27). In Paul, see Rom 5:3, 11; 8:23; 9:10; 2 Cor 7:7; 8:19; 2 Tim 4:8. It is found twice in the LXX (2 Macc 2:4; Sir 1:23), five times in Josephus, not at all in Philo or Epictetus, and once in the AF (1 Clem. 35:6, which adds *de* to a quotation of the *ou monon* of Rom 1:32).

(*periergoi*, meddlers in others' affairs). "Busybodies who talk nonsense" (NIV) reverses Paul's order but gives the cumulative sense.

Paul adds "saying things they ought not to,"[702] which can seem like unnecessary filler or piling on. In the background, though, is Jesus, who taught the gravity of people's words,[703] and Paul, whose speech-ethics credo called for saying "only what is helpful for building others up according to their needs, that it may benefit those who listen" (Eph 4:29).[704] Both Timothy (see 4:12) and Titus (Titus 2:8)[705] are admonished regarding their speech.

These younger widows were on a risky descent, dramatizing what can happen when resolve to follow Christ is replaced (recall v. 11) by willingness to pursue the more immediate and tangible personal gratification afforded by fellowship centered on less sublime matters.[706] Towner (following Marshall) thinks Paul's disapproval may relate to false teaching they were instrumental in spreading.[707] This charge cannot be verified, and nothing in the immediate context suggests that Paul viewed them as a formal doctrinal threat. They had simply reverted to lives emptied of the serious pursuit of Christ and were dragging others into their distractions. For pastoral leaders like Paul and Timothy who took note of individual lives, this is ample cause for dire concern.

14 Paul wants Timothy to steer younger widows away from the superficiality, if not decadence, into which too many have fallen. With the same creation mandate in the background as encountered earlier (see 4:4–5 and discussion above), Paul commends the holy pursuit of godliness in everyday living.

NIV's "So" translates *oun*. In the earlier three occurrences in 1 Timothy (2:1, 8; 3:2), *oun* serves to introduce a solemn inference from what precedes in order to lay out a vital course of action. The sense is "therefore on the basis of what I just said." Solemnity is confirmed by "I counsel" (*boulomai*), an expression that conveys strong resolve (in the PE see also 1 Tim 2:8; 6:9; Titus

702. Cf. Titus 1:11: "They are disrupting whole households by teaching things they ought not to teach." The word behind "ought" is *dei*; see table 15 and discussion at 3:2 above.

703. "For by your words you will be acquitted, and by your words you will be condemned" (Matt 12:37).

704. Cf. Col 4:6: "Let your conversation be always full of grace, seasoned with salt, so that you may know how to answer everyone."

705. Cf. Titus 2:1, 15 and the command to "speak" (*lalei*; NIV "teach") aright.

706. Schlatter, who thinks the widows have turned away from the faith (v. 12), not just broken a vow, comments aptly: "Paul viewed it as dangerous to go back on a course of action begun in the faith. It is not in a person's own power to determine whether they will truly believe or not; if they enter into faith, they must be diligent to preserve it" (*Die Kirche der Griechen*, 143). In other words, they were dependent on grace to embrace faith, and it is only by grace they will endure. To presume on grace by abandoning faith is to flirt with disaster.

707. Towner, *Letters*, 355.

3:8).[708] Too much is at stake here for Paul to be understood as offering just a neat four-point package of casual advice.[709] Younger widows wavering in their devotion to Christ should do the following.

First, be open to marriage. For Paul, marriage needs to be to another believer (1 Cor 7:39). Of course, he is not urging some immediate move to the first candidate encountered. He is speaking of the course of her life ahead. Rather than persist in frustrated desire, broken pledges, and undisciplined living (vv. 12–13), she should seek the solace and constructive possibilities offered by marriage in the Lord. This path will also confirm her in defiance of the antimarriage philosophy in the air at Ephesus (4:3).

Second, have children, if God grants, since they are God's gift (see Ps 113:9; 115:15; 127:3; 128:3). They are also a great responsibility and decades-long burden; Calvin comments, "When he speaks of bearing children, he sums up in one phrase all the annoyances comprised in rearing offspring."[710] This is an honest assessment of an important dimension of married life even (and especially?) in Christ, where there is daily opportunity and indeed necessity to learn the hard lessons of serving others rather than indulging oneself. See 2:15 on the noun form (*teknogonia*, child-bearing) of the verb used here ("have children"); there is soteriological benefit to the pursuit of everyday activities (like rearing children, if we are parents) rendered unto God.

Third, "to manage their homes." Verse 13 describes neglect if not abandonment of attention to domestic responsibilities. See discussion at Titus 1:5 on the household management implied there. The verb *oikodespoteō* used here refers to oversight of the household, not menial maintenance. This is the word's only occurrence in the NT. The noun form *oikodespotēs* (master or manager of a household) is much more common.[711] The classic biblical portrait is found in Prov 31. A woman was "in charge of what went on in the home."[712]

Fourth, "to give the enemy no opportunity [*aphormē*] for slander." In Gal 5:13 Paul writes of giving "opportunity [*aphormē*] for the flesh" (ESV).[713] There

708. Dibelius and Conzelmann (75, with n. 21) point out that the expression "is used in legislative regulations." The sense could be understood more in the direction of "mandate" or "command" than the therapeutic-sounding "counsel."

709. NIV adds "and" before "to give the enemy" near the end of v. 14, creating the appearance of a tidy series. But there is no "and" in Greek; Paul uses asyndeton (ungainly absence of conjunctions) for a more open-ended, wide-ranging effect. See also v. 10 above, where NIV adds "and" before "devoting herself," transforming conjunctionless -ing parallels into a more symmetrical series. In both cases, the change makes for smoother English. But it obscures Paul's (here) more brusque and staccato style.

710. Calvin, 260.

711. Twelve times in the NT.

712. Marshall, with Towner, 604.

713. Among NT writers, only Paul uses *aphormē*. See also Rom 7:8, 11; 2 Cor 5:12; 11:12.

his prescription is, "Walk by the Spirit, and you will not gratify the desires of the flesh" (5:16). In v. 14 his directive is for younger widows to live diligently as the (eventually) married women God calls them to be postwidowhood. Their preoccupation with the redemptive demands of living daily household life in a way pleasing to God will ensure a higher road than v. 13 (dissolute younger widows) depicted. It will also make them a creative partner in the creation mandate (Gen 1:28).

Otherwise "the enemy" will have an opening "for slander [*loidoria*]."[714] Who is this enemy? Does it represent the person or party behind the opposition to marriage (4:3)? If so, they might spread word that younger widows in the church who are not marrying represent a victory for their party. Some see other human opponents here;[715] still others see the devil.[716] Evidence does not permit a decisive choice. Paul does not want to bring ill repute on the household of faith from any quarter. The strategy he outlines will prevent that.

15 Logically this verse begins with *gar* (for). It signals that v. 15 is an explanation for why Paul has just spoken so bluntly and in considerable detail (relative to the length of 1 Timothy) about the younger widows. The reason is that "some have . . . already turned away to follow Satan." On Satan, see references and discussion at 1:20. On "turn away" (*ektrepō*), see discussion at 1:6.

"Some" (*tines*, pl. form of *tis*) "reflects a practice of not referring to opponents in the church by name but by using *tis* [meaning "someone, a certain person"]."[717] Paul uses *tines* (a pl. form of *tis*) seventeen times, always with a pejorative connotation, as table 21 indicates.

Table 21. Pejorative uses of *tines* (some)[718] in Paul

Passage	Occurrence of *tines* (some)
Rom 3:3	What if *some* were unfaithful?
Rom 3:8	Why not say—as *some* slanderously claim that we say . . . ?
Rom 11:17	If *some* of the branches have been broken off. . . .
1 Cor 4:18	*Some* of you have become arrogant.
1 Cor 6:11	And that is what *some* of you were.

714. See 1 Pet 3:9 for the only two other occurrences of *loidoria* (NIV "insult").

715. The word is so used in Luke 13:17; 21:15; 1 Cor 16:9; Phil 1:28; for human opponents by the same word in the LXX, see 2 Sam 8:10; Esth 8:11; 9:2; 1 Macc 14:7.

716. The devil is in view in 2 Thess 2:4; 1 Clem. 51:1; Mart. Pol. 17:1.

717. Marshall, with Towner, 365.

718. If "people" is present in the translation (2 Cor 3:1; 1 Tim 6:10), it is apparently only for stylistic reasons or clarity; a separate Greek word for "people" is absent.

Passage	Occurrence of *tines* (some)
1 Cor 10:7	Do not be idolaters, as *some* of them were.
1 Cor 10:8	We should not commit sexual immorality, as *some* of them did.
1 Cor 10:9	We should not test Christ, as *some* of them did.
1 Cor 15:12	How can *some* of you say that there is no resurrection of the dead?
1 Cor 15:34	There are *some* who are ignorant of God—I say this to your shame.
2 Cor 3:1	Or do we need, like *some* people, letters of recommendation to you or from you?
1 Tim 1:6	*Some* have departed from these and have turned to meaningless talk.
1 Tim 1:19	. . . holding on to faith and a good conscience, which *some* have rejected.
1 Tim 4:1	The Spirit clearly says that in later times *some* will abandon the faith.
1 Tim 5:15	*Some* have in fact already turned away to follow Satan.
1 Tim 6:10	*Some* people, eager for money, have wandered from the faith.
1 Tim 6:21	. . . which *some* have professed and in so doing have departed from the faith.

Seen in light of table 21, v. 15 contains a Pauline idiom not limited to addressing widows at Ephesus. Across a span of his epistolary discourse, rather than name names Paul summarizes the involvement of individuals in unfortunate activities with an indefinite plural pronoun. In some cases it may be convenient generalization. In others it may involve a situation where names are not known. In others, it may be gracious restraint to spare individuals the embarrassment of being called out personally. Or it may be reluctance to dignify individuals by the mention of their names.

Verse 15 sheds grim light on the discourse going back to v. 11. The problem addressed in this subsection is not trivial. "To follow Satan" can mean only apostasy. For men like Paul and Timothy who have devoted their lives to taking the gospel to the lost, the loss of any persons, and especially those thought to be members of Christ's body, to perdition would be agony (see, e.g., Rom 9:2–3; 2 Cor 11:29; Gal 4:11, 19–20). Paul wants Timothy to take the full measure of the danger facing the younger widows under his oversight lest the number giving up their fidelity to Christ grow as a result of his pastoral neglect. Paul also wants to highlight the importance of measures prescribed in the previous verse that can be means of grace to prevent the slide.

5. *Personal Caregivers of Widows (5:16)*

> 16 *If any woman who is a believer has widows in her care, she should continue to help them and not let the church be burdened with them, so that the church can help those widows who are really in need.*

16 Almost as an afterthought, Paul issues two final commands, each pertaining to a situation that must be inferred from the context. At issue: a "woman who is a believer [*pistē*]"[719] who "has widows in her care." This is a new scenario; earlier Paul spoke of widows cared for by either their family or the church. In the case of such a woman who cares for widows, Paul's command to Timothy is, first: "She should continue to help [*eparkeitō*][720] them." "Continue to" is inferred from the present tense of the imperative. "Should" is not Paul's observation of what ought to occur; he is issuing a third person command to Timothy that pertains to the believing supporter of widows. Nothing Paul has said in previous verses requires alteration of the effective care presently underway. In its way, then, this is a commendation of women who have already stepped up to take responsibility for a less fortunate group in the church. Not everything at Ephesus is imperiled or broken.

Paul's second command is for the church not to "be burdened with them," that is, with the widows and their care. "Burdened" (from *bareō*) is used six times in the NT; two of the other occurrences are in Paul (2 Cor 1:8; 5:4). Here it simply refers to whatever the charitable caregiver is expending (time? finances? room and board?) for the widows' upkeep. As vv. 4 and 8 indicate, the ideal is for families or people in the church with means to care for the church's needy, not to make the needy wards of the church when other means of relief are feasible. Paul knows the church will always have more people to care for than it has resources. Church relief (as opposed to church members taking the initiative to identify and respond to situations of real need) should be the last and not the first resort.

The last clause of the verse confirms that Paul is not simply trying to palm off care for widows onto individuals. He wants the church to be able to

719. For the adjective *pistos* used as a substantive for a believing individual, see Acts 16:1; 2 Cor 6:15; 1 Tim 4:10; Titus 1:6.

720. The verb is used twice in v. 10 (see discussion there). Apart from v. 10 and here, the verb does not appear in the NT.

reserve its resources to "help[721] those widows who are really in need." As in vv. 3 and 5, "really in need" translates *ontōs* (really, certainly). The church is not primarily a social relief agency, though Paul clearly conceives such ministry as a significant component of its mission. When widows (for example) would otherwise be destitute, it is entirely within the purview of congregational care for their need to be alleviated. Of 1 Timothy's 113 verses, 14 (12.38%) are devoted explicitly to Paul's concern for widows' welfare (i.e., 5:3–16). As indicated earlier, this emphasis speaks to Paul's understanding of pastoral ministry as response to real-life needs, both personal and congregational. It is also a counter against the idea that Paul was a misogynist. It is also sensitive to the view of God present in the OT and in Jesus's teaching prioritizing the care of those often overlooked and victimized (i.e., widows and orphans). Finally, it confirms the view of ministry hinted at in Eph 4:12, namely, that the ministry of the church is not primarily what the paid staff perform; rather, it is the outreach of God's "people for works of service." Families and women of means, not the church as a whole, should care for the church's widows wherever possible. "By requiring well-endowed Christians to fulfill their responsibilities . . . , Paul hopes to stretch the church budget to help those who really had no other means of support."[722]

When it comes to widows, Paul has given Timothy much to chew on to steer congregations in constructive directions regarding this perennially relevant social and individual opportunity to show the love the gospel proclaims, calls for, and enables. His commands and counsel are also suggestive for church outreach to analogous subgroups that may be more prominent in a given setting than widows (e.g., orphans, single parents with children as the result of divorce, refugees, the unemployed, victims of other local calamity or malady).

6. Elders (5:17–20)

> [17] *The elders who direct the affairs of the church well are worthy of double honor, especially those whose work is preaching and teaching.* [18] *For Scripture says, "Do not muzzle an ox while it is treading out the grain," and "The worker deserves his wages."* [19] *Do not entertain an accusation against an elder unless it is brought by two or three witnesses.* [20] *But those elders who are sinning you are to reprove before everyone, so that the others may take warning.*

721. The verb translated "help" is the same as the one translated "help" earlier in the verse.

722. Keener, *Bible Background Commentary*, 612.

Is the sudden shift from widows (vv. 3–16) to elders random? Perhaps, but there is more likely an earlier clue that hints at what vv. 17–20 contain. In v. 1 Paul spoke of "elder" in the singular using the same word (*presbyteros*) found in v. 17 in the plural. We suggested above that "elder" in v. 1 refers to the mature (in contrast to the youthful) grown men of the congregation. Verse 1 was a more general admonition regarding Timothy's treatment of men roughly his father's age or older. In vv. 17–20, using the same word, he probably does not posit a wholly different group of men. But he does single out those in church leadership. So while a part of this subsection (vv. 19–20) may have application to the mature men in general, its major focus is the men Timothy depends on for congregational oversight.

Such an analysis yields a chiasm that may reflect the sequence and structure of much of ch. 5.

A Elders, a significant subset of which is . . .
    B Older and younger women, a significant subset of which is . . .
    B′ Widows
A′ Elders in leadership

There may also be a conceptual explanation that helps explain Paul's focus and shifts. Mention of older and younger women in v. 2 gave occasion to single out a group within those women requiring special attention. Verses 3–16 provide direction. But the care and rationale outlined for widows will not happen by itself, and Timothy cannot oversee it all personally. Therefore, for the benevolences projected in vv. 3–16 to take place, subsidiary pastoral leadership will be key. That leadership is encompassed in the subgroup "elders," to which Paul now turns.

17 Verse 1 already spoke of "an older man" (*presbyteros*) in juxtaposition with younger men, then older and younger women. Now Paul speaks of "elders" (*presbyteroi*) in the plural. Hard evidence for the details of early church structure is notoriously scant, but what there is suggests that mature men (not flighty youths) had teaching and pastoral (not dictatorial) oversight duties in local house churches as the gospel went forth into the Roman world. Already in the early AD 40s, the church at Antioch sent aid for suffering Judean believers "to the *elders*" in the Judean churches "by Barnabas and Saul" (Acts 11:30). The elders evidently administered the aid. Later in the 40s, "Paul and Barnabas appointed *elders* . . . in each church" (Acts 14:23) they planted on Paul's so-called first missionary journey (Acts 13–14). These are surely the pastoral overseers. *Elders* along with apostles presided at the Jerusalem Council (Acts 15:2, 4, 6, 22, 23; 16:4). From Miletus near Ephesus on Paul's last known trip to Jerusalem, "Paul sent to Ephesus for the *elders* of the church" (20:17), who convened the next day (20:18). Throughout Acts, there are likewise leaders among the Jews called by the same term "elders" (4:5, 8, 23; 6:12; 23:14; 24:1; 25:15). The early church was, at it remains today in many respects, heavily (and generally positively) conditioned by its synagogue roots and its domestic location.[723]

The very reason Paul left Titus in Crete was so that he "might put in order what was left unfinished and appoint *elders* in every town" in accordance with Paul's directions (Titus 1:5).[724] Many would see "elders" implicit in the "the overseers and deacons" Paul mentions at Philippi (Phil 1:1).

At Ephesus, where in vv. 3–16 Paul has just outlined in considerable detail the ministry priority posed by widows, he now advises Timothy regarding those who will actually administer that (and other) pastoral care: key "elders." Some of them "direct the affairs of the church." "The affairs of the church" does not appear in Greek and is evidently inferred from the word translated "direct." That word, a perfect participle of *proistēmi* (manage, lead)[725] may suggest a settled and stable status quo, not a current and temporary ad hoc arrangement. These men are directing "well" (*kalōs proestōtes*), language almost identical to the household management exercised by overseers in 3:4 (*kalōs proistamenon*). Paul is not commending men merely by virtue of their gender and age.[726] The decisive factor, along with Paul's standing formal qualifcations, is the quality of their service.

Quality leaders are required for church ministry to flourish. Paul has just outlined a touchy issue: the care of widows. In the same way that in modern times building programs can create pressure and hard feelings between a pastor and a congregation, so it is easily imaginable that care of widows could be divisive—it was in Acts 6. Timothy must be ready to go to bat, not only for widows, but also for those who administer their care and who sustain congregations by their teaching and shepherding. This care means according them the respect they deserve for the work they will perform.

What is due these effective leaders is "double[727] honor." Other PE uses of *timē* (honor) are in 6:1 (respect due to masters), 6:16 (honor due to God); 2 Tim 2:20, 21 (household vessels and believers dedicated to "honor" in their function).[728] NIV's "are worthy of double honor" obscures the fact that Paul's

723. On the house church setting in the PE, see Laansma, 258.

724. The word *presbyteros* occurs in Paul's writings only in 1 Tim 5:1, 17, 19 and in Titus 1:5.

725. Used by Paul in the sense of leading or directing also in Rom 12:8; 1 Thess 5:12; 1 Tim 3:4, 5, 12. Significantly, the word connotes and can denote giving care or showing concern: Titus 3:8, 14. These verses and v. 17 discussed above contain all the Pauline occurrences.

726. Note Dibelius and Conzelmann, 78: "The evidence taken as a whole makes it impossible to see in the term 'presbyter' only a designation of age."

727. This adjective (*diplous*) occurs elsewhere in the NT only in Matt 23:15 and Rev 18:6 (twice).

728. *Timē* elsewhere in Paul: Rom 2:7, 10; 9:21; 12:10; 13:7; 1 Cor 6:20; 7:23; 12:23; Col 2:23; 1 Thess 4:4.

statement is a command, as in NRSV (and other translations): "Let the elders who rule well be considered worthy of double honor." Timothy's task in overseeing these elders is to do what is possible to avoid misunderstanding and abuse arising from fulfillment of their duties, including care of widows. They should be respected, not ignored or reviled.

While "honor" can refer to an honorarium, salary, or stipend (BDAG 1005 [3]), it can be asked, first, whether elders at this stage in the early church received monetary compensation,[729] and, second, whether Paul actually meant they should receive a double salary. This reading can perhaps not be ruled out, though "double" might be overstatement. Paul's point would be that they would deserve it, if it could somehow be granted them at a time when widows' needs are critical. Witherington (citing Collins and Fee) points out that "double" here could mean "both respect and remuneration."[730] The next verse (18) may be cited as evidence for remuneration, but it actually confirms from Scripture how much these elders deserve it, not that they are actually receiving it in literal form.[731]

Another possibility is that Paul is simply instructing Timothy to pray for, uphold, and give public recognition to elders thrust into the thankless task of administering relief (and associated arduous duties) where hard decisions must be made and resources are limited. This support would be "letting them be considered worthy" of whatever respect it is appropriate to accord them. "Be considered worthy" translates *axiousthōsan*, a passive verb from *axioō* (consider worthy).[732] Those counting the elders as worthy would be the people in the congregations, including other elders. Towner speaks of "community esteem."[733]

Another possibility is that, by "double" or "twofold," Paul is speaking of remuneration of elders who are bivocational. They have a nonchurch income source but also devote much time and energy to ministry and the preparation necessary for teaching and preaching (see below). "Double" denotes (1) their nonchurch wages and (2) whatever "honor" the church can afford to bestow on them.

Among these effective leaders is a still smaller group: "especially those whose work is preaching and teaching." "Especially" is found in Paul seven times

729. Keener, *Bible Background Commentary*, 612, answers yes, but not so as "making them wealthy, of course."

730. Witherington, 273–74.

731. See Quinn and Wacker, 450–51, 459–60 for thorough analysis of NT and AF references and the larger question of whether these elders received salaries. Their answer seems to be a guarded yes.

732. The only other Pauline use is 2 Tim 1:11. Elsewhere in the NT: Luke 7:7; Acts 15:38; 28:22; Heb 3:3; 10:29.

733. *CNTUOT* 899.

elsewhere.[734] "Those whose work is" translates a form of *kopiaō* (toil, labor; see discussion at 2 Tim 2:6: the "hard-working" farmer). "Preaching and teaching" translates forms of *logos* (word) and *didaskalia* (instruction, teaching). Both words involve verbal communication, but we lack evidence to assign precise functions to each term. Elders who are skilled, effective, and hard-working in these areas are always at a premium. Timothy must make sure they are affirmed in an enterprise that can be imperiled by discouragement from many quarters, including the elders' own native lethargy, the difficulty of the task, and the inability to see how the hard work of ministry done with integrity is worth it in the long haul.

18 Paul cites two sayings as "Scripture" (*graphē*) in support of the proposition in v. 17 that hard-working elders deserve high respect. The first is the four words of Deut 25:4 LXX: *ou phimōseis boun aloōnta* ("You shall not muzzle a threshing ox" [NETS]). Paul changes the word order so that the ox is mentioned first. But he uses the exact same four LXX words. Emphasis on the ox is appropriate, as the ox "by analogy stands for the laboring elders who are the main topic."[735] Earlier in dealing with the Corinthians, Paul had cited this verse,[736] which in its OT setting regulated treatment of oxen who were led across sheaves of grain on a threshing floor to separate the edible grain kernels from the straw (or chaff). They needed and deserved a little of the grain they produced to sustain their own output.[737]

Like rabbis of his time, Paul parlayed this practical farm wisdom into a life lesson applicable to those who labor for the gospel. God and Scripture speak here not only to the Mosaic community of old but equally to Christian believers—"this was written for us, because whoever plows and threshes should be able to do so in the hope of sharing in the harvest" (1 Cor 9:10; cf. Sir 6:19; Jas 5:7). This double application is entirely consistent with Paul's high view of the relevance of Scripture for believers in the church across the spectrum of his extant writings.[738]

The second "Scripture" Paul cites poses a problem for many in NT scholarship because it appears to call a line from a canonical Gospel *graphē* (Scrip-

734. See note at Titus 1:10. The idea that "especially" could mean "namely" here (so Witherington, 274) has been refuted by V. Poythress, "The Meaning of μάλιστα in 2 Timothy 4:13 and Related Verses," *JTS* 53 (2002): 523–32.

735. Towner, "1–2 Timothy and Titus," 899.

736. See 1 Cor 9:9–10.

737. Luther calls this oxen passage "pure allegory" and "a beautiful allegory" (348, 349). Actually, it is probably nothing more subtle than arguing from lesser to greater: if oxen benefit from their prescribed labor, why should not elders?

738. On Paul's view of Scripture, as well as Jesus's, see relevant essays in Carson, ed., *The Enduring Authority of the Christian Scriptures* (e.g., C. Blomberg, "Reflections on Jesus' View of the Old Testament"; D. Moo and A. Naselli, "The Problem of the New Testament's Use of the Old Testament," with reflections on the use of Deut 25:4 at 708–9).

ture).[739] The words from v. 18 "The laborer deserves his wages" come from Luke 10:7 (closely paralleled by Matt 10:10). There is a widespread academic conviction that there was no authoritative canon of NT writings as early as the first century, or even the second until perhaps very late. David Trobisch writes, "Scholars of the period concede that there was no established, authoritative entity during the middle of the second century CE that could have decided and enforced the use of a special edition of scripture among Christian churches."[740] Hermann von Lips goes farther: "Around 200 CE, important theologians show that the basic structure of the NT canon begins to take on form."[741] (This is a small part of the argument for dating 1 Timothy, like the other PE, much later than Paul's lifetime: the historical Paul could never have quoted a line from Luke's Gospel as "Scripture.") Consequently, many commentators regarded the second "Scripture" as simply an oral citation of something like Jesus said (or could have said).[742]

More recent scholarship has shown the likelihood, if not the necessity, of granting that Paul "must refer to written text relative to both citations offered" in v. 18.[743] Swinson argues from a range of considerations (word meaning; discourse analysis; parallel uses of *graphē* in Philo, Josephus, the LXX, the NT, and the AF) that Paul regarded certain writings circulating already in his day as canonical Scripture on par with the OT, among them Luke's Gospel. Parallel to Swinson's research on Paul, R. Deines has argued for Matthew's awareness of his Gospel's scriptural character (like OT books). Deines extends this judgment beyond Matthew: "I am quite convinced that it would be possible to demonstrate for nearly all writings in the New Testament that they were intended to be Scripture-like."[744] M. Kruger has confirmed many of Swinson's findings in a weighty study of his own.[745]

739. Cf. Dibelius and Conzelmann, 79: the verse "designates a saying of Jesus as a portion of Scripture." So also Bassler, 100.

740. D. Trobisch, "Canon III: Formation of the New Testament," *EBR* 4:899.

741. H. von Lips, "Canon IV: Christianity," *EBR* 4:903. For more positive assessment of the evidence for a much earlier existence of NT writings regarded as canonical, see, for example, Schnabel, "The Muratorian Fragment." He argues for a second-century date for the Muratorian Canon, adding, "The Four Gospel canon can be established for the early 2nd century without recourse to the [Muratorian] Fragment" (253).

742. See, for example, Collins, 146; Johnson, *First and Second Letters to Timothy*, 278; Mounce, 310–11, Witherington, 275.

743. Swinson, *What Is Scripture?*, 179.

744. R. Deines, "Did Matthew Know He Was Writing Scripture? Part 2," *EJT* 23.1 (2014): 3–12; see also part 1, *EJT* 22.2 (2013): 101–9. See also C. Hill, *Who Chose the Gospels?* (Oxford: Oxford University Press, 2010), as well as Hill's essay "'The Truth above All Demonstration': Scripture in the Patristic Period to Augustine," in Carson, *The Enduring Authority of the Christian Scriptures*, 43–88.

745. M. Kruger, "First Timothy 5:18 and Early Canon Consciousness: Reconsidering a

In any case, Paul bases his counsel to Timothy about the high value of elders' work on what he takes to be God's word written (see 2 Tim 3:15–17). Commenting on the Scripture citations of both v. 18 and v. 19, Towner concludes, "Definite quotation of the OT [as well as Jesus's enscripturated teaching] was intended to ensure that the authority of the instructions and the gravity of the situation were properly understood."[746]

19 Paul continues to show personal concern for elders under Timothy's leadership. Towner thinks the catalyst for vv. 19–20 is the false teaching in the air in Ephesus.[747] While this setting probably conditions everything Paul writes in 1 Timothy, the more immediate context for his counsel regarding elders in these verses may suggest also the rough-and-tumble he knows elders must endure in matters like care of widows (see vv. 3–16). When some people receive special assistance from the church, others may grumble. Despite admirable growth in the early Jerusalem church, "the Hellenistic Jews among them complained against the Hebraic Jews because their widows were being overlooked in the daily distribution of food" (Acts 6:1). The apostles appointed others to address the problem—which means they would also have taken the heat. Verse 19 assumes a scenario in which elders faced accusations perhaps like the deacons (as they are often regarded) in Acts 6 had to field.

As in v. 18, Paul appeals to Scripture and perhaps also to Jesus's teaching, as well as tradition in churches he had founded to furnish guidance for Timothy. He anticipates "an accusation [*katēgoria*] against an elder." The word translated "accusation" occurs elsewhere in the NT only at John 18:29 and Titus 1:6 (see discussion there). Outside the NT it often carries a formal "judicial connotation and a legal sense."[748] Paul's command is directed to Timothy: he should not receive[749] such charges unless[750] they can be adequately documented. What would that look like?

Paul reverts to an ancient (yet timeless) mode of establishing facts: testimony. "Witnesses" must come forward, tell what they see and/or know, and let their claims be subjected to scrutiny. One voice for or against someone is not sufficient to convict of wrongdoing. The background for this outlook is (as

---

Problematic Text," in Dow, Evans, and Pitts, *The Language and Literature of the New Testament*, 680–700.

746. *CNTUOT* 901.

747. *CNTUOT* 900.

748. Quin and Wacker, 464.

749. From *paradechomai*, used in five other NT passages: Mark 4:20; Acts 15:4; 16:21; 22:18; Heb 12:6. This is the only imperatival use.

750. "Unless" translates the expression *ektos ei mē*. It is found in 1 Cor 14:5 and 15:2 but nowhere else in the NT or in the LXX, Philo, Josephus, the AF, the Apologists, or Epictetus. See BDF §376.

in v. 18) both Moses and Jesus.[751] As to Moses, both Deut 17:6 and Deut 19:15 call for witnesses as necessary to establish culpable actions. Deuteronomy 17:6 deals with the death sentence, Deut 19:15 "for any iniquity, or for any fault, or for any sin which" a person may commit. It is the Deut 17 text that Paul follows more closely in v. 19.[752]

As to Jesus, he was content to abide by the Mosaic witness rule: "But if I do judge, my decisions are true, because I am not alone. I stand with the Father, who sent me. In your own Law it is written that the testimony of two witnesses is true. I am one who testifies for myself; my other witness is the Father, who sent me" (John 8:16–18). Jesus uses the same basis (Deut 19:15) for establishing facts in disputes among this followers (Matt 18:16). Towner observes that the principle of multiple witnesses is reflected frequently "in various practical and eschatological situations . . . in the teaching of the early church."[753] The same scruples are evident in Josephus and at Qumran.[754] Paul himself had appealed to Moses's teaching on this point at Corinth (2 Cor 13:1).

In short, v. 19 tasks Timothy with protecting elders in their range of duties, perhaps especially their administration of care for widows: "Accusations must be properly examined and not uncritically accepted."[755] Barrett notes wisely, "No man is so exposed to back-biting and reproach as the minister who discharges his office faithfully."[756]

20 Not all elders in all disputes will prove free of wrongdoing. Verse 20 assumes a scenario in which accusations against elders ("those elders who are sinning") have been assessed and proven true.

But it should be noted that "elders who are sinning" is an interpretation of *tous harmartanontas*, "the ones who are sinning." Some commentators (going back to Chrysostom and Origen) have viewed "the ones who are sinning" as nonelders in the church,[757] perhaps the ones who bring unjustified accusations against the elders (v. 19). This interpretation "cannot be excluded as impossible."[758]

Most commentators today view the ones who are sinning as elders, in view of the emphasis on this group going back to v. 17. This interpretation will

751. Not surprisingly, the Pharisees were governed by the same Mosaic rule: "The Pharisees challenged [Jesus], 'Here you are, appearing as your own witness; your testimony is not valid'" (John 8:13).

752. For detailed exegesis, see Towner, "1–2 Timothy and Titus," 900–901.

753. Towner, "1–2 Timothy and Titus," 901. Note references to multiple witnesses in, for example, Matt 18:19–20; Mark 6:7; Luke 9:30, 32; 10:1; 24:13; John 20:12; Acts 1:10; Heb 6:18; Rev 11:3–4.

754. Towner, "1–2 Timothy and Titus," 901.

755. Keener, *Bible Background Commentary*, 612.

756. Barrett, *Pastoral Epistles*, 80.

757. See Quinn and Wacker, 465.

758. Barrett, *Pastoral Epistles*, 80.

be followed below. But even if Paul is not referring to the unjustified critics of the elders, there is an application here for that contingency, which does arise in churches. People who stir up trouble with false charges against church leaders can count on being confronted and, if need be, reproved. This process reflects a disciplinary mechanism going back to Jesus himself (Matt 18:15–20).

"Elders who are sinning" envisions leaders who should be honorable (v. 17) running afoul of accusation (v. 19) that turns out to be true. Timothy is to "reprove" them. Part of the twofold pastoral mandate (teaching, pastoral oversight; see 2:12) must at times extend to the activity denoted by the verb *elenchō* (reprove, rebuke, refute). It occurs eight times in Paul, five times in the PE (see 1 Cor 14:24; Eph 5:11, 13; in the PE 2 Tim 4:2; Titus 1:9, 13; 2:15; see commentary at those verses for further discussion). Pastoral overseers make mistakes. The gaffe of Peter and Barnabas in Antioch is a famous example from apostolic times (Gal 2:11–13). When Paul "saw that they were not acting in line with the truth of the gospel," he called them out "in front of them all" (Gal 2:14). This is probably what Paul has in mind for Timothy with "reprove before everyone."[759] Church leaders in Paul's view are subject to a high view of accountability. Their sin when discovered (and frequently before it is formally uncovered) often has immediate public effects. It is reasonable and restorative when matters can be set right in public view.[760]

Part of the benefit of public rebuke of church leaders' sin is "so that the others may take warning." "The others"[761] could be other elders, or it could be the rest of the faith community in general. "Take warning"[762] translates *phobon echōsin* (have fear). Paul sees a beneficial deterrent effect in the sins of elders (or their unjust accusers) being brought into the light. Fear may not be the noblest of motivators, but Paul often commends it as appropriate (Rom 11:20; 13:3, 4, 7; 2 Cor 5:11; 7:1, 11, 15; Eph 5:21, 33; 6:5; Phil 2:12; Col 3:22). It was part of his own experience in certain settings (1 Cor 2:3; 2 Cor 7:5).

Moreover, there is an OT basis for the scenario Paul envisions, and it too ends with deterrent fear among the faith community. After Deut 19:15 speaks of confirmation of wrongdoing "by two or three witnesses" (see 1 Tim 5:19), it goes on to describe the public trial if a witness proves to be false. The "unjust witness" (Deut 19:16 NETS) who has alleged wrongdoing must appear before the (innocent) accused and "before the Lord and before the priests and before the judges" (Deut 19:17 NETS). After inquiry, when the accuser is convicted

759. So also Witherington, 276.

760. Cf. Aquinas, 72: "An ecclesiastical judge ought to punish publicly so that others may be edified," citing Eccl 8:11 and Prov 19:25.

761. Paul uses *hoi loipoi* (the others, the rest) also in Rom 11:7; 1 Cor 9:5; Gal 2:13; 1 Thess 4:13.

762. Towner, *Letters*, 372n56, comments that this translation "perhaps minimizes the sense of 'dread of judgment' often associated with 'fear' in such contexts."

of his false testimony, then the community "shall do to him just as he connived to do to his brother. And you shall remove the evil one from yourselves" (Deut 19:19 NETS). The final outcome? "And the rest [*hoi epiloipoi*], when they hear, shall be afraid and will not add to act again according to this evil thing among you" (Deut 19:20 NETS). It is possible, if not indeed likely, that Paul's projection of outcome in 1 Tim 5:20 draws on his recollection of this Mosaic precedent.

Paul ends this four-verse subsection highlighting personal concern for the elders under Timothy's care on a strong note of realism. Church leaders are sinners, too, just like the members of the flock they oversee. Paul has already admitted his own "worst of sinners" status (1:15–16). Timothy should be protective of the elders (vv. 17–19) but not to be point of cronyism. In recent generations, and perhaps throughout the church's mottled history, too many church structures have covered up corruption by priests and pastors. God is not partial (see next verse), and to the extent possible neither should be those like Timothy who administer proceedings in God's household, the church. The fact that church discipline can be difficult and messy does not relieve leaders of the responsibility of seeking to replicate in their own setting the level of integrity and accountability that Paul called on Timothy to uphold, especially among their own ranks.

7. For Timothy: An Aside (5:21–25)

> [21] *I charge you, in the sight of God and Christ Jesus and the elect angels, to keep these instructions without partiality, and to do nothing out of favoritism.* [22] *Do not be hasty in the laying on of hands, and do not share in the sins of others. Keep yourself pure.* [23] *Stop drinking only water, and use a little wine because of your stomach and your frequent illnesses.* [24] *The sins of some are obvious, reaching the place of judgment ahead of them; the sins of others trail behind them.* [25] *In the same way, good deeds are obvious, and even those that are not obvious cannot remain hidden forever.*

21 "I charge you" (*diamartyromai*) is strong language. The verb is used by Paul elsewhere only at 1 Thess 4:6; 2 Tim 2:14; 4:1. It seems more likely that it marks a turn to address Timothy about matters concerning him personally than a conclusion to his remarks on elders (vv. 17–20), as in the NIV paragraphing. Beginning with a solemn charge, vv. 21–25 make sense as a unit rallying Timothy in various ways, fortifying him individually just as, in the discourse overall from 5:1 to 6:2a, Paul has been dealing with subgroups in some of their selected needs and challenges. Timothy has his needs and challenges too. With all he is placing on Timothy, Paul can sense sufficiently to feel the need to encourage him with direct address at this point before concluding the section with admonition regarding slaves (6:1–2a).

Paul's charge is "in the sight of God and Christ Jesus and the elect angels," wording that underscores its gravity.[763] Those three entities pretty much cover the whole heavenly host. The "elect" angels are those who serve God in contradistinction to those who fell (Jude 6; 2 Pet 2:4). They are associated with Christ's return and the final judgment.[764]

"In the sight of" translates *enōpion*, used ninety-four times in the NT and seventeen times in Paul.[765] "In the presence of" is often the sense. Paul invokes that presence elsewhere in the PE (1 Tim 6:13; 2 Tim 2:14; 4:1). Paul wants to impress on Timothy that both he, in writing, and Timothy, in receiving this letter, do so in God's very presence. God and all heaven are observers and judges of this interchange. Timothy dare not take the duties Paul is outlining lightly.

Paul's charge and solemn adjuration have a twofold aim. The first is that Timothy would "keep these instructions without partiality." "These instructions" translates the neuter plural pronoun *tauta* (these things). Paul refers most directly to what he has written going back to 5:1. Timothy must stand by what Paul has stated regarding widows and elders, as prickly as the issues may be. Paul's counsel has not been offered for Timothy's editing or selective implementation. "Keep" (*phyllassō*) is found eight times in Paul, twice referring to observing the Torah (Rom 2:26; Gal 6:13) and twice referring to God's protection of those who trust him (2 Thess 3:3; 2 Tim 1:12). Because God keeps his own, they can keep (or "guard": 1 Tim 6:20; 2 Tim 1:14) what he entrusts to them.[766]

Timothy's observance of Paul's apostolic guidance must be "without partiality." Partiality translates a form of *prokrima*, a NT hapax. It is a courtroom term and would describe a crooked procedure: deciding an issue in advance based on personal preference or taking sides. Justice is supposed to be blind, in God's household just as much as in a secular courtroom. Another NT word, *prosōlēmpsia*, also refers to "partiality" and is used more frequently. God does not show *prosōpolēmpsia*,[767] so neither should a pastoral leader like Timothy, though nothing is more tempting in some pastoral situations. James warns against partiality in matters of faith and regard for other people in a discourse that also refers to the care of widows and orphans (Jas 2:1; cf. 1:27). It is obvious that Peter and Barnabas showed partiality in their addled social dealings

763. Other passages in which God, Christ, or angels appear: Matt 16:27; Mark 8:38; Luke 9:26; 2 Thess 1:6, 7; Heb 12:22–24.

764. Knight, 238 (with numerous references).

765. In the PE eight times; see also 1 Tim 2:3; 5:4, 20; 6:12, 13; 2 Tim 2:14; 4:1.

766. A final use of *phyllassō* refers to Timothy's need to be "on guard" against Alexander (2 Tim 4:15).

767. See also Rom 2:11; Eph 6:9; Col 3:25; Jas 2:1, the only other NT uses of the word.

in Antioch (Gal 2:11–13). Paul wants Timothy to be circumspect rather than install himself as judge—it is God and his counsel (including Paul's apostolic guidance) that should steer Timothy, not his own best lights or the political pressures of the moment. Nor can he afford to privilege those he cares for in ways that will corrupt them by allowing them to languish and stray outside the bounds of what Paul has outlined.

Paul's second charge is that Timothy not be led by "favoritism." Keener comments that Roman law favored the powerful and wealthy; the OT[768] and Judaism did not.[769] Despite the status of Ephesus as a leading city of the Roman Empire, Paul insists on observing what God commends rather than what the dominant society favors. The participial construction places "do nothing out of favoritism" in a position that makes it explanatory of "keep these instructions without partiality." In other words, they are not two separate prohibitions in Paul's conception; rather, the second gives added texture to the first.[770] "Favoritism" (*prosklisis*) is a word found nowhere else in the NT. But it does crop up four times in the AF, all in 1 Clement, written just a generation after the PE. In one passage Clement calls on women to "show their love, without partiality [*mē kata proskliseis*] and in holiness, equally toward all those who fear God" (1 Clem. 21:7). In 1 Clem. 47:3 the phrase "split into factions" (*proskliseis . . . pepoiēsthai*) is language close to Paul's in v. 21. In both 47:3 and 47:4 Clement quotes Paul as using the word to denote the partisan divisions that had marked Corinth's churches from the beginning. He calls on the Corinthians to pray, "that we may be found blameless in love, standing apart from any human factiousness [*proskliseōs*]" (1 Clem. 50:2).

A pastoral leader needs to be a unifier, not a divider. "Favoritism" spoils all prospects of that ideal. In dealing with widows, elders, and all the related pastoral issues Timothy faces, his default posture needs to be holy equanimity, not shifting with the political winds, the favor of preferred personalities, or other unholy considerations. Only in this way will he keep his hands and conscience relatively clean before God and command the respect of those looking to him for guidance. As Barrett summarizes, "The purity of the ministry is of the deepest concern" for Paul, "and the way to preserve it" is for Timothy to keep the instructions Paul has given,[771] not just in ways he can justify but "in the sight of" the heavenly authority he serves.

768. Aquinas, 73, notes Exod 23:6: "Do not deny justice to your poor people in their lawsuits."

769. Keener, *Bible Background Commentary*, 612.

770. Marshall, with Towner, 620, citing Knight, does discern progression: "The first phrase says that one is not to come with pre-formed opinions, the second that one is not to be ruled by partiality to one party or the other." Yet, it would be too subtle to insist on absolute distinction between the two.

771. Barrett, *Pastoral Epistles*, 80.

22 On "laying on of hands," see commentary at 2 Tim 2:6. Jesus's gesture of laying on hands often brought healing or other blessing.[772] In Acts it signifies conveyance of divine sanction.[773] Paul placed his hands on those who first professed Christ at Ephesus (Acts 19:6). In 1 Tim 5:22 it serves as shorthand for Timothy commissioning new leaders.

In this context, Paul could be addressing the temptation to populate leadership ranks with yes-men (or women),[774] persons whom Timothy could count on to see things his way. Or Paul could have in mind pressure from others to appoint their cronies. Either option (and others imaginable) would violate Paul's call to impartiality (see previous verse). In 3:6 Paul warned against appointing a new convert as an overseer, because he could "become conceited and fall under the same judgment as the devil." But in v. 22 Paul's concern is with the integrity of Timothy's leadership, not the destructive effects of haste on those prematurely advanced, though that would not help Timothy's cause, either.

To recognize leaders who are not really qualified would be to "share in the sins of others."[775] Paul could be referring to the sins of those pressuring Timothy to appoint them. Or he could be thinking of the wreckage caused when people are placed in service when they are not really fit. Paul uses the word translated "share" (*koinōneō*) in other settings, always positive (Rom 12:13; 15:27; Gal 6:6; Phil 4:15). But sharing in "sins" (from *hamartia*) is another category. "The person who appoints is responsible for what the person appointed does while holding office."[776] Paul's admonition echoes a more generic concern that he voices elsewhere concerning guilt incurred by endorsing, directly or indirectly, the sins of others (Rom 1:32; Eph 5:11; cf. 2 John 11; Rev 18:4; on being held accountable for others' sins, see also Ezek 3:18; 33:6, 8).

Instead, Paul tells Timothy: "Keep yourself pure." On "pure" (from *hagnos*), see Titus 2:5.[777] Timothy and his leadership will be compromised if he gets in a hurry in the recognition process described in ch. 3. He may feel more help is needed, quickly, for demands posed by widows and elder issues. Paul encourages Timothy to resist the urge to overreact when to do so might create new problems and solve none.

23 Paul's personal concern for Timothy extends to his personal health. This practical care confirms that the close relationship implied in 1:2 ("my true son in the faith") and elsewhere is not merely rhetoric. Timothy's health was

772. Matt 9:18; 19:13, 15; Mark 5:23; 6:5; 7:32; 8:23, 25; Luke 4:40; 13:13.

773. Acts 6:5; 8:17, 19; 9:12, 17; 13:3; 19:6; 28:8.

774. Schlatter, *Die Kirche der Griechen*, 154, thinks the reference is to overseers or deacons.

775. "Others" (from *allotrios*) elsewhere in Paul: Rom 14:4; 15:20; 2 Cor 10:15.

776. Marshall, with Towner, 622.

777. Paul also uses the word in 2 Cor 7:11; 11:2; Phil 4:8.

evidently not ideal ("your frequent illnesses"). Was Timothy, "drinking only water," ascetically inclined himself? Was he "influenced by the Nazarite vow of Num 6:1–4"?[778] Was he "seeking to avoid the criticism of those influenced by the false teachers (4:3; some ascetics abstained from wine)"?[779] Clearly Paul thinks "a little wine" would be of medicinal value; elsewhere he calls attention to the danger of this drink used to excess.[780] It is also better avoided (in the same sense meat could be) when it is a detriment to others' progress in the gospel (Rom 14:21).

Witherington calls drinking wine in small amounts "standard medical practice of the day," citing Hippocrates, Plutarch, Pliny the Elder, and other sources.[781] It may be that Paul knew Timothy was prone to digestive upset when under stress, as this epistle pictures him, given the daunting threats it outlines and the nearly four dozen imperatives it issues. One can imagine Timothy contemplating tensions regarding care of widows, elder malfeasance, and staying objective (v. 21) and pure of heart (v. 22) and grumbling, "This all makes me sick to my stomach!" or "It's enough to give you ulcers!" Paul and Timothy had labored together long enough for Paul to know Timothy well.

We should probably understand the verse in this light. It is not a strange random extrusion into the discourse but part of the flow of Paul's expression of personal concern for Timothy under the pressures created by the responsibilities he carries. "It is part of the duty of a good minister to take reasonable care of his health in order that he may render effective service."[782] Paul points Timothy to one avenue in this direction.

24 Paul's words of encouragement to Timothy continue. He offers wise counsel probably in connection with the topic begun in vv. 21–22. First, Timothy needs to be totally aboveboard in dealing with issues like widows and elders and the related disciplinary matters that may arise (v. 21). Second, Timothy must exercise caution in appointing new leaders so as not to aid and abet their subsequent sin and compromise his own integrity (v. 22). Yet, these commands do not make Timothy's job any easier in a setting that may be putting a strain on Timothy's health (v. 23). So vv. 24–25 offer consolation: "In assessing people, errors are unavoidable." The next two verses put "the procedure Timothy is to execute in the context of divine judgment."[783] The weight of all these weighty matters is not so much on Timothy's shoulders as in God's hands.

778. Raised as a possibility by Knight, 240.

779. Keener, *Bible Background Commentary*, 612.

780. Eph 5:18; 1 Tim 3:8; Titus 2:3.

781. Witherington, 277. See also Towner, *Letters*, 376nn82–83.

782. Barrett, *Pastoral Epistles*, 81.

783. Towner, *Letters*, 376.

In dealing with wrongdoing, Timothy should remember that certain people's sins ("the sins of some") "are obvious." The word order emphasizes, and may constitute a rebuke of, these sinning people. Perhaps Paul refers to a recurring pattern he and Timothy had observed. Or perhaps these people had a history of transgression. "Obvious" (*prodēlos*) occurs only here, in v. 25, and in Heb 7:14 ("clear"). Paul means there is no mistaking these people's wrongdoing. It will terminate in their condemnation ("judgment"), but long before then and even now, their error is open to view. This situation is probably not news to Timothy; Paul may simply be commiserating with him over a depressingly common pastoral phenomenon.

"The sins of others trail behind them" translates *tisin de kai epakolouthousin*. This is a difficult clause whose details are glossed over in most commentaries, so a brief explanation will be offered here. *De* is adversative, implying a contrast between this clause and the preceding (implied by the semicolon in NIV). In combination with *de*, *kai* can be taken here as "similarly."[784] Just as certain people's obvious sins get their due in the end, so do the less obvious sins of others. *Epakolouthousin* means "to happen . . . in connection with someth." or "follow" (BDAG 358). The implied subject of *epakolouthousin* is the sins of certain people. *Tisin* (dative pl., here perhaps a dative of respect) corresponds to *tinōn anthrōpōn* (genitive pl.; "*some people's* sins") in the first half of the verse. Taking all these factors into consideration, the second half of the verse can be paraphrased: "But regarding certain other people, their sins follow them, yet with the similar outcome of judgment."

Whether sins are visible or hidden, they are all known to God and will be dealt with in his wisdom, grace, and justice. Timothy should neither ruin his health (v. 23) nor be derelict in his duties (vv. 22–23) but rather should take heart in what God will put right in due time.

25 It is important not to overdo the negative. Yes, sins visible and invisible (to human eyes) bedevil pastoral caregiving. But God will deal with them all (v. 24). And on the other side of the ledger, "likewise also" (*hōsautōs kai*; NIV "in the same way"), "good deeds are obvious." Timothy will observe not only heinous behavior but also exemplary. On "good deeds," see discussion of good deeds/works at Titus 1:16. Timothy must not become jaundiced or cynical. He must continue in his own right actions, if that is what Paul is commending in v. 25. Like believers before him, Timothy is susceptible to growing "weary in doing good" (Gal 6:9). Paul reminds him that his good actions will be evident, at least to God and others with eyes to see. Even hidden acts will receive final reward, "for at the proper time we will reap a harvest if we do not give up" (Gal 6:9). As Jesus put it, "Your Father, who sees what is done in secret, will reward you" (Matt 6:4). Timothy should take heart in his

784. See BDAG 213 (5.b).

dedication to do right, even when it seems nonproductive or exposes him to criticism or even persecution.

Or Paul may be speaking more directly not of Timothy's acts but of actions of obedience to God by those under his oversight. Pastoral service should never, but sometimes does, lead to a mocking attitude toward sincere acts of devotion or concrete expressions of piety (one form of "good works"), since there is much hypocrisy. ("Piety" itself has become a term of derision in some quarters.) Scorn for documentable sin (v. 24) can segue into contempt for people who commit such sins and then seep over to contaminate a pastor's regard for people in general, even those who do good. Doctrines like human depravity can be overextended and blot out equally true considerations such as human beings made in God's image. This is a toxic brew, especially if combined with pastoral self-righteousness, and then perhaps multiplied when pastoral coworkers conspire in their sense of indignation against those they serve.

Paul has already built into his testimony an ongoing consciousness of personal shortcoming (1:13–16). This frank assessment enabled him, in the face of discerning and dealing with evil, not to elevate himself over others, but to find in God and Christ (hence the doxology in 1:17) resources for nurturing humility and harboring hope. It is this hope that Paul models for Timothy in v. 25. He will see (and perform) righteous acts relevant to disciplinary issues, elder appointment, and ministry to widows. He should not lose faith in the God who is at work both to will and to do what honors him (see Phil 2:13) through followers like those under Timothy's care and in Timothy's own life.

But the situation is even more hopeful than that. There are also good works "that are not obvious." Timothy does not see them, or he performs them in secret, and they may never come to light in this life. But in the end they will be recognized (Matt 10:26; Luke 8:17; 12:2). Paul's guarded appeal to the final judgment begun in v. 24 continues. Ministry proceeds under many auspices, but one that is indispensible is eschatology, for therein lies all ultimate Christian hope. God will exonerate and reward all good works done in faith good and true. On this note, symmetrical with Paul's charge in the presence of "God and Christ Jesus and the elect angels" (v. 21), Paul concludes his honest, personal, businesslike, but upbeat aside to Timothy—except for one more matter he must touch on.

8. Slaves (6:1–2a)

> [1]*All who are under the yoke of slavery should consider their masters worthy of full respect, so that God's name and our teaching may not be slandered.* [2]*Those who have believing masters should not show them disrespect just because they are fellow believers. Instead, they should serve them*

even better because their masters are dear to them as fellow believers and are devoted to the welfare of their slaves.

1 Having reflected on pressing priorities regarding widows, elders, and Timothy himself, Paul now has brief counsel for slaves (*douloi*).[785] Paul regarded himself and Timothy as *douloi* of Christ (Phil 1:1). "All"[786] signals that this same status holds true for every person in this social class who is under Timothy's pastoral guidance. The emphasis on the individual that has characterized this subsection going back to 5:1 continues. "Yoke of slavery" is a term found in classical Greek writers.[787] Jesus used "yoke" as a metaphor for being his disciple.[788] Slavery was onerous and undesirable, but it was universal across the Roman Empire and indeed across most civilizations until fairly recent times. It is currently still by no means eradicated. In hierarchical societies like that of Ephesus, "where most people were born into their predetermined niches in the social complex, slaves were simply at the bottom of a long continuum of varying levels of subordination based on birth."[789]

Paul urged slaves who could attain freedom to do so (1 Cor 7:21). He called on Philemon to receive his escaped slave Onesimus back as a brother (Phlm 16).[790] Yet, like other NT figures (including Jesus), Paul's immediate goal in ministry was not revolutionary change of the social order: it was preaching and teaching the gospel for the sake of establishing enclaves of Christian believers and thereby ultimately redeeming the world.[791] "Christianity did not understand itself to be a revolutionary movement even through its teachings had clear reformatory implications."[792] In due course Christian doctrine and practice could and did challenge corrupt institutions like slavery (though societies free from slavery are still corrupt because of pervasive human sin and oppression by other means).

785. See also Eph 6:5–6; Col 3:22.

786. Greek *hosoi*, not the usual word for "all" (*pas*) but here its equivalent (see BDAG 729 [2]). Paul uses this word only here in the PE but ten other times elsewhere: Rom 2:12 (twice); 6:3; 8:14; Gal 3:10, 27; 6:12, 16; Phil 3:15; Col 2:1.

787. See BDAG 429. "Yoke" (*zygos*) and "slavery" (*douleia*) are closely associated in 2 Chr 10:14; 1 Macc 8:18 LXX.

788. Matt 11:29, 30. See also Acts 15:10 (the "yoke" of a faulty understanding of the Torah).

789. Thomas Sowell, "The Real History of Slavery," in *Black Rednecks and White Liberals* (San Francisco: Encounter Books, 2005), 169. For literature on slavery, see also Towner, *Letters*, 379n3; more broadly (and with references to historical studies of the Roman Empire), Johnson, *First and Second Letters to Timothy*, 288–90).

790. On NT teaching regarding slavery, see T. Schreiner, *New Testament Theology* (Grand Rapids: Baker Academic, 2008), 794–800.

791. See James Hamilton, "Does the Bible Condone Slavery and Sexism?," in *In Defense of the Bible*, ed. S. Cowan and T. Wilder (Nashville: B&H, 2013), 343.

792. Bassler, 103.

To say that "the Pastorals endorse the cruelty of Graeco-Roman society without reflection"[793] may be technically true (depending on how one defines "reflection"), but it is, first, anachronistic. Known social orders free of slavery did not exist. It would be like condemning today's church a thousand years from now because it did not speak out against traffic deaths. Second, there are estimated to be some 45 million slaves in the world currently; that is not appreciably fewer than would have existed in the Roman Empire. Third, it appears to assume the superiority of contemporary social orders. We are less cruel and would not condone such practices. Yet, the twentieth century was the most brutal in human history, measured by loss of life in war and genocide. The pace does not seem to be slowing at present. Or consider persecution of Christians. One agency says that 1,207 Christians a year die as martyrs.[794] That's about 3.3 a day. By another reckoning 90,000 die a year.[795] That's 247 a day. The larger figure is projected to continue through 2025, then increase to 100,000 annually through 2050.[796] How civilized is modern civilization, in which 200 million women cope with genital mutilation (most under the aegis of the world's second largest religion)?[797]

In light of the low moral ground modern commentators occupy, PE and other New Testament passages should get credit for calling for and enabling revolutionary ties between slaves and their owners, not criticism for failing to leave a clear record of direct condemnation of then-global economic and social orders.

Slaves in the church "should consider[798] their masters[799] worthy of full respect." The form of the Greek verb is a third person imperative; *GNC* translates "slaves ought to." This is the same notion of "respect" (*timē*) accorded to elders (see 5:17 and discussion there). Paul knows that "masters" can be overbearing and that servitude is a thankless station in life (see also Luke 17:7–9). Yet, the most disastrous slavery is bondage to sin, which leads to death (Rom 6:16, 20), and Christ frees every last person who follows him from that inglorious end. That freedom puts life in perspective. The calling of slaves in Ephesus,

793. Davies, 89.

794. Open Doors, www.opendoorsusa.org. They limit their numbers to eyewitness accounts.

795. Center for the Study of Global Christianity, Gordon-Conwell Theological Seminary. See Mendy Belz, "Numbers Matter," *World Magazine*, February 18, 2017, 32. They include all who have died as the result of being Christians, including those killed in war.

796. Johnson, Zurlo, Hickman, and Crossing, "Christianity 2017," 50.

797. For the 200 million figure, see P. Belluck and J. Cochrane, "Unicef Report Finds Female Genital Cutting to Be Common in Indonesia," *New York Times*, February 4, 2016.

798. Paul used the same word (*hēgeomai*, to consider, regard) in 1:12. It is found in nine other Pauline passages: 2 Cor 9:5; Phil 2:3, 6, 25; 3:7, 8 [twice]; 1 Thess 5:13; 2 Thess 3:15.

799. See the next verse for more on this word (*despotēs*).

then, like that of all believers, is to honor God where they find themselves. For slaves, it means honoring their masters. Paul will describe a particular instance of this more fully in the next verse.

One immediate concern Paul voices is "that God's name and our teaching may not be slandered." "God's name"[800] is "a powerful expression of his personal rule and activity"[801] and refers to his full being, authority, and majesty. Slaves in the church who discredit their masters would also discredit the Son of God, whom they have confessed as their Lord. This would cause God and apostolic teaching to be spoken ill of ("slandered,"[802] Paul's charge against fellow Jews in Rom 2:24). Timothy should minister to slaves in the congregation in such a way that they recognize and avoid this trap. The temptation to despise, malign, and give minimal service to masters was no doubt just as compelling as contempt for employers is for many today.

2a Some slaves would find themselves in the seemingly favorable position of having "believing[803] masters." "Master" (*despotēs*) occurs in Paul two other times.[804] The word denotes a person in charge, in this case the owner of one or more slaves. Just as some slaves professed faith in Christ, so did some owners (as Paul's letter to Philemon dramatizes). There could be a temptation for slaves to take advantage of those they served because of their new relationship as brothers (or sisters) in the household of faith. Paul commands with a third person imperative that could be translated, "Let them not regard their masters with contempt"[805] just because they are now siblings in God's household of faith in Christ.

On the contrary (*alla*), they are commanded to serve all the more[806] diligently (*douleuetōsan*, ESV "let them render their service as slaves"; *GNC* "they are to serve them all the more readily"). Why? Paul replies that the masters are worthy of this respectful service precisely because they are (fellow) believers (*pistoi*). Also, they are "dear" (from *agapētos*, beloved), which NIV renders

800. Greek *onoma*. Its only other PE use is in 2 Tim 2:19 (see discussion there). The "name" of God (or Christ) is referred to elsewhere in Paul in Rom 1:5; 2:24; 9:17; 10:13; 15:9; 1 Cor 1:2, 10; 5:4; 6:11; Eph 5:29; Phil 2:9, 10; Col 3:17; 2 Thess 1:12; 3:6.

801. *NIDNTTE* 3:517.

802. Greek *blasphēmeō*, used in the PE also at 1:20; Titus 2:5; 3:2. See commentary at these verses.

803. Greek *pistos* (an adj. meaning "faithful"; used as a noun, as here, "one who believes"). For other uses of the same word as a substantive to refer to believers in the PE, see 1 Tim 4:3, 10, 12; Titus 1:6. For a possible parallel elsewhere in Paul, see Eph 1:1.

804. 2 Tim 2:21 (of God); Titus 2:9.

805. Greek *kataphroneō*. It occurs in the PE only one other time (4:12; see discussion there).

806. The comparative element is provided by the adverb *mallon* (more, rather) preceding the imperative *douleuetōsan*.

"dear to them," that is, to the slaves. Paul could also be speaking of their favored status before God—God has accepted them as his "beloved," and their slaves (who have likewise become objects of God's redemptive love) should do no less.

Paul further describes these masters as "devoted to the welfare of their slaves." Johnson stresses here how the wording means the masters are either receiving a "benefaction" (*euergesia*)[807] from their slaves (Johnson's view) or providing a benefaction to their slaves (NIV's interpretation). Commentators are divided on the direction of the benefaction. What is definite is that in that setting, slaves and masters are in a mutually dependent relationship, each (potentially) deriving a benefit from the other, just as they equally do (or can) provide a service to each other. Paul wants that relationship to be sweetened, not soured, by the presence of Christ's gospel grace in the master-slave interchange.

Recent commentators like Johnson and Towner (who devotes twelve pages to vv. 1–2) agree that, contrary to the appearance that Paul in vv. 1–2 is reinforcing culture's norm of slaves simply knowing their status and maintaining it nobly, he is rather "reversing the roles of slaves and masters and speaking of slaves as benefactors."[808] This perspective alters the understanding implied by NIV's focus on the masters' devotion to their slaves: "They should serve them even better *because their masters* are dear to them as fellow believers and *are devoted to the welfare of their slaves.*" Towner's paraphrase highlights the difference: "Instead slaves should serve their masters even better because those who receive the slaves' benefaction are believers and loved (by God/by the slaves)."[809]

In either interpretation it could be argued that a Pauline Christology and theology of the cross are in evidence. In the NIV rendering, slaves' possible resignation or even resentment is transformed by their masters' reception of grace and (arguably) the slaves' reception of the promise of the gospel that they "will receive an inheritance from the Lord as a reward. It is the Lord Christ [they] are serving" (Col 3:24). This promise is foreshadowed by their masters' devotion to their slaves' welfare, because of which (along with their love for their masters) the slaves serve them heartily. In Towner's and Johnson's understanding, slaves are already in the driver's seat by virtue of their realization that the one who is truly greatest in gospel living is the one (like a lowly slave) who

807. Johnson points out that this word "universally bears the sense of benefaction within the ancient system of patronage" (*First and Second Letters to Timothy*, 284).

808. Towner, *Letters*, 387; Johnson, *First and Second Letters to Timothy*, 283–84: "Paul is using conventional honor/shame language in a manner subversive of the system itself."

809. Towner, *Letters*, 390. Towner draws on parallel thought in Seneca (*On Benefits* 3.18–20) and by Jesus (Luke 22:25–27).

serves their master to God's glory, period, not just those who serve masters who "are devoted to the welfare of their slaves" (NIV), which may have been a rarity, even under the best of church circumstances.

IV. FINAL CLARIFICATION AND EXHORTATION (6:2B–21)

This last major section of the epistle bears comparison with the letter's opening (1:3–20). "Most scholars now admit that the structure is intentional,"[810] in the sense that Paul recalls the notes he sounded at the start and wants to echo and extend those as he concludes. Each division contains six features, interspersed with slight variation.

Table 22. Opening and closing of 1 Timothy compared

Opening feature	Closing feature
1:3 Charge to stay at Ephesus	6:2b Charge to teach and uphold the faith
1:4–7 Issue (false teachers) and commendation of love	6:3–6 Issue (false teachers) and commendation of godliness
1:8–10 Proper use of the OT (law)	6:7–10 Proper regard for money (see also vv. 17–19)
1:11–16 Testimony: Paul was saved by Christ, not law	6:11–15a Appeal: Timothy should lay hold of eternal life in Christ, who also made the good confession
1:17 Doxology	6:15b-16 Doxology
1:18–20 Application: charge to Timothy confirmed, with warning regarding those who have rejected the faith	6:17–19 Application: charge confirmed to the wealthy under Timothy's leadership and to Timothy himself, with warning regarding those who have rejected the faith

The rough but evident symmetry in the epistle's opening and closing confirms the consistency of Paul's intent from beginning to end: to stabilize and rally Timothy. It also illustrates the point that pastoral care never occurs in a vacuum: Timothy will fulfill Paul's aim for him, if he does, in the face of opponents (like the law-twisters; ch. 1) or misguided people in the church who suppose the point of their (claimed) pursuit of godliness is material gain (ch. 6). It also reminds

810. Towner, *Letters*, 390.

readers of an undercurrent informing all Paul undertakes: the transforming conviction of God's radiant gloriousness, with eternal life in his presence a controlling motivator for every aspect of the believer's life. Finally, at the epistle's conclusion as at its onset, Paul points to the disaster of lax or errant appropriation of the Christian message. The line from Hymenaeus's and Alexander's blasphemies (1:20) to the godless chatter and notions of the wayward "some" (6:21) is direct and has the effect of subordinating all Paul writes to the cause of God's and Christ's supremacy over all that opposes the truths of the faith.

"These things" that Timothy is "to teach and insist on" (6:2b) will lead to steadfastness in "the faith," for which Timothy is to contend (v. 12) in the face of those departing from it (v. 21)—a sad reality that may help explain why Timothy would ever have considered departing from Ephesus (1:3) in the first place.

A. False Teachers and the Love of Money (6:2b–10)

> [2]. . . *These are the things you are to teach and insist on.* [3]*If anyone teaches otherwise and does not agree to the sound instruction of our Lord Jesus Christ and to godly teaching,* [4]*they are conceited and understand nothing. They have an unhealthy interest in controversies and quarrels about words that result in envy, strife, malicious talk, evil suspicions* [5]*and constant friction between people of corrupt mind, who have been robbed of the truth and who think that godliness is a means to financial gain.* [6]*But godliness with contentment is great gain.* [7]*For we brought nothing into the world, and we can take nothing out of it.* [8]*But if we have food and clothing, we will be content with that.* [9]*Those who want to get rich fall into temptation and a trap and into many foolish and harmful desires that plunge people into ruin and destruction.* [10]*For the love of money is a root of all kinds of evil. Some people, eager for money, have wandered from the faith and pierced themselves with many griefs.*

2b The words "These are the things you are to teach and insist on" serve both as a conclusion to the previous section and as the opening to this one. "These things" (*tauta*)[811] looks back on 5:1–6:2a, but it also prepares the way for what Paul is about to lay down by way of response to anticipated challenge (v. 3: "If anyone teaches otherwise . . .").

"Teach" (*didaske*) and "insist on" (*parakalei*) both render imperative verbs. The verb (*didaskō*) or noun (*didaskalia*) for teaching occurs some

811. The same near demonstrative plural pronoun is found in 1 Timothy elsewhere at 3:14; 4:6, 11, 15; 5:7, 21; 6:11.

twenty times in the PE (see commentary Introduction, IX.D), with eleven of these in 1 Timothy.[812] It is an obvious central emphasis of the letter, which is understandable in a movement begun by a man often called Rabbi[813] (teacher), and now furthered by his follower Paul, who received rabbinic training (Acts 22:3) and obviously plies teaching gifts. But the centrality of teaching is not primarily a function of Jesus's and Paul's personalities or backgrounds: it is inherent in a redemptive initiative calling for faith based on hearing. Teaching must occur if those who have heard are to pass along what they received. The process is perhaps epitomized in 2 Tim 2:1: "The things you have heard me say in the presence of many witnesses entrust to reliable people who will also be qualified to teach others."

As Paul nears the end of this epistle, he wants to emphasize Timothy's call and pastoral responsibility to teach, and to do so in accord with what Paul and other apostles have received.

Timothy is not only to teach but to "insist on." The same word (from *parakaleō*) is translated here "urge" (ESV, NABRE, NRSV), "exhort" (GNV, ISV, JUB, NET), and "encourage" (HCSB, LEB, NLT).[814] It is not enough to impart information. Pastoral teaching is zealous for the sake of those taught. It is also highly motivated by the unique substance and redemptive potential of the message conveyed. Paul spoke of a compulsion to make the message known and of woe if he did not (1 Cor 9:16). "Knowing the fear of the Lord," Paul's aim was to "persuade others" (2 Cor 5:11), not just to inform them. Timothy's goal as a pastoral teacher is to instruct but also to encourage appropriation of the truths duly learned. That is why a parallel verse (4:11) states, "*Command* and teach these things." "Insist on" in v. 2b should be seen as nearly synonymous[815] with the verb *parangellō* (to charge, command), which also dots 1 Timothy (1:3; 4:11; 5:7; 6:13, 17). Paul places before Timothy a most urgent matter. His best didactic skills and suasive gifts are called for.

3 "If anyone [*ei tis*] teaches otherwise" describes a likely hypothetical scenario.[816] Paul often uses "if anyone" language in negative situations: "If anyone destroys God's temple" (1 Cor 3:17); "If any of you think you are wise

812. The verb: 2:12; 4:11; 6:2; the noun: 1:10; 4:1, 6, 13, 16; 5:17; 6:1, 3.

813. See Matt 26:25, 49; Mark 9:5; 10:51; 11:21; 14:45; John 1:38, 49; 3:2, 26; 4:31; 6:25; 9:2; 11:8.

814. Used also in the PE at 1 Tim 1:3; 2:1; 5:1; 2 Tim 4:2; Titus 1:9; 2:6, 15. See discussion in commentary.

815. Noted also by Knight, 248.

816. See Wallace, *Greek Grammar*, 706, who notes this clause as an example of *ei* + indicative not always referring "to something particular." The indefinite pronoun *tis* signals that this is a projection of what Timothy may encounter, not a description of what he actually faces at the moment. The subjunctive marker *mē* in the next clause ("*does not* agree") confirms the general and hypothetical (though not unlikely) nature of what Paul warns against.

by the standards of this age" (1 Cor 3:18); "If anyone is not willing to work" (2 Thess 3:10 ESV). The same expression can also be positive: "If anyone aspires to the office of overseer" (1 Tim 3:1 ESV); "If any woman who is a believer has widows in her care" (5:16). Here it is negative because it precedes the subversive activity of teaching "otherwise." The verb *heterodidaskaleō* (to teach wrongly, teach what is false, teach false doctrine) appears elsewhere in the NT only in 1:3. Its position there and in the present verse serves to confirm that wrong or false teaching is a prevalent concern from this epistle's start to finish.

The hypothetical false teacher also "does not agree to the sound instruction of our Lord Jesus Christ." "Agree to" translates a form of *proserchomai*, a word used eighty-six times in the NT but only here in Paul. It normally means to approach (e.g., a person) or arrive (e.g., at a place). But it can also refer to approaching a deity or devoting oneself to a philosophy for the sake of full compliance with it. Epictetus, for example, envisions justifying himself before his (Stoic) god by asking: "Have I not always approached [*proselthon*] you with a cheerful countenance, ready to do your commands and to obey your signals?" (*Discourses* 3.5.9).[817] Paul draws on that sense here; he frets about the person with whom Timothy will have to deal who is not devoted to the teaching Timothy is charged to represent and to administer in the community that learns and lives by it.

"Sound instruction" is one of the great themes of the PE (see commentary Introduction, IX.D; see also earlier in 1 Tim 1:10). The Greek here could also be translated "agree to the sound words of our Lord Jesus Christ," all the more, since Paul has just drawn on such words in 5:18.[818] Either way, Paul warns against teaching and any teacher out of compliance with Christ's own teaching and the Christology that his teaching and earthly career imply.

Coordinate with "to the sound instruction of our Lord Jesus Christ" are the words "to godly teaching." Paul is equally concerned about (1) lack of conformity to instruction by, from, and about Christ and (2) failure of subsequent "teaching" (*didaskalia*) to be in accordance with (*kata*) *eusebeia* (godliness; see commentary Introduction, IX.B). Paul envisions a comprehensive and coherent body of understanding extending from what Jesus gave and represents to what Paul apprehends and has founded faith communities upon. This teaching

817. See also Epictetus, *Discourses* 1.26.9; 2.17.3; 3.5.12; 3.21.14; 3.26.13.

818. See Witherington, 283n442: "It would seem to be some teaching of Jesus himself, perhaps even a collection of such teaching." A written gospel, for example, would meet this description. See also Rom 16:25; 1 Thess 1:8; 2 Thess 3:1; Col 3:16, all of which mention the proclamation or word (*logos*) of Christ; cf. Schlatter, *Die Kirche der Griechen*, 160n1. Note also Guthrie's observation (123): "Spicq, who considers that Luke's Gospel is here meant, favours Schlatter's opinion that it is difficult to believe that Paul could so speak of the words of Jesus if no gospel existed in the community, Acts 20:35 furnishing an illuminating parallel."

produces living suffused with God and honoring to God through Christ—hence "godly teaching."

Verse 3 puts Timothy on alert against the likely influence of teachers and teachings out of sync with all he has seen from Paul in co-ministry with him over the past decade, as well as with "these things" (v. 2a) Paul has restated and reinforced in the epistle up to this point.

4 The protasis (if clause) in v. 3 now finds its apodosis (then clause) in a fairly detailed characterization of the hypothetical but not unlikely teacher who strays from the norms upon which Paul and Timothy agree.[819] The point could be manifold. First, this graphic if somewhat cryptic description could help Timothy recognize such dangerous aberration when he encounters it. Second, it could forewarn Timothy not to be taken in by these views if they happen to be packaged slickly, advanced skillfully, or find such a hearing among believers at Ephesus that Timothy might be tempted to follow along. Paul's description will predispose Timothy to healthy skepticism. Third, it provides a foil for the positive benefit of true gain (v. 6), contentment (v. 8), and pursuit of higher aims (vv. 11–14) to be commended later.

"Conceited" describes the possible pitfall of a new convert (3:6; see discussion there of the word in Philo and Josephus) and the wicked in the last days, including the present (2 Tim 3:4). The word could describe someone mentally ill[820] and may have that sense here, according to A. Malherbe (cited under *typhoō* in BDAG 1021 [3]); an illness metaphor also lies behind "unhealthy interest" later in the verse. The verb's perfect form describes the false teacher's characteristic disposition. Paul enlarges on "conceited" by adding that the person is bereft of understanding. By placing "nothing" first in its clause, Paul may be implying "understands absolutely nothing," a hyperbolic but telling charge.

What is rather the case (note *alla* in Gk. after "understands nothing") is sinister when compared with Paul's irenic understanding of the gospel's aim as "love, which comes from a pure heart and a good conscience and a sincere faith" (1:5). The false teacher is ill with, or has "a morbid craving for,"[821] "controversies and quarrels about words." On "controversies," see discussion at 2 Tim 2:23 and Titus 3:9, the only other occurrences of the word (*zētēsis*) in Paul. The word implies an inquiry that becomes contentious (as in John 3:25; Acts 15:2, 7). The false teacher has a sick obsession with stirring up disagree-

819. NIV translates "they are conceited. . . . They have an unhealthy interest." This rendering avoids the generic (but in some views gender-specific) "he." In Greek, however, the verbal forms are singular.

820. Saarinen, 100, sees the reference here to "a psychopathic character" with "a one-sided obsession."

821. See entry for *noseō* (be sick, ailing) in BDAG 678.

ment, which involves disputes "about words" (from *logomachia*), a word found in the NT only here (see 2 Tim 2:14 for the likewise singular occurrence of the verb form *logomachein*). It seems the false teacher's forte is stirring the pot in an ill-informed and dissension-creating manner.

The result is a fivefold collection of calamities,[822] the first four of which round out v. 4. First is "envy" (*phthonos*), which occurs nine times in the NT and five times in Paul,[823] with two of those occurrences in the PE (see Titus 3:3). Doctrinal controversies can create envy in various ways—some may envy the false teacher's influence or the apparent advantage of what the false teaching brings. When new teaching arises, there can easily be wistful resentment (envy) among those not (yet) part of the new movement but who can see its attraction. Alternately, a false teacher and his following may be full of envy of the majority whom they seek to convert, or of a leader among the majority like Timothy or Paul (see Phil 1:15, 17).

Second, "strife" (*eris*) occurs eight other times in Paul and is rendered in the NIV some half-dozen different ways: "strife" (Rom 1:29), "dissension" (Rom 13:13), "quarrels" (1 Cor 1:11), "quarreling" (3:3), "discord" (2 Cor 12:20; Gal 5:20), and "rivalry" (Phil 1:15). Whereas the Pauline mandate is "to keep the unity of the Spirit through the bond of peace" (Eph 4:3), the false teacher's calling card is obstreperous division.

Third, "malicious talk" (pl. of *blasphēmia*) is found two other times (both sing.) in Paul (Eph 4:31; Col 3:8). The verbal form plays a slightly larger role in the PE (see 1 Tim 1:20; Titus 2:5; 3:2). Paul refers to slanderous, abusive, or otherwise destructive verbal expression. It may or may not be denunciatory of God or Christ; only the context can determine, and what some view as blasphemy (like Jesus forgiving sins; Luke 5:21), others may recognize as valid. When true doctrine is defied, an inevitable entailment is unfavorable depiction of it by the allegedly fresh construal. If it is not the teaching that is inveighed against (see, e.g., Acts 28:22), it may be the teacher (as Christ was charged with blasphemies: Matt 26:65; Mark 14:64; Luke 5:21; John 10:33), which may be the error of a certain Alexander who did Paul harm and "strongly opposed [Paul's] message" (2 Tim 4:14).

Fourth, "evil suspicions."[824] The adjective "evil" (*ponēros*) is common in the NT (seventy-eight occurrences, thirteen of them in Paul, three of these in the PE [see also 2 Tim 3:13; 4:18]). Much rarer is the word translated "suspicions" (*hyponoia*), the noun form of a verb (*hyponoeō*) that means to think

822. Marshall, with Towner, observes that the literary construction is one in which "vices are related to their origin" (640).

823. See Rom 1:29; Gal 5:21; Phil 1:15.

824. Cf. Sir 3:24 NETS, where the same word combination in the singular is translated "evil fancy."

suspiciously or to suspect. Paul appears to have in mind speculative or fanciful convictions that are harmful in their claims or effects, some of which will be detailed in the next verse.

5 The language and logic of the verse present challenges. Marshall's characterization of the first half furnishes a helpful road map: "If people lose hold of the truth of the gospel, they become corrupt in mind and turn to quarrels that engender strife."[825]

"Constant friction" (*diaparatribē*)[826] is the fifth of Paul's negative characterizations of the false teacher and the quarrels he sparks, beginning in v. 3. There is no "and" in Greek; the rhetorical stream runs straight from "evil suspicions" (v. 4) to "constant friction." The last word in the series may be "particularly significant" and serves to sum up the four that precede.[827] The outcome of the warped teaching in vv. 3–4 is a continual fractious meltdown.[828]

This friction, perhaps the summation and culmination of the vices preceding it, has a baleful threefold effect.[829] First, people's thinking is corrupted (from *diaphtheirō*).[830] The divisive churning produced by "controversies and quarrels about words" (v. 4) impairs[831] the ability to observe clearly and reason logically, the "mind" (*nous*),[832] which is the faculty behind human observation and judgment. Paul flags this hazard elsewhere in the PE with respect to Jannes and Jambres (2 Tim 3:8: "men of depraved minds") and to Jewish false teachers at Crete, whose "minds and consciences are corrupted" (Titus 1:15). When Christ and gospel graces (v. 3) are spurned in favor of human theories and polemics (v. 4), clear thought is the first casualty. In a religion that depends on being "transformed by the renewing of your mind" (Rom 12:2), clouded thought is counterproductive.

These same dynamics not only ruin good thinking but also replace what the gospel message brings with the wranglings and animosities Paul has just described—people are "robbed [from *apostereō*] of the truth."[833] The verb means

825. Marshall, with Towner, 642.

826. "This is the only occurrence in ancient literature" of this word (Johnson, *First and Second Letters to Timothy*, 293). A related word *paratribai* is found in Polybius, *Histories* 2.36.5.

827. Marshall, with Towner, 641.

828. See BDF §116.4: "constant disputations."

829. Aquinas (79) sees three lamentable conditions: "The first pertains to a defect of natural light, the second to a defect of knowledge, the third to the vice of inordinate affections."

830. Paul uses this verb only one other time: to describe the "wasting away" of the believer's outward body in life while the inner person is "being renewed day by day" (2 Cor 4:16).

831. MM 157: the word is "a perfective compound" that "denotes usually a completed process of damage."

832. The word occurs nineteen times in Paul, three times in the PE.

833. This thought is paralleled in Titus 1:14, which speaks of "those who reject the truth."

to cheat or deprive others of what is theirs by rights.[834] God "wants all people to be saved and to come to a knowledge of the truth" (2:4), and the church is "the pillar and foundation of the truth" (3:15), but the people Paul describes have been defrauded of both truth (which here refers to the gospel)[835] and its benefits.

A third negative outcome is the flawed supposition that "godliness is a means to financial gain." At least this is what the false teacher (v. 3) and those he influences "think."[836] But Paul has already pointed out in this verse that their thinking is skewed and empty when it comes to substance—it is void of truth. It is little wonder, then, that they replace a conception of "godliness" mediated by Christ, who establishes eternal fellowship with God, with one that equates it with "financial gain" (*porismos*).[837]

It is important to note that the word translated "financial gain" does not in itself denote fantastic wealth or attainment of opulence.[838] The health-and-wealth teaching that has spread around the world in recent generations is not the best analogy for what Paul refers to, though Paul will shortly bring up the desire to "get rich" (v. 9). A better comparison might be with the mistaken notion of gospel faith Paul challenges at Corinth. The Corinthians (or those peddling "the word of God for profit" there [2 Cor 2:17]) were replacing Paul's theology of the cross (the only means of glimpsing true godliness) with a human doctrine of personal advancement (a sure means of squelching godliness). It is not a fixation with obscene wealth that Paul rejects; his objection here is more subtle. Wherever people think that the gospel message is primarily about better quality of life, personal well being, or gain as measured in a materialist human consumer society, they run afoul of Paul's strictures here.

What Paul objects to in his words to Timothy is that the false teacher and teaching (v. 3) have reduced "godliness" (*eusebeia*) to mere "financial gain," the procurement of material prosperity. Something fundamentally transcendent has been replaced by the mundane; human aims and pragmatic needs have supplanted the longing for God and fulfillment with God that separates humans from animals. The birthright of a gospel inheritance has been sold for a bowl of stew (like "Esau despised his birthright" [Gen 25:34]) or hog feed (like the prodigal son [Luke 15:16]) by comparison, as Paul sees it. He points to a better way in coming verses.

6 Paul defines godliness (*eusebeia*) in a way that sets it apart from the false conception against which he warns Timothy (vv. 3–5). Such godliness is

834. Paul uses the word three other times: 1 Cor 6:7, 8; 7:5.

835. Marshall, with Towner, 642.

836. Paul uses the word two other times: 1 Cor 7:26, 36.

837. The word occurs twice in the LXX (NETS): Wis 13:19 ("means of livelihood"); 14:2 ("gain"). *GELS* defines it as "pecuniary gain" (578).

838. Note Philo's twelve uses, which mostly pertain to procuring daily necessities.

"great gain" indeed, for it is accompanied by (*meta*; NIV "with") "contentment" (*autarkeia*). The definition of this word and how it qualifies "godliness" are key to Paul's positive thrust.

Autarkeia occurs one other time in the NT: "And God is able to bless you abundantly, so that in all things at all times, having all that you need [*autarkeia*], you will abound in every good work" (2 Cor 9:8). *Autarkeia* is translated here "what one needs." ESV translates "sufficiency." In this verse Paul refers primarily to external support: God will bless the Corinthians with what they require. The sole use of the word in the LXX conveys the same sense: "Happy is the man whom God remembers in due proportion to sufficiency [*autarkeia*]; if man has too much, he sins" (Pss Sol 5:15 NETS). As the proverb has it: "Give me neither poverty nor riches, but give me only my daily bread" (Prov 30:8). These passages taken together describe broadly the ideal of external *autarkeia*.

In 1 Tim 6:6 Paul refers to inner *autarkeia*. When used in that sense, the word refers to being content and self-sufficient. He uses the adjectival form of the same word when he writes, "I have learned to be content [*autarkēs*] whatever the circumstances" (Phil 4:11; this is its only NT occurrence).[839] Major philosophical schools of the era (Stoics and Cynics) deemed this disposition a prized virtue, with an emphasis on harmony with circumstances (Stoicism) or autonomy from support by others (Cynics). "One of the most common doctrines of philosophers and those influenced by them was contentment: people should be self-sufficient, recognizing that they need nothing other than what Nature has given them."[840] Their understanding of this ideal is conveyed by the English term "self-sufficiency."

Yet, Paul was neither a Stoic nor a Cynic.[841] Paul's "very strong . . . sense of grace precludes . . . the Stoic notion of total self-determination."[842] He did not believe in an autonomous self, since (unlike Greek philosophers) he believed in one God, the creator of the world and its inhabitants, upon whom all depend and with whom all may enjoy fellowship through faith in Christ (recall 1 Tim 2:3–6). He did not prize human reason as the ultimate source of truth, as did the Greeks, but believed in God's very words (*ta logia tou theou* [Rom 3:2]) the Scriptures as the source and norm of truth accessible to humans. To live on this earth in the fullest sense is to have what the Scriptures foretold and commend: Christ (Phil 1:21). For Paul this, or rather he, is "the secret of being content in any and every situation, whether well fed or hungry, whether living in plenty or in want" (Phil 4:12). This statement does not describe a man

839. It is found six times in the LXX: 4 Macc 9:9; Prov 30:8; Sir 5:1; 11:24; 31:28; 40:18.

840. Keener, *Bible Background Commentary*, 613.

841. So also, with references to the philosophers, Marshall, with Towner, 644–45.

842. Bassler, 110.

sufficient in himself (Cynics) or in harmony with Nature and indifferent to circumstances (Stoics). It rather describes a person for whom "the Lord [i.e., Christ] is near," so that he can reassure other believers who know that nearness, "The peace of God, which transcends all understanding, will guard your hearts and your minds in Christ Jesus" (Phil 4:5, 7). These verses express both contentment in the Pauline sense and its source.

The false teaching at Ephesus did not promote Christ to such an end, as demonstrated by the fruit Paul lists in vv. 4–5. Their "godliness" is of a different source and quality from the "great gain" godliness (*eusebeia*) that the PE so frequently commend, which, it is now clear, is "godliness with contentment" with Christ and his benefits. Paul furthers understanding of this conviction in coming verses.

7 This verse (with its reference to "we") gives a reason (*gar,* for) for Paul's and Timothy's contentment with living out Christ—true "great gain," rather than pursuing the ideals and material *porismos* (gain) championed by the false teaching.

"We brought nothing into the world"[843] is self-evident from the account in Genesis of human origins and confirmed every time a baby is born. As Job observed, "Naked I came from my mother's womb, and naked I will depart" (Job 1:21). This truth is paralleled in other ancient writings both Jewish (Philo) and Greco-Roman (Seneca). Since we brought nothing into the world—our acquisition of personal possessions is not essential to life in its most basic sense—it is possible that such acquisition does not furnish the key to well-being in life.

The second half of the verse is just as self-evident. It is supported by Eccl 5:14 LXX, which restates and extends Job's wisdom: "Just as he came out from his mother's womb naked, he will return to go as he came, and he will not take anything for his toil that may go in his hand" (NETS).

Verse 7 overall confirms the wisdom of what v. 6 commends, which was a repudiation of the notion in v. 5 that "godliness is a means to financial gain." That is a flawed conception. Birth and death both illustrate the tenuous relation between life and material goods. Paul wants to relativize (not trivialize or eliminate)[844] the importance of earthly acquisitions, since he observes people

843. Quoted by Polycarp in *Phil.* 4:1: "But the love of money is the beginning of all troubles. Knowing, therefore, that we brought nothing into the world and cannot take anything out, let us arm ourselves with the weapons of righteousness, and let us first teach ourselves to follow the commandment of the Lord." For discussion of Polycarp's use of 1 Timothy and Paul's letters more generally, see Johnson, *First and Second Letters to Timothy*, 298–300. Johnson concludes that (1) Polycarp does draw from 1 Timothy, and (2) he regarded it (along with other Pauline letters he cites) as written by Paul. Polycarp also "assumed that his readers would recognize the words as those of Paul" (300).

844. See Towner, *Letters*, 400: "While he does not devalue human earthly life in any sense, he does force the reader to view it in temporary terms."

tempted to enlist God in their material quest. Paul essentially echoes Jesus's warning that "not even when one has an abundance does his life consist of his possessions" (Luke 12:15). True godliness relishes life in a deeper vein.

The grammar of v. 7 presents a challenge in that the second half starts with *hoti* (because). Johnson renders "because neither can we take anything out of it" but admits the Greek wording "is very awkward."[845] After listing nine different proposals, Marshall concludes that none "is wholly satisfying.[846] He suggests the translation "We brought nothing into this world, because we cannot even take anything out," and he points to Barrett's more periphrastic rendering: "There was no point in bringing anything into the world with us, because we shall not be able to take anything out."[847]

A possibility mentioned but dismissed by Marshall is that the *hoti* introduces words regarded by Paul as a citation.[848] This may deserve more consideration. It is implied by the way the clause and v. 8 are printed in NA^{28}: as confessional, traditional, or even poetic material. (Notice the endings in the three inset lines in NA^{28}: *metha, mata, metha*. And in all three cases the accented syllable is the same [antepenult] and sounds roughly the same.) But no extant source contains these words. Yet, what they express is paralleled in various sources. Possibly the lines were known to Paul as colloquial wisdom in one of the many social settings he had frequented in his travels.

The challenge in wording does not jeopardize the general force of the statement's wisdom. Birth and death both teach that it would be folly to pin even a life philosophy, let alone Christian theology, on such a fleeting hope as material acquisitions.

8 "Food" (*diatrophē*, also more broadly "sustenance") is a common word.[849] So is *skepasma* (clothing), though both words occur only here in the NT. Other words do occur that mean the same thing. The realities to which Paul refers are not lofty or obscure.

What is elusive is the ideal he names: contentment with no more than life's basics. "We will be content" translates a form of *arkeō*. In the active voice it means to satisfy, to furnish what is necessary, as in 2 Cor 12:9: "But he said to me, 'My grace is sufficient [*arkei*] for you, for my power is made perfect in weakness.'"[850] In the passive, as here, it means to be satisfied with something.[851]

845. Johnson, *First and Second Letters to Timothy*, 294.

846. Marshall, with Towner, 648.

847. Barrett, *Pastoral Epistles*, 84. See also Towner, *Letters*, 400.

848. Marshall, with Towner, 647, option *e*. Cf. Gal 6:7–8.

849. 1 Macc 6:49 LXX; twelve times in Josephus and numerous other references in BDAG 238.

850. The other active uses in the NT: Matt 25:9; John 6:7; 14:8.

851. The other passive uses in the NT: Luke 3:14 (soldiers content with wages); Heb 13:5; 3 John 10.

Heb 13:5 conveys a closely related sentiment: "Keep your lives free from the love of money and be content [*arkoumenoi*] with what you have, because God has said, 'Never will I leave you; never will I forsake you.'" Consciousness of God's presence (like his grace in 2 Cor 12:9) plus life's basics are rich fare.

It is important to note that this is not an adaptation of an ideal of Hellenistic philosophy. Nor is it an endorsement of poverty.[852] It is rather an application to the situation at Ephesus of what Paul stated more expansively in Rom 8:35 and is in fact an entailment of his theology of the cross and union with Christ: trouble, hardship, persecution, famine, nakedness, danger, sword—no such things can separate the believer from God's care, in the form of "the love of God that is in Christ Jesus our Lord" (Rom 8:28), in this world and the next.

The false teaching Timothy faces has, among its other shortcomings, elevated "financial gain" (v. 5) to a level that ironically proves its bankruptcy. "A religiosity that made the accumulation of wealth either the point of profession or the proof of righteousness is deeply inimical to the spirit of Paul's teaching."[853] If God does grant wealth, and if a believer has not sold his or her soul to acquire it, Paul will later give directions for its proper utilization (see on vv. 17–19 below).

9 A keen observer of world Christianity notes, "Every society has its own versions of Elmer Gantry, people who use religious deception as a money-making tool."[854] An African reviewer of a major monograph on global evangelicalism notes that this study shows that "money, power, and influence . . . constitute important values" in this movement.[855] "A new crop of charismatic entrepreneurs who challenge the Western missionary mind-set that equated poverty with spirituality now lead some of the largest conservative evangelical churches" in the regions studied. Economic "opportunity and upward mobility" are central in this "new Christianity."[856]

The allure of material plenty is understandable and irrepressible. Paul glimpses a first-century precursor of it at Ephesus and counsels Timothy regarding its dangers. His colorful depiction points to a threefold calamity and ultimate demise awaiting those gripped by inordinate pursuit of wealth.

Paul uses the word translated "want to" (*boulomai*) nine times. All but once (1 Cor 12:11) he refers to something he desires or requests.[857] "Get rich" sounds crass and can refer metaphorically to over-the-top wealth (1 Cor 4:8, referring to the Corinthians' arrogant sense of their own spiritual attainment).

852. As Towner, *Letters*, 401, notes, citing Marshall and Stott.

853. Johnson, *First and Second Letters to Timothy*, 304.

854. Philip Jenkins, "When Does Faith Become Fraudulent?," *ChrCent*, August 3, 2016, 45.

855. The monograph: Offutt, *New Centers of Global Evangelicalism.*

856. J. Kwabena Asamoah-Gyadu, review of *New Centers of Global Evangelicalism in Latin America and Africa*, by S. Offutt, *IBMR* 40.2 (April 2016): 193.

857. Elsewhere in the PE, see 2:8; 5:14; Titus 3:8.

But in two of Paul's uses it refers to wealth God bestows (Rom 10:12) or that Christ gave up in order to grant to believers (2 Cor 8:9). It is both possible and desirable for believers "to be rich in good deeds" (v. 18).

By "rich" in v. 9 Paul has in mind those running with the orientation described in vv. 3–5. They have neither sought nor grasped the deepest riches of sufficiency in Christ, attended by quite modest material provision if that is what God grants (vv. 6–8). The ferment of bad teaching and corrupted thinking leads them to seek gratification in religiously justified material acquisition. Paul projects where this is apt to lead them.

First, they "fall into temptation." On "fall" (from *empiptō*), see 3:6–7, the only other occurrences of the word in Paul. In literature more widely it "often depicts the unexpected and unfortunate entrance into an experience or condition that is better avoided."[858]

Paul uses the word translated "temptation" (*peirasmos*) twice in 1 Cor 10:13.[859] Using the cognate verb, Paul expresses concern that "in some way the tempter had tempted you" (1 Thess 3:5), a reminder that Satan works behind the scenes to draw the faithful away from God's best intent for them. This drawing away is happening at Ephesus, which causes Paul to warn against an unhealthy desire for wealth. Aquinas comments that riches tempt, insofar as they "allure and lead to other sins."[860] "Things perceived to be needs multiply, and the longing for pleasures gains force."[861]

Second, they also fall into "a trap." See almost identical language in 3:7, referring to the need of a would-be overseer to be of good repute. Here Aquinas's comment is that riches "envelop in a snare, since riches are a temptation for those who do not have them, but a snare for those who do, since they do not willingly return that which they have taken."[862]

Third, they also fall "into many foolish and harmful desires." This may be seen as the result of the previous two steps of descent. The key word here is "desires" (from *epithymia*).[863] Desire is God-given; Jesus himself possessed and expressed it (Luke 22:15). But like the mind that God likewise gives and that can be corrupted (v. 5), desires can be "foolish" (*anoētos*,[864] a word suggesting "mindless" or the opposite of what marks a wise person). Desires can also be "harmful" (*blaberos*), a NT hapax. Epictetus uses it to denote the danger posed

858. Towner, *Letters*, 402.

859. Paul's only other use, Gal 4:14, refers to a trial or ordeal.

860. Aquinas, 81.

861. Schlatter, *Die Kirche der Griechen*, 165.

862. Aquinas, 81.

863. The word occurs nineteen times in Paul, six of these in the PE. See 2 Tim 2:22; 3:6; 4:3; Titus 2:12; 3:3.

864. Six NT occurrences; see elsewhere Luke 24:25; Rom 1:14; Gal 3:1, 3; Titus 3:3 (see discussion of word uses there).

by wolves (*Discourses* 1.3.7) or other wild beasts (2.10.14). In the modern setting one might think of rich athletes, celebrities, politicians, or, in some quarters, church leaders with seemingly endless money and the risky, self-destructive behavior to which wealth sometimes leads.

These desires "plunge people into ruin and destruction." The word translated "plunge" occurs one other time in the NT, describing how the waves almost sank a fishing boat (Luke 5:7; cf. Epictetus, *Discourses* 3.2.18). In its one LXX occurrence it describes the treacherous drowning of some 200 people (2 Macc 12:4). Paul envisions harmful desires torpedoing the unwary and sending them down to "ruin [*olethros*][865] and destruction [*apōleia*],"[866] two words that are here probably synonymous.[867] They describe present deleterious effects "which last into the next life."[868] Eschatological judgment is the ultimate end.

In sum, Paul reminds Timothy, in graphic terms relevant to his field of service at Ephesus, of what the sacred writings they had known from youth (see 2 Tim 3:15) taught: "One eager to get rich will not go unpunished" (Prov 28:20). This is not because material goods are evil but because, in the scenario Paul envisions, God in Christ has been set aside, or the truth of who he is has been perverted, in a move to gratify desires by lesser means.

10 Paul extends the line of thought begun in the previous verse. "For" (*gar*) signals that v. 10 serves to explain v. 9. Why do people follow their urge to get rich and then plunge to destruction? Paul's answer in v. 10: *philargyria*—the love of money.[869]

Paul was not the first to detect the danger lurking in this love. An ancient proverb called *philargyria* "the capital city all of evils."[870] Paul replaces "capital city" with "root" but otherwise quotes the proverb. He joined others in recognizing that "the dream of wealth can gain a demonic hold over a person or a nation. In its bib[lical] context . . . the saying is grounded in a person's relationship with God. Like Adam and Eve's grasping after the forbidden fruit in the garden of Eden, a person's selfish amassing of material possessions sug-

865. Used elsewhere in the NT only by Paul: 1 Cor 5:5 (destruction of flesh by Satan); 1 Thess 5:3 (eschatological destruction at Christ's return); 2 Thess 1:9 (everlasting punishment, "shut out from the presence of the Lord").

866. Used eighteen times in the NT, five times in Paul: see also Rom 9:22; Phil 1:28; 3:19; 2 Thess 2:3.

867. Towner, *Letters*, 403.

868. Marshall, with Towner, 651.

869. On the issue of money here and throughout the PE, see V. Verbrugge and K. Krell, *Paul and Money: A Biblical and Theological Analysis of the Apostle's Teachings and Practices* (Grand Rapids: Zondervan, 2015), esp. ch. 11.

870. Diogenes Laertius, *Vitae* 6.50; see also *HCNT*, which traces the saying to Stobaeus, *Anthology* 3.417 (= III.10.37).

gests that life is no longer being accepted thankfully from the hand of God. Love of money erects a selfish dividing wall against God and our neighbors; it is the germ of total alienation from God."[871] In calling love of money "a root," Paul recognizes that it is often concealed from view and that it gives rise to ills and evils that grow out of it. It often serves as the hidden motivation driving behaviors that at first glance have other sources or aims. When Jesus taught "You cannot serve both God and money" (Luke 16:13) and religious zealots listening sneered, who would have known they were not only apparently earnest and pious Pharisees but *philargyroi*—lovers of money (Luke 16:14)? Jesus responded, "You are the ones who justify yourselves in the eyes of others, but God knows your hearts. What people value highly is detestable in God's sight" (Luke 16:14).

Insight into something like this very truth[872] enables Paul to identify the craving for financial wherewithal that drives "some people" (*tines*; see table 21 and discussion at 5:15). They are "eager for money."[873] "Eager" is from the same word (*oregō*) used by Paul in 3:1 about the person who "aspires" to be an overseer.[874] All humans have drives. The trick is to tap into the right source for fueling and the right goals for directing them. When the root of drives is greed, the result will be negative. Paul observes two results.

First, people rooted in money-love "have wandered from the faith." This statement assumes they had connection to the faith, an indication that in vv. 9–10 Paul harks back to those close enough to the church to be plaguing it with the conviction that "godliness is a means to financial gain" (v. 6). Such a belief already diverges from true godliness, as vv. 6–8 explain. They had "wandered from the faith," in the words of v. 10.

"Faith" here is the *fides quae* (see discussion at 1:19), the core content or substance of Christian doctrine or teaching. People may think they can combine loyalty to God with devotion to mammon. But to start down that path is already to stray from Christ's narrow "road that leads to life" (Matt 7:14). The word translated "wandered" (*apoplanaō*) is used only one other time in the NT: in Mark 13:22, where "false messiahs and false prophets" threaten to lead astray (*apoplanan*) "even the elect." Desire for wealth can have the same effect.

871. *NIDNTTE* 4:608.

872. For the theory that the passage is more amenable to a Marxist analysis, see Krause, 126–27, who asserts that "the letter writer's class location and ideological agenda against his opponents are clear."

873. More precisely, the Greek indicates that their desire is directed toward *philargyria*—they crave the desire that seeks fulfillment in finances. But "Death and Destruction are never satisfied, and neither are human eyes" (Prov 27:20). The desire never grants the gratification it appears to offer.

874. On the positive side, the same word describes those "longing for a better country—a heavenly one" in Heb 11:16. There are only three NT uses of the word.

Schlatter explains: "You cannot make your goal the acquisition of money and at the same time receive direction for your will and actions from the faith."[875] For the faith sets a different goal for those who embrace it.

Second, people rooted in money-love have "pierced themselves with many griefs." The placement of "themselves" in Greek is at the head of the clause, which may emphasize their own role and culpability in caving in to money-love's siren song. "Pierced" translates a form of *peripeirō*, a NT hapax, which means to impale.[876] The image is arresting, not to say gruesome. A desire so alluring lances those who give in to it "with many griefs [from *odynē*]."[877] Yet, it is self-inflicted woe.

So concludes a section that began, "These are the things you are to teach and insist on" (v. 2b). Paul has dispensed a world of pastoral wisdom, much of it diagnostic. In the letter's concluding section he will exhort Timothy what to do with it.

B. Final Charge to Timothy (6:11–21)

> [11] *But you, man of God, flee from all this, and pursue righteousness,*
> *godliness, faith, love, endurance and gentleness.* [12] *Fight the good fight of*
> *the faith. Take hold of the eternal life to which you were called when you*
> *made your good confession in the presence of many witnesses.* [13] *In the*
> *sight of God, who gives life to everything, and of Christ Jesus, who while*
> *testifying before Pontius Pilate made the good confession, I charge you*
> [14] *to keep this command without spot or blame until the appearing of our*
> *Lord Jesus Christ,* [15] *which God will bring about in his own time—God, the*
> *blessed and only Ruler, the King of kings and Lord of lords,* [16] *who alone is*
> *immortal and who lives in unapproachable light, whom no one has seen*
> *or can see. To him be honor and might forever. Amen.* [17] *Command those*
> *who are rich in this present world not to be arrogant nor to put their hope*
> *in wealth, which is so uncertain, but to put their hope in God, who richly*
> *provides us with everything for our enjoyment.* [18] *Command them to do*
> *good, to be rich in good deeds, and to be generous and willing to share.*
> [19] *In this way they will lay up treasure for themselves as a firm foundation*
> *for the coming age, so that they may take hold of the life that is truly life.*
> [20] *Timothy, guard what has been entrusted to your care. Turn away from*

875. Schlatter, *Die Kirche der Griechen*, 166.

876. See Josephus, *Jewish War* 3.296 (run through with swords); 4.425 (with Roman arrows).

877. The word occurs elsewhere in the NT only in Rom 9:2: "I have great sorrow and unceasing *anguish* in my heart."

godless chatter and the opposing ideas of what is falsely called knowledge,
21 *which some have professed and in so doing have departed from the faith.*
Grace be with you all.

11 The first word, "but" (*de*), marks a major shift in the direction of the discourse. So does "you," which is a personal pronoun of direct address that marks the PE.[878] Yet another dramatic touch is the words "man of God," which in Greek are preceded by an untranslated interjection that could be rendered "O!" (see also 6:20). It occurs in Paul for rhetorical effect in diatribes or when, as here, he conveys great passion.[879] The heightened tone indicates that Paul is ramping up to leave final and lasting impressions.

"Man of God," which receives little note in some commentaries,[880] is changed to "person of God" in Witherington's translation.[881] This is the only time the expression occurs in the NT. For Jews like Paul and Titus, it would resonate with the same words that appear in over sixty passages of the LXX.[882] Moses is "the man of God."[883] So are various prophets like Shemaiah (1 Kgs 12:22), Elijah (1 Kgs 17:18, 24; 2 Kgs 1:9–13), Elisha (2 Kgs 8:4), and David (2 Chr 8:14; Neh 12:24, 36). Paul's language evokes a startling correlation between figures in OT times who received unusual commissionings (on Timothy's call, see v. 12) and enablements from God and his young(er) understudy Timothy.

This correlation is unlikely to indicate that Paul saw Timothy as a new Moses, Elijah, or David. But it does invest Timothy's role and position with the gravity of a tradition in which God leads his people through chosen shepherds and teachers of his word. And since "Timothy is addressed as a leader whose way of life is to be an example to all believers," there is a sense in which all believers are summoned by these words. What Paul writes is "to be followed by all of God's people," albeit "especially by their leaders," starting with Timothy.[884]

Both v. 11 and v. 12 are dominated by imperatives. "Flee" refers to the evils cited in the previous section and perhaps in the whole epistle to this

878. See also 2 Tim 1:18; 2:1; 3:10 (see commentary for discussion), 14; 4:5, 15; Titus 2:1.

879. The other Pauline occurrences: Rom 2:1, 3; 9:20; 11:33; Gal 3:1.

880. For example, Johnson, *First and Second Letters to Timothy*, 305. For thorough treatment, see Marshall, with Towner, 656–57.

881. Witherington, 291.

882. Dibelius and Conzelmann, 87, deny the tie between Timothy and "the image of the 'man of God' which the OT suggests." This separation is plausible if the PE are non-Pauline and "Paul" and "Timothy" are constructs. But if the PE are from the Paul and Timothy (both Jewish) found in the NT documents, the association between "man of God" and the dozens of LXX passages that contain the phrase is somewhat likely.

883. See in the LXX Deut 33:1; Josh 14:6; 1 Chr 23:14; 2 Chr 24:6; 30:6; 1 Esd 5:48; Ezra 3:2. See also Towner, "1–2 Timothy and Titus," 902.

884. Marshall, with Towner, 657.

point. Paul uses the word (*pheugō*) only three other times, most notably in 2 Tim 2:22: "Flee the evil desires of youth" (see commentary there for discussion).[885] There are things to engage and confront, and there are things with which one deals by giving a wide berth. The pseudogodliness of materialist ministry (v. 5) and money-love (v. 10) ranks among the latter.

"Pursue" following "flee" displays what may be called Paul's positive ethic. Avoiding or repudiating the bad may be necessary, but it is seldom an end in itself. The gospel empowers pursuit of the excellent in personal communion with God, not just forbidding wrong based on God's law, a moralistic conception of what relationship with the God of Abraham, Isaac, and Jacob in Christ calls for.[886] For every No! in Paul there is generally a corresponding and relational Yes![887]

Paul's Yes here is sixfold, perhaps corresponding loosely to the vices listed in vv. 4–5.[888] For the pursuit of righteousness, faith, and love, see commentary at 2 Tim 2:22, where Paul names the same priorities. Righteousness can be viewed as living out what union with Christ through faith imparts to the believer, as in Phil 1:11: "filled with the fruit of righteousness that comes through Jesus Christ—to the glory and praise of God." "Righteousness" and "faith" "sum up comprehensively the ethical and spiritual outlook of the PE."[889] "Love" is sometimes placed first by Paul (1 Cor 13:13; Col 3:14), but Christ's righteousness and faith in him are the means for that love to be poured out into believers (Rom 5:1, 5). Different settings call for emphasis on now one, now another of the communicable attributes of God conveyed through the gospel.

To these Paul adds "godliness" (*eusebeia*), already mentioned repeatedly in this letter.[890] He also adds "endurance" (*hypomonē*), a critical posture if Timothy is to fulfill Paul's overarching command to remain at Ephesus (1:3). Elsewhere Paul points to his own endurance (2 Tim 3:10; see commentary there for additional Pauline references and discussion) and instructs Titus to confirm older men in this characteristic (Titus 2:2). Finally, Paul also calls Timothy to the pursuit of gentleness (*praupathia*), a word found only here in the NT. It conveys "the opp[osite] of an overbearing attitude" (BDAG 861).

885. See also 1 Cor 6:18; 10:14; both of which, however, are plural in form and not singular as here, addressed to Timothy.

886. This same moralism is also at the center of Islam: see Michael Cook, *Forbidding Wrong in Islam* (Cambridge: Cambridge University Press, 2003). The generally negative portrayal of historic Christianity in this book, however, is to be regarded with caution.

887. Note, for example, in Ephesians: no to falsehood, yes to speaking truth (4:25); no to anger, yes to reconciliation (4:26; the Stoics just called for apathy); no to stealing, yes to work supporting benevolent acts (4:28); no to degrading speech, yes to encouragement (4:29).

888. So Johnson, *First and Second Letters to Timothy*, 305.

889. Marshall, with Towner, 658.

890. See 2:2; 3:16; 4:7, 8; 6:3, 5, 6. See also commentary Introduction, IX.B.

Johnson renders "a generous temper."[891] "Gentle" can imply weak, but it can also suggest strength deployed with sensitivity and empathy. Paul likely means the latter.

The cluster of six characteristics worthy of Timothy's pursuit are for the most part Pauline staples in his writings, in the life he lived, or both. For example, although he does not use the word for "gentle" elsewhere in his known writings, he uses a synonym (*epieikēs*) when stating overseer qualifications (3:3), and he uses yet another synonym in instructing Titus to direct believers "always to be gentle [*praütēs*] toward everyone" (Titus 3:2). He commends gentleness with these or other words in other passages.[892] As for his life, while we cannot interview witnesses regarding how Paul was received, he does describe the desired effect of his presence: "Even though as apostles of Christ we [i.e., Paul, Silas, and Timothy] could have asserted our authority. Instead, we were like young children among you. Just as a nursing mother cares for her children, so we cared for you. Because we loved you so much, we were delighted to share with you not only the gospel of God but our lives as well" (1 Thess 2:6–8).

In this context, we can regard Paul's six targets for Timothy's pursuit as an informal summary of a few of the main graces the gospel imparts to those who receive and walk in it over the course of time. To do justice to these six (and others closely related) would be the business of a theology of Paul. But Timothy, having ministered with Paul and been taught by Paul, did not need a structured exposition. Just a few of the main headings of the Pauline synthesis were sufficient to impress him with Paul's will regarding how he should *act* (not merely think or believe) in light of the epistle thus far.

12 Following "flee" and "pursue" come two more action mandates: "fight" and "take hold."

Regarding fighting "the good fight of faith," see commentary at 2 Tim 4:7, where Paul testifies that he has done just that. But for Timothy at this point, his greatest service and hardest strivings may still lie before him. Hence Paul's rallying words.

Johnson's translation "engage the noble athletic contest for the faith" is creative but too insistent on preserving the athletic metaphor (clearly present, e.g., in 1 Cor 9:25). Johnson also sees only "noble" here in *kalos* (good, beautiful, noble);[893] in a battle context, the sense could easily be "valiant." The Greek words translated "fight" (*agōnizomai* [verb: to fight, struggle, compete]; *agōn* [noun: a fight, struggle, competition]) are also used in warfare contexts: "Jesus said, 'My kingdom is not of this world. If it were, my servants would fight

891. Johnson, *First and Second Letters to Timothy*, 306.

892. See 1 Cor 4:21; 2 Cor 10:1; Gal 5:23; Eph 4:2; Phil 4:5; Col 3:12.

893. Barrett's "great race" is also apt (85). Quinn and Wacker opt for "fine": "Contend in the fine contest . . . you made that fine profession" (518–19; see also 529–31).

[*agōnizomai*] to prevent my arrest by the Jewish leaders'" (John 18:36). Timothy is not in a race or game against the evils at Ephesus so much as serving as "a good soldier of Christ Jesus" (2 Tim 2:3).[894] At stake is "the faith," the message he is charged to promulgate and the doctrine he has been trained to pass along faithfully. "This command has to do with doctrine,"[895] not just courageous action with religious sincerity.

Regarding "eternal life," see 1:16 (note references in commentary above) and Titus 1:2 (note additional discussion) and 3:7 (more discussion). This is not merely a duration of life in the age to come but a quality of life in the present age. "Take hold" (*epilabou*) here means to fully appropriate (see also v. 19 below; these are the only Pauline uses of the word).[896] It is one of only two aorist imperatives in 1 Timothy (the other is "guard" in 6:20), all others being present. The root word *epilambanomai* can convey just as violent an image as the word-group associated with fighting.[897] Paul is calling for pursuit (v. 11) that is proactive, aggressive, and tenacious. The picture of Jacob wrestling with God, so to speak, comes to mind (Gen 32:22–32), or Abraham sweating it out in sacrificing Isaac (Gen 22:1–19), or any of the saints in Heb 11 who went to their grave striving and hoping but unrequited in this life. Or there is the NT heritage of Jesus's followers who "left everything."[898]

Paul calls on Timothy, in a word, to live radically in the light of the age to come ("eternal life"). His own testimony in Phil 3:8–14 is an excellent commentary on the orientation and effort he expects from Timothy as he presses on "toward the goal to win the prize for which God has called [him] heavenward in Christ Jesus" (Phil 3:14).

As Paul was called heavenward, so Timothy was called to "eternal life" when he made his "good confession in the presence of many witnesses." Many attempts have been made to imagine exactly what Paul refers to. Belleville, for example, imagines "a profession of faith before the local authorities," drawing on Heb 13:23 and mention of Timothy's release from prison.[899] NIV's "when

894. Otherwise Keener, *Bible Background Commentary*, 614, who favors the imagery of a track meet. For oscillation between the two images, including the expression "we must not shrink when we are engaged in the greatest combat [*ton agōna ton megiston agōnizomenois*], but we must even take blows [*plēgas*]," see Epictetus, *Discourses* 3.25 (quote from 25.2). His argument is that sometimes a "contest" (*agōn*) is not just a contest but mortal conflict.

895. Ryken, 269.

896. See Guthrie, 127.

897. This word is used, for example, in Acts this way: "They *seized* Paul and Silas and dragged them into the marketplace to face the authorities" (16:19); "Then the crowd there *turned on* Sosthenes the synagogue leader and beat him" (18:17); "*Seizing* Paul, they dragged him from the temple" (21:30).

898. For example, Matt 19:27; Mark 10:28; Luke 5:11, 28.

899. Belleville, 120.

you made your good confession" points to a temporal setting, but the wording could also stress purpose. Eternal life was "that for which" (*eis hēn*) Timothy was called, and the same words could be assumed after the subsequent "and" (*kai*): ". . . and for which you confessed." The point is not a certain day and protocol in an initiation ceremony but Timothy's motivation. Or to turn it around, Paul is calling to mind God's promise and assurance that moved Timothy to begin the trek that has landed him in challenging if not dire straits at Ephesus.

Marshall is probably correct that, despite all the commentary speculation, "there is no indication that" Timothy's "good confession" "was anything more than a confession of Jesus Christ as Lord."[900] It was a good (or noble or valiant: *kalos*) testimony, just as he is now summoned to a valiant fight. Moreover, it was made "in the presence of many witnesses." This could be the motivation of prospective shame: what will they think if you falter now? But it could also be corroboration of his confession's validity: it was a public commitment to things not done in a corner (Acts 26:26), to Jesus who made "the good confession" himself (v. 13 below), affirmed by the presence of witnesses (in both OT and NT a validation of an event's truth) already in the body of Christ who welcomed the new addition.

The "many witnesses" image should be seen not as motivation to avoid shame but as a reminder of a noble heritage (already in Timothy's spiritual DNA from his mother and grandmother; 2 Tim 1:5). This heritage helps make an invisible God (see v. 16 below) and a promised (but not yet fully realized) future more real and relevant to everyday decisions and actions than the unpleasantries that pastors must often navigate, whether by fleeing, pursuing, fighting, seizing, or some combination of them all.

13 In Greek the first words are "I charge you." The complementary infinitive does not come until the first word of v. 14: "to keep."[901] For clarity the NIV moves "I charge you" to the end of v. 13. This change may ease comprehension for some English readers, but the emphasis of the original, at the outset of the verse, bears notice. Paul leans heavily on Timothy with yet another recourse to a key word-group appearing repeatedly in this epistle: *parangellō* (verb: to charge, command with force; see 1:3; 4:11; 5:7); *parangelia* (noun: a stern order

900. Marshall, with Towner, 661. This understanding would comport with Paul's sole use of *homologia* (confession) outside of 1 Tim 6; see 2 Cor 9:13. Barrett, *Pastoral Epistles*, 87, accepts Calvin's view (which Marshall rejects) that Timothy's "confession" "was not that which is expressed in words, but rather what is actually performed; and that not in a single instance merely, but throughout his whole ministry." There is much to say for this understanding, and there may be some of both explanations latent in Paul's words to Timothy. Aquinas (85) pictures Paul telling Timothy, "you acknowledged the good fight in your consecration, when you were ordained to the episcopate." Dibelius and Conzelmann, 88, see in this confession "baptism or 'ordination.'"

901. For similar use of this verb, followed by appeal to Christ, followed by the action called for, see 1 Cor 7:10; 2 Thess 3:6, 12.

or command; see 1:5, 18). Knight sees Paul's apostolic authority implied in this choice of words.[902] Viewed in conjunction with the ca. four dozen imperatives in the epistle, Paul's "I charge you" in v. 13 is the rhetorical equivalent of grabbing Timothy by the shoulders and giving him a heartfelt and bracing shake.

Four additional components of this verse reinforce the tone of gravity and encourage awareness of high stakes. First, with "in the sight of [*enōpion*][903] God," Paul seeks to impress on Timothy that he, in writing, and Timothy, in receiving this letter, both do so in God's very presence. God and all heaven are observers and judges of this interchange. Timothy dare not regard Paul's charge lightly.

Second, the God in whose presence Paul issues his charge "gives life [from *zōogoneō*][904] to everything." This wording combines with mention of "eternal life" (v. 13) to underscore that present life, as well as the future, is under God's sway, dependent on his sustenance, and subject to his assessment.[905] That God gives life to all things (*ta panta*)[906] is closely related to the confession that he is "the living God," a formulation found over two dozen times in the NIV. Paul himself voices this conviction repeatedly.[907] Since he is the living God, he is also God of the living, as Jesus asserted.[908] Paul wants Timothy to weigh this truth fully.[909] Some see here "a deliberate opposition to the imperial cult," since emperors demanded recognition as the upholder of their subjects' lives.[910]

Third, the word *enōpion* (in the presence of, in the sight of) is understood in Greek before the words "Christ Jesus." In other words, "Christ Jesus" stands in parallel with "God" at the start of the verse, and *enōpion* applies to

902. Knight, 265.

903. See 5:21 for additional discussion. The word also appears in 1 Tim 2:3; 5:4, 20; 6:12; 2 Tim 2:14; 4:1. There are nine other Pauline uses outside the PE.

904. The word occurs two other times in the NT (Luke 7:19; 17:33) but with a slightly different meaning.

905. Schlatter points here to God giving life not only in creation but also in the resurrection (*Die Kirche der Griechen*, 168).

906. Cf. 1 Cor 12:6 ("the same God who works all things"); Eph 1:11 (God, "who works all things after the counsel of His will"); 1:23 ("the fulness of Him who fills all [things]"); 3:9 ("God, who created all things"). Translations all NASB (1977).

907. Acts 14:15; Rom 9:26; 2 Cor 3:3; 6:16; 1 Tim 3:15; 4:10; see also Heb 3:12; 9:14; 10:31; 12:22; Rev 7:2.

908. Matt 22:32; Mark 12:27; Luke 20:38.

909. God's grandeur as creator and sustainer of all things living is also an emphasis of Paul's Athenian speech: see Acts 17:25–30, which contains both an assertion (all life has its root in God) and entailment (v. 30: "now he commands all people everywhere to repent").

910. Quinn and Wacker, 532, citing Spicq. Also Schlatter, *Die Kirche der Griechen*, 169: "Rome's claim to power and Jesus' lordship stand in opposition, and this conflict determines the situation of the church and the duty of its leaders and workers."

them both. It is not some generic or universal God that Paul appeals to, as one finds, for example, in Epictetus, who uses the word "God" over two hundred times—but often in the plural, signaling that he, like most of his Hellenistic contemporaries, is a polytheist. He sounds a bit like Paul, but then radically unlike him, when he writes: "We are all sprung from God in an especial manner, and . . . God is the father both of men and of gods" (*Discourses* 1.3.1).[911]

For Paul, Christ Jesus is the definitive and saving manifestation of God (of which only one exists). He is also the sole mediator between God and humans (1 Tim 2:5). Socrates may have thought and spoken like he knew himself to be "a relative of the gods,"[912] but this conviction was mistaken, both as to divinity's number and divinity's identity. Timothy's connection with Christ Jesus, to which Paul appeals, is a strong incentive to heed his words.

Fourth is a mention that Christ "testifying before Pontius Pilate made the good confession." Christ paved the way for what Timothy himself must do (recall Timothy's "good confession" in v. 12). Mention of the Roman governor who ruled over Judaea (AD 26–36) and presided over Jesus's trial and execution reminds Timothy that this was a public event that occurred in real history; it is not just a religious conviction with tenuous or no tie to lived-out life in the Roman Empire and its major eastern city, Ephesus.[913] Before Pilate, Jesus stated clearly who he was (Luke 23:3),[914] at great peril to his life, humanly speaking. Now at Ephesus Timothy has the opportunity to state clearly who he takes Jesus to be, whatever threats and loss he might face in doing so. Paul "draws a parallel between Jesus appearing before a hostile ruler and Timothy (and Paul) bearing witness before hostile people inside and outside the church."[915] It is unnecessary to decide whether Paul has in mind Jesus's act of testifying or the content of his profession;[916] from the Gospels we learn details affirming both, and neither can be ruled out in Paul's admonition to Timothy.

Verse 13 sets the stage for what Paul will actually command Timothy, stating at the end of the verse (NIV), "I charge you. . . ." It does so with Paul

911. See also 2 Macc 10:28; 14:18, 43; Isa 7:13; Philo, *Husbandry* 145; *Planting* 175; *Life of Moses* 1:318; *Every Good Person Is Free* 133; *Embassy to Gaius* 194; Josephus, *Jewish Antiquities* 6.368.

912. Epictetus, *Discourses* 1.9.22, 24.

913. Johnson, *First and Second Letters to Timothy*, 308, observes here "an interest in the human Jesus roughly proportional to that found in Paul's undisputed letters."

914. It is not clear why Johnson, *First and Second Letters to Timothy*, 308, states that "the Synoptic Gospels do not have Jesus speaking before Pilate."

915. Marshall, with Towner, 663.

916. Both Marshall, with Towner, and Johnson, *First and Second Letters to Timothy*, 307, downplay the content of what he professed. But just because Paul did not highlight it (would he have needed to?) does not mean he was unsure of it or thought it less important than Jesus's willingness to testify itself.

appealing to God the Father and his courageous, confessing Son to ensure that Timothy will take full and careful note.

14 This verse in conjunction with the preceding one constitutes a blanket imperative for Timothy to follow through on all this epistle presents him with, what Johnson calls "the entire commission that Timothy has received from Paul."[917] It also points to incentive for doing so.

The combination of "keep" (*tēreō*) and "command" (*entolē*) occurs some dozen times in the NT, but only here in Paul.[918] Paul uses a form of *entolē* some thirteen other times, to speak of:

1. OT commandments (Rom 7:8, 9, 10, 11, 12, 13; 13:9; Eph 6:2)
2. God's commands in general (1 Cor 7:19; Eph 2:15)
3. his own apostolic instruction, which is "the Lord's command" (1 Cor 14:37; cf. Col 4:10)
4. "the merely human commands of those who reject the truth" (Titus 1:14)

In v. 14 Paul his in mind the third classification, backed by classifications 1 and 2. As Timothy well knows, Paul has a distinct apostolic call and authority, which he draws on here in summoning Timothy to abide by what he is writing to him. It can be regarded as a command, given the prominence of Paul's "charge" to Timothy throughout 1 Timothy (see discussion of previous verse). Even if Paul has in mind the contextually more proximate directive to fight the good fight and make the good confession (v. 12), these imperatives themselves cannot be separated from the dozens of other commands Paul issues in 1 Timothy. "This command," accordingly, refers to "everything entrusted to Timothy" and is analogous to "what has been entrusted to your care" in 6:20.[919]

Being "without spot [*aspilos*]" before God is an important aspiration to other NT writers, too (Jas 1:27; 2 Pet 3:14; cf. Eph 5:27). This status is possible through faith in Christ, who in his death was "a lamb without . . . defect [*aspilos*]" (1 Pet 1:19). The unnegated form of the word[920] describes the wicked who revel in the daytime (2 Pet 2:13): "Their idea of pleasure is to carouse in broad daylight. They are blots [*spiloi*] and blemishes, reveling in their pleasures while they feast with you."

917. Johnson, *First and Second Letters to Timothy*, 308. So also Towner, *Letters*, 414. Montague, 129 (along with others) relates Paul's command to "the entire Christian gospel: 'All that I have commanded you' (Matt 28:20)." Since the entirety of the message of 1 Timothy can be understood as pastoral application of the gospel, the difference between the two views is not great.

918. The combination occurs also in Matthew's Gospel (once), John's Gospel (four times), 1 John (five times), and Revelation (two times).

919. Dibelius and Conzelmann, 89.

920. That is, *aspilon* with the alpha privative removed: *spilos* (stain, blot).

Being "without blame" or reproach (*anepilēmptos*) is a qualification for overseer (3:2; see discussion in commentary there) and a desideratum for believers under Timothy at Ephesus: they must not "be open to blame" (5:7) because of neglect of widows. There are no other NT uses of the word. Together with "without spot," these two adjectives (Gk. "spotless and blameless") describe what Timothy ought to be aiming for when Christ appears (if that should occur on Timothy's earthly watch).

"Appearing" translates a form of *epiphaneia* (appearing, manifestation), the word for Christ's second coming that he expresses in his other writings mainly with the word *parousia*.[921] *Epiphaneia*[922] is said to be a technical term that "refers to a visible and freq[uently] sudden manifestation of a hidden divinity, either in the form of a personal appearance, or by some deed of power or oracular communication by which its presence is made known" (BDAG 385). It is found once in 2 Thess 2:8, describing the gloriousness of Christ's *parousia* (second coming). Otherwise, it is found only in the PE (see also 2 Tim 2:10; 4:1, 8; Titus 2:13 [see discussion in commentary]). *Epiphaneia* lays stress not just on arrival but on the resplendent or dazzling or stunning appearance of what or who arrives. The word has a rich background in both Jewish and Hellenistic history.

Paul's word choice is apt, for it is "our Lord Jesus Christ" whose arrival Timothy needs to be prepared to welcome. Johnson comments, "It is striking how often this unusually full title appears in eschatological contexts,"[923] listing as examples 1 Thess 5:9, 23, 28; 2 Thess 2:1, 14; 3:18. He could have added 1 Cor 1:7, 8. But the rich designation "our Lord Jesus Christ" is found nearly four times more frequently in some twenty other passages, in which reference is to matters like justification (Rom 5:1), reconciliation (Rom 5:11), ecclesial unity (Rom 15:30; 1 Cor 1:2, 10; Eph 6:24), Christian perseverance (1 Cor 15:57) and hope (1 Thess 1:3; 2 Thess 2:16), God's praiseworthiness (2 Cor 1:3; Eph 1:3; 5:20; Col 1:3), Christ's cross (Gal 6:14), and Christ's words (1 Tim 6:3).

As Paul appeals to Timothy to "keep this command," he highlights Christ's appearing. But it is an appearing whose gloriousness is radiant precisely as the culmination of numerous other aspects of his person and work that have created a people who live awaiting his return, whether they eventually celebrate it in this age or the next.

15 "Which" refers to "the appearing" in v. 14. "God" is not explicitly stated in Greek in either v. 15 or v. 16 but is the only being to whom the de-

921. For *parousia* in Paul, see 1 Cor 15:23; 16:17; 2 Cor 7:6, 7; 10:10; Phil 1:26; 2:12; 1 Thess 2:19; 3:13; 4:15; 5:23; 2 Thess 2:1, 8, 9.

922. For scholarly literature, see Towner, *Letters*, 415n50. Note also his extensive discussion (416–20).

923. Johnson, *First and Second Letters to Timothy*, 308.

scription could apply. His absence rhetorically corroborates the mystery of invisibility and other attributes Paul extols.

Paul speaks first of the timing (*kairos*) of Christ's appearance. *Kairos* also appears in the PE at 2:6; 4:1; 2 Tim 3:1; 4:3, 6; Titus 1:3 (see table 25 and discussion). The word here (in the pl., perhaps reflecting the span of times over which God holds sway) does not so much refer to a day and hour (although that would be implied) but the time frame—it is in God's hands. Jesus warns that his disciples three times in Matthew alone (24:36, 50; 25:13) that they will not know the precise timing of final events. When Jesus tells his disciples, "It is not for you to know the times or dates [from *kairos*] the Father has set by his own [from *idios*] authority" (Acts 1:7), two of the words he uses (italicized) are echoed by Paul in v. 15, where "in his own time" translates *kairois idiois*.

Paul wants Timothy to live in keen awareness and anticipation of Christ's glorious appearing (v. 14). But Timothy cannot become distracted by wondering when that will be, for its timing is up to God and him alone to "bring about" (from *deiknymi*).[924] Paul models the correct conviction on the presumed eve of his own execution: he speaks of the reward in store for him "on that day—and not only to me, but also to all who have longed for his appearing [*epiphaneia*]" (2 Tim 4:8). Timothy is to nurture and feed off this longing without becoming discouraged that it is not fulfilled as soon as he might wish.

The link in Paul's outlook between the sure but unknown timing of Christ's return, on the one hand, and praise of God, on the other, has been clarified in research on another well-known Pauline doxology: Rom 11:34–35. Andrew Naselli explains that Paul reflects the conviction there (drawn in large measure from the OT) that "God is incomprehensible in the sense that no one can fully understand him (11:34a). At least four theological implications follow: (1) humans cannot understand everything; (2) God is not obligated to explain anything; (3) Christians must humbly believe and cherish what God has revealed; and (4) God deserves praise for what he does and does not explain."[925] These implications, if shared by Paul and Timothy, as is likely, given the length and depth of their shared experience in ministry,[926] shed light on the persuasive force of Paul's assertion in v. 15 regarding "his own time."

At the end of v. 16 Paul will climax vv. 15–16 with laud for God. Leading up to this ending, Paul surveys God's majesty (relevant to his governance of all times) with three clauses, each beginning with *ho* (the). The first two clauses complete v. 15.

924. The only other Pauline usage: 1 Cor 12:31. BDAG 214 (1) shows the word is often used "of apocalyptic visions" and "direction to transcendent matters."

925. A. Naselli, *From Typology to Doxology: Paul's Use of Isaiah and Job in Romans 11:34–35* (Eugene, OR: Pickwick, 2012), 161.

926. Timothy was present as Paul dictated Romans: Rom 16:21.

First, God is "the blessed and only Ruler." Paul has already (1 Tim 1:11) called God who entrusted the gospel to him "blessed," *makarios*, the word used by Jesus to describe God's favor in the Beatitudes. The OT usually speaks of God's blessing, not his status as "blessed."[927] In the Roman world the word referred to fortune's favor. In LXX usage it describes "those who have a right relationship with God." Philo stresses that "only the deity attains to blessedness."[928] Paul affirms an analogous exaltation of deity, though with a supercharged consciousness because of God's appearance in Christ that Philo (whose inspiration here was Platonic philosophy) did not share.

God is not only the "blessed" but also the "only" Ruler (*dynastēs*).[929] The singularity of God is axiomatic throughout all Scripture, marking a radical distinction between Gentiles (overwhelmingly polytheist) and both Jews and Christians. The Shema declares, "The LORD is one" (Deut 6:4). Numerous OT writers address God, "Who is like you?" in marveling at his uniqueness, notably Exod 15:11: "Who among the gods is like you, LORD? Who is like you—majestic in holiness, awesome in glory, working wonders?" (see also Deut 33:29; Pss 35:10; 71:19; 89:8). Paul's conviction of God's oneness is confirmed in Rom 3:30; 1 Cor 8:4, 6; Gal 3:20; Eph 4:6; 1 Tim 2:5; and many other statements that speak of him in terms like "the living and true God" (1 Thess 1:9). There is, has been, and can be no other.

Second, lending further depth to God's place as "Ruler" is the description "the King of kings and Lord of lords." In Scripture "king of kings" describes Nebuchadnezzar—he ruled over all his subject rulers (Ezek 26:7). Daniel confirms his status: "Your Majesty, you are the king of kings" (Dan 2:37). But in the same verse he continues: "The God of heaven has given you dominion and power and might and glory."[930] There are earthly potentates like Nebuchadnezzar. And then there is God over all. Later in the same conversation Nebuchadnezzar exclaims to Daniel, "Surely your God is the God of gods and the Lord of kings" (Dan 2:47). Other OT passages call God "Lord of lords" (Deut 10:17; Ps 136:3).

It is this conviction into which Paul taps. "Whatever forces there are in the universe are subject to God."[931] "He shapes the world's course of events and

927. But see Neh 9:5: "Blessed be your glorious name, and may it be exalted above all blessing and praise." This wording reflects the MT; the LXX is "Bless the Lord, our God, from everlasting and to everlasting" (NETS).

928. *NIDNTTE* 3:207.

929. Found elsewhere in the NT only at Luke 1:52 (Mary extolling God in the Magnificat) and Acts 8:27 (describing the Ethiopian eunuch's status as royal agent). In the LXX, see, for example, Sir 46:5; 2 Macc 12:15; 3 Macc 5:51.

930. As Aquinas, 87, affirms: other rulers have power "through participation, but only God possesses it in himself essentially."

931. Marshall, with Towner, 667.

reigns over all kings and rulers."[932] For Paul this conviction would be doubly true, for in Jesus's humiliation and exaltation Paul has seen God's sole sovereignty manifest in history (Phil 2:5–11).[933] It would also be doubly significant for Timothy. Not only would it invite him into the doxology Paul has begun to intone here, it also would serve the apologetic function of affirming that it is to God "to whom alone mortals owe obedience and adoration" (note the same strategy in 2:1–5).[934] This mind-set encourages Timothy to allow God's grandeur to relativize his circumstances.

16 The third of three clauses affirms God's greatness. He is the Ruler-King-Lord par excellence (v. 15), and he is likewise the one "who alone is immortal" (cf. 1:17). Death cannot touch him. *Athanasia* (immortal) appears in the NT elsewhere only in 1 Cor 15:53 (twice), 54. For NT-era convictions about death, see *NIDNTTE* 2:404–6. Philosophers and religions had no solutions, only coping mechanisms that often amounted to thin means of denial. The fear and horror of death remained. God exists above human desperation and can therefore be Savior from it, which in Christ (and particularly in Christ's resurrection: 1 Cor 15:55–57, drawing on Isa 25:8; and Hos 13:14) he shows himself to be. Affirmation of God's immortality may not be as much appropriation of "the language used of gods and emperors" in Hellenism[935] as extrapolation from Christ's victory over death to the God who performed it.

Existence beyond death's grasp is glossed by "who lives[936] in unapproachable[937] light." God's association with light[938] is nearly as ubiquitous in Scripture as is insistence on his uniqueness. Along with "unapproachable" it suggests moral purity along with utter transcendence. It is not simply God who is unapproachable; it is rather the effulgence, the radiant outward rim, of his holy splendor, conceived as fatal to errant humans (cf. Heb 12:18–21 [the terrifying gloom yet light of fiery Sinai]). Paul's blinding at his conversion is also suggestive (Acts 9:9; 22:11). "The idea" is "that the light is so bright that people cannot gaze at it[939] or so intense that it burns

932. Schlatter, *Die Kirche der Griechen*, 170.

933. Cf. Rev 17:14, where the Lamb is "Lord of lords and King of kings"; 19:16, where the rider on the white horse has written "on his robe and on his thigh . . . this name written: KING OF KINGS AND LORD OF LORDS."

934. Collins, 167.

935. So Marshall, with Towner, 667.

936. Paul uses the same verb, *oikeō* (to live, dwell), of God's Spirit living in or among believers in Christ: Rom 8:9, 11; 1 Cor 3:16.

937. *Aprositos*, a NT hapax.

938. See, for example, Gen 1:3–5; Job 33:28; Pss 18:28; 118:27; Isa 60:19; Acts 26:18; 1 John 1:5; Rev 22:5.

939. Cf. Paul's recollection of his blinding: "I saw a light from heaven, brighter than the sun, blazing around me and my companions. We all fell to the ground" (Acts 22:13–14).

them up."[940] Yet, because of a mediator (1 Tim 2:5), Paul can celebrate this attribute: "For God, who said, 'Let light shine out of darkness, made his light shine in our hearts to give us the light of the knowledge of God's glory displayed in the face of Christ" (2 Cor 4:6). In Christ there is access and welcome into what otherwise would remain inaccessible and fatally daunting.

"Whom no one has seen or can see" underscores God's transcendence. Paul continues his doxological appeal for Timothy to remain steadfast (vv. 13–14). This conviction also affirms the wonder and magnificence of the gospel he and Timothy are pledged to minister, which (as 2 Cor 4:6 in the previous paragraph affirms) brings God into redemptive view. Just as eternal life is both later and now (v. 12), God is both beyond human sight and revealed in Jesus.[941] This is part of the wonder of Timothy's "good confession." Towner mentions that "whom no one has seen or can see" "is based on Exod 33:20 and may be a loose reworking of it, adding, "Texts in this category apparently have no overt intention of drawing the audience back into the OT narrative world or of appealing to the authority of the OT."[942] But coming from the OT-steeped Paul and with his primary target reader his fellow Jew Timothy, it seems more likely that Paul intended, and Timothy would have caught, the allusion.

Concluding the verse is "To him be honor and might forever. Amen." See 1:17 for a close parallel and discussion of "honor" (*timē*); see 5:17 for more on the word itself.[943] "Might" (*kratos*) occurs in Paul three other times (Eph 1:19; 6:10; Col 1:11).[944] Other NT writers use it in doxologies (1 Pet 4:11; 5:11; Jude 25; Rev 1:6; 5:13). This "might" is everlasting, "forever" (from *aiōnios*, eternal). It partakes of God's immortality and as a resource for those he favors is inexhaustible.

Honor is what Timothy and all creation owe God. Might is what he possesses that makes any other response to him except honor inexplicable folly. *Amēn* is Paul's affirmation that he affirms what is true of God and pledges himself to give it full credence and obeisance. His testimony is tacit invitation for Timothy to follow suit.

17 While the doxology of vv. 15–16 may have served well as the letter's end, Paul has more to say. Possibly mention of wealth earlier (vv. 9–10), followed by exhortation to Timothy to lay hold of eternal life (v. 12), prompts him to underscore how the rich, too, need to "lay up treasure for themselves

940. Marshall, with Towner, 668. See also Heb 12:29: "Our 'God is a consuming fire.'"

941. The paradox is expressed perfectly in John 1:18.

942. *CNTUOT* 902.

943. Note also Neudorfer's excursus in *Zweiter Brief an Timotheus*, 288–90.

944. See *NIDNTTE* 2:739–42.

. . . for the present age"[945] (v. 17) and "take hold of the life that is truly life [i.e., eternal life]" (v. 19). This brief admonition for the sake of the rich is notable for its positive and measured tone. It is a tribute to Paul's pastoral concern for a subgroup (in addition to those mentioned earlier: widows, elders, slaves) that it can be tempting either to favor (Jas 2:1) or to excoriate (Jas 5:1). Paul does neither; he rather administers to them implications of the gospel message.[946] If Timothy can keep the rich from self-destructing and help them direct their resources in the right directions, it will be a great boost to his goal of remaining at Ephesus (see 1:3).

"Command" is the fifth and final occurrence of the verb *parangellō* (to command, charge) in 1 Timothy (see discussion at v. 13 above). Three of these target Timothy (4:11; 5:17; 6:13); here as in 1:3 the charge is to be passed along to others, in this case, those who "are rich in this present world."[947] Timothy is to forbid two sterile course of actions (arrogance and placing hope in riches) but then to commend some five better alternatives. This is another example of the positive ethic glimpsed earlier (see commentary on 6:11 above). The gospel message is not about ethical negativity or denigration of God's good gifts (recall the demonic, anti-enjoyment views mentioned in 4:1–3) but rather productive and redemptive application of them. One such gift consists in abundance of resources, whether in income or in holdings.

Marshall points out that "social stratification was a common problem in early Christian congregations."[948] Is there any time or place where this is not a problem, at least potentially? Without some measure of resources, a congregation has no means to sustain itself or care for others. Jesus's own band of disciples required the support of at least somewhat wealthy women (Luke 8:3). In this sense the rich are a blessing and in the long run a desirable component in a stable and lasting congregation.

But the rich may be accustomed to telling others what to do or otherwise throwing their weight around. Their prosperity may tempt them to look down on others. It is not their wealth that is sinful but how they have permitted their wealth to corrupt them. Paul tells Timothy to command them "not to be arrogant" (from *hypsēlophroneō*, a NT hapax). The word carries the sense of self-exaltation. The OT taught that "by exalting themselves and in self-gratification relying on their own strength," the proud "place themselves in opp[osition] to

945. Cf. Gal 1:4: "the present evil age."

946. For a Marxist view of this section, see Krause, 130–32, who draws from the passage that "the church's belief and practices are always politically and economically involved, and that even the seemingly purest motivations are connected to the vagaries of everyday material existence and class struggle" (131–32).

947. For near equivalents to Paul's expression "in the present world," see Rom 3:26; 11:25; 2 Cor 8:14. For the identical words, see Titus 2:12.

948. Marshall, with Towner, 668–69.

God and call forth Yahweh's humbling intervention."[949] Paul's counsel would help "faithful Christians who are wealthy and not guilty of greed"[950] (as in vv. 9–10 above) avoid this tendency.

Timothy is also charged to counsel the rich not to "to put their hope in wealth," for it is "uncertain." Another way of wording this warning would be "hope in wealth's uncertainty."[951] Paul has already reminded Timothy, "We have put our hope in the living God" (4:10; see discussion of "hope" there and in 5:5), who is the opposite of uncertainty. The difference in outcome is decisive. Wealth's advantages are limited and fleeting. But the benefits of God, who "richly provides[952] us with everything for our enjoyment,"[953] are not. The enjoyments that wealth may afford are not in themselves incompatible with God, for true enjoyments have their source in him. But a danger lurks: "Give me neither poverty nor riches. . . . Otherwise, I may have too much and disown you and say, 'Who is the LORD?'" (Prov 30:8–9). Wealth and its concerns may blot out consciousness of God.

The wealthy therefore need to learn how to live with their eye on God more than on their wealth, a skill that may well require pastoral guidance, admonition, and encouragement, in addition to fiscal expertise and prudence. Paul is providing Timothy resources for his ministry to those with wealth here. "The issue is not whether one had wealth but whether one used it for oneself or for others."[954]

18 "Command" is carried into the NIV from near the beginning of v. 17, although the imperative is not actually restated here. By not restating the command, the rhetorical feel is of a list of positive outcomes the rich can attain, not on Timothy's need to be in their face. Timothy's task as pastor is to create space for God's people (and in this case esp. the wealthy) to respond to God's gospel call; it is not to serve as a moralizing policeman. That list consists of five aims for those who are committed to Christ and wealthy to pursue. Four are set forth in v. 18.

Here and throughout this section, Marshall's counsel bears notice: "On the whole, simply redistributing the existing wealth will not make for a vast change in the lives of the poor; the solution generally lies in increased productivity and ensuring that the poor get their fair share of the proceeds."[955] This is

949. *NIDNTTE* 4:580.

950. Zehr, 124.

951. See BDF §165.

952. "Provides" is from *parechō*, used elsewhere in Paul at Gal 3:17; Col 4:1; 1 Tim 1:4; Titus 2:7.

953. "Enjoyment" translates a form of *apolausis*, a word found elsewhere in the NT only in Heb 11:25 ("the fleeting *pleasures* of sin").

954. Keener, *Bible Background Commentary*, 613.

955. Marshall, with Towner, 670.

especially wise counsel if "fair share of the proceeds" includes not only income but also the responsible decisions and labor that produce income. It is also important to note that Paul's concern is not one-dimensional, that is, concern solely or primarily for the poor. No doubt they are on his mind and heart (cf. Gal 2:10). But they are one of many goals and concerns for which Timothy's congregation(s) and their wealthy bear responsibility.

1. "Do good." The verb (from *agathoergeō*) is found only one other time in the NT, where it describes God providing the good things of rain and crops (Acts 14:17). An almost identical word is used more widely (though not by Paul) and confirms how important "doing good" is as an aspect of following Christ.[956] Wealth holds potential for creating various effects. God, who is pro-enjoyment (v. 17), wants those effects to be in line with his own moral perfection, that is, goodness. The wealthy need to act ("do") in keeping with God's will and expectation.

2. "To be rich in good works." Marshall observes that the term "riches" "is always used pejoratively of human wealth in the NT." That negative feel contributes to an irony here, for "rich" (*plousios*) is a highly positive term. As Marshall also points out, the adjective "rich" "is used of God . . . and his generosity."[957]

"Rich in good deeds" is even more arresting in that Paul does not use an adjective but an infinitive (from *plouteō*, to be wealthy). He is not telling Timothy what the rich must be but what they are to do. In that respect "be rich in good deeds" simply restates "do good" in the previous clause. See table 26 and discussion of "good deeds" at Titus 1:16. The translation "rich in good works" may be preferable, especially in settings where cheap grace or antinomian tendencies have advanced, for Paul's *en ergois kalois* (NIV "in good deeds") does not denote occasional meritorious acts of mercy or goodness ("good deeds" in American English) but the "good works" that Scripture as a whole enjoins on God's people who walk in the power of Christ's Spirit by the gospel.

Accordingly, the challenge for the rich is not to be on the lookout for "good deeds" they can elect to perform with their money; it is rather to live the transformed life Paul speaks of in a passage like Rom 12:1–2. The result will be a wealth, a habitual productive pattern, of *erga* (works) that are "good" because they grow out of relationship with God and conform to the ethics commended by the Scriptures. Jesus laid a foundation for this understanding in warning those "not rich toward God" (Luke 12:21).

3. "And to be generous." There is no "and" in Greek. In fact, there are no conjunctions at all between "but" (*alla*) in v. 17 and "so that" (*hina*) in v. 19. The literary device in play here, probably intuitive rather than intentional on

956. That is, *agathopoieō* (to do good); see Luke 6:9, 33, 35; 1 Pet 2:15, 20; 3:6, 17; 2 John 11.

957. Marshall, with Towner, 671, 322 (with over a dozen NT references).

Paul's part, is asyndeton, a style of writing that omits conjunctions that could easily be inserted. As noted above, the result (in Gk.) is a list-like feel. The terse formulation creates a collage of expectations, a portrait of character and behaviors for Timothy to set before the wealthy under his care.

"Generous" translates *eumetadotos*, a NT hapax and a rare word elsewhere. Another translation suggestion is "ready to impart."[958] It is combined with the infinitive of "to be" (*einai*) to maintain the parallel with "to do good" and "to be rich." Paul wants Timothy's people with financial means not to be slack or grudging but to be quick to step up and put their potential to good use. "Readily giving, magnanimous" gives the sense.[959]

4. Again, there is no "and" in Greek. One descriptor follows another in rapid-fire succession. "Willing to share" (from *koinōnikos*) is defined as virtually synonymous with the preceding word, "generous" (BDAG 553). The idea is not stingy but liberal. In a number of passages where Philo uses the word, "community-minded" or "sociable" or having "social affection" describes his thrust.[960] Epictetus's six uses all run in the same direction.[961] We are justified in positing an added dimension to "willing to share," an expression that calls attention to the person sharing; such willingness to share should be steered by affection and concern for the community of which he or she is part, or for individuals regarded as part of that community.[962] This conviction comports with the observation that a communal outlook is common to the *koin-* word group.[963] Timothy needs to remind the rich and help them live out the fact that they are not the center of the world; those around them who are different from them (but who are bound to them by the tie of faith) are equally important in God's view of things.

19 In Greek there is no new sentence here. It begins rather with the fifth in a series that began in the previous verse.

5. Timothy's word to the rich (see "Command those who are rich . . ."; v. 17) is to be laying up "treasure for themselves" of a particular type (see below). This phrase translates a participle from a verb (*apothēsaurizō*) that is a NT hapax. Yet, a simpler (uncompounded) form (*thēsaurizō*) means the same thing (to accumulate, gather, save up something) and is used eight times, including a declaration in Jesus's Sermon on the Mount: "Do not *store up* for yourselves treasures on earth" (Matt 6:19; cf. Luke 12:21). Paul uses the word for

958. MM 263.

959. *NIDNTTE* 2:709.

960. For example, Philo, *Special Laws* 2.104; 4.120; *Flight* 11; *Preliminary Studies* 71.

961. For example, Epictetus, *Enchiridion* 36.1: "At a feast, to choose the largest share is very suitable to the bodily appetite, but utterly inconsistent with the social spirit [*to koinōnikon*] of an entertainment." See also *Discourses* 1.23.1; 1.28.20; 2.10.14; 2.20.13; 3.13.5.

962. So also Collins, 171.

963. See *NIDNTTE* 2:706–13.

storing up wrath (Rom 2:5; cf. 2 Pet 3:7) and money (1 Cor 16:2; 2 Cor 12:14; cf. Jas 5:3). The word in 1 Tim 6:19 may be rare, but the concept is commonplace.

Distinct in v. 19 is the outcome of this accumulation: "a firm foundation for the coming age." "Coming age" harks back to v. 17: "this present world," which could also be translated "age" (*aiōn*). Verses 17–19 as a unit are permeated by an eschatological conviction. We live in an "age" when wealth is commonly regarded and used one way. But Christians live in the light of an age that has not yet fully arrived. Yet, that future age[964] is normative for the present one in Jesus's teaching (e.g., the wise man building on rock [Matt 7:24]) and in the Bible's narrative overall. Living out God's generosity[965] now is a "firm foundation" (*themelion kalon*) for what lies ahead.

On *kalos* (good, beautiful, noble, here "firm"), see table 12 and discussion at 2:3. On *themelios* (foundation), see 2 Tim 2:19 and discussion there. Paul knows a God who "is able to guard what [he has] entrusted to him until that day," that is, the full arrival of the age to come (2 Tim 1:12). Good works, shared resources, and other benevolences of the rich may seem squandered and lost in this life (and Paul is not calling for indiscriminate or reckless giving). But actually in God's reckoning such acts serve to construct a "firm foundation," whose utility and glory will be revealed "in his own time" (v. 15).

The five aspects of Paul's "command" in v. 17 culminate in an already/not yet promise that applies the same "take hold of . . . eternal life" logic found in v. 12. Those rich in this age should construct a firm foundation for the coming one, "so that they may take hold of the life that is truly life." These words can hardly mean, essentially, "so that they may go to heaven when they die." The reference is not exclusively to "eternal life" as a solely future prospect. Their actions and use of wealth should rather reflect in the present a full measure of awareness of the eternal realities that earthly life, significantly but merely, foreshadows.

"Take hold of" is the same verb used in v. 12 (*epilambanō*). "Truly" (*ontōs*)[966] occurs in the PE elsewhere only at 5:3, 5, 16, referring to those who are "truly" widows.[967] Much of life is not "truly" life at all from the standpoint of eternity; it is overabsorption into the everyday: "Be careful, or your hearts will be weighed down with carousing, drunkenness and the anxieties of life,

964. "The coming age" in v. 19 translates *to mellon*, "the coming," with "age" supplied from an understood *aiōn* (translated "world") back in v. 17. For other forms and uses of *mellō* in the PE, see 1:16; 4:8; 2 Tim 4:1.

965. Schlatter, *Die Kirche der Griechen*, 172n1, observes how frequently Paul speaks of God's "riches" and observes that, for Paul, "God behaves like a rich man."

966. Some ancient MSS contain *aiōniou* (eternal) instead, and a few contain both words. The harder reading (*ontōs* is relatively rare in Paul) is likely to be original in view of its superior external attestation.

967. In Paul, see also 1 Cor 14:25 ("God is *really* among you!"); Gal 3:21 ("then righteousness would *certainly* have come by the law").

and that day will close on you suddenly like a trap" (Luke 21:34). The rich have means and, if they are not careful, also hearts for such dissolute living and distraction. They should be wary and opt instead for "life that is truly life."[968] Helpful here will be a pastoral guardian like Timothy who lives in that very conviction and so as a matter of course can help make it decisive factor in the decisions and lives of the believers he oversees and instructs.

20 A second emphatic "*O*" (not translated in NIV) sets off the epistle's final words. Paul addresses Timothy with pathos. See 6:11 for the parallel "O man of God" (NIV again leaves "*O*" untranslated). Paul's final charge to Timothy[969] is twofold and rich in substance. He does not just bawl out commands.

"Guard the deposit" would be one way to render NIV's "guard what has been entrusted to your care." By placing "the deposit" (from *parathēkē*) first in its clause, Paul may intend to emphasize it. For discussion of "deposit," see commentary at 2 Tim 1:12, 14. Schlatter finds "entrusted with the sacred oracles" (Rom 3:1) to be the closest parallel in Paul.[970] He describes it as a term that pictures a ruler entrusting what he owns to an administrator. For "guard" as an imperative, see commentary and discussion at 2 Tim 1:14; 4:15. See also discussion above at 5:21.

The expression can be compared to "fight the good fight" in v. 12: both require soldier-like readiness, rigor, loyalty, savvy, and, where necessary, counteraggression. Timothy is not to pick fights; he is, indeed, to avoid them. Paul's counsel in all three of the PE can be summed up in part under the rubric, "If it is possible, as far as it depends on you, live at peace with everyone" (Rom 12:18). But it is not always possible. When issues and enemies require, Timothy has to "guard what has been entrusted." Polemical sections of Paul's other letters (esp. in, e.g., Galatians and 2 Corinthians) and passages like Eph 6:10–20 ("put on the full armor of God") serve as examples. So do commands Paul gave to overseers early at Ephesus like "keep watch," "be shepherds of the church of God," and "be on your guard" (Acts 20:28, 31). Timothy, like loyal pastors through the centuries, will sometimes find himself saying with the Psalmist, "I am for peace; but when I speak, they are for war" (Ps 120:7; cf. Eccl 3:8; Mic 3:5). He cannot simply cave in. Guarding in the sense Paul intends "is active rather than a passive task."[971]

"What has been entrusted" to Timothy's care is, minimally, all that Paul has written to him in this epistle. It is a tall order, but none of it is insignificant. More broadly, it is the gospel message and the concerns of "God's household, which is the church of the living God" (3:15), that define the ambit of the

968. For "life" (*zōē*) in the PE, see also 1:16; 4:8; 6:12; 2 Tim 1:1, 10; Titus 1:2; 3:7. In all PE occurrences it centers on, or at least draws on the promise of, life in the coming age.

969. One imperative (guard) and a dependent adverbial participle (from *ektrepō*) in Greek; two imperatives (guard, turn away from) in NIV.

970. Schlatter, *Die Kirche der Griechen*, 173n1.

971. Towner, *Letters*, 431.

defensive perimeter that "guard" suggests. Johnson relates the deposit to "the way of life found in the 'healthy teaching' that accords with the good news."[972] This summary is apt as long as the way of life, the doctrine that informs it, and the historical truth that the good news consists in are not abstracted away from each other, or "way of life" (behavior, ethics) made to be the sole real issue. Marshall understands the deposit to be "clearly the gospel . . . , i.e. the whole of the apostolic teaching" that was being disputed by the false teachers.[973]

Simultaneous with "guard" Timothy must "turn away." See discussion of the word (*ektrepō*) at 1 Tim 1:6; 5:15; 2 Tim 4:4. This is a reverse image of the problem that helped precipitate the need for Paul to write this letter: "Some have *departed from*" gospel teaching and its aims "and have *turned to* meaningless talk" (1:6); indeed, "some have in fact already *turned away* to follow Satan" (5:15; italicized words translate forms of *ektrepō*). Now Paul advises Timothy to employ the same device of making a conscious turn, but on the basis of gospel truth, and in a Godward direction. There are times and occasions that call for study, dialogue, and positive engagement. But there are other settings when refusal to play along is required. A pastor's energy and time could be totally absorbed in taking with seriousness what boils down to vapid babble and fantasy. That is the situation Paul envisions here.

Specifically, Paul speaks of "godless chatter." The word translated "godless" (*bebēlos*, vile, profane) is applied to Esau in Heb 12:16; all other NT uses occur in the PE (see 1:9, 4:7; and esp. 2 Tim 2:16, where the identical expression "godless chatter" occurs). "Chatter" translates a form of *kenophonia* (empty noise). With *bebēlos* one could suggest the paraphrase "obscene racket." No matter what the aberrant teaching, someone in the Christian community needs to assess and deal with it. Irenaeus's voluminous interaction with gnostic views (much of it holding his nose) in the late second century comes to mind as a necessary analytical and apologetic service. Paul heard out and replied to the Athenian philosophers (Acts 17). But this is not the regular (or feasible) calling of most pastors in most settings. Timothy is not an academician up against ideas that might provide fruitful topics for a dissertation leading to a degree or for another journal article. He is instructing and shepherding God's people. In the division of labor under God's providence, he must "turn away from" the "godless chatter" of which Paul speaks.

"The opposing ideas of what is falsely called knowledge" likely refers in more detail to the "godless chatter."[974] Johnson sees both expressions as referring here to "generalized slander."[975] While older commentators often related this false "knowledge" to a religious orientation that came to be called Gnosticism,

972. Johnson, *First and Second Letters to Timothy*, 311.

973. Marshall, with Towner, 675. For other possibilities, see, for example, Twomey, 110.

974. Note that one article, *tas*, modifies both "chatter" and "opposing ideas."

975. Johnson, *First and Second Letters to Timothy*, 311.

Keener speaks for many in observing that "this interpretation is unnecessary; many philosophers made claims to 'knowledge' which other philosophers considered false."[976] Towner points to issues and texts involving "knowledge" at Qumran, not a source of gnostic views.[977] Johnson cites nearly two dozen other references to *gnōsis* (knowledge) in Paul's writings, few of which could possibly be referring to the "second-century Christian elitist movement"[978] that made esoteric lore and counterscriptural claims the basis of an anti-Christian theosophy. From the beginning of the epistle Paul has been writing against people teaching false doctrines (1:4). Their bogus claims, and others like them, are what Paul has in mind in v. 20. A recent summation of "Gnosis, Gnosticism" concludes that while "Gnostic overtones" have been detected in various expressions and words found in Paul's writings, "there is no evidence that anything like a coherent gnostic system of thought existed in the 1st century" that could have "served as a source for such ideas" in Paul.[979] It can only be said that Paul had in mind "a particular teaching which could be differentiated from that of the church."[980]

This is not to deny, of course, that Paul's remarks on this subject were (and are) relevant when gnostic ideas and claims surface, as they did in early church history and in some forms continue to appear regularly in the West.[981]

21 Paul concludes on a businesslike, almost laconic[982] note. The last hint of triumph was ascription of praise to God (v. 16). Since then, and to the end, Paul wraps up with carefully aimed words that seal his intention for Timothy to "stay there in Ephesus" (1:3). Luther concludes his 1 Timothy lectures as follows: "You have in this epistle the establishment of the bishop," that is, the overseer or pastor spoken of in ch. 3, "and what he should do to take special care of the Word so that it remains pure."[983] Timothy's job at Ephesus is to apply and administer this counsel.

"Which" in v. 21 refers to the bogus "knowledge" in the previous verse. On "some" (*tines*), see table 21 and discussion at 5:15. On "professed," see 2:10 and discussion there; the same word has the meaning "promised" in Titus 1:2; Rom 4:21; Gal 3:19. The views from which Timothy needs to "turn away" (v. 20)

976. Keener, *Bible Background Commentary*, 615.

977. Towner, *Letters to Timothy and Titus*, 433.

978. Johnson, *First and Second Letters to Timothy*, 312.

979. Einar Thomassen, "Gnosis, Gnosticism II: New Testament," *EBR* 10:344. Cf. Davies, 99: "There is, then, no unambiguous evidence that the opponents, whether present or future, are understood to be Gnostics." Those who date the PE well into the second century (and not written by Paul) will naturally take a different view on this issue.

980. Dibelius and Conzelmann, 92, who hold, however, that that teaching was gnostic.

981. See Dibelius and Conzelmann, 345–58, 361–63, 363–69.

982. Collins, 174, observes that the final farewell in 1 Timothy ("Grace be with you") is the shortest in all the NT letters.

983. Luther, 384.

are on the march. People are professing allegiance to them and no doubt living in ways that are as wrongheaded as the doctrines they have accepted. For this reason it is urgent that Timothy guard what he has received and thereby build up Christ followers in the faith.

There is urgency because, with respect to that faith, that body of true Christian doctrine that the PE so repeatedly affirm, people have "departed" (from *astocheō*). This statement repeats what Paul will later write in 2 Tim 2:18 regarding persons who "have departed from the truth." There he gives this example of their views and its outcome: "They say that the resurrection has already taken place, and they destroy the faith of some." Such departure does not involve petty matters. The only other NT use of the word has already been encountered at 1:6: "Some have departed from [love, which comes from a pure heart and a good conscience and a sincere faith (1:5)] and have turned to meaningless talk." See discussion there.

Retention is always an issue in movements, even if they eventually become institutions, and the church from the beginning was no exception. Some left Jesus because of his teachings (John 6:66); others disapproved of his direction (John 11:8, 16); in the end his closest followers could no longer stay in alignment with his mission (Matt 26:56). Some followers doubted after he had been raised from the dead (Matt 28:17). Paul will later report regarding the region of which Ephesus was the capital city, "You know that everyone in the province of Asia has deserted me, including Phygelus and Hermogenes" (2 Tim 1:15). Departure from Jesus, from Paul, and from the movement that began in their lifetimes was a constant of that era.

There has always been churning, ingress and egress, surrounding the household of faith. Paul did not have to elaborate; Timothy had been with him at places like Corinth, where aversion to the gospel message—in the church—seems to have been as strong as, if not stronger than, its attraction. Yet, they remained committed to the fellowship of ministry they shared. This epistle remains as evidence, as well as precedent for those still heeding the call to "stay there" in their place of service today.

The great enabler in it all is "God the Father and Christ Jesus our Lord," in whose name Paul offered Timothy the blessing of "grace, mercy and peace" many lines earlier in 1:2. Paul closes with a shorthand version of that blessing here, since "grace" encompasses the whole of God's favorable disposition to great sinners like Paul and Timothy who are still unworthy yet, through faith, effective leaders. "You all" in NIV reflects that Paul's last word (*hymin*, you) is plural, not singular.[984] Timothy receives this letter as servant of Christ's body and not a solitary agent.

984. Most minuscule MSS contain the singular "you." But based on the principle of the harder reading (the sing. makes perfect sense in an epistle written to an individual), and in view of strong external evidence (א A F G P 33. 81 bo), the plural is more likely to have been original.

The Letter of
2 TIMOTHY

The Text and Title of 2 Timothy

Like 1 Timothy, the text for 2 Timothy is attested by thirteen uncials, eleven minuscules, and two lectionaries (*l* 249 *l* 846) that likewise contain Titus. These twenty-six documents are "consistently and frequently cited" in the Nestle-Aland apparatus.[1] Numerous additional Greek (and Latin) witnesses could be listed, but they would add nothing significant to this sizable collection of ancient documents deemed foundational by specialists in the field for determining with relative certainty what the original author of 2 Timothy composed.[2]

In the NIV translation, the only footnote pertaining to the Greek text is at 2 Tim 4:19: the Greek text reads "Prisca," known to be a shortened form of "Priscilla" (BDAG 864). There is little dispute about the wording of the original manuscript of this epistle. While there will always be debates about how words and passages in 2 Timothy should be interpreted, what the original author or authors first wrote will be regarded as generally established for purposes of this commentary. Textual critics still debate the precise original wording of the Greek text of 2 Timothy in some fifteen places. Eight of these are of purely antiquarian interest,[3] including various subscriptions (titles). In all cases Timothy is the recipient, and in no subscription is another author mentioned besides Paul.

In all of 2 Timothy there are eight variant readings to which the United Bible Societies assigns a rating in their four-letter system of A (virtually cer-

1. *The Greek-English New Testament*, xxvii. For the listing of witnesses in 2 Timothy, see xxix.

2. In recent years a few scholars have argued that our knowledge of the original texts of the New Testament writings is fundamentally partial and uncertain. For a sample response to this minority but significant voice, see, for example, Daniel B. Wallace, "Has the New Testament Text Been Hopelessly Corrupted?," in *In Defense of the Bible: A Comprehensive Apologetic for the Authority of Scripture*, ed. S. Cowan and T. Wilder (Nashville: B&H, 2015), 139–63.

3. See Bruce Metzger, *A Textual Commentary on the Greek New Testament* (London: United Bible Societies, 1975), 653–56. See on variants at 2 Tim 2:3; 3:8, 11, 16; 4:16, 19, 22 (two variants).

tain) to D (evidence is divided). These variants are found at 1:11; 2:14, 18, 22; 4:1, 8 (all rated C) and at 4:10, 22 (rated B). A few of these will be touched on in the comments below. None of the variants in 2 Timothy is so disputed as to be given a D rating.

Outline of 2 Timothy

- I. Greeting and Reasons for Writing (1:1–18)
  - A. Greeting (1:1–2)
  - B. Thanksgiving (1:3–5)
  - C. Appeal for Loyalty to Paul and the Gospel (1:6–14)
  - D. Examples of Disloyalty and Loyalty (1:15–18)
- II. Priorities for Timothy (2:1–3:9)
  - A. The Appeal Renewed (2:1–13)
  - B. Dealing with False Teachers (2:14–3:9)
    - 1. Strategy for the Situation at Hand (2:14–18)
    - 2. Leadership Wisdom in the Face of Opposition (2:19–21)
    - 3. Personal Priorities for Pastoral Effectiveness (2:22–26)
    - 4. Withstanding the Suction of Terrible Times (3:1–5)
    - 5. Features and Creatures of Folly (3:6–9)
- III. Concluding Reminders, Instructions, and Greetings (3:10–4:22)
  - A. A Final Charge to Timothy (3:10–4:8)
    - 1. Resources (3:10–17)
    - 2. Responsibilities (4:1–8)
  - B. Personal Remarks (4:9–18)
  - C. Final Greetings (4:19–22)

Commentary on 2 Timothy

I. GREETING AND REASONS FOR WRITING (1:1–18)

This section, the entirety of ch. 1, identifies the author (vv. 1–2), greets the reader and expresses gratitude (vv. 3–5), and reminds the reader (Timothy) of his giftedness for ministry (vv. 6–7). The reminder segues into a complex appeal for Timothy to "join . . . in suffering for the gospel" (v. 8), partially on theological grounds (vv. 9–10) but also in light of autobiographical considerations Paul cites (vv. 11–18). The whole section exudes calm, yet also pathos and at times a wistful pensiveness, all of which makes sense in light of what Paul eventually discloses. As he writes, we learn that Paul is in chains (2:9) and in the midst of legal hearings (4:16), which he expects to end in his execution (4:6–8).

A. Greeting (1:1–2)

> [1] *Paul, an apostle of Christ Jesus by the will of God, in keeping with the promise of life that is in Christ Jesus,* [2] *To Timothy, my dear son: Grace, mercy and peace from God the Father and Christ Jesus our Lord.*

1 Paul's opening words here, as in all his letters, "follow the format of most Greco-Roman letters of his day."[1] "Paul, an apostle of Christ Jesus by the will of God," sounds unremarkable to Christian ears, most likely because these opening words are virtually identical with those of four other Pauline letters

1. Thomas R. Schreiner, *Interpreting the Pauline Epistles*, 2d ed. (Grand Rapids: Baker Academic, 2011), 13.

(1 Corinthians,[2] 2 Corinthians, Ephesians, Colossians). Several other letters contain the words "Paul" and "apostle" in their opening (Romans, Galatians, 1 Timothy, Titus). But the prepositional phrase "by the will of God" is a rarity. In all the New Testament, this expression occurs only in the openings of five Pauline letters (including 2 Timothy) and in two other places: Rom 15:32, where Paul expresses the wish to "come to you with joy, *by God's will*," and 2 Cor 8:5, to laud the Macedonians for giving "themselves first of all to the Lord, and then *by the will of God* also to" Paul. One seeks in vain to find the words "by the will of God" (*dia thelēmatos theou*) in the sizable corpus encompassing the LXX, Philo, Josephus, and the AF.[3]

The opening, then, is a place where PE usage (thought by many to be so non-Pauline as to preclude Paul as their author) perfectly mirrors a feature of writings widely affirmed as Pauline (Romans, 1–2 Corinthians, Ephesians, Colossians), and a linguistically obscure feature at that. We are dealing here either with deft and subtle imitation (whether for noble or for deceptive purposes) or Paul's own reflexive and unique style and theological understanding.

In addition to authorship, the phrase "by the will of God" may have relevance for three additional considerations. First, is *authority*. Paul's leadership in the early Christian decades owes most, in his thinking, not to personal qualifications, political skill, or other purely immanent factors but to God's direct intervention in the world and in Paul's life. We may think here, for example, of his dramatic conversion, which included personal conversation with the risen Jesus (Acts 9), or his explicit reference to his apostleship being a divine and not a human matter (Gal 1:1: "Paul, an apostle—sent not from men nor by a man, but by Jesus Christ and God the Father, who raised him from the dead").

The second consideration is *personal relationship with God*. "God" is not a religious cipher or symbol for Paul but a living being who has disclosed himself indelibly to Paul in ways that were and remain unique (see, e.g., Eph 3:4–5; 2 Cor 12:2–7a). "By God's will" in light of this epochal revelational disclosure points to an intensely personal consciousness of divine purpose and impetus in Paul's mission and interactions. It has its correlate in Jesus's filial consciousness.

The third is *strong tie to Jesus*. Whereas some propose that Paul founded a religion that Jesus never envisioned or would have sanctioned, "by the will of God" in v. 1b cements the tie between Paul as an "apostle of Christ Jesus" (v. 1a) and "the promise of life that is in Christ Jesus" (v. 1 c), a tie inclusive also of God the Father that is reiterated by the wording of v. 2 (see below). As Jesus pointed to himself as the sole and unique mediator between God and humans

2. In 1 Cor 1:1 Paul adds the word "called": "Paul, called to be an apostle. . . ."

3. It is found in Justin, *Apology* 1.63.27, referring to Jesus Christ, "now, by the will of God, having become man for the human race."

(Matt 11:27; John 14:6; cf. 1 Tim 2:5), Paul begins this letter on a strong christological note that is grounded, in his thinking, securely in the will of the one and only true and living God and his personal intention as sovereignly disclosed to Paul (who by all accounts was not seeking and did not initially welcome it).

"The promise of life that is in Christ Jesus" may have been vivid as Paul faced death (4:6). It may be related to the "promise" Paul sees in Christ "for both the present life and the life to come" (1 Tim 4:8), not just one or the other. (On "eternal life," see also Titus 1:2 and the discussion below.) What Paul writes to Timothy will equip him for temporal duties before him no less than for heavenly existence beyond.

2 On "Timothy," see Introduction, VIII.B. The words of this verse are identical to 1 Tim 1:2 (except there Paul calls Timothy not "my dear son" but rather "my true son in the faith"). The Greek could be rendered "beloved child" (*agapētō teknō*). While Timothy is no doubt a "dear son" to Paul in their joint allegiance to Christ and close personal ties over the years, the wording also calls to mind the beloved-by-God status of those who by his grace call on his name for forgiveness and find new life. Paul endures "everything for the sake of the elect" (2:10), of which he will shortly remind Timothy. Here at the letter's outset Paul reminds Timothy of God's sovereign and merciful claim on him, for Timothy is a Spirit-led and adopted "beloved child" of the Father (see Rom 8:14–17), as well as Paul's cherished spiritual son (1 Cor 4:17). The two perspectives—dear to Paul and beloved by God—are not mutually exclusive but interdependent. Underlying Paul's "dear" is more than mere human sentimentality.

Saarinen rightly points out that Paul calling Timothy his child is "the opposite of subordination." Rather, "Timothy inherits the theological legacy of Paul and is thus supposed to have authority in the church."[4]

Paul's greeting of "grace, mercy, and peace" is paralleled in Paul's letter openings only in 1 Tim 1:2 (see discussion there); in every other Pauline letter he opens with "grace and peace."[5] Specifics of Timothy's pastoral setting as Paul writes are scant; in the main they must be inferred from 2 Timothy. But in all pastoral situations "grace" is needed for the saving message of Christ to go forth (as, e.g., one observes the progress of gospel-engendered *charis* [grace] in Acts 4:33; 6:8; 11:23; 13:43; 14:3, 26; 15:11; 18:27; 20:24, 32: the advance of the church via the gospel message is dependent on the operation of divine grace). Mercy (*eleos*),[6] too, is a key pastoral ingredient, as it is fundamental to personal

4. Saarinen, 120.

5. In Gal 6:16 Paul writes in concluding, "Peace and mercy to all who follow this rule—to the Israel of God."

6. The word occurs twenty-seven times in the New Testament, ten times in Paul, five times in the PE.

salvation (Titus 3:5; cf. Rom 9:23; Eph 2:4–5), Gentile reception of the gospel (Rom 11:31; 15:9), and God's eschatological favor on judgment day (2 Tim 1:18), all integral facets in the church's ministry of evangelism and the care of souls.

Finally, "peace" in Paul's writings (ten times total, five times in the PE) as a greeting may be seen as a virtual invocation of God's presence, as he is a "God of peace" (Rom 15:33; 16:20; Phil 4:9; 1 Thess 5:23; cf. Heb 13:20) who grants "the peace of God" (Phil 4:7), which Paul will later admonish Timothy to "pursue," along with "righteousness, faith, and love" (2 Tim 2:22). As a stabilizing presence and gratifying goal, few divine attributes are more basic to ministry than God-wrought *shalom*. Jesus pronounced those blessed who embody and promote "peace" (Matt 5:9), "for they will be called" just what Paul calls Timothy: "children of God."

Paul's prospective pronouncement of blessing is from Paul's hand but more fundamentally "from God the Father and Christ Jesus our Lord." The single preposition *apo* (from) stresses the common origin of the blessing, from two persons who are yet one being. Nor is it from a distant shadowy cosmic deity, but from the "Father," who with Christ is "our" Lord. This is the covenantal language of God and a people in close relationship richly attested in many Old Testament passages ("our God" occurs 218 times in the NIV Old Testament) and elsewhere in Paul's writings.[7]

B. Thanksgiving (1:3–5)

> [3]*I thank God, whom I serve, as my ancestors did, with a clear conscience, as night and day I constantly remember you in my prayers.* [4]*Recalling your tears, I long to see you, so that I may be filled with joy.* [5]*I am reminded of your sincere faith, which first lived in your grandmother Lois and in your mother Eunice and, I am persuaded, now lives in you also.*

3 Prayer (in this case of thanksgiving) after an opening greeting was standard protocol in letters of Paul's era and culture. Drawing on work by Schubert, O'Brien, and Wiles, Schreiner observes that "Paul's thanksgivings and intercessory prayers often signal the major themes in the letters and thus demand careful analysis."[8] Paul's words in this verse and section highlight heritage.

There is, first, the heritage of ancestry. Paul expresses thanks by using the same term *charis* (grace) that appeared in v. 2. *Charis* as blessedness segues

7. "Our Lord" is found fifty-two times in Paul (NIV). In Paul's writings the expression is absent from Philippians, Titus, and Philemon.

8. Schreiner, *Interpreting the Pauline Epistles*, 16.

into *charis* as gratitude;[9] "thanksgiving and blessing cannot be strictly separated."[10] Paul is grateful that he serves[11] God from within a long and established lineage, "as [his] ancestors[12] did." Jesus alluded to this redemptive heritage with the words "salvation is from the Jews" (John 4:22). Through "the people of Israel" God has provided for world redemption things like "adoption to sonship . . . , the divine glory, the covenants, the receiving of the law, the temple worship and the promises," to say nothing of the patriarchs and in terms of "human ancestry . . . the Messiah, who is God overall, forever praised!" (Rom 9:4–5). Paul, like Timothy, serves the God who has acted to furnish all this grace. Their common commitment to him is the foundation upon which Paul builds the encouragement and counsel of this letter; it is theocentric in orientation (like all the PE; see Introduction, II–III).

Paul's gratitude and service are "with a clear conscience."[13] Acts records a similar conviction in Paul (23:1; 24:16). "Conscience" is mentioned frequently in the PE and often in Paul, who uses the word twenty times, most often in the Corinthian correspondence.[14] Conscience can be "seared" (1 Tim 4:2) or "corrupted" (Titus 1:15). But when "clear,"[15] it can also be an impetus to love (1 Tim 1:5) and faith (1 Tim 1:19). Though as he writes he is "chained like a criminal" (2 Tim 2:9) and could easily succumb to feelings of fear or guilt, he reminds Timothy of the purity of moral and spiritual awareness that accompanies faithful gospel service, not because people approve but because God stands behind those who trust in him (cf. 1 Cor 4:4: "My conscience is clear, but that does not make me innocent. It is the Lord who judges me"). This assurance furnishes fortification within.

Growing out of Paul's sense of ancestry and clear conscience, he continually prays for Timothy ("night and day constantly"). It is unnecessary for Paul to point out that his ancestral consolation is Timothy's, too, as Timothy's own

9. *Charis* as thanksgiving or gratitude is not unusual in Paul (Rom 6:17; 7:25; 1 Cor 10:30; 15:57; 2 Cor 2:14; 8:16; 9:15; Col 3:16).

10. David Pao, *Thanksgiving: An Investigation of a Pauline Theme* (Leicester: Apollos, 2002), 82n71.

11. Greek *latreuō*. The word occurs twenty-one times in the New Testament, four of those times in Paul: see also Rom 1:9, 25; Phil 3:3.

12. Greek *progonos*, a word used elsewhere in the New Testament only at 1 Tim 5:4. In the LXX it appears primarily in the Maccabean writings, often in the sense of the spiritual heritage of forebears: see, for example, 2 Macc 11:25; 3 Macc 6:28; 4 Macc 5:29; 9:2. The word is common in Philo and Josephus but absent from the AF.

13. In 1 Tim 3:9 clear conscience is a qualification for deacons. On "conscience" in Paul, see *DPL* 153–56.

14. Altogether, "conscience" appears thirty times in the New Testament.

15. Here Paul uses the adjective *katharos* (clean, pure). In other New Testament passages the adjectives *agathos* and *kalos* (both mean "good") are used, usually with little appreciable difference in meaning. NIV "clear conscience" rightly defers to English idiom.

maternal background is Jewish (see v. 5; cf. Acts 16:1). Against this backdrop Paul moves to a second aspect of Timothy's heritage.

4 Paul and Timothy have a shared history of life and ministry that is extensive enough to have generated strong emotional ties. Paul appeals now to this heritage of personal relationship. He mentions Timothy's "tears." Word may have reached Paul of grief or other calamity in Timothy's life. Perhaps he refers to a rough patch in Timothy's ministry or some other crisis. We simply do not know particulars. But Paul's language is "intensely personal and emotional."[16] In response to Timothy's woe Paul does not sit passively or idly. He is already in constant prayer (v. 3). In addition, he holds out the prospect of reunion. Paul and Timothy have leaned on each other in the past—this is implied by the Pauline letters that open with mention of Timothy (i.e., 2 Corinthians, Philippians, Colossians, 1–2 Thessalonians, Philemon). They have a track record of mutual support. Paul longs[17] for this rapport to be reestablished face to face. Later in the letter he takes steps to ensure that it will (4:9).

For now, it is enough to acknowledge Timothy's duress, assure him of empathy, and anticipate the joy of Timothy's eventual arrival. Paul mentions joy frequently (twenty times) in his other letters but only here in the PE. Anticipation of joy forms part of the heritage that causes Paul to give thanks (v. 3). He knows he will be not merely touched by but "filled with joy."[18] Here is a practical instance of Paul living out his own already/not yet eschatology, as he is distressed that Timothy is "not yet" consoled (implied by Timothy's "tears"), yet confident and content with the "already" reality of their reunion in due course.

5 A third motivation for Paul's gratitude is family faith. In broad terms, all in the church are siblings sharing the same Father God and in that sense constitute the household of God (1 Tim 3:15). They are family in that they share a de facto God-family tie. But in some cases the kinship of shared loyalty to Jesus (cf. Mark 3:33–35) is matched by the blood kinship of family members. Among Jesus's followers were the brothers James and John (Mark 3:17), as well as Andrew and Simon (John 1:40). His disciples eventually included his mother and his brothers James and Jude. Paul recalls not only Timothy's tears (2 Tim 1:4) but also Timothy's faith (v. 5), particularly in the forms it assumed "first" (*prōton*) in Timothy's grandmother Lois and mother Eunice.[19] It is be-

16. Towner, *Letters*, 452.

17. From Greek *epipotheō*, which Paul uses in six other passages, usually to express interpersonal ardor (Rom 1:11; 2 Cor 9:14; Phil 1:8; 2:6; 1 Thess 3:6) but once to express eschatological longing (2 Cor 5:2).

18. On joy in Paul, see Matthew Elliott, *Faithful Feelings: Emotion in the New Testament* (Leicester: Inter-Varsity, 2005), 172–75. For other references to filling with joy in Paul, see Rom 15:13; 2 Cor 7:4; Phil 2:2.

19. These are both Greek names, which were common among Jews in the Roman Empire (Laansma, 130).

cause of them, it seems, that Paul can later write to Timothy that "from infancy you have known the Holy Scriptures," through which he received the wisdom needed "for salvation through faith in Christ Jesus" (3:15).

The strength of Timothy's faith lies not only in its family heritage; Paul calls it "sincere" (from *anypokritos*). Of the New Testament's six occurrences of this word, four are in Paul.[20] Outside the PE Paul twice describes love (*agapē*) by this adjective (Rom 12:9; 2 Cor 6:6), which Danker glosses with words like "without pretense, unfeigned, genuine."[21] Timothy was no less committed to Christ than was Paul (1 Cor 16:10) nor any less solicitous for the welfare of the churches and "the interests . . . of Jesus Christ" (Phil 2:19–22).

Another clue to the quality of Timothy's faith may lie in Paul's statement that it "lived" in his grandmother (perhaps mentioned first out of respect for age)[22] and mother. The word translated "lived" (from Gk. *enoikeō*) is found only in Paul in the New Testament. Paul uses it to speak of the Spirit indwelling believers (Rom 8:11; 2 Tim 1:14), God living in the midst of his people (2 Cor 6:16, adapted from Lev 26:12), and "the message of Christ" dwelling lavishly among the Colossians (Col 3:16). In Paul, *enoikeō* describes divine, dynamic, and transforming presence. The faith of Timothy's maternal forebears was not passive, merely external, or pro forma but deep and alive. "Lived in" (NIV) is accurate though perhaps a little bland.[23] No wonder Timothy's appropriation of this faith (not shared, it seems, by his father; Acts 16:1, 3)[24] resulted in a fidelity and fervor that Paul found matched by few if any even among his distinguished coworkers (Phil 2:20).

Paul is "persuaded" (*pepeismai*) that the same faith continues to be present in Timothy. First person use of the root verb *peithō* is limited in the New Testament to one Pauline statement in Acts (26:26) and seven other uses in Paul's letters (Rom 8:38; 14:14; 15:14; Gal 1:10; 5:10; Phil 2:24; 2 Tim 1:12). The expression is curious (lit. "But I am convinced that [the same faith dwells] also in you."). Given short life spans in antiquity, perhaps the grandmother if not also the mother have already departed this life ("lived in" is aorist, which in itself does not prove Paul's reference is to the past, though it would be appropriate if he is not referring explicitly to the present). They persevered to the end. Now it is Timothy's turn to be as steadfast. Paul is optimistic ("persuaded").

20. Outside Paul: Jas 3:17 (referring to wisdom); 1 Pet 1:22 (referring to fraternal affection [*philadelphia*]).

21. F. W. Danker, *The Concise Greek-English Lexicon of the New Testament* (Chicago: University of Chicago Press, 2009), 38.

22. Or perhaps she was closer to Paul's own age than Timothy's mother.

23. Other options include "dwelt" (KJ21, ASV, *GNC*, DLNT), "was alive" (NIRV), "filled" (NLT), and "came to live" (NTE).

24. Thus he "did not undertake Timothy's biblical training," although "godly instruction should come from the father and mother (Prov 1:8)" (Spencer, 83).

But will Timothy vindicate this trust? Paul does not take it for granted as he moves next to call on Timothy to follow their dedicated lead.

C. Appeal for Loyalty to Paul and the Gospel (1:6–14)

"Loyalty to Paul" (NIV heading above) needs to be understood in the sense of "loyalty to what claims Paul's loyalty." For these verses do not call for a loyalty to Paul himself, as if he commanded Timothy's allegiance and deserved his recognition, but rather to the Lord (v. 8), the gospel (v. 9), the apostolic "pattern of sound teaching" (v. 13), and "the good deposit" Timothy has received (v. 14). It is a Christocentric and gospel-centered appeal that points beyond Paul for its substance and high value.

> [6] *For this reason I remind you to fan into flame the gift of God, which is in you through the laying on of my hands.* [7] *For the Spirit God gave us does not make us timid, but gives us power, love and self-discipline.* [8] *So do not be ashamed of the testimony about our Lord or of me his prisoner. Rather, join with me in suffering for the gospel, by the power of God.* [9] *He has saved us and called us to a holy life—not because of anything we have done but because of his own purpose and grace. This grace was given us in Christ Jesus before the beginning of time,* [10] *but it has now been revealed through the appearing of our Savior, Christ Jesus, who has destroyed death and has brought life and immortality to light through the gospel.* [11] *And of this gospel I was appointed a herald and an apostle and a teacher.* [12] *That is why I am suffering as I am. Yet this is no cause for shame, because I know whom I have believed, and am convinced that he is able to guard what I have entrusted to him until that day.* [13] *What you heard from me, keep as the pattern of sound teaching, with faith and love in Christ Jesus.* [14] *Guard the good deposit that was entrusted to you—guard it with the help of the Holy Spirit who lives in us.*

6 "For this reason"[25] refers to Paul's confidence regarding Timothy's faith, rooted as it is in ancient family heritage. He is betting that Timothy will prove as steady as the women who grounded him in the faith so that he will not falter or fold. But this confidence assumes Timothy will follow through on the good

25. This prepositional phrase is sparsely attested in the LXX; outside of one use in 1 Esd 2:17, it appears only six more times, all in the Maccabean writings. It is found in Josephus only three times, in Philo a dozen times, and in the AF not at all. Other New Testament occurrences of *di' hēn aitian* (for which reason, because of which): Luke 8:47; Acts 22:24; 2 Tim 1:12; Titus 1:13; Heb 2:11.

work begun in him (see Phil 1:6; 1 Thess 5:24). Paul opts only to "remind"[26] Timothy of "the gift" he has received. Like his suasive strategy in dealing with Philemon (Phlm 8–9), Paul draws on the indicative of what he knows the gospel message has implanted in Timothy, not some authoritative force vested in Paul, much less psychological or emotional manipulation.

"The gift of God" (*to charisma tou theou*) may refer to the Holy Spirit (see v. 7), to the spiritual enablements he bestows (see 1 Tim 4:14 and discussion), or to both. In the New Testament's only other occurrence of this exact phrase, Paul uses it to refer to "eternal life in Christ Jesus our Lord" (Rom 6:23). *Charisma* ("gift," often as the result of God's grace [*charis*]) is a signature Pauline term.[27] Timothy has received something free and powerful from God[28] that can make all the difference in a situation where timidity may be a temptation (see v. 7) and suffering may be called for (see v. 8) in order for Timothy to stay true to what has been entrusted to him (vv. 13–14). The Spirit or other bestowals or visitations from God (see 4:17) give impetus for ministry. But his gifts call for reception and intentional response (see Eph 5:18; 1 Thess 5:19). In this case the need is for Timothy to relight or stir up[29] a devotion that Paul apparently sees as burning low.

The verticality of this gift—"from God"—is complemented by a social horizontality: the means of bestowal was "through[30] the laying on of [Paul's] hands." In the Old Testament this symbolic action was a sign of dedication to the Lord's service (see, e.g., Num 8:10; 27:18). Christ often touched in connection with healing. R. Banks describes the laying on of hands as "a multiple-purpose procedure" in the early church, signifying reception of the Spirit (Acts 8:17; 9:17), restoration to fellowship or possibly appointment to spiritual office (1 Tim 5:22), or "commissioning for itinerant service (Acts

26. From *anamimnēskō*, found six times in the New Testament total; in Paul, elsewhere at 1 Cor 4:17; 2 Cor 7:15. Other uses: Mark 11:21; 14:72; Heb 10:32.

27. Except for one occurrence, in 1 Pet 4:10, its other sixteen New Testament occurrences are in Paul's writings: besides 2 Tim 1:6, Rom 1:11; 5:15, 16; 6:23; 11:29; 12:6; 1 Cor 1:7; 7:7; 12:4, 9, 28, 30, 31; 2 Cor 1:11; 1 Tim 4:14. There are six AF occurrences: 1 Clem. 38:1; Did. 1:5; Ign. *Eph.* 17:2; *Smyrn.* 0 (Greetings) (twice); *Pol.* 2:2.

28. Cf. Wright, 85, with stress on both the power of leadership and the quality of love required to exercise it by the Spirit (not "spirit" as in Wright).

29. From *anazōpyreō*, a New Testament hapax. MM 33 reports that the word is "vouched for in the common speech of the day." It occurs twice in the LXX, once of Jacob's spirit reviving when he saw his long lost son Joseph (Gen 45:27), and again of the spirit of the people when Simon spoke to them encouragingly (1 Macc 13:7). The word is absent from Philo, occurs five times in Josephus, and is used twice in the AF, of renewed faith in God (1 Clem. 27:3) and of "new life through the blood of God" (Ign. *Eph.* 1:1).

30. Dibelius and Conzelmann, 98, comment: "The preposition 'through' . . . must not be accorded too much importance. The grace is not yet understood as an habitual disposition transferred from person to person."

13:2; cf. 2 Tim 1:6)."[31] We cannot point to a known event Paul may have in mind in the v. 6 reference. It makes sense to see Paul reminding Timothy of what must have been a powerful moment in their mutual spiritual progress, ecclesial involvement, and personal relationship. Human physical contact can be virtually sacramental in its reinforcement of the reality of divine favor and equipping for tasks greater than flesh alone can undertake.[32]

7 Paul gives motivation for Timothy to rekindle the gift God entrusted to him (v. 6). In Greek this verse begins with the negative *ou* (not). Paul contrasts what God has *not* given to believers with what he has.

On the negative side, "the Spirit God gave us does not make us timid" (NIV). This is a rendering echoed by CEV ("God's Spirit doesn't make cowards out of us") and TLB ("For the Holy Spirit, God's gift, does not want you to be afraid of people"). Most translations, though, view the subject in Greek as "God" (in Gk., nominative with the article) not "Spirit" (accusative without an article). Most English translations run in the direction of HCSB's "For God has not given us a spirit of fearfulness" (so also, with variations, KJV, ESV, NASB). Some agree that God is the subject and "spirit" the direct object but view "spirit" as a reference to the Holy Spirit: "For God did not give us a Spirit of fear" (NET).

The NIV translation can be justified by the discourse flow. Since v. 6 speaks of "gift" and evokes a sense of the Holy Spirit's operation, it is reasonable to tweak "God has not given us a spirit" (which can be understood as "the Spirit") in v. 7 to the NIV's "the Spirit God gave. . . ." Even if we prefer the more straightforward "God has not given us a spirit of timidity" (NASB), the spirit thus received from God is surely because of the working of the Holy Spirit.

Paul's point to Timothy, on the negative side, seems to bear in mind his tears (v. 4), unlikely to be a sign of bravery, and seek to rally him to a fresh confidence in God. Whatever Timothy's specific *gift* (v. 6), what "the Spirit . . . *gave*" him (v. 7) is incompatible with fearfulness[33] (*deilia*, a New Testament hapax; but see cognates in, e.g., Matt 8:26; Mark 4:40; see also Rev 21:8). Paul's words diplomatically[34] challenge Timothy to frank self-assessment.[35]

31. *DPL* 135.

32. See also discussion at 1 Tim 5:22.

33. "Fearfulness" (conveyed in the New Testament most frequently by *phobos*) is the definition of *deilia* suggested in *GELS* 141 to cover its nine LXX uses. NETS renders its LXX occurrences with "faintness" (Lev 26:36; cf. 2 Macc 3:24), "cowardice" (1 Macc 4:32; 4 Macc 6:20; Ps 88:41), "dread" (2 Macc 6:19; Sir 4:17), "terror" (of death; Ps 54:5), and "timidity" (Prov 19:15). It appears forty-one times in Philo and fourteen in Josephus, in both of whose writings *phobos* is far more common (Philo 131, Josephus 148). *Deilia* occurs only two times in the AF, *phobos* thirty-nine times. MM does not list the less common word.

34. He writes in the first person plural ("us"), not with an accusatory "you."

35. For recognition of the fear factor in ministry by Chrysostom, Tertullian, and Calvin, see Twomey, 120.

On the positive side, God furnishes resources that can galvanize Timothy. In the NIV rendering, the Spirit provides these things. In other translations, God gives a "spirit" suffused with this brief but potent list of attributes: "power, love and self-discipline." Either way, fear is displaced by vastly superior qualities that can not only lift Timothy out of his mire but equip him to be of service to those who look to him (as Timothy looks to Paul) for pastoral direction.

Timothy can give that direction, and maintain his own, through God giving, first, power (*dynamis*). This common Pauline word (forty-five occurrences) is found in all his letters except 1 Timothy, Titus, and Philemon. He writes most often of "the power of God"[36] or of God's Spirit.[37] He also speaks of "Christ the power of God" (1 Cor 1:24). Divine power to save lies in the gospel message (Rom 1:16), "the message of the cross" (1 Cor 1:18). Timothy needs fortification, with which God is both replete and generous.

God also gives *agapē* (love), even more frequent in Paul (seventy-one occurrences) than "power." Paul had earlier written to Timothy that "love" was a central aim of his apostolic ministry (1 Tim 1:5), precisely because it had (along with grace and faith) been "poured out abundantly" on him (1 Tim 1:14). In reminding Timothy of what God gives, Paul speaks from vivid personal experience. He also indirectly reminds him of the highest priority set by Christ (see, e.g., Matt 22:37–40), a priority Paul famously affirms himself in 1 Cor 13. The close connection between God's giving and his love is as basic to early Christian teaching, and hence Paul's rallying words here, as John 3:16: "God so loved . . . that he gave."

God also gives a spirit (or Spirit) of "self-discipline" (*sōphronismos*, a New Testament hapax).[38] Fear or distraction can take control in the complexities of ministry or the intimidation of settings hostile to gospel service. The resulting stress can be paralyzing or can tempt to flight. God's Spirit imparts steadiness. "Do not be afraid" is a signature dominical exhortation in the Gospels.[39] Paul concisely erects a bulwark against craven lassitude with his appeal to God's gifting.

8 Here begins a sentence that in Greek runs for 105 words, to the end of v. 12. Paul waxes eloquent, signified by the versification in NA[28], which highlights the rhetorical elegance of vv. 9–10. Verse 8 inaugurates this impressive and memorable passage.

36. Rom 1:16; 1 Cor 1:18, 24; 2 Cor 6:7; 2 Tim 1:8.

37. Rom 15:13, 19; Gal 4:29.

38. But see nine occurrences of the cognate *sōphrosynē* (self-control) in the LXX: Esth 13:3; 2 Macc 4:37; 4 Macc 1:3, 6, 18, 30, 31; 5:23; Wis 8:7; note also the same word in the New Testament (Acts 26:25; 1 Tim 2:9, 15).

39. Jesus speaks these words in Matt 10:26, 28; 28:10; Luke 12:4, 32; John 14:27, and implies them in many other places, especially by his characteristic fearlessness.

"So" translates *oun*,[40] a conjunction that signals an inference from the preceding. In light of what God furnishes Timothy (v. 7), he should put behind him any lack of zeal for the gospel and instead reaffirm his partnership with Paul, even if it means suffering.

"Do not be ashamed of the testimony" recalls Paul's "I am not ashamed of the gospel" (Rom 1:16). The word translated "ashamed" (*epaischynomai*) is found in Paul only in Romans (see also Rom 6:21) and 2 Timothy (see also 1:12, 16). He appears to be summoning Timothy to boldness in two respects. First is regarding the *martyrion* (testimony) "about our Lord." Paul uses this word elsewhere.[41] There was an ancient tradition among God's people that facts were established by multiple (lit. "two or three") witnesses (Deut 17:6; 19:15). Jesus reaffirmed this principle (Matt 18:16, 20), and Paul was among those who carried it forward into early church life (1 Cor 14:29; 2 Cor 13:1; 1 Tim 5:19; cf. Heb 10:28). Whereas "witness" or "testimony" today can mean one's unique personal inner religious experience, its biblical usage points to a sharing of publicly observed phenomena. Jesus did not die for sin in secret, nor were his resurrection appearances viewed only by a select few off in hiding (see 1 Cor 15:1–8; Acts 1:3). After being told by Jesus, "You will be my witnesses" (Acts 1:8), Peter and John spoke of what they had "seen and heard" (Acts 4:20).[42] Timothy needs to be open and forthright about what had been proclaimed across the Roman world (and beyond) for some three decades by the time Paul writes 2 Timothy.[43]

G. Couser has argued that "the testimony about our Lord" in v. 8 should be understood as "the testimony the Lord *bore*, in his words and life, to the saving plan of God." The Greek certainly allows this understanding, and in support Couser points especially to "the importance of the words and acts of Christ (past, present, future) throughout" 1 and 2 Timothy.[44] In any case, NIV's "the testimony about our Lord" should not be viewed in a way that would exclude reference to Jesus's own testimony in his multifaceted ministry.

It is understandable that Timothy might be tempted to act "ashamed" of Paul the Lord's "prisoner."[45] It was neither safe nor simple to identify with

40. It appears 499 times in the New Testament, 111 times in Paul, and 7 times in the PE. The only Pauline letter from which *oun* is absent is Titus.

41. That is, 1 Cor 1:6; 2 Cor 1:12; 2 Thess 1:10; 1 Tim 2:6.

42. See testimony regarding what was "seen and heard" (NIV) in Luke 7:22; John 3:32; Acts 22:15; 1 John 1:3.

43. On the early missionary thrust of testimony to Jesus, see Schnabel, *Paul and the Early Church*.

44. G. Couser, "'The Testimony about the Lord,' 'Borne by the Lord,' or Both? An Insight into Paul and Jesus in the Pastoral Epistles (2 Tim 1:8)," *TynBull* 52 (2004): 316.

45. See Neudorfer, *Zweiter Brief an Timotheus*, 87–90, for details of the arrest and incarceration process Paul would have experienced.

those under imperial indictment; for someone to make such identification was courageous and commendable (see v. 16; Heb 10:32–35). The power, love, and self-discipline given by God (v. 7), however, should steel Timothy for rising to the challenge of even costly identification with Paul, as Timothy had already done many times over more than a decade of laboring with him. Yesterday's moral victories are launching pads, not the end game; divine grace is more than sufficient to empower Timothy to step out in open support of the gospel cause yet again.

Paul knows that such support will be difficult and risky: "join with me in suffering."[46] These five words in the NIV translate just one in Greek: *synkakopathēson*.[47] One might render this word literally, "Co-suffer!" It is the first formal imperative[48] of some thirty-three that appear in 2 Timothy. Paul has laid a gracious rhetorical foundation before now moving into harder things Timothy needs to hear. Is Paul perhaps even being curt? While scanning the clause in English highlights the specter of Timothy's suffering, in Greek what catches the eye is not the one-word imperative (though the distinctive word registers) but the five words following: literally "for the gospel according to the power of God." The weight of words falls on the gospel, on God, and on his power. (On "power," see previous verse.) "Rather than crediting or validating" the humiliation of associating with Paul, Timothy is exhorted to express his solidarity with the man who was his father in the faith (1:2; 2:1).[49]

9 Verse 8 speaks of being "ashamed," and v. 12 speaks of "no cause for shame." These verses bookend a section rallying Timothy to overcome any sense of gospel opprobrium. Paul seizes on the ultimate justification for human action: God. NIV begins a new sentence in v. 9, which gives the impression of a hard break at the end of v. 8. In Greek there is direct and full flow from "by the power of God" (v. 8) to "who saved and called us" (direct rendering of the beginning of v. 9).

The motivational effect of vv. 9–11, leading up to a climactic assertion of "I am not ashamed" of the gospel in v. 12 (with the implication that Timothy

46. The claim of Bassler (131) that this suffering is "with Paul, not suffering with Christ" assumes an absolute distinction that cannot be sustained, given the christological focus of the PE. Paul's very life was lived in and with Christ (Gal 2:20), whether he lived or died (Phil 1:20–21). His call to Timothy to join him in suffering was a call to join him in fellowship with Christ, not to support him in a christless ego trip.

47. This verb occurs only here and in 2:3 in the New Testament. A conceptually similar word is found in Heb 11:25. For both words, see BDAG 951.

48. While subjunctive in form, "do not be ashamed" earlier in v. 8 is a de facto imperative. Hellenistic Greek most commonly used the "prohibitive subjunctive" when forbidding an action using the aorist form of a verb. See Wallace, *Greek Grammar*, 487.

49. Trebilco, Caradus, and Rae, 29.

should not be, either), is achieved by elegant, theologically laden testimony to (1) what God has done and (2) what God has shown.[50]

As to God's doing, he "saved" Paul and Timothy and all believers ("us"). (On "saved," see Introduction, IX.A.) Bracketed with this saving action and intensifying it is another act of God: he "called us to a holy life." "Holy life" translates *klēsei hagia*, literally, "holy calling." "Calling" (*klēsis*)[51] in BDAG 549 is not defined as "life" but as "invitation to experience of special privilege and responsibility, *call, calling, invitation.*" BDAG adds that it refers almost exclusively to "divine initiative." This invitation should lead to holy living, but Paul is reminding Timothy of God's outreach, not human reflex. The glorious vision Paul begins to unfold here is not of how humans should live ("a holy life") but of God's remarkable, effectual, and ennobling summons to deliverance, worship, and service.

If Timothy might be inclined to look to himself so as to transcend shame and be willing to suffer for the gospel, Paul discourages the impulse to seize on human resources by adding that God's saving and summoning work is "not because of anything we have done but because of his own purpose and grace." (See Titus 3:5 and discussion for a similar affirmation.) Timothy may be feeling inadequate for bearing the onus of gospel duties. But he did not, in the end, get himself into this fix: God did; it was "his own" intention. Timothy's situation did not come about "according to" (*kata*) human achievement or qualification but "according to" (*kata*) divine "purpose[52] and grace." The energy and plumb line for Timothy's duties lie entirely in God. From experience Paul knows there is great freedom (e.g., from self-reliance) and promise in this understanding. What God began, he can carry out (Phil 1:6; cf. 1 Thess 5:24). Timothy should be wary of imagined self-limitations.

God has not only acted in saving and calling; he has also given grace. Paul highlights the transcendent origin of grace and its conferral on believers, as it "was given us in Christ Jesus before the beginning of time." "Was given" (*dotheisan*) is a passive participle behind which stands divine initiative and sufficiency. Again Timothy's gaze is directed not to himself but to a heavenly

50. Barclay, *Paul and the Gift*, 571, sees this verse as presenting works as "moral achievements" and thus constituting a "contextual shift" away from the real Paul. But given the theo- and Christocentricity of the discourse, it is also possible to see here integral links with—and no devolution from—Pauline teaching outside the PE.

51. The word occurs in the New Testament in ten other passages, most of them in Paul's writings: Rom 11:29; 1 Cor 1:26; 7:20; Eph 1:18; 4:1, 4; Phil 3:14; 2 Thess 1:11; Heb 3:1; 2 Pet 1:10. In the AF, too, it always refers to God's call or summons rather than to the life lived in response to it: 1 Clem. 46:6; Barn. 16:9; Herm. Mand. 4.3.6; Sim. 8.11.1.

52. The word can refer to human purpose or plan: for example, Acts 11:23; 27:13; 2 Tim 3:10. But Paul most often uses it of God's purpose in calling to salvation (Rom 8:28), in election (Rom 9:11; cf. Eph 1:11), and in his eternal redemptive plan "accomplished in Christ" (Eph 3:11).

horizon, namely, to eternity itself, in which the mystery of divine favor toward underserving creatures[53] is rooted.[54] Temporal difficulties are daunting, but they pale next to eternity's glories and mysteries,[55] in which Timothy has been invited to participate, for now through earthly pastoral service. See Titus 1:2 for additional relevant discussion.

In v. 9 having impressively rehearsed what God has done in saving, calling, and shedding grace, Paul now moves to affirm what God has shown.

10 In Paul's formulation here, bestowal of grace took place long ago (v. 9). Divine election was purposed before time began (cf. Eph 1:4: "before the creation of the world"). "Now" (v. 10) that grace "has been revealed." Awareness and effects of it have reached a new level. "Revealed" translates a form of the verb *phaneroō*, a word that can refer to disclosure of something divinely wrought (see, e.g., Mark 4:22; John 2:11; 3:21; 9:3; 17:6; 21:1, 13). Paul uses it this way nearly two dozen times and in one other PE passage (1 Tim 3:16: "appeared in the flesh"). The revelation of Christ Jesus that should uplift Timothy came "through the appearing" (see also 1 Tim 6:14; Titus 2:11, 13; 3:4 and discussion below) of "our Savior" (see Introduction, IX.A).

The Savior's "appearing" is riveting in itself. But Paul reminds Timothy that the potency of the incarnation lies in two things he effected through his coming. First, he "destroyed death." Similar language occurs in 1 Cor 15:26 and Heb 2:14. Second, he "brought life and immortality to light." "Brought . . . to light" (a form of Gk. *phōtizō*) is used by Paul elsewhere of divinely wrought disclosure (1 Cor 4:5; Eph 1:19; 3:9; cf. use of the same word in John 1:9; Heb 6:4; 10:32; Rev 18:1; 21:23; 22:5). Paul continues to stress not Timothy's resources or the work set before him but the resources faith can access in Jesus's death-destroying and light-disseminating ministry. Bringing "life and immortality to light" seems at least in part to be a reference to Jesus's resurrection, announced in the apostolic preaching.

"Through the gospel"[56] may refer to the good news of what Jesus did, its proclamation by figures like Paul and Timothy, or both. Perhaps the gospel does bring disapproval and "shame" to Timothy (see v. 8) as he seeks to minister it and to uphold Paul, despite his incarceration. But offsetting Timothy's

53. For a reminder of Paul's view of humans, and why grace so frequently elicits his praise, see Rom 3:9–20.

54. For some, what Paul says is no divine mystery, because it is viewed as a false statement. See, for example, Twomey, 124: in v. 9 "there is no place . . . for a theory of predestination according to which only some are saved, for God's perfect mercy requires the granting, universally, of eternal life."

55. Cf. Paul's use of "time" (*chronos*) in Rom 16:25: "the revelation of the mystery hidden for long ages past [*chronois aiōniois*]."

56. This precise phrase occurs in the New Testament only here and in 1 Cor 4:15; Eph 3:6; 2 Thess 2:14.

misgivings about the gospel should be the epochal illuminating effects of this reality and of testimony to it by apostolic leaders like Paul—and in times past by Timothy, his faithful coworker. Paul is not, then, informing Timothy of something new but rather giving him the opportunity to recommit to what he has already long affirmed.

11 Mention of the gospel (v. 10) calls forth a declaration of Paul's dedication to it, as explaining why he suffers the things he does (v. 12).

Paul "was appointed"[57] to gospel service, which he breaks down here into three components or functions: herald, apostle, and teacher. He refers to the same three roles in 1 Tim 2:7, with the additional note that he is "a true and faithful teacher of the Gentiles";[58] see discussion there. This range of duties comports with the statement God made when Paul received the Spirit, "This man is my chosen instrument to proclaim my name to the Gentiles" (Acts 9:15; cf. "apostle to the Gentiles" in Rom 11:13; Gal 2:8). Paul may be making the point that the grand truths he is highlighting (2 Tim 1:8–10) are not just interesting facts. Rather, they are incendiary assertions that impel those who internalize them as the God who accomplishes and makes known his truths claims some hearers (like Paul and Timothy) to be mediators of this gospel to others, as unpopular or risky (and hence causing suffering) as this office might be. Though Timothy was not an "apostle" like Paul, his duties were similar as a pastoral teacher (4:2) and an "evangelist" (4:5). Timothy's proximity to Paul marks him as quasi-apostolic. Paul's example might move Timothy toward Paul's level of courage and fidelity, especially with his imminent demise in view.

12 The lengthy sentence that began in v. 8 continues and in v. 12 terminates. Paul links v. 12 to v. 11 with the prepositional phrase "for which reason" (*di' hēn aitian*).[59] Because of his role as herald, apostle, and teacher, he states, "I am suffering as I am."

Paul's service to Christ and the gospel (v. 10) drew opposition, just as it did for his fellow gospel-followers—forms of the same Greek word *paschō* (I suffer) appear at 3:12 (referring to all believers) and at 2 Cor 1:6; Phil 1:29; 1 Thess 2:14; 2 Thess 1:5 (referring to duress or persecution in the Corinthian, Philippian, and Thessalonian communities, respectively). "If one part" of Christ's body "suffers [*paschei*], every part suffers with [*sympaschei*] it" (1 Cor 12:26). Far from rosy prosperity expectations, the Pauline gospel could and did usher in a world of woes to those who received it. Paul catalogues his own

57. The two other New Testament uses of the verb *tithēmi* to denote divine designation of someone for a task or to a status are Heb 10:13 (God's enemies "made" a footstool for the Son's feet) and 1 Pet 2:8 (those who disobey the gospel message are "destined" for the condemnation they receive).

58. Most MSS read "teacher of Gentiles" in 2 Tim 1:11. NA[28] editors consider absence of the words from א* A I 1175 to be decisive.

59. See discussion with footnote at 2 Tim 1:6 above.

battle scars in 2 Cor 11:23–12:10. "Suffering as I am" (Gk. lit. "these things I suffer") likely refers to Paul's prison status, including the specter of execution in a setting where false friends betrayed and many deserted him (v. 15; see also 4:14–16).

But (NIV "Yet"; the Gk. word is a hard adversative) Paul will not give in to a sense of shame (see v. 8[60] for discussion of the concept and its challenge for Timothy). He gives a twofold reason, a rationale no doubt pitched to buoy up Timothy. First, Paul claims a personal knowledge of God in Christ: "I know whom I have believed."[61] God is faithful[62] and does not let down those who look to him. This existential and relational conviction offsets Paul's suffering, making it perhaps not only bearable but in its way a ground for thanksgiving (cf. Acts 5:41). Timothy's faith, of course, is in the same God. Later, Paul will relate his graphic sense that, in his current trial, "the Lord stood at my side and gave me strength . . . and I was delivered from the lion's mouth" (4:17). Such consciousness gives rise, second, to hope or confidence about the future, about which a prisoner facing execution could scarcely fail to reflect. Knowing God as Paul does, he is "convinced that he is able to guard" what Paul has "entrusted to him." Here he uses the word *parathēkē*, which means "property entrusted to another, *deposit*" (BDAG 764). The word occurs only two other times in the New Testament (1 Tim 6:20; 2 Tim 1:14; see discussion there).

With this word Paul could refer to what he has placed in God's hands, such as his daily existence and eternal destiny. This meaning is suggested by the NIV's "what I have entrusted to him." But it may rather point to what God has entrusted to Paul in terms of the gospel message[63] and faithful apostolic teaching.[64] Paul writes literally *parathēkē mou*, "my deposit," as he writes elsewhere of "my gospel,"[65] the gospel message and its entailments entrusted to him.

Paul's point is that he has received a message to preserve and promulgate. It has brought him to a trial that will cost him his life. But God is with him in it all and will not permit either God's investment in Paul or Paul's commitment to God's trust to be squandered. There affirmations are all calculated to arouse Timothy's sentiments of loyalty, to Paul and to Christ whom Paul preached, as well as to the apostolic message being passed along to Timothy (see 2:1–2).

60. The same verb for being ashamed, *epaischynomai*, occurs in both v. 8 and in v. 12.

61. Reference to believing in the perfect tense and active voice is attested elsewhere in Paul only at Titus 3:8. It is more common in Acts (15:5; 16:34; 18:27; 19:18; 21:20, 25) and in the Johannine writings (John 3:18; 6:69; 8:31; 11:27; 16:27; 20:29; 1 John 4:16; 5:10).

62. See, for example, Deut 32:41; 1 Cor 1:9; 10:13; 2 Cor 1:18; 2 Thess 3:3.

63. So Neudorfer, *Zweiter Brief an Timotheus*, 105: the expression denotes "the gospel itself."

64. Affirmed by Swinson, *What Is Scripture?*, 81–82, citing Towner, Mounce, and others.

65. Rom 2:16; 16:25; 2 Tim 2:8.

For God will vindicate Paul at the final judgment (1 Cor 3:13; 2 Cor, 5:10), whatever opposition to him the gospel message may attract. This assurance underlies his reference to "that day" (see also 2 Tim 1:18).[66] On this day Paul envisions "the crown of righteousness, which the Lord, the righteous Judge, will award to me . . . and not only to me, but also to all who have longed for his appearing" (4:8). That number will include Timothy if he receives Paul's words as the apostle clearly intends and hopes.

13 The long and complex sentence (vv. 8–12) having ended, Paul makes his point with only the second imperative in the letter (the first was in v. 8): "keep . . . the pattern of sound teaching!" "Keep" translates a form of *echō*, which can mean "holding fast to matters of transcendent importance" (BDAG 420). "Pattern"[67] is the first word of the sentence, which may suggest emphasis. Woodenly rendered the verse reads as follows: "The pattern keep of healthy words." In contrast, in all three of the other passages where Paul uses *echō* as an imperative, the complement or object of the imperative is stated first, as the following table indicates:

Table 23. Uses of *echō* as an imperative in Paul's letters
The imperative is underlined. The object or complement of the imperative is in italics.

Passage	Greek text	Wooden rendering
Rom 14:22	*sy pistin [hēn] echeis kata seauton eche*	you, the faith [which] you have *as your own personal conviction* hold
1 Cor 7:2	*hekastos tēn heautou gynaika echetō kai hekastē ton idion andra echetō*	each husband *his own wife* let him have relations with and each wife *her own husband* let her have relations with
Phil 2:29	*tous toioutous entimous echete*	*such individuals* [as] *highly esteemed* hold
2 Tim 1:13	*hypotypōsin eche hygiainontōn logōn*	*the pattern* keep *of healthy words*

66. "That day" is the eschatological day of judgment frequently in the Gospels (Matt 7:22; 24:36; 26:29; Luke 10:12; 17:31; 21:34), as well as in Paul (2 Thess 2:3) and Peter (2 Pet 3:12).

67. Greek *hypotypōsis*. The word appears elsewhere in the New Testament only at 1 Tim 1:16. It is absent from the LXX and Josephus and occurs only once in Philo. The word can also mean "outline," the sense it carries as the title of a lost work of Clement of Alexandria, *Hypotypōses* (Outlines), mentioned in Eusebius, *Church History* 2.15.

Perhaps Paul intends emphasis in the first three passages, too. Or maybe it is just Paul's style to let the command to "have" or "keep" something trail the thing one is to "have" or "keep," in this case "the pattern."[68] In that case, no special emphasis should be assigned to the word order.

What is certain is that this pattern consists of "sound teaching" (lit. "healthy words"; see Introduction, IX.D). Paul does not have in mind some arbitrary selection of unrelated facts but a saving and life-transforming body of doctrine. Paul appears to refer to something similar in Rom 6:17: "But thanks be to God that, though you used to be slaves to sin, you have come to obey from your heart the pattern[69] of teaching that has now claimed your allegiance." Timothy has listened to and served with Paul for a decade now. He will have heard much from Paul (NIV: "what you have heard from me"; virtually repeated in 2:2; cf. 3:14) about many subjects in many circumstances in various locations. In addition, there is the substance of Paul's previous letter, 1 Timothy, and possibly others that have not survived. Paul draws on this body of instruction and lore now.

The verse ends "with faith and love in Christ Jesus." Paul could mean that this faith and love should accompany or somehow define Timothy's keeping "the pattern." Or Paul could be referring to the "faith and love in Christ Jesus" that Timothy exercised when he "heard from" Paul. In either case, the phrase reminds us that Paul is not referring to sheer recall of information. Keeping the apostolic counsel and living as a disciple—hearing and acting and thereby learning—are activities that involve trust (in God or in Christ) and the affective response to God and others denoted by *agapē* (mentioned elsewhere in 2 Timothy in 1:7; 2:22; 3:10).

14 This verse substantially repeats the previous one. "Guard the good deposit"[70] also echoes almost verbatim the closing of 1 Tim 6:20 (lit. "guard the deposit"; NIV "guard what has been entrusted to your care"). The parallel elements between v. 14 and v. 13 are:

v. 14	guard	the good deposit	with the help of the Holy Spirit
v. 13	keep	the pattern of sound teaching	with faith and love in Christ Jesus

68. In the five Gospel occurrences of *echō* as an imperative, *echō* precedes its object, as in Mark 11:22 (*Have* faith in God); see also Mark 9:50; Luke 14:18, 19. The other two examples of this construction in the New Testament (Jas 1:4; 2:1) follow Paul's pattern.

69. From Greek *typos* (model, pattern, form).

70. The words "that was entrusted to you" are not in the Greek text. They are added in NIV (as well as ESV and other translations), presumably to make clear that Paul is talking about the gospel message and the teachings that accompany it.

"Guard" (from *phylassō*) occurs as an imperative five other times in the New Testament. The passages, with things/person to guard against, are Luke 12:15 (greed), 1 Tim 6:20 (false knowledge), 2 Tim 4:15 (Alexander the coppersmith), 2 Pet 3:17 (deception), 1 John 5:21 (idols). The early church was not always a haven of security and harmony but was plagued with constant threats. Leaders like Timothy were tasked with maintaining clear kerygmatic and pedagogical direction. "Sound teaching" (v. 13) and "the good deposit" (the body of doctrine Timothy as an apostolic subaltern had inherited; see also 2:2) were key elements in this enterprise.

Timothy alone will not be up to the task, Paul realizes. Success hinges on God's support. He is present with those who serve him by his spiritual but real presence through faith in Christ. "With the help of the Holy Spirit"[71] is descriptive of the fulfillment of Jesus's promise to be with his disciples always (Matt 28:20). "Faith and love" (v. 13) are no less part of the picture. But these can be viewed as human initiatives. Timothy requires more than flesh and blood can furnish. "Unless the Lord builds the house, the builders labor in vain" (Ps 127:1). The indwelling Holy Spirit is the essential partner in any effective ministry team or assignment.

On the Holy Spirit in the PE, see Introduction, V. In the same way that faith (see v. 5) and the word about Christ (Col 3:16) are alive in believers, God himself by the Spirit indwells his people. He "lives in" (see discussion of "lived in," from Gk. *enoikeō*, in v. 5 above) each one personally and connects them corporately to Christ, making the many into one (1 Cor 12:13–14). As an ecclesial leader, Timothy is called on to unite disparate elements (various individuals) into a worshiping and ministering entity. "'Guarding' the gospel is not done alone but with the help of the Holy Spirit, who is the ultimate gift entrusted to the believer."[72]

The individual sense of the Holy Spirit's indwelling should not overshadow the possible sense of "in us" in v. 14. The Greek expression in the plural can be translated distributively: "among us; in our midst." Paul may not have in mind so much that the Holy Spirit is "in" Timothy and him, true though that be, as that God's sanctifying, protecting, and unifying presence can always be relied on across the relational ties and actual geography of Crete and all other places where Christ is confessed. This is an important consolation and stabilizer for a leader recently in tears (v. 4) who is now being called on to suffer (v. 8; see also 2:3) alongside his mentor, who is slated for execution.

Furthermore, it is not only Timothy who needs the Holy Spirit to face his challenges: Paul likewise depends on the Spirit's suasion to dispose Timothy to take heart and direction from these words.

71. Literally, "through the Holy Spirit."

72. Trebilco, Caradus, and Rae, 41.

D. Examples of Disloyalty and Loyalty (1:15–18)

There is a direct rhetorical connection between 1:14 and 2:1, for both verses exhort Timothy to be faithful and strong. Verses 15–18 are something of an interlude or parenthesis. It is as if, after exhorting Timothy to fidelity to the faith in v. 14, Paul in v. 15 thinks of people who were not faithful. Yet at the same time, v. 16, there is Onesiphorus, who upheld and lived out his Christian confession. Paul wishes him well (v. 18) and uses mention of him to encourage Timothy by their shared recollection of Onesiphorus's work for the gospel at Ephesus.

> [15] *You know that everyone in the province of Asia has deserted me,*
> *including Phygelus and Hermogenes.* [16] *May the Lord show mercy to*
> *the household of Onesiphorus, because he often refreshed me and was*
> *not ashamed of my chains.* [17] *On the contrary, when he was in Rome, he*
> *searched hard for me until he found me.* [18] *May the Lord grant that he will*
> *find mercy from the Lord on that day! You know very well in how many ways he helped me in Ephesus.*

15 The "You know that" construction is analogous to constructions in other Pauline letters.[73] Timothy should stay true to apostolic teaching (v. 13) and "the good deposit" he received (v. 14). Verse 15 sheds a ray of light on two men who have done otherwise, Phygelus and Hermogenes. Nothing more is known of Phygelus; there is even dispute about the spelling of this rare name.[74] MM terms him "a Christian," but if he "deserted" Paul, that label would seem to be conjectural. The verb translated "deserted" (from *apostrephō*) can denote decisive rejection (as in 2 Tim 4:4; Titus 1:14; Heb 12:25). The name Hermogenes is better attested in antiquity,[75] but apart from this reference, he does not appear in the New Testament.[76] Believers and even ministers today may recast or abandon the core gospel message because of various pressures, but from Phygelus and Hermogenes we learn that such moves have a hoary heritage (see also 1 Cor 4:9–13; 2 Cor 4:7–12; 1 John 2:19).

Both men were among inhabitants of the Roman province of Asia, whose capital was Ephesus (see Introduction, VII.A). In saying "everyone" in Asia had deserted Paul, he must have meant "most,"[77] for Onesiphorus (see v. 16) was likely from Ephesus (v. 18) and supported Paul. Paul is being frank with Timothy, baring his heart with this painful admission. "This is hardly the

73. That is, Phil 1:6; 1 Thess 4:15; Siebenthal, *Griechische Grammatik*, §141d.

74. MM 677; BDF §42.3.

75. MM 255.

76. The name is attested in Josephus, *Against Apion* 1.216.

77. Cf. Collins, 215: "The expression is in any case hyperbolic."

sort of detail a later pseudepigrapher writing in Paul's name would have made up about the end of his ministry."[78]

16 Paul commends Onesiphorus (mentioned also in 4:19), who rose to the occasion, despite Paul's chains as he languished in Rome (for Paul as a prisoner, see v. 8 above). Prisoners relied on help from relatives or friends. Onesiphorus provided it, the word order[79] perhaps stressing the frequency of this assistance. Paul prays for God's "mercy" on his behalf as a result. (For "mercy" in Paul, see Titus 3:5.) If Onesiphorus was the head of this "household," he may have been a man with a residence large enough to host Christian meetings in Ephesus, where Paul had earlier contact with him (v. 18). Perhaps, though, he was just a household member, whether family or slave, in which case Paul's prayer is for those who permitted Onesiphorus to act on his benevolent impulses toward Paul. His refusal to be "ashamed"[80] of Paul's incarceration models for Timothy the courage to transcend any tendency he might have to lie low because of being "ashamed" (v. 8) or feeling "shame" (v. 12). By "refreshed," Paul may refer to hospitality.[81] But Onesiphorus's encouragement might also have been of a nontangible nature. Visits, friendship, and the ministry of prayer can mean a great deal to a wizened Christian worker in captivity. Paul had learned to flourish with or without his physical needs being met (see Phil 4:11–13). In any case, Onesiphorus furnished repeated, laudable relief ("relief" being a prominent word in the discussion in BDAG 75 of the word translated "refreshed").

17 These gestures of assistance were possible because Onesiphorus "searched hard" and found Paul in Rome. "Hard"[82] implies zeal, determination, persistence, which Siebenthal sees as borne out also by Paul's use of a durative verbal form here.[83] Further details are unknown. Perhaps he was a man of means on business travel to the imperial capital city and sought out Paul while he was there. Or he may have been an underling of the household doing something of his master's bidding. He might have traced Paul's whereabouts via the network of local Christians (see the many names of Roman believers listed in Rom 16; these were known to Paul although he had never been in Rome, indicating that Christians in various population centers knew of each other by report).

18 Paul repeats his call for God's mercy on Onesiphorus, this time with an eye to "that day" (see discussion at v. 12 above and esp. n. 66 on p. 364).

78. Keener, *Bible Background Commentary*, 618.

79. That is, *pollakis* (often) is the lead word in its clause.

80. Greek *epaischynthē*. On the relative rarity of an indicative aorist form without augment, see Siebenthal, *Griechische Grammatik*, §71g.

81. Keener, *Bible Background Commentary*, 618.

82. Greek *spoudaiōs* occurs elsewhere in the NT only at Luke 7:4; Phil 2:28; Titus 3:13.

83. Siebenthal, *Griechische Grammatik*, §194m. The durative connotation inheres in the lexical meaning.

Paul has no doubts about the full sufficiency of Christ's work to deliver from judgment those who trust in him (in addition to v. 12 and 2 Tim 4:8, see Rom 8:1 and Phil 1:6). But he is also conscious that the working of divine grace impels the faithful to faithfulness until the end.[84] So Paul's plea for divine mercy does not seek to ward off an unpredictable bitter end for Onesimus but rather to see him fortified in the present in ways that will sustain his valuable ministrations (including outreach to Paul) to such an extent that they will enjoy even eschatological validation (cf. 1 Cor 3:10–15).

Years earlier Paul labored three years in Ephesus (Acts 19–20), and that may be when Onesiphorus "helped" Paul. "Helped" translates a form of Greek *diakoneō*, a verb appearing eight times in Paul's writings, always with the connotation of spiritual or gospel service.[85] The noun cognate underlies the English word "deacon." It does not mean Onesiphorus was a deacon, but it does imply that the help he gave Paul was not merely humanitarian aid, as valuable as that can be. Paul saw and no doubt felt the hand of God in Onesiphorus's efforts, which Timothy knew "very well" (*beltion*). Paul uses a word that occurs only here in the NT but is common in Hellenistic Greek of the era (BDAG 174).[86]

II. PRIORITIES FOR TIMOTHY (2:1–3:9)

The previous section (1:1–18) established friendly but purposeful rapport with Timothy. Much of the discourse repeated familiar Pauline doctrines regarding the work of the Spirit (1:7), the ministry of Jesus and God's power (1:8), God's call and grace in Christ (1:9), Christ's death-destroying and light-generating accomplishment (1:10), and much more. In other words, following a pattern well-established in other letters, Paul leads off 2 Timothy with a "theological" section rich in description of God's saving work (as in Rom 1–11 or Eph 1–3). He emphasizes the indicative, how much God has done to enable the ministry Paul and Timothy have long shared and that now, with Paul's impending death, Timothy will have to spearhead (1:13–14).

Paul now moves to application and appeal (as in Rom 12–15 or Eph 4–6). Of the thirty-three imperatives found in 2 Timothy, only three occur in ch. 1.[87] Fourteen occur in the section ahead. This does not mean that Paul will leave

84. See Thomas R. Schreiner and Ardel B. Caneday, *The Race Set before Us: A Biblical Theology of Perseverance and Assurance* (Downers Grove, IL: InterVarsity Press, 2001).

85. Rom 15:25; 2 Cor 3:3; 8:19, 20; 1 Tim 3:10, 13; Phlm 13.

86. On the grammar, see Siebenthal, *Griechische Grammatik*, §§50b, 242a.

87. 1 Tim 1:8, 13, 14.

theology behind as he moves now to ethics. The two are always intertwined in Paul, because it is the nature of theological truth in Christian understanding that it affects daily life and practical behavior. But the course of action necessary for Timothy will receive increasing emphasis. Paul's initial appeal will be deepened and extended (2:1–13). And he will sharpen the focus by moving beyond Timothy's need for fortitude.

Paul will highlight the challenges Timothy and those in his churches face from false teachers and teachings. This advice is significant in itself; as the old saying has it, forewarned is forearmed. But Paul will move beyond describing problems to prescribing responses. The section ahead, then, is rich both in its profiles of hazards and in tactics suggested for Timothy's survival and flourishing. Of necessity, if the leader goes down, congregations will face dire consequences. Paul has no intention of letting that happen after his demise if there is any way he can head it off.

A. The Appeal Renewed (2:1–13)

> [1] *You then, my son, be strong in the grace that is in Christ Jesus.* [2] *And*
> *the things you have heard me say in the presence of many witnesses en-*
> *trust to reliable people who will also be qualified to teach others.* [3] *Join*
> *with me in suffering, like a good soldier of Christ Jesus.* [4] *No one serving*
> *as a soldier gets entangled in civilian affairs, but rather tries to please*
> *his commanding officer.* [5] *Similarly, anyone who competes as an athlete*
> *does not receive the victor's crown except by competing according to the*
> *rules.* [6] *The hardworking farmer should be the first to receive a share of the*
> *crops.* [7] *Reflect on what I am saying, for the Lord will give you insight into*
> *all this.* [8] *Remember Jesus Christ, raised from the dead, descended from*
> *David. This is my gospel,* [9] *for which I am suffering even to the point of*
> *being chained like a criminal. But God's word is not chained.* [10] *Therefore*
> *I endure everything for the sake of the elect, that they too may obtain the*
> *salvation that is in Christ Jesus, with eternal glory.* [11] *Here is a trustworthy*
> *saying: If we died with him, we will also live with him;* [12] *if we endure, we*
> *will also reign with him. If we disown him, he will also disown us;* [13] *if we*
> *are faithless, he remains faithful, for he cannot disown himself.*

1 The second person singular "You" of direct address to start a sentence occurs six times in the PE[88] and only once elsewhere in Paul (Rom 14:10, where it is rhetorical). In the PE it conveys emphasis[89] and solemnity. This is the only

88. 1 Tim 6:11; 2 Tim 3:10, 14; 4:5; Titus 2:1.
89. Laansma, 156.

time Paul writes "my son" in the PE, a further indicator that particular gravity attaches to what he is about say.

It is important that Timothy find strength, so Paul bids him to "be strong."[90] This verb (from Gk. *endynamoō*) occurs seven times in the NT and is closely associated with Paul. Four times it refers to strength Paul received: Acts 9:22; Phil 4:13; 1 Tim 1:12; 2 Tim 4:17. Once Paul uses the word to describe how God fortified Abraham (Rom 4:20), and again the same verb to exhort the Ephesians to "be strong in the Lord and in his mighty power" (Eph 6:10). God who possesses power[91] also readily disposes it. Paul does not voice a random hope but invokes a tested and true divine resource that can surely stabilize and put backbone into Timothy.

That God does so, Paul knows and urges, is by "the grace that is in Christ Jesus." This exact expression occurs nowhere else in the NT. Campbell explains it as follows: "Grace pertains to, and in no small measure characterises, the realm of Christ. Being within this realm, Timothy is to be characterised by the grace with which the realm of Christ is itself characterised."[92] But how would this strengthen him? Elsewhere Paul writes, "It is by grace you have been saved, through faith" (Eph 2:8). Grace, available via personal relationship with Christ Jesus, mediates God's saving resources. Whatever Timothy might need to face his challenges—and both 1 and 2 Timothy bristle with references to them—"grace" is the shorthand Paul uses here to summarize God's limitless undeserved means of coming to his aid, bearing him through difficulties, and making his labors fruitful.

One thing is certain: Paul is commending Timothy to a source of empowerment that transcends mere flesh and blood, whether Paul's, Timothy's, their joint moxie, or that of Timothy and any congregational support he may enjoy. When Paul asks elsewhere, "Who is equal to such a task?" (2 Cor 2:16), he makes it clear that ministers such as he and Timothy are not "competent in ourselves to claim anything for ourselves, but our competence comes from God" (2 Cor 3:5). Grace, too, comes from God, and God alone. The appeal that begins with 2 Tim 2:1 is, accordingly, comprehensively theocentric in conception.

2 Paul has already urged Timothy, "What you heard from me, keep as the pattern of sound teaching, with faith and love in Christ Jesus" (1:13). Now, "in the grace that is in Christ Jesus" (2:1), Timothy is to recall Paul's words, impart them to faithful listeners, and orient them to convey Paul's message and teaching to others.

90. NIV translates the verb form as middle voice. The other possibility is passive voice. In that case, the sense would be "be strengthened," and the active agent would be God. In this context either interpretation seems possible.

91. Paul speaks of "power of God" in Rom 1:16; 1 Cor 1:18, 24; 2 Cor 6:7; 2 Tim 1:8.

92. Campbell, *Paul and Union with Christ*, 109–10.

The opening words of v. 2 could be translated "the things you heard from me through many witnesses." Those "things" would surely include the preaching of Paul like that recorded in Acts and his teaching as preserved in his extant epistles. Timothy had "heard" from, indeed had been hand-trained by, Paul, and hearing is the quintessential posture through which God's redemption comes to his people (see Deut 6:4; Rom 10:17; Gal 3:2, 5). Jesus's work centered on preaching and teaching is in line with this emphasis. Redemption had certainly come to Timothy, not in some isolated desert experience but in the community of other believers, including fellow Pauline coworkers ("witnesses" to the saving gospel message) like Luke, Silas, and Titus, or "Lucius, Jason and Sosipater," Paul's "fellow Jews," whom Paul names as present with him along with Timothy as he dictated Romans (Rom 16:21). Paul reminds Timothy, then, that his ministry had been bold and public, not timid (see 2 Tim 1:7) and concealed. It was corroborated by many other people over many years and in varied locales. As Guthrie puts it, what Timothy is to pass on "has a variety of witnesses to bolster up Timothy's own recollections."[93] Timothy should stand accordingly tall. Such encouragements all may be seen as part of the "grace" referred to in v. 1.

In addition, Paul's call is not for Timothy simply to be proactive and vocal. It is to speak in keeping with what he has heard. Keener calls attention to the passing on of hallowed conviction in rabbinic and Greek philosophical circles.[94] But they were scandalized by what Paul and Timothy embraced and proclaimed (cf. 1 Cor 1:23). Paul rejoiced when people became "obedient from the heart to the standard of teaching to which [they] were committed" (Rom 6:17). Paul reminds Timothy that his message is not self-devised but given to him to internalize, validate by personal practice, and then publicize.

One of Jesus's most celebrated directives is Matt 28:18–20: his followers are called to be disciples in order to make disciples. Paul had lived out this pattern, making a disciple of Christ out of Timothy. In 1 Tim 1:18 Paul wrote of a command he had "given" (from Gk. *paratithēmi*) Timothy for his strengthening. He uses the same word here to describe what Timothy should "entrust" to the followers of Christ under his direction.

These persons are to be "reliable" (*pistois*). The word conveys integrity in matters of faith and Christian obedience. They will be faithful to what they have received, not just for their own sake and benefit but so that they "will also be qualified to teach others." "Qualified" (Gk. *hikanoi*) means they will be up to the task, competent, deserving of what Timothy will delegate to them (cf. uses of the same word in 1 Cor 15:9; 2 Cor 2:16; 3:5). Calvin comments wisely, "It is right to render the word 'faithful' [NIV 'reliable'], since there are but

93. Guthrie, 150–51. For other, less likely options, see Guthrie, 150.

94. Keener, *Bible Background Commentary*, 618.

few concerned to perpetuate and conserve the remembrance of the doctrine entrusted to them." He continues: "Many are motivated by different kinds of ambitions, some by greed, some by malice and some are held back by their fear of danger, so that here special faithfulness is required."[95] Paul expects Timothy to give heed not only to his fidelity to apostolic instruction but to that of those he instructs.

3 For the second time (see 1:8 and discussion there), Paul calls Timothy to join him "in suffering." Paul will mention his suffering yet again in 2:9 and then in 4:5 will urge Timothy himself to suffer. Following Christ exposes believers to persecution (3:12), which Timothy, "like a good soldier of Christ Jesus," should be prepared for. He should not be trimming his sails in ways that will enable him to avoid it, if by avoidance his faithfulness in ministry is jeopardized.

The notion of early Christian persecution has been alleged to be largely a fabrication. In her book *The Myth of Persecution: How Early Christians Invented a Story of Martyrdom*, Candida Moss argues that biblical and postbiblical accounts of Christians actually suffering physically are for the most part trumped-up retellings of Maccabean or pagan martyrdoms as if they had happened to this or that Christian figure. Moss's revisionism has been adequately refuted.[96]

Persecution even unto death, recurrent throughout the history of the church, has again become a prominent feature of Christian experience in many locales in recent generations.[97] Dietrich Bonhoeffer is a reminder from the Nazi era, and he was not alone. In Africa and Asia,[98] in various Muslim lands,[99] in mainland China,[100] and beyond, Christians have constantly rediscovered

95. Calvin, 306.

96. C. Moss, *The Myth of Persecution* (San Francisco: HarperOne, 2013). See, for example, N. Clayton Croy, review of *The Myth of Persecution: How Early Christians Invented a Story of Martyrdom*, by Candida Moss, *RBL* 10 (2013), available at www.bookreviews.org/pdf/9158_10095.pdf.

97. As representative of a large literature, see Brian J. Grim and Roger Finke, *The Price of Freedom Denied: Religious Persecution and Conflict in the Twenty-First Century* (Cambridge: Cambridge University Press, 2011).

98. See Mark Noll and Carolyn Nystrom, *Clouds of Witnesses: Christian Voices from Africa and Asia* (Downers Grove, IL: IVP Books, 2011). Suffering looms large in many of the accounts.

99. See, for example, Nik Ripken, *The Insanity of God* (Nashville: B&H, 2013); Isaiah Majok Dau, *Suffering and God: A Theological Reflection on the War in Sudan* (Nairobi, Kenya: Paulines Publications Africa, 2002).

100. Liao Yiwu, *God Is Red: The Secret Story of How Christianity Survived and Flourished in Communist China*, trans. Wenguang Huang (New York: HarperOne, 2011). This is not an account of Christian sufferings per se, but the story of one of the most dramatic surges in Christian conversions in all of history, which cannot be told without repeated and sometimes graphic reference to persecution. See also Ian Johnson, *The Souls of China: The Return of Religion after Mao* (New York: Pantheon, 2017), 12, 162, 329, 334, 398.

the grim gloriousness of Jesus's promise, "Be faithful unto death, and I will give you the crown of life" (Rev 2:10 ESV).

Paul had witnessed (and supported) Stephen's stoning (Acts 7:58) and was no stranger to suffering himself (2 Cor 11:23–12:10). In 2 Tim 2:3 Paul exhorts Timothy to fresh readiness to exercise faithfulness to his Savior and Master whatever the cost or loss of personal comfort or advantage.[101] The simile of a soldier who is exposed to wounding or even death as a standard feature of his vocation is only barely metaphorical.

4 In vv. 4–6 Paul points to three examples of fruitfulness in service that is costly. First, a soldier avoids entanglement in nonmilitary matters, though he might be tempted to various distractions, whether for financial gain or to relieve the monotony of daily barracks life. In Paul's example, the soldier has his heart set rather on pleasing his commanding officer. Julius Caesar relates how his men rose to acts of great valor in battle when they saw their commanding officer draw near. There is, for example, the account of the standard-bearer of the Tenth Legion, who, "after supplicating the gods that the matter might turn out favorably to the legion," if the soldiers would only disembark bravely from their ships and join battle, exclaimed, "Leap, fellow soldiers, unless you wish to betray your eagle to the enemy. I, for my part, will perform my duty to the commonwealth and my general."[102] Or the motivation to please might be in hope of a reward from their commander.

Paul calls on Timothy to shun distractions and pay intense attention to his commander, the Lord Jesus. Not all of Christian life or service is like war by any means. Nor is Christ as military commander a dominant NT image. But it is present, as in Rev 19:11, which describes one on "a white horse, whose rider is called Faithful and True. With justice he judges and wages war." In certain situations, and apparently the one in which Paul views Timothy, faithful ministry bears martial characteristics.

5 Paul depicts the Christian life for "anyone"[103] as being not a leisure or spectator activity but like athletic competition. Rigorous training is necessary; the "victor's crown" is the goal (see also 4:8), which implies the approval of the judge. Timothy cannot be content with an approach to ministry that is distracted, casual, self-indulgent, or cowardly. For Paul's example in pursuing the "crown," see 1 Cor 9:24–27.

There is also no victory without "competing according to the rules." In serving Christ, the first rule is self-denial, with the possibility of earthly loss (see Jesus's call for disciples to "take up their cross": Matt 10:38; 16:24; Mark

101. See Ken Gire, *Shaped by the Cross: Meditations on the Sufferings of Jesus* (Downers Grove, IL: IVP Books, 2011).

102. Julius Caesar, *Gallic Wars* 4.25; 8.4.

103. On the "if" construction, see Siebenthal, *Griechische Grammatik*, §282d.

8:34; Luke 9:23). So this example, like those in vv. 4 and 6, is an oblique summons to readiness to suffer. As Schlatter comments: "Self-directed service to Jesus is invalid; it is not up to us to determine how we will please him. Rather, obedience is the root of all genuine, fruitful service."[104] That obedience may lead the servant of God in directions they would rather not go.

6 A third example of selfless and arduous service is "the hard-working farmer [*geōrgos*]." The farmer is a familiar image in Jesus's parables. Outside the Gospels (where the word occurs fifteen times), however, the word appears in the entire NT only here and in Jas 5:7. As for "hard-working," while the Gospels make some reference to toil of various sorts, thirteen of the NT's twenty-one uses of forms of *kopiaō* (I toil) occur in Paul's writings. The word's sole use in Acts occurs on the lips of Paul, describing his ministry labors: "In all things I have shown you that by *working hard* in this way we must help the weak" (Acts 20:35). In Paul it is a word that describes arduous work in gospel ministry.[105]

It is the *hard-working* farmer (and no other) who puts himself in the best position to enjoy the fruit of his labor. The point is not the obvious fact that farming normally results in harvest, but that only the farmer who exerts himself fully and perhaps painfully fully attains his purpose. Like vv. 4 and 5, v. 6 gives a word picture of what joining with Paul "in suffering, like a good soldier of Christ Jesus" (v. 3), entails. Like Jesus in his parables, Paul in these illustrations draws lessons about devotion to God from settings of everyday life.

Historically speaking, "these verses are important because they bear witness to the development of a ministry which presumably was (unlike Paul's) a full-time occupation, and was supported financially by the Church."[106] Barrett cites 1 Cor 9:4–15 in support. It was recognized early on in the apostolic church that pastoral service ("prayer and the ministry of the word"; see Acts 6:4) is a task and office worthy of a congregation's ample support (1 Tim 5:18).

7 The examples of the soldier, the athlete, and the farmer (vv. 4–6) do not seem lofty or obscure. Why, then, does Paul underscore Timothy's need to "reflect on"[107] what he has just written, and what further "insight" is needed from "the Lord"?

104. Schlatter, *Die Briefe*, 211.

105. See Rom 16:6, 12 (twice); 1 Cor 4:12; 15:10; 16:16; Gal 4:11; Eph 4:28; Phil 2:16; Col 1:29; 1 Thess 5:12; 1 Tim 4:10; 5:17.

106. Barrett, *Pastoral Epistles*, 102.

107. The verb *noeō* (I direct my thinking toward, recognize) occurs fourteen times in the NT. A number of times Jesus uses it to refer to the understanding that his hearers need and (most often) lack (e.g., Matt 15:17; 16:9, 11). In the LXX, and hence in John 12:40 (a quotation of Isaiah), the word often connotes spiritual understanding: "He has blinded their eyes and hardened their hearts, so they can neither, see with their eyes, nor *understand* with their hearts, nor turn—and I would heal them." Apart from Jesus's use of the word and one verse in Hebrews (11:3), Paul is the only NT writer to employ it (see Rom 1:20; Eph 3:4, 20; 1 Tim 1:7).

One possibility is the reluctance Timothy surely felt to pursue ministry in such a way that it would put him on a collision course with suffering. But that has been a theme throughout the letter (1:9, 12; 2:2) and will continue to be an emphasis (2:9; 3:11–12). Paul's directions to Timothy in this letter are inherently challenging, but to this must be added the likelihood of unpleasant consequences, not for sin or otherwise doing the wrong thing, but precisely for doing the right thing.

In other words, a statement like 2:2, which might seem like a generic reminder to make disciples, takes on a grave weight when evangelizing and equipping others may well bring the discipler into the same legal quandary that Paul, facing execution, must contend with. Paul is reminding Timothy of the theology of the cross.[108] Timothy must not skate quickly over Paul's examples of the soldier, athlete, and farmer but take them to heart as they bring home the nonnegotiable necessity of joining with Paul in suffering (2:3).

As for why divine "insight" may be needed, Paul may be aware that Timothy must go beyond simple literary comprehension of this epistle. He must heed Paul's summons to suffer, if necessary, as God's own counsel to him. As Jesus realized that God opened Peter's heart and mind one day (Matt 16:17), and as in the case of Lydia "the Lord opened her heart to respond to Paul's message" (Acts 16:14), so Paul knows that Timothy requires divine visitation for the full impact of Paul's counsel to sink in with the desired effect. In that case, this verse makes implicit reference to the Holy Spirit, otherwise a rarity in 2 Timothy (see 1:7, 14).

Trebilco, Caradus, and Rae point plausibly to an element of "mystery" in Paul's counsel that Timothy should take pains to "reflect," while it is "the Lord" who "will give . . . insight": "Understanding significant matters as far as God's way and kingdom is concerned requires God's gift of revelation, but it is revelation in the context of a thinking and grappling mind, not just revelation 'out of the blue.' Here Paul expresses the unique combination of the divine and the human that is integral to all revelation and the conveyance of the knowledge of God and his ways to the human mind."[109]

8 Kelly is probably correct that Paul mentions "Jesus Christ, raised from the dead," as a reminder that "even he had to walk the way of the cross and taste death before being exalted." It is less clear that "Son of David" is "irrelevant in the context,"[110] or that this verse and those following should be interpreted primarily as pre- and probably non-Pauline "traditional" or "creedal" language.[111]

108. This interpretation is more likely than the suggestion that Timothy will be thinking hard here about "his honorarium from the community" (Kelly, 176).

109. Trebilco, Caradus, and Rae, 57.

110. Kelly, 177; cf. Twomey, 138–39. See the attempt to account for it below.

111. So Collins, 222–28.

Christ's resurrection "from the dead" declares his deity (see Rom 1:4). Death did not defeat the Son of God, so his follower Timothy who has trusted in him need not fear when suffering looms. "Jesus Christ" occurs six times in the PE (see also 1 Tim 6:3, 14; Titus 1:1; 2:13; 3:6). More commonly (over two dozen times) Paul uses "Christ Jesus."[112]

The meaning of Christ ("anointed one") connects Jesus with David, Israel's ancient ruler, from whom Jesus descended. David was a regal and powerful conquering warrior and king. Victory is in Jesus's earthly bloodline, despite the suffering that ended his life. As ruler over all, including death, Christ in David's lineage receives the kingdom promised to his forebear (2 Sam 7:1–16) and administers its benefits to all nations, right down to individual followers like Timothy (cf. Matt 10:30). It should be recalled that Timothy, like Paul, was of Jewish descent.

Preaching of the gospel in Acts refers to David.[113] This is also true of one of Paul's few recorded evangelistic sermons.[114] It is therefore not surprising that in celebrating the gospel, David's name should crop up.

"This is my gospel" (NIV and with variations many other newer translations) might give the impression that Paul's gospel message, the core of what he preached, was Jesus "raised from the dead, descended from David." Certainly the resurrection and Jesus's ancestry (underscored in the Gospel genealogies) were integral to the saving message. But Paul makes it clear that it was Christ's death for sin, the cross, that is ground zero of Christ's saving work (1 Cor 1:18). Yes, it were for naught without the resurrection (Rom 4:25). But the price for sin was paid on Golgotha, by which those who believe receive God's righteousness in exchange (2 Cor 5:21).

A different understanding of Paul's wording would hew closer to the Greek "according to my gospel." That is, Paul's cruciform gospel message, whose call to Timothy places him in the way of suffering, is quite in accordance with Christ, whose faithfulness left him dead—but then restored. As counterintuitive as it might seem to many in cities like Rome or Ephesus that a scion of some long-dead Israelite king holds the keys to hope and life in the midst of hardship and even death, Paul and Timothy share the conviction that he does. "By identifying Jesus as a descendent of David, Paul declares that the gospel is rooted in history."[115] Serving Christ whatever the cost is eminently justified, though at present Timothy needs to "remember." He needs to call these matters intentionally to mind. They are not Paul's gospel message proper,

112. In Paul's letters outside the PE, "Jesus Christ" occurs seventy-three times, "Christ Jesus" sixty times.

113. Acts 2:25, 29, 34; 7:45; cf. 1:16; 4:25.

114. Acts 13:22, 34, 36; cf. 15:16.

115. Zehr, 178.

but they are completely consistent with, and give vital substance to, the theology of the cross at the heart of that message.

9 "For which" implies that Paul is suffering for his gospel message, which is undoubtedly true. It could also be translated "for whom," with the antecedent being Jesus Christ. In that case, Paul's stress would be more relational—Christ himself, with whom Paul enjoys personal communion, has everything to do with Paul's present straits. In the end, he is what makes the unbearable bearable (see Phil 4:13). Timothy should call him to mind for the sake of readiness in whatever his pastoral labor demands of him.

The word Paul uses for "suffering" occurs elsewhere only in 2 Tim 4:5 and Jas 5:13.[116] It means to endure hardship or adversity. The Greek word translated "criminal" occurs elsewhere in the NT only in Luke's account of Jesus's crucifixion as he hung between two "criminals" (Luke 23:32, 33, 39). The point of the verse is that Paul's fidelity to Jesus Christ, to which he is summoning Timothy, has led him to a distressing extremity. The implication is that Timothy must be prepared for whatever unwelcome attention his faith in Christ may bring upon him.

The verse concludes on a fortifying note. The saving word of which Paul and Timothy are ministers "is not chained." The NIV translation ("chained . . . "not chained") preserves the same play on words as the Greek (*desmōn . . . ou dedetai*). Those who proclaim the word may come to grief, incarceration, and even execution. God's word remains mobile, spreading "rapidly" (2 Thess 3:1) and enduring forever (1 Pet 1:23–25). "Ironically, Paul had bound . . . followers of the Way in Damascus, but now he was bound himself for the same reason he bound others."[117] On "the word of God," see commentary below on Titus 2:5. The expression occurs ca. forty times in the NIV.[118] It points to the totality of God's verbal self-disclosure, whether verbal or written. The apostolic message did not exist, historically speaking, apart from Old Testament writings that prepared the way for it and New Testament writings that quickly took shape as the gospel went forth. So while Paul may be speaking of God's saving message proclaimed, his understanding of "the word of God" should not be set at a distance from or in opposition to the canonical Scriptures.

10 Paul's extended exhortation for Timothy to persevere continues. "Therefore" probably draws on the twofold truth (see v. 9) that (1) it is because of Christ that Paul is suffering, and (2) the divine word that confirms his Savior status is unfettered. As a result, Paul is ready to go through anything—because

116. In the AF it appears only in 2 Clem. 19:3. It is found eight times in Philo and twenty-eight times in Josephus.

117. Spencer, 101.

118. In the NT, see Luke 8:11; John 10:35; Acts 6:7; 17:13; Rom 9:6; 1 Cor 14:36; 2 Tim 2:9; Titus 2:5; Heb 4:12; 1 John 2:14; Rev 19:13.

Christ did. Tacit is Paul's teaching that, by Christ's presence (his Spirit), his followers receive the same enabling to overcome mortal obstacles that he did (Rom 8:11). For a reminder that Paul was not talking theory here but alluding to commitment he had exhibited on many occasions, see 2 Cor 11:23–12:10. Neudorfer brings out the connections between Paul's suffering in this passage and other Pauline texts like Col 1:24 and Eph 3:13, concluding, "The circle of Pauline statements on this theme enlarges, the more we concern ourselves with it."[119]

"Endure" (*hypomenō*) is used by many in the NT to denote perseverance in the faith (by Jesus: Matt 10:22; 24:13; by Paul: Rom 12:2; 1 Cor 13:7; by the author of Hebrews: 10:32; 12:2, 3, 7; by James: 1:12; 5:11). Paul will use the word again in v. 12 (see below). The noun cognate (endurance, perseverance) is used sixteen times by Paul, thrice in the PE (1 Tim 6:11; 2 Tim 3:10; Titus 2:2). Paul understood and modeled a pursuit of God and service for God that called for stamina, risk-taking (in light of often adverse circumstances), steadiness, and consistency. Mercurial enthusiasm and flashy heroics were no more his style than they were Jesus's, according to Gospel records.

Paul could be counted on to expend steady, all-out effort "for the sake of the elect."[120] It bears repeating that Paul is not here idly reciting his merits but is seeking to inform and rally Timothy to analogous self-investment in gospel service. The proclamation of the gospel fulfills God's promises to all his people in all times. The fact that God elects (chooses) recipients of his covenant blessing (Deut 7:6; Jer 3:14; John 15:16; Rom 9:11; 11:7; 2 Pet 1:10) works together with the offer of salvation to all who believe (John 3:16; Rom 9:33; 1 Tim 2:4; 1 Pet 2:6). Paul has confidence that God will save his people, and a universal (but not universalistic) conception of who those people will turn out to be. Shockingly, from his former Pharisaic perspective, and an electrifying revelation in the early church (see Eph 3:4–6), many will be from the Gentile population among which he had long labored and Timothy was resident. (For "the Gentiles" in the PE, see 1 Tim 2:7; 4:17; other Pauline writings contain over two dozen references to the expression.)

Paul's ultimate commitment to his gospel calling was so that "they too," the full gamut of God's elect, "may obtain" salvation,[121] not only its temporal benefit of present communion with Christ but also "eternal glory." Paul's gaze rises above his prison setting and uncertain fate, and so should Timothy's.

119. Neudorfer, *Zweiter Brief an Timotheus*, 134.

120. Saarinen, 136, observes that "in the Pauline epistles, this word depicts those who believe in Christ (Rom 8:33; 16:13; Col 3:12)." There is truth to this comment, but the word implies more. With "elect," Paul denotes those "chosen" by God (NIV translation in Rom 8:33; 16:13; Col 3:12). They believe, but that response is a trust predicated on God's choice.

121. On "salvation," see commentary Introduction, IX.A. *Sōtērias* (salvation) is in the genitive case because the verb *tynchanō* (obtain) takes its object in the genitive.

11 On "trustworthy saying," see Introduction, IX.C. The same expression is found in 1 Tim 3:1 and Titus 3:8, with an expanded version in 1 Tim 1:15 and 4:9. Towner notes that, "with the formula, Paul emphasizes the authentic correspondence of the saying and its authority with the apostolic tradition, the (his) gospel, the sound teaching, and so on."[122] Paul affirms the doctrine he and Timothy share and stand for, over against the opposing teaching Timothy (and Titus) faces (see 1 Tim 1:3; 2 Tim 2:14–18; Titus 1:11). With an eye to the "trustworthy saying" passages, B. Paul Wolfe states: "Paul wrote with the presupposition that the apostolic tradition is the norm for the church and amounted to an extension of the scope of Scripture."[123]

In the verse at hand, Paul uses "Here is a trustworthy saying" to summarize the following set of rallying words (vv. 11–13) for Timothy to embrace suffering, if necessary, in the course of faithful pastoral labor, the point of much of 2:1–10. Now Paul clinches his appeal. Buttressed by the epigrammatic statements of vv. 11–13, Timothy will be positioned to receive the imperative-loaded counsel in the verses ahead.

"Died with him . . . live with him" calls to mind Paul's conviction that Christ's crucifixion was at the same time also that of each person who trusts in him. "Our old self was crucified with him so that the body ruled by sin might be done away with, that we should no longer be slaves to sin" (Rom 6:6; cf. Gal 2:20). In Timothy's case, such "sin" might be the pastoral failure to stand up for gospel teaching as he ought. Paul has a preemptive remedy for such fearful behavior. It is the doctrinal exhortation, "Now if we died with Christ, we believe that we will also live with him" (Rom 6:8). Those are not quite the exact words of 2 Tim 2:11, but almost. "Died with" in v. 11 is *synapothnēskō*, a word used in the NT elsewhere only in 2 Cor 7:3. "Live with" (*syzaō*) is likewise found otherwise only in Rom 6:8; 2 Cor 7:3.

Few NT writers are as explicit as Paul in linking practical living with Jesus's death, a shared death that holds in it the sure promise of life "with him." The future tense in v. 11 ("we will also live") points to the age to come. Timothy has a sure hope, even if[124] his faithfulness is at the cost of his life. But the benefits are not solely "not yet," lying in the future. They are at work already, as Timothy ponders Paul's epistle and will presumably heed these words. With divine help in understanding (see v. 7), they can be a potent force in the present to galvanize him for facing his daunting challenges.

12 The verse divisions in vv. 11–13 are hardly ideal. The first half of v. 12 belongs conceptually with v. 11; it is an extension of v. 11's positive affirmation.

122. Towner, *Letters*, 142.

123. B. P. Wolfe, "The Sagacious Use of Scripture," in Köstenberger and Wilder, *Entrusted with the Gospel*, 215.

124. On the conditional construction, see BDF §372.2a.

Verse 12b is negative, as is v. 13. This means that the reader must be prepared for a 180 degree shift in discourse flow halfway through v. 12.

In the first half, Paul affirms the advantage of the perseverance to which this passage urges Timothy. On "endure," see discussion of v. 10 above. Here in v. 12 Paul refers to steadfastness, diligence, faithfulness, courage, and the like in the face of challenge and threat, whether his chains and impending execution or Timothy's personal doubts and opponents. Those who lay hold of grace (v. 1), "remember Jesus Christ" (v. 8), and persevere "will also reign with[125] him," which means enjoy fellowship with Christ in the age to come (see Rev 5:10, 22:5). Aquinas explains, "We shall attain the kingdom together with Him," citing Matt 5:10: "Blessed are those who are persecuted because of righteousness, for theirs is the kingdom of heaven."[126] For Paul, and he hopes for Timothy, this is clearly a future promise with present effect.

The second half of v. 12 is not so rosy. The alternative to perseverance is betrayal and its consequences. God knows and keeps his own (see v. 19). But those who show by their beliefs and actions that Christ is not their Lord cannot expect God's approval, in this age or the next (see Matt 7:21–23). Ministers like Timothy are called to a high level of fidelity.

The verb translated "disown" (*arneomai*) is prominent elsewhere in connection with Jesus:

> But whoever *disowns* me before others, I will *disown* before my Father in heaven. (Matt 10:33)
>
> But whoever *disowns* me before others will be *disowned* before the angels of God. (Luke 12:9)
>
> Then Jesus answered, "Will you really lay down your life for me? Very truly I tell you, before the rooster crows, you will *disown* me three times!" (John 13:38)
>
> You *disowned* the Holy and Righteous One and asked that a murderer be released to you. (Acts 3:14)

Paul uses the same word to speak of denying the faith (1 Tim 5:8), denying the power of godly living (2 Tim 3:5), denying God (Titus 1:6), and, positively, denying "ungodliness and worldly passions" (Titus 2:12).

125. Paul uses the same verb (*symbasileuō*, reign with) in 1 Cor 4:8, its only other NT occurrence. It is found also in the AF, as Polycarp echoes 2 Tim 2:12 in writing, "If we prove to be citizens worthy of him, we will also reign with him—if, that is, we continue to believe" (*Phil.* 5:2).

126. Aquinas, 115.

Peter denied (or disowned) Christ (Matt 26:70, 72) but was restored. Paul persecuted the church and was forgiven (1 Tim 1:13). So Paul is aware that God can forgive those who turn their back on him (or his Son). But it is dangerous to presume on this forgiveness (see Rom 6:1, 15; cf. Heb 12:17). Paul knows Timothy may be tempted to compromise, then console himself that God will understand and forgive. Paul's rhetoric here heads off that line of rationalization. Violation of God's expectations can result in his irrevocable displeasure (see 2 Chr 36:16; Prov 29:1; Jer 30:13). Jesus's frequent teaching about hell is a reminder of this sobering truth. Paul is essentially echoing to Timothy the counsel David shared with Solomon: "If you seek [the Lord], he will be found by you; but if you forsake him, he will reject you forever" (1 Chr 28:9).

In the next verse, Paul intensifies the warning.

13 "Faithless" translates a verb (*apisteō*) used eight times in the NT by a wide range of authors (Mark 16:11, 16; Luke 24:11, 41; Acts 28:24; Rom 3:3; 1 Pet 2:7). From one point of view, the default setting of the human world is to lack the kind of faith God calls for—"the whole world is under the control of the evil one" (1 John 5:19).[127] Humans on the whole do not place their faith in the creator and redeemer God (Rom 1:18–23). But God calls for and deserves full trust. He is and "remains faithful." God's faithfulness is axiomatic across the whole of the Bible (Deut 7:9; Ps 31:5; 1 Cor 1:9; 10:13; 2 Cor 1:18). Human unbelief in no way nullifies it (Rom 3:3–4).

Paul's words to Timothy can be taken as consoling, as if he were saying, "Even if you are faithless, Timothy, God (or Christ) remains faithful and will forgive you" (see 1 John 1:9).[128] And it is true that "no human unfaithfulness or apostasy" can shake "the perpetual and unchangeable truth of Christ."[129] But it is a mistake to assert here "the impossibility of divine denial."[130] In that case, the message of v. 13 would be that no matter what Timothy does, it makes no difference. But such a conclusion defies the logic of the discourse.

It is more likely that Paul is plainly stating the danger Timothy faces if he does not heed Paul's words (though Paul is confident he will) and apply himself to his ministry responsibilities with fresh vigor.[131] God's character is unchanging (Mal 3:6; Heb 13:8). He warns the person who hears God's promises and invokes "a blessing on themselves, thinking, 'I will be safe, even though I persist in going my own way,' for they will bring disaster on" themselves (Deut 29:19). He calls his people to the faithfulness and holiness that mark their God,

127. Cf. Gal 1:1: "the present evil age."

128. So, for example, Johnson, *Letters to Paul's Delegates*, 69; Dibelius and Conzelmann, 109: we have here "the thought of God's faithfulness to the covenant (Rom 3:2f.)."

129. Calvin, 311–12.

130. Saarinen, 138.

131. So Calvin, 312.

who is both lenient and severe: "Consider therefore the kindness and sternness of God: sternness to those who fell, but kindness to you, provided that you continue in his kindness. Otherwise, you also will be cut off" (Rom 11:22). For God "cannot disown himself."

These passages echo Jesus's warning regarding those who do not "remain" in him and "bear much fruit" (John 15:5): "If you do not remain in me, you are like a branch that is thrown away and withers; such branches are picked up, thrown into the fire and burned" (John 15:6). It also helps account for the intensity with which Paul pursued the prize for faithful service (1 Cor 9:27).

Verse 13, then, makes no unusual or esoteric assertion. It is in large measure a summary of God's stance toward his people (and the world at large) across the generations of his dealing with them in OT times. While Christ has brought much that is new, the God he mediates (1 Tim 2:5) has not changed his nature, lowered his expectations, or lessened his ability to shepherd errant and faltering humans up onto plateaus of loyalty, self-sacrifice, and ministry that transcend their own unaided potential. It is this ancient, rugged hope in a God of fortifying substance that caps Paul's appeal to Timothy in vv. 1–13.

B. Dealing with False Teachers (2:14–3:9)

In 2:1–13 Paul has been reminding Timothy of his calling and of God's resources and expectations. Now the spotlight swings to Timothy's mandate of "reminding God's people" (v. 14) of these matters in the face of false teachers and the havoc they cause. This is the lengthiest section in 2 Timothy in terms of the NIV headings; in a concentrated torrent it reflects Paul's primary concerns for Timothy in his situation and contains the epistle's central counsel. Numerous instructions appear for Timothy personally, amid directions for God's people.

1. Strategy for the Situation at Hand (2:14–18)

Paul begins this lengthy section dealing with false teachers (2:14–3:9) by specifying how Timothy can flesh out, in the current adverse circumstances, the kind of counsel Paul has already offered. Timothy should "be strong in the grace that is in Christ Jesus" (2:1). He should join with Paul in suffering (2:3). He should "remember Jesus Christ, raised from the dead, Son of David" (2:8). These are powerful rallying words. But what would it look like to implement them? In 2:14–18, Paul frames answers to that question. Right understanding and presentation of "the word of truth" are central.

> [14]*Keep reminding God's people of these things. Warn them before God against quarreling about words; it is of no value, and only ruins those who listen.* [15]*Do your best to present yourself to God as one approved, a worker who does not need to be ashamed and who correctly handles the word of truth.* [16]*Avoid godless chatter, because those who indulge in it will become more and more ungodly.* [17]*Their teaching will spread like gangrene. Among them are Hymenaeus and Philetus,* [18]*who have departed from the truth. They say that the resurrection has already taken place, and they destroy the faith of some.*

14 Paul's previous words of exhortation and warning to Timothy (2:1–13) have immediate application to those Timothy shepherds. "God's people" is absent from the Greek, but they would be the recipients of what Paul instructs Timothy to do.

Timothy's instructions are twofold. First, he should remind. Jesus used a form of the same word (*hypomimnēskō*) to promise his disciples that the Holy Spirit would "teach you all things and . . . remind you of everything I have said to you" (John 14:26). Paul tells Titus, "Remind the people" (Titus 3:1). Three other early church leaders state that they will "remind" or "call attention" to matters their congregants need to know (2 Pet 1:12; 3 John 10; Jude 5). Often people do not require new information so much as fresh exposure to what they have already learned. This need requires leaders who can balance appreciation for the novel with cultivation of unchanging norms and graces.

Second, Timothy should "warn them before God."[132] The grammar makes it clear that "before God" refers to Timothy first of all: he should be keenly aware of the gravity of his responsibility. God is both enabling and observing Timothy's leadership. The expression "before God" or "in the presence of God" is not uncommon in Paul (Rom 14:22; 1 Cor 1:29; 2 Cor 4:2; 7:12; Gal 1:20; 1 Tim 5:4). In the PE it can be used with dramatic emphasis: "I charge[133] you, *in the sight of God* and Christ Jesus . . ." (1 Tim 5:21; cf. 1 Tim 6:13; 2 Tim 4:1). That emphasis is likely present in v. 14.

Timothy's reminders and warnings should serve especially to limit "quarreling about words" (see also 1 Tim 6:4).[134] Yes, there are times when it is right and necessary to assert exactly what words do and do not mean (see Matt 22:31–32). Debate and decision regarding matters of faith and practice have always been unavoidable in the life of the church (see Acts 15:1–21). But

132. Many later MSS contain *kyriou* (Lord) rather than *theou* (God). The evidence is fairly evenly divided, and the sense of the passage does not change significantly with either reading.

133. On the underlying Greek word *diamartyromai*, see discussion at 4:1 below.

134. On the possible imperatival infinitive, see BDF §389, who prefer a different reading.

at times it can be "of no value" and ruinous not only for those engaging in it but also for "those who listen." Timothy's mandate is gentle instruction and rescue of the unwary from "the trap of the devil" (v. 26). If people's zeal or poor judgment leads them into quarreling, it is his responsibility either to end it or to steer it in constructive directions.

The construction of the last clause ("it is of no value, and only ruins those who listen"), using *epi* first with the accusative and then with the dative, is subtle. Danker suggests that both uses connote an objective: word disputes are useless "for" any good purpose, and their effect tends to a ruinous outcome (*katastrophē*, cognate with English "catastrophe") for the hearers.[135] Towner follows BDF §235.4 in seeing the second part as connoting result. He also rightly points to v. 18 as an example of such a disastrous outcome: "They say that the resurrection has already taken place, and they destroy the faith of some."[136]

With v. 14, Paul serves notice in the first sentence of this section that Timothy's task is not mundane and bureaucratic but fraught with eternal consequences, both for Timothy and for those entrusted to him. This is not melodrama but recurrence of Paul's deep concern for pastors in their oversight of the church. In three years of service in Ephesus, Paul "never stopped warning each" of the elders (or pastors) "night day with tears" (Acts 20:31; cf. 20:27-31). He is no less passionate to urge Timothy to utmost effectiveness, as the next verse confirms.

15 "Do your best" is a call to act immediately, decisively, and with zeal. The underlying verb *spoudazō* is used by Paul both in the PE (see 2 Tim 4:9, 21; Titus 3:12) and elsewhere (Gal 2:10; Eph 4:3; 1 Thess 2:17). Timothy needs to make Paul's instructions his highest priority. We might also translate "Spare no effort" or "Tackle this no matter what."[137]

As in v. 14, where Paul depicted Timothy "before God," so here he urges Timothy to "present" or commend himself "to God." The idea is perhaps most familiar from Rom 12:1, where Paul urges readers with the same word "to offer [their] bodies as a living sacrifice, holy and pleasing to God" (see also Rom 6:13, 16, 19). Living for God is not a theoretical ideal or religious aspiration: it is an actuality realized by the way one takes up the responsibilities God lays upon a person. Timothy faces them in abundance. His priority is to discharge them "as one approved [*dokimon*]." Paul is conscious that "it is not the one who

135. Danker, *Concise Greek-English Lexicon*, 140.

136. Towner, *Letters*, 519n17.

137. KJV's translation "Study to show thyself approved" has fallen out of favor with a shift in the meaning of "study," which, when the KJV appeared (1611), meant to strive or be diligent. But the idea that ministers need to study if they hope to gain God's approval is inadvertently salutary.

commends himself who is approved [*dokimos*], but the one whom the Lord commends" (2 Cor 10:18).[138] God himself is the indispensable element in true and lasting ministry,[139] and Paul wants to ensure that Timothy transcends the trap of mediocrity by passing muster before God himself.

It is important that Timothy be reminded, not only of the high standard to which the gospel calls him and for which it equips him, but also of who and what he is. Church leaders serve many functions and may harbor various self-images, not all of them accurate or helpful. Paul reminds Timothy he is a "worker" (*ergatēs*).[140] The word is familiar from Gospel passages like Matt 9:37 ("Then he said to his disciples, 'The harvest is plentiful but the workers are few'") or Luke 10:7 ("the worker deserves his wages"), which Paul quotes in 1 Tim 5:18. People can be "workers" of evil and woe (note Paul's use of the same word with negative qualifiers in 2 Cor 11:13 ["deceitful workers"] and Phil 3:2 ["evildoers"]). Timothy's task is one of arduous productive labor, grinding out hard-won gains like a tradesman or farmhand.

But what are his aim and his task in this work? The aim is to meet God's approval as an "unashamed" worker. The word appears only here in the NT and is rarely found elsewhere. Earlier Paul urged Timothy "not to be ashamed of the testimony" about Christ or Paul (2 Tim 1:8). Paul affirmed Onesiphorus because he was not "ashamed" of Paul in his incarceration (1:16). And Paul resisted the urge to languish in "shame" because of his chains (1:12). He is simply calling Timothy to the level of self-confidence and good conscience that all-out engagement for Christ generates.

Timothy's task as depicted here is word-centered: "who correctly handles the word of truth" (see related discussion at 2:9 above regarding "God's word" and discussion below at Titus 2:5). Paul will warn against another, less noble word in v. 17. While the exact phrase "word of truth" occurs in the NIV only here and at Ps 119:43 and Jas 1:8, this is surely a word or message closely associated with God who has spoken to his people by Scripture (2 Tim 3:16), as well as by his Son (cf. Heb 1:2). Elsewhere in the PE, God's created bounty "is consecrated by the word of God and prayer" (1 Tim 4:5), Timothy is told to "preach the word" (2 Tim 4:2), and Titus should instruct so that "no one will malign the word of God" (Titus 2:5). From the beginning, the apostolic ministry has centered on the word of God (Acts 6:2, 4), and Paul throughout is passing along this heritage. Timothy's faithful discharge of teaching and

138. Other occurrences of *dokimos* in Paul: Rom 14:18; 16:10; 1 Cor 11:19; 13:7.

139. Cf. 1 Cor 3:7: "So neither the one who plants nor the one who waters is anything, but only God, who makes things grow."

140. See commentary Introduction, VI. See also Harold Mare, "The Pauline Work Ethic," in *New Dimensions in New Testament Study*, ed. Richard N. Longenecker and Merrill C. Tenney (Grand Rapids: Zondervan, 1974), 357–69.

other proclamation of the word will, through "the grace that is in Christ Jesus" (v. 1), garner God's approval. Such aproval assumes that Timothy "correctly handles"[141] it.[142]

16 Juxtaposed against "the word of truth" (v. 15), which Timothy is to minister aright, is "godless chatter" (see also 1 Tim 6:20), which he is to "avoid" (see also Titus 3:9, the only other use of this word in the NT in this sense).

This "chatter" is talk that is vapid, perhaps profane, and in any case "devoid of Christian content" (BDAG 539). Since Christian faith is so intertwined with preaching and other verbal information exchange, distortions of and challenges to it will most often take the shape of unacceptable verbal claims and expressions. This reality is borne out in any number of NT epistles. Romans warns against people who "by smooth talk and flattery . . . deceive" (16:18). At Corinth, Paul must confront "how these arrogant people are talking" (1 Cor 4:19). The ministry of Jesus as the Gospels report it is dominated by his tacit and sometimes explicit correction of people's erroneous religious outlooks, which, compared to Jesus's prophetic announcements, qualify as "godless chatter." Timothy was not facing some novel strategy of opposition to his ministry as he sought to further what Paul called earlier "the testimony about our Lord" (1:8).

Schlatter comments that the profane nature of the chatter shows that "its concocters have no concern for honoring God." But their blasphemies set in motion a progression. Schlatter continues: "When deep inside himself man chokes off reverence for God, he exalts himself against him with growing confidence and increasing pride. Emancipation from the fear of God and from gratitude toward God quickly gain momentum."[143]

Something like what Schlatter describes is evident as the verse unfolds. The people Timothy should "avoid" are in error and getting worse. Calvin depicts the situation colorfully: the course of these babblers "is like a labyrinth or rather a deep whirlpool, from which there is no escape and into which men plunge deeper and deeper."[144] While Paul writes nothing about labyrinths or whirlpools, Calvin evidently takes note of the future tense verb, which denotes ongoing progression; the prepositional phrase (*epi pleion*),[145] which NIV renders "more and more"; and the babblers' worsening condition of godlessness

141. BDAG 772 explains the word *orthotomeō* as meaning to "guide the word of truth along a straight path." On the word construction, see BDF §119.1.

142. On the unpopularity of this notion today in the form of preference for practical maxims, not doctrinal formulations, see Neudorfer, *Zweiter Brief an Timotheus*, 181–82.

143. Schlatter, *Die Kirche der Griechen*, 241.

144. Calvin, 314.

145. The phrase is found elsewhere in the NT only at Acts 4:17; 20:9; 24:4; 2 Tim 3:9. On the construction, see BDAG 849.

(*asebeia*; see discussion at Titus 2:12).[146] The babblers are certainly not headed anywhere Timothy wants to follow, nor does he want those under his pastoral direction to be subverted by them. Paul's counsel to give them a wide berth is wise and reasonable.

17 "Their" refers to the ungodly babblers in the previous verse. "Teaching" translates *logos*, the same word used in the phrase "word [*logos*] of truth" in v. 15. Timothy faces a situation in which there are dueling teachings: those of Paul and his disciples such as Timothy, and those who have a different interpretation of matters pertaining to Jesus. This errant teaching is anything but stagnant and moribund; in fact, Paul warns that it is like a wasting disease that spreads. The Greek word for "gangrene" could refer to various spreading diseases and underscores the repulsive nature of this particular "godless chatter" (v. 16). Collins terms the use of such a practical example "a characteristic ploy of Hellenistic rhetoric,"[147] but it is hard to see what is technically rhetorical about it: all three PEs stress healthy teaching (see Introduction, IX.D). Teaching that is unhealthy naturally seems analogous to disease. It is simply a straightforward if slightly jarring metaphor more than a ploy, which implies some level of disingenuousness or deception.

Another reason "ploy" may not fit is that Paul is not creating a rhetorical situation but responding to a real one, as the personages of Hymenaeus and Philetus indicate. Saarinen suggests they are "gnostics who claimed that they have already left the material world and their body in their conversion and are thus resurrected."[148] This could be the case only if 2 Timothy is dated well into the second century, when Gnosticism can be shown to have existed. "Their teaching" indicates they have influence, and it is complicating reception of the word Paul and Timothy uphold. Nothing more is known of Philetus. As for Hymenaeus, many hold that he is probably the same person mentioned in 1 Tim 1:19–20, who abandoned the faith and forfeited a good conscience. Paul "handed [him] over to Satan to be taught not to blaspheme" (1 Tim 1:20). As Paul writes 2 Timothy, it appears that this restorative action toward Hymenaeus has not yet borne the fruit Paul no doubt hoped, as the next verse underscores.

18 "Departed" translates a form of *astocheō*, a word that occurs elsewhere in the NT only at 1 Tim 1:6 and 6:21.[149] It connotes departure "from moral or spiritual standards" (BDAG 146). In nonreligious texts it refers to a projectile missing its mark.[150] Hymenaeus and Philetus have turned aside from

146. BDAG 871 notes that, when *prokoptō* (I advance, progress) is used as here, the word describing the nature or direction of the progress (*asebeias*) is in the genitive.

147. Collins, 232.

148. Saarinen, 143.

149. It is found twice in the AF: 2 Clem. 17:7 and Did. 15:3.

150. See Danker, *Concise Greek-English Lexicon*, 59. There are three such occurrences (not noted in Danker) in Josephus: *Jewish War* 2.159; 4.116; 5.61.

"the truth," a reference no doubt to the body of teaching referred to frequently as "truth" in the PE (see Introduction, IX.D).

Wherein lies their error? The verse could be translated, "They go astray by saying. . . ." Their error lies in seeking to inform others when they are in darkness themselves (cf. 1 Tim 1:7). Not only are they talking out of turn: what they say is false, so false that they not only mislead, but "they destroy the faith of some." They do so by twisting the meaning of one of the most fundamental claims of the good news about Jesus Christ: not just that he died for sinners, but that he rose from the dead and effects moral transformation in the lives of those who trust in him (see Rom 8:11).

The false assertion of Hymenaeus and Philetus that "the resurrection has already taken place" is not a statement about Jesus's resurrection itself. It is about the meaning of his resurrection for his followers. Some in the early decades of church life illegitimately applied the Bible's end-time teaching (eschatology) in a manner called "acute realized eschatology."[151] In this view, the future is *now*. Believers *already* enjoy the full benefit of God's eternal forgiveness. So live however you wish! Your soul is already saved forever, so what you do with your body doesn't matter. Some think this outlook was a factor at Corinth, causing Paul to write sarcastically, "Already you have all you want! Already you have become rich! You have begun to reign—and that without us! How I wish that you really had begun to reign so that we also might reign with you!" (1 Cor 4:8). This outlook might help explain the involvement of Corinthian church members in incest (5:1–5) and prostitution (6:12–20). It is possible that Hymenaeus and Philetus were also denying the bodily nature of believers' final resurrection, which was an absurd if not revolting notion in some Hellenistic understanding (cf. Acts 17:32).

An understanding of the resurrection this twisted is tantamount to a denial of it. No wonder "the faith of some" is being destroyed. NIV's "destroy" translates a form of *anatrepō*. The same word is used in Titus 1:11, also of the disastrous results of false teaching. The only other NT use is in John 2:15, when Jesus "overturns" the tables of the money changers. Hymenaeus and Philetus were not just misdirected doctrinally but were functioning as a two-man wrecking crew of the fragile faith of first-generation believers under Timothy's care.

2. *Leadership Wisdom in the Face of Opposition (2:19–21)*

As Paul continues to advise Timothy on dealing with false teachers (2:14–3:9), he has wisdom to share in view of antagonists like Hymenaeus and Philetus

151. Johnson, *Letters to Paul's Delegates*, 75.

(v. 17) and their aberrant activities (v. 18). To keep from either over- or under-reacting, Timothy needs perspective on the ominous scenario facing him, in which people "who have departed from the truth" (v. 18) are getting a hearing in an apostolic church in which truth matters a great deal. By the time Paul writes the PE (AD 60s), he has spent over thirty years ministering the gospel message in the face of sometimes lethal opposition. It will be recalled, for example, that no sooner had Paul (then Saul) converted to Christ and "baffled the Jews living in Damascus by proving that Jesus is the Messiah" (Acts 9:22) than there arose "a conspiracy among the Jews to kill him" (9:23). Paul escaped only by being smuggled out of the city by night (9:25; cf. 2 Cor 11:32–33). Shortly afterward, when in Jerusalem Saul "talked and debated with the Hellenistic Jews" about Jesus, "they tried to kill him" (Acts 9:29).

There is no evidence that Timothy is facing death threats (though Paul's exhortations to suffer [1:8; 2:3] imply some level of danger). But it is never easy to uphold the gospel when ideologues and their notions appear to gain traction in the church. As a result of Paul's extensive experience, he has several comments to offer that will help Timothy deal constructively with opposition, plus (beginning in v. 22) position himself not only to survive but to flourish in the unenviable circumstances that vv. 17–18 describe.

> [19] *Nevertheless, God's solid foundation stands firm, sealed with this inscription: "The Lord knows those who are his," and, "Everyone who confesses the name of the Lord must turn away from wickedness."* [20] *In a large house there are articles not only of gold and silver, but also of wood and clay; some are for special purposes and some for common use.* [21] *Those who cleanse themselves from the latter will be instruments for special purposes, made holy, useful to the Master and prepared to do any good work.*

19 What Timothy sees is the threat of false teachers and teaching (vv. 17–18). What he needs to "remember" (see v. 8) and remind God's people (v. 14) is that God has the situation under control. He "knows those who are his," and his people have standing orders to "turn away from wickedness." Timothy can confidently minister in light of God's good oversight. Even in the face of resurrection-denial and soul-destruction (v. 18), God's reign is not destabilized.

"God's solid foundation" is axiomatic in an understanding of God that views him as a sovereign administering an eternal kingdom, into which Paul, Timothy, and others are entering by means of faith in the gospel. It will be recalled that Acts represents Paul as summing up his first missionary journey with the words, "Through many tribulations we must enter the kingdom of God" (14:22). One of those who heard Paul's preaching in those days would have been Timothy (Acts 16:1; for Timothy's recollection of those times, see 2 Tim 3:10–11).

As Paul writes 2 Timothy, "kingdom" is still one of the convictions that joins him with Timothy in their faith in Christ: "I charge you in the presence of God and of Christ Jesus, who is to judge the living and the dead, and by his appearing and his kingdom: preach the word" (2 Tim 4:1–2). The only explicit Pauline reference to Jesus as "king" occurs in Paul's other letter to Timothy (1 Tim 1:17; 6:15). Clearly an underlying assumption about Jesus for Paul and Timothy is that Jesus reigns sovereign over his people and all the world. That reign, "his kingdom" (2 Tim 4:1), is at the core of Paul's eternal hope as he faces execution and seeks to rally and assure Timothy: "The Lord will rescue me from every evil deed and bring me safely into his heavenly kingdom. To him be the glory for ever and ever. Amen" (2 Tim 4:18).[152] No wonder Paul can allude without further explanation to "God's solid foundation."

Four significant linguistic features of v. 19 merit mention. (1) "Nevertheless" translates a word found elsewhere only in the writings of John, James, and Jude.[153] The meaning is not in doubt, but the distribution of occurrence is a reminder that an author's use of words can be random and unpredictable—caution is advised in disqualifying the PE as Pauline because they use words not always found in other Pauline letters. (2) A similar observation can be made regarding the word translated "solid," found only here in Paul but present in other NT books.[154] (3) "Foundation" is a word used both elsewhere by Paul and by other NT writers.[155] For Paul, Christ is the cornerstone of God's edifice (Eph 2:20; cf. 1 Cor 3:11). The foundation is firm because Christ is rock-solid. (4) The perfect-tense verb form Paul uses to affirm that God's foundation "stands" seems to have present force.[156] No particular importance attaches to the perfect use in this instance.[157]

God's foundation as depicted here is marked by a twofold seal. "Seals were used to identify objects and particularly to indicate ownership."[158] Both of the identifying "inscriptions" are from Scripture. They both constitute warnings that Hymenaeus and Philetus are not going to fool God, who is the judge of their errant doctrine and behavior. "The Lord knows those who are his" is a direct quotation of Num 16:5 LXX.[159] Moses in a showdown with Korah and

152. This and the previous paragraph are adapted from Yarbrough, "The Kingdom of God in the New Testament," 148.

153. *Mentoi*. See John 20:25; 21:4; Jas 2:8; Jude 8.

154. *Stereos*. See Heb 5:12, 14; 1 Pet 5:9.

155. *Themelios*. See Luke 6:48, 49; 14:29; Heb 6:1; 11:10; Rev 21:14, 19. In Paul: 1 Cor 3:10, 11, 12; Eph 2:20; 1 Tim 6:19.

156. See Wallace, *Greek Grammar*, 579–80.

157. For similar uses of *hestēken*, see John 1:26; Heb 10:11; Jas 5:9; Rev 12:4.

158. Knight, 415; cf. Keener, *Bible Background Commentary*, 619.

159. Paul does replace "God" (*ho theos*) in the LXX with "Lord" (*kyrios*). On the use of the OT in the PE more broadly, see Hanson, 139–41.

others warns that God will make the final determination of who teaches and lives truly. Paul is saying to Timothy that, in upholding the gospel message of the resurrection and its meaning, he can count on God's sanction and the eventual ousting of Hymenaeus and Philetus and their sympathizers, if not in this age, then in the next. Jesus's warning comes to mind that "on that day" (i.e., the day of judgment) he will say to some who trafficked in his name and service, "I never knew you" (Matt 7:22–23).

Technical commentaries relate the second seal, "Everyone who confesses the name of the Lord must turn away from wickedness," to various OT or OT apocryphal passages: Isa 26:13; Lev 24:16; Ps 6:9; Sir 17:26.[160] Most suggestive seems to be Num 16:26–27, in which Moses warns God's people: "'Move back from the tents of these wicked men! Do not touch anything belonging to them, or you will be swept away because of all their sins.' So they moved away[161] from the tents of Korah, Dathan and Abiram. Dathan and Abiram had come out and were standing with their wives, children and little ones at the entrances to their tents." If this is indeed the background, Paul draws on an incident where people are told "Move back!" to remind Timothy of his and the people's need to "turn away from wickedness."

In sum, for the weightiest of reasons, namely, that God's word says so, "the concrete application" for Timothy and his situation is that "they turn away from the errors of thought and practice of those" like Hymenaeus and Philetus "who have gone astray from the truth."[162]

20–21 Paul moves from a sublime source (Israel's Scriptures) of leadership wisdom in the face of opposition to the most mundane imaginable: household articles, including refuse receptacles.

"Large house" suggests some great residence of the rich. Such a house contains vessels[163] made of costly material like gold and silver. Their value and purpose would be highly esteemed. In contrast, there would be wooden articles or clay pots. Wood could be fashioned into, say, a coat hangar. Clay pots might hold water or vinegar (John 19:29) or for that matter garbage. In that case, they were nothing special.

Many commentators see a connection here with Rom 9:21,[164] where the same expression ("some . . . for special purposes and some for common use") is found. There may indeed be a connection, but it seems more likely

160. See Towner, *Letters*, 534–36; Collins, 236; Knight, 416.

161. A form of the same verb (*aphistēmi*) is used when Paul in 2 Tim 2:19 says "turn away."

162. Knight, 417.

163. From *skeuos*. It can refer to possessions, an object or container, or a human being carrying out some function or mission (see Acts 9:15), among other things.

164. "Does not the potter have the right to make out of the same lump of clay some pottery for special purposes and some for common use?"

that Paul is drawing an everyday, commonsense analogy for Timothy regarding the church, "the household of God" (1 Tim 3:15). Some of its members are distinguished in makeup and function. Others are of quite common or even dishonorable composition.[165] Paul may be characterizing Hymenaeus and Philetus and their movement as less than honorable in their convictions and goals.

On the bright side, people can turn out to be like vessels "who cleanse themselves" (v. 21).[166] The reference is actually singular: "If anyone cleanses himself or herself. . . ." Paul may have Timothy foremost in mind. If Timothy cleanses himself from things that defile (NIV: "from the latter"), he or those he influences can be commended. "Things that defile" might encompass the doctrines and deeds of Hymenaeus and Philetus and their followers.

The fourfold favorable outcome of repudiating these things for Timothy or those under his leadership are that he and they will become a vessel or instrument (sing. in Greek).

1. "For special purposes" (NIV). This wording borders on evangelical cliché. The Greek is simply "for honor." This might be for an esteemed purpose, a noble calling or assignment, in God's "large house" (world, kingdom, or church; see v. 20). Or it might refer to the eschatological destiny of those who "cleanse themselves" (see references to "honor" in Rom 2:7, 10).

2. Timothy or others will be "made holy." Paul uses this word to describe how the Holy Spirit (Rom 15:16), Christ (1 Cor 1:2; Eph 5:25), both Christ and the Spirit (1 Cor 6:11), and God the Father (1 Thess 5:23) set apart believers in Christ for his purposes. Just as God himself is holy, distinct by nature and character from creation and the fallen world order, association with him in Christ results in transformation by and reflection of his communicable attributes in this life. This process should be distinguished from sanctimonious behavior to project a religious self-image (cf. Matt 6:1).

3. Timothy or those under his care will be "useful to the Master," which refers to God in his total control and oversight. The word for "Master" is translated elsewhere in the NIV as "Sovereign Lord"; see Luke 2:29; Acts 4:24; 2 Pet 2:1; Rev 6:10; cf. Jude 4 ("Sovereign"). Paul uses the word translated "useful" to describe people valuable for his own ministry (Mark: 2 Tim 4:11; Onesimus: Phlm 11). An example of this in Paul's own experience is his "being poured out like a drink offering" (2 Tim 4:6).

165. The thought is, of course, close to Paul's talk of "members" of the body of Christ, just like parts of our own bodies, having more or less honorable regard for each other (1 Cor 12:12–29).

166. The expected word would be a form of *katharizō* (thirty times in the NT, three times in Paul). Instead, Paul uses a form of *ekkathairō*, used in the NT elsewhere only at 1 Cor 5:7: "Cleanse out the old leaven" (ESV).

4. Timothy or those under his care will be "prepared to do any good work." "Any" could be translated "every." Paul means any and all acts of loyalty to God that their walk in Christ might require. Just as Hymenaeus and Philetus's orientation dooms them to destructive results for them and others, those who "cleanse themselves" have happy prospects of achieving the purpose for which grace through faith (cf. Eph 2:8–9) came to them: "For we are God's handiwork, created in Christ Jesus to do good works, which God prepared in advance for us to do" (Eph 2:10). In keeping with God having "prepared in advanced" certain "good works" for his people's flourishing and his glorification, 2 Tim 2:21 assures Timothy that, by avoiding folly and pursuing what God bestows (see v. 22 below), they will be "prepared" to honor him by living out his will.

3. *Personal Priorities for Pastoral Effectiveness (2:22–26)*

The previous section conveyed wisdom for someone in Timothy's position to negotiate his tasks in the face of opposition (2:19–21). The assurances and insights offered there were no doubt of value for the first reader. But all the information and principles in the world mean nothing without what in athletics is called "execution." That is, skills and savvy are not merely rehearsed or sharpened but are actually deployed in a game situation. Paul now moves from mostly general and thematic exhortations[167] to pointed directives regarding the focus, tactics, and rationale Timothy needs to incorporate in his shepherding and oversight activities. This is not "what you should do if" but what must actually be true of Timothy and his actions if he is to perform his duties consistent with the gift (1:6) and commission (2:2) entrusted to him.

> [22] *Flee the evil desires of youth and pursue righteousness, faith, love and peace, along with those who call on the Lord out of a pure heart.* [23] *Don't have anything to do with foolish and stupid arguments, because you know they produce quarrels.* [24] *And the Lord's servant must not be quarrelsome but must be kind to everyone, able to teach, not resentful.* [25] *Opponents must be gently instructed, in the hope that God will grant them repentance leading them to a knowledge of the truth,* [26] *and that they will come to their senses and escape from the trap of the devil, who has taken them captive to do his will.*

22 Timothy's first priority is simultaneously to pull back and to advance. These actions are denoted by the present imperatives "flee" and "pursue," respectively.

167. Thus far in 2 Timothy, imperatives have appeared in the following verses: 1:8, 13, 14; 2:1, 2, 3, 7, 8, 14, 15, 16, 19.

"Flee" (*pheugō*) occurs as an imperative five times in the Gospels[168] and three other times in Paul.

> *Flee* from sexual immorality. All other sins a person commits are outside the body, but whoever sins sexually, sins against their own body. (1 Cor 6:18)
>
> Therefore, my dear friends, *flee* from idolatry. (1 Cor 10:14)
>
> But you, man of God, *flee* from all this [i.e., the pursuit of wealth], and pursue righteousness, godliness, faith, love, endurance and gentleness. (1 Tim 6:11)

The thought is straightforward, even if the mandated response can be difficult: there are acts that are heinous, immoral, unlawful, or otherwise contrary to God and good; therefore escape while you can! As Sir 21:2 states, using the same verb form, "As from before a snake, flee from sin, for if you approach, it will bite you; its teeth are lion's teeth, destroying people's lives." The same action is called for seven times in the AF,[169] though always in the second person plural rather than singular.

Timothy is to flee "the evil desires of youth."[170] "Desires" (*epithymiai*) as a noun in Paul almost always describe negative behaviors or impulses. Paul sees them "as an expression of the sin which rules man."[171] Galatians 5:16 speaks of "the desires [*epithymian*, sing.] of the flesh" (NIV). The list of examples there is graphic: "sexual immorality, impurity and debauchery; idolatry and witchcraft; hatred, discord, jealousy, fits of rage, selfish ambition, dissensions, factions and envy; drunkenness, orgies, and the like" (Gal 5:19–21). Paul evidently associates some of these, or misdeeds like these, particularly with youthfulness. He wants Timothy to put distance between any possibly inclination toward them and his daily life and service.

But the ethic Paul calls for is not simply one of sin negation. "If you are led by the Spirit, you are not under the law" (Gal 5:18), which certainly is or can be true of Timothy (see Introduction, VIII.B). Timothy is to substitute

168. Matt 2:13; 10:23; 24:16; Mark 13:14; Luke 21:21.

169. Passages and thing(s) to flee from: Ign. *Trall.* 11:1 (wicked offshoots that bear deadly fruit); *Phld.* 2:1 (division and false teaching); 6:2 (the evil tricks and traps of the ruler of this age); 7:2 (divisions); *Smyrn.* 7:2 (divisions); *Pol.* 5:1 (wicked practices); Did. 3:1 (evil of every kind and from everything resembling it).

170. In addition to BDAG 670 references to one occurrence each of *neōterikos* (youthful) in the AF ("youthful appearance") and in the OT Apocrypha ("youthful amusement"), see Josephus, *Jewish Antiquities* 16.399: "youthful vanity."

171. *NIDNTTE* 2:243.

illicit longing with the pursuit of "righteousness, faith, love and peace." It is as simple as Paul's dictum elsewhere: "Do not be overcome by evil, but overcome evil with good" (Rom 12:21). If Timothy will "walk by the Spirit," he "will not gratify the desires of the flesh" (Gal 5:16). Paul gives comparable counsel to the Philippians (Phil 4:8), underscoring the connection between their spiritual progress and his tutelage, something that would have been self-evident for Timothy: "Whatever you have learned or received or heard from me, or seen in me—put it into practice. And the God of peace will be with you" (Phil 4:9).

The course of action Paul prescribes is not solitary in nature but a project in which believers uphold each other ("along with[172] those who call on the Lord out of a pure heart").[173] "Believers" is actually putting it weakly; the participle translated "those who call on the Lord" is the form of a verb (*epikaleō*) often used to describe deep and even desperate appeal to the Lord. An example would be Stephen "calling on" Christ "while they were stoning him" (Acts 7:59; cf. 9:14, 21; 22:16). In a different context, the same word describes Paul's "appealing" to Caesar.[174]

Paul calls on Timothy to "pursue" godliness not in some vague sense but on the model of others in the early church who sought God and found him (see other references to "calling on" God in Rom 10:12, 13, 14; 1 Cor 1:2; 1 Pet 1:17) through radical embrace of the gospel message rejected by so many, then and now. Although Paul addresses Timothy as a leader, he understands the younger man's particular challenges and how much any Christian leader is in need of the same gospel graces that he proclaims to others.

23 The pursuit of "righteousness, faith, love and peace" (v. 22) may involve difficult tactical decisions. One such decision is which conflicts to engage and which to work around. Paul counsels Timothy to stay out of "foolish and stupid arguments." This counsel resonates with a lode of wisdom that glimmers in Proverbs:

> A hot-tempered person stirs up conflict, but the one who is patient calms a quarrel. (Prov 15:18)

> Starting a quarrel is like breaching a dam; so drop the matter before a dispute breaks out. (Prov 17:14)

172. BDF §227.3 stresses that this is peace "in company with," not "peace with," as if Timothy were here experiencing friction with "those who call on the Lord." Many MSS contain the word "all" before "those who call on the Lord." Overall, however, there is strong external evidence for the shorter reading.

173. The exact expression "from/out of a pure heart" (*ek katharas kardias*) is found elsewhere in the NT only at 1 Tim 1:5 and 1 Pet 1:22 (some MSS). It is probably something more theologically grounded than "complete sincerity" (Kelly, 189).

174. Acts 25:11, 12, 21, 25; 26:32; 28:19.

> Whoever loves a quarrel loves sin; whoever builds a high gate invites destruction. (Prov 17:19)

> It is to one's honor to avoid strife, but every fool is quick to quarrel. (Prov 20:3)

Like James, who advised a ready ear, a slow tongue, and rarely anger in arriving at "the righteousness that God desires" (Jas 1:19–20), Paul directs Timothy to recuse himself from unproductive disputes.

"Foolish" (from *mōros*, cognate with English "moron") is used to describe short-sighted or corner-cutting people (like "the foolish man" [Matt 7:26]) and ill-advised actions in Matthew's Gospel (5:22; 23:17; 25:2, 3, 8). It is a word that also comes to the fore when Paul addresses the Corinthians (1 Cor 1:25, 27; 3:18; 4:10). For more on "foolish . . . arguments," see discussion at Titus 3:9, where the same Greek words appear (translated "foolish controversies" in NIV).

The word translated "stupid" (*apaideutos*) in v. 23 is a NT hapax. It occurs eighteen times in the LXX, many of those occurrences in Proverbs (5:23; 8:5; 15:12, 14; 17:21; 24:8; 27:20).[175] NETS consistently translates it "uneducated" or "uninstructed." Timothy has probably already learned by now, but Paul takes pains to remind him of how "uneducated" or ignorant religious disputes can be whether inside or outside the church. Do not even start down that road.

Paul's reasoning is straightforward: such disputes "produce quarrels." On "quarrels," see Titus 3:9. The other two NT uses of the word are 2 Cor 7:5 and Jas 4:1. Quarreling is seldom compatible with the pursuit of "righteousness, faith, love and peace" called for in 2 Tim 2:22. Moreover, it will hinder execution of the tasks and outlook set forth for Timothy in vv. 23–26.

Admittedly there is a tension in this matter. At the same time Timothy should stay out of certain kinds of conflicts in some and perhaps most situations, he should "fight the good fight of faith" (1 Tim 6:12), publicly rebuke elders who are sinning (1 Tim 5:20), guard the good deposit (2 Tim 1:14), suffer like a military combatant (2 Tim 2:3), and perform other proactive if not aggressive functions. No pastor can or should always avoid disputes; to do so is to ensure that wolves will take over the flock (see Acts 20:28–30). The Gospels support an interpretation of Jesus as a sinless man, but they are at the same time a study in the conflicts he engaged in. The key in 2 Tim 2:23 may be "foolish and stupid." Some arguments are of the no-win variety. It takes pastoral wisdom steered by divine guidance, whether through Scripture or Spirit or human advisers, to recognize them when they arise and to act (or not) accordingly.

24 Paul refers to Timothy indirectly as "the Lord's servant [*doulos*,

175. See also Wis 17:1; Sir 6:20; 8:4; 10:3; 20:19, 24; 22:3; 51:23; Zeph 2:1; Isa 26:11.

slave]."[176] Paul calls himself a "servant of God" (Titus 1:1), using the same word. He calls Timothy and himself "servants of Christ Jesus" (Phil 1:1). He calls himself a "servant" of Christ Jesus (Rom 1:1), of Christ (Gal 1:10), and of the Corinthians (2 Cor 4:5). It is clearly a significant descriptor for what it means to know and follow Jesus. All believers are called to be "servants" of God and "slaves to righteousness" (Rom 6:19), but here the term refers to Timothy in his pastoral capacity. As an application of the "flee . . . pursue" strategy in v. 22, Timothy should resist the impulse to be "quarrelsome" and instead should exercise spiritual oversight that is kind, instructive, and not resentful, even in the face of provocation. "More sinners come to the Lord through a pastor's love than through words of condemnation."[177]

NIV aptly chooses cognate English words (quarrels, quarrelsome) to render cognate Greek words (*machē*, *machomai*) in vv. 23–24. Jesus said blessed are the peacemakers (Matt 5:9). A related word (*amachos*) is used to describe a pastoral qualification (1 Tim 3:3: "not quarrelsome") and the need for every Jesus follower "to be peaceable" (Titus 3:2). Paul's assertion in 2 Tim 2:24 that irascible behavior is disallowed is consistent with the Christian's personal ethos profile outlined in the NT generally. Belligerency or militancy is modeled by no NT spiritual leader, nor is aggressive or menacing behavior a fruit that Paul sees issuing from the work of the Holy Spirit (Gal 5:22–23). Such behaviors are indeed lumped in with "the acts of the flesh," which include "hatred, discord, jealousy, fits of rage, selfish ambitious, dissensions, factions, and envy" (Gal 5:19–21). If Timothy is ministering Christ by the suasion of his Spirit, contentiousness should be absent.

Timothy's interface with others should not be reactive and prejudicial but rather impartial. That is the weight of "to everyone" in 2 Tim 2:24, which could also be rendered "to all." Pastors cannot reserve civility only for certain persons they favor. Timothy should display evenhandedness in four ways, three of them laid out in v. 24.

First, "the Lord's servant" (in this case Timothy) should be "kind" (*ēpios*). Philo uses this word to describe God in his merciful disposition (*Life of Moses* 1.72).[178] The adverbial form of the word appears in the AF, again referring to God: "The Father, who is merciful in all things, and ready to do good, has compassion on those who fear him, and gently [*ēpiōs*] and lovingly bestows his favors on those who draw near to him with singleness of mind" (1 Clem. 23:1). In contemporary parlance Paul is saying that Timothy should be approachable and affirming.

176. For extended treatment, see M. Harris, *Slave of Christ* (Nottingham, UK: Apollos, 1999).

177. Zehr, 159.

178. See also Josephus's single attestation to the word: *Jewish Antiquities* 19.265.

Second, he should be "able to teach" (*didaktikos*), a word used elsewhere in the NT only at 1 Tim 3:2. This ability is self-evident if Timothy takes seriously Paul's mandate to "entrust" apostolic instruction "to reliable people who will also be qualified to teach others" (2 Tim 2:2). Effective instruction is paramount in a religion focused on discipleship.

Third, "the Lord's servant must not be . . . resentful [*anexikakos*]," another NT hapax. BDAG (77) suggests the idea here that a Christian leader (such as Timothy) should exercise restraint and patience, even if wronged. Justin Martyr uses this word to describe how Christians should appropriate Jesus's teaching on turning the other cheek by "being patient of injuries [*anexikakous*], and ready to serve all, and free from anger" (*Apology* 1.16). Pastoral caregivers face, and may be tempted to fall into, misunderstanding and malice. Paul calls Timothy to establish a buffer zone of magnanimity in interpersonal relationships.

25 A fourth requirement for "the Lord's servant" shifts from character traits (gentle, not resentful) and a competency (able to teach) in v. 24 to an activity. Paul knows that the Christian leader will seldom be free from opposition. Being maligned and reviled can in fact be a sign that one is squarely in the center of God's service (cf. Matt 5:11–12), and though this may not be the daily fare of most faithful pastors, times of turbulence inevitably arise. People opposing Timothy should encounter in him a laid-back but sharpened pedagogy that seeks to inform, though not in a haughty or high-handed manner.

In speaking of opponents being "instructed" in v. 25, Paul uses a form of *paideuō* (educate, instruct) that resonates with a cognate, negated word translated "stupid" (*apaideutous*, uneducated, uninstructed) and describing arguments that Timothy needs to avoid in v. 23. An antidote to wrongheaded disputes can be proactive instruction that anticipates and heads off misunderstanding or distortion of Christian teaching. Pastors who neglect their calling to ambitious study and effective instruction may be creating their own enemies by their malpractice.

On the positive side, God may "grant them repentance." This distinctive formulation[179] is found elsewhere in the NT only at Acts 5:31 (God exalted Christ "that he might bring Israel to repentance") and 11:18 ("even to Gentiles God has granted repentance that leads to life"). Similar constructions[180] depict repentance resulting in forgiveness of sins (Mark 1:4; Luke 3:3; 24:47) and salvation (2 Cor 7:10). In 2 Tim 2:25 the outcome is "knowledge of the truth." Collins calls such knowledge "the technical term used in the Pastorals to designate the community's understanding of the truth" and refers also to 3:7; 1 Tim 2:4; Titus 1:1.[181]

179. That is, a form of *didōmi* (I give, grant) plus *metanoia* (repentance).

180. That is, *metanoia* followed by the preposition *eis* (for, unto, resulting in).

181. Collins, 242.

Schlatter comments on how similar this understanding of repentance is to Paul's talk of man's "unrepentent" heart in Rom 2:5 and God's gift of "eternal life" to those who turn to him (Rom 2:7). Neither in Romans nor in 2 Timothy are faith and repentance depicted as discrete actions performed as conditions to produce a state of salvation. "Since Paul saw in that which takes place in man [to save him] the working of the divine word, conversion too is part of the divine gift which comes to those out of whose error the word of Christ liberates."[182] Timothy may hold out hope[183] for God to effect such transformation of his opponents through his patient instruction.

Similarly to Schlatter, Aquinas notes that the idea of God granting repentance "excludes the error of Pelagius who said that the gifts of grace are from our own merits." He continues: "Even the principle of good things, namely, repentance, is given by God," citing Lam 5:21 and Prov 19.[184]

The "truth" to which repentance opens knowledge most likely pertains to the message about Jesus and salvation of which Paul has been writing since the opening lines of this epistle and for the sake of which he was in chains as he wrote. The remarkable effect of this truth—liberation from satanic entrapment—is seen in the next verse.

26 If Timothy bears with opponents and God grants them repentance for knowledge of the truth (v. 25), a further possible effect is "they will come to their senses." Those six words translate the verb *ananēpsōsin*, a NT hapax. It is found several times in Philo and Josephus and means "to regain one's senses."[185] BDAG 68 notes that sometimes the connotation is "sobering up" after inebriation. Paul depicts people waking up and realizing they are ensnared by the devil—they need to be sprung from his trap.[186]

D. G. Reid[187] notes the interchangeability of "devil"[188] and "Satan"[189] in Paul. Paul speaks of entrapment by the devil also in 1 Tim 3:7. However named, he is "the supernatural adversary of God and his purposes."[190] Paul depicts Timothy's adversaries as dreadfully confined and neutralized by this being, "who has taken them captive." The word used could be rendered "live-

182. Schlatter, *Die Kirche der Griechen*, 249–50.

183. On the construction *mēpote dōē* (NIV "in the hope that [God] will grant"), see BDF §370.3.

184. Aquinas, 125. The Proverbs reference seems an error; see rather Isa 26:17–18 and the commentary notes (213).

185. Philo: *Allegorical Interpretation* 2.60; Josephus: *Jewish Antiquities* 6.241; *Jewish War* 1.619.

186. For DSS analogies, see Collins, 243.

187. In *DPL* 864.

188. In the PE, note also 1 Tim 3:6, 7.

189. In the PE, note 1 Tim 1:20; 5:15.

190. Reid in *DPL* 863.

trapped."[191] The devil is a merciless adversary. But the God who grants repentance (v. 25) can also grant liberation from his clutches. In that case, Timothy's opponents will no longer be detained "to do his will" instead of the will of God.

Paul's counsel to Timothy is a reminder of the great truth of Christian liberty. Jesus pictured those lacking faith in him as enslaved—they needed to affirm the truth regarding him in order to be set free (John 8:32). He came "to proclaim freedom for the prisoners" (Luke 4:18), drawing on a theme from Isaiah with roots in Israel's release from its Egyptian house of bondage. The gospel message brings creation and humans with it "into the freedom and glory of the children of God" (Rom 8:21). Paul states that "where the Spirit of the Lord is, there is freedom" (2 Cor 3:17) and that "it is for freedom that Christ has set us free" (Gal 5:1). Liberation from unrighteousness opens up the capacity for God to permeate one's life (Rom 6:18) and to produce fruit in keeping with repentance (Matt 3:8).

All of these ambitious and salubrious outcomes Paul wishes for Timothy's opponents under Timothy's wise and cautious instruction. Paul knew the Proverbs, which states, "When the Lord takes pleasure in anyone's way, he causes their enemies to make peace with them" (Prov 16:7). It was his hope that Timothy, by the wise pastoral practices and outlook outlined in 2 Tim 2:22–26, might find divinely granted favor with those apparently out of sympathy with his leadership. Timothy must not take opposition more personally than necessary but realize people may simply be living out their loyalty to a cruel taskmaster from whom they can be freed only by Christ in whose name Timothy serves.

4. Withstanding the Suction of Terrible Times (3:1–5)

These verses show that Paul envisioned deteriorating social conditions in times ahead. But these conditions are to some extent already present and making an impact on Timothy, as indicated by the commands in vv. 1 and 5 that Timothy should take note and act in response to them. Also, Paul links future deterioration with false teachers, whose effect Timothy must already counteract (vv. 6–9). So the warnings in vv. 1–5 pertain not only to future developments but to Timothy's current setting.

An alternate understanding of the passage (with reference also, one surmises, to the women in v. 6) is that a fictitious Paul was "encouraging the Christian men in Ephesus to help him mount a more successful defense against his opponents by tapping into their patriarchal fears" by raising the specter of "Home

191. *Ezōgrēmenoi*; see BDAG 430.

Breakers."[192] The hypothesis fails, though, if Paul was the author, since he writes to Timothy as pastor of a church of both men and women, not just men. It may also be asked whether either Paul or a fictitious post–New Testament writer could have found "patriarchal fears" to play on, even subliminally. And even if they could have, does this passage show any real signs of exploiting that rhetorical and psychological angle? If shady religious teachers are in fact deceiving women and thereby destabilizing one or more congregations, that is a real pastoral issue for the whole church to take note of, not a ploy to play on anyone's fears.

Jesus chided listeners, "How is it that you don't know how to interpret this present time?" (Luke 12:56). Later, when his disciples sought to nail down the relation between the present and end times, Jesus reminded them, "It is not for you to know the times or dates the Father has set by his own authority" (Acts 1:7). It is never easy for followers of Jesus to maintain balance between too much emphasis on the present without due regard for future matters, on the one hand, and so much attention to the future that the present is neglected or wrongly diagnosed, on the other. In vv. 1–5 Paul seeks to alert Timothy to end-time indicators in the present and how Timothy should respond to them. Laansma captures the effect through his comment that what can be "a source of deep discouragement for the servant of the Lord—difficult times—should be a cause of deepened resolve and, indeed, hope since this is precisely what the Lord has told us to expect."[193]

> [1]*But mark this: There will be terrible times in the last days.* [2]*People will be lovers of themselves, lovers of money, boastful, proud, abusive, disobedient to their parents, ungrateful, unholy,* [3]*without love, unforgiving, slanderous, without self-control, brutal, not lovers of the good,* [4]*treacherous, rash, conceited, lovers of pleasure rather than lovers of God—*[5]*having a form of godliness but denying its power. Have nothing to do with such people.*

1 NIV "mark" translates the singular imperative *ginōske* ("Know!"), the same form used in Socrates's celebrated "Know thyself!" The form occurs only here in the NT.[194] Philo uses Socrates's very expression to teach attainment of salvation and relates self-knowledge to "what Moses teaches us in many passages where he says, 'Take heed to thyself.'"[195] Paul, however, does not commend self-knowledge (and it may be asked whether Moses did, either). He rather calls attention to current social and moral conditions as manifest in human

192. Twomey, 154 ("Home Breakers" is the section heading on that page).

193. Laansma, 184.

194. It is also rare in the LXX: see Judg 4:9; Prov 24:12; 29:20.

195. Philo, *On the Migration of Abraham* 8.

behavior, always significant for someone in Timothy's position as a gospel minister.

These "last days"[196] are not only future times, when things will worsen (Matt 24:21–31), but also the present. As Neudorfer notes, "'Last days' precede the definitive last day; they will be characterized by negative alterations in human (and Christian?) behavior among themselves and against God."[197] Schlatter observes that Paul's grim projection may indicate that Paul's arrest preceded "the bloody events in Rome in AD 64," referring to Nero's persecutions.[198] Knowledge of those events may have conditioned his counsel to Timothy. These "last days," also called "later times" (1 Tim 4:1), were present with Christ's coming (Heb 1:1–2), intensified with his resurrection and the Spirit's powerful arrival (Acts 2:17, drawing on Joel 3:1), and continue until his return. Paul is about to describe, then, conditions as they will be but also already are.[199] They will be "terrible"[200] because of the base and brazen qualities people exhibit already.

2 In vv. 2–5 Paul lists nineteen qualities (some reckon eighteen) of the evildoers whose presence bears out that "terrible times" (v. 1) are at hand. For similar lists of evil and its misdeeds, see 1 Tim 1:8–11; Matt 15:17–20; Rom 1:29–31; 1 Cor 5:9–11; 1 Pet 4:3–4; Rev 21:8; 22:15. Cruse observes that "lists of vices and virtues appear in all the Pauline letters except 1 Thessalonians, 2 Thessalonians and Philemon."[201] Cruse counts five functions of the lists; 2 Tim 3:2–5 is the sole list devoted to advising a young pastor.

Lists of virtues and vices dot both Jewish and Hellenistic writings in the Second Temple and NT periods. Some see the background for the lists as Hellenistic, others as Jewish. Cruse notes that, if Paul is lifting vv. 2–5 more or less wholesale from another source, it is important not to overinterpret qualities found there "as if they were intended to be accurate descriptions of the conduct of those to whom they refer."[202] Rather, "The global impression is what is important."[203] Berger views the whole of 3:1–10 as stereotypical rhetoric.[204]

196. For OT and Second Temple parallels, see Keener, *Bible Background Commentary*, 620.

197. Neudorfer, *Zweiter Brief an Timotheus*, 186.

198. Schlatter, *Die Kirche der Griechen*, 251n2. For a colorful depiction of Nero, see Montague, 205.

199. "Will be" translates a future form of *enistēmi*, a word used elsewhere in the NT almost exclusively by Paul: see also Rom 8:38; 1 Cor 3:22; 7:26; Gal 1:4; 2 Thess 2:2. It also occurs in Heb 9:9.

200. The word is used elsewhere in the NT only in Matt 8:28, where it describes how "violent" the two Gadarene demoniacs were. It occurs eleven times in the LXX, all but one (Isa 18:2) in the Apocrypha. It is used over a hundred times each in Philo and Josephus, reflecting the extreme accounts they narrate and also at times their hyperbole.

201. *DPL* 962.

202. *DPL* 963.

203. Collins, 246.

204. Berger, 817.

There is no evidence, however, that Paul borrowed these terms from any known author or list. A man who could remember as many names and personal details as Paul dictates in Rom 16 could easily single out a dozen or more qualities of gnarly people, the likes of which he had encountered in abundance over the years. While we should not suppose Paul was necessarily predicting the precise negative traits of particular individuals Timothy would encounter, there is no reason to minimize or overlook the rich if somewhat revolting specifics Paul describes. The value to Timothy would be that, having been forewarned regarding "terrible times," he would also be prepared in advance to encounter correspondingly terrible people. Mounce concludes that in this list Paul is in fact "thinking of the eschatological evil that has infiltrated the Ephesian church" Timothy serves.[205] If so, the evil is taking human form.

It is possible that "lovers of themselves" is a category under which the subsequent vices are subsumed. Aquinas thinks Paul "first gives the root of their iniquity; second, its diverse species."[206] Guthrie thinks the first two characteristics, "lovers of themselves, lovers of money," constitute "the key to the rest of the list." He explains, "Moral corruption follows from love falsely directed."[207] This connection is hard to deny. Yet, it is also possible that the list is simply sequential, a sweeping glance across the barren moral landscape of natural lives untouched by the vivification of God's saving and transforming work.

In the remainder of v. 2, Paul lists[208] eight negative traits.

1. "Lovers of themselves."[209] The gospel enables love for God and for others; "whoever loves others has fulfilled the law" (Rom 13:8). But Paul describes some whose deepest affection is set on the self, whether individually or corporately. Timothy knew better; when Paul wrote Philippians, he commended Timothy as exemplary in his concern for the Philippians' welfare and added, "For everyone [else] looks out for their own interests, not those of Jesus Christ" (Phil 2:21). In self-love under Christian auspices, Christ is not explicitly denied, just effectively displaced. This is the subtle deception of narcissism, the excessive love of self.[210] Collins speaks here of "crass egocentrists."[211]

2. "Lovers of money." The word (*philargyros*, money-loving) is used only

205. Mounce, 543.

206. Aquinas, 127.

207. Guthrie, 168–69.

208. On the construction, which involves asyndeton, see BDF §460.2.

209. *Philautos* (love of self) is a NT hapax.

210. Jonathan Edwards saw self-love as a fundamental human flaw; see Bruce W. Davidson, "Narcission: The Root of All Hypocrisy in the Theological Psychology of Jonathan Edwards," *JETS* 57.1 (March 2014) 135–45.

211. Collins, 247. For Hellenistic parallels, see *NW* 994–97.

here in the NT.[212] Jesus spoke of this as a problem of certain Pharisees "who loved money" and "were sneering at Jesus" when he said one could not serve both God and mammon (Luke 16:14). Paul saw lust for money as one of humans' major besetting sins: "For the love of money[213] is a root of all kinds of evil" (1 Tim 6:10; see discussion there). Jesus said, "Beware, and be on your guard against every form of greed; for not even when one has an abundance does his life consist of his possessions" (Luke 12:15 NASB). The warning is as timely now as in Jesus's and Paul's world.

3. "Boastful." The same word (*alazōn*) appears in Rom 1:30 (and nowhere else in the NT).[214] The word can also be rendered "arrogant, audacious." The verb for "boasting" (*kauchaomai*) is frequent in Paul and usually negative, except when "boasting" or placing confidence in God (2 Cor 10:17) or Christ (Gal 6:14). Overall, the NT attitude toward haughty verbal self-promotion is summarized in Jas 4:16: "As it is, you boast in your arrogant schemes. All such boasting is evil." The sole AF occurrence of the word (1 Clem. 57:2) discourages boastfulness of the tongue on this ground: "For it is better for you to be found small but included in the flock of Christ than to have a preeminent reputation and yet be excluded from his hope." For Clement as for Paul, there are not only temporal but eschatological implications for such behavior.

4. "Proud." Paul uses this word (*hyperēphanos*) in Rom 1:30. It occurs three other times in the NT (Luke 1:31; Jas 4:6; 1 Pet 5:5). James and Peter quote the word from the LXX, where it occurs over three dozen times. Nearly a dozen denunciations of the arrogant in various Psalms employ this word.[215] God's opposition to the proud is axiomatic in OT and NT alike; it seems to be a human fault in all places and times. This does not mean that Timothy may simply sigh and resign himself to it, for God just as assiduously responds to it. The pastoral call is to shepherd people away from embrace of this vice.

5. "Abusive." The root word, *blasphēmos*, can be used for speech that maligns people, God, or both—Acts 6:11 uses it to describe "blasphemous words against Moses and against God." Paul describes himself with the same word in saying he "was once a blasphemer and a persecutor and a violent man" (1 Tim 1:13). Collins notes that the noun form "appears in many Hellenistic lists of vices as a general description of anti-social behavior."[216] LXX uses tend to stress malignment of God rather than humans. This is also true of the noun form (*blasphēmia*) in its eighteen NT occurrences. Paul may be saying that

212. In the LXX it occurs only in 4 Macc 2:8. Here reason and obedience to Torah can become "lord" (*kyrios*) over "one's own bent" (NETS).

213. Condemned also in 4 Macc 1:26, the only use of the word in the LXX.

214. In the LXX, see Prov 21:24; Job 28:8; Hab 2:5.

215. See LXX Pss 17:28; 88:11; 93:2; 100:5; 118:21, 51, 69, 78, 122; 122:4; 139:6.

216. Collins, 247.

these people are slanderous in their speech generally, whether about God or about other people.

6. "Disobedient to their parents." This behavior violates the commandment to honor one's parents (Exod 20:12; Deut 5:16; cf. Matt 15:4; 19:19; Eph 6:2; 1 Tim 5:8). "Love and obedience toward parents was one of the most central virtues of antiquity,"[217] but Paul points to many not living up to the ideal. On "disobedient," see discussion at Titus 1:6 (*anypotaktos*), 16. The word for "disobedient" in 2 Tim 3:2 is *apeithēs*.[218] Jesus called for loyalty to himself above parents (Matt 10:37), yet he critiqued gratuitous abandonment of responsibility for parents in their old age (Mark 7:8–13).[219] He cared for his mother until the end (John 19:26). Absence of love and relational responsibility (like respect for parents) within families and among family members is a token of "terrible times" (v. 1).

7. "Ungrateful." This word (*acharistos*) begins a series of four words beginning with alpha (here alpha privative, meaning "un-" or "non-"), then *diabolos* ("slanderous") in v. 3, then three more words beginning with alpha. The author shows creative flair in vocabulary. The only other use of "ungrateful" in the NT is near the end of the Lukan Sermon on the Mount, where Jesus notes that God "is kind to the ungrateful and wicked" (Luke 6:35). All LXX uses of the word are in the Apocrypha.[220] Philo says that "Noah found grace in [God's] sight, when all the rest of mankind appearing ungrateful were about to receive punishment" (*That God Is Unchangeable* 74).[221] The word occurs ten times in Josephus but is absent from the AF. The concept is not obscure: people who should be thankful, whether to God or to others, are neither. Fundamental to both OT and NT spirituality is the posture called for by Paul: "Give thanks [= be grateful] in all circumstances; for this is God's will for you in Christ Jesus" (1 Thess 5:18). In the OT this exhortation often takes the form of encouragement to praise (over a hundred times in the LXX). The world stands under God's wrath, Paul writes, because "although they knew God, they neither glorified him as God nor gave thanks to him" (Rom 1:21). People are frequently ungrateful, despite all that God provides.

8. "Unholy." The word (*anosios*) appears elsewhere in the NT only at 1 Tim 1:9. God is holy and calls for holiness on the part of his people. To be

217. Keener, *Bible Background Commentary*, 620.

218. Found also in Luke 1:17; Acts 26:19; Rom 1:30; Titus 3:3. In the LXX, see Num 20:10; Deut 21:18; Sir 16:6; 47:21; Zech 7:12; Isa 30:9; Jer 5:23. Philo speaks of disobedience (*apeithēs*) to parents in *Drunkenness* 17, 93, 95 and in *Virtues* 208.

219. On the dialectic and its solution, see Peter Balla, *The Child-Parent Relationship in the New Testament and Its Environment* (Tübingen: Mohr Siebeck, 2003).

220. 4 Macc 9:10; Wis 16:29; Sir 29:16, 25.

221. See also Philo, *That God Is Unchangeable* 48; *Life of Joseph* 99; *Embassy to Gaius* 60.

unholy is to fail to appropriate the God-resemblance (see Matt 5:48; Eph 5:1) that gospel reception and transformation bring about. Philo combines use of "unholy" with a description of lack of gratitude:

> Every impious [*anosios*, unholy] man supposes that what he thinks and understands is owing to the bounty of his intellect . . . ; that what he sees is the gift of his eyes . . . , what he hears of his ears, what he smells of his nostrils, and so that each of his outward senses bestows on him those perceptions which are in accordance with them. Again, [man supposes] that it is the organs of the voice which endow him with the capacity of speaking, and that there is actually no such thing as a God at all, or at all events that he is not the primary cause of things. (*Confusion of Tongues* 123)

This attitude contrasts sharply with Paul's ascription of all things (and esp. the desirable) to God: "For from him and through him and for him are all things. To him be the glory forever! Amen" (Rom 11:36). Timothy must be prepared to encounter people with very different convictions.

3 Paul continues his rapid-fire confirmation of the seamy characteristics of people Timothy will encounter in these "terrible times" (v. 1). Timothy is not newly hatched into the world, so these features will not surprise him. The list should rather be viewed as shoptalk between two ministry veterans, the older fortifying the younger and both commiserating over the plight of people (including themselves), yet affirming the triumph of God and the gospel, even over the pathological tendencies of human beings.

The listing of eight lamentable characteristics begun in v. 2 continues in v. 3, which adds six more.

9. "Without love." The word *astorgos* means bereft of natural affection. BDAG 146 offers translations like "hardhearted, unfeeling, without regard for others." Paul uses the same word in Rom 1:31. It points to abject godlessness, since love is at the core of God's identity and of what he calls for from people—in particular, from his people. A capacity for love is part of the image of God; when people suppress it and even replace it with the opposite, it is a sign of a hard and sinister turn away from their Creator.[222]

10. "Unforgiving." This word (*aspondos*) is a NT hapax.[223] Philo uses it nearly three dozen times[224] to refer to a person or situation that is intractable—no solution or reconciliation is possible. A related, positive word is

222. For the problem at present, see V. Kuligin, *Snubbing God: The High Cost of Rejecting God's Created Order* (Wooster, OH: Weaver Book Company, 2017).

223. It is, however, a variant reading in many MSS of Rom 1:31 (e.g., $\aleph^2$ C D^2 K L P Ψ [33] 81 etc.).

224. See also three uses in Josephus: *Jewish Antiquities* 4.264; 15.146, 220.

"treaty" (*spondē*). The "unforgiving" person is one who refuses to work toward settlement of a grievance or disagreement.

11. "Slanderous" (*diabolos*). The idea conveyed here is close to what the word "abusive" in v. 2 described (see discussion above). Paul (and probably Timothy) would have known the command "Do not go about spreading slander among your people" (Lev 19:16).[225] In v. 2 the stress was on the outrageous nature of the language; here it is more on the accusatory or adversarial nature of what is said. As a noun, the word is used to refer to the devil (in Paul, see Eph 4:27; 6:11; 1 Tim 3:6, 7; 2 Tim 2:26), whose role as liar and accuser is well known. Paul uses the same word in 1 Tim 3:11 ("malicious talkers") and Titus 2:3 ("slanderers").

12. "Without self-control." They lack sufficient limits and restrictions on their passions. Proverbs 27:20 (LXX) uses the same word, italicized in this translation: "An abomination to the Lord is . . . the untaught person, *unable to control* the tongue." Sometimes there is no restraint where there needs to be. A related, positive form of the word (the adj. *enkratēs*) is used in Titus 1:8 (an elder must be "disciplined"). A similar related noun form (*enkrateia*) is a fruit of the Spirit (Gal 5:23; see also same word in Acts 24:25; 2 Pet 1:6).

13. "Brutal." Like several words in this list, it is a NT hapax. Nor does it occur in the LXX or AF. Philo uses it some dozen times in contexts where "savage, untamable, unmerciful, cruel" are apt translations. In NT history one might think of the Roman governor's brutality in slaughtering hapless Galilean worshipers (Luke 13:1), or of the greedy cynicism of Felix as he kept Paul imprisoned on phony charges for two years, hoping for a bribe from Paul (Acts 24:26) or, barring that, political favor from the Jews (Acts 24:27).

14. "Not lovers of the good." BDAG 157 stresses the social implication of this epithet—they have no interest in the public welfare. Combined with the previous dozen-plus characteristics, this word intensifies the portrait of people not only despicable in personal qualities but enemies of good and of common social interests that make peaceable civic life possible, tolerable, and perhaps even enjoyable. The word itself (*aphilagathos*) is rare in the NT era (but attested in papyri; see MM 98). Its meaning is not in question because the positive form (*philagathos*, used in Titus 1:8) is common—people were known and extolled for acting in the interest of others, as one expects in reasonably healthy social settings. Timothy has to be ready to encounter the opposite in the course of his ministry labors.

4 With four more negative human characteristics, Paul brings this long list closer to completion. If he seems to be rubbing it in, bear in mind that Jesus lists over a dozen sins in a comparable compilation (Mark 7:21–23). And Philo

225. Mentioned by Aquinas, 128.

lists well in excess of *one hundred* in a single 155-word riff.[226] By that measure, Paul is terse and restrained.

15. "Treacherous." This translation of a form of *prodotēs* (traitor, betrayer) preserves symmetry with other words in the list, which are mostly adjectives. Yet, it is not an adjective but a noun: "[These people are] traitors, betrayers." "Treacherous" (NIV) certainly captures the thought, but the wording is perhaps even more denunciatory. The two other NT uses of the word describe Judas, "who became a *traitor*" (Luke 6:16), and those who were about to stone Stephen ("*betrayers* and murderers" of "the Righteous One"; Acts 7:52 NASB). Paul is not flagging insignificant foibles or describing abstract qualities.

16. "Rash." The word (*propetēs*) describes behavior that is reckless and hasty (see also Acts 19:36). It rhymes with the word before it (*prodotēs*). All three LXX occurrences describe precipitous speech:

> The mouth of the *reckless* brings ruin near. (Prov 10:14)
>
> He who is *rash* with his lips will bring terror upon himself. (Prov 13:3)
>
> He who is *reckless* in his speech will be hated. (Sir 9:18)

There is no way of knowing whether Paul limits the ill effect of this quality to damaging talk, but even if so, combined with the other traits, it is a menacing quality. Like others, it might well apply to those mentioned a few verses later, "teachers" who "oppose the truth" (v. 8).

17. "Conceited." The same word occurs elsewhere in the NT only at 1 Tim 3:6 and 6:4. It was used widely outside the NT to describe people who were overly impressed with their own knowledge. Again, the usage here could be foreshadowing mention of false teachers in verses just below. Or Paul could be drawing on past encounters known to him and Timothy like the people described in 1 Tim 1:7, who aspired to lead others but did not know enough to recognize that their purported knowledge was a flimflam.

18. "Lovers of pleasure rather than lovers of God." Whereas God calls people to love him (Deut 6:5) and to "have no other gods before [him]" (Exod 20:3), Paul here describes persons who enthrone their own self-gratification. The close-but-contrasting sound of the two main words in this clause

226. Philo, *On the Sacrifices of Cain and Abel* 32. To give just a sample of what happens to the person who chooses to "become a votary of pleasure" (Colson translation adapted): "You will be . . . colorless, immoderate, insatiable, insolent, conceited, self-willed, mean, envious, calumnious, quarrelsome, slanderous, greedy, deceitful, cheating, rash, ignorant, stupid, inharmonious, dishonest, disobedient, obstinate, tricky, swindling, insincere, suspicious, hated, absurd, difficult to detect, difficult to avoid, destructive, evil-minded, disproportionate, an unreasonable chatterer. . . ." This is less than a fifth of Philo's list.

(*philēdonoi* [pleasure lovers], *philotheoi* [God lovers]) signals that Paul is wrapping up this summation of problem people with rhetorical polish. The word translated "lovers of pleasure" appears nowhere else in the NT, and neither does "lovers of God." But the starkness and tragedy of the disjunction is plain: they have their priorities precisely backward. If they sought God, they would gain a relational standing that dwarfs the satiation of carnal appetites (see Matt 6:33; Luke 12:31). Instead, their desire is bent in a direction that can only frustrate them and constitute a hazard to others in danger of becoming their victims. For an example of sexual unrestraint threatening others in a congregation, as well as attracting God's judgment, see 1 Thess 4:6–8. "Lovers of pleasure," however, cannot be limited to sexual expression but applies to the full range of human drives that, pursued to excess and without Scripture's guidance and the Spirit's direction, lead to the barren human condition Paul describes.

5 A final descriptive assessment of people Timothy must prepare to face concedes their religious appearance but insists on their deficient condition. While this verse could be a summation of the eighteen qualities listed in vv. 2–5, we will treat it as the final characteristic in the series.

19. With "having a form [*morphōsis*] of godliness," Paul uses the same construction found in Rom 2:20: "having the form [*morphōsis*] of knowledge." These are the only two uses of *morphōsis* in the NT.[227] "Clearly the meaning of the word here is 'outward appearance'; the people in view are false believers, claiming to be godly, but 'as far as the faith is concerned, are rejected' (3:8)."[228] On "godliness," see Introduction, IX.B. Both Jesus and Paul warn elsewhere of wolves in sheep's clothing (Mark 7:15; Acts 20:29).

Their godly appearance is belied by the previous eighteen characteristics, which establish their true character. There is a "power" in the living, active presence of God through the gospel message that transformed Paul from a persecutor to a worshiper of Christ (1 Tim 1:16). Paul has already spoken of it earlier, as God's Spirit was said to give "power, love, and self-discipline" (1:7), and as Timothy is called to join Paul "in suffering for the gospel, by the power of God" (1:8). Paul and Timothy both know well that they would have neither redeemed standing nor a gospel voice were it not for the working of God's power.

These power-denying pretenders must present real danger to Timothy, as Paul says quite directly, "Have nothing to do with[229] such people." This com-

227. The word is absent from the LXX, Philo, Josephus, and the AF. It is found some eight times in Irenaeus as he explains aspects of gnostic cosmology and doctrine.

228. *NIDNTTE* 1:341.

229. The present imperative is a form of *apotrepō* (I turn away from), the only use of this word in the NT. It is a near synonym with *ektrepō*, which appears five times in the NT, four of those in the PE: 1 Tim 1:6; 5:15; 6:20; 2 Tim 4:4.

mand is striking, for a few verses earlier Paul counseled Timothy to instruct opponents gently, "in the hope that God will grant them repentance leading them to a knowledge of the truth" (2:25). Why should he now write off "such people"?

Perhaps the people referenced in 2:25 were still open to the gospel's truth. In contrast, vv. 1–5 describes a time (including the present) and people that he and Timothy both face and whose access to truth has been barred, not first of all by false teaching and argument (see next section) but by ethical collapse. Oden offers a contemporary analogy in those who are "deliberately unholy and still go to church, covetous and still say morning prayers, blasphemers and still repeat perfectly the Apostles' Creed; they may be treacherous and still remain on the church board, haters of good and still give lip service to God."[230]

With fresh guidance from the informal taxonomy Paul has provided, Timothy is in position to sidestep any potential downward pull of their influence on him and others in the Christian community. More details about these people, their tactics, their destructive effects, and their futility appear in the next four verses.

5. Features and Creatures of Folly (3:6–9)

These verses continue to describe a subset of people "in the last days" (v. 1), a time that in considerable measure includes Paul and Timothy's present. But whereas vv. 2–5 furnished a list of negative characteristics of ungodly people, vv. 6–9 specify why Timothy should "avoid" them (v. 5) and what the outcome of their folly is apt to be. In particular, Paul calls attention to conniving pastoral imposters (and their victims) who, in terms of moving God's interests forward, "will not get very far" (v. 9). "Deception always loses in the long term."[231] Timothy should certainly not follow their lead and in fact needs to give them a wide berth.

> [6] *They are the kind who worm their way into homes and gain control over gullible women, who are loaded down with sins and are swayed by all kinds of evil desires,* [7] *always learning but never able to come to a knowledge of the truth.* [8] *Just as Jannes and Jambres opposed Moses, so also these teachers oppose the truth. They are men of depraved minds, who, as far as the faith is concerned, are rejected.* [9] *But they will not get very far because, as in the case of those men, their folly will be clear to everyone.*

230. Oden, 76–77.
231. Zehr, 196.

6 This verse begins with two important clues as to why Timothy should "avoid" the people described in vv. 2–5: (1) they have skilled and toxic leaders, and (2) their leaders are on the offensive.

NIV chooses not to translate the inferential conjunction *gar*, which, if translated, would make the start of the verse read, "*For* they are the kind. . . ." In other words, v. 6 explains *why* Timothy should avoid "such people." He should avoid them because in their ranks (*ek toutōn*, from them) are leaders just as base as they are. The threat these figures pose as a result of their defective character will become clear as these verses unfold. Verse 6 stresses their present sneaky, malevolent tactics. Paul asserts that Timothy needs to avoid them because they are not seeking God's kingdom or the gospel's progress at all but only their own warped designs. There is a conceptual tie here with what "the elder" John advises believers in another setting regarding their interaction with false teachers: "If anyone comes to you and does not bring this teaching, do not take them into your house or welcome them. Anyone who welcomes them shares in their wicked work" (2 John 10–11). For both John and Paul, in this situation the watchword is "avoid," not embrace or parley with.

These leaders are not passive or perhaps seeking guidance from an apostolic associate like Timothy. They are on the offensive. They "worm their way into homes." The verb here (*endynō*, sneak in) is rare in Greek literature, but a near synonym appears in Jude 4 ("certain individuals . . . have *secretly slipped in* among you"). Sneaky usurpers also appear in Gal 2:4 ("false believers had *infiltrated* our ranks"). Subverting "homes" is particularly destructive in an age of house churches. But Paul decries not only where they are wreaking havoc but of whom they are taking advantage.

The expressions "loaded down" and "swayed" describe "gullible women." Some find this term "derogatory" (see BDAG 208), and in some contexts it may be. In other contexts it is complementary, connoting attractiveness or endearment.[232] In any case, it is tragically true that people across the board are susceptible to spiritual deception, men as well as women; in any given time and place, women will be among the ones who fall prey. It is unfounded to brand Paul's statement as "a cultural stereotype . . . intended to defame the opponents as teachers who could only persuade people who were incapable of recognizing the truth."[233] It is just as likely that Paul was speaking from the standpoint of personal observation. A study of Mary Baker Eddy (1821–1910), founding thinker of Christian Science, may serve to illustrate a gullible woman (blithely following her own convictions rather than Scripture and historic

232. Spencer, 122.

233. Bassler, 161. As Bassler notes elsewhere (189), "The use of stereotypical features in polemics does not automatically preclude their relevance; one simply cannot assume such relevance."

Christian teaching) misleading others, like the author of the study who extols and defends her.[234] Paul's term may not be derogatory but a description of facts on the ground. And it is not as if Paul lets those who are misleading them (apparently men) off the hook.

These men "gain control over" them, a word connoting forcible capture.[235] The women are being pursued and played for dupes. Because of the heavy weight of sins and tyrannical "evil desires,"[236] what they need is pastoral help and gospel rescue. It could and does happen to all kinds of people. What they get courtesy of the sneaky leaders whose ranks Timothy is told to "avoid" is quite different, as the next verse shows.

7 Description of the "weak women" of v. 6 continues. Targeted by duplicitous religious opportunists, they are "always learning." Like "burdened" and "led astray" (v. 6), "learning" is neuter in Greek, which matches the grammatical gender of the word translated "weak women." Learning itself is a good thing; recent research argues that it was a major unifying characteristic of early Christian congregations, which were primarily learning communities.[237] Since Jesus called and made disciples and then sent them forth to make disciples of all peoples, teaching them to do all Jesus commanded (see Matt 28:19–20), this unifier is not surprising. Paul reminded Timothy of his duty to take what he had learned from Paul and "entrust [it] to faithful men who will be able to teach others also" (2 Tim 2:2).

To learn is a mark of a disciple (a word that means "learner") of Jesus. But learning under Christian auspices should lead somewhere. Paul describes a situation in which people are "always learning"[238] but "never able to arrive at a knowledge of the truth." "Knowledge of the truth" is a PE refrain (see the same expression at 1 Tim 2:4; 2 Tim 2:25; Titus 1:1). It describes a saving understanding of the gospel message, resulting in a personal relationship with God through faith in the risen Christ. These women, despite "always learning," have not arrived at a resolution to the weight of sin and the tyranny of certain

234. Annette Kreutziger-Herr, "Eddy, Mary Baker," *EBR* 7:357–62.

235. The same verb (*aichmalōtizō*, I take captive) occurs in Luke 21:24; Rom 7:23; 2 Cor 10:5.

236. See discussion of *epithymia* (desire, lust) at 2:22 above. "Evil desires" above is apt to encompass more than sex. It would include the whole range of sinful neuroses and insecurities that tempt someone (in this context, a woman) to open the door to a perceived strong or attractive person (in this case, unscrupulous spiritual leaders) to address their ills or at least meet perceived needs. Many factors, not sexual lust alone, play into such situations: failure to seek and find fulfillment in Christ on the part of such women; pride and the drive for affirmation or domination on the part of such men. Analogous situations exist and tragically unfold, it seems, across the sweep of church history and societies everywhere.

237. Smith, *Pauline Communities*.

238. The verb *manthanō* (I learn) appears fifteen times in the Pauline corpus: Rom 16:17; 1 Cor 4:6; 14:31, 35; Gal 3:2; Eph 4:20; Phil 4:9, 11; Col 1:7; 1 Tim 2:11; 5:4, 13; 2 Tim 3:14; Titus 3:14.

passions (see v. 6). This is opposite to the effect of the freedom announced in the gospel message (Gal 5:1). It is also opposite to the effect that servants of the gospel like Paul or Timothy would seek to bring about through pastoral measures like prayer, sound instruction, and wise oversight. The destructive fallout of "those who creep into households and capture weak women" explains the verve with which Paul calls them out and characterizes their work in the next two verses.

8 The first words ("Just as") followed later by "so also" mirrors a construction common in the LXX (173 times) but rare elsewhere.[239] "Jannes" and "Jambres" were the names assigned in Jewish tradition to the court magicians who opposed Moses before Pharaoh (Exod 7:11–12);[240] their names do not appear in the OT. Philo retells the story as it was remembered from a first-century viewpoint among Alexandrian Jews:

> So now the marvelous sight [of Moses's staff turning into a serpent and swallowing the magicians' serpents] thus exhibited to [Pharaoh and the other Egyptians] wrought a fear in the soul of every one of these wicked and malicious men, so that they no longer fancied that what was done was the trick or artifice of men, devised merely for deceit; but they saw that it was a more divine power which was the cause of these things, to which all things are easy. But when by the evident might of what was done they were compelled to confess this, they still were not the less audacious, clinging to their original inhumanity and impiety as to some inalienable virtue, and not pitying those who were unjustly enslaved [i.e., the children of Israel in slavery], nor doing any such things as they were commanded by the word of God. And though God himself had declared his will to them by demonstrations clearer than any verbal commands, namely, by signs and wonders, still they required a yet more severe impression to be made upon them, and it was necessary for him to rise up against them with still greater power; and accordingly, those foolish men [like Jannes and Jambres], whom reason and command could not influence, are corrected by a series of afflictions: and ten punishments were inflicted on the land.[241]

The account above, which reflects imaginatively on the biblical narrative, may be like the recollection shared by Paul and Timothy of the famous Exodus

239. The construction is *hon tropon . . . houtōs* (just as . . . so also). It occurs only nine times in Philo, nine in Josephus, and four in the AF. The first part of the expression (*hon tropon*), roughly equivalent to *kathōs*, occurs in the NT at Matt 23:37; Luke 13:34; Acts 1:11; 7:28 (a LXX quotation); 15:11; 27:25.

240. For details, see Collins, 252; *NW* 1001.

241. Philo, *Life of Moses* 1.94–95.

incident. Jannes and Jambres are named central figures of the long-forgotten cast who, with the whole court of Pharaoh, stood against Moses because they had no respect for the God he claimed to represent.[242]

In a similar way, Paul warns about certain leaders among those with showy godliness but who deny its power (v. 5) and lead the weak astray (vv. 6–7). Their error is threefold. First, they "oppose[243] the truth." See comment on v. 7 regarding "knowledge of the truth." These leaders have not grasped the gospel, nor can those under their sway hear it aright.[244] By leading many into darkness, they oppose Christ's beckoning into the light.

Second, they have "depraved minds." The word translated "depraved" appears only here in the NT but is frequent in the LXX. It describes the moral "ruin" of the earth before the flood (Gen 6:12).[245] It also describes eschatological cosmic destruction (Isa 13:5; 24:1). These leaders are not innocently misinformed but deep in the throes and service of evil.

Third, they are "rejected" when it comes to "the faith."[246] These leaders should be instructing and encouraging others in the truths of the gospel. Instead, when assessed by standards implicit in confession of the crucified and risen Jesus ("the faith"), they are failures. The word translated "rejected" (*adokimoi*) is translated "unfit" in Titus 1:16 (see discussion there). Its opposite (*dokimos*) denotes someone approved by God (see 2 Tim 2:15; cf. 1 Cor 11:19; 2 Cor 10:18) or by humans (Rom 14:18). These leaders' actions mark them as acceptable to neither.

9 "Those men" refers to Jannes and Jambres (previous verse). God through Moses stopped them dead in their tracks. Paul assures Timothy that the same fate awaits the errant leaders.

First, "they will not get very far." This translates a negated verb (*prokoptō*)[247] meaning to progress. They will not progress or advance. Paul qualifies this

242. For further details (including reconstruction of the original document), see A. Pietersma, *The Apocryphon of Jannes and Jambres the Magicians* (Leiden: Brill, 1994), which argues that the account arose in Egypt Jewry under Roman rule, perhaps during the first century AD. "The author of *Jannes and Jambres* may be seen to be aiming his barbs at the [Roman] authorities using . . . a biblical tale from Pharaonic times as his vehicle" (58). Paul may be alluding to information in a currently popular story in circulation for an illustration of the behavior of gospel detractors whom Timothy faces, possibly in the same way Jude refers to the Assumption of Moses (Jude 9) or the Book of Enoch (Jude 14–15).

243. Paul uses the word (*anthistēmi*) in five other places: Rom 9:19; 13:2; Gal 2:11; Eph 6:13; 2 Tim 4:15.

244. Cf. Jesus's accusation (Matt 23:13): "You shut the door of the kingdom of heaven in people's faces. You yourselves do not enter, nor will you let those enter who are trying to."

245. Cited also in Philo, *That God Is Unchangeable* 140.

246. For the construction *peri tēn pistin* ("concerning the faith"), see also 1 Tim 1:19 and 6:21, the only other occurrences in the NT.

247. It occurs six times in the NT, five of those times in Paul. See Luke 2:52; Rom 13:12; Gal 1:14; 2 Tim 2:16; 3:13.

word with a prepositional phrase translated "very far" (*epi pleion*; see discussion at 2:16 above). Paul is not saying they will be completely ineffective. He has already mentioned "weak women" as preys of their targeting. Paul is saying their success will be spotty at best.[248] Timothy should certainly not be demoralized by their inroads. Their days and progress are numbered.

Paul is confident that the false leaders' influence is limited, second, "because their folly will be clear to everyone." "Folly" (*anoia*) can also be translated "stupidity" (2 Clem. 13:1) or "madness" (Irenaeus, *Against Heresies*, 1.0[Preface].2). Irenaeus uses it specifically of doctrinal innovators who have fallen into "an abyss of madness [*anoias*] and of blasphemy against Christ." The word occurs thirteen times in the LXX. Three examples (translation of *anoia* in italics):

> The wisdom of the smart will become familiar with their ways, but the *folly* of fools misleads. (Prov 14:8)
>
> *Folly* clings to the heart of a young boy, but the rod and discipline are far away from him. (Prov 22:15)
>
> Put away anger from your heart, and divert pain from your body, for youth and *lack of understanding* are vanity. (Eccl 11:10)

This folly, Paul continues "will be clear[249] to everyone." Perhaps Paul is confident in the grounding of most believers,[250] in God's ability to preserve them from such error (cf. 1 Tim 1:12), in Timothy's prowess as a pastoral leader, or in some combination of these factors. Or perhaps he feels that the false leaders' gifts and skills for widespread hijacking of the churches in question are inadequate. In any case, Paul has paid them the respect of mention and warned Timothy explicitly of the danger they pose. Still, he should not overreact against or obsess over them. Their credentials pale when set next to those of a true apostle such as Paul, when weighed against the inevitable failure of all who rise up against God and the gospel, and when compared with Timothy's resources for success in faithful ministry. All these things Paul will mention in the next section.

248. Collins, 253, calls attention to the Stoic view expressed by Epictetus (*Discourses* 2.17.4), who uses the same verb (progress, advance) "to express moral and intellectual growth." But Paul relates the failure of these figures to their opposition to the truth (v. 8), not to their lack of human development.

249. Greek *ekdēlos*, only here in the NT. It is, however, widely attested in Greek literature prior to and concurrent with the NT; see BDAG 300.

250. Notice John's optimistic counsel in 1 John 2:27, despite "those who are trying to lead you astray" (v. 26).

III. CONCLUDING REMINDERS, INSTRUCTIONS, AND GREETINGS (3:10–4:22)

A. A Final Charge to Timothy (3:10–4:8)

In the wake of a lengthy section placing accent on false teachers (2:14–3:9), Paul now shifts the focus to what Timothy knows and has received. He is more than adequately provisioned for the situations facing him (3:10–17), so that as a "servant of God" he is "thoroughly equipped for every good work" (3:17). In light of this provision, Paul can and does adjure Timothy (4:1–8) to "discharge all the duties of [his] ministry" (4:5). Paul's impending demise, track record, and tenacious hope (4:6–8) provide a template for Timothy to meet his own challenges head-on with courage.

Following poignant personal appeal to Timothy, Paul shares a series of loosely connected requests, descriptions of his current conditions, warnings, and assurances (4:9–18). These are followed by greetings, some from Paul (4:19) and some from those with him (4:21). Paul concludes with his usual allusions to the Lord and to his grace (4:22).

1. Resources (3:10–17)

The previous section stressed "terrible times" and equally intimidating people that Timothy faces. Now Paul moves to remind Timothy of the resources he possesses for the pastoral tasks entrusted to him. Goliath taunted David with the words, "Am I a dog, that you come at me with sticks?" (1 Sam 17:43). As Timothy contemplated the prospects for the tiny church's flourishing in the vast and resistant Roman world, and his chances for ministerial success, he must have felt a little like David with a slingshot. But he must not underestimate the conditioning he has received and the tools he possesses. Recounting trials of the Russian church under the Mongols (1237–1348), Timothy Ware says of St. Stephen, bishop of Perm (?1340–96), who worked as a missionary among the Zyrian tribes: "He spent thirteen years of preparation in a monastery, studying not only the native dialects but also Greek, to be the better fitted for the work of translation."[251]

Timothy has spent years of preparation, not in a monastery, but in public life as a servant of the gospel while under Paul's direct or indirect influence. He does not need to learn a new language, at least in the short term. Moreover, he is grounded in the same Scriptures from which Jesus taught and to which Paul constantly appeals. Both of these factors and more should buoy Timothy with

251. Timothy Ware, *The Orthodox Church* (London: Penguin Books, 1997), 83.

hope, even though "evildoers and imposters will go from bad to worse" (v. 13). Whatever his feelings of inadequacy, Timothy has the equipping he needs.

> 10 *You, however, know all about my teaching, my way of life, my purpose,*
> *faith, patience, love, endurance,* 11 *persecutions, sufferings—what kinds of*
> *things happened to me in Antioch, Iconium and Lystra, the persecutions I*
> *endured. Yet the Lord rescued me from all of them.* 12 *In fact, everyone who*
> *wants to live a godly life in Christ Jesus will be persecuted,* 13 *while evildoers*
> *and impostors will go from bad to worse, deceiving and being deceived.*
> 14 *But as for you, continue in what you have learned and have become*
> *convinced of, because you know those from whom you learned it,* 15 *and*
> *how from infancy you have known the Holy Scriptures, which are able to*
> *make you wise for salvation through faith in Christ Jesus.* 16 *All Scripture is*
> *God-breathed and is useful for teaching, rebuking, correcting and training*
> *in righteousness,* 17 *so that the servant of God may be thoroughly equipped*
> *for every good work.*

10 "You, however" is an emphatic expression.[252] It occurs when Paul seeks to rivet Timothy's attention (see v. 14; 2:1; 4:5; see also 1 Tim 6:11; Titus 2:1). Timothy should not be intimidated by the opponents and problems mentioned in previous verses. He should rather ponder and pursue Paul's teaching and example.

"Know all about" implies deep familiarity with. Paul regards Timothy as a close and loyal follower. He uses the same verb (*parakoloutheō*) in 1 Tim 4:6 to describe Timothy as an astute pupil of apostolic teaching. Luke uses the word to describe how he "carefully investigated everything" as he prepared to write his Gospel (Luke 1:3). Paul does not offer cheap assurance but draws on Timothy's grounding over a decade or more and in fact over his whole life from childhood (note 2 Tim 3:15). This stock of ingrained lore can now stabilize him against the push of opponents and problems.

Paul lists nine things, seven of them in v. 10, that Timothy has followed closely and that can now make a difference in his and the gospel's favor. The list begins with "my," and that possessive pronoun marks all nine points in the list as describing convictions or experience of Paul. This is confirmed as Paul sums them up in v. 11 with "what kinds of things happened to me." The nine items (no doubt more could have been mentioned) that should stabilize and guide Timothy into his personal and pastoral future are as follows.

1. Paul's "teaching" (*didaskalia*). See commentary on Titus 1:9; 2:1, 7, 10. Paul uses the same word elsewhere frequently in writing to Timo-

252. Greek *sy de*. It is used by Jesus (Matt 6:6, 17; Luke 9:60), by James (Jas 4:12), and elsewhere by Paul (Rom 11:20; 14:10).

thy.[253] For today's reader, the PE, along with Paul's other ten NT epistles, convey the breadth and depth of this body of conviction, richly informed by divine revelation (see, e.g., Rom 16:25–26; Gal 1:11–12; Eph 3:3–6). For Timothy, our two known Pauline letters to him certainly epitomize that teaching. So do other Pauline letters, particularly those in which Timothy is named alongside Paul as author (2 Corinthians, Philippians, Colossians, 1 and 2 Thessalonians, Philemon). Even if he did not actually cowrite these missives in the fullest sense, he surely was aware of and endorsed the teaching they contained.

2. His "way of life." Paul's teaching, like Jesus's, was not only for thought but for life. A term used by outsiders for the early Christian movement was "the way" (*hē hodos*),[254] referring to an actual path, road, or route but then also serving as a metaphor for conduct or way of life (BDAG 691). Here, however, Paul uses a word found nowhere else in the NT.[255] Clement of Rome uses it twice to describe Christian conduct (1 Clem. 47:6; 48:1). Paul's teaching was borne out of and validated by the Christ-centered and missional life he lived.

3. His "purpose" (*prothesis*). Paul refers to his resolve, the iron will he exhibited from the time of his conversion to live out the implications of Jesus's messiahship. Jesus taught, "No one who puts a hand to the plow and looks back is fit for service in the kingdom of God" (Luke 9:62), and Paul spoke of plowing as a metaphor for the Christian life (1 Cor 9:10). While he was surely not a sinless follower of Jesus (1 Tim 1:15–16), Paul seems to have wavered little. The consistent and courageous "purpose" he exhibited is a model for Timothy to emulate.

4. His "faith." This factor refers to the personal commitment to Christ that Paul and Timothy shared (see 1 Tim 1:2: "To Timothy, my true son in the faith"). Such faith has an objective component (*fides quae creditur*, the faith that is believed) and a subjective one (*fides qua creditur*, the exercise of faith). Here the accent may be placed on Paul's personal trust in God, but for Paul that never rules out the truths that constitute the core of biblical revelation and Christian confession. First Timothy 3:16 presents a sampler of those truths.

5. His "patience" (*makrothymia*). This is an attribute of God (Rom 2:4; 9:22) and of Christ (1 Tim 1:16), but also a trait of Paul (and Timothy) as Paul represents them to the Corinthians (2 Cor 6:6). It is a fruit of the Spirit (Gal 5:11) and a trait of God's people (Eph 4:2; Col 1:11; 3:12). Paul will later stress Timothy's need for it (2 Tim 4:2). There are times when any Christian is tempted to give up or take shortcuts. Paul had shown to Timothy a stead-

253. See 1 Tim 1:10; 4:1, 6, 13, 16; 5:17; 6:1, 3; 2 Tim 3:16; 4:3.

254. See, for example, Acts 9:2; 19:9, 23; 24:14, 22.

255. *Agōgē*. It is found six times in the LXX: Esth 2:20; 10:3; 2 Macc 4:16; 6:8; 11:24; 3 Macc 4:10.

fastness that bespoke belief that time is on God's side; his followers, as they toil mightily for him, can gamely await and expect his deliverance. That is Pauline patience.

6. His "love." The word (*agapē*) appears seventy-one times in Paul's letters and is absent from none of them. The God Paul serves is "the God of love" (2 Cor 13:11). Paul lived a life driven by that love: "Christ's love compels us" (2 Cor 5:14). He called for love from believers ("Do everything in love" [1 Cor 16:14]) and offered it to them ("My love to all of you in Christ Jesus" [1 Cor 16:24]). When thinking of Paul and what Timothy had learned from him about life in Christ and in service for Christ, Timothy would surely rank this depth and quality of love as one of his foremost impressions.

7. His "endurance" (*hypomonē*). This word is found two other times in the PE (1 Tim 6:11; Titus 2:2) and thirteen times in Paul's other writings.[256] Paul will shortly mention sufferings. Elsewhere he writes that such sufferings produce *hypomonē*, which can be translated "endurance" or "perseverance" (as in Rom 5:3). He is also about to confirm to Timothy that all believers can expect suffering in connection with the Christian life (see 2 Tim 3:12). Paul's model of "endurance" is important because it shows Timothy that Paul is not calling him to anything he has not already experienced extensively himself.

11 This verse begins with the last two of the nine facets of Paul's teaching and life to which Paul calls Timothy's attention as part of his final charge to him. Stabilizing and guiding Timothy into his personal and pastoral future are the following two additional factors.

8. Paul's "persecutions" (a form of *diōgmos*). Paul uses this word (italicized below) alongside others (i.e., trouble, hardship, *persecution*, famine, nakedness, danger, and sword) to describe what shall *not* separate believers from Christ's love (Rom 8:35). The same word appears in a list of what might seem to weaken Paul, but actually made him strong: weaknesses, insults, hardships, *persecutions*, difficulties (2 Cor 12:10). The Thessalonians endured "*persecutions* and trials" (2 Thess 1:4). Outside of Paul's writings, the word occurs five other times in the NT: Jesus promises "persecutions" (Matt 13:21; Mark 4:17; 10:30), and Acts recounts two examples (8:1; 13:50). Hostile reception and violent reaction were part of the mix as the gospel message first went forth. Paul and those who received his message were often at the epicenter of experiencing those unhappy but blessed consequences of faithfulness to God.

9. His "sufferings." Twice in its sixteen NT occurrences, this word (a form of *pathēma*) is translated "passions" (Rom 7:5; Gal 5:24). More commonly it refers to Christ's suffering (2 Cor 1:5; Phil 3:10; Col 1:24; Heb 2:9, 10; 1 Pet 1:11; 4:13; 5:1) or to believers suffering in connection with their commitment to Christ (so here, in 3:11; also Rom 8:18; 2 Cor 1:6, 7; Heb 10:32; 1 Pet 5:9).

256. Rom 2:7; 5:3, 4; 8:25; 15:4, 5; 2 Cor 1:6; 6:4; 12:12; Col 1:11; 1 Thess 1:3; 2 Thess 1:4; 3:5.

This pattern of usage confirms that Jesus's habit of faithfulness to the Father, with the implication that his followers ought to live as he did (see 1 John 2:6), often had baleful results. Yet, it created a fellowship (Phil 3:10) that was as unavoidable (see 2 Tim 3:12) as it was alarming. In reminding Timothy of his sufferings, Paul is commending to Timothy one of the hardest and yet noblest aspects of Christian belief: Jesus's followers do not add to what Jesus did for them on the cross, but they are called to live out the implications of the cross in their daily lives.

In the remainder of the verse, with mention of "Antioch, Iconium and Lystra," Paul most likely draws on a recollection of events described in Acts 13:13–14:23. These verses summarize Paul's so-called first missionary journey, during which he and Barnabas brought the gospel message to the region of Timothy's upbringing, resulting in his eventual enlistment as Paul's coworker (Acts 16:1–5). Paul was stoned and left for dead (Acts 14:19–20) and experienced much opposition during this time. Collins views this scenario as legendary and then heightened in this retelling by "the apocalyptic scheme" of the author (for Collins: not Paul) of 2 Timothy.[257] Another possibility is that Paul recalls what Luke (in Acts) faithfully narrates and what Timothy would have heard about, and possibly even witnessed, since he was resident in that locale hardly more than a decade previous, assuming Paul's authorship of 2 Timothy.

Such harsh events and memories might tempt a writer to self-glorifying or self-pitying reminiscence. Instead, Paul extols Christ for what he "endured."[258] "The Lord rescued me from all" the ill treatment he experienced in those momentous months. These words do not mean deliverance from all harm and pain. It means rather that the Lord kept him from death and empowered him for continued ministry. He lived (barely) to serve (and suffer, yet prevail) another day. As God upheld Paul, he can likewise strengthen Timothy in his demanding situation.

12 The words "everyone . . . will be persecuted" echo Jesus's promise that following him means taking up one's cross (Matt 10:38; 16:24). They also repeat Paul's conclusion from over a decade earlier: "We must go through many hardships to enter the kingdom of God" (Acts 14:22), words perhaps uttered in Timothy's hearing. Christian conviction lived out publicly in Paul's time attracted opposition resulting in persecution. Physical suffering by Christians may lessen in given locales as increasing percentages of a population affirm gospel belief and practice. Through much of history, Jesus's promises of persecution (John 15:18–21; 16:33; cf. 2 Tim 2:3) have found fulfillment in various quarters.

257. Collins, 257–59.

258. This word (from *hypopherō*) is used elsewhere in the NT only at 1 Cor 10:13 and 1 Pet 2:19.

These words are verified daily in many locations of the church of the twenty-first century, as Brian Grim and Roger Finke have shown.[259] For the claim that accounts of Christian persecution through history are largely fabrications, see discussion of 2 Tim 2:3 above. In (relatively safe and stable) Western settings, it is often asked: why do we not see such persecution? The personal question is raised: where is persecution in my own life? And how can Christians not currently suffering persecution assist those who are?

This is not the place for a full response, but four points may be mentioned. First, K. Greene-McCreight has written tellingly on contemporary martyrdom. She draws effectively on the church father Jerome: "Not all Christian martyrs lose their lives in their witness. In the fifth century, St. Jerome made a distinction between different types of martyrs. Red martyrs (or wet martyrs) are those who lose their lives for the sake of the name of Jesus. They are 'red' because their own blood was spilled in their refusal to deny Christ. White martyrs (or dry martyrs) are those who embrace the cruciform life in the humdrum of their own daily walk. For most of us, our lives do not require the shedding of our own blood."[260] "Everyone . . . will be persecuted" is not a mystery in too many Christian enclaves worldwide today. Those believers are under duress, and none is exempt.

Readers in safe zones who puzzle over how Paul's statement can be valid for them may find help in the red martyr/white martyr distinction above, helpfully fleshed out in Greene-McCreight's essay. Her many-sided findings cannot all be recounted here, but a core of her conclusion sheds light on an approach to 2 Tim 3:12 that does not merely dismiss it as either pseudepigraphic melodrama or counsel not relevant to socially comfortable readers:

> Suffering is simply part of our fallen condition. It is already part of our lives. Afflictions surround us: loss of loved ones, failing health, dashed hopes and dreams. When we place this suffering at the foot of the cross, we may be able to point beyond ourselves to the God who redeems our griefs and draws us into the light of his presence. We might in this way serve as white martyrs, signposts and witnesses to Christ. This kind of living into our afflictions can forge in us gifts of patience, hope, compassion, and peace that can witness to Christ in powerful ways. Thus we can give voice to Christ, who went to the cross in silence.[261]

Another way of viewing Greene-McCreight's point is to recall the experience of Dietrich Bonhoeffer. He ended his life, many would say, as a red

259. Grim and Finke, *The Price of Freedom Denied.*

260. K. Greene-McCreight, "United in Suffering: Martyrdom as Christian Vocation," *ChrCent*, September 30, 2015, 32.

261. Greene-McCreight, "United in Suffering," 34.

martyr—but not until April 9, 1945. One could argue that preceding his (and most?) red martyrdoms was a lengthy testing and preparation period of white martyrdom. Small risky acts of obedience grew into a larger core of proven character and grounding in the gospel's eternal hope (cf. Rom 5:3–5). Someone faithless in small things is unlikely to find the courage and commitment to exercise faithfulness in something large that results in arrest, torture, or execution (cf. Luke 16:10). Second Timothy 3:12 is certainly not a projection that every true Christian will suffer red martyrdom, but rather recognition that faithful servants of Christ will undergo testing and trials in the course of their daily duties that will often be costly to what they hold dear, and that will prepare them for increasing degrees of sacrifice, pain, and even personal injury and death if God's path for them must lead, as it did for Bonhoeffer, in that direction.

Second, the importance of prayer should not be underestimated, the self-abnegation of intercessory travail for the sake of another. Those who are not currently persecuted can through prayer help uphold those who are not being spared. Persecuted Christians often testify that they felt prayer and survived their rigors because of it. Furthermore, prayer may result, in the course of time, in redemptive participation in persecution. Plenty of Christians have through prayer decided to enter hazardous situations where other believers are suffering. They then know firsthand the truth of 2 Tim 3:12. Prayer is a means God used to get them there. Had they not prayed, humanly speaking, they would never have gotten beyond musing, "Why is there no persecution in my life when this verse seems to promise it?"

Third, Paul writes of wanting "to live a godly life in Christ Jesus." The words can be mouthed emptily to describe status quo churchianity with little real commitment and no risk of persecution. But taken in Paul's setting and with Paul's meaning, the will to live "godly . . . in Christ Jesus" bespeaks a nothing-held-back commitment to be as true to Christ as the cost may require in the course of expanding and deepening commitment to him. It is unlikely that there is any setting in the world today where such discipleship commitment will not result in social disapproval, perhaps family friction, and quite possibly painful complications involving matters like relationships, career opportunities, professional prospects, financial fortunes, and (increasingly) criminal prosecution.

Fourth, pastoral leaders do well to ask whether they approximate the cruciform pedagogy modeled by Paul. There is obviously a personal cost to seek to do so. Christian leaders will never be able to help God's people stand strong for Christ in difficult places if they are not living out Gal 2:20 (leading to 2 Tim 3:12) in their own lives. Do people we disciple or otherwise instruct learn to live bravely and faithfully enough that they might attract persecution in the places God leads them and then be able to stand when it comes? Part of Paul's orientation for new church members seems to have been preparation for the worst: "In fact, when we were with you, we kept telling you that we would be persecuted. And it turned out that way, as you well know" (1 Thess 3:4).

In sum, it should not be taken to be a curse when God spares his people from the "persecutions" so near Paul and Timothy in their setting. There should not be survivors' guilt but rather gratitude. The high likelihood, however, does need to be affirmed that every life dedicated to Christ in any social setting will in the course of time attract unwelcome resistance and result in unwanted pain. It may not be the stake or beheading, but it is possible that beginning of a path of faithfulness will lead to a martyr's glory. Even if it does not, Paul's persecution promise does have application for all who take their desire to "live godly" with a seriousness that hands them over fully to the good but distressingly demanding hand of the God who inevitably presses his people beyond what they might wish in his work of redemption throughout the world.

13 On the one hand, there is noble and sometimes heartbreaking suffering for one's Christian confession (v. 12). On the other, "evildoers and impostors" will flourish with seeming impunity. In the Scriptures to which Paul will shortly refer Timothy (see v. 15 below), this lamentable situation is already foreshadowed: see Job 12:6; Pss 37:1, 7; 92:7; Hab 1:13; Mal 3:15; see also Job 21:7–15; Ps 73:3–12. Second Timothy 3:13 does not describe a new development but a facet of the human dilemma in all places and times. "Evildoers" could be translated "evil men" (with women perhaps implied, too). "Imposters" is the translation of a word (*goēs*) often referring to a cheat or swindler (see BDAG 204); it appears only here in the NT.[262] Paul may have in mind the Jannes-and-Jambres types (v. 8), who circulate cultivating the appearance of religious servants but whose effect is to trip up the weak and unwary.

"Go from bad to worse"[263] uses the same verb (*prokoptō*) found in 2:16 and 3:9 (see discussions above). Here Paul adds to the verb a prepositional phrase to heighten the sense of progression.[264] Friends of the gospel will get hammered (v. 12), while foes and charlatans will be piling up gains in the course of "deceiving and being deceived."[265]

262. In the AF it is used once and translated "magicians" (Diogn. 8:4). For the notion of "wizard" attaching to the word, see MM 130.

263. This statement should not be read as an unerring prediction that every generation is worse than the preceding one. The point is rather that evil people (say, Hitler in the 1920s, or an internet stalker who later goes on to kidnap and kill) may well become more diabolical over the course of time.

264. The same prepositional phrase "for the worse" (*epi to cheiron*) is found five times in Josephus, two of those times in conjunction with the same verb (*prokoptō*) used by Paul: *Jewish Antiquities* 20:214; *Jewish War* 6.1.

265. For parallels in both Hellenistic and Jewish writers (e.g., Philo), see Dibelius and Conzelmann, 119.

On "being deceived," see discussion of "deceived" at Titus 3:3, where the stress is on deception as the universal human condition unless gospel liberation arrives. The Titus reference underscores that Paul is not predicating of these people anything that was not also true of him and Timothy before they switched their lives' loyalty to Christ. The doleful picture of people digging themselves deeper and deeper into arrears with God in the last times (see 3:1) calls to mind Jesus's description of busy but oblivious people ignoring prophetic summons (in the days of Noah) and sinning away their day of grace (see Matt 24:37–38; Luke 17:26–27; cf. 1 Pet 3:20: "those who were disobedient long ago when God waited patiently in the days of Noah").

The point of 2 Tim 3:13 is that, even in the face of persecution (v. 12) and the flourishing of the unscrupulous, Timothy can take heart. The next verses prescribe a strategy for Timothy (v. 14) along with the basis of that strategy (vv. 15–17).

14 "But as for you" repeats the construction Paul used in v. 10 above. Paul employs the same expression at key junctures in Romans (11:17, 20; 14:10). He addresses Timothy personally and particularly. His pointed counsel: "continue." The imperative form of *menō* (remain, abide, continue) occurs some seventeen times in the NT but only one other time in the second person singular (Luke 24:29).

To "continue" implies that Timothy has already been engaged in a certain pattern. That pattern involves what he had "learned" and "become convinced of." The verb for "learn" here is cognate with the noun for "disciple." Paul uses the same verb to warn the Romans regarding "those who cause divisions and put obstacles in your way that are contrary to the teaching you have *learned*" (16:17). He reminds the Ephesians of "the way of life you *learned*" (4:20). He urges the Philippians, "Whatever you have *learned* or received or heard from me, or seen in me—put it into practice" (4:9). Jesus is undoubtedly the master teacher of NT times, but the early Christian community flourished as the learning activity he set in motion continued in the wake of initial gospel reception. Here Paul recalls Timothy to his customary didactic focus. Servants of Christ never outgrow their need for studied faithfulness to the basic components of their confession.

Timothy has not only learned but "become convinced." He has been brought to a level of full faith. Paul may be thinking of God's work through the Scriptures (see next verse) in Timothy's mind and heart. The goal of gospel instruction is not merely information but real-life assurance: Luke's Gospel is written so the reader "may know the certainty of the things you have been taught" (Luke 1:4). The verb translated "convinced" (*pistoō*) is a NT hapax,[266]

266. It is found some eighteen times in Philo and twice in the AF. Clement writes of the apostles, "Having therefore received their orders and being fully assured by the resurrection

but the concept is by no means rare or obscure. At a time when Paul knows he is passing from the scene, Timothy is to "continue" in the things Paul has entrusted to him (see 2 Tim 2:2), his learning leading to an understanding that elicits from him firm commitment.

Timothy's understanding and conviction stem in part from knowledge of the people[267] who were instrumental in explaining and confirming him in the faith: "because you know those from whom you learned it."[268] In the next verse Paul will refer to Timothy's infancy, so he may have in mind his mother and grandmother (see 1:5) and their part in Timothy's religious instruction. Surely Paul is also thinking of his own role as Timothy's mentor over the years. But these and any other human instruments are at best accessories to the state at which Timothy has arrived; he is not some mindless imitator of other people's beliefs. As the next verse shows, he has availed himself of the persuasive force of words that transcend mere human origin and wisdom (cf. 1 Thess 2:13; Rom 3:2). These are words that have brought together and sustained a people over millennia. This is the source of Paul's confidence that his exhortation for Timothy to "continue" is not in vain.

15 This verse contains the second part of why Timothy should "continue in what [he has] learned and have become convinced of" (v. 14). The first reason is "those from whom" he gained his instruction. The quality of their lives and the truths they confessed commend a similar course to Timothy. Now Paul comes to a second reason: his grounding in "the[269] Holy Scriptures." "From infancy" refers to his upbringing under a Jewish mother and grandmother (see 1:5; Acts 16:1). Instruction in the Torah was mandated by the rabbis for Jewish boys at age five (*m. 'Abot* 5:21). More fundamentally, the LXX states, "The testimony of the Lord is reliable, making infants wise" (Ps 18:8 [MT 7]), using the same distinct word for "making wise" that Paul does (see below). God's testimony is for Paul preeminently his written word. That word has benefit even for "infants," which may refer to the redemptive family setting that respect for God's word may establish for children's upbringing, leading them eventually to personal saving faith. Or it may refer metaphorically to all human as "infants" in comparison to God's infinite knowledge. In either case,

---

of our Lord Jesus Christ and full of faith [*pistōthentes*] in the word of God, they went forth with the firm assurance that the Holy Spirit gives, preaching the good news that the kingdom of God was about to come" (1 Clem. 42:3).

267. "From whom" in v. 14 is plural.

268. "It" is plural in the original, as is "what you have learned" earlier in the verse. The translation could run "the things you have learned" and "from whom you learned them." Paul has in mind a range of insights, not some solitary lump truth.

269. The Greek codex א omits "the" and is followed by a few other MSS. Whether the article is included or not, Paul's reference can only be to what we know as the OT, along with any other writings known to us as part of the NT.

Timothy has been a beneficiary of the scriptural grounding that conditioned his life from earliest memory.

"Holy Scriptures" (our OT writings) were the foundation of Jewish identity and hence (by the Second Temple period) synagogue activity. The Torah gave direction, the Prophets heritage and conviction, and the Psalms (and other "Writings" such as Proverbs) resources for guidance, prayer, and corporate song. Timothy would have been the beneficiary of OT commands to teach children the Scriptures of the Jewish faith (Deut 6:7; Pss 71:17; 78:5–6). Paul had firsthand knowledge of these matters from his own upbringing in Jerusalem (Acts 22:3) and Jewish heritage (2 Cor 11:22; Phil 3:5). Since Paul appears to cite Luke 10:7 as Scripture in 1 Tim 5:18 (see discussion there), "the Holy Scriptures" may include some of the NT writings, too. God's word in written form has typically played a foundational role in awakening his people to faith and then sustaining them in that faith's exercise, as Paul here exhorts Timothy. Despite pessimism in some quarters regarding Scripture's "holy" status,[270] many concur that what Paul says is no less true today, whoever the reader or hearer and whatever the locale.

The Scriptures Timothy has come to know have the ongoing capacity[271] to impart redemptive wisdom—"to make [him] wise for salvation." (On "salvation," see commentary Introduction, IX.A.) "To make wise" translates a form of *sophizō*, a word used in the NT elsewhere only in 2 Pet 1:16.[272] In 2 Cor 3:13–16 Paul describes the bane of minds darkened, despite the gospel's light. Speaking of his (and Timothy's) fellow Jews, he refers to a "veil" that "remains when the old covenant is read" (2 Cor 3:14). This barrier to understanding "has not been removed, because only in Christ is it taken away." Yet, Paul adds, "But whenever anyone turns to the Lord, the veil is taken away" (2 Cor 3:16). Timothy obviously has had this experience (as did Paul, dramatized in Acts 9:18 when the scales fell from his eyes), which is likely at the core of the making "wise for salvation" Paul describes.

For Paul is not thinking of some merely rational or even sapiential breakthrough in knowledge per se on Timothy's part. He refers rather to understanding that arises "through faith in Christ Jesus" (= "turns to the Lord" in 2 Cor 3:16). Paul uses the expression "faith in Christ Jesus" in some passages

270. See, for example, Harvey, *Is Scripture Still Holy?* He answers his question largely in the negative.

271. A possible inference from the present participle form (*dynamena*) translated "are able."

272. Ignatius writes to the Smyrnaeans (1:1), "I glorify Jesus Christ, the God who made you so wise [*sophisanta*], for I observed that you are established in an unshakable faith, having been nailed, as it were, to the cross of the Lord Jesus Christ." The word occurs twenty times in the LXX (ten times in Sirach). It is rare in Josephus (three times) and hardly more common in Philo (five times), who always uses it in the negative sense of sophistry.

(Gal 2:16; Col 1:4; 1 Tim 3:13) and "faith in Jesus Christ" in others (Rom 3:22; Gal 2:16; 3:22). The word order constitutes no discernible difference for interpretation.[273] Taken as a whole, the entirety of 2 Timothy calls on its recipient to exhibit a high level of comprehension and response. This is possible, Paul affirms, by the scriptural truth that has long steered Timothy, as well as the relationship of trust in Christ that transforms Scripture from dead letter (see again 2 Cor 3 and discussion in previous paragraph) to elevating, liberating, and energizing force.

16 Verses 16–17 are abrupt in that they appear without any conjunction or connecting particle. They are dropped like an anvil into the flow of discourse, which gives them special emphasis. Paul essentially provides a footnote to his mention of "the Holy Scriptures" in v. 15. He does not want Timothy to overlook (1) Scripture's' divine origin, (2) its utility,[274] or (3) its necessity for the challenges Timothy faces and the life in God that he seeks to live. Each of these elements will be taken up below.

A preliminary question needs to be addressed. Should it be "all Scripture" (most translations) or "every Scripture" (some commentators, along with AMP, ASV, GW, NET, WEB)? There is no real difference if the whole of Scripture is in mind; "all" would simply emphasize the whole, and "every" would stress each part. A difference is implied, however, by NEB's "Every inspired Scripture,"[275] which raises the question whether in Paul's thinking some Scripture might *not* be "inspired." Saarinen, for example, thinks this is the case: all Scripture "should probably not be read to mean 'everything in the sacred writings' so that the inspiration of every word or sentence should be assumed."[276]

Wallace argues that the NEB rendering is "highly suspect." He gives two contextual reasons and five grammatical ones. The fifth grammatical reason alone seems sufficient to call NEB in question. Wallace points out that "all Scripture is God-breathed" is in Greek an adjective-noun-adjective construction. Based on some fifty similar expressions in the NT or LXX, the evidence overwhelmingly supports Wallace's deduction that "in πᾶς ['all' or 'every'] + noun + adjective constructions in equative clauses the πᾶς, being by nature as definite as the article, implies the article, thus making the adjective(s) following the noun outside the implied article-noun group, and, therefore,

273. The two PE occurrences (1 Tim 3:13; 2 Tim 3:15) use a construction with the name in the second attributive position, which may underscore Christ as the object of faith. But such a focus is hardly minimized in the other passages.

274. Dibelius and Conzelmann, 120, play the divine origin off against Scripture's utility and conclude that "the emphasis of the passage doubtless lies . . . on the usefulness." This minimizing of Scripture's divine origin lacks basis in the text. It is better to take with equal force all that Paul says here of the Scriptures.

275. As in Barrett, *Pastoral Epistles*, 114.

276. Saarinen, 156.

predicate."[277] Paul's wording should not be taken "to contain a hint that certain passages of Scripture are not inspired."[278] Towner, who translates "every [text] of Scripture," observes: "The scope is extensive, leaving no text of 'scripture' unaccounted for."[279] Saarinen's proposal that inspiration does not refer "to the most comprehensive unit (the canon) nor to the smallest unit (word or sentence), but to the middle-sized unit (*graphē* as text or individual book)"[280] is untenable grammatically. Zehr adds a contextual consideration: "Given the context in which the deviant teachers interpreted some parts of Scripture as myths (1 Tim 1:4) and the similar grammatical construction in 1 Timothy 4:4, Paul likely intends to emphasize that Scripture in its entirety is inspired of God."[281]

Looking now in more detail at Scripture in Paul's view, we consider first its divine origin. "God-breathed" (*theopneustos*) "denotes not the manner of the inspiration of Scripture but rather its source."[282] This makes "God-breathed" more accurate than "inspired" as a translation. The expression is unusual in English, but the word was equally rare in Greek literature generally. It is not found elsewhere in Scripture, though the notion of Scripture's divine origin is powerfully expressed by the statement that the Scripture did not have "its origin in the human will, but prophets, though human, spoke from God as they were carried along by the Holy Spirit" (2 Pet 1:21). "The Holy Spirit spoke" in the writings of OT leaders and writers like David (Acts 1:16; see also Acts 4:25). By extension this understanding applies to NT writings as well (see 2 Pet 3:15–16). God has chosen to reveal himself not only in nature (Ps 8:1, 3; Rom 1:20) and human moral awareness (Rom 2:15) but also supremely by spoken and written human language. This verse, then, helps underwrite the doctrine of verbal inspiration. This doctrine does not downplay human action in Scripture's authorship but affirms Scripture's ultimate origin in God, who gave it. "Because Scripture comes from God, it is therefore true, and because it is true, it is therefore profitable."[283] Witherington states, "Certainly Paul believes that these words have authority because they are God's words, spoken of course in human words and through human beings, but reflecting God's character, and so are truthful and trustworthy."[284] Because the Scriptures are "more than

277. Wallace, *Greek Grammar*, 313–14: *pasa* ("all," adj.) *graphē* ("Scripture," noun) *theopneustos* ("God-breathed," adj.). The verb "is" in English is supplied from the context.

278. Kelly, 203. Kelly affirms the same view as Wallace.

279. Towner, *Letters*, 587.

280. Saarinen, 156.

281. Zehr, 207.

282. Mounce, 566.

283. Mounce, 566.

284. Witherington, 360n254.

human literature . . . , this also has implications for interpretation."[285] The Bible is not just a collection of writings like any other.

The second aspect of the value of Scripture is its utility; Paul describes it as "useful [*ōphelismos*, beneficial, profitable]." This adjective appears in the NT only three times (see also 1 Tim 4:8; Titus 3:8), though the verb cognate *ōpheleō* is more common, occurring fifteen times, including four times in Paul.[286] Paul employs understatement here. If the Scriptures truly are "holy," with the rootedness in Almighty God that "holy" implies (2 Tim 3:15), to say no more than that they are "useful" is about like saying God himself is useful.[287] What Paul means is they have value, and as *holy* Scripture that value is unparalleled and indeed essential to the Christian pastoral task.

Paul touches on Scripture's unique benefit in four dimensions.[288] This is not an exhaustive list but typical pastoral applications of God's word of which he sees fit to remind Timothy. It is useful, first, for *didaskalia* (teaching; see commentary Introduction, IX.D). Paul uses this word elsewhere (Rom 12:7; 15:4; Eph 4:14; Col 2:22) but emphasizes it in the PE (see discussion at 2 Tim 3:10 above). Pastors are undershepherds (1 Pet 5:2) of the Great Shepherd (1 Pet 5:4), who, when he saw people in their disarray, had compassion and taught them (Mark 6:34; see also Matt 9:36). Pastoral teaching involves many strategies and sources; it assumes a personal relationship with Christ on the part of the pastor and a call from Christ to serve as pastor in the body of Christ. But the cognitive and pedagogical foundation for what pastors feed their minds and souls with and commend to their people and the world is the Scriptures.

Scripture is useful, second, for "rebuking." (See discussion of the verb form of this word in Titus 1:13.) The word (*elegmos*) occurs only in here in the NT but twenty times in the LXX, where to fail to reprove is a sign of contempt (Lev 19:17). In Western self-esteem cultures, pastoral rebuke may be a paradoxical and unwelcome notion. Is the role of the minister not rather to accept, affirm, and encourage? In a biblical outlook like Paul's that stresses divine holiness and human imperfection, the need not only for acceptance but also for love that cares enough to confront when necessary is obvious

285. Laansma, 198.

286. Rom 2:25; 1 Cor 13:3; 14:6; Gal 5:2.

287. Cf. Neudorfer, *Zweiter Brief an Timotheus*, 229, who stresses not just that Scripture functions a certain way but that what it conveys is reliable.

288. NIV translates "for" just one time: "for teaching. . . ." NIV also tidies up the expression by inserting the conjunction "and." Paul states the word translated "for" (*pros*) four times, lending discrete emphasis to each application or dimension. His omission of "and" avoids the impression that he is giving a complete, four-point summary of the usefulness of Scripture. He rather alludes in an informal but fulsome manner to a cluster of important ways that Scripture is integral to the pastoral task.

and will be welcomed (at times) by those truly seeking God. Paul uses the related verb form of "rebuke" (*elenchō*) frequently. He writes to Christians at Ephesus, "Have nothing to do with the fruitless deeds of darkness, but rather *expose* [= rebuke] them" (Eph 5:11). Elsewhere he counsels Timothy to "rebuke" sinning elders (1 Tim 5:20) and to "rebuke and encourage" in his preaching (2 Tim 4:2). "Rebuke" is also a staple in Titus's repertoire of pastoral duties (1:9, 13; 2:15). On what basis does any pastor stand in undertaking such a daunting responsibility? It is the Scriptures that furnish guidance and divine authority for servants of that word to perform this necessary function.

Scripture is useful, third, for "correcting." This NT hapax is used twice in the LXX, denoting spiritual restoration that extends to God's physical protection (1 Esd 8:52) and civic reconstruction under Simon Maccabeus (1 Macc 14:34).[289] Pastors do not merely rebuke: they restore and point in corrective directions. "If convicting is regarded as a negative measure, the activity that follows, 'correcting,' is positive, aiming at the goal of recovery."[290]

Paul commends Scripture, fourth, for its value in "training in righteousness." "Training" translates *paideia*, a word not common in the NT[291] but found over a hundred times in the LXX, especially in the wisdom literature (e.g., Proverbs) and the Prophets (notably Jeremiah). In ancient Hellenistic settings the word was common in contexts speaking of children's upbringing and education.[292] Several LXX passages contain "training" (or "discipline") and "righteousness" in proximity.[293] Paul's point cannot be regarded as obscure: Scripture is a primary resource for inculcating the acts and habits that will reflect God's own character (his "righteousness") in relationship with his people. The biblical and Jewish background of Paul's counsel is more likely than the theory that the PE author is dependent on Hellenistic philosophy,[294] which did not view either Scripture or a single God as source or motivation for either education or ethics.

Paul could have said many more things about the use of Scripture in pastoral labor. His own uses (see *CNTUOT*) are richly illustrative, surely left their mark on Timothy as he observed Paul, and no doubt furnished a lens for Timothy to flesh out as he read this letter with Paul's terse four-point summary. Likewise, interpreters take various approaches in unpacking Paul's statement. Aquinas serves as a suggestive example: "The effects of Scripture are fourfold: regarding the speculative reason, to teach the truth and to reprove falsity

289. The word is frequent in Philo (twenty-nine times) but not in Josephus (twice). It is not found in the AF but is used once by Irenaeus (*Against Heresies* 1.9.2).

290. Towner, *Letters*, 591.

291. Found elsewhere only at Eph 6:4; Heb 12:5, 7, 8, 11.

292. MM 474; Johnson, *First and Second Letters to Timothy*, 421.

293. Prov 16:17; Wis 8:26; 18:7; Bar 4:13.

294. Cf. the claim of Davies, 57.

[= NIV 'for teaching, rebuking']; regarding the practical reason, to free one from evil and to lead him to good [= NIV 'correcting and training in righteousness']."[295] Neudorfer underscores the similarity between Paul's regard for Scripture and that of Jesus.[296]

But enough has been said to move from v. 16 to the "so what" of Paul's concluding reminder about Scripture's high value.

17 Paul asserts here the outcome of Scripture's origin and utility. He stresses its effect on Timothy: he will be able to rise to meet whatever challenge presents itself—"be thoroughly equipped." Most translations render separately the second word of the verse in Greek *artios* (BDAG 16: "complete, capable, proficient") and the last word, the participle *exērtismenos* (equipped, fitted out for something). ESV is an example: "that the man of God may be complete [*artios*], equipped [*exērtismenos*] for every good work." NIV combines the two ideas: "so that the servant of God may be thoroughly equipped for every good work." "Thoroughly" is justified not only by combining the two expressions but also by the perfective verbal aspect of the participle. Still, the NIV rendering results in a rhetorical de-emphasis, as Paul's wording stresses what the Scripture's effect is (1) on what the servant of God is and then (2) how that person is equipped. The two notions are closely related but need not be collapsed together.

"Servant of God" translates Greek "man of God" (see 1 Tim 6:11 and comments), the only other place in the NT the Greek term appears. The phrase is used over sixty times in the LXX to refer to figures including Moses, Samuel, Shemaiah, Elijah, Elisha, several unnamed prophets, and David. Like Timothy,[297] these men were called to leadership through prophetic gifting (see 2 Tim 1:6; also 1 Tim 1:18; 4:14). The expression would be meaningful to Timothy with his OT knowledge (2 Tim 3:15), though it has relevance to all who share Timothy's faith in Christ (again, v. 15) and recognize the God who gives Scripture (v. 16). By "thoroughly equipped," Paul refers to Timothy's grounding in Scripture and his grasp of its wide range of pastoral applications typified in v. 16. "The understanding of the scriptures (i.e. of the OT) . . . makes the leader of the congregation fit for the fight against the false teaching."[298]

Because "for every good work" begins with the same preposition (*pros*, for) as the four benefits of Scripture in v. 16, it is possible that Paul is using the phrase to summarize those four benefits. They are provided by Scripture, but

295. Aquinas, 137.

296. Neudorfer, *Zweiter Brief an Timotheus*, 242.

297. For arguments that "the servant of God" here does not refer, in the first instance, to any and all believers, but to Timothy and others like him in particular, see Towner, *Letters*, 592–93.

298. Dibelius and Conzelmann, 120.

God uses means for the realization of those benefits: those who minister the Scriptures, that is, pastoral leaders like Timothy who teach, rebuke, correct, and train. Barrett understands "every good work" more generically: the expression "denotes any of the useful tasks that fall to a minister's lot."[299] Perhaps Paul is speaking generically, yet still mindful of the pastoral utility of the Scriptures he has just detailed in their particular relevance to Timothy's flourishing as Paul passes from the scene.

2. *Responsibilities (4:1–8)*

Paul's final charge to Timothy continues. "The image of a solemn ceremony, recalling that of a court, whether judicial or regal, is evoked" as Paul "outlines this charge."[300] He moves from reminding Timothy of the resources at his command in 3:10–17 (Paul's teaching and example, Timothy's godly heritage and understanding, the Scriptures) to the duties devolving on Timothy at this critical juncture in the unfolding history of the fledgling church. Because God is a redeeming God, ever at work in an unruly world (see John 4:34; 5:17), his servants like Paul and Timothy do more than tally up their resources and blessings: they strategize how to use them for God's purposes and glory. Paul now reminds Timothy of mandates being passed on to him with force and urgency in relation to God and the Scriptures he has just mentioned and to the saving message he has been called to live out and promulgate.

> [1]*In the presence of God and of Christ Jesus, who will judge the living*
> *and the dead, and in view of his appearing and his kingdom, I give you this*
> *charge:* [2]*Preach the word; be prepared in season and out of season; cor-*
> *rect, rebuke and encourage—with great patience and careful instruction.*
> [3]*For the time will come when people will not put up with sound doctrine.*
> *Instead, to suit their own desires, they will gather around them a great*
> *number of teachers to say what their itching ears want to hear.* [4]*They will*
> *turn their ears away from the truth and turn aside to myths.* [5]*But you, keep*
> *your head in all situations, endure hardship, do the work of an evangelist,*
> *discharge all the duties of your ministry.* [6]*For I am already being poured*
> *out like a drink offering, and the time for my departure is near.* [7]*I have*
> *fought the good fight, I have finished the race, I have kept the faith.* [8]*Now*
> *there is in store for me the crown of righteousness, which the Lord, the*

299. Barrett, *Pastoral Epistles*, 115. Towner, *Letters*, 594, states that the phrase "draws on Hellenistic ethical categories." Many note a parallel with Epictetus, *Discourses* 3.21.15 (e.g., BDAG 359; Witherington, 361).

300. Collins, 265.

righteous Judge, will award to me on that day—and not only to me, but also to all who have longed for his appearing.

1 In Greek the verse begins, "I charge [you, i.e., Timothy]." Like 3:16–17, 4:1 is unconnected by conjunction or particle to the discourse preceding it. The abruptness lends emphasis to Paul's declaration. The word *diamartyromai* (NIV "I charge") is used only four times in Paul's letters (see also 1 Thess 4:6; 1 Tim 5:21; 2 Tim 2:14). It is more common in the LXX (twenty-five times). In Paul it always connotes stern admonition, usually in light of eschatological realities. NIV's "I give you this charge" is semantically apt, but the "you" is added. In the LXX, when the person charged is mentioned, the sense is normally a testimony against that person or group:

> I call sky and earth to witness against you [*diamartyromai hymin*] today that by destruction you will perish. (Deut 4:26 NETS)
>
> I call both sky and earth to witness against you [*diamartyromai hymin*] today. (Deut 30:19 NETS)
>
> And he sent prophets to them to turn them back to the Lord, but they did not listen. And they bore witness against them [*diemartyranto autois*], and they did not listen. (2 Chr 24:19 NETS)

Paul, however, is not testifying against Timothy, though also not directly testifying to him. He is rather signaling utmost solemnity in what he is about to urge (vv. 2 and beyond); he speaks as in God's very presence. Paul's declaration is as weighty as analogous expressions used in the LXX and coming from Moses, Ezekiel, Jeremiah, Nehemiah, and even God himself (Pss 49:7; 80:9).

The gravity of Paul's urging is clear also in his calling as witnesses both God and Christ Jesus.[301] Collins comments, "Jewish tradition demands a pair of witnesses in a judicial procedure (Deut 17:6; 19:15)."[302] On "before God," see comments on 2:14. Here he adds reference to Christ's glorious appearing[303] "to judge the living and the dead." As Paul is prepared to stand before God to give account of his life (4:8), he wants Timothy to exhibit the same readiness—not first of all so he can die well, however, but so that he will be motivated to proclaim the gospel as he ought (see v. 2).

301. Aquinas, 139, raises the question: "But since Christ is God, why does the Apostle use here the phrase *before God and Jesus Christ*?" His answer: "*Before God* means the Father, and *Jesus Christ* means the Son. For the Father is the font of the divinity" (italics in original).

302. Collins, 268.

303. On "appearing" (*epiphaneia*), see comments on Titus 2:13.

As an inducement to faithfulness, Paul mentions not only Christ's "appearing" but also "his kingdom." In the PE, "kingdom" (*basileia*) occurs only one other time (2 Tim 4:18).[304] It will be recalled that Acts represents Paul as summing up his first missionary journey with the words, "Through many tribulations we must enter the kingdom of God" (Acts 14:22). One of those who heard Paul's preaching in those days would have been Timothy (Acts 16:1). Paul's appeal in 2 Tim 4:1 shows that, late in Paul's life, "kingdom" is still one of the convictions that joins him with Timothy in their faith in Christ. The only explicit Pauline reference to Jesus as "king" occurs in Paul's other letter to Timothy (1 Tim 1:17; 6:15).[305] Clearly an underlying assumption about Jesus for Paul and Timothy is that he reigns sovereign over his people and all the world. That reign, "his kingdom," is at the core of Paul's eternal hope as he faces execution and seeks to rally and assure Timothy, as 4:18 indicates: "The Lord will rescue me from every evil attack and will bring me safely to his heavenly kingdom." Both Christ's future reign (his appearing) and his present (and eternal) reign argue for Timothy to remain hopeful and faithful in his duties, foremost among which is proclamation as the next verse indicates.

2 This verse has two prominent features. One is the imperative to "preach the word." S. Stout has based an entire Pauline theology of preaching on this verse in its immediate context.[306] The other feature is four additional imperatives that give directions that will make Timothy's preaching possible and effective. A rough correlation may be observed between this verse and 3:16–17, where the Scripture was highlighted and then four uses of it were noted. Now the Scripture is again highlighted, but in terms of what Timothy needs to do with it. He needs to preach it. And to give that preaching direction, Paul calls to readiness and to a clear sense of what and how this proclamation needs to be administered.

"Preach" (from *kēryssō*) was one of Paul's customary verbs for his own gospel proclamation.[307] "It calls attention to the prophetic side of Christian

304. For other occurrences in Paul, see Yarbrough, "The Kingdom of God in the New Testament," 143–51.

305. Christ's reign over all is implicitly asserted every time Paul refers to him as Lord (*kyrios*). That is, infrequent mention of Christ as "king" or of his "kingdom" is less significant than is sometimes argued. To acknowledge Christ's lordship as Paul did is to stand in full continuity with the kingdom Jesus preached. Paul's *kyrios* is the kingdom's ruler (king).

306. S. Stout, *Preach the Word: A Pauline Theology of Preaching Based on 2 Timothy 4:1–5* (Eugene, OR: Pickwick, 2014), xv: "The central governing activity of the ministry of the Apostle Paul is the oral proclamation of the Gospel of Christ. All other activities in his ministry are subservient to this over-riding concern, and they find meaning only if preaching is primary."

307. The other word for preaching: *euangelizō* (preach the gospel): 1 Cor 9:16; 15:1, 2; 2 Cor 11:7; Gal 1:8, 16; 4:13.

ministry."[308] The word appears in the PE only one other time (1 Tim 3:16). Paul and those associated with him preached "the message concerning faith" (Rom 10:8), "Christ crucified" (1 Cor 1:23; cf. 15:11; 2 Cor 11:4; Gal 2:2), "Jesus Christ as Lord, and ourselves as your servants for Jesus's sake" (2 Cor 4:5), and "the gospel of God" (1 Thess 2:9). "The word" (from *logos*) Timothy is to preach should in Paul's intention no doubt hew to the lines Paul has already established over decades of missionary and church planting activity.

Paul's concern is not just that Timothy preach but that he "be prepared"[309] to do so. He needs to have his mind fixed on this task and be attentive to it (so BDAG 418). The following phrase helps explain why: "in season and out of season." Timothy's task is to preach when it is easy and productive and also when it is not. Timothy's past experience with Paul would offer graphic examples, as Timothy was with Paul in some situations that Paul addresses with ease and optimism (see Phil 1:1; 1 Thess 1:1; 2 Thess 1:1). In other situations Paul (aided by Timothy) faced "many adversaries" (1 Cor 16:9–10). The word must go forth under all circumstances, not just favorable ones. Timothy "is to get on with it and not let circumstances determine whether he does it or not."[310]

And what should this preaching aim to achieve? Three additional imperatives flesh out Paul's counsel. Each ends with the suffix *-son*, lending rhetorical polish to varied vocabulary.

1. "Correct" (*elenxson*) is the verb form of the noun translated "rebuking" (*elegmos*) in 3:16. Pastoral preaching must often help people stay on their desired path by addressing errant tendencies. The preacher or spiritual counselor must not only disseminate information or offer engrossing talks but actually deter digression and herd sheep back toward where they belong, to the extent verbal suasion (and other pastoral tools like prayer and encouragement) can help effect such redirection. (Paul would also view the Holy Spirit's work as key.)
2. "Rebuke" (*epitimēson*) is a verb used only one other time in the NT epistles (Jude 9) but frequently in the Synoptic Gospels to describe Jesus's action.[311] Jesus taught his disciples to "rebuke" one another, forgiving when there is repentance (Luke 17:3). Timothy's preaching ministry should not only "correct" but, when necessary, confront with stern reproof.

308. Zehr, 216.

309. From *ephistēmi*, a verb found in Paul only two other times (1 Thess 5:3; 2 Tim 4:6) and carrying a wide range of meanings. It appears eighteen other times in the NT, all in Luke-Acts.

310. Witherington, 365.

311. See Matt 8:26; 12:16; 17:18; Mark 1:25; 3:12; 4:39; 8:30; 9:25; Luke 4:35, 39, 41; 8:24; 9:21, 42, 55.

3. "Encourage" (*parakaleson*) is a word that can approximate the meaning of "correct" or "rebuke," but it may also convey a more nurturing sense. It is used 109 times in the NT, 54 of those times in Paul (see discussion at Titus 1:9). Over a dozen times in Paul's writings, he uses this word to denote strong encouragement or admonition: see his "I urge/plead/appeal . . ." in numerous contexts.[312] Paul has already exercised this duty in his own "preaching" to Timothy in an earlier letter (1 Tim 1:3; 2:1). Timothy's preaching should be suffused with heartfelt, affirmational appeal that will confirm in listeners that their pastor cares and that there is much at stake.

All of Timothy's preaching with its variegated functions should proceed "with great patience and careful instruction." "Great" translates a form of *pas* (all, every, much) and here conveys the idea of entire, full, complete. Timothy's patience and instruction should not be piecemeal or partial. Halfhearted pastoral preaching is a contradiction in terms. On "patience" (*makrothymia*), see discussion on 3:10 above. Paul has already called Timothy's attention to Christ's "patience" in bringing Paul to faith: "I was shown mercy so that in me, the worst of sinners, Christ Jesus might display his immense patience [*makrothymian*] as an example for those who would believe in him and receive eternal life" (1 Tim 1:16). Timothy should exercise similar grace in addressing his hearers. As he does so, he may reasonably expect analogous results.

"Careful instruction" (*pasē . . . didachē*) highlights the didactic side of pastoral preaching worthy of the name. For discussion of the word *didachē* (instruction, teaching), see commentary at Titus 1:9. Jesus called disciples (learners); he did not merely assemble audiences. Pastors are not merely orators. In his preaching, Timothy is to embrace, live, and impress the teaching he has received from the Scriptures (3:15–17) and others (such as Paul) who have taught him so he can teach others (see 2:2 and discussion there). Combined with patience, sound instruction will ground God's people so they can withstand the challenges of which the next two verses speak.

3 Paul speaks of a future that in some respects has already arrived[313] and is still with us today. On "time" (*kairos*), see discussion at Titus 1:3. Paul used the same word in the plural earlier: "There will be terrible times in the last days" (3:1; see discussion there; see also 1 Tim 4:1). In the Scriptures of which Paul has just reminded Timothy (2 Tim 3:15–17), "there is a time for everything" (Eccl 3:1), not all of it good. The OT is replete with episodes of rebellion against God's

312. See Rom 12:1; 15:30; 16:17; 1 Cor 1:10; 4:16; 16:12, 15; 2 Cor 2:8; 10:1; 12:19; Eph 4:1; Phil 4:2; Phlm 9, 10.

313. See Dibelius and Conzelmann, 120: "In 2 Tim 4:3, as in 1 Tim 4:1ff, it is obvious that the future which 'Paul' predicts is already a present reality for the situation of the letters."

word and the prophets who delivered it. Paul foresees adverse circumstances for Timothy and his preaching. He now details his apprehension.

The Greek word order highlights "sound doctrine," the very thing Timothy (like Titus; see Titus 1:9, 13; 2:1, 2 and discussion there; see also Introduction, IX.D) is charged to affirm, inculcate, and defend. Sound doctrine encompasses and reaffirms the "instruction" in v. 2. The fellowship of God's people thrives on shared certainties regarding Christ and the Scriptures that mediate knowledge of God to them. And yet, "the time will come when people will not put up with" what Timothy is bound to teach them. "Put up with" (*anechō*) translates a signature Pauline word.[314] Jesus "put up with" people skeptical of him (Matt 17:17; Mark 9:19; Luke 9:41). In the LXX the same word depicts God enduring the provocation of wayward Israel (Isa 42:14; 46:4). Timothy will find, as he no doubt already knows, that people in the church do not always return the favor to those who preach Jesus.

Rather than crave what is best for them (see 1 Pet 2:2), the people of whom Paul warns "will gather around" themselves leaders of a different ilk. The Greek wording emphasizes "their own desires" as playing a leading role in this. The word for "gather around" (*episōreuō*) is a NT hapax and implies collecting more than is needed. Just one dubious teacher is too many, but these people heap up a surplus. This "great number" of purported teachers will appear to outweigh the testimony of a solitary leader like Timothy, whose words are not calculated to satisfy the "desires" (*epithymias*)[315] of hearers but to be faithful to teaching he had received (see 1 Tim 6:20; 2 Tim 1:14), just as the apostle Paul sought to uphold what had been entrusted to him (1 Cor 4:1; Gal 2:7; 1 Thess 2:4; 1 Tim 1:11; Titus 1:3). Christ did not come to please himself (Rom 15:3), and he spoke as God directed, not as his audience preferred (see John 7:17; 8:28; 12:49). Paul essentially commends to Timothy both the warning and the opportunity conveyed by Jesus's words: "Whoever speaks on their own does so to gain personal glory, but he who seeks the glory of the one who sent him is a man of truth; there is nothing false about him" (John 7:18). Paul wants Timothy above all to be a man of truth.

Almost as an afterthought, Paul concludes the verse with words that could be rendered "scratching/tickling the hearing" (NIV "say what their itching ears want to hear"). This participial phrase is depicted as the activity of those who heap up the opportunistic teachers, who in essence prostitute themselves. In that sense it is an exercise in self-gratification. BDAG 550 comments that the expression is a figure of speech describing religious voyeurism "that looks for interesting and juicy bits of information. This itching is relieved by

314. *Anechō* occurs nine other times in Paul: 1 Cor 4:12; 2 Cor 11:1 (twice), 4, 19, 20; Eph 4:2; Col 3:13; 2 Thess 1:4.

315. See discussion of this word at 2:22 above.

the messages of the new teachers." In the twenty-first-century West, examples abound with books and speakers garnering followings (and often profits) based on views regarding eschatology, sexual behavior, theories or purported discoveries proving the Bible is not true or needs radical reinterpretation, sensational religious experience, including wealth acquisition through faith, and other titillating claims, like describing what it is like to die and go to heaven. Paul's words are a reminder that such fascinations are nothing new. North America and other relatively affluent regions, with their consumerist and often narcissistic social orders, decreasing biblical literacy, and lack of appetite for features of the gospel and God as presented in Scripture, are prime venues for such activity. Through electronic means the West's deceptions and delusions find ready recipients worldwide. The antidote would lie, not in denouncing the West, but in rediscovering the message Paul and Timothy preached and living accordingly.[316]

4 Concurrent with collecting of desirable teachers (v. 3), the same people will engage in a two-step move that is resistant to the preaching Paul calls for from Timothy. This is underscored by a construction (*men . . . de*) that means "on the one hand . . . on the other hand." This ties in a neat bow, so to speak, an elegant literary pattern in which peculiar (but in vv. 3–4 consistent) word order serves to emphasize the tawdriness of the desires of those Timothy will face. This rearrangement of NIV phrases in vv. 3–4 reflects the actual Greek word order:

> with sound doctrine people will not put up . . .
> to suit their own desires they will gather around them . . .
> from the truth (on the one hand) they will turn their ears away . . .
> to myths (on the other hand) they will turn aside

To "turn . . . ears [*akoēn*, hearing] away" is a disastrous move when salvation comes through "hearing" (see Deut 6:4; Rom 10:17; Gal 3:2, 5; 1 Thess 2:13). Jesus insists that "whoever has ears" had better hear (Matt 11:15; Mark 4:9; Luke 14:35b; see Mark 4:23), not shop for a more favorable message elsewhere. In the OT, prophets who pleased their listeners were usually false ones (see Jer 6:14; 8:11; Ezek 13:10, 16; Mic 3:5). For discussion on turning from the truth and turning aside[317] to "myths" instead, see commentary at Titus 1:14, where Paul also mentions myths. Collins speaks of "a negative conversion" (from gospel faith to preference for fables) and underscores that hundreds of years prior to NT times, "the Greeks were aware of the differences between

316. For an exercise in taking the "itching ears" warning out of context and reading "the Pastor's [i.e., Paul's] own words in judgment against him," see Twomey, 173–75.

317. "Turn aside" translates a form of *ektrepō*; see discussion at 1 Tim 1:6.

myths and truth."[318] Keener has documented both gullibility and skepticism toward miracles in the NT era;[319] people in Paul's time were not necessarily any more uncritical of purported miracles and other supernatural claims than are people today. It is ironic and telling that in the West, leading NT scholars like F. C. Baur (1792–1860) have built their entire reading of the NT on the assumption that its fundamental empirical and theological claims are mythical.[320] This move has had fateful consequences for church orders built on this conviction and for whole nations in which churches have turned to doctrines based on modern philosophers[321] rather than on Christ and other messengers sent from God.

5 "But you" followed by one or more commands[322] is a PE pattern (see also 1 Tim 6:11; 2 Tim 3:14; Titus 2:1). Here it sets up a clear contrast between the spiritual promiscuity of people defining their religion by "their own desires" (v. 3) and a leader like Timothy.

"Keep your head" translates a form of *nēphō*, found in the NT five other times.[323] The word can denote sobriety rather than drunkenness. More broadly, it expresses freedom from "excess, passion, confusion," and other imbalances (BDAG 672). In the AF it can express moral clarity[324] or the self-control of an athlete.[325] The expression "the fog of war" has been associated with Prussian military analyst Carl von Clausewitz and his book *On War*;[326] those with pastoral experience can attest to something like "the fog of care of

318. Collins, 270.

319. In Keener, *Miracles,* see chs. 1–4. esp. 1:87–96.

320. In Martin Bauspiess, Christof Landmesser, and David Lincicum, eds., *Ferdinand Christian Baur und die Geschichte des frühen Christentums,* WUNT 333 (Tübingen: Mohr Siebeck, 2014), see Stefan Alkier's observations on the extent to which Baur's core convictions are often little more than early "epistemologically based variants" of Rudolf Bultmann's "demythologization strategies" (286; for differences, see 306; Baur views the NT miracles not as historical events but "as biblical ideas in poetic forms of presentation" [307]). Both Baur and Bultmann treat Paul's sober truth claims as mythical, despite Paul's precisely opposite testimony.

321. Dorrien, *Kantian Reason and Hegelian Spirit,* points to the seminal roles played by Kant, Schelling, Schleiermacher, and Hegel. Note also the moving testimony of a Bultmann student who, after years of advocating his hermeneutic, (re)discovered Scripture and its transforming message: www.gracevalley.org/teaching/eta-linnemann-testimony.

322. The expression *not* followed directly by an imperative appears in Paul at Rom 11:17, 20; 14:10; 2 Tim 3:10.

323. 1 Thess 5:6, 8; 1 Pet 1:13; 4:7; 5:8.

324. "Let us be clear-headed [*nēpsōmen*] regarding the good, for we are full of much stupidity and wickedness" (2 Clem. 13:1).

325. "Be sober [*nēphe*], as God's athlete" (Ign. *Pol.* 2:3).

326. For important qualifications on the accuracy of this attribution, see, for example, Eugenia C. Kiesling, "On War without the Fog," *Military Review* 85.11 (September–October 2001): 85–87.

souls." Uncertainties regarding what to do may abound. There can be temptations to cut corners, panic, or just quit. Paul urges Timothy once more, as he has already done frequently both in this letter and 1 Timothy, to get a grip. "In all situations" stresses that Timothy needs to implement this across the board. As Paul nears the end of the epistle, it probably also serves as a blanket statement covering eventualities in Timothy's work that Paul either could not foresee or did not have energy or space to address.

"Keep your head" is a present imperative;[327] the next three commands are aorist. Johnson calls them "mutually interpretive."[328] They specify three overlapping domains in which Timothy must maintain composure and exercise balanced leadership. It is not easy to see just why Paul singles out these three matters. It is tempting to speculate that Timothy should "endure hardship" because he is prone to evade it, "do the work of an evangelist" because he is inclined to skirt it, and "discharge all" his ministry duties because he might skip some. But none of this can be verified.

It is more fruitful to observe that these three commands serve to restate or summarize what Paul's own life in ministry has exemplified, as well as what he has already commended to Timothy in this epistle. Paul is about to talk of his own death; here is how Timothy may carry on the work with integrity in his mentor's absence.

"Endure hardship" commands what Paul has described as his own experience in jail—but God's word continues its free course of movement (2:9; see discussion there). He has already called Timothy to join him in "suffering for the gospel" (1:8), to be strong in grace (2:1), and to be prepared for persecution (3:12). The call to hardship repeats an established theme of this epistle.

"Do the work of an evangelist" should be kept free of associations with "evangelists" in the sense of hip (or folksy traditional) itinerant preachers with jets, advance teams, big budgets, and live streaming to remote campuses. The word *euangelistēs* (evangelist), which appears elsewhere in the NT only twice (Acts 21:8; Eph 4:11), means simply a proclaimer of the gospel's good news. It is likely that Paul has in mind the preaching he commanded Timothy in 2 Tim 4:1: "Preach the word." In his work as pastor and overseer, Timothy should make known the *euangelion* (good news) of which Paul has already spoken (1:8, 10; 2:8). "The work of an evangelist" is not some flashy specialty but the meat-and-potatoes of regular pastoral instruction and spiritual over-

327. Towner, *Letters*, 606, comments that the verbal aspect here "may underline the normality of this requirement"; it is a standing order for every situation. See Mounce, 576: "The surrounding eight imperatives are all aorist; the shift to . . . the present tense here is appropriate for a general admonition." Current debates on verbal aspect may call such conclusions in question; for orientation, see, for example, ch. 5 in C. Campbell, *Advances in the Study of Greek* (Grand Rapids: Zondervan, 2015); more broadly, Porter, *Linguistic Analysis*.

328. Johnson, *Letters to Paul's Delegates*, 96.

sight. The opening verses of 1 Cor 15 verify how fundamental the work of gospel iteration was in Pauline understanding, even in an established congregation. The core message of Christ's death and resurrection in accordance with the Scriptures must remain at the heart of all Timothy undertakes.

None of the above should be taken as criticizing countless humble "evangelists" around the world, now and in the past, who are appointed by their churches to preach the gospel to the unconverted, full or part time, often in very challenging circumstances. "The work of an evangelist" includes their work, though it is rightly understood as a pastoral ministry in its own right for deployment within local church ministry, as well as an outreach tool for engaging the lost. To "do the work of an evangelist" only within the church would be coals to Newcastle, but evangelism without organic connection to the church would suggest an orphaned evangelist and evangel.

As for "discharge all the duties of your ministry," these seven words could be expressed in just three: "fulfill your ministry." "Fulfill" (from *plērophoreō*) is a word used only once in the NT outside of Paul's writings.[329] Here it means to carry out completely; to leave nothing undone; to execute tasks with the high standards and fidelity to Christ that Paul has called for throughout the epistle. In v. 17 Paul will use the same word to describe how he "fully proclaimed" the gospel message with God's help and was thus spared from the lions. Timothy should be faithful unto death in every aspect of his *diakonia* (service, pastoral labors, ministry), the same word Paul uses to describe his work for the Lord (1 Tim 1:12; 2 Tim 4:11). Mounce calls it "the call to sacrificial service."[330] This is a call, then, to complete vocational faithfulness rather than the minimalist mentality of a hireling.

6 The first word, "For," confirms that the commands of the previous verse, and indeed the entire admonition stretching back to v. 1, have Paul's demise in mind. "Already being poured out like a drink offering" (eight words) translates just two words in Greek. One is *ēdē* (already), which occurs in the PE three times (see also 1 Tim 5:15; 2 Tim 2:18), about the same rate of use found in the other ten Pauline letters (eleven times). The other word, from *spendō* (to offer a drink offering or libation), could be either middle or passive voice. If the former, Paul is stressing his involvement and perhaps consent: "I am pouring out myself." If passive, as NIV translates, the stress is that Paul is being acted upon, and perhaps by God, who has brought Paul to this sobering juncture.

Paul's "being poured out" (*spendō*) is explained with reference to Hellenistic sources in BDAG 937. The picture is of a libation poured out to pagan deities, a ubiquitous phenomenon in the Roman world.[331] But an equally

329. See Luke 1:1. Other Pauline occurrences: Rom 4:21; 14:5; Col 4:12; 2 Tim 4:17.

330. Mounce, 577.

331. For references, see Bassler, 171. She thinks the language here is so similar to Phi-

possible background is Hebrew history and the Jewish world reflected in the LXX, where the word occurs nineteen times, beginning with a drink offering poured out by Jacob (Gen 35:14). David pours out to the Lord water he will not drink because it was procured for him at mortal risk by his soldiers (2 Sam 23:16; 1 Chr 11:18; 4 Macc 3:16). This incident is also noted in Josephus (*Jewish Antiquities* 7.314), who uses the word a dozen other times. The God acknowledged by Paul and Timothy is a God who calls for sacrifice, not only in OT ordinances but in NT fulfillments and applications like Paul's "offer your bodies as a living sacrifice" (Rom 12:1). Paul has lived out this mandate over the years, which has landed him where he now sits as he writes or dictates: death row.

Moreover, there is in Jewish thinking by Paul's time (perhaps under Stoic influence) the notion that such sacrifice has a steeling and calming effect. Josephus asserts that pouring out wine unto God "is the pledge of fidelity and mutual confidence among men; and puts an end to their quarrels, takes away passion and grief out of the minds of them that use it, and makes them cheerful" (*Jewish Antiquities* 2.66). When David poured out the water before the Lord, he showed the power of reason over desire (4 Macc 3:16). "For the temperate mind can conquer the compulsions of the passions and quench the flames of frenzied desires. It can overpower bodily agonies even when they are extreme and by the nobility of reason spurn all domination by the passions" (4 Macc 3:17–18).

There is little reason to think Paul's self-sacrifice is a Stoic gesture; there is better basis to understand it as an application of his own principle of presenting one's body a living sacrifice, which is itself a manifestation of his theology of the cross (see Gal 6:14). As Paul notes that his time of "departure"[332] is near, his demeanor is not frantic or fatalistic but composed and in harmony with an ancient tradition (sacrifice, even self-sacrifice, with confidence in God for the outcome) well-established among God's covenant people.[333]

7 In staccato fashion Paul makes three almost perfectly symmetrical declarations. Each begins with the direct object and concludes with a perfect tense verb. The word order in Greek runs:

> the good fight I have fought
> the race I have finished
> the faith I have kept

---

lippians that it shows the author "relied on that letter for his language and, to some extent, his thought." Another possibility is that Philippians and 2 Timothy share a common author.

332. *Analysis*, a NT hapax. The word could refer to "loosening" and came to be a euphemism for death. See also, for example, 1 Clem. 44:5.

333. See, for example, Exod 32:31; 2 Sam 24:17; Isa 53.

This distinct yet plain structure emphasizes the stark fact that Paul has reached the end of the line. Yet, the rhetoric is not gloomy but nobly upbeat. "Good fight" and "the faith" repeat what Paul admonished Timothy earlier: "Fight the good fight of the faith" (1 Tim 6:12). Paul practices to the end what he has long commanded Timothy. The motif of strenuous striving using this particular word (*agōnizomai*, strive, fight, contend) sweeps from the Gospels into Paul's letters in a fascinating arc through the NT's seven other occurrences:

> *Make* every effort [*agōnizesthe*] to enter through the narrow door, because many, I tell you, will try to enter and will not be able to. (Luke 13:24)
>
> Jesus said, "My kingdom is not of this world. If it were, my servants would fight [*ēgōnizonto*] to prevent my arrest by the Jewish leaders. But now my kingdom is from another place." (John 18:36)
>
> Everyone who competes [*agōnizomenos*] in the games goes into strict training. They do it to get a crown that will not last, but we do it to get a crown that will last forever. (1 Cor 9:25)
>
> To this end I strenuously contend [*agōnizomenos*] with all the energy Christ so powerfully works in me. (Col 1:29)
>
> Epaphras, who is one of you and a servant of Christ Jesus, sends greetings. He is always wrestling [*agōnizomenos*] in prayer for you, that you may stand firm in all the will of God, mature and fully assured. (Col 4:12)
>
> That is why we labor and strive [*agōnizometha*], because we have put our hope in the living God, who is the Savior of all people, and especially of those who believe. (1 Tim 4:10)
>
> I felt compelled to write and urge you to contend [*epagōnizesthai*] for the faith that was once for all entrusted to God's holy people. (Jude 3)

While affirming a God who is sovereign in all things, Paul is faithful to Jesus (and to the Pauline heritage established in other epistles) in affirming all-out effort to lay hold of the salvation Jesus won. Paul's wording—with insinuations of rigor, competition (with movements and persons hostile to the gospel's spread and flourishing), and dangerous risk—bears emphasis and reflection. Some fights are not pointless or frivolous violence but necessary and "good."

Paul's mention of "race" (*dromos*) as a metaphor for the course of life reflects Luke's depiction of Paul's language on two occasions in Acts (13:25;

20:24).[334] Otherwise the word is absent from the NT. Paul's reference to "the faith" likely refers to the core content of Christian belief; see comment regarding *fides quae creditur* at Titus 1:4. Paul has not allowed the "deposit" (1:14) of Christian truth to be watered down or adulterated.[335]

8 "Now" translates *loipos*, a word used by Paul elsewhere to mean "in any case, otherwise, as far as everything else is concerned" (e.g., 1 Cor 1:16; 4:2; 2 Cor 13:11; 1 Thess 4:1). In summing up, his thoughts turn to what he knows is stored up[336] for him "on that day" (see also 2 Thess 2:3; 2 Tim 1:18), the day of final reckoning, with punishments and rewards depending on one's relationship to Christ (see 1 Cor 3:11–15).[337] The future form "will reward" confirms the eschatological viewpoint. He views his impending martyrdom as "no cause for shame," because, in his words, "I know whom I have believed, and am convinced that he is able to guard what I have entrusted to him until that day" (1 Tim 1:12). Jesus spoke of "that day" over a dozen times, both as judgment (Luke 21:34) and as a joyful time of reward (Luke 6:23) and reunion with his disciples (Matt 26:29).

This relational consideration informs the meaning of "the crown of righteousness." Victors, whether kings (see Rev 6:2) or athletes (2 Tim 2:5), received the *stephanos*,[338] a wreath expressing honor, achievement, and recognition. In Paul's view, to cite words from another early church leader, Christ is "now crowned with glory and honor because he suffered death, so that by the grace of God he might taste death for everyone" (Heb 2:9). The righteousness available through him via faith in the gospel (see Rom 1:16–17) enables participation in the victory he won. With victory comes reward.

Paul may have had in mind reward for a righteous life, a reward consisting of righteousness, a reward bestowed justly by "the righteous Judge," or some combination of these. "Probably it is best not to distinguish too rigidly between" such possibilities.[339] "The righteous judge" is Christ (note "his appearing" at the end of the verse; also Acts 10:42; Jas 5:9), yet not without the presence and sanction of "the righteous Judge" named as God in the LXX.[340]

Reward is in store not just for Paul or other apostles but for "all who have longed for his appearing." "In athletic competition there can be only one winner, but here all are victors, at least all who endure to the end, for in heaven there is no competition."[341] Those with this deep longing include Timothy

334. See also the same word used once by Ignatius (*Pol.* 1:2).

335. See Towner, *Letters*, 613–14, for discussion.

336. *Apokeimai*; see also Luke 19:20; Col 1:5.

337. For Augustine's wrestling with this text, see Barclay, *Paul and the Gift*, 89n22.

338. The same word is used elsewhere in Paul in Phil 4:1 and 1 Thess 2:19.

339. Towner, *Letters*, 615.

340. Ps 7:12 (*ho theos kritēs dikaios*); 2 Macc 12:6.

341. Berger, 819; whether Paul banned competition from heaven may be left open.

and those he oversaw, so this vision could serve as a boost for them as their doughty leader was passing from the scene. On "appearing" and longing for it, see comments on Titus 2:13. "Have longed" translates a verbal form of *agapaō* (to love). Christ's followers await his return with settled but ongoing ardor, living conscious of what they have been entrusted with and how important it is that they render it back to God in their daily decisions and actions. Berger calls the rugged perseverance reflected in this verse "an integral part of the faith as Paul understood it" and evidence of Paul's authorship.[342] For the reward in this, and also the tragedy of laxity or forgetting about the master's return, see, for example, Matt 24:42–53; cf. 1 John 3:1–3. The ultimate reward will be union with Christ (see v. 18).

B. Personal Remarks (4:9–18)

In addition to asking Timothy to come soon and bring needed items, Paul shares news about associates whom they have in common, some who are friends and some who are foes (vv. 9–15). He also comments on the trial process underway (vv. 16–18). The tone overall is mixed, neither overwhelmingly optimistic nor unremittingly negative. Definite bright spots as Paul gives Timothy a sort of status report on certain persons are Timothy himself, whom Paul longs to see; Crescens, Titus, and Tychicus, who are out on assignment; Luke, who is Paul's sole current helper; and Mark, whom Paul hopes Timothy will bring with him. On the downside, Demas has acted dishonorably in Paul's view, and a certain Alexander who has done damage to Paul's cause also poses a threat to Timothy, who should watch out for him.

Collins sees this section as filled with "name-dropping," viewing it as "a feature of deuteropauline literature" that is absent from "the authentic Pauline correspondence."[343] Most of Rom 16 would counter this view, and plenty of names are mentioned along the way in other letters viewed as undoubtedly Pauline (see, e.g., Timothy, Apollos, Stephanus, Fortunatus, Achaicus, Aquila, Priscilla, all named in the final verses of 1 Corinthians). There is nothing either non-Pauline or historically unlikely about the persons and situations alluded to in this section. Johnson comments that "the percentage of known personal names to unknown is remarkably high," higher than the percentages in Philippians and Romans.[344]

As for Paul's legal status, there has been a "first defense" (v. 16), some sort of preliminary hearing, at which Paul felt quite alone. Yet, he felt the Lord

342. Berger, 820.

343. Collins, 276.

344. Johnson, *Letters to Paul's Delegates*, 98.

still with him for the sake of fulfilling his mission and goal (v. 17). The passage closes on a strong note of confidence, including a doxological flourish (v. 18).

> [9] *Do your best to come to me quickly,* [10] *for Demas, because he loved this world, has deserted me and has gone to Thessalonica. Crescens has gone to Galatia, and Titus to Dalmatia.* [11] *Only Luke is with me. Get Mark and bring him with you, because he is helpful to me in my ministry.* [12] *I sent Tychicus to Ephesus.* [13] *When you come, bring the cloak that I left with Carpus at Troas, and my scrolls, especially the parchments.* [14] *Alexander the metalworker did me a great deal of harm. The Lord will repay him for what he has done.* [15] *You too should be on your guard against him, because he strongly opposed our message.* [16] *At my first defense, no one came to my support, but everyone deserted me. May it not be held against them.* [17] *But the Lord stood at my side and gave me strength, so that through me the message might be fully proclaimed and all the Gentiles might hear it. And I was delivered from the lion's mouth.* [18] *The Lord will rescue me from every evil attack and will bring me safely to his heavenly kingdom. To him be glory for ever and ever. Amen.*

9 "Do your best" translates an aorist imperative form of *spoudazō*, a verb that can mean to hurry, to expedite a process, or to exercise zeal and urgency in fulfilling an obligation (BDAG 939). The verb is used eleven times in the NT, most frequently by Paul (see also Gal 2:10; Eph 4:3; 1 Thess 2:17; 2 Tim 2:15; 4:21; Titus 3:12).[345] Paul wants Timothy to spare no pains and make every effort. Paul was under arrest and suffering as a result (see 1:12). Imprisonment in any form is rarely pleasant, and Paul is conscious of people moving away from him and even from the gospel (see 1:15; 4:10, 14). A visit from trusted coworker Timothy would be a great uplift. The last word in the verse, "quickly" (*tacheōs*) underscores the urgency. Collins views this word as "an epistolary cliché";[346] if so, the historical Paul favored the same convention (see the same word in 1 Cor 4:19; Gal 1:6; Phil 2:19, 24; 2 Thess 2:2). It appears elsewhere in the PE only in 1 Tim 5:22.

10 "For" implies that Paul will now give one or more reasons why he feels acute need for Timothy's speedy arrival. The first matter he raises concerns Demas. Only a few years previous, he was a loyal coworker alongside Paul's valued lieutenant Luke (Col 4:14; Phlm 24). He has "deserted" Paul, who used the same word to describe the not uncommon Christian lot in life: "persecuted, but not abandoned [= deserted]" (2 Cor 4:9). He means that God does not abandon those whose faithfulness leads them into dire straits for

345. Outside of Paul, see Heb 4:11; 2 Pet 1:10, 15; 3:14.

346. Collins, 277.

Jesus's sake. But people, including fellow believers once deemed trustworthy, may prove fickle. Demas is a case in point.

Demas tripped up on inordinate affection for "this world." Whether this was an act of apostasy is uncertain.[347] Calvin's gracious analysis is attractive though not verifiable: "We are not to suppose that he completely denied Christ and gave himself over again to ungodliness or the allurements of the world, but only that he cared more for his own convenience and safety rather than for the life of Paul."[348] The "world" Demas loved is not *gē* (planet earth, humanity) or *kosmos* (the created universe viewed with or without its inhabitants). Paul does not disparage Demas for embodying a positive view of the created order. Paul refers rather to the current *aiōn* (age, era, as in "the Age of Reason"). Every time and place has its tone and trends. Those who follow Christ seek to love his priorities and "appearing" (see 4:8); they heed the command, "Do not conform to the pattern of this world [*aiōn*]" (Rom 12:2).[349] The message of the lordship of Christ is "not the wisdom of this age [*aiōn*] or of the rulers of this age [*aiōn*], who are coming to nothing" (1 Cor 2:6). Paul uses the same word with this meaning in two other PE passages (1 Tim 6:17; Titus 2:12). Whereas the Christian mandate is to love God and your neighbor as yourself, Demas has set his affection at least to some extent on this crumbling world order, not the kingdom of God. We do not know why he went to Thessalonica or what he may have sought there.

"Crescens" occurs nowhere else in the NT. Since nothing more is known of him, the question of just where "Galatia" was can be left undetermined, as well.[350] On Titus, see commentary Introduction, VIII.A. Dalmatia lay in southwest Illyricum (modern Croatia), where Paul had evangelized some years previous (Rom 15:19). Since both Galatia (the Roman province in modern Turkey) and Dalmatia were sites of Paul's earlier work, perhaps these men were being sent there from Paul to strengthen or extend what had been established earlier.

11 Paul has been describing movements of a few of Timothy's colleagues. Now he describes an aspect of his own setting: only Luke is with him. This need not be a sinister suggestion that everyone else has turned away: some (see previous verse) have been sent out on assignment. Paul may simply be

347. Towner, *Letters*, 623, says "apostasy as such does not seem to be in view."

348. Calvin, 340. For comment on Calvin's view and other interpretations, see Twomey, 186.

349. For a classic statement of how Christians are fully part of the world and society, yet also profoundly noncompliant with its inexorable overreach, see Diogn. 5, epitomized in 2 Tim 4:5: "They live in their own countries, but only as nonresidents; they participate in everything as citizens, and endure everything as foreigners. Every foreign country is their fatherland, and every fatherland is foreign."

350. For extra-NT references to Crescens, see Towner, *Letters*, 623n19. In the same note, Towner thinks Galatia is the Roman province evangelized by Paul and Barnabas in Acts 13–14; Quinn and Wacker (802–4) instead favor Gaul, the region in present-day France and Belgium conquered for Rome by Julius Caesar.

verifying his need for Timothy because other coworkers are in short supply. Luke's presence with Paul (also Demas's) during an earlier imprisonment (Col 4:14; Phlm 24) has already been noted. What is clear, and will become clearer still (2 Tim 4:16), is that at present Paul is not surrounded by an abundance of active supporters. In that situation the presence of a trusted companion like Luke serves as a profound encouragement. Some suggest Luke as author of this letter (and perhaps other of the PEs).[351]

Also mentioned is Mark, likely "the cousin of Barnabas" who was with Paul during an earlier imprisonment (Col 4:10; cf. Phlm 24). He and Paul evidently reconciled after a falling out years earlier (Acts 15:37–39). Wherever Timothy is when he receives this letter and its summons to hurry to Paul's side (2 Tim 4:9), he should bring Mark when he comes. This request implies that Mark is already with Timothy, or perhaps that Timothy will be able to pass by Mark's location on his way to see Paul.

Paul's remark that Mark is "helpful" (*euchrēstos*) in Paul's "ministry" (*diakonia*) is notable on two counts. First, it speaks to Paul's poise and tenacity in the face of mortal peril. On the one hand, his execution may be imminent (v. 6). For many, such a prospect would have been paralyzing; fear can be a great immobilizer (see John 20:19; Heb 10:32–39). On the other hand, he has been in, and then out, of incarceration many times before (2 Cor 11:23). He refuses to roll over in fear or passive self-pity but continues to place his life at God's disposal for ministry. Second, *euchrēstos* occurs also in 2 Tim 2:21 and Phlm 11 (and nowhere else in the NT). While no final conclusions can be drawn from three appearances of the word, its presence here is consistent with Paul's known usage elsewhere.

12 Tychicus joins Crescens and Titus (v. 10) as coworkers whom Paul has dispatched elsewhere, in this case to Ephesus. See commentary on Titus 3:12, which also mentions Tychicus. Long a coworker of Paul and courier of two earlier letters (Ephesians and Colossians), he receives no expanded reference either because his purpose in Ephesus would have been self-evident to Timothy, or because there was no need to burden Timothy with further specifics at this point. The verb for "sent" (*apostellō*) is used frequently in the Gospels (e.g., Matt 10:5; Mark 6:7; Luke 4:43), in Acts (e.g., 8:14; 11:30; 19:22), and (less frequently) in Paul (Rom 10:15; 2 Cor 12:17) to describe evangelistic or missionary labor. Collins notes that this description of Tychicus "underscores the missionary character of early Christianity and the prominence of the church in Asia."[352] It is not clear that this mere mention[353] justifies calling

351. For the unlikelihood of Luke's authorship, see Marshall, with Towner, 817. For investigation of possibilities, see Knight, 48–52.

352. Collins, 281.

353. See Marshall, with Towner, 818: "rather casual."

his work in Ephesus an "apostolate"[354] unless a very low bar is set for what apostolate signifies. If Timothy is at Ephesus when he receives this letter, Paul mentions Tychicus to assure Timothy that he can safely depart to join Paul, for his replacement is on the way.[355]

13 Assuming Timothy will comply with the request to come speedily (v. 9), Paul lists two items he needs. Timothy would pass through Troas in traveling from Ephesus to Rome. Paul visited Troas in earlier times and ministered there (Acts 16:8, 11; 20:6–12; cf. 2 Cor 2:12). "Cloak"[356] refers to a heavy garment like a blanket with a hole in it to fit over the head. Paul needed it with winter coming (2 Tim 4:21). Nothing more is known of Carpus. Fellows suggests he "may have been Paul's host in Troas."[357]

"Scrolls" and "parchments" could be Paul's own notes and records. They could also include portions of OT Scriptures and what later would become NT Scriptures. If this is the case, the request verifies the unsurprising fact that Paul remained a reader and thinker devoted to the ministry of the word until the end. Verification of the documents' contents, however, is not possible; as Johnson states: "In short, we know that Paul requested materials to read and probably also materials for writing, but nothing more than that." Johnson does concede, though, that biblical documents may have been intended.[358]

Collins sees here a symbolic statement of "a desire to have available for eventual transfer to Timothy the symbols of his ministry, namely, the mantle and the books." He proposes that the author of 2 Timothy, who was not Paul but someone he calls "the Pastor," may have remembered OT stories about Moses, Joshua, Elijah, and Elisha and drawn on their motif of "the transference of prophetic power" to prepare "the way for the later ordination ritual in which vestments and the Scriptures are given to the newly ordained."[359] Considerable imagination is required to see all these details implied in such a laconic and offhand request. Marshall points to similar requests in comparable circumstances in the writings of both William Tyndale and Dietrich Bonhoeffer; his conclusion is reasonable: "The most likely explanation is that the reference is historical. The cloak was required for winter in a Roman prison; the books may be Scriptures and the parchments are personal documents."[360]

354. Collins, 281–82.

355. Calvin, 340; Witherington, 378.

356. For the complex history of the interpretation of this object in German-language scholarship, which has tried to understand it symbolically under the assumption that a pseudepigrapher was using it to "mean" something, see Neudorfer, *Zweiter Brief an Timotheus*, 270–72.

357. R. Fellows, "Name Giving by Paul and the Destination of Acts," *TynBul* 67.2 (2016): 261.

358. Johnson, *First and Second Letters to Timothy*, 441, 440.

359. Collins, 283, 284.

360. Marshall, with Towner, 820–21.

14 The name "Alexander" appears six times in the NT. It was a common name, and two of the references are to men in Jesus's time and setting (Mark 15:21; Acts 4:6). Of the others, at least three are associated with someone in Ephesus (Acts 19:33 [two times]; 1 Tim 1:20). Commentators argue persuasively that the figure in 1 Tim 1:20, who with Hymenaeus had been "handed over to Satan" for defecting from Christian faith, is the same one mentioned here.[361] It is even possible that he is also the Alexander of Acts 19:33, though this is speculation. He may have lived in either Ephesus or Troas, which could account for Paul's mention of him here, since Timothy either is or could be in either or both of these cities as he prepares to travel to Paul.

Alexander, a tradesman who worked in metals,[362] had done "a great deal of harm" to Paul. BDAG 332 comments that, with the word *endeiknymi* (show, demonstrate), "Alexander the coppersmith is cast in an especially bad light through the use of diction that characterizes him as one at odds not only with Paul but Gr[eco]-Rom[an] culture." What was the "harm"?[363] Some have suggested that Alexander was instrumental in Paul's arrest. But we have no specifics. If he is continuing the pattern implied in 1 Tim 1:20, Paul may be thinking of the damage Alexander has done to the gospel cause so dear to Paul rather than to Paul personally. "The Lord will repay" (see same word in 4:8) expresses certainty.[364] There is nothing Paul can do but bear the situation with hope and grace, but there is no hint that Alexander will get away with his machinations. God's recompense for both good and evil is a prominent teaching of Jesus (see, e.g., Matt 6:4; 16:27) that also left its imprint on Paul (Rom 2:6).

15 Paul warns Timothy to "guard" against Alexander. Paul uses the same word (*phylassō*) to assure the Thessalonians that God will "protect" them (2 Thess 3:3). Timothy should "keep" or "guard" what has been entrusted to him (1 Tim 5:21; 6:20; 2 Tim 1:12, 14). Defensive measures are sane and necessary against some threats and people. Evidently Alexander is not someone to fool with. Trusting God, a forte of Paul that he consistently commends to his understudies like Timothy and all readers of his letters, is not incompatible with realistic wariness, given some people's traits and track record.

The basis for Paul's warning is the recollection that Alexander has in the past "opposed" the "message" that Paul (or Paul and Timothy) stood for. "Opposed" is the same word used of Jannes, Jambres, and other false teachers

361. See, for example, Towner, *Letters*, 630–31; Mounce, 593. But see Joel B. Green, "Alexander," *ABD* 1:151–52.

362. The word translated "metalworker" (*chalkeus*) could refer to specialization in particular metals, like copper or gold, but also could denote a blacksmith with a more general focus (BDAG 1076).

363. For *kaka* (evil, evil things), see also Luke 16:25; Acts 9:13; Rom 3:8.

364. Marshall, with Towner, 822.

in 2 Tim 3:8. Paul uses it in his other writings.[365] "Strongly" (*lian*) is in emphatic position and underscores Alexander's destructive capacity. "Message" translates a plural form of *logos* (word) and may be understood as the wide range of specific matters about which Paul spoke and taught, not merely some bland, simplistic summation.[366] Timothy, like Paul and the whole early church, had staked their lives on these "words" and the saving truths they conveyed.[367] Opposing or undercutting those words amounted to obstruction of God's redeeming presence in the world. Calvin can be at his best in passages like this; he comments that, in contrast to the next verse, where Paul expresses compassion for those who failed to defend him, "Alexander had risen up against God with malice and sacrilegious audacity and was openly attacking the truth he had once confessed, and such wickedness deserves no mercy."[368]

Paul's objection to Alexander and exhortation to Timothy do not reflect some petty or personal narrowness on Paul's part; they rather reflect apostolic conviction that to oppose the gospel message is the gravest of errors and an affront to Christ's lordship. While there are some "opponents" whom Timothy should gently instruct (2 Tim 2:25), Alexander is by his own choosing in a different category.

16 Paul's "first defense" was perhaps a pretrial arraignment. Possibly Alexander (previous verses) had a hand in Paul's arrest. Since he is still captive, the outcome must have been unfavorable. Like Jesus in his extremity (Luke 23:34) and Stephen at his stoning (Acts 7:60), Paul forgives those have seriously wronged him and in so doing condemned themselves. To stand alongside a man accused of a capital offense might have been risky; Paul understands this reluctance. He still counted friends around him (see v. 21) and has not descended into Elijah's abyss of supposing no faithful servants of God remain but him.[369]

"Defense" (*apologia*) is a word associated with Paul in seven of its eight NT uses (see also Acts 22:1; 25:16; 1 Cor 9:3; 2 Cor 7:11; Phil 1:7, 16; the exception is 1 Pet 3:15). "Came to my support" translates a form of *paraginomai*, which nearly always means simply to appear or show up (see Paul's only other use:

365. See Rom 9:19; 13:2; Gal 2:11; Eph 6:13.

366. Other plural uses of *logos* in the PE, with NIV translation of "words" italicized: 1 Tim 4:6 ("nourished on the *truths* of the faith"); 1 Tim 6:3 ("does not agree to the sound *instruction* of our Lord Jesus Christ); 2 Tim 1:13 ("the pattern of sound *teaching*").

367. Note the plural of *logos* to refer to Jesus's teachings in just one of the Gospels (Matt 7:24, 26, 28; 10:14; 19:1; 26:1), climaxed perhaps by two Matthean statements: "For by your words you will be acquitted, and by your words you will be condemned" (12:37); "Heaven and earth will pass away, but my words will never pass away" (24:35). The edifice of gospel truth is composed of numerous specific and essential components.

368. Calvin, 342.

369. See 1 Kgs 19:10; Rom 11:1–5.

1 Cor 16:3; it is frequent in the Gospels [fourteen times]). MM 481 comments that the idea of assistance or support comes from the dative pronoun *moi* (to me, for me), not from the verb itself.

One way or the other, Paul felt left in the lurch, which the next clause confirms: "everyone deserted me." Paul did not renege on his convictions but held to them and faced the consequences; he did not peg the truth of the gospel to popular reception, even among ostensible fellow believers. On earlier talk of desertion, which was more general and did not pertain to his trial,[370] see 1:15 and commentary there. Paul uses the same word for "desert" (*enkataleipō*) in 4:10 with reference to Demas. Despite the grave disappointment of feeling alone at his hearing, Paul pronounces an absolution: "May it not be held against them." These seven words translate only three in Greek, at the heart of which is the only optative form of *logizomai* (regard, consider, reckon) among the forty uses of the word in the NT. Paul's statement coheres with this teaching elsewhere that Christian love "keeps no record of wrongs" (1 Cor 13:5). The passive voice of the verb points to God, who would be the one to hold desertion "against them," that is, against other believers who might well have stood by his side. Paul asks that God show them his mercy.

17 The first word "But" (*de*) sets up a contrast between fickle people (v. 16) and "the Lord." Paul states a primary reason for his poise as he stood trial alone: God was with him. There are reverberations here with Ps 22 (LXX Ps 21); Paul, "like Jesus, entered the Psalm of messianic travail [i.e., Ps 22] . . . and came out of the other end of it (or would do so) in the strength of the Lord's presence."[371] Other LXX texts use the same verb for "stood" (*paristēmi*) to express divine presence. For example, the Lord "stood beside" Moses as he received the new stone tablets at Sinai (Exod 34:5). Second Temple conviction is voiced in Wis 19:22: "For in all things, O Lord, you magnified your people and glorified them and did not disregard them, standing by them in every time and place." God's people are set apart by the personal presence of their God, who is present to preserve them in the face of danger. This is as basic to biblical faith as the immortal Twenty-Third Psalm: "Yea, though I walk through the valley of the shadow of death, I will fear no evil: for thou art with me" (Ps 23:4 KJV). "Lord" refers to the risen Christ, who in Paul's postresurrection understanding fills the role played by YHWH for his forebears under OT auspices. Christ promised to be with his followers always (Matt 28:20), and Paul clings to this conviction.

The Lord did more than just show up: he fortified Paul ("gave me strength"). The same verb (*endynamoō*,[372] strengthen, empower) describes

370. So Johnson, *First and Second Letters to Timothy*, 442 (with caution).

371. See Towner, *Letters*, 641, with extensive argumentation.

372. It appears seven times in the NT, always in connection with Paul.

Saul's strengthening right after conversion (Acts 9:22), Abraham's confirmation in faith (Rom 4:20), and Paul's empowerment in an earlier imprisonment (Phil 4:13; cf. 1 Tim 1:12). Using the same word, Paul commends God's strengthening to the church (Eph 6:10) and to Timothy (2 Tim 2:1). In the next generation, as his own trial and martyrdom approach, Ignatius will extend and apply Paul's logic using a similar expression: "But in any case, 'near the sword' means 'near to God'; 'with the beasts' means 'with God.' Only let it be in the name of Jesus Christ, so that I may suffer together with him! I endure everything because he himself, who is the perfect human being, empowers me" (*Smyrn.* 4:2).[373]

It should be noted that Ignatius was empowered, not to evade the "beasts," but to identify fully with Christ in enduring whatever he was called on to face. Eventually the beasts won, in earthly terms. While Paul tells Timothy in v. 17, "I was delivered[374] from the lion's mouth"[375] and was no doubt happy to report it, indications are that eventually the grace of preservation morphed into the grace of martyrdom for Paul, as it did for Ignatius. Paul has already faced and reflected on this contingency (Phil 1:20–21). The sobering possibility of dying for Christ was as fundamental to Paul's theology of the cross as were the joyful possibility and necessity of living for Christ.

So Paul was strengthened, not for miraculous and sensational deliverance, but for an entirely different sort of purpose: that "through" (*dia*) him the apostolic "message" (*kērygma*)[376] of salvation in Christ "might be fully proclaimed." Neudorfer calls attention to the combination of humility (he served not by his own strength) and apostolic self-consciousness (it had been incumbent on him at all costs to take the gospel to the Gentiles) here.[377] Technically, the verb Paul chooses (*plērophoreō*; see discussion of the same word in 4:5) connotes completion, fulfillment, not proclamation. But in conjunction with "message" Paul must have in mind a full, or fully faithful, rendering of it. A second aspect of the purpose behind the Lord's presence and strengthening is that "all the Gentiles might hear it." On Paul as "apostle to the Gentiles," see Rom 11:13; Gal 2:8; 1 Tim 2:7. Paul is in Rome, not some backwater outpost; what happens to him there will echo across the Roman Empire. In that sense his witness to Christ under trial will ensure maximal reach at the nerve center

373. Ignatius uses Paul's verb in a genitive absolute construction: *autou me endynamountos tou teleiou anthrōpou.*

374. From *hryomai* (to save, deliver). See discussion in next verse.

375. Possibly a metaphorical expression referring not to actual lions but to Nero (Spencer, 152).

376. The word is used by Paul elsewhere in Rom 16:25; 1 Cor 1:21; 2:4; 15:14; Titus 1:3. More frequently he spoke of his message using not a noun but the verbs *kēryssō* (I proclaim; eighteen times) or *euangelizō* (I preach the good news; nineteen times).

377. Neudorfer, 283.

of the Gentile populace to which he had been called to devote his gospel labors for over two decades. Paul saw "a divine reason for" his arrest: "He could fulfill the mission that God had given him from the start on the Damascus Road to proclaim the gospel to the Gentiles even before the empire's highest dignitaries (Acts 27:24)."[378]

Hearing is all-important for Paul because it is a primary means of grace that constitutes God's people and bestows on them saving faith (Deut 6:4; Rom 10:17). Even if "all" did not receive it, Paul's courageous witness would help ensure that they had the chance.

18 "The Lord will rescue [future of *hryomai*, rescue, save, deliver] me" needs to be seen in light of v. 6: "the time of my departure is near." Paul expects death soon. God can deliver from danger and death: "He has delivered [aorist of *hryomai*] us from such a deadly peril, and he will deliver [future of *hryomai*] us again. On him we have set our hope that he will continue to deliver [future of *hryomai*] us" (2 Cor 1:10).[379] Even in death the believer is not separated from Christ (Rom 8:35–37). Paul believes in the resurrection, not only of Jesus in the past, but of believers in the future (1 Cor 15:51–57). Such a hope is displayed here.

Hope in God's future deliverance expressed with the same verb *hryomai* is expressed frequently in the LXX (NETS translation of *hryomai* in italics):

> I *will deliver* you from slavery. (Exod 6:6)
>
> He *will rescue* me from my powerful enemies and from those that hate me. (Ps 17:18 [MT 17])
>
> An angel of the Lord will encamp around those who fear him and will rescue them. (Ps 33:8 [MT 7])
>
> Treasures shall not profit the lawless, but righteousness *shall deliver* from death. (Prov 10:2)
>
> Which of the gods of all these nations *has delivered* [aorist] his land out of my hand, that God *should deliver* Ierousalem out of my hand? (Isa 36:20)
>
> I *shall rescue* them from the hand of Hades. (Hos 13:14)

In light of such LXX passages, Paul's expression of confidence in God's future saving work is an example of the same recourse to Holy Scripture of which he

378. Witherington, 381.

379. For other uses of *hryomai* in Paul, see Rom 7:24; 11:26; 15:31; Col 1:13; 1 Thess 1:10; 2 Thess 3:2; 2 Tim 3:11; 4:17.

reminded Timothy earlier (3:15). From another viewpoint, Johnson notes the strong echo of the Matthean Lord's Prayer here (Matt 6:13).[380]

"Every evil attack" covers any deed or incident that might be contrived to Paul's disadvantage, whether the devil's "schemes" (Eph 6:11) or "trap" (1 Tim 3:7; 2 Tim 2:26), the work of those like Alexander (4:14), or the timidity of fellow believers (4:16).

"Will bring me safely" refers to Christ's work of redemption that ensures the believers' arrival in "his heavenly[381] kingdom," that is, in heaven. "Bring safely" translates a form of *sōzō* (save, deliver), used here as a synonym for *hryomai* (see examples above). On the close connection between "saved" and "justified" in Paul, see Titus 3:7 and commentary there.

Paul's confidence in the Lord's rescue and heaven thereafter leads him to doxology: "To him be glory for ever and ever."[382] Ascription of glory (*doxa*) or other indicators of supernal quality that belong to God alone receive frequent enough mention in Paul[383] to suggest he was preoccupied with this image and aspect of God and Christ. Academicians may haggle over the ideas they associate with Paul's language about God, but Paul pondered a reality like that described in Isa 6 or 2 Pet 1 (the transfiguration). The Damascus Road experience, which would have etched the Lord's blinding radiance on Paul's memory,[384] had come in space and time, and in preparation for a costly commission: what would the reality be in God's eternal dimension (cf. 1 Cor 2:9) and as eternal reward? The "amen" confirms Paul's assurance or at least professed resolve and invites Timothy to join him in sober acknowledgment of divine excellence, even in the face of loss of earthly life.

C. Final Greetings (4:19–22)

In terse concluding remarks touching on people and places dwarfed by the transcendent image in the previous verse, Paul requests that greetings be conveyed to his longtime associates Priscilla and Aquila and to the household of a certain Onesiphorus. He passes along word of two coworkers whom Timothy must have known. He underscores his need for Timothy to visit him soon and adds greetings from four named individuals plus other unnamed

380. Johnson, *First and Second Letters to Timothy*, 443.

381. For the other eleven Pauline uses of *epouranios* (heavenly), see 1 Cor 15:40 (twice), 48 (twice), 49; Eph 1:3, 20; 2:6; 3:10; 6:12; Phil 2:10.

382. On *eis tous aiōnas tōn aiōnōn* (for ever and ever), see Harris, *Prepositions and Theology*, 95.

383. See also Rom 1:25; 9:5; 11:36; 16:27; 2 Cor 1:20; Gal 1:5; Eph 3:21; Phil 4:20; 1 Tim 1:17; 6:16.

384. Acts 9:1–19; 22:3–16; 26:9–18.

"brothers and sisters" (v. 21). He concludes with a benediction for Timothy personally and then another for the church (v. 22). Though the epistle has been addressed to Timothy, the shift to the second person plural in the final word (*hymōn*, "you all") reminds readers that it "belongs to the entire church," so that "its charges, its warnings, and its promises are ours and as poignant as ever."[385]

Towner wisely comments that we see in these remarks "more of the human side of the writer." He continues: "At the end, he is concerned for the friendships that he has made over the years, and desires that these friends know of his continued feelings for them in the hardest of times."[386]

> [19] *Greet Priscilla and Aquila and the household of Onesiphorus.* [20] *Erastus stayed in Corinth, and I left Trophimus sick in Miletus.* [21] *Do your best to get here before winter. Eubulus greets you, and so do Pudens, Linus, Claudia and all the brothers and sisters.* [22] *The Lord be with your spirit. Grace be with you all.*

19 Passing along greetings (using the verb *aspazomai*, welcome, greet) is not uncommon in letters of Paul (Rom 16:3–16; 2 Cor 13:13; Phlm 23–24) and of other early Christians (Heb 13:23–24; 1 Pet 5:13–14). Priscilla (diminutive of Priska)[387] and Aquila must be near Timothy and perhaps in Ephesus. This married couple is encountered first in Acts 18:2, which states that the husband was a Jew from Pontus in Asia Minor. At some point they became Christians, as is clear from other NT references (Acts 18:18, 19, 26; Rom 16:3; 1 Cor 16:19).

Out of a total of six references in the NT, Priscilla is named first four times (Aquila is first in Acts 18:2; 1 Cor 16:19). Towner joins many in recent years in finding it "striking" that Priscilla is *ever* mentioned first, but six references with a 4:2 split is a slender database. Perhaps the four times she is mentioned first point to higher "social status or greater importance in the church's ministry."[388] Yet, Knight's suggestion that Paul is being courteous is not (contra Towner) "historically improbable." Knight also quite reasonably suggests that NT usage "may reflect [Paul's] gratitude in that the couple's hospitality toward him involved her in considerably more work."[389] Another possibility is that Paul (and Luke) simply resonated with Priscilla and out of admiration or affection sometimes named her first. Or perhaps she had attention-getting traits, appearance, or skills in the trade she shared with Aquila (like Paul they were

385. Laansma, 219.
386. Towner, *Letters*, 649.
387. See BDAG 864.
388. Towner, *Letters*, 651.
389. Knight, 475, 476.

tentmakers) that made her stand out. Luke's use of the diminutive (Paul always uses the more formal Priska) may point to an unmistakable pluck, charm, or competence. Maybe Aquila had a flat personality by comparison. Or perhaps Aquila, heeding Paul's word to the Ephesians (Eph 5:25), so elevated his wife by his love for her that those who knew them sometimes viewed her first in the relationship just like Aquila did.

In any case, like Jesus seemed to have drawn important comfort from Lazarus, Martha, and Mary, Paul had a rich association with this couple who stayed with him, no doubt buoyed him, and perhaps (in part through prayer) anchored him till the end. He wants Timothy to make sure they know this. It may be significant that they are the first people he mentions in this section; perhaps that indicates they were as close to Timothy as they were to Paul.

On Onesiphorus, see remarks at 1:16–18. These are the only NT references to him. Paul's greeting could be directed to his "household" as a way of including him and all his family (and perhaps associated house church). Or Paul may know that Onesiphorus is away, or even deceased, yet wishes to greet those who are still present.[390] Another possibility is that Priscilla and Aquila are somehow making common cause with Onesiphorus and his family circle (the meaning of "household" here), so it is appropriate for Paul to greet them all at once.

20 "Erastus" appears only two other times in the NT (Acts 19:22; Rom 16:23). For those who view 2 Timothy as pseudepigraphic, Trevor W. Thompson's verdict might seem plausible: "The author of 2 Timothy likely borrowed the name from Romans and employed it as part of a literary fiction designed to create an aura of verisimilitude."[391] Thompson also argues that that Erastus of Acts 19 and the Erasmus of Rom 16 cannot have been the same person. Evidence is not conclusive,[392] but Marshall's conclusion that all NT references refer to the same Corinthian named as a city administrator in Rom 16:23 cannot be ruled out.[393]

Trophimus was an Ephesian who worked with Paul earlier (Acts 20:4; 21:29), accompanying him to Jerusalem with the collection for the stressed believers there. He would have heard Paul's sermon on the Miletus beach near Ephesus (Acts 20:17–38). Now it seems in Paul's recent travels that Trophimus has taken ill. Paul knew that God sometimes allows "weaknesses [a word cognate with 'sick' in 2 Tim 4:20], insults, hardships, persecutions, and calamities" (2 Cor 12:10). None of these is pleasant, and most people are spared most of them most of the time. Yet, the unwanted, including sickness, comes. This is in part because when a believer is "weak" or sick, then by God's aid that same

390. Cf. Marshall, with Towner, 828.

391. Trevor Thompson, "Erastus," *EBR* 7:1126.

392. Montague, 208: "We will probably never know for sure."

393. Marshall, with Towner, 828–29. So also Collins, 290; Laansma, 218.

person may in fact be in a place of great strength. Paul does not despair but mentions the case to Timothy, perhaps just for information about a mutual friend, perhaps for Timothy's prayer consideration, and perhaps most likely for both.

21 In 2 Tim 1:4 Paul spoke of his strong desire to see Timothy. He repeated this wish in 4:9 and added that Timothy should come "quickly." Now he states Timothy should arrive "before winter." Paul's strong faith in God did not reduce his sense of dependence on fellow believers in previous verses, and his long-term co-labor with Timothy did not lessen the need he felt for the younger man's presence during what Paul understood as most likely his last days. Regarding Paul's reference to "before winter," sea lanes were closed from around early November until early March because of storms. If Timothy did not arrive soon, Paul might not survive long enough to see him at all.

The four names mentioned appear nowhere else in the NT. The first three are male and the last female. Mounce suggests "they were leaders in the Roman church" but gives no reason for the assertion.[394] Since Paul passes on their greetings to Timothy, one wonders why they did not support Paul at his trial (v. 16). Perhaps they lacked social standing to make any difference in such a situation, or perhaps it would have exposed them to inordinate danger to appear to stand at Paul's side. Paul does not feel it necessary to account for these details with Timothy. The NIV implies that Eubulus sends greetings first, and then so do others. But this is merely to jazz up the flat diction of the Greek, which reads simply, "Eubulus, Linus, Claudia, and all the brothers [i.e., men and women who are believers] greet you." The Greek verb is singular because in a series, the verb usually takes its number from the nearest subject nominative.

Eubulus is a common Greek name,[395] but nothing more about this person is known. The next three names are Latin. The name Pudens is attested outside the NT,[396] but later references add nothing shedding historical light on 2 Timothy. Irenaeus says that Linus served as the first bishop of Rome, followed by Anacletus and Clement (*Against Heresies* 3.3.3). If Linus here in the text was this bishop, Paul shows no signs of recognizing such prominence but simply includes him in a list of names. Claudia was a common name with possible royal associations,[397] but the significance of this possibility for the person named here is uncertain.[398]

394. Mounce, 601.

395. Collins, 291; Trevor Thompson, "Eubulus," *EBR* 8:166–67.

396. MM 531.

397. Collins, 292.

398. For concise assessment of the ancient references and their value, see Ray Van Neste, "Claudia," *EBR* 5:398–99: "In the end, there is far too little evidence to make any certain

22 Paul ends the epistle by wishing for Timothy the Lord's presence with his spirit—in other words, that Timothy would personally know and sense that Christ is with him. "Grace be with you all" shifts to the plural, evidently addressing Timothy's fellow leaders (like Priscilla or Aquila; v. 19) or perhaps his congregation (as in 1 Tim 6:21: "Grace be with you all"; cf. Titus 3:15). Paul's final word to Timothy confirms that Timothy does not stand before God or his congregation alone but as a member of the body of Christ. Paul commends to Timothy the same individual yet ecclesial consciousness that bears up Paul in his final days of intermingled grave concern yet eternal hope.

---

identification of the Claudia mentioned in 2 Tim 4:21." For additional reflection on the names in this verse, see Neudorfer, *Zweiter Brief an Timotheus*, 297–98.

The Letter of TITUS

The Text and Title of Titus

As was the case for 1 and 2 Timothy, modern translations are based on a stable and reliable text, for Titus is attested most prominently by two papyri (P^{32} P^{61}),[1] sixteen uncials (א A C D F G H I K L P Y 048 088 0240 0278),[2] eleven minuscules (33 81 104 365 630 1175 1241 1505 1506 1739 1881), and two lectionaries (*l*249 *l*846). These thirty-one texts are "consistently and frequently cited" in the Nestle-Aland apparatus.[3] Numerous additional Greek (and Latin) witnesses could be listed, but they would add nothing significant to these nearly three dozen copies deemed foundational by specialists in the field for determining with relative certainty what the original author of Titus composed.

In the NIV translation, there are no footnotes on the Greek text (as there are, e.g., at the end of the Gospel of Mark or at 1 John 5:8), an indication that there is little dispute about the wording of the original manuscript of this epistle. While there will always be debates about how words and passages in Titus should be interpreted, what the original author or authors first wrote will be regarded as generally established for purposes of this commentary.

Textual critics still debate the precise original wording of the Greek text of Titus in a dozen places. Six of these are of purely antiquarian interest,[4] though the last of these bears comment: Metzger notes that there are, technically speaking, ten different "titles" to this epistle (commonly preserved as "subscriptions," or final comments to the manuscripts). These range from "To Titus" to "To Titus, Written from Nicopolis" to "The Epistle of the Apostle Paul

1. P^{32} dates to around AD 200 and contains Titus 1:11–15; 2:3–8. P^{61} dates to around AD 700 and contains Titus 3:1–5, 8–11, 14–15. See *The Greek-English New Testament*, 1583, 1585. See also Marshall, with Towner, 8–11; J. K. Elliott, *The Greek Text of the Epistles to Timothy and Titus*, Studies and Documents 36 (Salt Lake City: University of Utah Press, 1968).

2. א, a fourth-century MS, also called Sinaiticus, contains the earliest complete copy of the PE; see Towner, *Letters*, 9.

3. *The Greek-English New Testament*, xxvii. For the listing of witnesses in Titus, see xxix.

4. See Metzger, *Textual Commentary* (1994), 584–87. See on variants at Titus 1:9, 11; 2:5, 7; 3:9, 15.

to Titus the First Appointed Bishop of the Church of the Cretans, Written from Nicopolis of Macedonia." Such divergences and bits of lore commonly accumulated as scribes copied manuscripts over the centuries. The information may or may not be verifiable. What is consistent in all copies (not only Greek but also Coptic and Syriac) is that Titus was the recipient. This would have been evident from Titus 1:4, just as Paul's status as writer (not always noted in the "titles" of other ancient manuscripts) is evident from the epistle's first word.

In all of Titus there are only four variant readings to which the United Bible Societies assigned a rating in their four-letter system of A (virtually certain) to D (evidence is divided). These variants are found at 1:4, 10; 3:1 (all rated C) and 3:15 (rated B). Each will be treated in the comments below.

Outline of Titus

I. Greeting (1:1–4)
II. Confirmation of Titus's Mission (1:5–9)
III. Description of the Gospel's Opponents (1:10–16)
IV. Summary for Pastoral Direction (2:1–10)
V. Motivation for Ministry (2:11–15)
VI. Standing Orders for Believers (3:1–11)
VII. Closing Requests and Blessing (3:12–15)

Commentary on Titus

I. GREETING (1:1-4)

Paul follows the letter-writing style of his locale and era in beginning this epistle: he states his name. Other elements of a typical prescript were the addressee's name (in this case Titus),[1] a greeting, a blessing, and a prayer. In this epistle Paul dispenses with the prayer. But even more fundamentally, compared with other Pauline openings, this one is unusual, as the third column of table 24 indicates. "Titus begins with one of the longest, and most complex, salutations of the canonical Pauline corpus."[2]

Table 24. Pauline prescripts

Pauline epistle and first word	Addressee(s)	Number of Greek words between Paul's name and the addressee(s)
Romans: "Paul"	To all in Rome	71
1 Corinthians: "Paul"	To the church of God in Corinth	11
2 Corinthians: "Paul"	To the church of God in Corinth	10
Galatians: "Paul"	To the churches in Galatia	25

1. On Titus, coworker of Paul, see commentary Introduction, VIII.A.

2. Twomey, 190.

Pauline epistle and first word	Addressee(s)	Number of Greek words between Paul's name and the addressee(s)
Ephesians: "Paul"	To God's holy people in Ephesus	6
Philippians: "Paul"	To all God's holy people in Christ Jesus at Philippi	5
Colossians: "Paul"	To God's holy people in Colossae	14
1 Thessalonians: "Paul"	To the church of the Thessalonians	4
2 Thessalonians: "Paul"	To the church of the Thessalonians	4
1 Timothy: "Paul"	To Timothy my true son in the faith	14
2 Timothy: "Paul"	To Timothy, my dear son	13
Titus: "Paul"	**To Titus, my true son in our common faith**	**46**
Philemon: "Paul"	To Philemon our dear friend and fellow worker	7

Only Romans has a lengthier prescript than Titus, with Galatians a distant third. Between the first word of this epistle ("Paul") and the name of the recipient ("Titus"), Paul sandwiches a wealth of historical and doctrinal information.

Details of these data will emerge in discussion of individual verses below, but a preliminary observation is in order. This lengthy prescript foreshadows the substance of the epistle. Spencer asserts that "all the components of the letter are present in microcosm in the introduction."[3] Prominent in the prescript is, first, "God," a word that occurs five times in the first four verses[4] and is implied even more frequently. "Jesus Christ" (v. 1) and "Christ Jesus (v. 4) join "God" in bracketing the prescript fore and aft. "Savior" is also a significant repeated word (vv. 3, 4).

3. Spencer, 6.

4. Unless otherwise noted, word counts are based on NA[28] as determined by Accordance 11 Bible Software.

The second prominent word is "faith," and not just the word alone but the two prepositional phrases in which it appears. Paul writes "to further the faith of God's elect" (v. 1), to Titus his "true son in our common faith" (v. 4). There is symmetry in the original that translation may obscure, as this transliteration indicates:

> v. 1: to further the faith of God's elect = *kata pistin eklektōn theou*
> v. 4: in our common faith = *kata koinēn pistin*

The underlined words in isolation can be rendered "in accordance with faith" (so, e.g., KJV, ASV, GNV, JUB). The NIV translates slightly differently because of contextual considerations.[5] But this should not hide the prominence of "faith," just like "God," at the beginning and end of the prescript. And viewed more broadly, "faith" turns out to be one of the most frequently occurring nouns in Titus, appearing six times. Only the nouns "God" (13x), "work" (8x), and "Savior" (6x) rival "faith" in frequency of appearance. Thus Paul serves notice at the outset that he writes to ensure that God and faith receive their due in the ministry with which Titus has been entrusted.

> [1]*Paul, a servant of God and an apostle of Jesus Christ to further the faith of God's elect and their knowledge of the truth that leads to godliness—*[2]*in the hope of eternal life, which God, who does not lie, promised before the beginning of time,* [3]*and which now at his appointed season he has brought to light through the preaching entrusted to me by the command of God our Savior,* [4]*To Titus, my true son in our common faith: Grace and peace from God the Father and Christ Jesus our Savior.*

1 Paul identifies himself as "a servant [*doulos*] of God."[6] This is slightly unusual; in Paul's other letter prescripts, only in Romans and Philippians (where he pairs himself with Timothy as "servants") does he call himself a "servant."[7]

5. For defense of the NIV handling of *kata* as "to further" rather than "in accordance with," see Harris, *Prepositions and Theology*, 159–60. For the understanding of "according to," see Dibelius and Conzelmann, 131.

6. Some commentators stress the "slave" connotation of *doulos* (e.g., Gloer, 19–20), as do many translations and paraphrases: CEB, JUB, LEB, MSG, NET, TLB, TLV. For extended treatment, see Harris, *Slave of Christ*.

7. In the Romans and Philippians passages Paul calls himself a servant of "Christ Jesus." R. H. Williams, *Stewards, Prophets, Keepers of the Word: Leadership in the Early Church* (Peabody, MA: Hendrickson, 2006), 86, thinks this wording constitutes evidence that that is the real Paul, while in Titus 1:1, in contrast, "the pseudo-Pauline author has Paul introduce himself as God's slave." But this argument is hardly compelling, in part because it minimizes the extent to which "Christ Jesus" and "God" overlap in Paul's thought and language. To be servant of one is at once to be a servant of the other.

In this he joins Peter (2 Pet 1:1: "a servant . . . of Jesus Christ"), James (Jas 1:1: "a servant of God"), and Jude (Jude 1: "a servant of Jesus Christ"). Jesus taught that those who count as leaders among his disciples are to regard themselves as the servants, even slaves, of others (Matt 20:27). With Paul's opening words he confirms his endorsement of Jesus's leadership philosophy. But this is not menial self-effacement or a self-denigrating slur. Paul is a servant "of God," who uplifts those who are lowly for his sake, as Jesus's teaching in the Beatitudes makes clear (Matt 5:1–12). Paul will dispense apostolic counsel in this epistle. But he does so by presenting Jesus Christ as Lord, not himself, and Paul as a servant for God's sake (see 2 Cor 4:5).

Being a "servant" does not contradict but helps define what Paul means by being "an apostle of Jesus Christ." The construction[8] may imply that yes, Paul is a servant—but that fact should not detract in any way from his apostolic rank. Paul had been called by Christ, who made known to him at his conversion that he was "a chosen instrument" to testify to Christ before all, both Gentile and Jew (Acts 9:15). By the time Paul writes to Titus, he has been living out this calling for three decades. It is second nature for Paul to affirm this by referring to himself as an apostle here. The only Pauline letters in which Paul does not open with this self-designation are epistles in which he begins by listing himself with coworkers.[9]

Paul's servanthood and apostleship have a particular and twofold goal. First, they are "to further the faith of God's elect." Paul's life had long centered on enduring "everything for the sake of the elect, that they too may obtain the salvation that is in Christ Jesus, with eternal glory" (2 Tim 2:10). Paul calls believers by this same word "elect" (*eklektos*) in Rom 8:33 and Col 3:12 (where it is translated "those whom God has chosen"). This designation has ancient grounding in God's sovereign and gracious choice of a redeemed people through the calling of Abraham and his descendants (Gen 12; see also Rom 9:11; 11:28). Jesus likewise called his followers, particularly those who remain faithful through great trial, "the elect" (Matt 24:22, 24, 31). In broad biblical perspective, few concepts are more basic to the identity of God's people than being chosen by God. Whatever Paul writes in this letter, it will extend and solidify that identity.

A second goal of Paul's servanthood and apostleship pertains to "their knowledge of the truth that leads to godliness,"[10] with "their" referring to

8. Paul does not use the simple "and" (*kai*) to link "servant" and "apostle" in v. 1 but *de*, which could give a concessive force to "servant of God."

9. See Phil 1:1 and Phlm 1 (with Timothy); 1 Thess 1:1 and 2 Thess 1:1 (with Silas and Timothy).

10. "Their" is inferred from the context. "Truth" in Greek is anarthrous; on the possibly "arbitrary" usage of the article here, see C. F. D. Moule, *An Idiom Book of New Testament Greek*, 2d ed. (Cambridge: Cambridge University Press, 1994), 112.

God's elect. This knowledge (see discussion below in v. 4) can also be understood as "in accordance with godliness."[11] It is not vague or random piety but has a norm. Such "godliness" (*eusebeia*; see commentary Introduction, IX.B) is a prominent theme in 1 Timothy (2:2; 3:16; 4:7, 8; 6:3, 5, 6, 11; also 2 Tim 3:5). At roughly the same time of the AD 60s, Peter exhorted his readers to this same quality of character (2 Pet 1:3, 6, 7; 3:11). Such "godliness" is the practical expression, the living out in real life situations, of the knowledge of God that easily veers off into abstract conviction that is mentally stimulating but practically barren. In contrast to a merely theoretical, confessional, or speculative "truth" (note 2 Tim 3:7: "always learning but never able to come to a knowledge of the truth"), Paul writes to commend "knowledge of the truth" that will make a difference for his readers' religious disposition, which affects their everyday affairs, relationships, and actions. This practical emphasis paves the way for Paul's stress on works in later sections of this epistle. Paul may be using "truth" in a way that foreshadows a polemical or apologetic stance toward opponents of his apostolic status or message.[12]

2 The practical godliness Paul calls for has a theological basis—more precisely, an eschatological one. It rests on "the hope of eternal life."[13] This comment refers first of all not to hope as "an inward disposition" but to "the object of hope."[14] Yet, this objective expectation produced a subjective conviction. "Deep within the mind and imagination of most first-century Jews lay the belief that world history itself is divided into two 'ages': the present age and the age to come."[15] As a Jew, and drawing from the Old Testament, Paul carried the conviction that beyond this world lay another, already inhabited and prepared by God. Consistent with this perspective Jesus (also a Jew) promised "eternal life" to his followers (Matt 19:29) and "eternal punishment" to others (Matt 25:46), which John's Gospel in particular stresses.[16] Paul speaks of "eternal life" explicitly in Romans (2:7; 5:21), Galatians (6:8), and 1 Timothy (1:16; 6:12). And Paul often has "eternal life" in mind when he does not use the expression, as when he speaks about resurrection (see, e.g., 1 Cor 15). It is not surprising that he opens this letter with reference to such a fundamental aspect of Christian belief. P. Jeon goes so far as to say that "the hope of eternal life" is the main theme of this entire epistle, especially

11. Gloer, 29: "'according to godliness,' i.e., a life pleasing to God." So also Calvin, 353.

12. Marshall, with Towner, 122, 168.

13. On the grammar of the clauses, see BDF §469; N. Turner, *Syntax*, vol. 3 of *A Grammar of New Testament Greek* (Edinburgh: T&T Clark, 1963), 325.

14. Harris, *Prepositions and Theology*, 76, with appeal to similar constructions in Col 1:4–5; 1 Pet 1:4.

15. Wright, 139.

16. See John 3:15, 16, 36; 4:14, 36; 5:24, 39; 6:27, 40, 54, 68; 10:28; 12:25, 50; 17:2, 3.

insofar as Paul calls to Titus to "exhort and reprove to commendable works according to" this hope.[17]

Paul's reference to eternal life reminds Titus at the outset of the otherworldly dimension of his very this-worldly assignment. Titus has responsibilities on Crete. Like a pastoral overseer anywhere, he faces tangible and tawdry obstacles in the form of "rebellious people" (Titus 1:10), the unholy urges that guide them, and the deleterious effects they produce. Moreover, Christians of all people are acutely conscious of their own past lives, when they too were "foolish, disobedient, deceived and enslaved by all kinds of passions and pleasures" (3:3). Nor, in Paul's writings, are Christians perfect in all their ways at the present time; otherwise, Paul's ethical counsel would be either superfluous or tantamount to the charge that his churchly readers were as yet actually outside the pale of God's saving grace. But the faith and knowledge given believers in the gospel message introduce a transforming dynamic because they rest on what pertains to the age to come—God and his promises, which are already powerfully at work at the present time. Consciousness of this truth is necessary for Titus to face his situation with the optimism and courage that his concrete circumstances require. Adolf Schlatter comments: "Man cannot conjure up the hope of eternal life by his thoughts and moods; it requires a firm basis in God's action. It can only arise from the facts of the divine reign."[18] The future God promises is more powerful in this fallen world than the seemingly intractable evil and setbacks than can easily darken church leaders' vision, skew their judgment, and extinguish their hope.

Paul can concretize the implications of an invisible future because the God of whom Scripture speaks "does not lie."[19] This truth is axiomatic in the Old Testament: "He who is the Glory of Israel does not lie" (1 Sam 15:29); "God is not human, that he should lie" (Num 23:19). He is rather "the God of truth" (Ps 31:5 KJV, HCSB, NLV; Isa 65:16). This is also axiomatic for Paul:[20] "Let God be true, and every human being a liar" (Rom 3:4). So Paul refers Titus to "the hope of eternal life" (see discussion at Titus 3:7 below) with complete assurance because, as the eternal sovereign being who cannot lie (cf. Heb 6:18), God and his promises cannot possibly fail. Moreover, "this leads to a knowledge of the truth: not just guesswork, not just humans groping in the dark to try to discover something about God,

17. P. Jeon, *To Exhort and Reprove: Audience Response to the Chiastic Structures of Paul's Letter to Titus* (Eugene, OR: Pickwick, 2012), 1, 127, and throughout.

18. Schlatter, *Die Briefe*, 245.

19. Note parallel (without definite article) to *ho apseudēs theos* ["the nonlying God"] in Euripides, *Orestes* 364; see *NW* 1012.

20. As it was for Plato (*Republic* 2.382e; *NW* 1012): "There is nothing for the sake of which God could lie." But Socrates spoke within a polytheistic framework of "the gods."

but revealed truth you can stake your life on."[21] God's fidelity to truth and fact, and its salubrious effects on those who trust in his promises, would stand in stark contrast to the chicanery of the deities of Greco-Roman mythology.[22] "Indeed the only foundation of all religion is the unchangeable truth of God."[23]

God's promises pertain not only to the coming age but to eternity past, "before [*pro*][24] the beginning of time." The prickly present that Paul and Titus must negotiate as spiritual leaders is bracketed by God's steadfastness at the start and finish of all that is historical, social, and earthly. Paul's affirmation here that "God . . . promised" eternal life "before the beginning of time"[25] echoes his reminder to Timothy that saving grace "was given us in Christ Jesus before the beginning of time" (2 Tim 1:9). Eternal life and Jesus Christ, prior to this age and after it terminates, are intertwined as benefit and benefactor. Both are guaranteed by an utterly truthful and therefore dependable God who dwells not only in but beyond time.[26] Abraham was "fully persuaded that God had power to do what he had promised" (Rom 4:21). Paul had stood trial "because of my hope in what God has promised" (Acts 26:6). Paul's opening words lay the foundation for this to be Titus's stance, too. (On eternal life, see also Titus 3:7 and discussion below.)

3 Paul's conviction regarding God's steadfastness pertains not only to what God promised but to what he has "now" revealed.

There is a critical time element to God's revelatory activity. "At his appointed season" translates a plural form of *kairos*, "season," a word often connoting the aptness of the hour[27] rather than the chronological location of an event (see BDAG 497). Paul uses the plural form eight times, listed in table 25.

21. Wright, 141.

22. Baugh, 98.

23. Calvin, 354.

24. Wallace, *Greek Grammar*, 379, classifies this as one of about a dozen "significant passages" in the New Testament using the preposition *pro*. See also Harris, *Prepositions and Theology*, 185.

25. J. H. Bernard, *The Pastoral Epistles* (repr., Grand Rapids: Eerdmans, 1980), 155: "The promise was made before time was, in the eternal purpose of God."

26. Cf. Quinn, 65: "before the beginning of time" refers to "the timeless order in which God himself lives in contrast to the . . . countless ages through which his creatures have come and gone."

27. Here and at Gal 6:9; 1 Tim 2:6; 6:15, Wallace, *Greek Grammar*, 157, suggests "something like 'at just the right moment.'"

Table 25. Plural use of *kairos* in Paul

PASSAGE	NIV TRANSLATION OF *KAIROS* UNDERLINED
Gal 4:10	You are observing special days and months and *seasons* and years!
*Eph 1:10	. . . to be put into effect when the *times* reach their fulfillment—to bring unity to all things in heaven and on earth under Christ.
*1 Thess 5:1	Now, brothers and sisters, about times and *dates* we do not need to write to you.
*1 Tim 2:6	. . . who gave himself as a ransom for all people. This has now been witnessed to at the proper *time*.
1 Tim 4:1	The Spirit clearly says that in later *times* some will abandon the faith and follow deceiving spirits and things taught by demons.
*1 Tim 6:15	. . . which God will bring about in his own *time*—God, the blessed and only Ruler, the King of kings and Lord of lords.
2 Tim 3:1	But mark this: There will be terrible *times* in the last days.

In speaking of God's "appointed season," Paul reflects usage in the passages in table 25 marked with an asterisk (*). They reflect "the Pauline philosophy of history as expressed in the Pastoral Epistles."[28] God is at work in human history, which he superintends in his own ways and for his eternal purposes. (Ramsay finds a parallel here in Homer's *Illiad*.) At the center of that purpose is Christ. As Ramsay states with regard to Titus 1:2–3, "The promise of God, given and published long ago, had never been rightly understood until its true meaning was declared through the crucifixion."[29] Paul reminds Titus of the epochal, cosmic, and temporal "cross"-road at which he and the Cretan churches stand.

In this "season"—a time period covering roughly the life of Jesus and the apostolic age—God "brought his word [*logos*] to light," in the words of NIV84.[30] This assertion could refer to how God has fulfilled Old Testament Scripture,

28. Ramsay, 137–41.

29. Ramsay, 141.

30. NIV inserts "which" at the beginning of v. 3, referring to the "eternal life" mentioned in v. 2. It is this eternal life "which now . . . [God] has brought to light through the preaching" (v. 3). This translation either omits *ton logon autou* (his word) or collapses it into "the preaching." NIV84 does better justice to Paul's admittedly awkward phrasing: "and at his appointed season he brought his word to light. . . ."

since Paul can use *logos* to refer to it (Rom 9:6, 9; 13:9; 1 Cor 15:54; Gal 5:14). Or it could refer to the gospel message: "For the message [*logos*] of the cross is foolishness to those who are perishing, but to us who are being saved it is the power of God" (1 Cor 1:18). "The *word* here is the preached word by means of which God in Christ is made known."[31] Since the message is foretold in the Old Testament, there is not a sharp distinction between the two.

God's "word" surged into public view "through the preaching entrusted to" Paul.[32] Paul is of course not suggesting that he is the only person to have preached Christ in his time. But he may be harking back to the awareness conveyed to him via Ananias at Paul's conversion: "This man is my [God's] chosen instrument to proclaim my name to the Gentiles and their kings and to the people of Israel. I will show him how much he must suffer for my name" (Acts 9:15–16). Certainly the Pauline mission thrust forth the gospel message with an enormous force and effect, particularly in the vast sweep of the Roman Empire.[33] And this was at great personal cost to Paul (see 2 Cor 11:23–33). The mystery of the ages as it related to Christ's mission had been disclosed to Paul in a manner that distinguished him even among the other apostles (see Eph 3:2–9). This being "entrusted"[34] is a significant marker across a sweep of Paul's writings: as a Jew whose race had long been "entrusted with the very words of God" (Rom 3:2), Paul via Christ's calling had gone a giant step further: he had been entrusted with a stewardship (1 Cor 9:17), with "the task of preaching the gospel to the uncircumcised" (Gal 2:7), "with the gospel" (1 Thess 2:4), and with "the gospel concerning the glory of the blessed God" (1 Tim 1:11). He reflects this same consciousness in his opening words to Titus.

With "brought to light," Paul has in mind the direct revelatory work of God. How else would he fulfill his promise? *Who* else could bring it about? It could occur only by revelation, by which God had made known his divine attributes (Rom 1:9), his righteousness (Rom 3:21), his saving mystery (Rom 16:26), hidden human motives (1 Cor 4:5), the fragrance of the knowledge of Christ (2 Cor 2:14), and much else. In the PE Paul uses the same verb in 1 Tim 3:16 ("He appeared [was revealed] in the flesh") and 2 Tim 1:10 ("[grace] has now been revealed through the appearing of our Savior, Christ Jesus"). Titus can have confidence because gospel ministry does not need to invent a marketable commodity but merely commend what God has already fully made known.

31. Hanson, 170 (italics in original).

32. On the construction involving the passive voice of *pisteuō*, see Harris, *Prepositions and Theology*, 233.

33. Schnabel, *Paul and the Early Church*, 923–1485.

34. Scripture references in this sentence all translate a form of *pisteuō* in the passive voice.

The "command [*epitagē*][35] of God our Savior," which resulted in Paul preaching, surely relates to the "command" by which he became an apostle (1 Tim 1:1; see also references to Paul's conversion above). More fundamentally, it can hardly be separated from the mystery "now revealed and made known through the prophetic writings by the command [*epitagēn*] of the eternal God, so that all the Gentiles might come to the obedience that comes from faith" (Rom 16:26), in the outworking of which Paul as "apostle to the Gentiles" was a central figure. Both he and Titus serve a movement and a Savior[36] far greater than pressing issues to be faced in Crete.

4 After a bracing series of theological and historical affirmations and qualifiers, Paul finally comes to the epistle's addressee: "To Titus."[37] He is Paul's "true son," which likely implies that Paul had a hand in Titus's coming to faith. Paul uses similar language of Timothy (1 Tim 1:2). "True" here is not the opposite of "false," as if Paul might have treacherous sons, too; it rather refers to Titus's authenticity—he is genuine in his conviction and service; as a disciple and coworker, he is the real thing (cf. Phil 2:20, 22 regarding Timothy). Paul elsewhere refers to himself as the "father" of those who received Christ through his missionary or pastoral efforts (1 Cor 4:15; cf. 1 Thess 2:11; Phlm 10). Paul's expression of fatherly nurture is a reminder that the religion he represents, like the God he serves, has love as both inner essence (1 John 4:8) and outward marker (Matt 22:34–40).

Paul and Titus share a "common faith." This shared commitment certainly includes their experience of believing in Jesus,[38] what theologians call *fides qua creditur* (personal faith that is placed in something or someone). But it likely refers still more to the substance of what both have believed in, the *fides quae creditur*, or core content of the Christian faith. The extent to which God—Father, Son, and Holy Spirit—pervades the PE was explored at the beginning of this commentary (see Introduction, III–V). Knowing him is not only experiential and relational; it has cognitive dimensions. Thus Paul has spoken of "knowledge" (*epignōsis*) in vv. 2 and 3 in conjunction with faith. In biblical parlance the two are inseparable, in contrast to a common Western understanding that views "faith" as antithetical to "knowledge." The glue binding Paul and Titus is "the faith that was once for all entrusted to the saints" (Jude 3), faith with cognitive substance (e.g., that God exists; that he created the world; that he rules over all things; that he sent his Son, who died for sin and rose from the dead; that he gave Scripture by inspiration). This common

35. MM 247: "The use of the word in Paul to denote a *divine* command . . . is in accord with its technical use in dedicatory inscriptions."

36. On "Savior" in the PE, see commentary Introduction, IX.A.

37. On Titus, see commentary Introduction, VIII.A.

38. Witherington, 105.

faith has implications for ministry and life, some of which Paul will unfold in this epistle. That he can do so with such confidence in Titus's understanding and receptivity is a tribute to a "common faith" that Christians have affirmed since earliest generations. It is more than mental "knowledge," and it is not merely confessed assent. But neither is it nothing but a shared, undefined, inner religious experience called "faith."

Testimony to this common faith concludes the epistle's opening section: "Grace and peace from God the Father and Christ Jesus our Savior."[39] Necessary, universal, and revealed aspects of Christian knowledge of God here include God's identity as Father and Son, his incarnate self-disclosure through Jesus Christ, his role (both as Father and as Son) as Savior, and his redemptive benefits extended to this fallen world: "Grace and peace." As Paul prepares to launch into the meat of his directions to Titus, his starting point is, first, the "grace" that brings salvation (Titus 2:11) and justifies sinners (3:7). It is also the "peace" (in the Old Testament *šālôm*) that Christ has brought to the world through his reconciling death (see Eph 2:14–16). Both grace and peace flow from Father and Son. Titus's task upon reading this epistle will be to administer those benefits amid churches beset by ills and hankering for direction. True to his calling as servant of God and apostle of Christ (v. 1), with brevity but with power, Paul will give counsel for realization of that same grace and peace.

II. CONFIRMATION OF TITUS'S MISSION (1:5–9)

To understand this section, it is necessary to look ahead in the epistle. In v. 10 Paul will point to "many rebellious people." In fact the whole next section (vv. 10–16) will furnish a profile of the pastoral problem Titus faces in the form of some people who are "full of meaningless talk and deception" (v. 10). What is Titus to do? Paul tells him: "You . . . must teach what is appropriate to sound doctrine" (2:1). That is not all Titus must do. For example, like any Christian, he must mind the integrity of his own personal life before God. He must select good leaders, "elders," a term roughly synonymous with the "overseers" spoken of in 1 Tim 3.[40] He must encourage people in the churches.

39. Some MSS (including A C^2 K L 81, the Textus Receptus, and others) insert "mercy" (*eleos*) after "grace." Metzger, *Textual Commentary* (1994), 584, notes that Paul definitely writes "grace, mercy, and peace" in 1 Tim 1:2; 2 Tim 1:2. On this basis scribes may have added "mercy" to Titus 1:4. But "mercy" could also have been present originally, with some early scribes opting for the familiar Pauline "grace and peace."

40. Saarinen, 172: "not very different offices."

But for him in that time and place, teaching is the essential core of the ministry he has received from God.

Yet, Titus is just one individual. Crete is a large place (see Introduction, VII.B) with many towns. This implies many congregations. Titus needs help. He must identify, confirm, and equip leaders. Otherwise the "rebellious people" will have their way. They will destroy faith, souls, and churches. The congregations' daily existence and longer-term mission will run aground.

Paul does not intend to see these things happen. The "peace" he wished Titus in v. 4 is not a limp-wristed passivity that lets matters take their natural aberrant course. Even after thirty years of apostolic service, his philosophy of Christian ministry is far from a bored "Whatever." He no doubt knows the promise that the gates of hell will not prevail against the church (Matt 16:18; see, e.g., Rom 16:20; 2 Cor 2:11). But God frequently uses human means to fulfill his (or Jesus's) promises. Paul is one of those means, and now Titus, as his coworker, must be another. Central to the future of Christ's churches in Crete is the quality and character of pastoral leadership they receive. In this section Paul will underscore what that involves for the situation at hand and in significant measure for churches in all times.

> [5]*The reason I left you in Crete was that you might put in order what*
> *was left unfinished and appoint elders in every town, as I directed you.*
> [6]*An elder must be blameless, faithful to his wife, a man whose children*
> *believe and are not open to the charge of being wild and disobedient.* [7]*Since*
> *an overseer manages God's household, he must be blameless—not overbearing, not quick-tempered, not given to drunkenness, not violent, not*
> *pursuing dishonest gain.* [8]*Rather, he must be hospitable, one who loves*
> *what is good, who is self-controlled, upright, holy and disciplined.* [9]*He*
> *must hold firmly to the trustworthy message as it has been taught, so that he can encourage others by sound doctrine and refute those who oppose it.*

5 In the Introduction we suggested that Paul most likely left Titus in Crete following a visit to the island after his first Roman imprisonment. Paul has moved on to another site, from which he now writes, perhaps Nicopolis (3:13). But there is no particular reason to think that our knowledge of Paul's place of writing is crucial for what he counsels Titus.

What is crucial is that Titus heed what Paul "directed" him to do. This same word (from *diatassō*) describes how God "directed" Moses regarding details of the tabernacle construction (Acts 7:44). The word can have imperial or military connotations, as when Caesar Claudius "ordered" the Jews to leave Rome (Acts 18:2) or when soldiers gave and received orders concerning Paul's custody while under arrest (Acts 23:31; 24:23). The word describes Jesus's instruction of the Twelve before they were sent out to preach (Matt 11:1). It also describes orders Jesus gave in other settings (Luke 8:55; 17:10). Nor is it foreign to Paul, as it is used in three places in 1 Corinthians:

> This is the rule I *lay down* in all the churches. (7:17)
>
> In the same way, the Lord has *commanded* that those who preach the gospel should receive their living from the gospel. (9:14)
>
> And when I come I will *give* further *directions*. (11:34)

So even though "as I directed you" comes at the end of the verse and might appear to be an afterthought, it was not a phrase apt to encourage complacency in Titus. It might rather connote urgency,[41] if not slight pique, as in the idiom "Like I good and well told you!"

What had Paul told him? The reason[42] Titus was left on Crete is not exactly clear. Was it a single task stated in two stages: (1) to "put in order what was left unfinished" and (2) to "appoint elders in every town"? Or did Paul view those as substantially different matters? Various options could be argued, but we will view (1) as a blanket directive and (2) as a primary means of achieving it. The unfinished matters (the Gk. is pl.) on Crete were more wide-ranging than just appointing pastoral leaders. But for various reasons, some of which will emerge below, until the pastoral pool could be enlarged, enhanced, or both, Paul's command to "put in order" what was awry or lacking had only dim prospects of effective implementation.

The word translated "put in order" could also be understood as "correct"; it occurs nowhere else in the New Testament and is in fact rare across the whole sweep of ancient Greek literature. It does occur in one inscription—dating to the second century on the island of Crete (BDAG 371)! The phrase "what was left unfinished" translates a form of a word (*leipō*) that is found elsewhere in Paul's writings only in Titus 3:13. Apparently Paul was aware of issues on Crete that he had not been able to resolve personally. This is hardly surprising; the work of the ministry is never done, and Crete was a large island (over 3,000 square miles) with many cities. One of those issues is surely leadership cultivation. The other is perhaps best thought of as involving the

41. The possibly emphatic use (but, see Turner, *Grammar of New Testament Greek*, 37) and position of the pronouns *egō* and *soi* in front of the verb "directed" should also not be overlooked.

42. The relatively rare *toutou charin* ("for this reason") occurs in the New Testament elsewhere only in Eph 3:1, 14; in the LXX only in 1 Macc 13:4; and not at all in the AF. It occurs very sporadically in Philo and Josephus. On the telic use of *charin* (see also Titus 1:11; Jude 16), see S. E. Porter, *Verbal Aspect in the Greek of the New Testament, with Reference to Tense and Mood* (New York: Peter Lang, 1989, 1993), 263n12.

range of topics that Paul touches on elsewhere in the letter as it unfolds, like dealing with opponents, instructing the faithful, encouraging household and relational godliness, instilling eschatological hope, and more.[43]

In any case, Titus is to "appoint elders in every town." There is a parallel between "every town" (*kata polin*) here and "each church" (*kat' ekklēsian*) in Acts 14:23, which speaks of elders being appointed as pastoral leaders during Paul's first missionary journey.[44] Each local congregation and every locale needs such figures. These are most likely leaders for recently planted congregations. But they could also be pastors of newer or renewed, primarily Pauline churches carrying out their work amid congregations already present when Paul first made contact with people on the island. Arguing against this possibility is Paul's policy "to preach the gospel where Christ was not known, so that I would not be building on someone else's foundation" (Rom 15:20). Yet, perhaps by this time in the expansion of the Christian message it was not always possible for the purview of Paul's preaching and the mission spillover of churches in areas he or his followers had evangelized to be kept hermetically sealed from the geographic spread of congregations hailing from other quarters. And, if Paul's description of some of the behavior of Cretans around if not in certain churches is accurate, there was a de facto need to restart what had evidently strayed from gospel moorings at least here and there.

In any case, quality leadership, an obvious concern for Jesus, who poured himself into the Twelve to provide the initial administrative core of the Christian movement, was no less critical in the ecclesial and missional outlook of Paul. Titus is to locate and "appoint" fit individuals. "Organization has its place in building up the kingdom of God, but virtues that conform to the nature of God take higher priority."[45] "Appoint" does not carry quite the same strongly ecclesial overtones as our word "ordain."[46] But the word translated "appoint" (from *kathistēmi*) often does mean "put in charge" (Matt 24:45, 47), assign chief responsibility (Acts 6:3, speaking of the duties delegated to table-servers), or place in high and holy office (Heb 5:1; 7:28; 8:3). "Ordain" may not be a totally inappropriate description of what Paul directs Titus to do, depending on what is understood in current settings by "ordain," which may or may not reflect assumptions and practices of New Testament times. Still, Titus is in charge of putting others in charge.

43. Calvin, 356–57, sees here "Paul's modesty in freely allowing someone else to complete what he has begun. And even though Titus is greatly his inferior, he does not refuse to have him . . . put finishing touches to his own work. This should be the disposition of all godly teachers, not that each should selfishly strive to have everything done as he wants it, but they should help each other."

44. See Spencer, 11.

45. Ngewa, 323.

46. Mounce, 387, suggests a black/white distinction between the two concepts.

6 But what kind of people, Titus could wonder, should be appointed as elders? The rest of this section (vv. 6–9) answers that question. Titus probably already had a fair notion: he had been in Christian service for some years (see Introduction, VIII.A). He would have had occasion to observe and participate in various ministerial and missionary duties as Paul's coworker. It should not be thought that the 129 words (in the NIV) of these four verses represent a comprehensive account of pastoral character, behavior, aptitude, and qualification. Paul rather should be regarded as hitting key high points. Much more could be said, but these are some basic nonnegotiables that he wants to remind Titus not to neglect. Titus had perhaps never before served in precisely this capacity of congregational leadership development, and therefore Paul repeats some ABCs of one of Titus's primary present responsibilities.

"An elder must be blameless." This is critical, since Paul repeats it in v. 7.[47] "Blameless" (*anengklētos*) cannot mean sinless or morally perfect, as Paul knows that all humans fall short of God's glory (Rom 3:23). It can also hardly mean a wonderful person in the sight of all, having a life "which offers no convincing evidence of wrongdoing."[48] This would go against Jesus's teaching that his followers will be disliked and opposed by at least some people at least some of the time.[49] Paul says the same thing to Timothy: "Everyone who wants to live a godly life in Christ Jesus will be persecuted" (2 Tim 3:12). Persecution implies accusation of wrongdoing. It would also be contrary to the assumption of this very epistle, which addresses the problem and reality of people straying from apostolic faith and practice. Self-evidently, such people would not consider Paul, Titus, and others who represent their viewpoint as blameless, for they oppose key tenets of their convictions and are trying to push alternate views. For convinced pagans and Jews alike, no one who espoused the untenable views of Paul's gospel could be considered blameless (see 1 Cor 1:18–23).

The only two other New Testament passages that contain this word suggest another possibility for explaining what Paul has in mind. First, Paul assures the Corinthians that Jesus Christ "will also keep you firm to the end, so that you will be blameless on the day of our Lord Jesus Christ" (1 Cor 1:8). Paul is not saying the Corinthians are presently perfect; his epistle to them is proof of the contrary. They are not even blameless in Paul's assessment, from a doctrinal and ethical point of view. He is rather speaking of them as believers "in Christ." As those who have believed and received the grace of the gospel (see 1 Cor 1:4–6), they possess a righteousness through faith that assures them of God's present, as well as eschatological, exoneration. They are blameless in God's sight by virtue of the sufficiency of Christ's death for their sake.

47. The same word is applied to deacons in 1 Tim 3:10.

48. Quinn, 85.

49. See, for example, Matt 5:11; John 15:18–21.

Second, Paul tells the Colossians that God "has reconciled you by Christ's physical body through death to present you holy in his sight, without blemish and *free from accusation*" (Col 1:22). The words in italics translate the Greek word for "blameless" in Titus 1:6, 7. Again, Paul is not predicating sinless perfection of the Colossians or suggesting that they are above all criticism in how they live—Paul himself is critical of them (Col 2:20). He is rather speaking of their standing in God's sight by virtue of their "faith in Christ Jesus and . . . the love [they] have for all God's people" (Col 1:4). They have received the gospel message, it is transforming them, and this work of God's word confers a status of blamelessness upon them in God's sight.

To be blameless as a pastoral candidate in Titus 1:6–7, therefore, could have to do with living in the present in a way that is consistent with what the grace of the gospel confers on those who believe and receive it. Both 1 Corinthians and Colossians bristle with ethical injunctions that imply how the readers' blameless status theologically ought to manifest itself practically. Paul is likewise telling Titus that pastoral candidates must exhibit strong signs of the presence of the divine grace that transforms their lives in godly directions.

Specifically, they should be blameless as regards ground zero of their real-world existence. This starts with the integrity of their marriage. A candidate should be "faithful to his wife" (see also 1 Tim 3:2). While this condition would rule out polygamy in that setting, it is unlikely to be what Paul had in mind. Nor is this an implicit command that a pastoral leader must be married (it seems Paul was not: 1 Cor 7:7; 9:5), or that he cannot have remarried after a wife's death or a divorce.[50] He is assuming that candidates who are mature adults will probably be married. What is the quality of their character when it comes to marital loyalty, including sexual purity? For most if not all human males, this is a litmus test of their character in every other domain of their lives, at least as far as God is concerned, who sees the heart. Jesus set forth a high standard for his would-be followers when he said that to look on a woman lustfully is tantamount to a liaison with her (Matt 5:28). This is not a swipe at sexual activity but a confirmation of its sanctity in lawful matrimony, a given in Old Testament teaching and subsequent Jewish tradition. Paul endorses marriage in 1 Cor 7, 1 Tim 4:3–4, and elsewhere. The precise sentiment of "faithful to his wife" is set forth powerfully in Scripture (Prov 5:15–20):

> Drink water from your own cistern,
> running water from your own well.
> Should your springs overflow in the streets,
> your streams of water in the public squares?

50. All these possibilities are weighed and plausibly called in question by Towner, *Letters*, 250–51, especially n. 42. But see Mounce, 388.

> Let them be yours alone,
> never to be shared with strangers.
> May your fountain be blessed,
> and may you rejoice in the wife of your youth.
> A loving doe, a graceful deer—
> may her breasts satisfy you always,
> may you ever be captivated by her love.
> Why, my son, be intoxicated with another man's wife?
> Why embrace the bosom of a wayward woman?

Paul is insisting, then, on a candidate whose relationship with God is such that his commitment to his wife reflects the love and fidelity that the law requires[51] and that grace enables. If a candidate shows signs of loving his wife like Christ loved the church (Eph 5:25), this is probably what Paul wants Titus to look for.[52] The robust love for God and people that is the lifeblood of pastoral care should be fueled by the discipline and joy of married love in the pastor's personal life.

To this brief but telling marital marker is then added the requirement of having children "who believe and are not open to the charge of being wild and disobedient." The stress here is presumably on dependent children, not so much those who are now adults themselves. The intent is surely not to insist that the candidate have more than one child,[53] though the wisdom attained through multiple children can be most salutary for pastoral work. As in the economy of his brief epistle Paul assumes that candidates will have wives, he is assuming that at least by some point they will have children. In that likely event, just as his relationship with his wife says much about the integrity of a man's Christian confession, so does his relationship with his children. Elsewhere Paul speaks of the need for fathers not to deal harshly with their children (Col 3:21). Jesus warned of dire consequences for causing children to stumble (Matt 18:6; Mark 9:42; Luke 17:2), confirming the high premium God places on them in general. How much truer this would be of one's own children. From the onset of gospel proclamation, the good news did not target only adults but the welfare of whole households: "The promise is for you and your children" (Acts 2:39). Fit pastoral candidates, Paul is indicating to Titus, will reflect the grace of the gospel not only in love for their wives but in the kind of ties with their children that result in the latter's embrace of their parents' relationship with God, not their rejection of it. Their children should "believe." The word could also be translated "be faithful." In that case, Paul

51. See Exod 20:14, 17: "You shall not commit adultery. . . . You shall not covet your neighbor's wife."

52. So Gloer, 35: "An elder must be faithful to his wife."

53. See Mounce, 388.

would be speaking of their inward and outward compliance with the terms and expectations of the gospel message.

"Not open to the charge [*katēgoria*] of being wild and disobedient" could refer to a formal accusation, whether in a civil court or in the congregation. The same word is used when Paul tells Timothy, "Do not entertain an *accusation* against an elder unless it is brought by two or three witnesses" (1 Tim 5:19).[54] There was an expectation that congregants would comply with standards set by their leaders (1 Thess 5:12; Heb 13:17). A candidate whose children were under formal disciplinary proceedings should probably wait till these matters resolve themselves before seeking pastoral office. Likewise, if a child faces criminal charges in the societal legal system, this may not be the time for dad to be presenting himself to assume pastoral responsibilities. The distraction for him and his wife, and opprobrium of the general citizenry, would be crippling for his reputation and concentration until matters were resolved. It would also distract from the attention to a child most necessary precisely at a time when he or she is facing such dire personal circumstances.

A less restrictive but not unrelated understanding is possible. "Wild" connotes engagement in debauched behavior or gross dissipation—note the only other New Testament uses of the word in Eph 5:18 and 1 Pet 4:4. "Disobedient" is likewise a strong word, found in 1 Tim 1:9, where it appears alongside descriptors like "lawbreakers . . . , the ungodly and sinful, the unholy and irreligious; . . . those who kill their fathers or mothers, . . . murderers." The word does not describe penny-ante transgression or the foibles of youth. The word will also appear in Titus 1:10 to describe the "many rebellious people" who threaten the very integrity of the Cretan churches (see further discussion of the word "disobedient" there). Dedicated and self-conscious opposition to gospel witness and behavior is implied. In each individual case[55] it would be a judgment call for Titus and other leaders, but the fitness of a pastoral candidate cannot be totally divorced from his track record as a believing and faithful head of his own household. Paul's words to Timothy bear repeating, "If anyone does not know how to manage his own family, how can he take care of God's church?" (1 Tim 3:5)

This is a delicate matter, since Jesus taught that his message would divide households, including parents and children (Luke 12:53). Paul's compressed counsel should be applied with sagacity and compassion, not wooden casuistry.[56] Binding biblical principles found elsewhere must be factored in, for exam-

54. Otherwise, the word appears in the New Testament only in John 18:29: "So Pilate came out to them and asked, 'What *charges* are you bringing against this man?'"

55. NIV begins v. 6, "An elder must be blameless"; the Greek reads, "If anyone is blameless," pointing to the case-by-case purview of Paul's policy.

56. See Balla, *The Child-Parent Relationship in the New Testament and Its Environment.*

ple, "The child will not share the guilt of the parent, nor will the parent share the guilt of the child" (Ezek 18:20). But between a view so stringent that no person, finally, could qualify for pastoral office—who, in the end, is blameless, with equally angelic children?—and ministerial tracks today that are largely blind to people's domestic lives and even degenerate histories, there is surely middle ground. Paul's counsel here is relevant to determining its location.

7 From what Paul states in v. 6, he makes an inference[57] that forms the substance of v. 7. This inference parallels v. 6 by restating the requirement of blamelessness on the part of a pastor or pastoral candidate, here using the word "overseer" (*episkopos*). This is evidently a near-synonym for "elder" in v. 6. Overseers "must be blameless." The word "must" (*dei*) and this grammatical construction[58] often imply moral necessity or even divine compunction (e.g., Rom 1:27; 8:26; 12:3; 1 Cor 8:2; 15:25, 53; 2 Cor 5:10; see also table 15 and discussion at 1 Tim 3:2 in this commentary). If it was not already clear to Titus, Paul now reiterates that this is an iron-clad necessity.

The reason comes at the end of the clause: such a person "manages God's household." Paul stresses[59] that *God* is the determining element in this; the person serves at *God's* behest. The word "household" (*oikonomia*) envisions a divinely ordained and superintended domain (e.g., 1 Cor 9:17; Eph 1:10; 3:2, 9; Col 1:25; 1 Tim 1:4) in which God delegates certain responsibilities to a chosen servant (cf. 1 Cor 4:1). The pastor is not merely a social worker or religious organizer, nor is such ministry viewed from the standpoint of human self-actualization or the self-directed deployment of spiritual gifts. The character, presence, and active will of God in the pastoral mission lay the highest necessity of probity on Titus and prospective appointees. Paul's point could have to do with the notion of God as judge in all this. He could also have in mind the high stakes and spiritual nature of the conflict churches face on Crete—the sanctity, if not survival, of God's work in the form of the church there is at stake, and divine resources are required for those who answer the bell to uphold God's truth and interests.

For that reason, Paul lists a series of disqualifiers. In popular language, these are no-brainers, immediate warning flags for Titus as prospective pastoral workers come into view. This is not a comprehensive list, but it furnishes a composite sketch of the kind of person who may be safely eliminated from the list of volunteers or recruits to take up pastoral duties in the Cretan setting.

First, they must not be "overbearing" (*authadēs*). This Greek word appears only here and in 2 Pet 2:10 (of those said to be "bold and arrogant

57. The Greek conjunction *gar* in v. 7 denotes an inference from what precedes.

58. See Porter, *Verbal Aspect*, 488, with n7.

59. In Greek the word order may emphasize God as the manager rather than the household being managed.

[*authadeis*]" and "not afraid to heap abuse on celestial beings") in the New Testament. In the LXX it is found three times and connotes self-centered and audacious behavior (Gen 49:3, 7; Prov 21:24). It appears in the first verse of Clement of Rome's letter to Corinth and describes the reckless and "arrogant" people that have caused schism there (1 Clem. 1:1). "Arrogant" seems the sense of the word too in the four other AF passages in which this relatively rare word is found (Did. 3:6; Herm. Sim. 5.4.2; 5.5.1; 9.22.1). Pastors need to be proactive and bold in witness and service. But such forthrightness cannot cross over the line to self-importance and a sense of superiority or entitlement over others. Aristotle, too, condemns this quality,[60] but does so because it violates his ideal of the golden mean. The "overbearing" person seeks to please only himself or herself, which is just as undesirable as living only to please others. The proper position is safely between the two extremes, according to Aristotle. This is not bad counsel, but the basis for it is very different than for Paul.

Second, they must not be "quick-tempered." This word appears only here in the New Testament; in the LXX it is found four times and is translated (NETS) "irascible" (Ps 17:49 [48]), "irritable" (Prov 21:19), "passionate" (Prov 22:24), and "quick-tempered" (Prov 29:22). Like many of the qualifications (or disqualifications) Paul mentions, this one is rooted primarily in common sense, as a hothead is unlikely to prosper in the Christian care of souls. "It is to one's honor to avoid strife, but every fool is quick to quarrel" (Prov 20:3). The evil of unbridled impulse is a prominent feature in Old Testament narrative (e.g., Moses striking the rock; the insane fury of King Saul toward his son Jonathan and David) and wisdom literature (e.g., Prov 29:8, 11; 30:33), teaching the lesson that "human anger does not produce the righteousness that God desires" (Jas 1:20). Rage is likewise condemned in Hellenistic moralism, which in Stoic form prized freedom from all affect whatsoever.[61] Pastors need not become Stoics, but of all people they should not readily or frequently lose their temper.

Third, they must not be "given to drunkenness." The expression occurs in the New Testament elsewhere only in 1 Tim 3:3 and is self-explanatory. To have access to intoxicating drink may be a sign of God's blessing,[62] but more often the Old Testament warns of its misuse (e.g., Prov 20:1; 21:17; 23:20, 31; 31:4). Paul's general injunction "Do not get drunk on wine, which leads to debauchery. Instead, be filled with the Spirit" (Eph 5:18) applies particularly to a church leader.

Fourth, they must not be "violent." As with the previous word, this one occurs in the New Testament elsewhere only in 1 Tim 3:3. Jesus taught the

60. Aristotle, *Magna Moralia* 1.29.1192b30–37; see *NW* 1013.

61. See Plutarch, *Moralia* 454b–c; *NW* 1015.

62. Prov 3:10: "Then your barns will be filled to overflowing, and your vats will brim over with new wine."

virtue of peacemaking (Matt 5:9), and James taught that "peacemakers who sow in peace raise a harvest of righteousness" (Jas 3:18). A person quick with his fists, who is "pugnacious" or a "bully" (see BDAG 826) whether literally or psychologically, is unripe for candidacy for pastoral ministry.

Fifth, their hearts must not be set on the acquisition of "dishonest gain." As with the previous word, this one occurs in the New Testament elsewhere only once, in 1 Tim 3:8 (qualification for deacons). It is one thing to earn your wage, and Paul upheld fair recompense for church leaders (1 Cor 9:12; 1 Tim 5:17–18). Jesus worked with his hands for a living until his public ministry began, from which time he apparently relied on the largesse of supporters, including generous women (Luke 8:3). But it is another to have one's heart shot through with greed, a vice as roundly condemned by Jesus and Paul as any.[63] Paul had "learned the secret of being content in any and every situation, whether well fed or hungry, whether living in plenty or in want" (Phil 4:12). He saw this "secret" as a discipline and disposition essential to pastoral care, as well.

According to Polybius (second century BC) Crete was a place noted for greed:

> In all these respects the Cretan practice is exactly the opposite [of the Spartans']. Their laws go as far as possible in letting them acquire land to the extent of their power, as the saying is, and money is held in such high honor among them that its acquisition is not only regarded as necessary, but as most honorable. So much in fact do sordid love of gain and lust for wealth prevail among them, that the Cretans are the only people in the world in whose eyes no gain is disgraceful. . . . The Cretans, on the other hand, owing to their ingrained lust of wealth are involved in constant broils both public and private, and in murders and civil wars.[64]

This greed and its attendant ills may or may not have been a factor at the time Paul writes. But the possibility of a strong streak of culpable acquisitiveness in the Cretan soul and psyche is at least a historical possibility.[65] If so, it links them with many cultures and individuals at the present time. Ngewa points to the problem in Africa of pastors who are "motivated more by the offerings people bring than by concern for people's souls"; "they paint their greed in the

63. Jesus on greed, for example: Matt 23:35; Mark 7:22; Luke 11:39; 12:15; Paul on greed: Rom 1:29; Eph 5:3; Col 3:5; 1 Thess 2:5.

64. Polybius, *Histories*, 6.46.1–5.

65. See Jeon, *To Exhort and Reprove*, 123: Paul furnishes Titus "a vivid description of God" in the epistle's opening verses to challenge his readers "to reject their cultural norms, which not only accepted deceit but to some degree encouraged it."

colors of Scripture."[66] This is understandable, for health-and-wealth teaching has long been exported abroad from figures in the West and appeals, it seems, to many people in all times and places.

8 Offsetting the five disqualifiers in the previous verse are six[67] positive character traits that Titus should seek out and affirm in pastoral candidates. It is not enough that they not be cads and scoundrels. The grace of the God they confess should have permeated their lives to the point that it produces an array of serviceable habits and strengths inherent to mature godliness. As in the case of the negative traits, Paul does not give a comprehensive list but furnishes enough components for a helpful character sketch, a working model of what Titus is after when seeking pastoral material.

"Hospitable" denotes a readiness that should mark everyone in the church (Rom 12:13) but is doubly requisite for its pastoral leaders (see also 1 Tim 3:2). At the very least this practical openness should extend to other Christians; another apostle wrote, "Offer hospitality to one another without grumbling" (1 Pet 4:9). Yet, the purview is not only family and close friends: there was determination in the early church of the need for care for outsiders, too (Heb 13:2; cf. 3 John 8). There is basis for this broad scope in Jesus's teaching that his disciples should be openhearted not only toward loved ones but toward people in general (Matt 5:43–48). In 1 Clement, hospitality is commended on the basis of the examples of Abraham (10:7), Lot (11:1), and Rahab (12:1, 3).[68] However idealized, another AF source (Herm. Sim. 9.27.2) depicts pastoral hospitality as follows, speaking of "bishops" (or overseers) as "hospitable men, who were always glad to welcome God's servants into their homes without hypocrisy. And the bishops always sheltered the needy and the widows by their ministry without ceasing, and conducted themselves in purity always."

Closely tied to this social openness, and in fact necessary for hospitality to flourish in a pastor's household and in the church, is the quality of loving what is good (*philagathos*). This word is found nowhere else in the New Testament and only once in the LXX (Wis 7:22; loving the good is said to be part of the spirit of wisdom). It is absent from the AF, but Philo refers to it once to describe one of four qualities he sees necessary for administrative power; the other three are humility, the love of justice, and the hatred of iniquity (*Life of Moses* 2.9). Paul speaks of goodness (*agathōsynē*) in other passages (Rom 15:14; Gal 5:22; Eph 5:9; 2 Thess 1:11); a pastor should "love" the good not in an idle philosophical sense but by being passionate in embodying it and zealous to see that what is good flourish in and out of the church. There is a connection

66. Ngewa, 350.

67. Or seven, if one includes v. 9 (so Mounce, 385, 391).

68. Other examples: 1 Clem. 1:2; Herm. Mand. 8.1.10.

between this pastoral quality and the "good works" enjoined on Titus and the congregations elsewhere in the letter.

"Self-controlled" (from *sōphrōn*; RSV "master of himself") translates a word distinct to the PE in the New Testament (see also 1 Tim 3:2; Titus 2:2, 5), though related words are found elsewhere in Paul (Rom 12:3; 2 Cor 5:13; cf. Acts 26:25). Paul warned against belligerent impulsiveness in the previous verse. Old Testament wisdom counsels, "Do not be quickly provoked in your spirit, for anger resides in the lap of fools" (Eccl 7:9) and "A wise man keeps himself under control" (Prov 29:11 NIV84). In the LXX the word occurs only in 4 Macc, where NETS usually translates "temperate."[69] Whatever the theological, ethical, or interpersonal issue, whether public or private, the advisability for a church leader being steady and dependable, not at the mercy of pressures external to himself, is self-evident.

"Upright" (*dikaios*) is a word used seventeen times by Paul. It can mean "righteous" when applied to God (e.g., 2 Tim 4:8) or even to an Old Testament or New Testament believer (e.g., Rom 3:10; 5:7). In this particular list, however, NIV's decision to highlight the human ethical quality rather than a "righteous" status as such is reasonable—though it is striking that of the seventy-nine occurrences of *dikaios* in the New Testament, NIV translates "upright" only three times.[70] There is an argument to be made for not divorcing "upright" here from the "righteous" status that is so central to Paul's use of this word and cognates in other passages.

"Holy" is a quality attributed to God in Old Testament and New Testament Scripture. The word "holy" (*hosios*) is paired with "upright/righteous" (*dikaios*) in a few LXX passages (e.g., Deut 32:4; Ps 144:17; Prov 17:26; 21:15); the doublet may refer either to God or to a devout person. The two words overlap, and Paul is probably not thinking of two vastly different things. Only God, in the end, is truly "upright" and "holy," yet through faith these divine attributes can suffuse and transform gospel recipients. Titus should appoint to leadership only persons who evidence these elements in their character and lives.

The last quality Paul calls for in this rapid-fire sequence is "disciplined." The word (*enkratēs*, often translated "self-controlled") is found nowhere elsewhere in the New Testament, though the noun cognate is present.[71] It may carry a sexual connotation and was highly prized in Stoic ethics.[72] It appears three times in the AF, notably in Polycarp (*Phil.* 5:2), who states that "deacons must be blameless in the presence of [God's] righteousness, as deacons of

69. 4 Macc 1:35; 2:2, 16, 18, 23; 3:17, 19. Yet, in 15:10 NETS translates "self-controlled."

70. Besides Titus 1:8, see Luke 23:50 (of Joseph of Arimathea); Titus 2:12. ESV calls these persons "righteous."

71. Note *enkrateia* in Acts 24:25; Gal 5:23; 2 Pet 1:6 (twice).

72. Mounce, 391.

God and Christ and not of men: not slanderers, not insincere, not lovers of money, *self-controlled* in every respect, compassionate, diligent, acting in accordance with the truth of the Lord, who became 'a servant of all.'" Polycarp here includes "self-controlled" (translated "disciplined" in NIV) as part of a whole suite of character traits of a church leader, in this case deacons, but the purview and even particular elements are reminiscent of Paul's list in Titus. "Disciplined" in Paul's use here may serve to summarize the entire list of traits found in v. 8: without the last one, the presence or absence of the previous five could quickly be rendered moot. It has been remarked that it takes twenty years to build a reputation, but only five minutes to destroy it.

When one thinks ahead to the problems Paul will urge Titus to face in coming sections of this epistle, it is no wonder he commends self-control to him here. The troublemakers, the damage they have created, the shortcomings of the congregations needing to be shored up and furnished with leaders—it will try anyone's patience. Even those who do meet the fairly stringent standards Paul lays out will need to transcend any tendency to impulsiveness.

9 To the six qualities in v. 8 that pastoral candidates must have, Paul now summarizes what, looking ahead, under Titus's leadership they must do.

It boils down to one thing: "hold firmly to the trustworthy message as it has been taught." There is an obvious connection with the "trustworthy sayings" encountered frequently in the PE (1 Tim 1:15; 3:1; 4:9; 2 Tim 2:11; Titus 3:8), which at the very least point to Paul's sense of apostolic authority (see Introduction, IX.C) and his belief that this "message" is "trustworthy" in terms of faithfully representing the truth of the gospel of Christ.[73] "Hold fast" translates a form of *antechō* that can connote fierce attachment, like the greedy person's devotion to money rather than God (Matt 6:24; Luke 16:13).[74] There is a slightly weaker sense used in contexts of "help" for others (1 Thess 5:14), but even there the sense of engagement implied is "strong" (BDAG 87). While the word is absent from the AF, it is found nineteen times in the LXX. There God "takes hold" of judgment, wielding it like a dagger (Deut 32:41); wisdom will "cleave to" the person who seeks it with abandon (Prov 4:6). The person who "holds fast" to God's ways is blessed (Isa 56:2), yet even those who did "hold fast to the law" but did not know God personally were doomed to destruction (Jer 2:8).[75] Paul speaks of a settled and seasoned dedication that may even look fanatical to those not convinced of the truths that he and his coworkers like Titus and Timothy champion.[76]

73. Zehr, 252, comments that to "hold firmly to the trustworthy message as it has been taught" means "understanding the whole Bible interpreted through God's fullness of revelation in Jesus Christ, as set forth by apostolic teaching."

74. Cf. Marshall, with Towner, 165–66.

75. All quotations in the last two sentences from NETS.

76. It is not clear why Dibelius and Conzelmann, 133, call the translation "to hold fast"

For Paul, this devotion was not about fanaticism (note Acts 26:25), however, but about a message that lines up with[77] what has "been taught." Paul uses a word (*didachē*) that summarizes apostolic instruction in Acts (2:42; 5:28; 13:12; 17:19) and in his own ministry (Rom 6:17; 16:17; cf. 2 Tim 4:2). In the subapostolic age a whole document was dedicated to this theme, the Didache (in which the word appears in the title and in 1:3; 2:1; 6:1; 11:2). The "message" that pastoral leaders are charged to uphold is not theirs to invent, shape to their own demands, or edit to their preferences. They are to embrace, live, and impress the teaching they have received from an apostolic spokesman (in this case Paul) on their followers. What they have received, in turn, is the "trustworthy message" that Paul has preached for a generation and that saved their own souls, gave rise to local congregations on Crete, and now furnishes the ecclesial and missional agenda that Paul and Titus intend to delegate to pastoral workers.

Paul gives two broad justifications[78] for the intense loyalty to this "trustworthy message" that he insists on. First, the pastor has to be in a position[79] to "encourage others by sound doctrine" (see Introduction, IX.D). A form of the verb "encourage" occurs 109 times in the Greek New Testament (54 times in Paul) and can connote tender nurture (2 Cor 2:7; 7:6; 1 Thess 5:14) or stern entreaty (Phil 4:2; 2 Thess 3:12). Here it may carry variable weight, depending on the situation a pastoral teacher finds himself in. Paul himself uses it in different ways. The default modus operandi of the pastor is to be "encouraging," but that may mean one thing in a bereavement situation[80] and another at some point in a discipline case. Jesus's preaching and teaching were notoriously varied, depending on the message and the audience and the timeline of his life: he denounced on some occasions (e.g., Matt 23), was silent before Pilate, and spoke endearingly at the Last Supper. But while the mien of Jesus and Paul was flexible, their respective basic messages (which substantially overlapped)[81] did not flip-flop. Neither should the didactic core[82] of ministers laboring in their train (recall comments on the *fides quae* at v. 4 above).

Second, pastoral laborers must be in a position to "refute those who oppose it," "it" referring to the sound doctrine. The activity denoted by "re-

---

"very weak," especially when they suggest the gloss "to be concerned with something"—which seems even weaker.

77. The sense of *kata* with the accusative here.

78. Note the "both . . . and" (*kai . . . kai*) construction; Marshall, with Towner, 167.

79. Literally, "in order to be able [*dynatos*]." Siebenthal, *Griechische Grammatik*, §219, notes that this adjective ("able") is then complemented by the infinitives "to encourage" and "to refute."

80. See Isa 42:3; Matt 12:20.

81. See commentary Introduction, VIII.C.

82. Marshall, with Towner, 168, sees here "a fixed body of teaching."

fute" (*elenchō*) comes into view elsewhere in the PE (1 Tim 5:20; 2 Tim 4:2; Titus 1:13; 2:15; cf. 2 Tim 3:16 of Scripture's function). This requires loyalty to that doctrine on their own part. The PE are testimony to how little (even) a first-generation believer who had personally encountered the Lord risen from the dead felt he could presume on the steadfastness of (even) proven second-generation coworkers like Titus and Timothy. Given human nature and the ferocious antagonism of the fallen world order at times to the gospel decree (cf. 2 Cor 10:4; Eph 6:12), the counsel is always in order: "So, if you think you are standing firm, be careful that you don't fall!" (1 Cor 10:12). Paul's reminder of the need to refute is not a command to attack but a reminder of an aspect of ministry that transcends the competency of flesh and blood in itself. "Who is equal to such a task?" (2 Cor 2:16). Ministers had better know their stuff, including the limits of their knowledge, and have their helmets strapped on. Holding firmly to the message is a baseline necessary resolve.

So the elder must both "encourage" and "refute." Calvin's observation is apt: "A pastor needs two voices, one for gathering the sheep and the other for driving away wolves and thieves."[83]

But who is it who opposes the message? In the next section Paul will sketch a scenario with which he realizes Titus is already sadly familiar. This will provide background for taking up primarily positive instruction or theological affirmation for congregational members in the remainder of the epistle (Titus 2–3).

III. DESCRIPTION OF THE GOSPEL'S OPPONENTS (1:10–16)

In a sense the substance of the whole of the epistle turns on this section. It goes far toward explaining just why Paul is writing. We have already seen that a major aim is to support Titus in his mission of completing unfinished business in the Cretan churches and appointing elders (1:5). To that end Paul has given a concise but rich description of desirable qualities in pastoral candidates (1:6–9). He will subsequently set forth desirable qualities among various groups in the congregations (2:1–10) and explain why Titus's outreach to various groups holds such urgency and promise (2:11–15). Finally, he will give general directives for all believers (3:1–3), a rationale for their actions (3:4–8), and final warnings regarding controversies in the churches (3:9–11).

While all of these topics hold some inherent importance, the question remains why Paul chose this particular time to address these matters and took

83. Calvin, 361.

up just the subjects he did in the way he did. The section below may answer that question to a considerable extent. The immediate background to Paul's mostly positive directions are negative local developments or conditions in the form of troublesome people—the primary subject of the section at hand.

> [10] *For there are many rebellious people, full of meaningless talk and deception, especially those of the circumcision group.* [11] *They must be silenced, because they are disrupting whole households by teaching things they ought not to teach—and that for the sake of dishonest gain.* [12] *One of Crete's own prophets has said it: "Cretans are always liars, evil brutes, lazy gluttons."* [13] *This saying is true. Therefore rebuke them sharply, so that they will be sound in the faith* [14] *and will pay no attention to Jewish myths or to the merely human commands of those who reject the truth.* [15] *To the pure, all things are pure, but to those who are corrupted and do not believe, nothing is pure. In fact, both their minds and consciences are corrupted.* [16] *They claim to know God, but by their actions they deny him. They are detestable, disobedient and unfit for doing anything good.*

10 The first word "for" sets this paragraph in relation to the previous one. Paul has given directions to Titus regarding setting matters straight and appointing elders "for" the reason indicated in the next six verses.

There are, it seems, "many rebellious people"[84] creating disturbance in the congregations with which Titus is connected. "Many" translates *polloi* (note the idiom "hoi polloi") and carries a disapproving if not derogatory sense.[85] "Many" opposed Paul at Corinth (1 Cor 16:9), and "many" lived as enemies of Christ's cross (Phil 3:18). The problem of a numerically significant opposition was not a new thing for Paul.[86] Even if this group did not consist of hundreds or even scores, it does not take many energetic contrarians to create disruption.

The adjective "rebellious" (from *anypotaktoi*) carries the idea of not being subject to something or someone. In 1:6 it was translated "disobedient." Another New Testament use of this word is in Heb 2:8, which states that God has left nothing in the cosmos that is "not subject" to Christ. The only other New Testament occurrence is 1 Tim 1:9: "We also know that the law is made not for the righteous but for lawbreakers and *rebels*." The word is not found in

84. Many Greek MSS contain *kai* (which here could mean "even, indeed") after "many." Many MSS regarded as important by textual scholars omit it (e.g., ℵ A C P 088 and others). The difference for translation and interpretation is negligible. See Metzger, *Textual Commentary* (1994), 584–85.

85. For example, 2 Cor 3:17. In a later generation, see in the AF Papias 3:3.

86. Or other leaders of the era: see 2 Pet 2:2; 1 John 4:1; 2 John 7.

the LXX or AF and is found only once each in Philo (*Who Is the Heir?* 4) and Josephus (*Jewish Antiquities* 11.217).

Yet, the thrust of the word is hardly obscure—the people it describes are out of line, in Paul's view, with norms they should respect—and in any case Paul gives further qualification. He spotlights first what they do, and next who they are.

As to what they do, Paul calls them *mataiologoi*, which NIV translates "full of meaningless talk." This probably means they talk too much, and what they say is vacuous.[87] They "talk wildly."[88] Not only is their talk unprofitable: they mislead, Paul describing their effect as "deception." The word (from *phrenapatēs*) occurs nowhere else in the New Testament.[89] They are leading people astray by verbal means. Irenaeus uses a form of this word when he writes, "You see, my friend, the method which these men employ to *deceive* themselves, while they abuse the Scriptures by endeavoring to support their own system out of them" (*Against Heresies* 1.9.1).

Who are these people? Their profile takes on more clarity in the coming verses. And even then Paul is not giving a comprehensive account. What he does say is that these dissidents include "especially those of the circumcision group." They are Jewish. Not all of them; "especially" assumes a larger number of which they are a subset.[90] Perhaps they are the central figures in the movement that troubles Paul. The phrase "those of the circumcision" is not uncommon in the New Testament.[91] By synecdoche a distinctive aspect of Jewish practice, circumcision, is used to represent members of the entire ethnic group (see BDAG 807).

Paul has special zeal and affection for his fellow Jews (Rom 9:2–3). The Christian church owes its existence to the Jewish heritage (Rom 9:4–5; see also Rom 11; John 4:22). There is no taint of anti-Semitism here, as Paul himself is a Semite (2 Cor 11:22; Phil 3:5). But Paul thinks that God's promise to the Jews to send a savior was fulfilled in the coming of Jesus. In his day most Jews disagreed. Even some who confessed Jesus as Lord contributed to tension as the meaning of Jesus's fulfilled messiahship was worked out vis-à-vis Jewish

87. Polycarp uses the noun cognate (*mataiologia*), as well as Paul's "many," in calling his readers to serve God "leaving behind the empty and *meaningless talk* and the error of the many" (*Phil.* 2:1).

88. F. Young, *The Theology of the Pastoral Epistles* (Cambridge: Cambridge University Press, 1994), 8.

89. But see the cognate verb in Gal 6:3: "If anyone thinks they are something when they are not, they *deceive* [*phrenapata*] themselves."

90. See similar use of *malista* (especially) in Gal 6:10; Phil 4:22; 1 Tim 4:10; 5:8; and elsewhere; also Witherington, 119n92.

91. See Acts 10:45; 11:2; Rom 4:12; Gal 2:12; Col 4:11; see also Barclay, *Paul and the Gift*, 366n39.

customs and understanding of Old Testament passages and promises and traditions long attached to them (see, e.g., Isa 29:13; Mark 7:6–7). The Jerusalem Council (Acts 15) highlights a dispute that took place perhaps twenty years after Jesus's death. How Jews should relate to God's new-covenant activity was anything but self-evident in early decades of the Christian movement. Jews who profess faith in Jesus as Messiah today still wrestle with analogous questions.

It is entirely plausible, therefore, that Paul and Titus should encounter continuing turbulence related to Jewish influence on or in Crete's congregations. Comporting with this situation is attestation in sources outside of the New Testament of a large Jewish population on Crete in the first century. Josephus tells of a young man who "deceived" many Jews on Crete.[92] Philo writes of the numerous Jewish settlers in all quarters of the known world in his time, especially on the islands of Euboea, Cyprus, and Crete.[93]

11 Paul suggests a course of action for Titus and the leaders who do or will look to him for leadership: emanations from the "many rebellious people" must be squelched. "Must" here translates *dei* ("it is necessary"), a word that appeared above in v. 7 (see discussion there; see also table 15 and discussion at 1 Tim 3:2 in this commentary). Paul's use of the word here implies at least urgent necessity. The same can be said of the occurrence of the same word when Paul writes later in the verse of things they "ought not" teach. Moral compulsion works against what they are doing, but they lack the wisdom and perhaps the scruples to respect that fact. Titus and his associates must act.[94] Paul may or may not be implying some amount of divine necessity in these two phrases. But given the importance of stopping this deceptive teaching and its deleterious effects, the connotation cannot be ruled out. In that case, this is not merely a Pauline reaction but a divine priority.

The word "silenced" (from *epistomizō*) occurs only here in the New Testament and never in the LXX or AF. It is found once in Josephus, referring to a Roman legion under Varus whose presence in Jerusalem following the death of Herod the Great ca. 4 BC would "keep the Jews quiet."[95] Philo uses the word more frequently (seventeen times), often with the sense of bridling (as a horse, or an unruly passion) for a constructive purpose,[96] not merely preventing any and all audible activity. If Paul has this connotation in mind, silencing these individuals is not so much the final goal as a necessary preliminary to their

92. Josephus writes *exapatēsas*, related to *phrenapatēs* found in Titus 1:10 (*Jewish War* 2.103); the same story is told in his *Jewish Antiquities* 17.327 (cf. *NW* 1016).

93. Philo, *Embassy to Gaius* 282 (*NW* 1017).

94. On the syntax, see Siebenthal, *Griechische Grammatik*, §289j.

95. Josephus, *Jewish Antiquities* 17.251. See also MM 246, which calls the verb "rare."

96. Philo, *Allegorical Interpretation* 2.104; 3.128; *Agriculture* 88; *Special Laws* 1.193; 4.97.

repentance and subsequent positive, rather than subversive, involvement in congregations.

It would also be a short-term measure needed, lest they continue "disrupting whole households." "Households" could refer to domestic life-settings, the seat of family life, exclusively.[97] But since the early congregations were household churches, the tie between domestic household and local Christian assembly could be quite close.[98] The havoc needing to be checked, and malicious energy needing redirection, may have been playing out in homes, congregations, or both.[99]

The mode[100] of destabilization was noble: "teaching" (see Introduction, IX.D). From Moses to Ezra to Jesus to Paul, spiritual leadership among God's chosen people was exercised in part by didactic means. The problem with the activity of the "rebellious people" was not that they were teaching—Jesus commanded his disciples to teach others (Matt 28:19–20)—but *what* they were teaching and *why*.

As to *what* they taught, clearly it did not comport with the gospel or its implications as Paul and his churches everywhere understood these matters. Churches were founded by apostolic proclamation and pedagogy; Paul told the Romans: "Thanks be to God that, though you used to be slaves to sin, you have come to obey from your heart the pattern of teaching that has now claimed your allegiance" (Rom 6:17). But that command implies they could be brought down by the same means if the truth was misrepresented. Paul sensed this threat in the air on Crete. To do nothing would imperil the churches' mission, to say nothing of individual souls.

As to their motivation for teaching, it was "for the sake of dishonest gain." Paul speaks of "gain" (*kerdos*) positively in the only two other New Testament passages where this word is found (Phil 1:21; 3:7). Ignatius exhorts Polycarp, "Bear the diseases of all, as a perfect athlete. Where there is more work, there is much *gain*" (*Pol.* 1:3). There is nothing necessarily sub-Christian about things that make for human flourishing and divine approval, both of which count as "gain." But the gain Paul refers to in this case is "dishonest." The same word is translated "a disgrace" (1 Cor 11:6; cf. 14:35) and "shameful" (Eph 5:12) elsewhere in Paul.[101] It may imply financial gain, but that is not certain in Titus 1:11. It may simply mean unfair and deceptive advantage in support of an ignoble cause. For Paul, the damage

97. See in Paul 1 Cor 11:34, 35; 1 Tim 3:4.

98. See in Paul Rom 16:5; 1 Cor 16:19; Col 4:15; 1 Tim 3:15; Phlm 2.

99. Cf. Marshall, with Towner, 196–97.

100. Wallace, *Greek Grammar*, 630, lists this is an example of an adverbial participle of means.

101. Note also the related compound forms in 1 Tim 3:8; Titus 1:7; 1 Pet 5:2. They are all pejorative.

to souls and testimony would be disastrous enough. This verse amounts to shorthand, then, for what Paul told another audience more expansively, "I urge you, brothers and sisters, to watch out for those who cause divisions and put obstacles in your way that are contrary to the teaching you have learned. Keep away from them" (Rom 16:17). Or again: "In the name of the Lord Jesus Christ, we command you, brothers and sisters, to keep away from every believer who is idle and disruptive and does not live according to the teaching you received from us" (2 Thess 3:6). Paul's directive to Titus, as well as his resolve to uphold the redemptive core of the gospel, has close parallels in other Pauline missives.

12 Social generalizations can be pernicious—today we call them stereotypes—but they can shed light on what is happening in a particular setting. As Paul traveled from place to place, he no doubt observed certain tendencies among various populaces (as locals would have noted peculiarities about Paul as an outsider). On the one hand, he had learned to "regard no one from a worldly point of view" (2 Cor 5:16). In Christ, people become part of "the new creation" (2 Cor 5:17). But yet, on the other hand, these "rebellious people" were not conducting themselves in a way that encouraged Paul to think of them as being and acting "in Christ" insofar as they obstructed apostolic teaching. Paul apparently saw points of contact between their behavior and well-known motifs found in various literary sources of his day[102] that reflected negatively on the social and personal character of Cretans generally.

The fact that Paul was seeking to plant and stabilize churches in the region is proof enough that he did not denigrate or despise the inhabitants of Crete in toto. They were objects of God's love and candidates for gospel redemption just like all other humans. Paul will remind Titus that followers of Christ are no better (Titus 3:3).[103] But the propensity of some for undistinguished outlook and behavior was legendary. A third-century BC source states, "Cretans are thieves from way back, pirates; they never think along legal lines."[104] The lexicon of Hesychius of Alexandria (fifth century AD but drawing on older works and writings) contained the entry *krētizein* (to speak or act like a Cretan; cf. LSJ 995) with the definitions "to lie, to deceive" and an allusion to their reputation for these actions.[105] If, as the NA[27] cross-reference suggests,

102. C. A. Evans, *Ancient Texts for New Testament Studies* (Peabody, MA: Hendrickson, 2005), 395, lists the following possible background sources: Callimachus, *Hymn to Zeus* 8; Epimenides, *De oraculis*; Leonidas, *Anth. lat.* 3.369; Polybius, *Histories* 6:47. Quinn, 108–9, discusses many more. See also Dibelius and Conzelmann, 133.

103. Calvin, 349, thinks the whole letter "is not so much a private letter to Titus as a public epistle to the Cretans." If that is true, by mention of the weaknesses of some he is underscoring their need for the redemption promised in the gospel.

104. *Anthologia Graeca* 7.654 (*NW* 1024).

105. *NW* 1022.

Paul is citing the Cretan holy man Epimenides[106] (sixth or seventh century BC), "one of Crete's own prophets," this reputation was already centuries old at the time Paul wrote.

Whether with a note of irony,[107] resignation, or just the realism of a seasoned gospel messenger who has been there,[108] Paul draws on well-known traditions to remind Titus of the notoriety of Crete's inhabitants over the centuries. Many have noted their tendency to lie, to sink to animal excesses, and to be ruled by crude appetite[109]—they "are[110] always liars, evil brutes, lazy gluttons." It is far from an idyllic social setting. This does not mean that Titus should despair, demonize everyone, or lash out. It should rather inform his prayers for the believers and congregations, help him be a little philosophical about these tendencies if he encounters them, and steel him for the ministries among the congregations to which Paul will set him in subsequent sections of the epistle. Jesus reminded his disciples of the kind of people they were up against, yet were called to minister to (John 16:2–4). He did this in advance so his followers would "not fall away" (John 16:1). Paul's allusion may have an analogous purpose here.

13 Paul affirms the truth of conventional wisdom about Cretans, then urges on Titus an inference. "This saying"[111] of which Paul speaks is the prophetic utterance epitomized in v. 12. The word translated "saying" (*martyria*) appears thirty-seven times in the New Testament but primarily (thirty times) in the Johannine corpus (fourteen times in John's Gospel, seven times in the Epistles, nine times in Revelation). In Paul it is used elsewhere only in 1 Tim 3:7. In Acts Paul reports hearing the word from the Lord while praying in a trance in Jerusalem: "Leave Jerusalem immediately, because the people here

106. So also, for example, Young, *Theology of the Pastoral Epistles*, 9n8, who adds that he was one of seven celebrated sages of antiquity, "described as a prophet by Plato, Aristotle and Cicero."

107. Emphasized by Wright, 147–48. Stott, *The Message of 1 Timothy & Titus*, 181, notes that if Cretans "endorsed their prophet's statement, they condemned themselves; it they repudiated it, they made him the liar he said they were!" Cf. Young, *Theology of the Pastoral Epistles*, 9n8, who depicts the "famous logical puzzle" the statement presented: "If a Cretan says all Cretans are liars, how can it be true?"

108. Less likely is Kelly's claim, "The tone of the sentence suggests that he has had bitter personal experience on the island" (236). This implication cannot be ruled out, but since bitterness does not seem integral to the discourse overall, there is no need to posit it as the informing authorial sentiment here. The claim is about (some) Cretans, not Paul, and if some have strayed from Christian teaching, it is not necessarily bitterness to point to contributing factors.

109. For over two dozen ancient parallels, see *NW* 1017–27.

110. There is no verb in Greek; see Wallace, *Greek Grammar*, 55n59.

111. On the use of the article with the demonstrative, see Wallace, *Greek Grammar*, 242; more broadly, Siebenthal, *Griechische Grammatik*, §263a.

will not accept your *testimony* about me" (22:18). The word denotes an attestation of the way things are, or at least the way someone observes or thinks them to be. Paul adds his own confirmation to what the Cretan prophet said. The word translated "true" occurs nowhere else in the PE but does occur elsewhere in Paul (Rom 3:4; 2 Cor 6:8; Phil 4:8). As far as the stereotype goes, Paul tells Titus, it has some validity.

Given this fact, Paul draws an inference. "Therefore" translates a prepositional phrase[112] found five times elsewhere in the New Testament (Luke 8:47; Acts 22:24; 2 Tim 1:6, 12; Heb 2:11). Because of the validity of the witness, Titus should "rebuke" the troublemakers. This word is used in Luke 3:19 when John the Baptist points out Herod's sin in marrying Herodias. Paul uses it to refer to a necessary pastoral function: sometimes it is necessary to "reprove" church leaders publicly (1 Tim 5:20); pastors must not only preach but correct and "rebuke" (2 Tim 4:2); pastors must also encourage by sound doctrine and "refute" opponents of that doctrine (Titus 1:9). Paul underscores this action with the adverb "sharply," a word used elsewhere in the New Testament only in 2 Cor 13:10. NETS translates the word in Wis 5:22 (its only LXX occurrence) as follows: "Rivers will overwhelm them *relentlessly.*" Titus must leave no doubt but rather be decisive, forthright, and persistent in laying out the truth regarding what the troublemakers are twisting. Or in Wright's words, "He's going to have to be robust and be prepared to work with the people of Crete."[113] Working with people as a leader is a consensual enterprise, optimally, but at times must be adversarial. "Weak and tentative response to their misdeeds would only make the evil worse."[114]

The rebuke is not punitive or vindictive; it has a restorative aim: "so that they will be sound in the faith" (see Introduction, IX.D). Most likely "they" refers to the troublemakers. They are not outside the church but in it. They have gone astray, however, and threaten to take others with them. This outcome is unnecessary and unacceptable. As Titus does his job, there is hope they will return to the apostolic truth from which they have evidently strayed.

"They" could possibly refer, not to the troublemakers, but to those in the church they threaten to subvert. Then Paul's command would be especially for the sake of those who stand in the way of the harm the troublemakers can inflict. For the sake of the faithful, Titus must enter the lists of controversy.

112. The phrase: *di' hēn aitian*. On the construction, see Siebenthal, *Griechische Grammatik*, §289g. Synonymous with this phrase, also more common, is *dia touto* (sixty-four times in the New Testament, of which twenty-two are in Paul, including two occurrences in the PE: 1 Tim 1:16; 2 Tim 2:10).

113. Wright, 148.

114. Schlatter, *Die Kirche der Griechen*, 251.

In either case, to assuage and appease is to promote unhealthy doctrine, conceptual poison that will sicken those who swallow it. Paul's stance here assumes, of course, a model of Christian faith and practice for which doctrine is foundational. In our age, where biblical teachings and practices have frequently been abandoned and where pastoral care seems often to be construed as only affirming the errant and seldom confronting them, Paul's words pose formidable challenge and in fact are clearly rejected by many.

But Paul wants all to be "sound in the faith." The definite article before "faith" implies the content of Christian belief, the confessed or creedal substance. *What* is believed is no less important than *that* people believe. For false or unhealthy teaching does not uplift but misleads. The precise phrase "in the faith" is rare in the New Testament, occurring elsewhere only in 1 Cor 16:13; 2 Cor 13:5; 2 Pet 1:5. The reality it describes, of course, is affirmed frequently. The concept is basic to Jesus's command to teach "them to obey everything I have commanded you" (Matt 28:20) and Paul's notion of an apostolic doctrinal norm (Rom 6:17).

14 Paul defines the kind of "sound in the faith" he has in mind by depicting a twofold opposite. Those whom Titus confronts and stabilizes in faith will as a result "pay no attention to Jewish myths or to the merely human commands of those who reject the truth."

"Myths" are mentioned explicitly only four times in the New Testament (see also 1 Tim 1:4; 4:7; 2 Pet 1:16). The word (*mythos*) refers to fanciful tales in contrast to narrative grounded in fact (see BDAG 660). Hanson suggests that Paul speaks of "Gnostic theogonies propagated by Christian Jews,"[115] but if Paul is the author, distinctly Gnostic yarns were probably not yet current in the AD 60s.[116] Paul's objection would not pertain to Old Testament narrative, which he regarded as true and indeed the foundation of the good news he preached (see Rom 15:4; 1 Cor 10:1–11). By "Jewish myths" he would be referring to stories circulated by Jewish teachers or in Jewish circles that lacked credible basis in fact and that were distracting Christian congregants from doctrines they needed to affirm and live out. Dozens of extant documents might furnish examples. Quinn cites numerous Jewish and Hellenistic possibilities and helpfully points to their danger: "Myths were not just stories, or just stories about what had never really occurred; they were stories in which . . . their authors foisted their own immoral conduct on the gods or . . . enticed their hearers into evil acts on divine precedents."[117] He points out that Greeks and Romans themselves saw the folly and indeed danger of putting stock in

115. Hanson, 178.

116. *EBR* 10:344: "There is no evidence that anything like a coherent gnostic system of thought existed in the 1st century" that could have "served as a source for such ideas" in Paul.

117. Quinn, 110–12. See also Collins, 335, with references to Pindar, Strabo, and Philo.

fictional fantasies.[118] How much truer this would be for Paul, who saw in the story of Jesus (and its Old Testament precursors) the outworking of eternal redemption. The churches in Crete would be neutralized or tilt negatively if their members exchanged the wholesome substance of Scripture and apostolic proclamation for the pottage of speculative fictions. Paul warned Timothy in the Ephesian setting, "They will turn their ears away from the truth and turn aside to myths" (2 Tim 4:4). There is also the danger that attention to such myths by eroding Christian practice would boomerang, shredding the credibility of Scripture, as an AF source recounts: "When the pagans hear from our mouths the oracles of God [= the Scriptures], they marvel at their beauty and greatness. But when they discover that our actions are not worthy of the words we speak, they turn from wonder to blasphemy, saying that it is a myth and a delusion" (2 Clem. 13:3).[119]

This is all the more true if, as Paul's next point implies, these "Jewish myths" amount to or support "the merely human commands of those who reject[120] the truth." The only other time Paul speaks of "command" or "commandment" in the PE, it is a positive thing: "Keep this command without spot or blame until the appearing of our Lord Jesus Christ" (1 Tim 6:14). Elsewhere, too, in Paul "the commandment is holy, righteous and good" (Rom 7:12), speaking of what Scripture enjoins, and "the commandments" of the Decalogue are set forth in their relevance for believers (Rom 13:9; see also Matt 5:19). Paul is far from antinomian; he offers no commandment against commandments that are truly from God. But in Jesus's teaching there is wariness regarding what humans make of divinely revealed mandates: "You have let go of the commands of God and are holding on to human traditions" (Mark 7:8). This tendency in turn has roots in the Old Testament: "The Lord said: 'These people draw near me; they honor me with their lips, while their heart is far from me, and in vain do they worship me, teaching human commands and teachings'" (Isa 29:13 NETS slightly altered). Something analogous comes to the fore in Paul: "See to it that no one takes you captive through hollow and deceptive philosophy, which depends on human tradition and the elemental spiritual forces of this world rather than on Christ" (Col 2:8; see also Gal 4:3, 9; Col 2:20).

In instructing Titus to rebuke and subsequently reclaim for the faith some who have gone astray, there are echoes of earlier encounters and incidents in which "the truth" as conceived by Jesus and the Old Testament and in their train Paul was rejected. Whether this was rejection outright, as in 1 Cor 15, where the resurrection is doubted, or rejection by addition of tales

118. Quinn, 111.

119. This is the only occurrence of the word "myth" in the AF.

120. From the verb *apostrephō*; see discussion of 2 Tim 1:15.

and doctrines that nullify the gospel essence, as in Galatians or Colossians, is not made clear at this point in Titus. Either way, the problem does not seem limited to doctrine but extends also to ethics—practice and behavior—as the remaining two verses of the section make clear.

15 In the history of interpretation, "this verse is among the most widely appropriated from the Pastorals."[121] Paul contrasts two classes of people in order to highlight deficiencies of the Cretan troublemakers whom Titus needs to resist and correct. There is surface similarity to Philo's contrast between an "unclean" (*akathartos*) person who taints all he or she touches and "the actions" committed by good people, as such actions are "made better by the energies of those who apply themselves to them, since in some degree what is done resembles in its character the person who does it."[122] For Philo, however, the good derives from human virtue and ethical probity, while for Paul it is lack of gospel faith that corrupts and presence of such faith that sanctifies.

The first class are "the pure." Paul uses this word (*katharos*) adjectivally to refer to "clean" food (Rom 14:20), a "pure" heart (1 Tim 1:5; 2 Tim 2:22), and a "clear" conscience (1 Tim 3:9; 2 Tim 1:3). Here, however, it is a noun that denotes ethically upright persons. Paul often uses "righteous" to describe such individuals (e.g., Rom 1:17; 2:13; 5:7), as when he tells Timothy, "We . . . know that law is made not for the righteous [person]" (1 Tim 1:9). In Titus 1:14, however, he spoke of "Jewish myths" and specious regulations. Informing such tales and scruples would be hoary tradition grounded in the Torah about matters "clean" and "unclean," the same word group Paul uses in v. 15 to refer to the "pure." It may be the Jewish framework of the discussion that inclines him to refer to people in this way, a usage otherwise absent from his writings.[123]

To these "pure" persons, "all things are pure." It is easy to imagine the Cretan troublemakers declaring certain foods or practices off limits (cf. 1 Tim 4:4), whereas for Paul, the gospel liberates particularly non-Jewish believers from the necessity of many practices and traditions distinct to the various forms of Judaism prevalent in the first century. Or perhaps Paul had in mind the purity of gospel belief of most in the Cretan churches. Was this unaffected faith being tainted by unholy considerations seeping in via errant persons? To those sanctified by faith, Paul and Titus's teaching in its fullness is perfectly "pure."

121. Twomey, 197.

122. Philo, *Special Laws* 3.209; *NW* 1027–28. Cf. Seneca's attribution of weal or woe to deployment of inner attributes to prevail over external circumstances (*Epistles* 98.2–3; *NW* 1028). See also Dibelius and Conzelmann, 138.

123. Jesus speaks of "the pure [*katharoi*] in heart" (Matt 5:8), tells Pharisees to "give what is inside [the dish] to the poor, and everything will be clean [*kathara*] for you" (Luke 11:41), and tells his disciples, "You are already clean [*katharoi*] because of the word I have spoken to you" (John 15:3). In Acts, Paul uses this word to refer to himself (18:6; 20:26).

But there is the second class of persons, "those who are corrupted[124] and do not believe." Paul surely means they reject or disastrously tamper with the gospel. The word "corrupted" (from *miainō*) is not common in the New Testament, appearing elsewhere only three times (John 18:28; Heb 12:15; Jude 8). It occurs often in the LXX (128 times), 32 times in Leviticus, where it means to defile or make oneself "unclean" and thus not fit to appear before the Lord. Again, the "Jewish myths" and hence mythmakers Paul is dealing with may incline his word choice in this direction—these Cretans make bold to improve on the cleansing gospel, but they are actually reverting to the same uncleanness that was a problem going back to Moses's era. In claiming to improve on the apostolic gospel, everything they propound is tainted. They are "corrupted" by their disbelief.[125]

"Do not believe" is the NIV rendering of a signature Pauline expression that means "unbelievers." Outside of Paul's writings, this term (from *apistos*, unbelieving, faithless) appears in its noun usage only twice (Luke 12:46; Rev 21:8). But it is how Paul typically speaks of "unbelievers" (1 Cor 6:6; 7:12, 15; 10:27; 14:22; 2 Cor 4:4; 6:15; 1 Tim 5:8).

Nothing is "pure" for these persons. They do not affirm the apostolic message, which creates a domino effect that skews their judgment across the board. It is not just their counsel and political influence in Cretan churches that is a problem: "both their minds[126] and consciences[127] are corrupted."[128] Their behavior is pervasively self-destructive. Paul's concern is not solely for those loyal to Christ but also for the souls of those who have strayed. "Mind" here likely refers to rational faculty. "Conscience" is an organ of moral discernment that informs the human will and is informed by the value system to which one chooses to submit—whether, for Paul, either sin or righteousness (see Rom 6:16–18), as defined primarily by revealed Scripture and its fulfillment in Christ. Since these corrupted individuals do not accept the gospel,

124. Wallace, *Greek Grammar*, 437, suggests this Greek use of the passive is "the suppression of the agent for rhetorical effect."

125. Ovid, *Tristia*, 301–2, writes, "Anything can corrupt a perverted mind: everything's harmless in its proper place." See *NW* 1029. Ovid trivializes what some find morally questionable in his writings; Paul confirms the reality of a moral universe in which God is judge.

126. "Mind" (*nous*) is a characteristically Pauline word. Of its twenty-four New Testament occurrences, twenty-one are in Paul's writings (just three times in the PE: see also 1 Tim 6:5; 2 Tim 3:8).

127. This word (Gk. *syneidēsis*) also occurs in the New Testament primarily in Paul's writing. It is found thirty times in the New Testament, twenty times in Paul. (In its two Acts occurrences, the word appears on Paul's lips: Acts 23:1; 24:16.) Six of these occurrences are in the PE.

128. On the agreement of compound subject and verb in this construction (but not some others), see Siebenthal, *Griechische Grammatik*, §264a.

their consciences cannot derive the benefit of righteousness that the gospel believed imparts.

16 Paul summarizes the error of those who detract from the gospel message in ways that threaten the integrity of Christian congregations in Crete. Their deficiency has two aspects: (1) there is a disconnect between their confession and their behavior, and (2) they are unsuited to furnish leadership for God's people.

First, "they claim to know God." In Greek "God" is likely emphatic by means of placement first in the sentence. *God* is who they claim to honor and uphold. In their minds they act for his sake. "Claim" could be translated "confess" in the sense of a verbal statement of belief (see also Rom 10:9, 10; 1 Tim 6:12). These are not godless persons at all levels; quite the opposite, as they have a strong sense of knowing him.

The problem is that their "actions" constitute betrayal of their confession. The Greek word underlying "actions" is *ergon*, often translated "works" when in the plural, as here. It is a key word in Titus, occurring in seven verses. (It is found 169 times in the New Testament as a whole.) In Titus, only here does it have a negative connotation—and this is not because "works" in themselves are somehow bad. It is because the convictions informing the actions of these particular persons are wrong, producing unwholesome results. For this reason Paul will later exhort in the direction of sound or healthy doctrine.

Table 26 shows the centrality of "works" to the discourse in Titus in its central and closing portions.

Table 26. "Works" (from *ergon*) in Titus

NIV (TRANSLATION OF *ERGON* ITALICIZED)	COMMENT
1:16 They claim to know God, but by their *actions* they deny him. They are detestable, disobedient and unfit for doing *anything good.*	Faith that is confessed needs to align with actions. Works that God recognizes as "good" are a high priority for gospel believers.
2:7 In everything set them an example by *doing what is good.*	It is critical, as a church leader, that Titus set an example of being rich in good works (*kalōn ergōn*).
2:14 who gave himself for us to redeem us from all wickedness and to purify for himself a people that are his very own, eager to do *what is good*	Christ's intent in dying was in part to create a people zealous to perform "good works" (*kalōn ergōn*).

NIV (TRANSLATION OF *ERGON* ITALICIZED)	COMMENT
3:1 Remind the people to be subject to rulers and authorities, to be obedient, to be ready to do *whatever is good.*	Zeal for "every good work (*pan ergon agathon*) should be characteristic of Christians. Here the actions are in the social sphere and not merely in the church.
3:5 He saved us, not because of righteous *things we had done*, but because of his mercy.	"Works" (*ergōn*) are not a basis for God's gift of saving grace.
3:8 This is a trustworthy saying. And I want you to stress these things, so that those who have trusted in God may be careful to devote themselves to doing *what is good.* These things are excellent and profitable for everyone.	Paul places a high priority on Christians moving from profession of faith to "good works" (*kalōn ergōn*) that embody and express that faith. There is a redemptive gain and effect from such service.
3:14 Our people must learn to devote themselves to doing *what is good*, in order that they may provide for urgent needs and not live unproductive lives.	A central aim of Christian faith and life is "good works" (*kalōn ergōn*) in their practical expression and outcome.

In Titus 1:16 Paul underscores that the works in question do not commend those who perform them; they rather constitute denial of God. Jesus noted, "Not everyone who *says* to me, 'Lord, Lord,' will enter the kingdom of heaven, but only the one who *does* the will of my Father who is in heaven" (Matt 7:21). The problem of flawed confession, of the one who purports to know God "but does not do what he commands" (1 John 2:4), recurs across the sweep of biblical history. It is lamentable but hardly surprising to learn that it was part of the religious landscape as Paul and Titus contemplate ministry prospects on Crete. "Sound doctrine is not merely a propositional profession, but a conviction that illumines the mind so that it can become operative in virtuous behavior."[129] "Paul understands that orthodox proclamation without orthopraxy makes a mockery of the faith we proclaim."[130]

Paul concludes his depiction of these gospel detractors with a threefold critique. First, they are "detestable." The underlying Greek word (*bdelyktos*) occurs nowhere else in the New Testament. The LXX uses it to describe the

129. Saarinen, 176.
130. Gloer, 41.

heinous act of "acquitting the guilty and condemning the innocent," both of which are "detestable to God" (Prov 17:15, my translation; see also 2 Macc 1:27).[131] Clement of Rome uses the word to praise the Corinthians for their aversion to division in the church: "Every faction and every schism was *abominable* to you" (1 Clem. 2:6). And he warns against "detestable" behavior: "Seeing then that we are the portion of the Holy One, let us do all the things that pertain to holiness, forsaking slander, disgusting and impure embraces, drunkenness and rioting and *detestable* lusts, abominable adultery, *detestable* pride" (1 Clem. 30:1). Paul's concern fits well within both biblical and subapostolic admonition.

Second, they are "disobedient." People of this description are part of the background at Jesus's birth (Luke 1:17), in the vice-list of Romans (1:30), and in the coming (and already present) evil age (2 Tim 3:2). If, as Paul charges, these Cretans' knowledge of God is flawed and their actions inconsistent, they rightly deserve the label "disobedient."

Third, they are unsuited for "doing anything good" (see table 26 on "good works"). In Paul's thinking acts that honor God are those arising from fellowship with him—God is at work in believers' lives both to will and do what pleases him (see Phil 2:12–13). But these persons do not know God. They are therefore *adokimoi* ("unfit") for truly God-honoring responses to his gracious revealed will. Seven out of eight times this word appears in the New Testament, it occurs in Paul's writings and refers to morally or spiritually deficient persons or their (twisted) mental faculties.[132] It is entirely consistent with usage elsewhere that Paul warns Titus of the work and influence of such persons in the congregations over which he has oversight on the island of Crete.

IV. SUMMARY FOR PASTORAL DIRECTION (2:1–10)

Thus far in the epistle Paul has conveyed (theologically charged) greetings, reminded Titus of his mission, and sketched prominent features of key opponents. Grammatically, the discourse has been primarily in the indicative mood—Paul has been describing how things are or should be. There has been only one formal command (1:13: "rebuke them sharply").

As a whole, the epistle contains a total of fourteen formal imperatives, thirteen of which appear in Titus 2–3. Three may be set aside as time-bound

131. *CNTUOT* 913 points to the use of the cognate verb in Ps 13:1 LXX (14:1 ET).

132. The exception is Heb 6:8: "But land that produces thorns and thistles is *worthless* and is in danger of being cursed." The other Pauline occurrences: Rom 1:28; 1 Cor 9:27; 2 Cor 13:5, 6, 7; 2 Tim 3:8.

personal requests from Paul to Titus.[133] But the remaining ten, surveyed together, are important as highlighting the hortatory center of the epistle. Titus is rightly known as a *pastoral* letter. What *should* a pastor do, be, or both, from the standpoint of the apostle Paul? A brief epistle is not a wide-ranging pastoral manual. But viewing the imperatives specifically and as a whole yields at least a partial, textually grounded answer to that reasonable and important question.

Table 27. The pastoral mandate in Titus: Paul's 11 imperatives to Titus

Passage	Command to Titus (imperatives in italics)
1:13	This saying is true. Therefore, *rebuke* them sharply, so that they will be sound in the faith
2:1	You, however, must *teach* what is appropriate to sound doctrine.
2:6	Similarly, *encourage* the young men to be self-controlled.
2:15 (4x)	These, then, are the things you should *teach*. *Encourage* and *rebuke* with all authority. *Do not let* anyone *despise* you.
3:1	*Remind* the people to be subject to rulers and authorities, to be obedient, to be ready to do whatever is good,
3:9	But *avoid* foolish controversies and genealogies and arguments and quarrels about the law, because these are unprofitable and useless.
3:10	*Warn* a divisive person once, and then warn them a second time. After that, have nothing to do with them.
3:14	Our people must *learn* to devote themselves to doing what is good, in order to provide for urgent needs and not live unproductive lives.

Many of Titus's priorities would be given with his status as a Christ-follower, missionary companion of Paul, and church-planting overseer. Paul does not need to tell Titus to cling to gospel conviction, pray without ceasing, love God and neighbor, and dozens of other obvious priorities for a Christian generally, to say nothing of a church leader. He does, however, issue specific commands that shed light on the pastoral task in analogous situations today—Titus's

133. Titus 3:12, 13, 15. Two verses in the NIV translate *dei* with "must" and may therefore sound imperatival (1:7, 11). But in both passages the semantics of the discourse remains on the indicative side of the indicative-imperative divide.

setting can hardly be regarded as unique and nonrepeatable in all respects. Paul's commands to Titus continue to be imperatives for ministers now, to a considerable extent and allowing for situational particulars inherent to Crete or to a given setting currently. These imperatives are commands for Titus to:

rebuke (2x)
teach (2x)
encourage (2x)
not let people disregard[134] you
remind the people (to do three things)
avoid fruitless disputations
warn the divisive person
let people learn devotion to good works

The section begins, then, with an imperative edge,[135] as Paul begins to unpack what Titus can and should do (1) fully to utilize the vast resources that God's provision in the gospel makes available to him, and (2) diligently to deploy his leadership calling and skills for the sake of stabilizing and enhancing the work of ministry and mission in the Cretan congregations.

> [1] *You, however, must teach what is appropriate to sound doctrine.* [2] *Teach the older men to be temperate, worthy of respect, self-controlled, and sound in faith, in love and in endurance.* [3] *Likewise, teach the older women to be reverent in the way they live, not to be slanderers or addicted to much wine, but to teach what is good.* [4] *Then they can urge the younger women to love their husbands and children,* [5] *to be self-controlled and pure, to be busy at home, to be kind, and to be subject to their husbands, so that no one will malign the word of God.* [6] *Similarly, encourage the young men to be self-controlled.* [7] *In everything set them an example by doing what is good. In your teaching show integrity, seriousness* [8] *and soundness of speech that cannot be condemned, so that those who oppose you may be ashamed because they have nothing bad to say about us.* [9] *Teach slaves to be subject to their masters in everything, to try to please them, not to talk back to them,* [10] *and not to steal from them, but to show that they can be fully trusted, so that in every way they will make the teaching about God our Savior attractive.*

134. NIV translates "despise"; the sense is "disregard." See explanation in commentary on 2:15 below.

135. Moule, *Idiom Book*, 126, suggests that 2:1–10 may also contain imperatival infinitives, in effect extending the base infinitive "teach" in 2:1.

1 Paul gives direct instructions to Titus regarding his own top responsibilities. Paul's "response to the situation produces an emphasis on teaching which is approved."[136] The conjunction *de* ("so then" or perhaps "but"), translated as "therefore" in NIV, links the verse with previous sections. A contrast between what the mythmakers say and what Titus should say is possibly implied.[137]

First of all, Titus is to "teach." This imperative (from *laleō*) is generally defined as "speak, say, talk." BDAG does not include "teach" as a definition of the word. Many versions do not translate "teach" here:

> What you *say* must be in keeping with wholesome doctrine. (NEB)
>
> *Preach* the behavior that goes with healthy doctrine. (JB)
>
> *Speak* thou the things which become sound doctrine. (KJV)
>
> You must *speak* what is consistent with sound teaching. (HCSB)
>
> Yet, as for you, may the words which you *address* to others be such as to be in conformity with sound doctrine. (*GNC*)

Any of the above renderings is perhaps preferable to "promote the kind of living that reflects right teaching" (NLT), as the Greek verb *laleō* potentially overlaps more with teaching activity than with promoting some kind of living. And NIV is not off the mark in connecting "speaking" and "teaching" in this verse.[138] In a parallel passage (2:15) that likewise uses the verb for "speak," codex A reads *didaske* (second person sing. imperative for "teach"). Titus is a pastoral leader; such leaders are called to speak frequently in a didactic matter; their speaking is therefore often tantamount to teaching.

Yet, not all speaking, even of a pastoral leader, is "teaching" in the formal sense. Pastoral leaders "speak" a great deal in ways that would not normally be called teaching. Paul's command to Titus certainly extends to his teaching ministry, and by extension to the ministries of the pastors whose appointment he will oversee. But it also applies to his prayers, his personal interaction with others, and indeed all his verbal expression. "For the mouth speaks [*lalei*] what the heart is full of" (Matt 12:34). Paul's concern is not limited to what Titus "teaches" or preaches in the formal sense but extends to the fullest expression of who he is as a verbal and interactive man of faith

136. Young, *Theology of the Pastoral Epistles*, 75–76; cf. 77.

137. So Knight, 305.

138. Among translations that follow suit: RSV, NRSV, ESV. Both Luther and the Latin translate "speak."

and ecclesial leader.[139] (For additional discussion of *lalei* as "teach," see on Titus 2:15 below.)

Paul rivets Titus's attention with an emphatic pronoun of address: "You."[140] It marks a major shift in the discourse. Paul means business; Titus cannot take this lightly. With a similar construction Jesus tells John, "You—follow me!"[141] If Titus is going to identify, train, and appoint elders, he must be exemplary in all his speech. It must be "appropriate to" (*prepei*) "sound doctrine" (see Introduction, IX.D). The word means "fitting, proper," and has many parallels elsewhere.[142]

The standard for all Titus says, "sound doctrine," could also be translated "healthy teaching." "All trifles vanish away before solid teaching."[143] The previous section described a pathological situation in which misguided leaders wreak havoc in families, congregations, or both. False teaching is foundational to the maladies Paul diagnoses. The antidote is its opposite: "healthy" or "sound" instruction in the Christian faith. That is not all Titus must do. But if he fails at promoting that kind of teaching, any hope for healing of the ills in Cretan churches is slim. In following verses Paul will prescribe godly mien and behavior, the basis for which is the kind of teaching mentioned here and the patterns of speech of the godly leader who is called to deliver it.[144]

2 The remainder of this section is devoted to directives appropriate to various groupings of persons: older men (v. 2), older and younger women (vv. 3–5), young men, (v. 6), Titus himself (vv. 7–8), and slaves (vv. 9–10). It is common for this passage to be treated as stereotypical counsel on the model of alleged "household codes," but the basis for this analysis is shaky.[145] Even if Paul were using an established literary form, it would not restrict him from filling it with content grounded in apostolic ethics, itself informed by Old Testament Scripture, Jesus's teaching and self-disclosure, and the cognitive work of the promised Holy Spirit.[146] It would be rank hypocrisy for Paul to summon Titus (and Timothy) to uphold sublime "sound doctrine" and then dish up for them bland accommodations to cultural convention, as some

139. See Calvin, 368.

140. See similar constructions at 1 Tim 6:11; 2 Tim 2:1; 3:14; 4:5, 15. Formal equivalents in Rom 14:22 and Jas 2:3 are rhetorical, not actual personal address.

141. John 21:22 (my translation).

142. Other New Testament uses: Matt 3:15; 1 Cor 11:13; Eph 5:3; 1 Tim 2:10; Heb 2:10; 7:26.

143. Calvin, 368.

144. See Mounce, 408.

145. See Yarbrough, "Familiar Paths and a Fresh Matrix," 229–33.

146. This is surely part of what Paul has in mind when he mentions "the grace given" to him: Rom 12:3; 15:5; 1 Cor 3:10; Gal 2:9; Eph 3:7–8. It can also be regarded as inherent in his status as apostle, to which he calls attention dozens of times in his writings, including five times in the PE (1 Tim 1:1; 2:7; 2 Tim 1:1, 11; Titus 1:1).

understandings of the household codes claim. But this is hardly what Paul does here.

He first tells Titus how to instruct "the older men." This is a diplomatic translation of the plural for "old men." It appears only two other times in the New Testament. It refers to Zechariah as he asks the angel, "How can I be sure of this? I am an old man and my wife is well along in years" (Luke 1:18). And Paul applies this term to himself ca. AD 60, when he would have been around sixty years of age (Phlm 9). Life spans were short in antiquity: "The consensus of modern scholars is that life expectancy in the Roman Empire as a whole in our period fell in the range of twenty-five to thirty years, comparable with that of other preindustrial societies."[147] Of course there are always those who outlive statistical norms. There is evidence that Paul had in mind the age of about forty or fifty and upward.[148] Quinn too places the division between older and younger at about fifty.[149]

Titus is to minister in such a way that these men (probably rank-and-file church members rather than office-holding "elders" per se, which would be a different word) excel in four qualities. They should first be[150] "temperate," a word found elsewhere in the New Testament only in 1 Tim 3:2, 11. It is absent from the LXX and AF. Josephus uses it to laud the Old Testament priests, who, according to Moses's teaching, were to be "without spot, in all respects pure and *temperate*" (*Jewish Antiquities* 3.279). As in English, the word can connote freedom from intoxication by alcohol,[151] but by extension its sense is wise moderation in matters that sinful humans frequently pursue to excess. Paul has already talked about misguided moral and doctrinal tendencies afoot in the Cretan congregations; at the very least he is telling Titus to help older men deliver themselves from entrapment in these through lives informed by divine guidance, restraint, and pursuit of more noble ends.

Titus's second pastoral aim with these men is that they be "worthy of respect." The word occurs three other times in the New Testament (Phil 4:8; 1 Tim 3:8, 11). It refers to "that which is sublime, majestic, holy, evoking reverence."[152] A godly dignity should mark their character and shine forth from their lives.

Third, they should be "self-controlled." Paul uses this word to describe a qualification for pastors (see discussion at 1:8 above); otherwise, the word

147. Susan Treggiari, "Marriage and Family in Roman Society," in *Marriage and Family in the Biblical World*, ed. Ken Campbell (Downers Grove, IL: InterVarsity Press, 2003), 143.

148. The major ancient demarcations of age are given in Marshall, with Towner, 239.

149. Quinn, 129.

150. For the use of the infinitive *einai* to designate a predicate accusative, see Wallace, *Greek Grammar*, 190–92.

151. For example, Philo, *Allegorical Interpretation* 2.29; 3.210.

152. NIDNT 2:92.

is found in the New Testament only at 1 Tim 3:2 and Titus 2:5. Clement of Rome sends his letter to Corinth accompanied by men of this description: "We have also sent trustworthy and *prudent* men who from youth to old age have lived blameless lives among us, who will be witnesses between you and us" (1 Clem. 63:3). Justin Martyr uses the word to denote "*sound* reason" (*Apology* 1.2; cf. *Dialogue with Trypho* 4).[153] Fickleness, rash passion, and impulsiveness should be things of the past for men in this stage of life, now that they have made Christian confession and are engaged in Christian life and service.

Paul's fourth desideratum for Titus's elderly male echelon is for them to be "sound," or healthy, in three domains: faith, love, and endurance.[154] The word "in" before each of these (there is no "and" in Gk.) gives the effect of Paul pausing over them one by one, as if relishing the prospect of old and respected believers given over to these great, gospel-enabled practices. These are central Christian graces that, however, cannot be assumed to thrive where "sound doctrine" (v. 1) is threatened by errant views and their accompanying negative ethical effects. It is important that Titus stabilize and confirm the oldest and presumably most reliable elderly men in the Cretan congregations in all three domains so they may be sheet anchors against the winds of aberrant faith and practice that Paul writes to counteract. Paul's later theological reflections (e.g., 2:11–14; 3:3–7) will serve this end by giving additional grounding for his exhortations here.

3 Titus does not preside over a male-only club or fraternity of celibates; where there are elderly men in domestic and church settings, there will be elderly women too. The godly bearing of both groups is equally important for the flourishing of God's people. Paul gives directions for older women's comportment in the next three verses.

"Likewise"[155] signals that Titus owes this group the same pastoral attention that the older men[156] received (v. 2) and that the younger men likewise require (v. 6). Titus needs to "teach" the older women no less than the older men. The word "teach" does not actually occur either here or in v. 2; NIV infers it from the context, perhaps especially 2:1, where, however, "teach" is not in the Greek either. As Titus goes about his verbal interaction with congregations and

153. It is found thirty-one times in Philo and twenty-four times in Josephus. It was not, therefore, a rare or foreign thought in first-century Jewish ethical reasoning.

154. Wallace (*Greek Grammar*, 146) sees a dative of reference here: sound *with reference to* faith, love, endurance.

155. This adverb occurs nine times in the Synoptic Gospels and eight other times in Paul (Rom 8:26; 1 Cor 11:25; 1 Tim 2:9; 3:8, 11; 5:25; Titus 2:6.

156. The "older women" are presumably about the same age (see discussion at v. 3). The same word is used in 1 Tim 5:2: Timothy is to treat "older women as mothers . . . with absolute purity."

individuals, he should take special care to nurture the kinds of results among older women that these verses describe.

Paul refers to a range of four characteristics or tendencies: behavior, speech, appetite, and teaching competence. The first is the most general and may be an umbrella under which to regard the other three. The word for "the way they live" (*katastēma*; BDAG 527) means behavior or demeanor. "Paul is referring to all aspects of a Christian woman's bearing and appearance, in public and in private."[157] It occurs only here in the New Testament and not at all in the LXX. It occurs once in the AF, denoting the "demeanor" of a gentle bishop whom "even the godless respect" (Ign. *Trall.* 3:2). Josephus used the word to describe the poise and composure of Mariamne I when Herod the Great cruelly ordered her execution (*Jewish Antiquities* 15.236). "Outwardly visible bearing" seems to be the sense. In this regard elderly women are to be "reverent" (*hieroprepēs*; BDAG 470), another word that does not occur elsewhere in the New Testament, and only in 4 Macc in the LXX, once describing the noble spirituality of the first of seven brothers being martyred for their faith (9:25) and again describing the holiness or sanctity of the death throes of the sixth brother tortured to death in the same sequence (11:20). Titus is to encourage these women in the direction of truly sublime deportment.

This godly character and behavior, Paul continues, should play out as follows. First, in speech they should not be "slanderers." This is the feminine form of the word often translated "devil" when used in the singular[158] masculine form, which refers to Satan.[159] The sense of the word is to accuse, to speak against maliciously. In the PE such activity is condemned for the wives of deacons (1 Tim 3:11). The same term is used to describe degenerate people, men and women, in the terrible last days of which 2 Timothy speaks: they will be "without love, unforgiving, slanderous," and much more (or less; 2 Tim 3:3). From the Proverbs to Jesus's teaching to James and beyond, speech ethics are a central canonical concern for the people of God; Paul voices it here with regards to women whose conversation should build up and not tear down.

Paul moves from speech to appetite. There is no reason to think Paul was a teetotaler (1 Tim 5:23), but he is aware that intoxicating beverages can contribute to ruin (Rom 14:21; Eph 5:18).[160] Perhaps he knew of problems in this regard in Crete. Zehr points out that drunkenness was a problem among older

157. Ngewa, 362.

158. On use of the plural, see Wallace, *Greek Grammar*, 224.

159. See in the PE 1 Tim 3:6, 7; 2 Tim 2:26. In Paul elsewhere: Eph 4:27; 6:11.

160. On Old Testament awareness of wine abuse, see, for example, Gen 9:21; 19:33; Lev 10:9; 1 Sam 1:14; 2 Sam 13:28; Prov 20:1; 21:17; 23:20, 31; Isa 5:11; Jer 23:9; Dan 1:8; Joel 3:3; Amos 6:6; Hab 2:5. At least as many passages speak positively of prudent alcohol consumption, however.

women in both Hellenistic and Jewish circles.[161] Alcohol abuse and addiction are prominent among evils that seems to crop up in most places and times if one looks closely enough. These women should have no part in imbibing to excess. It would be ungodly in itself, as well as contrary to the sublime deportment called for earlier in the verse.

Paul's final expectation for older women is that they "teach what is good."[162] They have a discipleship function in the congregations. Paul will expand on this in the next two verses. Jesus's call to be and make disciples is for everyone in the church, not just one sex and not just a narrow selection of specially called and gifted persons. Some may and should have special gifts and training for this, but in the course of time virtually all believers of all ages can be of didactic assistance to Christian sisters and brothers and others outside the church for that matter. Here Paul seeks to inculcate that inclusive and evangelistically aggressive mentality with regards to the elderly women of the congregations of Crete.

NIV translates "*but* to teach what is good." The italicized word, absent in Greek, is a reasonable inference, given the flow of the discourse: the women should not be slanderers or drunks *but* teachers of the good. Few if any other translations (but see NLT) interpolate the adversative conjunction, the effect of which may be to place additional emphasis on the wine and speech problems and give the discourse a slightly moralistic tone—as if not slandering others or sousing oneself is tantamount to teaching what is good. Too much should not be made of the presence or absence of an adversative. But without "but" it may be clearer that Paul values the actual teaching role (not just the absence of gossip and drunkenness) in women who have reached the level of maturity assumed here. Translations taking this tack often begin a new sentence that underscores this emphasis: "They are to teach what is good" (ESV, RSV, NRSV, CSB); "They must teach what is proper" (CEV; cf. JB, NEB).

4 The traits and abilities cited in the previous verse are advantageous for all kinds of reasons in broad Pauline perspective. They glorify God (1 Cor 10:31). They constitute decent behavior (Rom 13:13). They contribute to wholesome talk that builds others up (Eph 4:29). They contribute to mutual encouragement and instruction in the faith (Rom 15:14). There are many valid applications Paul could make of what he has said in Titus 2:3.

The application Paul chooses is to the family (and by extension congregational) sphere. This is perfectly logical if the point of attack of the troublemakers on Crete is that "they are upsetting whole families" (1:11). The positive traits urged in Titus 2:3 are to be deployed by older women to contribute to

161. Zehr, 265.

162. Hanson (180) comments that the one-word adjective translated "to teach what is good" (*kalodidaskalous*) "appears to have been coined by the author."

God-honoring, Christ-reflecting attitudes on the part of "younger women"[163] toward their husbands and children. Paul uses the same descriptor for the "younger women" whom Timothy is to treat "as sisters, with absolute purity" in 1 Tim 5:2.

Specifically, older women are to "urge" (from *sōphronizō*) the younger. This word does not occur elsewhere in the New Testament, in the LXX, or in the AF but is found in Justin Martyr, Josephus (eleven times), and Philo (thirty-four times). The NIV84 translation "train" no doubt captured in English an aspect of what Paul intends. But that could come across as stilted and stifling if not pedantic and a bit demeaning. We "train" pets; is this Paul's drift? Emphatically not, it would seem, even from a glance at BDAG (986–87), where the meaning given is "to instruct in prudence or behavior that is becoming and shows good judgment, *encourage, advise, urge*." MM 622 points to the meaning "bring to one's senses," as if to wake someone up or give them a good shaking. The entire word group of which the verb translated "urge" is part is redolent of qualities like prudence, moderation, good judgment, reasonableness, rationality, and self-control. With the verb in v. 4 Paul urges Titus to steer older women toward inculcating certain admirable and beneficial qualities in younger women, not to "train" them in rote formalities, mere external actions, or (as the household code theory has it) cultural accommodation.

Paul has two goals for older women to keep in mind relative to the younger ones. First, the younger are "to love their husbands." NIV here is trying to render the infinitive "to be" plus an adjective that means "affectionate/loving toward one's husband."[164] Paul does not so much say what younger women should be "urged" *to do* as he presents *what kind of wife* a younger married woman should be encouraged *to be* by their godly older peers, who have the wisdom of years to draw upon. Jesus taught lifelong heterosexual monogamy (Matt 19:4–6), an institution often debased among God's Old Testament followers (note polygamy, adultery, fornication, and more recounted in the Old Testament) but at the same time protected (e.g., by commands against carnal violations of the marital covenant) and even celebrated (e.g., Prov 5; Song of Songs) in Old Testament history and Scripture. Paul envisioned deep and self-sacrificial love between spouses (Eph 5:22–33). Greco-Roman marriage was an institution facing many challenges in the first century,[165] much as it is in the

163. On the use of the article *tas* with the adjective *neas* (new, young) to denote "young women," see Wallace, *Greek Grammar*, 233.

164. The word (*philandros*, lit. "husband-lover") does not appear elsewhere in the NT, nor in the LXX, AF, or Josephus. It occurs once in Philo (*Rewards* 139).

165. See Ken M. Campbell, ed., *Marriage and Family in the Biblical World* (Downers Grove, IL: InterVarsity Press, 2003), esp. chapters by S. M. Baugh ("Marriage and Family in Ancient Greek Society"), Susan Treggiari ("Marriage and Family in Roman Society"), and

West today. Gospel reception can create strong, godly, and selfless relationships leading to vibrant marriages. That is what Paul is trying to encourage.

The grace and beauty of a loving wife are captured in a gravestone inscription dating from Hadrian's era (ca. AD 117–38). It contains the same word for "loving her husband" (*philandros*) found in Titus 2:4: "Julius Bassus to Otacilia Polla, his sweetest wife. *Loving her husband* and loving her children, she lived with him unblameably thirty years" (MM 668).

Along with the love for husbands, Paul urges that the same women be affectionate/loving toward children, presumably first of all their own. An age in which slaughter of the unborn through abortion is internationally rampant should not find it hard to imagine a situation in which mothers need to be called back to the protection and promotion of their children. The word for "lovers of children," like "loving toward husbands," is nonexistent elsewhere in the New Testament and LXX. But its meaning is not in question. Elsewhere in Paul fathers are charged not to "exasperate your children; instead, bring them up in the training and instruction of the Lord" (Eph 6:4). Paul does not offload the whole wagon of parental duties on wives. But if wives need their husbands' engagement, husbands need the fertile soil of children's hearts that are secure, strong, and joyful in their mother's loyalty and affection. This maternal integrity will not only facilitate parenting: it will unite wife and husband in the joint challenge of their children's daily care and confirmation in Christian faith. They can agonize in prayer as one over what is not falling into place; they can bask in conjugal joys as they see God's grace bearing fruit in their children's lives.[166] Attempts of enemies to ruin households (Titus 1:11) will be thwarted both short-term and long.

Titus can help effect all this by enlisting older women in the project. Their possible status as grandmothers will motivate them all the more to stir up daughters to do right in Christ by their spouses and offspring.

5 Paul continues to sketch the composite of what kind of young women the congregations' older women should be seeking to form by their example and counsel. Words like "teach" (vv. 1, 3) and "train" (v. 4 NIV84) could, on a quick surface reading, convey a sense of Pauline heavy-handedness and intrusiveness toward the personal lives of women. It should be noted again, however, that the command "teach" is absent from this section (v. 1 says "speak"; see commentary above and at 2:15 below). And the actions envisioned are to be performed, not by Paul, nor even by Titus, but by women. With great pas-

---

David Chapman ("Marriage and Family in Second Temple Judaism"). See also Winter, *Roman Wives, Roman Widows*.

166. For the challenges and joys of marriage for young adults in the current North American setting, see Owen Strachan, "Risky Families: Building a Legacy," in *Risky Gospel* (Nashville: Nelson, 2013), 95–114.

toral wisdom and tact, Paul instructs Titus to delegate the spiritual formation and daily lives of younger women to the believers best situated to encourage them. This is a fine example of Paul advising Titus in such a way that he will do precisely what Paul elsewhere urges as a central duty of pastors: "to equip [God's] people for works of service, so that the body of Christ may be built up" (Eph 4:12). Women no less than men are at the core of this ministry.

There are five traits the older women should aim to establish and enhance in their younger charges. The first is to be "self-controlled." This is a requirement for pastors (see 1:8 and commentary above; also 1 Tim 3:2), as well as for the older women themselves (Titus 2:2). For younger men as well, self-control is a first priority (v. 6).[167] People of the first-century Mediterranean world may have been less "expressive individualist"[168] than most Westerners today and more corporately oriented. But Paul, like other New Testament writers, envisions all people[169] struggling with unholy impulses and tendencies that Christ's gospel has the effect of checking and transforming in constructive directions. Paul calls here for younger women to be under the control of God's liberating presence and Spirit, not the tyranny of unregenerate human nature (see Titus 3:5–6), whose characteristic expressions would have been familiar to Titus from Paul's instruction elsewhere (see "the acts of the sinful nature" listed in Gal 5:19–21; even at that point Titus was Paul's coworker [Gal 2:1]). It is not a compliment when we say, in a North American idiom, that someone is "out of control." The older women under Titus's direction should minimize the occurrence of this blight in the lives and marriages of these younger women, in their relationships, and thereby in the congregations in which they serve.

A second desirable trait is "purity." In this word's eight New Testament occurrences, it can denote feminine chastity (2 Cor 11:2; 1 Pet 3:2), and that sense cannot be ruled out here. A Christian wife is to be faithful to her husband. More precisely, "in the context of this letter, the words do not refer to sexual abstinence (a position firmly opposed by the author), but to a wife's sexual fidelity to her spouse."[170] But it also carries the sense of moral or legal innocence (2 Cor 7:11) and theological or ethical excellence (Phil 4:8). The transcendent "wisdom" that James extols is "first of all pure" (Jas 3:17). This "purity" is not a trait reserved solely for women, as Timothy is told, "Keep yourself pure" (1 Tim 5:22). In fact, this quality is a priority for all believers in light of apostolic teaching on last things: "All who have this hope [of Christ's appearing] in him purify themselves, just as he [i.e., Christ] is pure"

167. Here Paul uses a verbal form; see commentary below.

168. A term popularized in Bellah et al., *Habits of the Heart*.

169. Including himself: 1 Tim 1:15.

170. Bassler, 196.

(1 John 3:3). In calling for younger women's "purity" Paul is calling for actualization of a lofty aspect of Christlikeness appropriate to their status as children of God in the covenant of marriage. This sterling character quality would be no less important for the unmarried.

A third trait to be passed from older to younger women is variously translated: "busy at home" (NIV, NEB); "working at home" (ESV; cf. JB); "workers at home" (CSB); "domestic" (RSV); "a good homemaker" (CEV). But NRSV best captures the nuance of the rare Greek word *oikourgos*: "good managers of the household."[171] Support for this meaning comes from use of the cognate verb *oikourgeō* by Clement of Rome in the next generation, as he praises the Corinthian church: "You instructed the young to think temperate and proper thoughts; you charged the women to perform all their duties with a blameless, reverent, and pure conscience, cherishing their own husbands, as is right; and you taught them to abide by the rule of obedience, and to *manage the affairs of their household* with dignity and all discretion" (1 Clem. 1:3).

Admittedly one cannot manage without working diligently, or if wealthy delegating that work (which properly done is still hard work). But Paul is not locking women up in the kitchen and cleaning supply closet. The Paul of the New Testament knows women moving about in public is normal (the Greco-Roman world was not a Taliban society) and conducive to social order and church growth (as in Lydia's case [Acts 16]) and ministry (as in the case of fellow workers like Euodia and Syntyche [Phil 4:2–3]). Nothing in the New Testament suggests that Paul (or Jesus) had a draconian intent to restrict women's public presence or movements, confining them perhaps to a harem of one. While there is truth in saying that Paul's direction to Titus reflects "the Semitic and Hellenic ideal" that "women . . . remain at home and discharge domestic duties" (BDAG 700), it is hermeneutically unwarranted to press this definition to mean that women must go nowhere else and do nothing besides this. The noble wife of Prov 31 is socially and commercially active as she "watches over the affairs of her household" (Prov 31:27).[172] Paul is not putting Cretan Christian women under marital house arrest but, as the NRSV recognizes, calling them to diligence in and full attention to the ordering of household matters.[173]

171. Cf. *GNC*: "to manage their households well"; also Neudorfer, *Titus*, 139–40 (with reference to Strabo, *Geographica* 10.4.20); Gloer, 56. Contra Twomey, 204, who claims the word "does not imply participation in decisions concerning the household economy."

172. Note the NETS translation of the LXX: "The way she ran her household was careful."

173. D. Sweeney notes how Jonathan Edwards's ministry would not have been possible, humanly speaking, without his wife, Sarah, assuming almost total management of their household and property affairs (*Jonathan Edwards and the Ministry of the Word* [Downers Grove, IL: IVP Academic, 2009], 66).

Many married women find this is one of their innate tendencies and strengths, while the living quarters of many single men indicate weak giftedness in this domain. Both Old Testament and New Testament criticize "the opposite tendency (i.e., to be a gadabout)"[174] on the part of some. Perhaps those who were "ruining whole households" were distracting women from necessary and by no means ignoble priorities of daily life. Titus's older women were to be on the front lines of counteracting this subversion.

"To be kind" is the fourth trait Paul commends. Why NIV translates "kind" for *agathos* ("good") is not clear.[175] There is a Greek word that clearly means "kind": *chrēstos*.[176] The word *agathos* is translated "good" when applied to Joseph of Arimathea (Luke 23:50) and Barnabas (Acts 11:24). These were men of exemplary courage and character. "Virtuous" might have been an equally defensible rendering. In fact, in a sense only God is "good" (Mark 10:18). 1 Clem. 3:5 speaks of the "good [i.e., exemplary] apostles." Admittedly, to say young women should "be good" in English sounds pedestrian and perhaps moralistic. But it is easier to imagine Paul thinking of excellence or exemplary virtue (as in the case of Barnabas and Joseph) than blandly calling for young women to be "kind" (besides NIV, see also RSV, ESV, NEB). Even less defensible are renderings that interpolate domesticity into the semantics: "good housewives" (TEV); "good homemakers" (HCSB).

Fifth, through the leadership of older women (v. 3), younger women are to "be subject to their husbands." The wording makes it clear that Paul means women's *own* husbands, not all married men generally. Much ink has been spilled in recent generations debating what "wives submit to your husbands" does and does not mean. Few notions attributed to Paul have been the target of so much ire since the sexual revolution of the 1960s. "Submit" translates a word that envisions a particular order or setting and calls for a person to fit into rather than obstruct or seek to opt out of that ongoing order. In a marriage, Paul is saying, wives should live in line with their husbands' loving leadership. Passages like Eph 5:22–33 make it clear that Paul envisions husband's interface with their wives as loving and even self-sacrificial. In 1 Cor 7:1–5 Paul states that, in their physical relationship, husbands and wives must meet each other's needs, not just their own, with neither privileged over the other. S. Tracy has shown the interbiblical limits of marital submission. He asserts on plausible exegetical grounds that a wife must *not* submit to her husband when obedience to him would:

174. Towner, *Letters*, 727n56. He points to Prov 7:11 and 1 Tim 5:13. Cf. 2 Thess 3:11.

175. "Kind" and "generous" are admittedly glosses for *agathos* in BDAG 4. But the examples given (Matt 20:15 and parallels) clearly have to do with monetary generosity and do not provide semantic justification for the same translation of *agathos* in Titus 2:5.

176. Used by Paul in Rom 2:4; 1 Cor 15:33; Eph 4:32.

- violate a biblical principle (not just a direct biblical statement)
- compromise her relationship with Christ
- violate her conscience
- compromise the care, nurture, and protection of her children
- enable (facilitate) her husband's sin

In addition, Tracy argues, "a wife must not submit to physical, sexual, or emotional abuse."[177]

The issue is too vast to be aired in detail here, but it is not exegetically compelling to convict Paul of complicity in brutal curtailment of wives' human rights or the enthronement of male whim and dictate over their wives' personal dignity and freedom. The previous four character traits mentioned in this verse are ennobling and praiseworthy when applied to women, just as they are to men. This fifth characteristic calls for Christian wives to give their husbands the space and respect to love them as Christ loved the church (Eph 5:25). Husbands will answer to Christ regarding whether and how well they live up to this expectation (see 1 Cor 11:3). As Tracy posits above, the broader sweep of biblical teaching (some in Paul's own writings) forbids applying these verses in a demeaning and stultifying manner.

Conversely, it is unnecessary to theorize some "social setting" that ruled Paul's thought and so remove the phrase "subject to their husbands" completely from the discussion table as a mandate for Christian wives in other places and times.[178] The words properly interpreted, in the doctrinal context of the New Testament, do not give husbands a license to suppress or oppress. They do assume a level of appropriation of divine love and grace to which relatively few spouses in any cultural setting may attain, with reasons varying by culture. In the West the problem could be heightened by theories of autonomous personhood that leave scant room for historic understanding of divine creation of male and female, the Christian covenant of marriage and its attendant reciprocal love, and God's prerogative to order relations in marriage in ways that will optimize his glorification and the mission of the church.

That mission furnishes the note on which Paul ends this verse and indeed this small section regarding how older women should be seeking to elevate the younger in God's household (vv. 3–5). If older women and younger women team up as Titus encourages, grounds will be lacking for maligning God's word. "Malign" translates a word used eight times in Paul, four times

177. S. Tracy, "What Does 'Submit in Everything' Really Mean? The Nature and Scope of Marital Submission," *TJ* 29.2 (2008): 306–9, 310.

178. As is the tendency, for example, in the preponderance of the essays in David Blankenhorn, Dan Browning, and Mary Stewart Van Leeuwen, eds., *Does Christianity Teach Male Headship? The Equal-Regard Marriage and Its Critics* (Grand Rapids: Eerdmans, 2004).

in the PE.[179] In Paul's writings it means to speak disparagingly of someone or something holy. "The word of God" here probably refers most directly to the apostolic message Paul upholds and delegates to workers like Titus and Timothy to preach and teach, but its ca. forty occurrences in the NIV point to the totality of God's self-disclosure, whether verbal or written. The apostolic message did not exist, historically speaking, apart from Old Testament writings that prepared the way for it and New Testament writings that quickly took shape as the gospel went forth. Acts depicts the progress of the gospel in terms of the growth of "the word of God."[180] Paul wants the godly character and conduct of Christian women young and old to be a winsome reflection of the church's message and Scriptures. This intention is essentially an application of Jesus's teaching to "let your light shine before others, that they may see your good deeds and glorify your Father in heaven" (Matt 5:16).

Oden notes that "Christianity has an important stake in the home, its right ordering, its decency, its love, its capacity to enable growth. If Christianity does not act to guide and enable these values, it will not show its social worth and will in the long run become justifiably discredited."[181] There is truth in this assertion, but Paul is not arguing solely from the basis of social utility. God created humans to "be fruitful and increase in number; fill the earth and subdue it" (Gen 1:28). In the biblical economy this mandate involves marriage and family. Godly domestic patterns undoubtedly send a message to a watching world, but more fundamentally they mark the doxological living patterns that enable the crown of God's creation (see Ps 8) to flourish, a concern in Paul because of its concern to Jesus[182] and to the Jewish heritage they shared.

6 Paul continues the pattern of naming a gendered age group and then prescribing desirable qualities or practices that Titus's verbal ministry and influence should promote. In v. 2 it was "older men" and in v. 3 "older women," and by their influence "younger women" too (vv. 4–5). Verse 6 turns to "the young men." The age span implied is from roughly mid-teens to around forty. The definite article (*tous*, the) could imply that Titus and Paul both know exactly who he is talking about—that is, "*those* young men"—whereas reference to older men and women, where the article was lacking, was more generic. But the use of the article could also be a stylistic variation without discernible semantic significance. The "similarly" of v. 6 is parallel to the "likewise" of v. 3; in Greek they are identical words.

179. From Greek *blasphēmeō*, cognate with the English word "blaspheme." See also 1 Tim 1:20; 6:1; Titus 3:2. In Paul elsewhere: Rom 2:24; 3:8; 14:16; 1 Cor 10:30.

180. Acts 4:31; 6:2, 7; 8:14; 11:1; 12:24; 13:5, 7, 46; 17:13; 18:11.

181. Oden, 118.

182. See Pennington, *Sermon on the Mount and Human Flourishing*.

Using only the second imperative of this entire chapter (the other was "speak," translated "must teach" by NIV in v. 1), Paul tells Titus to "encourage" the young men. Paul used the same word in 1:9, prescribing how elders must be in a position to "encourage others by sound doctrine and refute those who oppose it." Now Titus must exercise this function himself. It is "the younger men" whom he should target. This term is used in the PE elsewhere only in 1 Tim 5:1 ("encourage . . . younger men as brothers").

Titus's guidance should steer young men in the direction of being "self-controlled." The word connotes possessing mental and emotional composure; not being distracted; not impulsive but focused. The same word is used to refer to the (healed) Gerasene demonic (Mark 5:15; Luke 8:35), the "sober judgment" Christians should exercise (Rom 12:3), Paul being in his "right mind" for the sake of the Corinthians (2 Cor 5:13), and the recipients of 1 Peter, who are to be "sober-minded" for the purpose of prayer (1 Pet 4:7). A related word is used as a requirement for pastors (see 1:8 and commentary above; also 1 Tim 3:2), as well as for older (Titus 2:2) and younger (v. 5) women. *Everyone* in the church should exhibit this quality. But young men are susceptible to particular blandishments and allurements that detract from godward aims. Even lawful pursuits and callings may become objects of idolatrous devotion. Titus's challenge is to direct young men's intensity and energy in redemptive directions, tethering them to God's will and direction in their lives through the sound doctrine they receive.

But doctrine alone is not sufficient: Paul draws also on the force of Titus's example, as the next verse shows.

7 The words translated "in everything" in the NIV could be included with v. 6, as NEB: "Urge the younger men, similarly, to be temperate *in all things*."[183] Most translations, however, understand the words to open v. 7. Perhaps because Titus is himself a younger rather than older man in Paul's taxonomy, Paul glides seamlessly from "the younger men" of v. 6 to Titus (as one of their number), his example, and the means to maximize it.

"In everything"[184] that Titus is being told in this epistle, he is to "set[185] . . . an example" for those he leads and serves. NIV inserts "them" (absent from the Gk.), so that reference is primarily to the younger men, but Paul could be thinking of everyone touched by Titus's leadership. He is to present himself[186] as an exemplary model in his own behavior. "Example" translates *typos*, which

183. Supported by the comma after *panta* (all things) in NA[28]. So also Siebenthal, *Griechische Grammatik*, §184n: "to be discreet in every respect."

184. Moule, *Idiom Book*, 62, renders the Greek "in all respects."

185. The root word *parechō* (offer, show, furnish) occurs across the span of Paul's writings: see also Gal 6:17; Col 4:1; 1 Tim 1:4; 6:17.

186. Underscored not only by the reflexive pronoun *seauton* but also the middle form of *parechō*.

elsewhere refers to the "pattern" of teaching that the Roman church upheld (Rom 6:17), to Paul's "model" for the Philippians (Phil 3:17; cf. 2 Thess 3:9), and to the "model" that the Thessalonian believers were to churches in Macedonia and Achaia (1 Thess 1:7).[187] Paul tells Timothy that he is to "set an example for the believers in speech, in conduct, in love, in faith and in purity" (1 Tim 4:12). Christian leaders are player-coaches, not theoreticians who place burdens on people but "are not willing to lift a finger to move them" (Matt 23:4).

The way for Titus to set an example is through "doing what is good" (or "good works"; see table 26 and discussion at 1:16 above). Since "works" do not effect salvation (cf. 3:5: "righteous things we had done" in NIV), and since Paul cannot say everything at every point, these "works" are not enumerated and codified here. They may be thought of as whatever is right in God's sight, given the whole scope and wealth of biblical ethical teaching, especially that of Jesus and the apostles but also the Old Testament as Jesus and the apostles appropriated it and taught their followers. Such "works" are not merely ethical abstractions but concrete imperatives to be lived out as occasion arises. In pastoral labor, as well as in the believer's daily walk of discipleship, such occasions are constant. Elsewhere in this section, and even later in this verse, Paul stresses Titus's speech and doctrine. But those are incomplete and in fact incriminating of the speaker if Titus is not practicing what he preaches (cf. 1:16). Jesus vested his own credibility in the fact that he did not simply *speak* in his own interest: he *labored* for another: "Whoever *speaks* on their own does so to gain personal glory, but he who seeks the glory of the one who sent him is a man of truth; there is nothing false about him" (John 7:18). By a life rich in good works, Titus points beyond himself and his rhetoric to the God he serves and the Christ whose gospel he ministers.

Schlatter comments that, for Titus and all the groups he admonishes, their tasks consist "not in acquisition of some special knowledge, not in arriving at peculiar experiences of the divine grace, but in transformation of the daily affairs that fill up everyday living."[188]

A domain of good works in which Titus should excel is the "teaching" he offers (see Introduction, IX.D). It should have "integrity" (*aphthoria*), a rare word translated "incorruption" in LSJ[189] and "soundness" in BDAG.[190] The word may also imply moral purity, chastity.[191] What he speaks should have enduring quality and not be shaky. It should also exhibit "seriousness" (from

187. Other Pauline occurrences: Rom 5:14; 1 Cor 10:6; 1 Tim 4:12.

188. Schlatter, *Die Kirche der Griechen*, 257.

189. LSJ 289 lists only one other occurrence of the word (in the fourth-century writer Themistius).

190. BDAG 156 relates the word to *aphthoros*, a slightly more common synonym, for which it lists some dozen references.

191. MM 97, citing papyri, as well as Justin Martyr.

semnotēs), a word found in the New Testament elsewhere only at 1 Tim 2:2 ("holiness") and 3:4 ("full respect"). The serious situation in which the Cretan congregations find themselves calls for instruction of due gravity and reverence, in contrast to the profit-driven babble of detractors and troublemakers (see Titus 1:10–11).

8 Titus's teaching or "speech" should show a third quality: "soundness." While the verb cognate of this adjective (in Gk.) occurs eight times in the PE, this is the only time the adjective occurs in any New Testament epistle. It is found in ten Gospel passages and once in Acts, in every case referring to a person who is "healed" or "restored" or "made well." Words can cripple and harm, but Titus's discourse (*logos*) is to be restorative and healing; its "soundness" lies in its potential to strengthen and make whole. The result will be teaching that "cannot be condemned." This is close to concern voiced regarding women (v. 5) that the word of God not be maligned.

Why would there be worry that someone might condemn what Titus says? The second half of the verse hints at an answer. Paul speaks of "those who oppose" Titus. These words might refer to the troublemakers mentioned earlier (1:10) or to others who rally against the Christian movement. "Those who oppose" (NIV) is singular in Greek; Paul could have in mind a given sole opponent who arises, perhaps to lead others in opposition to apostolic teaching. If Titus is circumspect in his speech practices and patterns, any such opponents will be shamed[192] because they have nothing "bad"[193] with which to charge him.

9–10 Paul addresses the last class of individuals named in this section: slaves (*douloi*).[194] In Titus 1:1 (but not in the openings of 1 or 2 Timothy) Paul is a "slave" of God, as are all who labor in the pastoral vocation (2 Tim 2:24), but both passages use a metaphor. Paul writes here about literal slaves. They are to be compliant with ("subject to")[195] their masters "in everything," a phrase that occurs in Paul's writings nineteen out of the twenty-three times it is found in the New Testament.[196] It could also be translated "in all things." Paul himself provides commentary on this notion when he writes with parallel counsel to Timothy (1 Tim 6:1–2; see commentary there): "All who are under the yoke of slavery should consider their masters worthy of full respect, so that God's

192. For similar use of this verb, see 1 Cor 4:14; 2 Thess 3:14; MM 219.

193. Paul uses this word in Rom 9:11 and 2 Cor 5:10; otherwise it is attested in the New Testament only in John 3:20; 5:29; Jas 3:16.

194. For a characterization of slavery in the Roman Empire, see Neudorfer, *Titus*, 149–50. He points out that Crete was a hotbed of the slave trade because of the activity of pirates based on the island.

195. Probably not an imperatival infinitive but rather "an ellipsis of a verb of saying" (Wallace, *Greek Grammar*, 608; cf. BDF §389).

196. Five of these occurrences are in the PE: see also 1 Tim 3:11; 2 Tim 2:7; 4:5; Titus 2:10.

name and our teaching may not be slandered. Those who have believing masters should not show them disrespect just because they are fellow believers. Instead, they should serve them even better because their masters are dear to them as fellow believers and are devoted to the welfare of their slaves." Here in Titus, the upshot is that, broadly speaking, whether masters are believers or not, the default approach of slaves should be to serve their masters well. But how? Paul sets forth two positive-negative pieces of counsel.

First, slaves are to be well-pleasing rather than "to talk back to" their masters. "To try to please them" (NIV) translates a single Greek word rendered as "well-pleasing" in NIV84. The word occurs seven other times in Paul; in every case it refers explicitly to pleasing God.[197] That connotation can hardly be ruled out here, as Paul's general expectation is for all followers of Christ in all circumstances to live as unto the Lord. The same applies to slaves, as Paul states elsewhere: "Whatever you do, work heartily, as for the Lord and not for men" (Col 3:23 ESV). In the context he clearly has Christian slaves in mind. Not talking back (from *antilegō*)[198] is an obvious primary means for them to realize the goal of pleasing God.

Second, slaves are not to pilfer—they are "not to steal things from" their masters. The word (from *nosphizō*) can also mean to "keep back" something that belongs to others, a sin committed by Ananias and his wife in Acts 5:2, 3 (the only other time in the New Testament the word occurs). While Paul may be warning against thievery, he may also be thinking of what these slaves owe their masters in God's sight and what they must not therefore fail to present: a demonstration of forthright Christian faith backed up by concrete upright behavior. This will "show that they can be fully trusted."[199]

By this demonstration slaves will bear witness to the Christian witness: "they will make the teaching about[200] God our Savior attractive."[201] Just as they are subject to masters "in everything" (v. 10), their behavior will enhance the attractiveness of apostolic teaching "in every way." In Greek the words in quotation marks are identical in both v. 9 and v. 10. Paul has already mentioned "teaching" or doctrine three times in this epistle (see 1:9;

197. Rom 12:1, 2; 14:18; 2 Cor 5:9; Eph 5:10; Phil 4:18; Col 3:20.

198. Paul uses this word in Titus 1:9 to speak of "those who contradict"; otherwise it is found in his writings only in Rom 10:21.

199. But Wallace, *Greek Grammar*, 189–90, points out that most translations go in the direction of "showing forth all good faith." He suggests the sense "demonstrating that all [genuine] faith is productive." See also 312–13.

200. On the article here in the second attributive position, see Wallace, *Greek Grammar*, 215; he suggests it should be rendered as a relative pronoun. Siebenthal, *Griechische Grammatik*, §136e, renders it "the teaching of God, our Savior."

201. On "teaching," see commentary Introduction, IX.D. Likewise, on "Savior," see Introduction, IX.A.

2:1, 7); it is clearly a focal point. In this case the concern is evangelistic: he wants masters to be impacted by the gospel message. The comportment of Christian slaves is a primary way to encourage this gospel impact. Doctrine by itself can be lifeless and dull, but lived out nobly, it may work magnetically and give rise to admiration.[202] Then it may communicate the saving grace of the Christian message across even the kinds of social barriers that separated slaves and masters. God the Savior cares for both and uses every means possible to makes his presence known. One of these means is how believers live out their convictions wherever God places them. This is at least as true today for employees in the workplace as it was then in the economy of the Roman Empire.[203] It also has very direct relevance for the tens of millions of people who languish in slavery still in various regions of the world.

V. MOTIVATION FOR MINISTRY (2:11–15)

Paul has repeatedly urged on Titus the importance of sound teaching or doctrine (1:9; 2:1, 10). Beginning with this section, he models the practice of doctrinal exposition as a means of practical guidance and encouragement. In these verses Paul "speaks" (his command to Titus in 2:1, 15) in the manner that he urges Titus to conduct his own verbal interchange. In other words, these verses model and provide the foundation for the speaking Paul calls on Titus to engage in.

The first four verses of this section are read annually on Christmas Eve in churches that use the liturgical calendar.[204] And they do draw on the truth of the incarnation. Here, however, the stress is on *what* appeared, which is "the grace of God" (v. 11), not *who* appeared, namely, Jesus Christ.[205] God has shown forth his grace in such a way that it discourages certain behavior, enables uprightness, and implants a transcendent hope.

202. The verb translated "make attractive" in v. 11 is used to describe how the Jerusalem temple was "adorned" architecturally (Luke 21:5), how women should project their inner beauty outwardly (1 Tim 2:9), how women in Old Testament times made themselves beautiful (1 Pet 3:5), and how "the Holy City, the new Jerusalem," shines forth in splendor (Rev 21:2, 19).

203. See Neudorfer, *Titus*, 155, who stresses the passage's relevance to Christian employers and employees.

204. See M. Reiser, "Erziehung durch Gnade: Eine Betrachtung zu Titus 2,11–14," *Erbe und Auftrag* 69 (1993): 443–49.

205. For that reason Reiser's direct recourse (see previous note) to John 1 in connection with this passage, while homiletically effective, is not directly explicative of this particular Pauline discourse.

> 11 *For the grace of God has appeared that offers salvation to all people.*
> 12 *It teaches us to say "No" to ungodliness and worldly passions, and to live*
> *self-controlled, upright and godly lives in this present age,* 13 *while we wait*
> *for the blessed hope—the appearing of the glory of our great God and Sav-*
> *ior, Jesus Christ,* 14 *who gave himself for us to redeem us from all wickedness*
> *and to purify for himself a people that are his very own, eager to do what is*
> *good.* 15 *These, then, are the things you should teach. Encourage and rebuke*
> *with all authority. Do not let anyone despise you.*

11 The first word ("for") is significant. Paul is drawing an inference from the preceding section with its guidance for various social, age, and gender groupings. Why should Titus instruct people in these ways? Why should he think that, given the grim social setting and personal tendencies of many on Crete, pastoral presence and instruction will make any difference? Paul grounds his counsel to Titus in the manifestation of God's grace (*charis*).

Paul uses this word thirteen times in the PE. Six of those are at the beginning and end of each PE, whether as part of Paul's opening "grace and peace" formula (1 Tim 1:2; 2 Tim 1:2; Titus 1:4) or his closing "grace be with you" (1 Tim 6:21; 2 Tim 4:22) or "grace be with you all" (Titus 3:15).[206] "Grace" will receive mention a few verses later as the means by which believers are "justified" and "become heirs having the hope of eternal life" (3:7). Grace lies at the very heart of God's saving work.

This focus is borne out in other key PE passages, such as 1 Tim 1:14, where Paul says that, despite his former reprobate and homicidal religiosity, "the grace of our Lord was poured out on me abundantly, along with the faith and love that are in Christ Jesus." Another important parallel is 2 Tim 1:9, which links grace with God's purpose (from *prothesis*) and declares them both foundational factors in redemption and holy living. Lest Timothy see "grace" as some reactionary expedient on God's part, Paul adds in the same verse, "This grace was given us in Christ Jesus before the beginning of time." Like God and his eternal purposes, grace has its preexistent dimensions in God's character and will.

And yet it "has appeared" (Titus 2:11). Siebenthal notes the aorist form of this verb (*epephanē*) and observes, "The historical (indicative) aorist is used in the NT to describe, among other things, the unique, great facts of salvation history."[207] It is reasonable to see this as an expression of the Christian doctrine of incarnation. The underlying Greek word *epiphainō* in its four NT occurrences can mean to shine in a dark place (Luke 1:79; Acts

206. In 1 Tim 1:12; 2 Tim 1:3 Paul uses *charis* to mean "thanks, gratitude."

207. Siebenthal, *Griechische Grammatik*, §199b. Admittedly, other tenses and moods can convey the same meaning.

27:20) or to become manifest or gloriously visible, its meaning here (see also Titus 3:4).

This grace "offers salvation [*sōtērios*] to all people" (Titus 2:11).[208] Deliverance for all[209] is a possibility in principle, since the God of all has made his saving work known to all in sending Christ. "Just as the one sun and its light are for all human beings and their life, so the Father's grace ushers in the light of a new day for every human being without distinction."[210] In reality, and as Paul has already indicated to Titus, not all will welcome God's saving gesture in Jesus; some will actively oppose it (Titus 1:10, 15–16). Such opposition does not detract from the glory of what God has brought powerfully into being in the earthly sphere. It can and should motivate Titus, as it has for many years caught the imagination and steered the life of Paul.

Paul next highlights the transforming pedagogical effect linked with God's grace revealed.

12 This grace, Paul states, "instructs us."[211] "Instructs" does not translate the more common NT word for "teach" (*didaskō*, ninety-seven occurrences in the NT). Instead, Paul uses a form of *paideuō* (thirteen occurrences in the NT), a word frequently connoting the sort of education (e.g., Acts 7:22; 22:3), guidance, and even discipline associated with parental oversight, pastoral leadership (e.g. 2 Tim 2:25), or God's benevolent if sometimes painful supervision (e.g., 1 Cor 11:32; 2 Cor 6:9). Paul writes to instruct Titus, and Titus's call is to instruct others, but all alike from apostle to pastor to congregational member are equally schooled by divine grace.[212]

This instruction is for everyday living. Verse 12 can be rendered "teaching[213] us, in order that denying ungodliness and worldly passions *we might live*

208. More precisely, it reads "the saving grace of God has appeared"—*sōtērios* is an adjective modifying "grace," not the noun "salvation" (*sōtēria*). It therefore is not and cannot be "the predicate of the sentence" (contra Zehr, 280).

209. On the "generic force" of the construction, see Wallace, *Greek Grammar*, 253.

210. Quinn, 143. Calvin, 373, notes the contextual proximity of slaves (vv. 9–10) and states, "He does not mean [all] individuals, but rather all classes of men with their diverse ways of life," God having "condescended even to slaves." This move should make other classes even more ready to "embrace His goodness."

211. For the important role of grace in spurring to ethically aggressive lives in Calvin, fueled in part by Titus 2:11–14, see Barclay, *Paul and the Gift*, 124–28.

212. Dibelius and Conzelmann, 142, finds a contrast here with the true Paul: "In Paul the accent is placed upon justification, here upon education in the faith." But it is hard to rule out Paul's capability of thinking from both angles. For a fuller refutation of Dibelius and Conzelmann, see Laansma, 270.

213. *Paideuousa*, a dependent adverbial participle describing the guiding work of divine grace. The word was used to describe "the daily instruction and supervision of conduct of a minor," appropriate, since some Cretans Christians seem to have been "'minors' in the faith and needed to become more mature" (Spencer, 49).

in a manner that is self-controlled,[214] righteous,[215] and godly"[216] (translation of the main verb is in italics). NIV chooses to render "denying"[217] as "to say 'No' to" and as a main verb parallel with "to live." This is a perfectly legitimate translation but should not obscure the semantic effect of the Greek, which is to highlight God's intention of administering his grace so that practical living takes on distinctly gospel-generated and Christlike character (NIV "self-controlled, upright and godly").

Standing in the way of such living are "ungodliness and worldly passions." This caveat confirms that Paul was not earlier demonizing Cretans as if only they succumb to submoral living patterns: the bent of all humans is to languish in lamentable behavior and outlooks. The church needs to be warned of this danger as much as any local populace needs to be delivered from it. All alike require divine grace.

The noun "ungodliness" (*asebeia*; six occurrences in the NT) serves a key function in Romans, describing a major reason for God's wrath (1:18) and a major effect of God's saving work through "the deliverer," who will "turn ungodliness away from Jacob" (11:26, quoting Isa 59:20 LXX). In 2 Tim 2:16 "ungodliness" is portrayed as the outcome of "godless chatter." The word is also featured in Jude's description of those whom God will judge (Jude 15, 18).

"Worldly passions" makes use of two words that can be favorable or sinister. "Worldly" (*kosmikas*) is a positive term in Heb 9:1, where it describes the temple ("earthly sanctuary"). "Passion, desire" (*epithymia*) can also be neutral or positive (e.g., Phil 1:23). More frequently in the NT, however, human passion is linked with "a desire for someth. forbidden or simply inordinate, *craving, lust*" (BDAG 372).

God's grace defeats these traits or tendencies. As surely as it "has appeared" (Titus 3:11), it trains (v. 12), so that life can be different for those willing to deny "ungodliness" and the base drives leading to it. The Greek makes transparent the human volition required for grace to serve so nobly: whereas NIV implies that grace "teaches us to say 'No' . . . and to live" in certain ways, a better rendering makes people the subject of "denying" what is wicked and of living out what grace enables. As Jesus felt constrained to confront the "large crowds" flocking to him with the necessity of hating their

214. Greek *sōphronōs*, a NT hapax. But cognates appear frequently in Titus: *sōphroneō* (self-controlled; 2:6); *sōphronizō* (train, urge; 2:4); *sōphrōn* (sensible, self-controlled; 1:8; 2:2, 5).

215. Greek *dikaiōs*. The word appears only here in the PE but is found five times elsewhere in the NT: on the lips of a thief on the cross (Luke 23:41); in Paul's writings (1 Cor 15:34; 1 Thess 2:10); and in 1 Pet 2:23.

216. Greek *eusebōs*. The word appears elsewhere in the NT only at 2 Tim 3:12: "Everyone who wants to live a *godly* life in Christ Jesus will be persecuted."

217. *Arnēsamenoi*, taken as coordinate with "to live" (attendant circumstance) in the NIV, though it could be instrumental (CEB: "by rejecting ungodly lives and the desires of this world").

own kin and even life, taking up their cross (Luke 14:25–27) to receive the grace offered in his proclamation, so Paul here reminds Titus that grace is extended so that humans might extend themselves to lay hold of it. "So that we might start living godly lives" is the sense.[218] Grace may be "irresistible," as some formulations have it. But it is a theological mistake and pastoral misunderstanding to fail to warn people "not to receive God's grace in vain" (2 Cor 6:1). Only robust pursuit of grace appropriates it. Paul models, and urges on Titus, an understanding of grace that does not promote passivity but rather stirs to zeal even "in the present age," which in so many ways seems to be given over to evil (note Gal 1:4: "the present evil age") and its sinister would-be "ruler . . . *now* [i.e., in the present age] at work in those who are disobedient" (Eph 2:2).

Hanson objects that Paul's stress here on ethical probity ("to live sober, upright, and godly lives") betrays a non-Pauline writer: "It is hard to imagine anything more unlike Paul's fervent, far-reaching, and profound theology."[219] On the contrary, Hanson has failed to see the seamless flow from Paul's theology to its ethical realization, an emphasis of the whole of Scripture in which, because God is holy, his people are to live holy.

13 As Titus and those entrusted to his care lay hold of grace to "live self-controlled, upright and godly lives in this present age" (v. 12), they "wait for the blessed hope" (v. 13). "Wait" can sound like idleness or nonchalance, but the underlying word (*prosdechomai*)[220] taps into a rich and distinct religious phenomenon characterizing Judaism and early Christianity.

Table 28. Uses of *prosdechomai* analogous to Titus 2:13

Passage	Person(s) awaiting	Object awaited
Luke 2:25	Simeon	the consolation of Israel
Luke 2:38	Anna and others in Jerusalem	the redemption of Jerusalem
Luke 12:36	servants in Jesus's teaching about readiness	their master [returning] from a wedding banquet
Luke 23:51	Joseph of Arimathea	the kingdom of God

218. Wallace, *Greek Grammar*, 559, proposes an inceptive idea for the aorist *zēsōmen* (we might live).

219. Hanson, 184.

220. This verb occurs a total of fourteen times in the New Testament; Danker, *Concise Greek-English Lexicon*, 302, explains its prominent meaning as "look forward to in a receptive frame of mind."

Passage	Person(s) awaiting	Object awaited
Acts 24:15	Paul along with Jewish opponents seeking his condemnation	resurrection of both the righteous and the wicked
Jude 21	recipients of Jude's epistle	the mercy of our Lord Jesus Christ [for] eternal life

From table 28 it is clear that "wait" can describe a posture, not of passivity in the face of a fickle future (cf. *Waiting for Godot* in Samuel Beckett's absurdist play), but of dogged confidence in God and his sure promises, however remote they may seem at times. Table 28 attests, and Paul describes, a waiting that is proactive, alert, and expectant. It is ready to jump in and hasten, if possible, the coming of what it awaits (see 2 Pet 3:12). This is the readiness called for by Jesus in view of the return of the Son of Man and final judgment (see, e.g., Matt 24–25).

Here, however, it is not the sinister side of judgment that is awaited but "the blessed hope—the appearing of the glory. . . ." The em-dash replaces a Greek *kai* ("and") to indicate NIV's decision to take "hope" and "appearing" as appositional. They are not two different things but one and the same. The ultimate hope of Christians is here and now, in that Christ and his grace have already "appeared" (v. 11). Yet, there is a future dimension that should permeate their daily consciousness, expectations, and decisions. This "hope" is not barren (as many human hopes are) but "blessed" (*makarios*), an adjective that occurs fifty times in the NT and seven times in Paul (see also Rom 4:7, 8; 14:22; 1 Cor 7:40; 1 Tim 1:11; 6:15). For Paul it connotes a status that is elevated, even sublime, by virtue of its close association with God, who is himself "blessed" (1 Tim 1:11). Paul confirms the future aspect of God and his blessedness in writing to Timothy of Christ's "appearing . . . which God will bring about in his own time—God, the blessed and only Ruler" (1 Tim 6:14–15). For both Timothy and Titus, pastoral leadership needs to be suffused with eschatological conviction and expectancy in light of God's imminent personal arrival. Paul keeps alive a prominent stress of Jesus himself (see, e.g., Luke 21:34–36).

A daily fervent eye to the future is justified because of divine glory's "appearing." The word (*epiphaneia*) occurs six times in Paul (see also 2 Thess 2:8; 1 Tim 6:14; 2 Tim 1:10; 4:1, 8) and is partially synonymous with the more common term *parousia* (coming, appearing; twenty-four occurrences in the NT, fourteen in Paul; absent from the PE). But *epiphaneia* lays stress not just on arrival but on the resplendent or dazzling or stunning appearance of what or who arrives. Paul reminds Titus of "the *appearing* of the *glory.*" Something is just over the horizon (see Rom 13:12), and it is God's own blinding and transforming radiance, a unique possession of and gift to God's people (Rom

9:4).[221] This "ultimate revelation" (a component of Jewish, as well as early Christian, conviction) will "signal the end of the present age [see v. 12] and the beginning of the new one."[222]

Not just a new age but "the glory of our great God and Savior,[223] Jesus Christ," will appear. It is widely accepted that this is one of the several NT passages that ascribe full divinity to God the Son (see also John 1:1, 18; Acts 20:28; Rom 9:5; 2 Thess 1:12; Heb 1:8; 2 Pet 1:1; 1 John 5:20).[224] Most commentators in the history of the interpretation of this verse have understood it to be affirming Christ's full divinity alongside that of the Father.[225] Wallace shows that, along with 2 Pet 1:1, Titus 2:12 is "secure as any [verse] in the canon when it comes to identifying Christ as *theos*."[226] The glory that believers await is not merely the appearance of the invisible transcendent deity, "who lives in unapproachable light, whom no one has seen or can see" (1 Tim 6:16), Paul's depiction of God the Father. Nor is it simply Jesus resurrected showing up again like he did in the weeks following his death (see Acts 1:3), great though such an appearing would be. It is rather the denouement of the Trinitarian mystery which in the historical and material sphere has never been fully seen or comprehensively conceptualized. Evil and its proponents will be judged; God's kingdom and its subjects will be vindicated and exalted (2 Thess 2:5–12). Believers will see the Lord in whom they have trusted as he is and be made like him (1 John 3:2). All that Titus may have endured by way of hardship and deprivation will be forgotten in the magnificence of what the last day will reveal and the age to come will showcase. There could hardly be a greater motivation for ministry.

But not only these sure prospects lying in the future should spur on Titus and his flock: it is also the track record and intention of the one whose appearing they await.

14 The "who" is "our great God and Savior, Jesus Christ" of v. 13. He acted as Savior in many ways—by his identity as the eternal Son of God,[227] by

221. On God's glory in Paul, see R. Yarbrough, "Paul and Salvation History," in Carson, O'Brien, and Seifrid, *The Paradoxes of Paul*, vol. 2 of *Justification and Variegated Nomism*, 330–42. "Paul speaks of the glory of God more than any other New Testament writer" (Gloer, 67).

222. Keener, *Bible Background Commentary*, 629.

223. On "Savior" in the PE, see commentary Introduction, IX.A.

224. See M. J. Harris, *Jesus as God: The New Testament Use of Theos in Reference to Jesus* (Grand Rapids: Baker Books, 1992); D. Wenham, *Paul: Follower of Jesus or Founder of Christianity?* (Grand Rapids: Eerdmans, 1995), 118. See also Harris, *Prepositions and Theology*, 74. Fee, *Pauline Christology*, 442–46, argues against this consensus but unconvincingly (cf. Moule, *Idiom Book*, 109). The finding of D. Wallace regarding Sharp's canon (which applies to personal, sing., common substantives) seems decisive here; see his *Granville Sharp's Canon and Its Kin* (New York: Peter Lang, 2009), 81–82. See also n. 226.

225. Twomey, 211.

226. Wallace, *Greek Grammar*, 290.

227. See D. A. Carson, *Jesus the Son of God* (Wheaton, IL: Crossway, 2012).

his incarnation,[228] by his miracles,[229] by his teaching, by his founding of a community (the church) still prominent around the world, by his resurrection[230]—but especially in that "he gave himself." This is a signature Pauline expression, using either of two verbs:

> . . . who *gave* [*didōmi*] *himself* for our sins to rescue us from the present evil age. (Gal 1:4)
>
> I live by faith in the Son of God, who loved me and *gave* [*paradidōmi*] *himself* for me. (Gal 2:20)
>
> Christ loved the church and *gave himself up* [*paradidōmi*] for her. (Eph 5:25)
>
> . . . who *gave* [*didōmi*] *himself* as a ransom for all people. (1 Tim 2:6)

Like in 1 Tim 2:6 (see discussion there), Paul in Titus 2:14 uses a form of *didōmi*. Because of this selfless action (epitomized in Jesus's atoning death), Titus should be motivated for the ministry this epistle outlines and calls for.

Christ's selfless giving had a dual purpose. The first was "to redeem us from all wickedness." "Redeem" (from the verb *lytroō*)[231] implies purchase from a state of bondage or condemnation. People are in trouble—they need to be redeemed—because of their "wickedness" (*anomia*). Hardly a common word, it is part of the rich New Testament vocabulary of sin[232] and occurs there fifteen times in thirteen verses.[233] *Anomia* is the opposite of *dikaiosynē* (righteousness).[234] It denotes utter lawlessness, the inveterate state of humankind apart from God described by Paul in Rom 1:18–3:20. It may have been on rich display in the Cretan environment. The human

228. See Graham Cole, *The God Who Became Human* (Downers Grove, IL: IVP Academic, 2013).

229. Succinctly summarized in Keener, *Miracles*, 1:19–34.

230. See N. T. Wright, *The Resurrection of the Son of God* (Minneapolis: Fortress, 2003); M. Licona, *The Resurrection of Jesus: A New Historiographical Approach* (Downers Grove, IL: IVP Academic, 2010).

231. Other New Testament uses of the word: Luke 1:68; 2:38; 24:21; Heb 9:12. Paul uses a related word (*antilytron*, ransom) in 1 Tim 2:6.

232. See Christopher Morgan and Robert Peterson, eds., *Fallen: A Theology of Sin* (Wheaton, IL: Crossway, 2013).

233. In the Gospels only Jesus uses it (Matt 7:23; 13:41; 23:28; 24:12). Paul uses it seven times in six verses: Rom 4:7; 6:19 (twice); 2 Cor 6:14; 2 Thess 2:3, 7; Titus 2:14. It occurs also in Heb 1:9; 10:17; and in 1 John 3:4 (twice). It is used frequently in the LXX (over 200 times).

234. See Danker, *Concise Greek-English Lexicon*, 35.

condition would seem to be hopeless if God is infinitely holy and intent on judging the world. But Christ's self-giving sheds a ray of hope. The dark outrage of "all wickedness" is offset by the light of Christ's redemptive action.

Yet, Christ's act did more than remedy a malady: it constituted an activist following. He gave himself for nothing less than "to purify for himself a people that are his very own" (v. 14). Reference to purification is found over two dozen times in the Gospels, but Paul uses the verb "purify" (*katharizō*) only three times (see also 2 Cor 7:1 and Eph 5:26). It means to be cleansed from what defiles and then rendered fit. A right religious status is established or restored. Christ claims people as his "very own" (lit. "a people chosen, especial"; see BDAG 803). Paul expressed this same idea in referring to "God's elect" in Titus 1:1.

Christ's cleansing and claiming work has a distinct effect on those changed by it: they are "eager to do what is good" (v. 14). See table 26 at Titus 1:16 for the importance of good works in this epistle. Paul conceives of them, not as optional activities or even virtuous ideals for believers, but as the inevitable outworking of Jesus's signature saving action in the light of his resurrection, which in conquering death gives life to mortal beings (see Rom 8:11). The notion of a salvation through faith that generates zeal for good works is ubiquitous in Scripture and left its mark in the AF.[235]

Paul envisions not a dogged acceptance of religious commandments but a real zeal. "A people . . . eager to do what is good" could be rendered literally "a zealot[236] people when it comes to good works." While religious fervor can be misguided and dangerous, its absence is no less ominous. Paul praised it among fellow Jews (Rom 10:2a), and Jesus expressed disgust for its lack: he will spew the lukewarm Laodiceans out of his mouth (Rev 3:16). A hostile social environment like Crete can tempt the church to lie low, nurse its grievances, and turn inward. Paul calls for renewed attention to Jesus's death as a reminder that, in God's economy, the grain of wheat that dies yields an abundant harvest (see John 12:24). That harvest takes the form of lives actively fulfilling and surpassing God's commands and leading.

15 Paul restates and extends the counsel of 2:1. There he told Titus, "You . . . must teach [*lalei*] what is appropriate to sound doctrine." Here he writes literally "speak [second person sing. imperative of *laleō*] these things," that is, the things he has urged in 2:1–14.

235. Cf. 1 Clem. 33:1: "Let us hasten with earnestness and zeal to accomplish every good work [*pan ergon agathon*]"; Pol. *Phil.* 6:3: "Let us be eager with regard to what is good [*to kalon*]."

236. The word translated "eager" in NIV is not an adjective but the noun *zēlōtēs* (zealot, an ardent supporter). It is masculine accusative, in apposition to *laon* (people).

It is not clear why NIV (in both 2:1 and 2:15) translates the imperative with the indicative ("you . . . must" in 2:1; "you should" in 2:15). Perhaps the idea is that rhetorically these indicatives are imperatival. As the discussion in 2:1 showed, *laleō* need not mean "teach" but simply speak.[237] This verb in the imperative form occurs nine times in the New Testament; if it ever means "teach" per se, then it is only in Titus.

Table 29. Imperative uses of *laleō* (speak) in the New Testament

Passage	Greek transliteration	English translation
Mark 13:11	*kai hotan agōsin hymas paradidontes, mē promerimnate ti lalēsēte, all' ho ean dothē hymin en ekeinē tē hōra touto laleite· ou gar este hymeis hoi lalountes alla to pneuma to hagion.*	Whenever you are arrested and brought to trial, do not worry beforehand about what to *say*. Just *say* whatever is given you at the time, for it is not you speaking, but the Holy Spirit.
Acts 5:20	*poreuesthe kai stathentes laleite en tō hierō tō laō panta ta hrēmata tēs zōēs tautēs.*	"Go, stand in the temple courts," he said, "and *tell* the people all about this new life."
Acts 18:9	*Eipen de ho kyrios en nykti di' horamatos tō Paulō· mē phobou, alla lalei kai mē siōpēsēs,*	One night the Lord spoke to Paul in a vision: "Do not be afraid; *keep on speaking*, do not be silent."
1 Cor 14:28	*ean de mē ē diermēneutēs, sigatō en ekklēsia, heautō de laleitō kai tō theō.*	If there is no interpreter, the speaker should keep quiet in the church and *speak* to himself and to God.
1 Cor 14:29	*prophētai de dyo ē treis laleitōsan kai hoi alloi diakrinetōsan.*	Two or three prophets should *speak*, and the others should weigh carefully what is said.
Eph 4:25	*Dia apothemenoi to pseudos laleite alētheian hekastos meta tou plēsion autou, hoti esmen allēlōn melē.*	Therefore each of you must put off falsehood and *speak* truthfully to your neighbor, for we are all members of one body.

237. In its discussion of *laleō*, BDAG does not offer the gloss "teach" for any of the 296 occurrences in the New Testament. In the 95 uses of *laleō* in the AF, it never seems to mean "teach," though in 1 Clem. 13:1 Jesus's speaking is further defined as "teaching": "let us remember the words of the Lord Jesus, which he spoke [*elalēsen*] as he taught [*didaskōn*] gentleness and patience." This does not imply that *laleō* is synonymous with teaching but that speaking can be didactic in its aim or effect.

Passage	Greek transliteration	English translation
Titus 2:1	*Sy de lalei ha prepei tē hygiainousē didaskalia.*	You, however, must *teach* what is appropriate to sound doctrine.
Titus 2:15	*Tauta lalei kai parakalei kai elenche meta pasēs epitagēs· mēdeis sou periphroneitō.*	These, then, are the things you should *teach*. Encourage and rebuke with all authority. Do not let anyone despise you.
Jas 2:12	*Houtōs laleite kai houtōs poieite hōs dia nomou eleutherias mellontes krinesthai.*	*Speak* and act as those who are going to be judged by the law that gives freedom.

In the only direct parallel to Paul's imperatival use of *laleō* in the AF,[238] Ignatius writes to Polycarp: "Devote yourself to unceasing prayers; ask for greater understanding than you have. Keep alert with an unresting spirit. Speak [*laleō*] to the people individually, in accordance with God's example. Bear the diseases of all, as a perfect athlete. Where there is more work, there is much gain" (*Pol.* 1:3). This passage nicely situates the verbal dimension of pastoral ministry in a wide spectrum of attitudes and activities. It is not so much about teaching per se as some formal ecclesial event as about the kind of language in all settings that will make pastoral care most fruitful. It is possible that this why Paul used a form of "speak" rather than of "teach."

Titus's speech pattern, his speech ethics as it were, is required by Paul to serve to inform and "encourage and rebuke" (two more second sing. imperatives). These activities dominated the life of Jesus, are prominent in Paul's life and letters, and form the core of the pastoral mandate in the Pauline churches. The verb "encourage" (*parakaleō*) occurs 109 times in the New Testament, 54 times in Paul, and 8 times in the PE[239] (see discussion in passages above). There was much in Crete that was detestable and alarming. Titus's labor should promote a buoyant attitude, not a sense of fear, hopelessness, or defeat. It should encourage. "Men are not sufficiently reminded of their duty, unless they are also vehemently urged to do it."[240]

As for "rebuke," Paul has already used the same word in 1:9, 13 (see discussion there). As a command, the word occurs six times in the New Testament. Jesus taught, "If your brother or sister sins, go and *point out their fault*, just between the two of you" (Matt 18:15). Paul calls for reproving or

238. There are three imperatival uses of *laleō* in the AF; the other two are either plural (not sing.) or third person (not second). See Ign. *Rom.* 7:1 and Did. 15:3, respectively.

239. See also 1 Tim 1:3; 2:1; 5:1; 6:2; 2 Tim 4:2; Titus 1:9; 2:6.

240. Calvin, 375.

exposing evil deeds or evildoers in other contexts (e.g., Eph 5:11; 1 Tim 5:20; 2 Tim 4:2). While Christians generally and pastors in particular should be civil and even magnanimous in their dealings with others (see Titus 3:2–3), "nice" is not always optimal in the care of souls. The contemporary dogma of "tolerance" in particular calls for careful critique and definition.[241] As Paul wrote elsewhere, "Blessed is the one who does not condemn himself by what he approves" (Rom 14:22). Paul found it necessary to reprove Peter (Gal 2:11, 14). Most of his letters (most notably 1–2 Corinthians) contain passages that rebuke. Paul is not calling for anything from Titus that he has not modeled himself in the establishment and oversight of other congregational bodies. In any case, Titus "is not rebuking them on his own authority. God is the one who sets the standard for right conduct."[242]

Paul puts teeth in his directive to "rebuke" by adding "with all authority."[243] Normally the word (*epitagē*, used seven times in the New Testament, all in Paul)[244] refers to a command. The word has already been discussed at 1 Tim 1:1 and Titus 1:3. Here it is defined by BDAG (383) as the authority that stands behind (divine)[245] commands. It could, however, be understood as "with every command [Paul has given to Titus]." Titus should not pull any punches. Paul is an apostle of Jesus Christ (1:1), and Titus stands in a succession of those who lead in his name. While he should embody gracious treatment of others, he cannot waffle or let himself by pushed around by the ignorant or unruly.

Paul underscores this frank counsel with a parting insistence: "Do not let anyone despise[246] you." Maccabean martyrs "scorned" or "despised" or "disdained" their tortures and agonies (see use of the same word at 4 Macc 6:9; 7:16; 14:1). They stuck to their guns, despite heavy disincentives. Titus faces formidable adversaries. Paul does not specify names, though he may have certain persons in mind with the pronoun translated "anyone." Whatever face the adversaries take, Titus should trust God and his apostolic messenger in accordance with the counsel of this epistle.

241. See D. A. Carson, *The Intolerance of Tolerance* (Grand Rapids: Eerdmans, 2013).

242. Ngewa, 381.

243. "With all impressiveness" or "with confidence" (Dibelius and Conzelmann, 146) both fall short as possible glosses.

244. See other uses at Rom 16:26; 1 Cor 7:6, 25; 2 Cor 8:8; 1 Tim 1:1; Titus 1:3.

245. MM 247 notes that "Paul's use to denote a *divine* command . . . is in accord with its technical use in dedicatory inscriptions" (italics in original).

246. From Greek *periphroneō*, a New Testament hapax.

VI. STANDING ORDERS FOR BELIEVERS (3:1–11)

Whereas Titus 2 is divided clearly between paraenesis for different groups (2:1–10) and theological grounding for that paraenesis (2:11–15), this section of Titus 3 intertwines ethics and theology. Verses 1–3 and 8–11 deal with behavior, attitudes, and policies for Titus to observe and encourage. Verses 4–7 are a thick vein of soteriological lore that furnishes a basis for Paul's counsel. While Paul's paraenesis could be construed as ethical admonition suitable for people in general (see "for everyone"; 3:9), it is rather addressed to and intended for Christians—Paul means "everyone" who has received God's grace in Christ. "The people" (v. 1) whom Titus is to address have been "saved" (v. 5) and "justified" (v. 7). They "have trusted in God" (v. 8) in accordance with a high Christology and robust pneumatology (see commentary on vv. 4–7 below).

In this section Paul reminds Titus yet again (see already 1:16 and table 26 and commentary there), and not for the last time (see 3:14), of the high priority he attaches to a faith that moves decisively beyond assent to certain teachings, to tangible and effective response to God and his word by zeal for good works. While there are only eleven imperatives in all of Titus's forty-six verses (see table 27 at the introduction to 2:1–10 above), three of them occur in this section. This is not a pushy epistle in terms of frequency of occurrence of commands, but if there is ethical urgency anywhere, in this section it is on display. God's saving work (v. 5) has direct implications for how believers behave in the world. They should be devoted to doing the right and best thing in every situation (vv. 1–2, 8). This devotion includes pursuing harmonious relations with others (vv. 9–11). There are no illusions that that assignment will be easy or even doable, given the recalcitrance of some whom Titus will likely encounter.

> [1]*Remind the people to be subject to rulers and authorities, to be obedi-*
> *ent, to be ready to do whatever is good,* [2]*to slander no one, to be peaceable*
> *and considerate, and always to be gentle toward everyone.* [3]*At one time we*
> *too were foolish, disobedient, deceived and enslaved by all kinds of passions*
> *and pleasures. We lived in malice and envy, being hated and hating one*
> *another.* [4]*But when the kindness and love of God our Savior appeared,*
> [5]*he saved us, not because of righteous things we had done, but because of*
> *his mercy. He saved us through the washing of rebirth and renewal by the*
> *Holy Spirit,* [6]*whom he poured out on us generously through Jesus Christ*
> *our Savior,* [7]*so that, having been justified by his grace, we might become*
> *heirs having the hope of eternal life.* [8]*This is a trustworthy saying. And*
> *I want you to stress these things, so that those who have trusted in God*
> *may be careful to devote themselves to doing what is good. These things are*
> *excellent and profitable for everyone.* [9]*But avoid foolish controversies and*

genealogies and arguments and quarrels about the law, because these are unprofitable and useless. [10] *Warn a divisive person once, and then warn them a second time. After that, have nothing to do with them.* [11] *You may be sure that such people are warped and sinful; they are self-condemned.*

1 "Remind the people" is literally "remind them." Paul has in mind members of the communities of faith under Titus's oversight. He issues a similar directive to Timothy (2 Tim 2:14).[247] "Remind" implies prior knowledge, concerning which people need to refresh their memories. In this case the subject is civil government (bearing in mind that, in the Roman world, there was a religious dimension to all governmental authority—the modern secular state did not exist).[248] Jesus had been questioned on that point, resulting in his dictum: "Give back to Caesar what is Caesar's, and to God what is God's" (Matt 22:21). Paul's counsel may be seen as fleshing out Jesus's mandate, applying it to the social setting of the churches in Crete.

"Rulers and authorities" are those who constitute and enforce government. The expression is likely hendiadys; Paul frequently uses these terms in tandem to denote ruling powers, whether earthly or heavenly.[249] Here reference is to the former, as in Rom 13:1 ("authorities") and 13:3 ("rulers). Also in the Rom 13 passage, Paul uses the same word translated "be subject to" (*hypotassō*; see 13:1, 5) that is found in Titus 3:1. It appears also in 2:5, 9 (see discussion there). The people under Titus's spiritual care should live their lives in line with duly constituted governing powers, "ready[250] to do whatever is good" (lit. "every good work").

Paul uses an even stronger term than "be subject to" when he adds, "be obedient" (from *peitharcheō*).[251] Cretans had a reputation for lack of restraint. Christian witness, personal integrity, and corporate reputation would suffer if believers lived scofflaw lives. "The Romans hated nothing worse than cults they deemed seditious."[252]

247. Other New Testament occurrences of the verb *hypomimnēskō* (remind): Luke 22:61; John 14:26; 2 Pet 1:12; 3 John 10; Jude 5.

248. Rather, there was the imperial cult, which, though "but one religion among others, and in no way exclusive, still carried out persecutions in the name . . . of civic traditions involved in loyalty towards the emperor" (Robert Turcan, *The Cults of the Roman Empire*, trans. Antonia Nevill [Oxford: Blackwell, 1996], 340). There were also local religions and gods, which come into view repeatedly in Acts (e.g., 14:11; 17:18; 19:26; 28:11).

249. See 1 Cor 15:24; Eph 1:21; 3:10; 6:12; Col 1:16; 2:10, 15. For papyrus testimony to *archē* as "magistrate," see MM 81.

250. Greek *hetoimos*, a word appearing only three other times in Paul (2 Cor 9:5; 10:6, 16).

251. See Acts 5:29, 32. Otherwise, it is found only in Acts 27:21, for a total of four New Testament uses.

252. Keener, *Bible Background Commentary*, 630.

Paul's tone as this verse opens is pointedly terse; the NIV "and" in "rulers and authorities" is added for English literary flow, just as it was in some Greek manuscripts.[253] But Paul's diction here likely makes use of asyndeton, the omission of conjunctions for effect.[254] The staccato sequence signals that this is not breezy verbiage but critical counsel.[255]

Paul's directive implies that "rulers and authorities" are not commanding rebellion against God but generally fulfilling their God-ordained duties (see Rom 13:1–7). They are upholding social order. Above we noted situations where wives have biblical ground not to "submit to" their husbands (see discussion of Titus 2:5). The same undoubtedly holds true for believers in relation to government. Sometimes it is necessary to go against earthly authorities to uphold the divine will, as when the Hebrew midwives "feared God and did not do what the king of Egypt had told them to do" (Exod 1:17); when Moses defied Pharaoh (Exod 7–12); when Shadrach, Meschach, and Abednego would not bow down (Dan 3); when Daniel prayed, despite the king's edict (Dan 6); and when Peter and John kept preaching after being ordered to be silent (Acts 4:18–20). Over the past century history offers numerous examples of godly and (most think) justifiable civil disobedience on the part of Christians, whether Bonhoeffer in opposition to the Nazis, Corrie Ten Boom and her family hiding Jews from the same tyrants, North American Christians defying racial segregation laws during the civil rights movement of the 1960s, or Christian martyrs in numerous nations refusing to renounce their faith and paying the consequences of criminal penalty for their righteousness.[256]

Ngewa points out that, assuming Paul's martyrdom, "Paul himself would demonstrate by his death that when the state stands in opposition to God, it becomes time to obey God and not human authorities."[257]

Paul is not blindly ordering Titus to enforce lockstep adherence to civil rule no matter what. He is confirming that, under conditions like those in Crete at that time, Christians should be exemplary subjects, even in a pagan social order. The special grace they have received in Christ should enhance,

253. Metzter, *Textual Commentary*, 655.

254. See BDF §§458–64.

255. Bassler, 206, suggests that the language and "lofty, formal tone of the passage set it apart from the surrounding material and suggest an origin in the baptismal liturgy of the church." On another reading, such words are quite in line with the rest of Titus (and the other PE) and the pastoral counsel often issued by Paul.

256. See, for example, Grim and Finke, *The Price of Freedom Denied*. On mainstream Western media silence, see R. Shortt, *Christianophobia: A Faith under Attack* (Grand Rapids: Eerdmans, 2012). For examples of perseverance under suppression in China, see Yiwu, *God Is Red*. For numerous poignant contemporary examples of persecution, see Nik Ripkin, with Gregg Lewis, *The Insanity of God* (Nashville: B&H, 2013).

257. Ngewa, 394.

not curtail, their cooperation with the common grace of human government to the extent this is possible (see Rom 12:18).

2 While v. 1 promotes a social ethic, v. 2 applies theological insight to personal ethics with echoes of Jesus's "blessed are the peacemakers" (Matt 5:9). Paul calls for gracious deportment "toward everyone," not just toward friends or others in the church (see Matt 5:46–47). He discourages two negative tendencies and encourages two positive.

The negatives have to do with speech ethics and possible combativeness. As to speech ethics, Titus should remind believers (v. 1) "to slander no one." The Greek word (*blasphēmeō*), not uncommon in Paul's writings,[258] means to speak against someone or something maliciously. It is not only a Cretan but a human tendency to grouse, malign, complain, and commit other acts of verbal aggression, whether directly or behind others' backs. Jesus taught that human speech bears eschatological consequences (Matt 12:37). Paul has already commented on how grace and salvation (2:11) result in magnanimous lives (2:12). He now extends that conviction in reminding Titus how transformation of the heart shows itself in reform of the tongue. In an age when some are reluctant to call any act or viewpoint wrong,[259] Calvin's comment is helpful: "Not that he wishes them to condone the faults of ungodly men; he is condemning only the propensity to slander."[260]

As to combativeness, "to be peaceable" translates a form of *amachos*, a word that in the New Testament means not disposed to fight, quarrel, or be contentious.[261] Paul lists it among pastoral qualifications (1 Tim 3:3), its only other New Testament occurrence. A sharp tongue is often combined with an irascible spirit and confrontational behavior. These tendencies are inconsistent with confessing Christ as Lord and Savior. Titus's oversight should have the effect of discouraging their manifestation.

On the positive side, Cretan Christians are to be "considerate" (from *epieikēs*). In its other four New Testament uses, the word is translated in the NIV twice the same way[262] but as "gentle" in Phil 4:5 and 1 Tim 3:3. In the AF it carries the sense of magnanimity (1 Clem. 1:2) and moderation (1 Clem. 21:7), as well as gentleness (1 Clem. 29:1; Herm. Mand. 12.4.2), a sense it carries in the LXX when applied to God (Ps 85:5).[263] When combined with the

258. See also Rom 2:24; 3:8; 14:16; 1 Cor 10:30; 1 Tim 1:20; 6:1; Titus 2:5.

259. See Kuligin, *Snubbing God*.

260. Calvin, 377.

261. MM 25 lists the word's appearance on a gravestone inscription by a husband in memory of his wife. The word has a wider range of meanings in classical Greek (LSJ 78) and occurs in both Josephus (seven times) and Philo (eleven times) bearing these non–New Testament meanings.

262. Jas 3:17; 1 Pet 2:18.

263. "It is you, O Lord, who are kind and gentle [*chrēstos kai epieikēs*] and abounding in mercy to all who call on you" (NETS).

additional adjective "gentle" in Titus 3:2 ("always . . . be gentle"), the picture emerges of a person who is distinctly retiring and deferential to all people all the time. Pushed very far, this pattern could require the retooling of some personality types.

In the Greek, however, "always" is absent.[264] This is fortuitous in a religion that looks to Jesus as a model, for he was not *always* gentle himself.[265] Furthermore, while NIV translates "*be* gentle," the verbal idea in Greek is the more proactive "demonstrating, displaying" (from the participle of *endeiknymi*). God raised up Pharaoh to *display* his power (Rom 9:17); Christ *displayed* his patience in showing mercy to Saul of Tarsus (1 Tim 1:16). When combined with Paul's repeated insistence on ambitious exercise of good works (see table 26 and comments at Titus 1:16), it is doubtful he wants Titus to instill continuous bland timidity in those under his care. Their lives should rather be ongoing demonstrations of *praütēs*, which BDAG (861) explains as "gentleness" in the sense of "the quality of not being overly impressed by a sense of one's self-importance." Danker gives the sense as "a non-imperious attitude."[266] Paul is calling for behavior free of arrogance and proud cockiness, not a gentleness that is always deferential to everyone, a grotesque disposition that would define the Christian as a quailing caricature.

NIV does not help its cause with v. 2's final words "toward everyone." Most frequently "everyone" translates a form of *pas* (all, every) in the singular. Here however the Greek is plural; it can reasonably be rendered as "toward all persons." "Toward everyone" (esp. when combined with "always") could lend itself to an interpretation requiring weak deference toward every single person in all circumstances. The more expansive sense of the Greek (captured in RSV and WEB by "toward all men," in ESV by "toward all people," and in CSB by "to all people") is conveyed well (if idiomatically) by *The Message* in rendering both vv. 1 and 2: "Remind the people to respect the government and be law-abiding, always ready to lend a helping hand. No insults, no fights. God's people should be bighearted and courteous." The godly character traits called for in v. 2 should be chronically present in the lives of those Christ has redeemed (Titus 2:14) and expressed in ways that are situationally and interpersonally fitting, as well as psychologically and socially authentic.

3 The verse begins, semantically, with "for" (*gar*). The basis for the previous two verses is found in this verse and what follows. Titus should "remind the people" (v. 1) to live graciously and considerately toward others (v. 2), in view of their own mottled, if not motley, past (v. 3). Paul characterizes the

264. NIV may infer it from the present aspect of the participle *endeiknymenous*.

265. For example, in the temple cleansings, in debates with hostile opponents, and in other cases (such as with the Syrophoenician woman), Jesus's behavior was brusque.

266. *Concise Greek-English Lexicon*, 296.

seamy side of his and his readers' pregospel lives with seven colorful words or descriptive phrases. "The point is not, however, to portray unbelievers in unflattering terms but to remind believers of who they were in their very identity before God's saving act on their behalf."[267] Just like non-Christians, Paul and Titus had been the folllwing:

1. *anoētoi* (foolish). Jesus called his companions by this unflattering term (using the Gk. vocative case) on the Emmaus Road (Luke 24:25). Paul used it to jolt the Galatians (Gal 3:1, 3)[268] and to warn of the "foolish" desires attending the pursuit of wealth (1 Tim 6:9).[269] The word means to exercise poor judgment, to behave senselessly. The murderous opposition of Saul of Tarsus to Jesus's followers (Acts 9:1) exemplifies the trait.

2. *apeitheis* (disobedient). In its other five New Testament uses, it denotes unruly behavior in general (Luke 1:17; Titus 1:16), rejection of God's command (Acts 26:19), and rebellion against parents (Rom 1:30; 2 Tim 3:2). Those who follow Christ should be inclined to honor God-ordained norms, not defy them. Examples abound in the postmodern West (and elsewhere) of people even in the church who interpret religion as liberation from biblical prescription. This was a problem, however, already in apostolic times[270] and even before (see Mark 7:6–8).

3. *planōmenoi* (deceived). The verb on which this adjectival participle is based (*planaō*) is frequent in the New Testament (thirty-nine times). Paul uses it in the imperative ("Do not be deceived"; see 1 Cor 6:9; 15:33; Gal 6:7) and in warning Timothy about the dire moral direction of the present age (2 Tim 3:13). Analogous use is reflected nearly two dozen times in the AF; the image of errant and wandering souls is common in depicting the plight of humans outside of faith in Christ: "We were all deceived [*eplanēthēmen*] like sheep; each person was deceived [*eplanēthē*] in his daily living" (1 Clem. 16:6, my translation; see Isa 53:6).[271]

4. "enslaved by all kinds of passions and pleasures." This wide-ranging *nostra culpa* ("we are all guilty") recalls Paul's depiction of all humans as slaves of either sin or righteousness (Rom 6:16–19). "Passions and pleasures"[272] are not evil in themselves, but every time "passions" (*epithymiai*) are mentioned

267. Laansma, 284.

268. For the vocative use in the AF, see 1 Clem. 23:4; 2 Clem. 11:3; Herm. Mand. 10.2.1. It appears eleven times in the LXX, eight times in Philo, and seventeen times in Josephus, all confirming that human folly was abundantly in evidence in New Testament times.

269. The other New Testament use of the word (out of six total): Rom 1:14.

270. See, for example, 1 Pet 2:16; Jude 4.

271. For evidence of deceit, deceivers, and delusion in Second Temple Judaism generally, see Quinn, 202–3.

272. Greek *hēdonē*. The word occurs in only four other places in the New Testament: Luke 8:14; Jas 4:1, 3; 2 Pet 2:13.

in the PE,[273] the connotation is negative. God's grace (Titus 2:11) enables the escape of "worldly passions" (2:12) for the sake of living passionately (and with pleasure)[274] for God.

5. "We lived in malice and envy." This was how they spent their lives viewed over the course of time—the verbal form translated "lived" (from *diagō*)[275] means to pass through, to conduct one's life, languishing or flourishing depending on the circumstances. "Malice and envy" were not occasional lapses but their characteristic mode of deportment. Paul could easily draw on his own experience here as a persecutor of Stephen and others (see Acts 8:1; Gal 1:13–14).

6. *stygētoi* (being hated). BDAG (949) defines the root word as "loathsome, despicable." This is a New Testament hapax. In its only two AF occurrences the word describes people "hateful to God" (1 Clem. 35:6) and the "abominable" persons who sought to burn Shadrach and his friends alive (1 Clem. 45:7; see Dan 3). Philo uses it to describe adultery in God's eyes: "a detestable [*stygēton*] thing hated by God [*theomisēton*]" (*Decalogue* 131). In Titus 3:3 Paul describes people in their native decadence as God views them, apart from his mercy.

7. "hating one another." Ever since enmity (*echthra*) entered humanity in Eden (Gen 3:15 LXX), human relations have been strained, epitomized by Cain and Abel (Gen 4). Human life is no stranger to "idolatry and witchcraft; hatred [*echthrai*], discord, jealousy, fits of rage, selfish ambition, dissensions, factions" (Gal 5:20), and more. For Paul it is Christ, and only him, who reconciles Jew and Gentile alike to God "through the cross, by which he put to death their hostility [*echthra*]" (Eph 2:16). But as he writes to Titus, Paul has in mind Crete and its people's need for Christ. People unreconciled to God will gravitate toward tension and hostility, as history shows. Sadly, even in the wake of confession of Christ, people may live in animosity more than in hospitality and love.

Taken together, the seven deadly traits above are a slap in the face to Cretan Christians to jettison any complacency over presumed moral superiority in their admittedly tawdry social location. "The congregation must never forget that it once harbored the same thoughts about Jesus as his enemies did."[276] The warning would also apply to Titus, were he to feel himself better or less spiritually needy than those to whom he was called to reach out. Titus and those he led alike should regard recipients of their ministry with openness fueled by deep contrition at what they once were and how much they owe the one

273. See 1 Tim 6:9; 2 Tim 2:22; 3:6; 4:3; Titus 2:12.

274. See numerous passages in Psalms that speak of delight in God, nine times in Ps 119 alone. (See Ps 112:1, in which "fear of the Lord" = finding "great delight in [God's] commands.")

275. The word occurs in the New Testament elsewhere only in 1 Tim 2:2. It is found sixteen times in Philo, often with its New Testament sense (e.g., *Creation* 79; *Allegorical Interpretation* 3.125; *Preliminary Studies* 174). For the same meaning in the papyri, see MM 147.

276. Schlatter, *Die Kirche der Griechen*, 261.

who has forgiven them (see Luke 7:36–47). However bad the Cretans might be (Titus 1:12), Paul knows that he, Titus, and all believers are by nature and past deeds no better. Their only advantage is due to a person and work manifestly not their own, as the following verses show.

4 Offsetting the human state (previous verse) and in fact creating conditions favorable for human rescue are the divine being, attributes, and action.

His action is seen in something that has "appeared." The underlying Greek word *epiphainō* in its four NT occurrences can mean to shine in a dark place (Luke 1:79; Acts 27:20) or, in its meaning here, to become manifest or gloriously visible (see also Titus 2:11). Siebenthal,[277] while recognizing the nondescript, unmarked character of aorist form depiction of past events, observes that "the historical (indicative) aorist is used in the New Testament to, among other things, describe the singular great facts of salvation history [*Heilsgeschichte*]." This is not to deny that other tenses and moods may convey the same meaning. Representative examples (Titus references in bold) are found in table 30.

Table 30. Examples of historical (indicative) aorist

Aorist form, transliterated	Translation/action	References
heauton ekenōsen	he divested himself	Phil 2:7
etapeinōsen heauton	he humbled himself	Phil 2:8
apesteilen	he sent	e.g., John 3:17
epephanē	**there appeared**	**Titus 2:11; 3:4**
ephanerōthē	he/it was revealed	1 Tim 3:16; 1 John 1:2
edōken	he gave	John 3:16
paredōken	he gave up	Rom 8:32
apethanen	he died	1 Cor 15:3
heauton prosēnenken	he offered himself	Heb 9:14
ēgeiren	he rose	e.g., Acts 3:15
ēgerthē	he was raised	e.g., Rom 6:4
edoxasen	he glorified	Acts 3:13
hyperypsōsen	he exalted him highly	Phil 2:9

277. *Griechische Grammatik*, §199b.

The point of table 30 is not to encourage reversion to simplistic generalizations about the aorist[278] but to situate key claims found in Titus in their historical-theological, first-century setting. God, Christ, or both have acted decisively in a variety of ways to effect salvation. The appearing of divine "kindness and love" (3:4), like divine grace (2:11), is part of that saving divine action.[279]

Divine attributes highlighted in 3:4 are "kindness" (*chrēstotēs*) and "love"—not *agape*, as might be expected, but *philanthrōpia*. Both are depicted as attributes of "God our Savior." The ties in this verse with 2:11 suggests the author is thinking of God's "kindness and love" in the sending of his Son (the incarnation) to achieve the saving work depicted in vv. 5–7.

"Kindness" (*chrēstotēs*), which is used in the New Testament only by Paul, occurs ten times. In some cases it is an attribute of God (Rom 2:4; 11:22 [three times]; Eph 2:7).[280] In other cases it is an ethical expression of believers' union with Christ (2 Cor 6:6; Col 3:12). In one case it is both: as a fruit of the Spirit (Gal 5:22), "kindness" is both a divine quality and a human possibility through faith. In Titus 3:4 God's kindness serves as a contrast to the despicable behavior and traits people display (v. 3).[281]

The same is true for God's *philanthrōpia* (love), a word that occurs in the New Testament otherwise only in Acts 28:2: the islanders on Malta who took in Paul and others after shipwreck showed the shivering survivors "unusual *philanthrōpia*" (NIV "kindness"). It is common in the papyri (MM 668–69), where it often denotes gracious or humane treatment. In the AF the word appears once (Diogn. 9:2), in apposition to the words *chrēstotēs* (see reference to "kindness" above) and *agapē* (love): "The season arrived during which God had decided to reveal at last his goodness [*chrēstotēs*] and power (oh, the surpassing kindness [*philanthrōpia*] and love [*agapē*] of God!)." People menace each other, though each is as morally flawed as the other; God, who is without flaw, displays "kindness and love" in the work of Christ, described in the next verses.

5 A striking feature of this verse is the word order. After the adversative conjunction and dependent clause in the preceding verse ("But when the

278. Cf. Constantine Campbell, *Basics of Verbal Aspect in Biblical Greek* (Grand Rapids: Zondervan, 2008), 13.

279. Bassler, 183, claims that Paul's failure to mention other salvation-historical events like the exodus, the Sinai covenant, or God's promises to David mark this as a "static and isolated . . . illumination of God's plan of salvation," not a component in a salvation-historical continuum. But if Paul is the author, he is aware of these related events; he cannot list all of them every time he mentions that "the kindness and love of God our Savior appeared."

280. Saarinen, 191, translates it "goodness" and calls "the goodness of God" here "the paradigmatic good work that, in addition to its saving meaning, has an exemplary character," citing Marshall. But it is a divine attribute, not an act, and may have less an exemplary function here than a doxological one.

281. On "kindness" here, see also Barclay, *Paul and the Gift*, 449n1, 578.

kindness . . . appeared"), the reader might expect the immediate statement of a subject and verb, as in the NIV: "he saved us." But in Greek, fourteen words precede the verb that states "he saved."

These fourteen words express, first, a negative. (For the same assertion and rhetorical strategy see 2 Tim 1:10.) Paul reminds Titus that God "saved" (evidently the ministry of Christ is still in view) believers "not on the basis of works performed in righteousness which we did"—"which" referring back to "works." It is always good when people, and Christians in particular,[282] act morally and compassionately. But human acts can be performed "in righteousness" only when there is a personal relationship with the one true God who acted to save in Christ. Then and only then can there be talk of "works performed in righteousness," that is, acts of response to God and his word through union with Christ and leadership by the Holy Spirit. God does not save on the basis of the good things people may do, even though it is good when people do good things. While obedience to God's commands is never to be denigrated, in itself human obedience cannot establish a right relationship with God.

In the context of v. 5, Paul's disavowal of "righteous things we had done" (NIV) serves at least three purposes. First, it clears the ground for declaring the true basis of salvation, which he will shortly explain. Second, it restates the truth emphasized in Romans that God justifies the ungodly (4:5; see also 5:6)—Christ died for us "while we were still sinners" (Rom 5:8), not because people earn divine acceptance by some set or store of deeds done to deserve it. Third, it underscores the folly of supposing that Paul, Titus, or any Cretan Christians occupy high moral ground from which to look down on others around them (see Titus 3:3). The doleful diagnosis of Isa 64:6 comes to mind: "*All* of us have become like one who is unclean, and *all* our righteous acts are like filthy rags; we all shrivel up like a leaf, and like the wind our sins sweep us away." For Paul, ministry to Cretans requires profound consciousness that, outside of a "righteousness" not one's own, no one is any different from the worst Cretan.

Next in v. 5 and still prior to stating "he saved us," Paul then expresses a positive: "because of [*kata*] his mercy." The preposition *kata* can also carry the idea "according to, in keeping with." Salvation is not conferred based on some scale of human merit but according to the working of "his mercy." The placement of "his" in Greek before "mercy" may be emphatic, and if so, it may stress either the uniqueness of *this* God, the elevated quality of *this* mercy, or both. Of the twenty-seven times "mercy" appears in the New Testament, ten are in Paul, and five of those are in the PE.[283] The word is used over three hundred

282. See Jerram Barrs, *Delighting in the Law of the Lord: God's Alternative to Legalism and Moralism* (Wheaton, IL: Crossway, 2013).

283. Elsewhere in the PE: 1 Tim 1:2; 2 Tim 1:2, 16, 18. Elsewhere in Paul: Rom 9:23; 11:31; 15:9; Gal 6:16; Eph 5:24.

times in the LXX and is particularly frequent in the Psalms. God's mercy is axiomatic in the Old Testament. Not wanting to fail to elicit worship, Paul, in referring to mercy, taps into a deep and longstanding scriptural consciousness of gratitude and praise.

At last Paul comes to the core affirmation of the verse: "He saved us." The particular means of rescue cited are twofold, but because both are introduced with just one preposition (*dia*, through, by means of), they may be viewed as closely related: "through the washing of rebirth and renewal by the Holy Spirit." It is possible that "and" (*kai*) is ascensive here and might be rendered "even" or "indeed." In any case, God's saving work is described in the major effects it works on those who receive the gospel message with faith (see 1:1; 3:8).

Paul writes first of "the washing of rebirth,"[284] which is surely related to the divine regeneration of the human heart through faith in Christ alluded to in John 3:3–8. Water baptism is a recognition of and catalyst for this spiritual but real transformation. It is difficult, and unnecessary, to make a radical separation between the two.[285] "Renewal [*anakainōseōs*] by the Holy Spirit" may plausibly be related not only to what John the Baptist promised (Matt 3:11) and early Acts preaching recognized (Acts 1:5; 11:16)[286] but what Paul taught in 1 Cor 12:13: "For we were all baptized by one Spirit so as to form one body—whether Jews or Gentiles, slave or free—and we were all given the one Spirit to drink." The language of renewal is familiar from Paul elsewhere (2 Cor 4:16; Col 3:10), where Paul uses the verb *anakainoō*, cognate with the noun *anakainōsis* in Titus 3:5. When the "disobedient" (v. 3) come to faith, dramatic inner cleansing ("washing") and new moral and ethical potential result (see Rom 8:2, 11). Paul's point in this context, it will be remembered, is that Titus and Cretan believers should seek to connect with the surrounding non-Christian culture in a positive and gracious way (vv. 1–2), since they are not inherently superior (vv. 3), just recipients of divine largesse (vv. 4–5).

284. The Greek word *palingenesia* (regeneration) occurs elsewhere in the New Testament only at Matt 19:28, where Jesus describes human transformation at the resurrection of the righteous. In 1 Clem. 9:4 Noah is said to have "proclaimed a second birth [*palingenesian*] to the world by his ministry, and through him the Master saved [*diesōsen*] the living creatures that entered into the ark in harmony." See also Theophilus, *To Autolycus* 16, which speaks of "repentance and remission of sins, through the water and laver of regeneration [*dia hydatos kai palingenesias*]—as many as come to the truth, and are born again [*anagennōmenous*], and receive blessing from God."

285. For a measured interpretive paraphrase, see Calvin, 382: "God saves us by His mercy, and He has given us a symbol and pledge of this salvation in baptism, by admitting us into His Church and engrafting us into the Body of His Son." For vehement protest against separation of baptism from the redemption effected by God's saving act in Christ and word of that act, see Luther, 268–69.

286. A background in the Christian movement is more plausible than Hanson's efforts to find the meaning in Mithraism, the Stoics, and the Pythagoreans (191).

6 "Largesse" is not overstatement given the language here. The same verb for "poured out" (*ekcheō*) appears in Joel 2:28, 29 (LXX Joel 3:1), a verse quoted at Pentecost (Acts 2:17–18; see also v. 33) to describe the Spirit's lavish outflow. The adverb "generously" (*plousiōs*)[287] augments a picture of abundant overflow. Paul envisions an issuance of the Holy Spirit not by dabs and dribbles but in a full and rich stream. The use of the preposition *epi* in the phrase translated "on us" denotes "individuals or groups on whom some spiritual blessing comes or rests."[288] Paul uses the same image of copious outflow when he writes about "God's love poured out [*ekchynnō*][289] into our hearts through the Holy Spirit, who has been given to us" (Rom 5:5).

In an age of charismatic influence in the world church, thoughts may turn here to emotional enhancement of spiritual experience. In the first-century context, whatever people's emotional states, there is likely reference to the exhilaration of historically hostile parties finding the joy of mutual respect, charity, and joint service in Christ's name. We should think of unfeigned, divinely enabled acceptance of one another and worship side-by-side by Arab Christians today and persecuted Sudanese, or by Messianic Jews and Palestinians who confess Jesus as Lord, or by whites and blacks in regions of racial tension where community relations may have a rocky history but who are exercising reciprocal compassion as sisters and brothers in Christ, or by formerly warring tribes in Rwanda or elsewhere in a world where murderous conflicts have flared up. Yet, now believers find themselves improbably united by the reality of God's healing presence. As Christ was filled with love for Samaritans (see, e.g., John 4), for the city that slew him (Luke 13:33; 23:28), and for all others as typified by his forgiveness of both one who died next to him (Luke 23:43) and those who crucified him (Luke 23:34), and as God's mercy took Paul from a Christian-killer (Acts 9:1; Gal 1:23; 1 Tim 1:13) to a Christian evangelist, Titus and others on Crete can move from loathing and aversion in the face of Cretan morals to hopeful proclamation of the gospel that reconciles and personal apprehension of the joy of fellowship with people once estranged from God but now (like them) made part of Christ's body the church.

Mention that this is all "through Jesus Christ our Savior" lends a Trinitarian cast (see God in v. 4, the Spirit in v. 5) to this richly theological section. Although Paul has in mind the practical benefit and effect of the blessing God dispenses, he never lets readers forget that this is not an intellectual ideal or timeless truth or principle: it is the lived-out reality demonstrated and ac-

287. The word occurs four times in the New Testament: see also Col 3:16; 1 Tim 6:17; 2 Pet 1:11.

288. Harris, *Prepositions and Theology*, 138. Harris points out how the same construction is used in connection with the bestowal of the word of God, his kingdom, and his grace, as well as the power of Christ.

289. This word is an alternate form of *ekcheō*, used in Titus 3:6 (BDAG 312).

complished by God in Jesus Christ. Believers can never afford so to hype the blessing offered in the gospel that they lose the capacity for awe and reverence of the one cursed by God (Gal 3:13) for their blessing's sake.

7 The final verse of this brief theological flourish (vv. 4–7) concludes on the note of outcomes. Given the appearing of God's kindness and love (v. 4), his lavish washing and renewing not by human deeds but by his work (v. 5), and the work of Christ (v. 6), Paul highlights two results. First, believers are "justified by his grace." This phrase expresses a central Pauline teaching found frequently elsewhere, as table 31 indicates. It gives examples from the occurrences of the passive forms of the verbs "justify" and "save" in Paul[290] in which reference is made to human salvation by God.

Table 31. Passive voice occurrences of *dikaioō* (be justified) and *sōzō* (be saved) in Paul

Passage	Occurrence of passive voice
***dikaioō* (be justified)**	
Rom 3:20	Therefore no one *will be declared righteous* in God's sight.
Rom 3:24	All *are justified* freely by his grace.
Rom 3:28	A person *is justified* by faith.
Rom 4:2	If, in fact, Abraham *was justified* by works. . . .
Rom 5:1	Since we *have been justified* through faith. . . .
Rom 5:9	Since we *have* now *been justified*. . . .
1 Cor 6:11	But you were washed, you were sanctified, you *were justified.*
Gal 2:16	A person *is* not *justified* by the works of the law, but by faith in Jesus Christ . . . that we *may be justified* by faith in Christ . . . by the works of the law no one *will be justified.*
Gal 2:17	But if, in seeking *to be justified* in Christ. . . .
Gal 3:11	No one who relies on the law *is justified* before God.
Gal 3:24	. . . that we *might be justified* by faith.
Gal 5:4	You who are *trying to be justified* by the law. . . .
Titus 3:7	. . . *having been justified* by his grace. . . .

290. Passive forms of "justify" (*dikaioō*) occur some twenty times in Paul. Passive forms of "save" (*sōzō*) occur nineteen times. Table 31 lists only passages that refer to human salvation by God.

Passage	Occurrence of passive voice
***sōzō* (be saved)**	
Rom 5:9	How much more *shall* we *be saved* from God's wrath through him!
Rom 5:10	How much more, having been reconciled, *shall* we *be saved* through his life!
Rom 8:24	For in this hope we *were saved.*
Rom 9:27	Only the remnant *will be saved.*
Rom 10:9	If you declare . . . and believe . . . you *will be saved.*
Rom 10:13	Everyone who calls on the name of the Lord *will be saved.*
Rom 11:26	All Israel *will be saved.*
1 Cor 1:18	To us who *are being saved* it is the power of God.
1 Cor 3:15	. . . though only as one *escaping* through the flames.
1 Cor 5:5	. . . so that his spirit *may be saved* on the day of the Lord.
1 Cor 10:33	I am not seeking my own good but the good of many, so that they *may be saved.*
1 Cor 15:2	By this gospel you *are saved.*
2 Cor 2:15	For we are to God the pleasing aroma of Christ among those who *are being saved.*
Eph 2:5	It is by grace you *have been saved.*
Eph 2:8	For it is by grace you *have been saved*, through faith.
1 Thess 2:16	. . . in their effort to keep us from speaking to the Gentiles so that they *may be saved.*
2 Thess 2:10	They perish because they refused to love the truth and so *be saved.*
1 Tim 2:4	. . . who wants all people to *be saved* and to come to a knowledge of the truth.
1 Tim 2:15	But women will be *saved*[291] *through childbearing.*

291. Some think this is not eschatological salvation but physical protection in childbirth.

Table 31 shows several things. First, being "justified" and "saved" can be virtually synonymous in Paul (see Rom 5:9 under both *dikaioō* and *sōzō* above). Second, taken together, the word pair is fairly pan-Pauline—it occurs across a wide range of his letters. Third, *dikaioō* language is centered in Romans and Galatians, where the topic of justification was most germane to the issues Paul opted to address with those audiences; *dikaioō* language does not occur in 1–2 Timothy, though *sōzō* language does. Fourth, forms of the word *sōzō* do not strictly speaking appear in Titus, though the concept denoted by the word is everywhere assumed. *Dikaioō* language occurs only in 3:7, but in such an offhand way as to imply that Titus was familiar with the concept without needing an explanation of the word. Fifth, with "being justified by his grace" in 3:7, Paul is affirming in the most basic and comprehensive terms possible the fundamental terms of human redemption: God justifies "by his grace," which correlates with the less technical, more generic *sōzō* language found frequently elsewhere in Paul. "It is not surprising that Paul sounds this note to Christians living in the midst of the large Jewish population of Crete with the possibility that Judaizing tendencies may be present."[292]

The second result Paul highlights of the Spirit's outpouring (v. 6) is that believers "become heirs having the hope of eternal life." "Hope"[293] is not vague optimism but a stance of trust like that of Abraham (Rom 4:18) based on Scripture (Rom 15:4) and provided by God (Rom 15:13). On "eternal life," see also discussion at Titus 1:2 above.

The notion of being "heirs" is found elsewhere in Paul,[294] though only here in the PE. It has deep Old Testament roots, seen most notably in the noun form "inheritance" (*klēronomia*), found over two hundred times in the LXX. An example is when Israel is separating from Judah: "And all Israel saw that the king did not listen to them, and the people answered the king, saying, 'What share do we have in Dauid? And we have no inheritance in the son of Iessai'" (1 Kgs 12:16 NETS). A prophecy of Isaiah states, "Then you shall trust in the Lord, and he shall bring you up upon the good things of the earth and feed you with the heritage [*klēronomia*] of your ancestor Iakob, for the mouth of the Lord has spoken these things" (Isa 58:14 NETS). For Paul in New Testament terms, with fulfillment of messianic promises in Christ, believers are "heirs" of age-old promises made by this God to his people, who through faith now live in "the hope of eternal life" (see Titus 1:2 above). The assurance of a secure spiritual inheritance, the result of divine adoption (Rom 8:14–17), should empower Titus and Cretan believers to trust

292. Gloer, 83.

293. Fifty-six times in Paul. For "hope" (*elpis*) in the PE, see also 1 Tim 1:1; 3:14; 4:10; 5:5; 6:17; 2 Tim 2:25; Titus 1:2; 2:13.

294. See Rom 4:13, 14; 8:17; Gal 3:29; 4:7.

God for their future in the face of the possibly discouraging social situation faced in Crete.

8 On "trustworthy saying," see commentary Introduction, IX.C. Paul wants Titus "to stress these things," meaning the theological verities he has set forth in vv. 4–7. It is not only the "practical" directives of ch. 2 and of 3:1 but perhaps even more so their theological foundation that require emphasis. If Titus needs to be reminded of them, how much more the pastors and other believers on Crete who had not had the advantage of years of service with Paul?

The verb translated "stress" (from *diabebaioomai*) occurs in the New Testament elsewhere only in 1 Tim 1:7,[295] where false teachers "confidently affirm" distorted views. Paul does not want Titus to be tentative or timid about the gospel's theological substance but decisive and forceful. It is important and laudable that people "have trusted[296] in God." But the point of the gospel is not just assent to doctrinal truths (vital though that be) but existential appropriation of those truths.

Yet, it is not a blind or merely fervid activism that Paul has in mind but one informed by theological reflection. The word translated "may be careful" (from *phrontizō*) is a New Testament hapax; Danker explains it as "be mentally intent on, *concentrate on*" (his emphasis).[297] It occurs over a dozen times in the LXX, with meanings like "to think and give careful attention to" (Ps 39:18; Sir 50:4) and "to give thought to" (Job 23:15; 2 Macc 4:21).[298] In these cases the object of the verb is expressed in the genitive case, as "good works" (*kalōn ergōn)* is in Titus 3:8 (on "good works," see discussion and table 26 at 1:16). So while Paul's usage is unusual in the New Testament, it is by no means anomalous in Hellenistic Greek.[299] Ignatius (*Pol.* 1:2) uses a similar construction in the only AF occurrence of *phrontizō*, with the object likewise in the genitive case: "Focus on unity [*tēs henōseōs phrontize*], for there is nothing better."

Paul's language in 3:8 (cf. 3:14) takes an unusual turn, however, as "what is good" (*kalōn ergōn*) is the object, not of *phrontizō*, but of the middle infinitive translated by NIV as "devote themselves" (*proistasthai*).[300] This word occurs only eight times in the New Testament and only in Paul's writings.

295. The word is found twice in the AF (Papias 3:3; 6:1) and twice in Philo (*The Worse Attacks the Better* 38; *Decalogue* 130).

296. Greek *hoi pepisteukotes theō*. The perfect participle of *pisteuō* (believe) is found elsewhere in the New Testament only at John 8:31; Acts 15:5; 16:34; 18:27; 19:18; 21:20; 21:25.

297. *Concise Greek-English Lexicon*, 376.

298. See *GELS* 720–21.

299. Forms of *phrontizō* occur forty-nine times in Philo, forty-seven times in Josephus.

300. Middle infinitive uses of *proïstēmi* are not found in the AF or Philo. But see Josephus, *Jewish Antiquities* 7.93; 15.313; 20.1, 31, 162.

Usually it means to exercise leadership or management.[301] But here (and in 3:14) it means to have interest in[302] or to prioritize[303] the doing of good, which Paul has highlighted at various points in the epistle. Titus would have been expected to flesh out these commands according to the opportunities and needs presented by the local situation. Paul leaves a lot in Titus's (and God's?) hands in the economy of this brief epistle; what he is not shy about repeating is the need for active participation in the imperatives of faith in order to be taken seriously as possessors of faith ("those who have trusted in[304] God").

"These things" are the good works that Paul is urging Titus to make sure that the Cretan believers set a high premium on. Their behavior will benefit not only those performing such actions but also those in the world, to whom God calls the church to witness. "For everyone" is "for people" (*tois anthrōpois*), an expression inclusive of everyone, not just people in the church. Those whom the church might be tempted to despise (v. 3) are among those Paul calls on Christians to bless by their stellar comportment in society (vv. 1–2).

9 Paul returns to the issue addressed in 1:10–16: challenges and provocations facing Titus in Cretan congregations. "The stronger Jewish element in Crete may account for the stronger emphasis on law here."[305] Theological truths (vv. 4–7) and ethical probity (v. 8) are vital, but they can both be frittered away by feuding. Paul lists four things for Titus to avoid and the reason why.

Titus should avoid,[306] first, "foolish controversies." Neither word is common in the New Testament. "Foolish" (from *mōros*), always either on Jesus's lips[307] or in Paul's letters (1 Cor 1:25, 27; 3:18; 4:10; 2 Tim 2:23), occurs only eleven other times. "Controversies" (from *zētēsis*) occurs only six other times, referring to disputes about John's baptism (John 3:25), about the nature of the gospel (Acts 15:2, 7), about Paul's message (25:20), and about conflicts within the church (1 Tim 6:4; 2 Tim 2:23). There was never a golden age when the Christian message or its precursors in John the Baptist's or Jesus's preaching

301. With this meaning it occurs in the active voice: Rom 12:8; 1 Thess 5:12; 1 Tim 3:4, 5, 12; 5:17.

302. Danker, *Concise Greek-English Lexicon*, 300.

303. See *GELS* 587: "champion a cause."

304. On the construction, see Harris, *Prepositions and Theology*, 233–34. Harris comments (237) on the fact that "God is (relatively speaking) so infrequently held up as the object of faith (John 12:44c; 14:1a; Acts 16:34; Rom 4:3, 5, 17, 24; Gal 3:6; 1 Thess 1:8; Titus 3:8; Heb 6:1; 1 Pet 1:21) and Christ so frequently" in the New Testament writings. This imbalance "indicates that it is in Christ that God meets the individual in salvation. There are not two competing objects of human faith."

305. Hanson, 194.

306. The word (from *periïstēmi*) means "circumvent" and occurs with this meaning in only one other New Testament passage (2 Tim 2:16). With another meaning it is used in John 11:42; Acts 25:7.

307. Matt 5:22; 7:26; 23:17; 25:2, 3, 8 (always with reference to foolhardy people).

were not disputed. Most gospel ministry will run into opposition and conflict eventually. Paul is not ordering Titus to avoid all controversy, for that would require retirement from ministry. It is "foolish controversies" that Paul targets. Subsequent warnings of what to avoid fill out the picture of what these disagreements might entail.

Titus should avoid, second, disputations about "genealogies." Ancestral descent is of undoubted significance in a religion that traces human origins to Adam and Eve, covenantal redemption to Abraham, and the giving of divine guidance (*tôrâ*) to the world through Moses. Jesus claimed to be descended from God, which his detractors denied, grounding their legitimacy in the heritage of Moses and claiming Jesus was actually of Samaritan descent (John 8:48–59). Paul claimed that believers were children of Abraham (Gal 3), though some in the church (to say nothing of Jews outside) insisted that adherence to circumcision and the law of Moses were necessary for salvation (Acts 15:1, 5). Philo denied that Mosaic references to ancestry were historically significant: "But let no one who is in his senses suspect that the wise legislator recorded this [i.e., 1 Chr 7:14] as a historical genealogy, but it is rather an explanation of things which are able to benefit the soul by means of symbols" (*Preliminary Studies* 44). Titus lived in a time and was part of a movement of disputed origins. In the only other use of the word "genealogy" (*genealogia*) in the New Testament, Paul tells Timothy to instruct Ephesian believers not "to devote themselves to myths and endless genealogies," because "such things promote controversial speculations rather than advancing God's work" (1 Tim 1:4). Genealogies were not just an issue in Crete. Titus should take steps to avoid becoming enmeshed in debates about them.

Third, Titus should avoid "arguments [*ereis*]." The underlying word, *eris*, occurs only in Paul's writings in the nine times it is found in the New Testament. NIV translates it also "strife" (Rom 1:29; 1 Tim 6:4), "dissension" (Rom 13:13), "quarrels" (1 Cor 1:11) or "quarreling" (1 Cor 3:3), "discord" (2 Cor 12:20; Gal 5:20), and "rivalry" (Phil 1:15). The word also finds significant employment in the AF, often in contexts reminiscent of the Titus passage.[308] Harmonious relations are a challenge in every domain of human enterprise, and the church is no different in this respect. Paul knows that through grace mutual respect can replace contentious disagreement. But this exchange will require concerted effort on Titus's part.

So will, fourth, avoiding "quarrels about the law." This "quarrels" is literally "scribal battles," and the word translated "about the law" in NIV is from *nomikos*, an adjective meaning "pertaining to the law" or "learned in the law." In the New Testament's nine occurrences of the word it most frequently appears as a substantive and means "lawyer" in the sense of a Jewish scribe schooled in

308. See 1 Clem. 14:2; 35:5; 44:1; 46:5; 54:2; Ign. *Eph.* 8:1.

handling Mosaic law and its entailments.[309] Here it modifies a form of *machē*, which means battle or quarrel. Paul sounds another note reminiscent of Titus 1:10–16, in which "those of the circumcision group" (v. 10), were making trouble. Titus and the Cretan churches should avoid entanglement in pointless disputation that cannot have a happy ending. There is a time for "opponents [to be] gently instructed" (2 Tim 2:25), but there is also a time when those opponents are beyond the aid of dialogue and instruction (see Titus 1:11 and vv. 10–11 below).

Paul counsels this fourfold avoidance because the disputes he has in mind "are unprofitable and useless." To avoid misunderstanding here, it is important to observe how assiduously Paul strove in person and in his letters to overcome opposition to the gospel by suasion and to facilitate harmonious ties within and between churches. Most if not all of Paul's letters and his tenures in various locales can be understood as implementation of Christ's dictum "Blessed are the peacemakers" (Matt 5:9). The Jerusalem collection epitomizes Paul's impulse to bring those in Christ together, particularly across boundaries that tended to divide. But his own experience, Jesus's stormy relationship with many naysayers, and the whole history of the Old Testament prophets proved that men and women often insist on defying God, not being reconciled to him on God's terms as the gospel calls for (2 Cor 5:20: "Be reconciled to God"). As the psalmist lamented, "I am for peace; but when I speak, they are for war" (Ps 120:7). This experience was true of Jesus and likewise of Paul. Titus should reckon with more of the same and be prepared to engage by disengaging when necessary.[310] The next two verses describe when and how (v. 10), as well as why (v. 11).

10 Eight words in Greek swell to twenty in the NIV. The verse may be rendered literally as "a divisive[311] person after a first and second admonition reject."[312] This hypothetical person is evidently someone who absolutely will not abide by the gospel message and apostolic doctrine.

Many New Testament letters envision such persons or their influence. Acts 15 records an instance of group decision that amounted to rejection of a rival gospel interpretation or application. The years of Jesus's public ministry were marked by often spirited interaction with sometimes intractable opponents. "Have nothing to do with[313] them" (i.e., with the divisive person) prob-

309. See Matt 22:35; Luke 7:30; 10:25; 11:45, 46, 52; 14:3; Titus 3:13.

310. So also Neudorfer, *Titus*, 217.

311. The adjective *hairetikos* is a New Testament hapax. Along with "causing division," Danker, *Concise Greek-English Lexicon*, 10, suggests the gloss "self-promoting."

312. On the pathos of this situation from a pastoral standpoint, see Wright, 164–65.

313. The Greek verb *paraiteomai* occurs twelve times in the New Testament with some five different meanings (Danker, *Concise Greek-English Lexicon*, 267). It means "reject" or "have nothing to do with" only in 1 Tim 4:7; 2 Tim 2:23; Titus 3:10. It never conveys this meaning in

ably indicates what was later called excommunication: such individuals would not be welcomed as members in good standing of their local faith community. This status could include exclusion from the Lord's Table until they repented and were restored (see 1 Tim 1:20; 1 Cor 5:11–13; 2 Thess 3:14–15). Jesus gave instructions for dealing with people who condemn themselves by refusing to come to terms with their transgression (Matt 18:15–17). Redemptive exclusion may bring about honest reform; that goal, not punitive politics, should be viewed as Paul's intent for Titus here. The restorative intent of Paul's directive may lie behind use of the noun *nouthesia*,[314] rendered with the verb "warn" in NIV, which sounds menacing. But (as observed above) Paul writes literally of "a first and second *admonition*." Danker explains this as "advice offered in the interest of another's personal improvement,"[315] clearly a primary motivation behind Jesus's teaching in Matt 18:15.

We cannot, however, deny the ultimate need to defend church members and doctrine from perhaps well-meaning and earnest but sadly mistaken challengers to dominical and apostolic teaching. For this protection, strong measures can be required, which can always be interpreted as draconian by those who side with the divisive or by outside observers who do not identify with the zeal for truth reflected in the canonical writings[316] and shared by apostolic leaders commissioned by Jesus. Without that truth, the love that is the highest goal of Christian expression cannot flourish, either. Yet, part of that truth is that "church discipline should always be redemptive in nature,"[317] even when the redemptive action fails to stave off negative results, a contingency foreseen in the next verse.

11 Having explained when (in the event someone stirs up dissent) and how (by redemptive exclusion) Titus should respond to intransigent opposition (v. 10), Paul now states why this is fitting and necessary: Titus knows[318] (NIV "You may be sure . . .") two things about the kind of individual described

---

its seven LXX occurrences (see *GELS* 527) but often does in Philo (twenty-seven occurrences). The single AF occurrence resembles the PE sense: "For is it not unlawful to accept some of the things created by God for human use as created good but to refuse [*paraiteisthai*] others as useless and superfluous?" (Diogn. 4:2).

314. The word occurs three times in the New Testament: see also 1 Cor 10:11; Eph 6:4. MM 430 calls it "a comparatively rare and mostly late word." It is found four times in Josephus, thirty-seven times in Philo, and once in the AF, when Ignatius writes (*Eph.* 3:1), "For I need to be trained by you in faith, instruction [*nouthesia*], endurance, and patience." See Justin, *Apology* 1.67, for similar usage.

315. *Concise Greek-English Lexicon*, 243.

316. Twomey, 218–19, implies culpability on the part of "Paul" for being overly harsh.

317. Gloer, 90; "In each case, the purpose of discipline is redemptive and restorative!" (91).

318. Calvin (389) warns: Paul says "*knowing* that he is ruined. Let the bishop beware of yielding to his own passionate temper and treating with excessive hardship as a heretic someone he does not yet know to be such."

in v. 10. First, that person is "warped." The underlying Greek word *ekstrephō*, a New Testament hapax, means "turn aside, change entirely."[319] It is middle voice, which may underscore the subject's own role in the stance he or she has assumed; such people have "warped" themselves. The result is flagrant wrongdoing (they have become "sinful"). Their error is confirmed in their status of being "self-condemned" (*autokatakritos*), a New Testament hapax, though Jesus warns against self-condemnation using other words (Matt 12:37). It is the result of their own wrongdoing. They might blame Titus or Paul or the church or even God, but their woes are the result of their own stubborn stance and refusal to back down in the face of what they will not recognize as truer understanding.

VII. CLOSING REQUESTS AND BLESSING (3:12–15)

The final four verses issue closing directions (vv. 12–13), restate a central theme of the letter (v. 14), and pass along greetings (v. 15), concluding on the same note of grace with which the body of the letter began (1:4).

> 12 *As soon as I send Artemas or Tychicus to you, do your best to come to me at Nicopolis, because I have decided to winter there.* 13 *Do everything you can to help Zenas the lawyer and Apollos on their way and see that they have everything they need.* 14 *Our people must learn to devote themselves to doing what is good, in order that they may provide for daily necessities and not live unproductive lives.* 15 *Everyone with me sends you greetings. Greet those who love us in the faith. Grace be with you all.*

12 "Artemas or Tychicus" is perhaps marked out to be the courier of this epistle. Or perhaps this honor may have fallen to Zenas or Apollos (v. 13); at the time of writing or dictation, Paul may not yet have made the final determination. Nothing more is known of Artemas, which was a common name,[320] not to be confused with the female goddess Artemis.[321]

Tychicus was from the Roman province of Asia and accompanied Paul and others[322] on his last trip to Jerusalem, carrying the collection for the impoverished believers in Roman Syria (Acts 20:4). He had previously carried

319. Danker, *Concise Greek-English Lexicon*, 119.

320. Danker, *Concise Greek-English Lexicon*, 55.

321. See Acts 19:24, 27, 28, 34, 35.

322. That is, Sopater from Berea, Aristarchus and Secundus from Thessalonica, Gaius from Derbe, also Timothy, and then Trophimus, like Tychicus, from the province of Asia.

letters to the Ephesians and the Colossians; Paul calls him "the dear brother and faithful servant in the Lord" (Eph 6:21) and "a dear brother, a faithful minister and fellow servant in the Lord" (Col 4:7). He appears to have been with Paul in his final days, for Paul says he sent him to Ephesus at that time (2 Tim 4:12). He is reported to "have been the first bishop of Lystra."[323]

When the courier arrives, Titus is to make haste or spare no effort (*spoudason*; NIV "do your best"; see discussion of word at 2 Tim 4:9) to meet Paul in Nicopolis, where he has decided to spend the winter. The distance from Crete to Nicopolis is some 500 kilometers.[324] This city, capital of the province of Epirus, was located on the isthmus of the Bay of Actium in northwestern Greece. It had been founded by Augustus after his victory over Antony and Cleopatra in 31 BC. Titus will be free to vacate Crete and join Paul because, presumably, Artemas or Tychicus will have arrived to take his place at least temporarily as overseer of the Cretan churches. And Paul's letter to Titus, or a copy of it, will be available to furnish leadership reminders to Titus's replacements.

13 Titus should not only do his best to meet Paul in Nicopolis (v. 12): v. 13 requests Titus to help two people "on their way." One is Zenas, mentioned nowhere else in Scripture. "Lawyer" (*nomikos*; see discussion of this word in v. 9 above) or "scribe" signifies someone versed in Jewish law and tradition in the Synoptic Gospels. Here it likely refers to an expert in Greek or Roman law, though Torah expertise cannot be ruled out. The other person whom Titus is to help along is Apollos. This is likely the same Apollos mentioned ten other times in the New Testament.[325] Since he was from Alexandria, it is suggested that he and Zenas may have been heading in a southerly direction from Paul, to Crete, and then finally on to Alexandria.[326] This is only a possibility, however. Apollos was "a learned man, with a thorough knowledge of the Scriptures" (Acts 18:24), a reminder of the kind of leaders who made common cause with Paul in mission outreach and perhaps also an indicator of qualities found in Titus.

It is also possible that Zenas and Apollos are couriers of the letter to Titus.[327] When they reach Crete, Titus and the Christian community are not only to receive the letter from them but also to be proactive about helping them to their next destinations. The expression *spoudaiōs propempson* (NIV "Do everything you can to help . . . on their way") could be translated "diligently send along [with any assistance they need]."[328] It was not an age of credit

323. Schnabel, *Paul and the Early Church*, 1120.

324. Schnabel, *Paul and the Early Church*, 1287. Schnabel reckons this distance to be five to ten days by ship (1234).

325. Acts 18:24, 27; 19:1; 1 Cor 1:12; 3:4, 5, 6, 22; 4:6; 16:12.

326. Schnabel, *Paul and the Early Church*, 1286 (citing Mounce).

327. So Schnabel, *Paul and the Early Church*, and most commentaries.

328. See BDAG 873.

cards and electronic itineraries; traveling Christian workers were dependent on local generosity for their subsistence, unless like Paul they worked to support themselves. Paul emphasizes this reality by adding, "See that they have everything they need," which is literally "in order that they may lack nothing," with a possible emphasis on *nothing*.[329] Titus should support them in every respect. Despite the urgent tone and wide-ranging counsel of Paul's letter, Titus's attention cannot be only on himself and his churches; he is expected also to share Paul's heart for the wider spread of the gospel in regions beyond Crete. Missions does not detract from pastoral labor and oversight but is part of the lifeblood of those necessary local ministries.

14 One last time (see table 26 and discussion on 1:16 above), Paul calls for zeal in "doing what is good" (lit. "good works"). There are subtleties here, however. One is the way Paul describes "our people," using not the simple possessive pronoun "our" (*hēmōn*) but a form of the relatively rare word *hēmeteros*, found only six times elsewhere in the New Testament.[330] This may be unremarkable. But Paul may be implying a comparison between different groups: let *our* people (like those represented by Zenas and Apollos) do good. This suggestion is supported by *kai* (usually "and"), which could be rendered: "Let our people *too*. . . ." Or Paul could be saying: let *our* people (in contrast to others who are deficient in good works [1:16], or who are outside the Christian community and unconcerned about God's priorities), do good. In that case, this verse is not a flat or forgetful restatement of Paul's five earlier exhortations to do good but a distinct if not emphatic rearticulation of it.

An emphatic tone is supported by the imperative that begins the verse: "let them learn" (*manthanetōsan*). This is the last of the eleven imperatives found in Titus (see table 27 at the beginning of discussion of 2:1–10 above). This verb is cognate with the word "disciple" (*mathētēs*). Disciples cannot merely float along with community drift but "must learn" and then respond. With words reminiscent of v. 8 (see discussion above on the use of *proistēmi*, to be devoted), Paul wants the community under Titus's leadership to prioritize ethical expression of their confessed faith. "Sound doctrine involves living out the truth in everyday life."[331]

There is a goal stipulated for this zeal: their doing good is "for urgent needs." Harris renders this phrase "to relieve the pressing needs of others" and proposes cautiously that the Greek construction is one of "as many as 15 instances" in the New Testament "where *eis*" (in the construction *eis tas anankaias chreias*, NIV "for urgent needs") "could be construed as causal," a use of

329. In Greek "nothing" is the first word in its clause.

330. Acts 2:11; 26:5; Rom 15:4; 2 Tim 4:15; 1 John 1:3; 2:2. For a parallel in the time of Trajan, see MM 280.

331. Ngewa, 412.

this preposition omitted in standard reference works (and generally opposed by Harris).[332] It is not clear why NIV puts this after "in order to" when the Greek word order is "for urgent needs, in order that. . . ." Paul's point is that there *are* burning necessities that come along, Zenas and Apollos's requirements serving as present examples. An ethically lax or selfish community will not find it easy to rise to the occasion such visitors present. Years earlier, Paul had pointed to a Macedonian community where believers gave selflessly for a cause far beyond their own horizons (2 Cor 8:1–5). At that time he urged Titus to stir up the Corinthians to similar generosity based on the Macedonians' example (2 Cor 8:6; cf. 9:1–5). Paul drew on an important underlying principle grounded in the Old Testament: "Whoever sows sparingly will also reap sparingly, and whoever sows generously will also reap generously" (2 Cor 9:6; cf. Prov 11:24). All this is relevant background now for Titus's task, and the Cretans' responsibility, in the current setting.

The Cretan believers should learn to do good for meeting urgent needs in order that (*hina*) they "not live unproductive lives," literally "not be without fruit [*akarpoi*]." This Greek word can refer literally to trees without fruit (Jude 12), but its other six New Testament occurrences are metaphorical. The gospel message becomes "unfruitful" when choked out by worries and distractions (Mark 4:19). Paul warns of "fruitless deeds of darkness" (Eph 5:11). On the positive side, Jesus charged his followers to "bear much fruit" (John 15:8), and Peter gave instruction to keep believers "from being ineffective and unproductive [lit. 'unfruitful'] in your knowledge of our Lord Jesus Christ" (2 Pet 1:8). Paul's call to ethical productivity in Titus 3:14 is seen to have explicit parallels stretching all the back to Jesus and reverberating across the early decades of church formation. Living faith is more than nodding assent to some biblical assertions.

15 As Dietrich Bonhoeffer stressed in one of his best-known books, Christian existence is "life together"—with God in Christ, and with other believers. The community dimension was strong among Jesus and his followers and was only reinforced in the early days of gospel faith recorded in Acts, where believers "had everything in common" (Acts 2:44). This can be thought of primarily in material terms, but it grows out of things that transcend the material (Acts 2:41–43).

Some three decades later, as Paul completes this epistle, the pattern continues. He conveys greetings to Titus and other believers in Crete not merely from himself but from others with Paul who share his convictions and commitments. In a second sentence ("Greet those who love us in the faith") he expresses special affection for those who resonate with the apostolic faith Paul propounds and Titus labors to spread and uphold. There are

332. Harris, *Prepositions and Theology*, 90–91.

some who do not share that stance "who because of their sin" may "have left the church body."[333]

Social realities in Crete, human nature, and the resistance of a fallen world to God's kingdom will conspire to frustrate the harmonious relations and productive faith expression that the greetings in v. 15 celebrate. So Paul closes with the key to kingdom existence: "Grace be with you all"—not just to Titus, but to all who join him in worship and service to God and Christ their Savior. This shift to the plural may imply that Paul knew the letter would be read to the whole church.[334] Or it may simply acknowledge that, in writing to a leader with a pastor's heart, he was writing in large measure to a social collective and not some isolated ideologue. The true shepherd is one with the flock.

Paul's pronouncement of "grace" comes at or near the end of all his extant letters.[335] Many manuscripts add "amen" as the last word, though weighty witnesses omit it.[336] Paul and Titus had a long history; he did not need to school Titus here on the centrality and magnificence of gospel grace. Still, he has mentioned in this epistle that grace appeared in Christ and "offers salvation to all people" (2:11). By this same grace believers are "justified," that they "might become heirs having the hope of eternal life" (3:7). Grace will sustain Titus, Paul knows, in the difficult tasks he faces, as it linked believers across the stretches of the Roman Empire and beyond. It continues to transform those who receive the gospel message in all corners of the globe today as God's promise of redemption unfolds and "the appearing of the glory of our great God and Savior, Jesus Christ" (2:13) approaches.

333. Zehr, 318.

334. Köstenberger, 1.

335. See Rom 16:20; 1 Cor 16:23; 2 Cor 13:14; Gal 6:18; Eph 6:24; Phil 4:23; Col 4:18; 1 Thess 5:28; 2 Thess 3:18; 1 Tim 6:21; 2 Tim 4:22; Phlm 25.

336. For the evidence and discussion, see Metzger, *Textual Commentary* (1994), 587.

Index of Subjects

Index of Authors

Index of Scripture References

OLD TESTAMENT

NEW TESTAMENT

Matthew

John

Galatians

Philippians

Colossians

2 Timothy

Titus

Philemon

Hebrews

Index of Extrabiblical Literature